North American Plains	Eastern U.S.	Diablo Range Area	Western Meso-America	Eastern Meso-America	
Coal. Central Plains Vill. Late Woodland Period Hopewellian	Miss. Period: Moorehead, Fairmount, Patrick Woodland Period: Hopewell	Neomorphic Points: Southwest U.S. Farming, Eastern U.S. Pottery Archaeo-	Late Horizon: Aztec Second Interm. Period: Chichimec, Tula Middle Horizon: Xolalpan, Tlamimilolpa First Intermed. Period: Tzacualli	Late Post Classic Early Post Classic Terminal Classic Late Classic Middle Classic Early Classic Proto-Classic	1500 1000 A.D.
Archaic Period	Woodland Period: Adena Archaic: Savannah R., Late Lamoka	-morphic Points: Meso-Amer. Formative Influences	First Intermed. Period: Monte Alban I, Early Santa Maria Early Horizon: Early Ajalpan Initial Period: Purron Coxcatlán	Late Prec.: Chicanel Mid. Prec.: Early Mamom, Dili Early Precl.: San Lorenzo, Bajio, Ocos, Barra Pre-Formative Period: Earliest Pottery (?)	B.C. 1000 2000 3000
Archaic Period	Archaic Period: (Late) Morrow Mt. ↑ (Middle Arch.) ↑	Archaeomorphic Points	El Riego	Archaic Period: Chantuto ↑ Santa Marta	4000 5000 6000 7000
Paleo Indian Period: Itama Complex, Llano Complex	(Early Arch.) Paleo-Indian Period	Paleo Morphic Points	Early Ajuerea-	Archaic Period	8000
			Tlapacoya		

A hemispheric projection of New World area chronologies: North and Middle America (Front Endpaper) and Lower Central and South America (Back Endpaper). Each area column presents highly synopsized or selected archaeological-chronological data. The B.C.–A.D. dates on the charts are based largely on radiocarbon dates and are the uncorrected renderings of these dates. The heavy horizontal lines that run through the charts, at 10,000 B.C., 7000 B.C., 3000 B.C., and at the B.C.–A.D. division point, are for convenience in cross-column comparisons. No cultural periods, stages, or eras are intended. The purpose of the charts is to provide a rapid scan of absolute time scales and archaeological cultures in the Americas.

Chronologies in New World Archaeology

This is a volume in

Studies in Archeology

A complete list of titles in this series appears at the end of this volume.

Chronologies in New World Archaeology

R. E. Taylor

Department of Anthropology
University of California, Riverside
Riverside, California

Clement W. Meighan

Department of Anthropology
University of California, Los Angeles
Los Angeles, California

ACADEMIC PRESS New York San Francisco London

A Subsidiary of Harcourt Brace Jovanovich, Publishers

ACADEMIC PRESS, INC.
111 Fifth Avenue, New York, New York 10003

United Kingdom Edition published by
ACADEMIC PRESS, INC. (LONDON) LTD.
24/28 Oval Road, London NW1 7DX

Library of Congress Cataloging in Publication Data

Main entry under title:

Chronologies in New World archaeology.

(Studies in archeology series)
Includes bibliographies and index.
1. Indians--Antiquities--Addresses, essays, lectures. 2. America--Antiquities--Addresses, essays, lectures. 3. Archaeological dating--America--Addresses, essays, lectures. I. Taylor, Royal Ervin, II. Meighan, Clement Woodward,
E61.C55 970.01 78-2039
ISBN 0-12-685750-4

PRINTED IN THE UNITED STATES OF AMERICA

Contents

List of Contributors

Numbers in parentheses indicate the pages on which the authors' contributions begin.

Louis Allaire (431), *Department of Anthropology, University of Manitoba, Winnipeg, Manitoba, Canada*

Douglas D. Anderson (29), *Department of Anthropology, Brown University, Providence, Rhode Island*

Warren W. Caldwell (113), *Department of Anthropology, University of Nebraska, Lincoln, Nebraska*

James B. Griffin (51), *Museum of Anthropology, Ann Arbor, Michigan*

Wolfgang Haberland (395), *Hamburgisches Museum für Völkerkunde, Hamburg, Germany*

Robert F. Heizer (147), *Department of Anthropology, University of California, Berkeley, Berkeley, California*

Dale R. Henning (113), *Department of Anthropology, University of Nebraska, Lincoln, Nebraska*

Thomas R. Hester (147), *Department of Anthropology, University of Texas at San Antonio, San Antonio, Texas*

Edward B. Jelks (71), *Department of Sociology-Anthropology, Illinois State University, Normal, Illinois*

Gareth W. Lowe (331), *New World Archaeological Foundation, Brigham Young Foundation, Chiapas, Mexico*

Clement W. Meighan (223), *Department of Anthropology, University of California, Los Angeles, Los Angeles, California*

H. B. Nicholson (285), *Department of Anthropology, University of California, Los Angeles, Los Angeles, California*

Lautaro Núñez A. (483), *Departamento de Ciencias Sociales, Universidad del Norte, Antofagasta, Chile*

Arthur H. Rohn (201), *Department of Anthropology, Wichita State University, Wichita, Kansas*

Irving Rouse (431), *Department of Anthropology, Yale University, New Haven, Connecticut*

R. E. Taylor (1), *Department of Anthropology, University of California, Riverside, Riverside, California*

Paul Tolstoy (241), *Department of Anthropology, Queen's College, City University of New York, Flushing, New York*

Gordon R. Willey (513), *Department of Anthropology, Peabody Museum of Archaeology and Ethnology, Harvard University, Cambridge, Massachusetts*

Preface

This volume had its origin in a conversation between the editors, beginning with the thought: Would it not be very helpful if New World archaeologists had available a general summary of chronologies for the Western Hemisphere? The idea was triggered by our use of the comparable volume for the Old World (*Chronologies in Old World Archaeology*, edited by Robert W. Ehrich, University of Chicago Press, 1965) which has gone through many editions and serves as a basic reference work. Surprisingly, no comparable set of studies exists for the New World, and the necessity for it becomes increasingly evident as archaeologists seek to broaden their interpretations and theories. It is essential to higher level studies to control knowledge of the time placement of archaeological remains; neither studies of cultural change nor comparative analyses can have validity without fixing the archaeological remains in chronological order. Particularly for studies beyond the limits of a single site, the questions of chronology become critical for any comprehensive analysis.

But just as the archaeologists have reached a point of moving toward more general historical, functional, and processual analyses, the problems of controlling chronology have become much more intricate. Paradoxically, this results in part from the chronological information being vastly increased in both quantity and quality—the archaeologist has much finer chronological information available but it is often more difficult for him to find the information and use it critically. The expansion of archaeological study in all areas has made it impossible for the individual scholar to keep abreast of all the details of the developing regional chronologies. It is often a considerable task to control the chronology of the region in which the individual does his or her own fieldwork, and a great deal of research time must go into locating chronological details rather than seeking to expand conclusions to wider regions or more general problems than local ones.

Along with the general increase in archaeological studies there is the tremendous body of knowledge, still rapidly accumulating, to provide specific temporal data, the hard facts of chronology resulting from radiocarbon values, tree-ring counts, obsidian hydration results, and new and exploratory dating methodologies. Numerous lists and compendia of dates exist, some of them quite voluminous—*Radiocarbon*, for example, now in its nineteenth volume (1977), includes many thousands of individual dates and has published an index. These lists of dates, however, contain very little evaluation of the individual entries, and aside from the difficulties of finding the appropriate dating information, it is very difficult in many cases for the nonspecialist to make intelligent use of the dates without a detailed study of all the primary site reports. In other words, in order to understand the dates and the chronology, one often must study the total archaeology of a region. It is not unlikely that this alone has until recently inhibited and limited studies such as those concerned with, for example, relationships between the ancient centers of Mesoamerica and South America.

Even within individual countries and small geographic areas, problems of chronology require much of the archaeologist's time, and there are an increasing number of regional chronologies resulting from local conferences and symposia. These, unfortunately, are often unpublished or remain in local journals not widely available. It seemed to us, therefore, a most useful task to undertake the compilation of a general chronology for the whole of the New World, with a view toward providing a general reference work that can allow more ready understanding and comparison of chronological information for New World archaeology.

No single scholar has the expertise and first-hand knowledge to write such a volume, and our first task was to seek the collaboration of regional experts who had close knowledge of the chronological situation in their various areas. Our list was drawn up with the help and collaboration of Gordon Willey, who also agreed to write a general summation after seeing the individual articles, a task for which he is uniquely qualified since his textbooks on North and South American archaeology have required him to do his own personal grappling with the chronologies of all the areas considered in this volume. With the encouragement and great patience of these various scholars who not only agreed that a book of this sort would be useful but also agreed to undertake the writing of sections of it, the project has been developed to its present form.

One preliminary to the volume was presentation of a symposium discussion on New World chronology at the meeting of the American Association for the Advancement of Science in Washington (December, 1972). Several contributors to the volume presented preliminary papers on their subject areas, and from joint discussions with them and others attending the symposium a number of decisions were made about the nature and organization of the present book.

It should be made clear that while the present review is certainly one of the most detailed, comprehensive overall summaries of New World chronology that has been attempted, it cannot be expected to be a perfect tool for chronological studies. First of all, individual chapters have been prepared over a 5-year period. Chronological understanding changes rapidly as new evidence appears, and periodic future revisions will be necessary to incorporate new information and correct errors and uncertainties. Besides, the chapters are not the work of a committee but of individual scholars, all of whom would admit that despite all efforts to be comprehensive and judicious their knowledge is stronger in some parts of their analysis than in others. And finally, our areal coverage is subject to improvement in the future. Some authors have been asked to cope with very large and complex regions which might be better handled when subdivided into smaller units. There are also geographical gaps where it was impossible for us to get a comprehensive article for lack of a qualified specialist who could contribute to this volume. We are greatly appreciative of Gordon Willey's summary chapter for providing coverage of areas where the volume lacked a comprehensive article. Despite all the shortcomings, which will be corrected in future revisions, there is a reference tool of great value in having gathered together up-to-date knowledge of New World chronologies.

An editorial decision forced on us by the size of the book was to eliminate long lists of radiocarbon dates and extensive discussions of individual dates. Most of the authors prepared such data, and several of them submitted detailed analyses amounting to as much as half of their chapters. In a number of cases, therefore, the authors have been asked to present their evaluations without the opportunity of presenting the full evidence for their conclusions. This does not detract from the broad overview intended, but to the extent that it weakens individual discussions it should be stated that the abbreviation of date lists is the creation of the editors rather than the authors.

Dating Methods in New World Archaeology

R. E. TAYLOR

I. INTRODUCTION

The chronological structures currently used in New World prehistoric studies are the result of research conducted over the last seven or eight decades by a large and distinguished group of archaeologists. The development of a chronological perspective in American archaeology, however, cannot be accurately represented as a gradual incremental expansion of information over the whole period. Rather, an appreciation of the importance of the temporal dimension in New World archaeology tended to be somewhat retarded until well into the twentieth century.

Initially, the development of a prehistoric temporal framework in the Western hemisphere was handicapped by a lack of readily discernible archaeological horizon markers or stage designations (e.g., Stone, Bronze, and Iron "ages") which served so well the needs of European archaeologists during the nineteenth century as interim prehistoric temporal units. In addition, while Old World prehistorians were following up the change in world view typified in Darwin's *Origin of Species* and *Descent of Man* with increasing evidence of a much expanded temporal depth for man, in the New World similar claims were critically examined and largely rejected principally because of the absence of pre-*sapiens* skeletal materials. A legacy of this action was the creation of a strong reluctance to support any claim for man in the New World much older than a few thousand years. While there were some notable exceptions, this orientation held sway until the 1926 discovery at Folsom, New Mexico, of artifact material in undisputed association with extinct faunal remains within a Late Pleistocene geological context.

An additional inhibiting factor resulted from the fact that New World archaeological studies in the United States were, from the beginning, closely linked with American anthropology. The rejection of nineteenth century unilineal cultural evolutionism by American anthropologists under the leadership of Franz Boas and his students created a tradition that devalued an examination of culture change through time (Willey and Sabloff 1974:86–87). When attention was focused on chronological considerations, it tended to be limited to a correlation of archaeologically derived material with contact period ethnographically oriented material culture. While this situation temporarily inhibited the development of broad-scaled temporal perspectives, by the second decade of the twentieth century the introduction of stratigraphic excavation techniques and seriation studies (using variations in frequency of artifact style elements to infer the passage of time), especially in the southwestern region of the United States and in Mesoamerica, provided the most important stimulus for a concern with temporal relationships in the archaeological record.

Stratigraphic and seriational approaches soon became standard techniques in the investigation of archaeological materials. Local temporal sequences and local artifact complexes having temporal significance were developed. In some areas, cross-dating by the correlation of diagnostic artifact traits resulted in the development of regional sequences. The most widespread diagnostic artifacts would come to define "horizon styles," which permitted interregional comparisons. In certain areas, notably the Mayan area of ancient Mesoamerica, an indigenous writing and calendric tradition, when correlated with the Western calendar, provided limited dating evidence for both local and regional sequences in the first millennium A.D. period.

Beginning in 1901, A. E. Douglass, an astronomer interested in documenting past sun spot cycles, turned to the measurement of variations in the width of annual tree rings (Ferguson 1970). Concentrating on the southwestern United States, he had, by 1929, established a continuous dated tree-ring series running back to the beginning of the Christian era and thereby provided for archaeology one of the most precise dating methods to be found anywhere in the world—dendrochronology. Archaeologists in the U.S. Southwest had at their disposal a method that permitted them to structure a chronology of unrivaled accuracy and precision. For areas outside the Southwest, the period immediately before World War II saw the expansion and extension of local and regional chronologies into additional areas. The amassing of excavation data, and increased attempts to provide chronological ordering for these data, was especially exemplified in North America as a result of United States federal governmental support of archaeology during the period of the Great Depression.

Following World War II, the introduction of radiocarbon dating literally revolutionized the ability of New World archaeologists to provide relatively precise time placement for their materials. As Glyn Daniel has stated, "It is no exaggeration to say that the discovery of radiocarbon dating is the most important development in archaeology since the discovery of the antiquity of man (Daniel 1967:266)." Radiocarbon values were incorporated into existing chronological frameworks, with the result that both a lengthening and a shortening of numerous sequences, sometimes by thousands of years, was required. Radiocarbon dating, following its introduction in 1949, has become the principal chronometric method used in New World prehistoric studies. More than 20 years of research and utilization have created an increasingly comprehensive body of data pertaining to archaeological applications, contributed from a variety of research perspectives—so much so that the technique has come to occupy the position of what might be called a "standardizing" method, due to its worldwide applicability, its ability to utilize a wide spectrum of organic sample materials, and a situation in which the accuracy of newer dating methods in the process of development, have, in many cases, been validated or modified by comparison with radiocarbon determinations.

The outstanding success of radiocarbon, however, should not cause us to neglect the fact that post–World War II New World archaeology has witnessed the development and application of a number of physical dating methods to materials of archaeological significance. A review has noted nine operational chronometric techniques actively in use, with several additional methods in various stages of research and development (Taylor 1970). In addition, there are a number of secondary methods that can, in some situations, be employed to provide inferences concerning temporal relationships of archaeologically related materials.

Until recently, dating techniques have traditionally been divided into "relative" as opposed to "absolute" categories. Table 1.1, listing the major operational and experimental methods, has divided them into fixed-rate and variable-rate techniques. This terminology focuses upon the physical and/or chemical mechanisms used in the isolation of temporal increments and essentially agrees with Smiley's long standing suggestion to contrast time placement and relative placement methods (Smiley 1955). Time placement can be used to refer to the result of the application of fixed-rate process techniques, and relative placement to the application of variable-rate techniques. Calibrated variable-rate techniques, in addition, can be used for time placement purposes. It is important to note that, even when time placement results are being considered, each fixed-rate process method and calibrated

TABLE 1.1

Classification of Physical Dating Methods Used in Archaeology

I. *Operational*
   A. Fixed-rate processes (time placement)
      1. Radiometric: *radiocarbon, potassium-argon, fission track, uranium-actinium series*
      2. Biological: *dendrochronology*
      3. Geophysical: *archaeomagnetic orientation*
      4. Geological: *varve*
   B. Variable-rate processes (relative placement)
      1. Chemical: *obsidian hydration* (relative placement aspect), *FUN* (fluorine, uranium, nitrogen)

II. *Experimental*
   A. Fixed-rate processes (time placement)
      1. Radiometric: *thermoluminescence, electron spin resonance, alpha particle recoil*
      2. Geophysical: *archaeomagnetic intensity*
   B. Calibrated variable-rate processes (time/relative placement)
      1. Chemical: *obsidian hydration* (time placement aspect), *amino acid, fluorine diffusion*

variable-rate technique possesses unique and usually extensive sets of explicit or implicit assumptions and conditions that must be fulfilled *for each individual sample* if accurate data are to be generated. Of the nine operational chronometric techniques noted in Table 1.1, only two—dendrochronology and varve analysis—were in active use before 1950, and both of these methods had in common the problem of a severely restricted temporal and/or spatial application (Taylor 1976).

It is within the last decade or so that archaeochronometric studies can be said to have come of age, although the actual number of workers engaged in the field is still relatively small. An indication of this recent maturity is the appearance within the last decade of monographs and book-length summaries including, *Radiocarbon Variations and Absolute Chronology* (Olsson 1970), *Science and Archaeology* (Brill 1971), *The Impact of the Natural Sciences on Archaeology* (Allibone and Wheeler 1971), *Scientific Methods in Medieval Archaeology* (Berger 1970a), the second edition of *Science in Archaeology* (Brothwell and Higgs 1969), *Dating Techniques for the Archaeologist* (Michael and Ralph 1971), *Calibration of Hominid Evolution* (Bishop and Miller 1972), *Methods of Physical Examination in Archaeology* (Tite 1972) and *Dating in Archaeology* (Fleming 1976). Even a volume oriented to undergraduate audiences is available (Michels 1973).

Although there has been a relatively rapid expansion in the number of dating methods available to the archaeologist, only recently has there been expressed a concern over the development of a comprehensive interpretative framework into which data from various geophysical methods could be fed and evaluated. An early example of this type of concern was contained in a discussion by Meighan (1956) of problems revolving around the archaeologist's responsibility in the use of the radiocarbon method. He noted several areas wherein the archaeologist had specific responsibilities as a result of his collaborative relationship with those in the laboratories involved in the actual physical measurements. At that time, Meighan suggested that these responsibilities included such concerns as care in critically establishing and openly documenting the contextual cultural relationship and affiliations of the samples submitted for analysis and in completely eliminating reliance on single radiocarbon values. Over the last 15 years, especially in radiocarbon studies, an appreciation of the complexity and need for caution in the utilization of single "dates" has become increasingly evident.

In view of the rapid and increasing tempo of research activity in archaeological chronometrics, it seems appropriate to review recent major advances in the radiocarbon method, especially as it affects the precision and accuracy of the age determinations used by New World prehistorians. In addition, we will review developments in another important dating technique now coming into wider use—obsidian hydration—as well as discussing the status of two new experimental methods that exhibit great potential to provide even more comprehensive temporal controls for materials of interest to archaeologists—the amino acid and fluorine diffusion methods.

II. ADVANCES IN RADIOCARBON DATING

Clearly, the radiocarbon method is the most widely used isotopic dating technique in New World archaeology. Developed by W. F. Libby in the period 1946–1949 at the University of Chicago (Arnold and Libby 1949; Libby 1946, 1955, 1970, 1973; Libby *et al.* 1949), the principal assumptions on which the method was developed, all of which have subsequently been subjected to continuing scrutiny (Berger and Suess n.d.; Olsson 1970; Rafter and Grant-Taylor 1973) include (*a*) that the production of radiocarbon by cosmic rays has remained essentially constant over a period of sufficient length to establish a steady-state or equilibrium in the $^{14}C/^{12}C$ ratio in the atmosphere at least over the last 50,000–70,000 years, (*b*) that there has been complete and rapid mixing of radiocarbon throughout the various atmospheric, hydrospheric, and biospheric reservoirs, (*c*) that the total amount of carbon in these reservoirs has remained essentially constant, (*d*) that the decay constant (λ) of ^{14}C (which is related to the half-life by the expression $t_{1/2} = 0.693/\lambda$) can be measured to within a few percent, (*e*) that natural levels of radiocarbon can be measured by appropriate instrumentation to within 1–3%, and (*f*) that there has been no alteration in the carbon isotopic ratio except by decay within sample materials since they ceased to be a part of one of the carbon reservoirs (as at death).

In the decade of the 1950s, the principal *methodological* advance involved the substitution of gas or liquid scintillation counting methods in place of the original solid carbon approach. This development permitted, first of all, the maximum age range to be extended from ca. 25,000 years to between 40,000 and 50,000 years (75,000, utilizing enrichment procedures) and, second, an increase in the statistical precision of the age values cited (Grootes *et al.* 1975). By the inauguration of the journal *Radiocarbon* in 1959 (originally the *Radiocarbon Supplement* to the *American Journal of Science*), there were 36 radiocarbon laboratories operating, indicating the rapid wide acceptance of the method by that time. Throughout the 1960s the number of facilities continued to increase so that the number of active laboratories in 1976 stood at 98.

The relatively large number of workers engaged in radiocarbon studies since 1950, and the presence of a receptive group of collaborators among archaeologists and others, led to a number of studies bearing on a wide assortment of application-related problems in radiocarbon work. For the archaeologist these initially included, for example, the significance of the statistical character of radiocarbon data (Spaulding 1958), problems in the utilization of certain sample types and sample contamination (e.g., Bliss 1952; Olson and Broecker 1958) and variations between samples from different environments (Bender 1968; Chatters *et al.* 1969; Rubin *et al.* 1963).

From the point of view of the archaeologist, probably the most significant technical development in radiocarbon studies since the early 1960s involves an examination of the nature and magnitude of systematic anomalies in radiocarbon values when compared with known-age materials. These systematic variations in radiocarbon values—having both long and short term components—are known as "secular variation" or sometimes as the "de-Vries effect." Such variations indicate that one or more of the assumptions on which the ^{14}C method rests is not completely valid. Three types of reference data have been used in an attempt to calibrate the radiocarbon time scale. These include (*a*) historically known-age materials, (*b*) dendrochronologically known age materials, and (*c*) materials related to periglacial varve or lake sediment strata.

As early as the first series of radiocarbon determinations, the apparent discrepancy between certain radiocarbon values and the historically known-age early third millennium Egyptian materials was the occasion for comment (Libby 1963). However, due to the lower counting efficiency of the detection devices then in operation and the resulting relatively large statistical errors, the precise significance of the discrepancies could not be definitely evaluated. In the late 1950s the Heidelberg and Groningen laboratories, using the then newly introduced CO_2 gas counting technique, obtained radiocarbon determinations on a series of tree-ring samples (Munich 1957; deVries 1958). These data documented the suggestion that "radiocarbon years" and calendar, or sidereal, years could not be assumed to involve equivalent values. Because of the geophysical implications of these deviations, a number of additional workers confirmed their reality and, throughout the 1960s, extended back into time a knowledge of their magnitude (Damon *et al.* 1966, 1973; Michael and Ralph 1973; Ralph and Michael 1967, 1970; Ralph *et al.* 1973; Ralph and Stuckenrath 1960; Stuiver and Suess 1966; Suess 1965, 1967, 1970; Wallick 1973; Willis *et al.* 1960). At present, the most complete record of data pertaining to these variations derives from high precision radiocarbon determinations on dendrochronologically dated wood samples. These measurements have been made on the sequoias (*Sequoias gigantea*) and, most recently, on the bristlecone pine (*Pinus aristata*) of the White Mountains of eastern California by the Arizona, La Jolla, and Pennsylvania laboratories. Published bristlecone pine tree-ring data exist for the period back to almost 6300 B.C. with an expectation that an additional 1000-year segment will soon be added (cf. Ferguson 1973). An independently developed bristlecone pine tree-ring chronology from a different locality in the southern portion of the White Mountains has supported the accuracy of the Fergusson bristlecone tree-ring chronology at least back to 3535 B.C. (La Marche and Harlan 1973). Published radiocarbon determinations on dendrochronological samples now provide data reaching back to ca. 5500 B.C. (Ralph *et al.* 1973). Significant interpretative problems in the utilization of radiocarbon values are apparent when the ^{14}C dated tree-ring data are examined. If we ignore for the moment the *short-term* perturbations, the radiocarbon and dendrochronological values are in approximate agreement ($\pm$1–3%) for the period of the last 2000 years. However, as one moves backward in time from about the beginning of the Christian era, there is an increasing deviation in the radiocarbon values, so that by ca. 2000 B.C. ^{14}C values are registering ca. 200–300 years *too young*, and between 4000 and 5000 B.C. the deviation may be as much as 800 years.

The question of the nature of the major secular radiocarbon anomalies before ca. 5500 B.C. cannot, at present, be documented by the bristlecone pine data. It has been inferred, however, that the *long-term* characteristics of the DeVries effect may be estimated by reference to geomagnetic intensity data, since variations in the intensity of the earth's geomagnetic dipole field seems to have been identified as the principal cause of the long-term component of secular variation. Elsasser *et al.* (1956) had previously determined that a decrease in the intensity of the earth's dipole field was followed by an increase of the cosmic ray flux in the vicinity of the earth and therefore by an increase in the production rate of ^{14}C. Bucha presented data that strongly supported the existence of a correlation between the intensity of the earth's magnetic dipole moment and deviations observed in the bristlecone pine radiocarbon values (Bucha 1969; Bucha and Neustuphy 1967). He also assembled data bearing on the character of the intensity of the earth's dipole field for approximately the last 600,000 years in which the changes are presented as cyclic in nature with a period of approximately equal amplitude (Bucha 1967). The evidence seems to support the view that the long-term component of variability observed in the bristlecone ^{14}C data could best be characterized as describing a wave function and, thus, the temporal intervals of maximum and minimum deviation in atmospheric radiocarbon activity may then perhaps be extrapolated back to the present limit of the method at ca. 50,000 years. Any implementation of these extrapolations to provide "corrections" to the radiocarbon values on the order of the bristlecone pine data, however, would be premature and must await the development of a clearer consensus as to the specific nature and causes of the observed variability in ^{14}C activity over time, especially in view of the possible existence of an unusually large excursion of the geomagnetic field at ca. 30,000 radiocarbon years B.P. (Barbetti 1973). In addition to the variation in the earth's field intensity, other factors presently under consideration include fluctuations in atmospheric mixing rates, variations in solar cosmic-ray intensity, and variations in the solar wind (Yang and Fairhall 1973).

Two calibration curves utilizing summaries of the dendrochronology/radiocarbon data—one based on data generated by the La Jolla radiocarbon facility (Suess 1970) and a second plot assembled by the University of Pennsylvania's Museum Applied Science Center for Archaeology (MASCA)

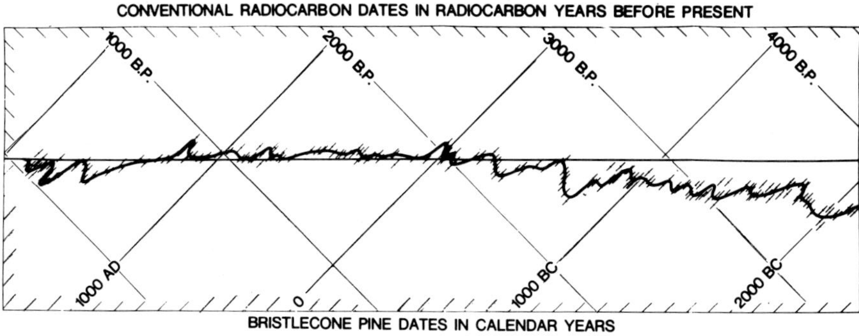

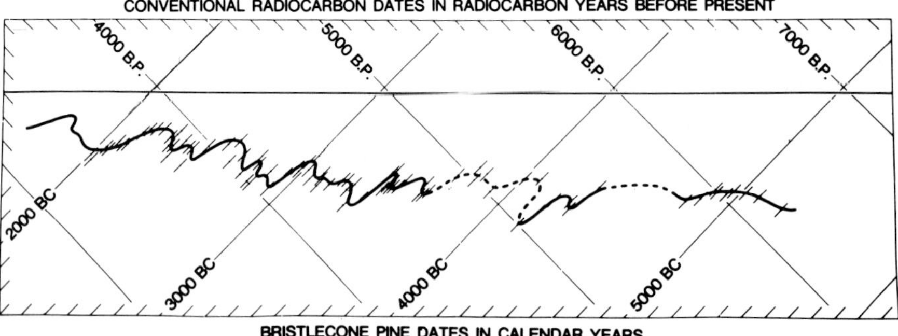

Figure 1.1. Relationship of radiocarbon and dendrochronological age of bristlecone pines after Suess (1970). Scale of plot has been inverted from original citation to permit comparison with Figure 2. ^{14}C half-life used 5568 years; point of origin of plot A.D. 1950.

(Ralph *et al.* 1973)—are presented here. In both the Suess (Figure 1.1) and the MASCA (Figure 1.2) data plots, the long-term component of the anomalies can be easily identified. In both plots, the solid horizontal line represents the ideal situation in which radiocarbon and calendar years would be equivalent, that is, any data point lying on that line would indicate that at that point in time radiocarbon and tree-ring (calendar year) values would coincide. Any point lying below the line would indicate that the radiocarbon values are "too young" with respect to tree-ring values, and, above the line, that the radiocarbon values are "too old." In both sets of data, the long-term component exhibits the characteristics of a wave function with a period of about 8500–9000 years and with a maximum deviation of ca. 8–10% centering about 4500–5000 B.C. calendar years. After smoothing the short-term oscillations, or "wriggles," both sets of data identify crossover points, or nodes, where radiocarbon years and sidereal years are in coincidence at ca. A.D. 700 (± 100) and 500 (± 100) B.C., although the later intersection coincides with a short-term excursus.

It is in the documentation of the nature of the short-term perturbations in radiocarbon values that the two sets of data are not in complete agreement, although there is agreement that there is a series of short-term episodes in

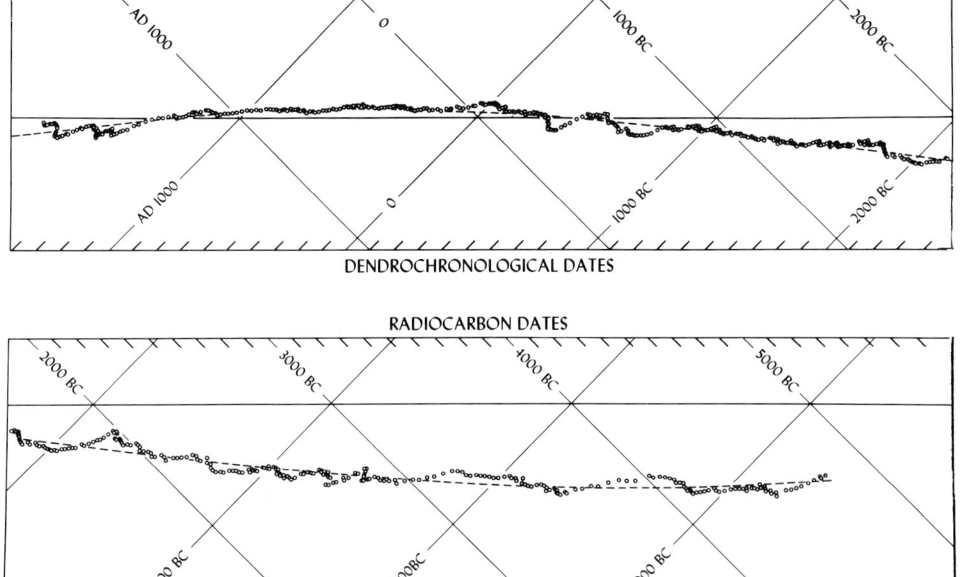

Figure 1.2. Relationship of radiocarbon and dendrochronological age of wood samples after Ralph *et al.* (1973). ^{14}C half-life used 5730 years; point of origin of plot A.D. 1950.

radiocarbon contents which generate an additional set of problems for the archaeologist in the utilization and interpretation of radiocarbon values (Farmer and Baxter 1973). In the Suess and MASCA plots, the interval of time from A.D. 1800 to the middle of the fourth millennium B.C. exhibits 12 major temporal episodes where radiocarbon values have multiple age equivalents. In these intervals, a given radiocarbon value may reflect two or more points in real time. Figure 1.3 provides an illustration of this problem on an expanded scale. The time period represents an interval on the radiocarbon scale of between 1950 B.C. (3900 B.P.) and 2350 B.C. radiocarbon years, based on Suess (1970). Note that if the radiocarbon value, for example 2050 B.C., were equal to the value given by the dendrochronological calibration, then the data points would lie along the horizontal reference line in Figures 1.1 and 1.2, that is, 2050 B.C. on the radiocarbon scale would equal 2050 B.C. on the bristlecone pine scale. Considering only a single calibrated equivalent point, a radiocarbon value of 2050 B.C. can be calibrated to a value of 2525

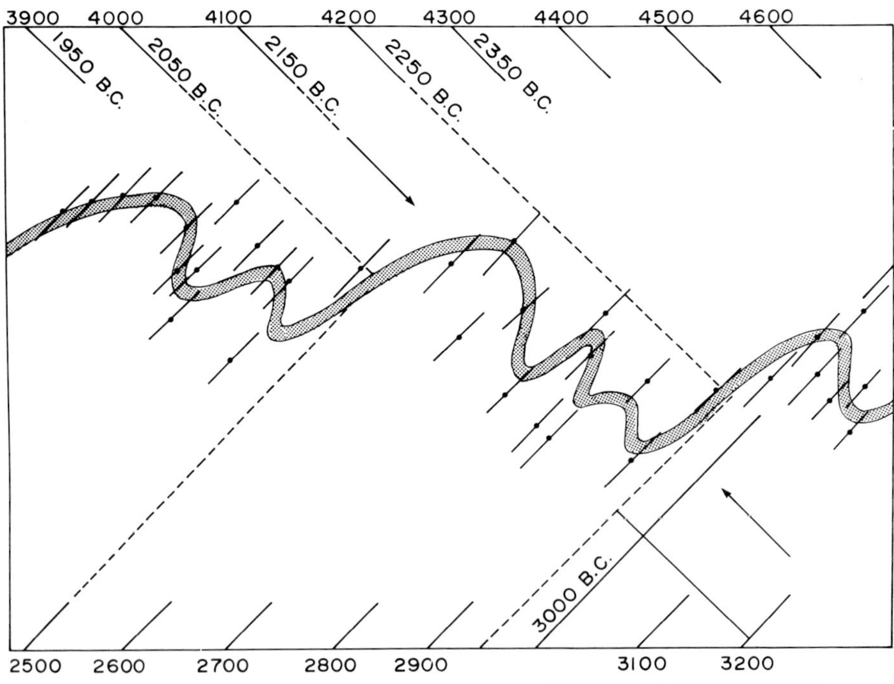

Figure 1.3. Relationship of radiocarbon and dendrochronological age of bristlecone pine samples for the period 3900–4300 radiocarbon years B.P. after Suess (1970). Scale of plot expanded from Figure 1.1. B.C. values associated with radiocarbon B.P. scale by subtraction of 1950 years. Note that value of 2150 (±100) B.C. radiocarbon years (arrows) cannot be calibrated to better than a range of 2500–2950 B.C. calendar years B.C. (dotted line relationship).

B.C. calendar or sidereal years. However, in looking again at the expanded scale in Figure 1.3, it will be noted that a radiocarbon value of 2150 (±100) years B.C. has been obtained on tree-ring dated wood samples that range in true age from ca. 2500 to 2950 B.C. This indicates, that, if a sample yields an age of 4100 radiocarbon years, then the true age of the sample material cannot be, at that point in time, isolated to better than a time interval of ca. 450 years. Thus, the tree-ring–radiocarbon values data may be used not only to identify the degree of deviation of the radiocarbon values from dendrochronologically determined values but also to identify the degree of maximum precision possible for a given temporal interval. The uncertain characteristics and magnitude of the short-term perturbations (or wriggles) in radiocarbon values may make their usage for chronological reconstructions somewhat problematical. However, Berger (1970b) has demonstrated the utility and necessity of short-term type corrections for accurate radiocarbon data analyses when applied to twelfth- to fourteenth-century European medieval archaeological materials. Since such variations reflect worldwide atmospheric conditions, such perturbation effects would obviously have a comparable effect on New World materials.

III. OBSIDIAN HYDRATION DATING

The utilization of the hydration phenomenon in obsidian to provide a chronometric method applicable to archaeological materials grew out of work carried out by Friedman, Ross, and Smith of the United States Geological Survey in the mid-1950s (Friedman and Smith 1958; Ross and Smith 1958). Their work centered on the examination of the relation of the water content of volcanic glasses to their physical and chemical properties and specifically the mechanisms involved in the formation of perlitic or hydrated obsidian glass. The application of this technique to archaeologically occurring materials was based on the fact that a freshly made surface of obsidian, such as a surface obtained by chipping in the manufacture of an obsidian artifact, will undergo chemical and physical changes as a result of the absorption of "water" from the surrounding environment. The hydration process begins immediately after a surface is exposed and theoretically continues at a constant rate until the present unless some factor intervenes to halt or modify the process.

The rate at which a hydration layer develops was initially evaluated in terms of a simple (Fick's first law) diffusion process in which the hydration front would be formed at a constant exponential rate with respect to time. The expression $x^2 = kt$, or $x = kt^{.5}$ [where x = depth of penetration of "water" (OH^-) in microns, k = an empirically derived temperature constant that is geographically variable, t = time in years] was used, and ages were calculated using this expression (Friedman and Smith 1960; Friedman *et al.*

1966). Since the temperature coefficient of the hydration rate was considered the principal variable, the dating potential of the method was operationalized by establishing obsidian hydration rates for six macroclimatic zones: Egypt, with two rates, one for trachytic and a second for rhyolitic obsidian; "Temperate No. 1," which included California, East Africa, Japan, the Near East, and the southwestern United States; "Temperate No. 2," which was essentially Mexico; the sub-Arctic; and the Arctic (Table 1.2).

Difficulties in the calculation of obsidian hydration dates using a simple diffusion formula approach became immediately apparent when the initial results were examined. Table 1.2 provides a summary of those data. It is interesting to note that the largest discrepancies between the assumed known dates of samples and the obsidian hydration "dates" occurred in those areas where the best archaeological controls were present. In the Maya area, for example, 85% of the hydration ages seriously conflicted with the dates assigned on the basis of the archaeological evidence. In the American Southwest, approximately two-thirds of the samples yielded unacceptable hydration values. Examination of Table 1.2 also reveals that the largest single lot of sample determinations were derived from Ecuador—229 in all. Of these, almost one-half were discarded as unacceptable. Under these conditions, there was understandable reluctance to accept a method in which 60%, on the average, of the "dates" were clearly anomalous when compared against the archaeological evidence.

As other investigators began to utilize obsidian hydration values for dating purposes, variant rate structures were reported. Clark (1964), working with California materials, presented data that described the rate function as $x = kt^{.75}$. Students of West Mexican prehistory, utilizing a relatively large corpus of obsidian hydration data and radiocarbon determinations, reported a hydration rate for the region that could be described as $x = kt$ (i.e., the hydration rate, at least in West Mexico, was linear) (Meighan *et al.* 1968a; Meighan 1974; Taylor *et al.* 1969). There was, however, continuing support for the concept of an exponential rate (Johnson 1969; Katsui and Kondo 1965) and a significant interpretative problem in the utilization of obsidian hydration dating for time placement purposes became apparent (Friedman and Evans 1968; Meighan *et al.* 1968b; Meighan 1970). Because of this, a significant percentage of the application of obsidian work through the 1960s involved its use for relative placement rather than time placement purposes where precise rate factors are not critical (Michels 1967).

The possibility that chemical variability would play a significant role in the physical and chemical mechanism involved in obsidian hydration was specifically recognized by Friedman and Smith when they established two rates for Egyptian obsidian, one for trachytic and another for rhyolitic obsidian. However, the possibility that this factor would be of general significance was minimized by them and by others (e.g., Johnson 1969), apparently because of the view that rhyolitic obsidian makes up the bulk of the world's obsidian

TABLE 1.2

Obsidian Hydration Studies: Character of Initial Data

	Scale/ Rate I[a]		Scale/ Rate II[b]		Total agreement			Disagreement													
	Scale	Rate[c]	Scale	Rate[c]	A	B	C	D	E	F	G	H	I	J	K	L	M	N	O	P	Q
Egypt (trachytic)	A	14.0			13	3	23.1	2		8										10	76.9
Coastal Guat.	B	11.0	A	11.0	64	35	54.7					6		23						29	45.3
Ecuador					229	104	45.4	10	2			11		102						116	54.6
Maya Area					47	7	14.9	39		1										40	85.1
Egypt (rhyolitic)	C	8.1	B	8.1	4	4	100.0													0	0.0
California	D	6.5	C	6.5	4	2	50.0								2					2	50.0
East Africa					28	2	7.1					2	1			2	17	1	3	26	92.9
Japan					15	10	66.7	3				2								5	33.3
Near East					72	6	8.3	24			1	2			21			18		66	91.7
U.S. Southwest					51	17	33.3	34												34	66.7
Oregon	D/E	[d]			14																
Mexico	E	4.5	D	4.5	11	4	36.4	5		2										7	63.6
Alaska (sub-Arctic)	F	.82	E	.9	8	4	50.0	1						3						4	50.0
Alaska (Arctic)	G	.36	F	.4	18	7	38.9	11												11	61.0

[a] Scale and rate from Friedman and Smith (1960).
[b] Scale and rate from Friedman *et al.* (1966).
[c] Rate expressed in microns squared.
[d] Rate not determined.

A = Total number tested; B = Satisfactory agreement between archaeological age and obsidian age based on assumed rate; C = Percentage of agreement; D = Unsatisfactory agreement unexplained; E = Unsatisfactory agreement due to natural chipping; F = Unsatisfactory agreement: no hydration; G = Unsatisfactory agreement: unworked; H = Unsatisfactory agreement: intrusive; I = Unsatisfactory agreement: poor obsidian; J = Unsatisfactory agreement: re-use; K = Unsatisfactory agreement: exposure to sun; L = Unsatisfactory agreement: hot springs; M = Unsatisfactory agreement: erosion of surface; N = Unsatisfactory agreement: burned; O = Unsatisfactory agreement: no comment; P = Total unsatisfactory agreement; Q = Percentage unsatisfactory.

sources and that all rhyolitic obsidian have essentially comparable chemical characteristics, especially with respect to SiO_2 content.

In the late 1960s, studies focusing on the chemical and physical characteristics of the hydration mechanism in obsidian were taken up by researchers at the University of California, Los Angeles, and more recently again by Friedman and Long (1976). The impetus for the UCLA work was generated by surveys of the literature bearing on the chemistry of glasses. One geochemical review volume noted, for example, that on the basis of the relatively small corpus of data available on diffusion constants in glasses, one should *not* expect the standard diffusion law to apply to the diffusion of water into a glass because this process involves an autocatalytic process in which water is the reactant as well as a catalyst (Weyl and Marboe 1964:720).

Aiello (1969) studied four separate obsidian assemblages in which chemical variability was thought to exist as an important factor in explaining anomalies in hydration results. In the first example, obsidian cache materials were examined from a context which allowed the assumption that all samples were of essential contemporaneous manufacture, were exposed to similar postdepositional environments, and therefore should manifest similar obsidian hydration values. However, the 17-member group of artifacts could be grouped into two assemblages based on their hydration values, with a mean value of 4.7 ± .33 μm for the low hydrating group and 6.2 ± .22 μm for the high hydrating group. The low and high groups could be distinguished chemically on the basis of differential compositions of iron. A second sample series utilized 21 obsidian points from a single 20-cm excavation unit which could be grouped into two categories of 10 and 11 specimens, respectively, on the basis of a characteristic color differentiation, differential hydration determinations of 1.8 ± .19 μm and 4.7 ± .24 μm, and chemical variability in the aluminum and iron compositions correlated with the two groupings. In a third example, obsidian samples previously measured by Clark (1964) were studied, and, although contemporaneity was expected, there was a discontinuity in the obsidian values obtained. Samples whose chemical composition was found to be essentially similar yielded hydration readings that were statistically similar. In contrast, a sample from the higher hydrating group could be differentiated in terms of all eight of the chemical components assayed.

In the same study, Aiello investigated the hydrating properties of a glassy species of fused shale. He observed what he believes to be two different rates of hydration operating within a *single* specimen. Hydration values differing by more than 1 μm were obtained from two different portions on the same artifact—segments clearly identified both on the basis of zoned differential color and on the basis of correlated differences in the aluminum, iron, and titanium concentrations in the two zones. While there is some danger in basing even tentative conclusions on a 1-μm amount of variability and in extrapolating this occurrence back to obsidian, the hydration mechanisms of fused shale and obsidian are probably essentially similar.

Using relatively well-dated (by associated radiocarbon determinations) obsidian samples from California and West Mexico, Kimberlin (1971) has suggested that the determination of a hydration rate will be valid only for a group of chemically homogeneous samples. In his study, a suite of obsidian artifacts grouped in terms of their trace-element chemistry and intrinsic water content, hydrated following the expression $x^3 = kt$, or $x = kt^{.33}$.

The most comprehensive evaluation of the presently understood chemical and physical characteristics of high alumina glasses (of which obsidian is one) in terms of their implications for obsidian hydration dating is being conducted by Ericson (Ericson 1975; Ericson and Berger 1976). His review of the relevant literature and his own experimental determinations have led him to conclude, both on theoretical grounds and as a result of a growing body of empirical evidence, that the concept that the hydration process in obsidian is solely a simple diffusion phenomenon can no longer be supported. Following Weyl and Marboe, he argues that "water" diffusion in obsidian is an autocatalytic process, with both diffusional and variable reaction characteristics dependent upon the internal structure and the initial and saturation concentrations of all the diffusing "water" species. He has isolated a set of physical and chemical factors relating to the structural characteristics of obsidian which he believes may have a systematic effect on the "water" diffusion rate, this is, hydration. Differential amounts of alumina (Al_2O_3) and alkali (Na_2O, K_2O), the silicon–oxygen ratios, and the specific volume of the obsidian are being used to study the bonding characteristics of the initial water as well as the reaction energies of different "water" species present in the obsidian in terms of free or bound hydroxyl groups.

Despite the broadened understanding of the complexities of the hydration process, as yet no comprehensive model that would allow a straightforward "correction" of obsidian hydration values as a function of physical and chemical constants is available. In the interim, the overwhelming weight of the evidence suggests that obsidians from separate geographic source localities which exhibit unique chemical characteristics such as that monitored by trace-element analysis, can hydrate at different rates, and, because of this, obsidian hydration rates must be considered source-specific. Two considerations follow from this observation: (*a*) source-specific hydration rates must be determined for individual obsidian sources in a given macroclimatic region, and (*b*) the source of each obsidian sample must be identified by appropriate trace element analysis, that is, "chemical fingerprinting." It is clear that the generalization of the hydration rate phenomenon for all obsidians even within a single macroclimatic–geographic zone is no longer appropriate and is probably a principal factor involved in the widely noted discordant results with which obsidian hydration dating has been plagued since its inception.

IV. EXPERIMENTAL METHODS

A. Amino Acid Dating

The question of the antiquity of *Homo sapiens* in the New World was one of the earliest "dating" questions of concern to students of American archaeology, and it continues to elicit highly contrasting opinions. In the early 1960s, radiocarbon values had been used to establish a temporal framework for man in the New World at least as early as the millennium between about 10,000 and 9000 B.C. In the early 1970s, collagen radiocarbon values on Paleo-Indian skeletal materials from California had adjusted the upper limit into the 20,000–25,000 radiocarbon years range (Berger *et al.* 1971). However, questions concerning the integrity of some samples, and problems associated with "contamination" of some of the bone collagen values, continued to be voiced. The need to develop an independent dating method on bone samples which could be compared with radiocarbon values and extend the dating range beyond the approximately 50,000-year range of ^{14}C was indicated.

The development of such a method had been under way for over 20 years by various workers, notably Abelson (1954), Hare (1962), and others of the Geophysical Laboratory of the Carnegie Institution of Washington and, more recently, by Bada and his collaborators at the University of California, San Diego. These researchers have been involved in studies concerned with temporal changes in the amino acid content of fossiliferous material as part of a broader inquiry into the geochemistry of amino acids. Such studies have generated suggestions concerning the utilization of changing ratios of certain amino acids and racemization (or epimerization) mechanisms to provide a chronometric methodology that may have the potential to provide temporal ordering for organic materials (e.g., bones, teeth, shell) for a portion of the Pleistocene beyond the range of radiocarbon potentially extending to several hundred thousand years, and to date bone and shell samples in the ^{14}C range that contain insufficient organics for a suitable radiocarbon analysis.

The foci of these investigations have variously combined basic geochemical and oceanographic interests (Bada 1972a; Bada and Schroeder 1972; Bada *et al.* 1970; Hare 1965, 1967, 1969, 1971; Hare and Abelson 1964, 1968; Hare and Mitterer 1967, 1969; Kvenvolden *et al.* 1970; Wehmiller and Hare 1971), as well as geochronometric–archaeochronometric interests (Bada 1972b; Bada and Helfman 1975; Bada and Protsch 1973; Bada *et al.* 1973b, 1974a,b; Hare 1974; Turekian and Bada 1972). Since the reaction rates are of a chemical nature, they are inherently extremely temperature sensitive, and amino acid studies on terrestrial and oceanic materials have also been applied to geothermometric questions (Bada *et al.* 1973a; Schroeder and Bada 1973).

Changes in the relative proportions over time of two or more of the approximately 20 amino acids commonly found as hydrolysis products of proteins, as a function of their differential thermal stability, were suggested initially as one mechanism that could be used to provide a chronometric indicator for bone, shell, and teeth materials. Hare's (1962) preliminary work bearing on the feasibility of this approach was applied to a series of radiocarbon-dated fossil shells of *Mytilus californianus* (from archaeological sites primarily located along the Southern California and Baja California coast) ranging from 400 to greater than 34,000 radiocarbon years B.P. Some differences could be detected in the 400-year-old shell as compared to recent shell material, and there was a positive correlation in the changing ratios of certain amino acids with time.

By studying the rates of amino acid reactions in the shell matrix at higher temperatures under laboratory conditions (Hare and Mitterer 1969), it was possible to extrapolate these rates to ambient temperatures and provide a means of determining the age and/or temperature of a particular fossil sample. Each amino acid has its own characteristic reaction rates (for decomposition, oxidation, racemization, etc.). As these rates are each independent functions of temperature, it is in theory possible to determine the age as well as the temperature history of a sample.

The utilization of the racemization process (or epimerization in the case of isoleucine) derives from a property of most amino acids that have two optical isomers designated as D and L enantiomers. Only L-amino acids are normally found in living organic systems. However, after death, the L form changes into the D form until an equilibrium condition is reached in which a racemic composition (i.e., containing equal amounts of the D and L enantiomers) is present. The work of Bada and his collaborators has provided the most extensive corpus of amino acid values to date utilizing predominantly the racemization reactions of isoleucine and aspartic acid.

The approach of Bada in dating fossil bone materials has been to eliminate the problem of evaluating average temperature conditions by using a "calibration" procedure in which the intrinsic rate of amino acid racemization for a particular site is determined by measuring the extent of racemization in a radiocarbon dated sample. After such a "calibration" step has been performed, other bone samples from the site or area can be dated using the calibrated racemization rate (Bada and Protsch 1972).

Bada has analyzed the aspartic acid racemization values for a series of Paleo-Indian skeletons from Southern and Central California (Bada and Helfman 1975). Ages ranging from ca. 27,000–48,000 year B.P. have been obtained on human bone samples from near San Diego, California (Del Mar,

Scripps, Batiquitos Lagoon) and a 70,000 year B.P. value has been reported on a sample from near San Jose, California (Sunnyvale Skeleton). Clearly such values, if subsequently supported by additional work, will require a reappraisal of widely held views concerning the antiquity of man in the New World.

Hare (1974) has questioned some of the assumptions under which Bada's values have been obtained. He calls attention to the potential variability in racemization rates brought about by differential amounts of leaching by groundwaters and argues that free amino acids are more racemized than the intact protein "so that leaching selectively leaves the protein-bound amino acids that are less racemized in the bone and carries away the more highly racemized free amino acids out of the bone into the groundwater and soil [1974:5]." He suggests that some published amino dates are off by an order of magnitude (Hare *et al.* 1974). Bada *et al.* (1974b) argue that concordance between collagen-based radiocarbon and aspartic acid racemization values mitigate against this possibility. The outcome of this dialogue will certainly be followed with interest by students of New World prehistory.

B. Fluorine Diffusion Dating

In most prehistoric New World societies, stone constituted a principal raw material from which artifacts were fabricated. Unfortunately this ubiquitous category of cultural materials has lacked a comprehensive direct physical dating method. The term *patination* has been used as a label to describe a spectrum of macrochemical and physical effects observed on various types of lithic samples. A number of efforts have been made to use the various surface alteration effects as temporal markers, but there has been a notable lack of success except under very specialized situations (Goodwin 1960, Hurst and Kelly 1961). It has been determined that there are a large number of causal agents and variable rates involved in cortical decomposition. Chemical and physical differences between and among samples and sample suites as well as unique environmental variables can combine to create a highly complex system in which time may not, in a majority of cases, be the most significant variable.

As we have noted, the hydration phenomenon in obsidian can be employed as a chronometric method of some utility. However, on a worldwide basis, the type of obsidian typically suitable for artifact manufacture is a relatively sparsely distributed resource. Once the, as yet unresolved, questions concerning obsidian hydration rate structures are resolved, the technique promises to provide very precise chronologies for those few regions (e.g., California and Mesoamerica) where obsidian was widely used. However, as an outgrowth of obsidian hydration studies, research has begun on a newly discovered fluorine diffusion phenomenon observed to occur in a wide spectrum of rock types (Taylor 1975). Like obsidian hydration, the dating potentiality of this method follows from the fact that a new surface would be created as a result of the chipping process used in the manufacture of an artifact. With the exposure of such a surface, fluorine in ionic form would begin to diffuse into the rock matrix with a rate structure somewhat analogous to that found in obsidian.

Fluorine is widely distributed in nature, dissolved in groundwater, but until the physiological effects of fluorine, especially in dental health, were recognized in the early and middle 1930s, fluorine determinations were not generally performed in water analysis. Since then, it has been determined that fluoride concentrations in natural groundwaters range from traces below detectable limits, that is $<.1$ parts per million (ppm), up to a reported maximum concentration of 67 ppm in South Africa, although water having concentrations of 10 ppm are rare and surface water seldom contains more than 1 ppm. Since it has been suggested that endemic cumulative fluorosis involving both dental (e.g., mottled teeth) and skeletal pathologies would appear in regions where fluoride concentrations consistently exceeded 20 ppm over a period extending beyond a few years, one can initially assume that unless such pathologies are reported in archaeologically derived skeletal populations, the average natural fluorine concentrations did not exceed ca. 20 ppm. In the United States, fluorine concentrations measured between 1948 and 1952 from well and spring water sources, ranged as high as 3.8 ppm in a South Carolina locality and 3.6 ppm in Wisconsin. However, the average values from the United States as a whole ranged from .1 to 1 ppm (Lohr and Love 1954a,b).

Investigation of the potential of using fluorine diffusion as a method for dating chipped lithic samples has been made possible by the use of a proton-induced nuclear resonant reaction, which allows diffusion measurements to be performed on a quantitative basis with an apparent accuracy of ca. .1–.2 μm and a resolution of ca. $\pm$ .05 μm (Taylor *et al.* n.d.). To date, about 40 fluorine diffusion profiles have been measured and identified in a broad spectrum of petrographic types, including igneous, sedimentary, and metamorphic samples.

The first suite of samples on which a completed set of measurements have been performed are associated with a radiocarbon-dated series of lithic complexes from the San Diego area of Southern California and, in order of age, were derived from the Diegueño (ca. A.D. 1000), La Jolla (3000–4000 B.C), and San Dieguito (5000–7000 B.C.) assemblages. A single sample from another San Diego locality (Bucannon Canyon) was examined to determine its relative age in relationship to the better-known sequence, since it has been suggested that the Bucannon Canyon materials were of significant antiquity (Middle Pleistocene?), far older than the San Dieguito materials. Figure 1.4 represents the results of the diffusion measurements plotted against the estimated age of the samples. A positive lineal relationship between the archaeologically estimated age and the fluorine diffusion values

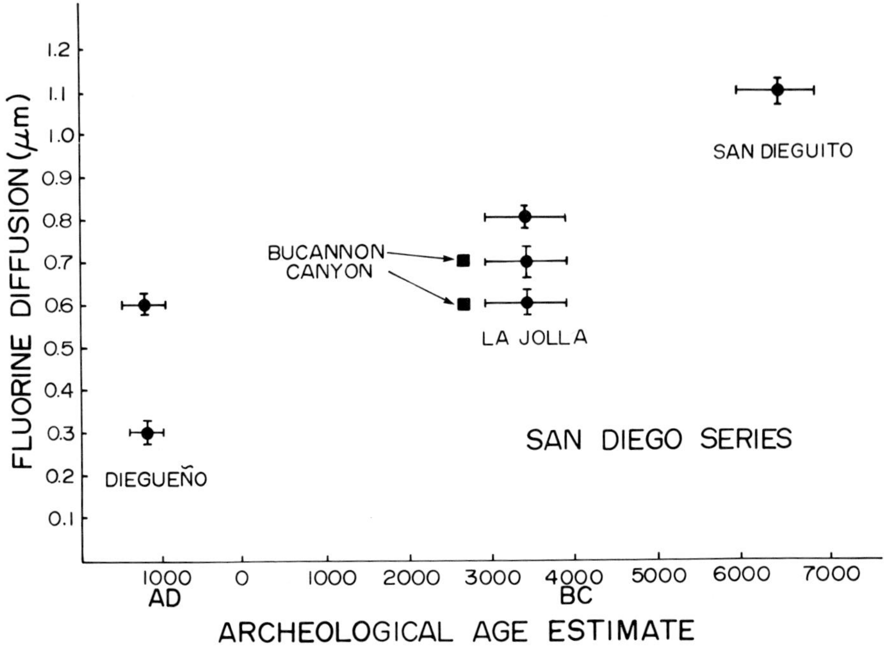

Figure 1.4. San Diego series fluorine diffusion values compared with archaeological age estimate of Diegueño, La Jolla and San Dieguito complexes. See Taylor (1975) and Taylor *et al.* (n.d.).

for the time period is indicated. A number of important questions involving the general applicability of the technique await further study, but even at this incipient stage of development the method can provide significant temporal insights not available from any other method. For example, the suggestion that the Bucannon Canyon sample should date to the Pleistocene does not seem to be supported in the case of this particular sample. Based on the fluorine diffusion data as presently available, the Bucannon Canyon sample seems to be associated in time with the La Jolla materials tested.

In the coming years, as additional studies are undertaken, we can look forward to the exciting prospect of having the ability to provide temporal controls directly on a wide spectrum of lithic artifact forms over the whole time range of hominid tool-making activity.

V. CONCLUSION

In American archaeology, the decade beginning about 1960 witnessed what some have labeled a "revolutionary" shift in theoretical perspectives on the part of a number of archaeologists (Adams 1968; Binford 1968, 1972; Binford and Binford 1968; Fitting 1973; Flannery 1967; Watson *et al.* 1971). The origins of the so-called "new archaeology," its long-range implications and ultimate significance will most certainly continue to be evaluated at some length. However, whatever the outcome of the dialogue, one would hope that at least a footnote will be allocated to what certainly was a significant factor involved in the reordered research priorities among students of New World prehistory. This is the ability independently to assign specific temporal frameworks to archaeological materials by the use of geophysical or geochemical techniques. The operation and validity of such techniques rest on assumptions and mechanisms completely removed from materials and phenomena normally studied by the archaeologist. This means that the analysis of cultural materials directly to derive chronology (e.g., seriation of ceramics) no longer merited the high priority that it had, heretofore of necessity, demanded. While other factors may be considered more critical in their immediate impact on theoretical archaeology over the last 15 years, the ability to establish temporal placement independently of the archaeologically derived cultural materials themselves can be looked upon as one supporting pillar in the foundation upon which more recent theoretical shifts in American prehistoric studies were developed.

Certainly, the establishment of chronological structures for archaeological materials is not an end in itself. Man in his few million years sojourn on this planet and few tens of thousands of years occupation of the Western Hemisphere has left, encoded in the organization of his physical remains, direct evidence of his evolving behavior patterns. For practically all of that time, it is the *only* direct evidence. Explaining why that development took the course that it did, presupposes an understanding of the rates of evolutionary change in that behavior. All archaeological studies, whether concerned with culture historic, processual, or strictly chronological issues, have as their ultimate goal a more complete and comprehensive understanding of what it was that made *Homo sapiens* the way he is.

BIBLIOGRAPHY

Abelson, P. H.
1954 Amino Acids in Fossils. *Science* **119:**576.
Adams, R. McC.
1968 Archeological Research Strategies: Past and Present. *Science* **160:**1187–1192.
Aiello, P. V.
1969 The Chemical Composition of Rhyolitic Obsidian and Its Effect on Hydration: Some Archaeological Evidence. Unpublished master's thesis, University of California, Los Angeles.
Allibone, T. E., and M. Wheeler (Editors)
1971 The Impact of Natural Sciences on Archaeology. *Philosophical Transactions of the Royal Society of London* **269:**1–185.

Arnold, J. R., and W. F. Libby

1949 Age Determinations by Radiocarbon Content: Checks with Samples of Known Age. *Science* **110**:678–680.

Bada, J. L.

1971 Kinetics of the Nonbiological Decomposition and Racemization of Amino Acid in Natural Waters. In *Non-equilibrium Systems in Natural Water Chemistry, Advances in Chemistry Series* **106**:309–331, Washington, D.C.: American Chemical Society.

1972a Kinetics of Racemization of Amino Acids as a Function of pH. *Journal of the American Chemical Society* **94**:1371–1373.

1972b The Dating of Fossil Bones Using the Racemization of Isoleucine. *Earth and Planetary Science Letters* **15**:223–231.

Bada, J. L. and P. M. Helfman

1975 Amino Acid Racemization Dating of Fossil Bones. *World Archaeology* **7**:160–173.

Bada, J. L., K. A. Kvenvolden, and E. Peterson

1973b Racemization of Amino Acids in Bones. *Nature* **245**:309–310.

Bada, J. L., B. P. Luyendyk, and J. B. Maynard

1970 Marine Sediments: Dating by the Racemization of Amino Acids. *Science* **170**:730–732.

Bada, J. L., and R. Protsch

1973 Racemization Reacting of Aspartic Acid and Its Use in Dating Fossil Bones. *Proceedings of the National Academy of Sciences* **70**:1131–1134.

Bada, J. L., R. Protsch, and R. A. Schroeder

1973a The Racemization Reaction of Isoleucine Used as a Paleotemperature Indicator. *Nature* **241**:394.

Bada, J. L., and R. A. Schroeder

1972 Racemization of Isoleucine in Calcereous Marine Sediments: Kinetics and Mechanism. *Earth and Planetary Science Letters* **15**:1–11.

Bada, J. L., R. A. Schroeder, and G. F. Carter

1974a New Evidence for the Antiquity of Man in North America Deduced from Aspartic Acid Racemization. *Science* **184**:791–793.

Bada, J. L., R. A. Schroeder, R. Protsch, and R. Berger

1974b Concordance of Collagen-Based Radiocarbon and Aspartic-Acid Racemization Ages. *Proceedings of the National Academy of Sciences* **71**:914–917.

Barbetti, M.

1973 Geomagnetic Field Behavior between 25,000 and 35,000 yr B.P. and Its Effect on Atmospheric Radiocarbon Concentration: A Current Report. In *Proceedings of the 8th International Conference on Radiocarbon Dating,* edited by T. A. Rafter and T. Grant-Taylor. Wellington, New Zealand: Royal Society.

Bender, M. M.

1968 Mass Spectrometric Studies of Carbon 13 Variations in Corn and Other Grasses. *Radiocarbon* **10**:468–472.

Berger, R.

1970a *Scientific Methods in Medieval Archaeology*. Los Angeles: University of California Press.

1970b The Potential and Limitations of Radiocarbon Dating in the Middle Ages: The Radiochronologist's View. In *Scientific Methods in Medieval Archaeology*, edited by R. Berger. Los Angeles: University of California Press.

Berger, R., R. Protsch, R. Reynolds, C. Rozaire, and J. R. Sackett

1971 New Radiocarbon Dates Based on Bone Collagen of California Paleoindians. *Contributions of the University of California Archaeological Research Facility* **12**:43–49.

Berger, R., and H Suess (Ed.).

n.d. *Advances in Radiocarbon Dating. Proceedings of the IX International Radiocarbon Conference*, June 20–26, 1976. Los Angeles and San Diego, California. In press.

Binford, L. R.
1968 Some Comments on Historical Versus Processual Archaeology. *Southwestern Journal of Anthropology* **24**:267–275.
1972 The New Archaeology—an American Archaeologist, Lewis Binford Gives His Opinion. *The Listener* (London) **87**:174–176.
Binford, L. R., and S. R. Binford (Editors)
1968 *New Perspectives in Archaeology*. Chicago: Aldine.
Bishop, W. W., and J. A. Miller (Editors)
1972 *Calibration of Hominoid Evolution*. Edinburgh: Scottish Academic Press.
Bliss, W. L.
1952 Radiocarbon Contamination. *American Antiquity* **17**:250–251.
Brill, R. H. (Editor)
1971 *Science and Archaeology*. Cambridge, Massachusetts: MIT Press.
Brothwell, D., and E. Higgs (Editors)
1969 *Science in Archaeology*. 2nd ed. London: Thames and Hudson.
Bucha, V.
1967 Archaeomagnetic and Paleomagnetic Study of the Magnetic Field of the Earth in the Past 600,000 Years. *Nature* **213**:1005–1007.
1969 Changes of the Earth's Magnetic Moment and Radiocarbon Dating. *Nature* **224**:681–683.
Bucha, V., and E. Neustuply
1967 Changes of the Earth's Magnetic Field and Radiocarbon Dating. *Nature* **215**:261–263.
Chatters, R. M., J. W. Crosby III, and L. G. Engstrand
1969 Fumarole Gaseous Emanations: Their Influence on Carbon-14 Dates. Washington State University, College of Engineering, *Research Division Circular* **32**:1–8.
Clark, D. L.
1964 Archaeological Chronology in California and the Obsidian Hydration Method: Part 1. *Archaeological Survey Annual Report,* University of California, Los Angeles **6**:141–209.
Damon, P. E., A. Long, and A. C. Gray
1966 Flunctuation of Atmospheric C14 Dating the Last Six Millennia. *Journal of Geophysical Research* **71**:1055–1063.
1970 Arizona Radiocarbon Dates for Dendrochronologically Dated Samples. In *Radiocarbon Variations and Absolute Chronology,* edited by I. U. Olsson. Stockholm: Almqvist and Wiksell.
Damon, P. E., A. Long, and E. I. Wallick
1973 Dendrochronologic Calibration of the Carbon-14 Time Scale. In *Proceedings of the 8th International Conference on Radiocarbon Dating*, edited by T. A. Rafter and T. Grant-Taylor. Wellington, New Zealand: Royal Society.
Daniel, G.
1967 The Origins and Growth of Archaeology. New York: Crowell.
Elsasser, W. E., P. Ney, and J. R. Winckler
1956 Cosmic-Ray Intensity and Geomagneticism. *Nature* **178**:1226–1227.
Ericson, J. E.
1975 New Results in Obsidian Hydration Dating. *World Archaeology* **7**:151–159.
Ericson, J. E., and R. Berger
1976 Physics and Chemistry of the Hydration Process in Obsidian II: Operational Implications. In *Advances in Obsidian Glass Studies: Archaeological and Geochemical Perspectives*, edited by R. E. Taylor. Park Ridge, New Jersey: Noyes Press. Pp. 46–62.
Farmer, J. G., and M. S. Baxter
1973 Short-Term Trends in Natural Radiocarbon. In *Proceedings of the 8th International*

Conference on Radiocarbon Dating, edited by T. A. Rafter and T. Grant-Taylor, Wellington, New Zealand: Royal Society.

Ferguson, C. W.
1970 Concepts and Techniques of Dendrochronology. In *Scientific Methods in Medieval Archaeology*, edited by R. Berger. Los Angeles: University of California Press.
1973 Dendrochronology of Bristlecone Pine Prior to 4000 B.C. In *Proceedings of the 8th International Conference on Radiocarbon Dating*, edited by T. A. Rafter and T. Grant-Taylor. Wellington, New Zealand: Royal Society.

Fitting, J. E.
1973 History and Crisis in Archaeology. In *The Development of North American Archaeology,* edited by J. E. Fitting. New York: Anchor Press.

Flannery, K. V.
1967 Culture History Versus Culture Process: A Debate in American Archaeology. *Scientific American* **217:**119–122.

Fleming, S.
1976 Dating in Archaeology: A Guide to Scientific Techniques. New York: St. Martin's Press.

Friedman, I., and C. Evans
1968 Obsidian Dating Revisited. *Science* **162:**813–814.

Friedman, I. L., and W. Long
1976 Hydration Rate of Obsidian. *Science* **191:**347–352.

Friedman, I. L., and R. L. Smith
1958 The Hydration of Obsidian Artifacts. *Transactions of the American Geophysical Union* **39:**515.
1960 A New Dating Method Using Obsidian. *American Antiquity* **25:**476–522.

Friedman, I. L., R. L. Smith, and W. Long
1966 Hydration of Natural Glass and Formation of Perlite. *Geological Society of America Bulletin* **77:**323–328.

Goodwin, A. J.
1960 Chemical Alteration (Patination) of Stone. In *The Application of Quantitative Methods in Archaeology*, edited by R. F. Heizer and S. F. Cook. New York: Viking Fund Publications.

Grootes, P. M., W. G. Mook, J. C. Vogel, A. E. deVries, A. Haring, and J. Kistmaker
1975 Enrichment of Radiocarbon for Dating Samples Up to 75,000 Years. *Zeitschrift Naturforsch* **30a:**1–14.

Hare, P. E.
1962 The Amino Acid Composition of the Organic Matrix of Some Recent Shells of Some West Coast Species of Mytilus. Unpublished doctoral dissertation, California Institute of Technology, Pasadena, California.
1965 Amino Acid Artifacts in Organic Geochemistry. *Carnegie Institution of Washington Yearbook* **64:**232–235.
1967 Amino Acid Composition of the Extrapallial Fluid in Mollusks. *Carnegie Institution of Washington Yearbook* **65:**364–365.
1969 Geochemistry of Proteins, Peptides, and Amino Acids. In *Organic Geochemistry,* edited by G. Eglington and M. T. J. Murphy. New York: Springer-Verlag.
1971 Effects of Hydrolysis on the Racemization Rates of Amino Acids. *Carnegie Institution of Washington Yearbook* **70:**256–258.
1974 Amino Acid Dating—A History and an Evaluation. *Museum Applied Science Center for Archaeology Newsletter* **10:**4–7.

Hare, P. E., and P. H. Abelson
1964 Proteins in Mollusk Shells. *Carnegie Institution of Washington Yearbook* **63:**267–270.

1968 Racemization of Amino Acids in Fossil Shells. *Carnegie Institution of Washington Yearbook* **66:**526–528.

Hare, P. E., and R. M. Mitterer

1967 Nonprotein Amino Acids in Fossil Shells. *Carnegie Institution of Washington Yearbook* **65:**362–364.

1969 Laboratory Simulation of Amino Acid Diagenesis in Fossils. *Carnegie Institution of Washington Yearbook* **67:**205–208.

Hare, P. E., D. J. Ortner, D. W. Von Endt, and R. E. Taylor

1974 Amino Acid Dating of Bone and Teeth. *Geological Society of America Abstracts* **6:**778.

Hurst, V. J., and A. R. Kelley

1961 Patination of Cultural Flint. *Science* **134:**251–256.

Johnson, L.

1969 Obsidian Hydration Rate for the Klamath Basin of California and Oregon. *Science* **165:**1354–1356.

Katsui, Y., and Y. Kondo

1965 Dating Stone Implements by Using Hydration Layer of Obsidian. *Japanese Journal of Geology and Geography* **36:**45–60.

Kimberlin, J.

1971 Obsidian Chemistry and the Hydration Dating Technique. Unpublished master's thesis, University of California, Los Angeles.

Kvenvolden, K. A., E. Peterson, and F. S. Brown

1970 Racemization of Amino Acids in Sediments from Saanich Inlet, British Columbia. *Science* **169:**1079.

La Marche, V. C., and T. P. Harlan

1973 Accuracy of Tree Ring Dating of Bristlecone Pine for Calibration of Radiocarbon Time Scale. *Journal of Geophysical Research* **78:**8849–8858.

Libby, W. F.

1946 Atmospheric Helium Three and Radiocarbon from Cosmic Radiation. *Physical Review* **69:**671–672.

1955 *Radiocarbon Dating.* 2nd ed, Chicago: University of Chicago Press.

1963 Accuracy of Radiocarbon Dates. *Science* **140:**278–280.

1970 Ruminations on Radiocarbon Dating. In *Radiocarbon Variations and Absolute Chronology,* edited by I. U. Olsson. Stockholm: Almqvist and Wiksell.

1973 Radiocarbon Dating, Memories and Hopes. In *Proceedings of the 8th International Conference on Radiocarbon Dating,* edited by T. A. Rafter and T. Grant-Taylor. Wellington, New Zealand: Royal Society.

Libby, W. F., E. C. Anderson, and J. R. Arnold

1949 Age Determination by Radiocarbon Content: World-Wide Assay of Natural Radiocarbon. *Science* **109:**227–229.

Lohr, E. W., and S. K. Love

1954a The Industrial Utility of Public Water Supplies in the United States, 1952. Part 1. States East of the Mississippi River. *Geological Survey Water-Supply Paper* **1299:**1–639.

1954b The Industrial Utility of Public Water Supplies in the United States, 1952. Part 2. States West of the Mississippi River. *Geological Survey Water-Supply Paper* **1300:**1–462.

Meighan, C. W.

1956 Responsibilities of the Archeologist in Using the Radiocarbon Method. University of Utah, *Anthropological Papers* **26:**48–53.

1970 Obsidian Hydration Rates. *Science* **170:**99–100.

1974 Prehistory of West Mexico. *Science* **184:**1254–1261.

Meighan, C. W., L. J. Foote, and P. V. Aiello
1968a Obsidian Dating in West Mexican Archeology. *Science* **160:**1069–1075.
1968b Obsidian Dating Revisited. *Science* **162:**814.
Michael, H. N., and E. K. Ralph
1971 *Dating Techniques for the Archaeologist*. Cambridge, Massachusetts: MIT Press.
1973 Discussion of Radiocarbon Dates Obtained from Precisely Dated Sequoia and Bristlecone Pine Samples. In *Proceedings of the 8th International Conference on Radiocarbon Dating,* edited by T. A. Rafter and T. Grant-Taylor, Wellington, New Zealand: Royal Society.
Michels, J. W.
1967 Archaeology and Dating by Hydration of Obsidian. *Science* **158:**211–214.
1973 *Dating Methods in Archaeology*. New York: Seminar Press.
Munich, K. O.
1957 Heidelberg Natural Radiocarbon Measurements I. *Science* **126:**194–199.
Olson, E. A., and W. S. Broecker
1958 Sample Contamination and Reliability of Radiocarbon Dates. *Transactions of the New York Academy of Sciences* **20:**593–603.
Olsson, I. U.
1970 *Radiocarbon Variations and Absolute Chronology*. Stockholm: Almqvist and Wiksell.
Rafter, T. A., and T. Grant-Taylor (Editors)
1973 *Proceedings of the 8th International Radiocarbon Dating Conference*. Wellington, New Zealand: Royal Society.
Ralph, E. K., and H. N. Michael
1967 Problems of the Radiocarbon Calendar. *Archaeometry* **10:**3–11.
1970 MASCA Radiocarbon Dates for Sequoia and Bristlecone-Pine Samples. In *Radiocarbon Variations and Absolute Chronology,* edited by I. U. Olsson, Stockholm: Almqvist and Wiksell.
Ralph, E. K., H. N. Michael, and M. C. Hann
1973 Radiocarbon Dates and Reality. *Museum Applied Science Center for Archaeology Newsletter* **9:**1–19.
Ralph, E. K., and R. Stuckenrath, Jr.
1960 Carbon-14 Measurements on Samples of Known Age. *Nature* **183:**1582.
Ross, C. S., and R. L. Smith
1958 Water and Other Volatiles in Volcanic Glasses. *American Mineralogist* **40:**1071–1078.
Rubin, M., R. C. Likins, and E. G., Berry
1963 On the Validity of Radiocarbon Dates from Snail Shells. *Journal of Geology* **71:**84–89.
Schroeder, R. A., and J., L. Bada
1973 Glacial-Postglacial Temperature Differences Deduced from Aspartic Acid Racemization in Fossil Bones. *Science* **182:**479.
Smiley, T. L.
1955 The Geochronological Approach. In *Geochronology,* edited by T. L. Smiley. *University of Arizona Bulletin Series* **26:**15–28.
Spaulding, A. C.
1958 The Significance of Differences between Radiocarbon Dates. *American Antiquity* **23:**309–311.
Stuiver, M., and H. E. Suess
1966 On the Relationship between Radiocarbon Dates and True Sample Ages. *Radiocarbon* **8:**534–540.

Suess, H. E.
1965 Secular Variations of the Cosmic Produced Carbon 14 in the Atmosphere and Their Interpretation. *Journal of Geophysical Research* **70:**5937–5952.
1967 Bristlecone-Pine Calibration of the Radiocarbon Time Scale from 4100 B.C. to 1500 B.C. In *Radiocarbon Dating and Methods of Low Level Counting.* Vienna: International Atomic Energy Agency.
1970 Bristlecone-Pine Calibration of Radiocarbon Time Scale 5200 BC to the Present. In *Radiocarbon Variations and Absolute Chronology,* edited by I. U. Olsson. Stockholm: Almqvist and Wiksell.

Taylor, R. E.
1970 Chronological Problems in West Mexican Archaeology: An Application of a Dating System Approach in Archaeological Research. Unpublished doctoral dissertation, University of California, Los Angeles.
1975 Fluorine Diffusion: A New Dating Method for Chipped Lithic Materials. *World Archaeology* **7:**125–135.
1976 Science in Contemporary Archaeology. In *Advances in Obsidian Glass Studies: Archaeological and Geochemical Perspectives,* edited by R. E. Taylor. Park Ridge, New Jersey: Noyes Press. Pp. 1–21.

Taylor, R. E., R. Berger, C. W. Meighan, and H. B. Nicholson
1969 West Mexican Dates of Archaeological Significance. In *Occasional Papers of the Museum and Laboratories of Ethnic Arts and Technology* No. 1. University of California, Los Angeles.

Taylor, R. E., F. S. Spear, and B. Dunn
n.d. A Dating Method for Chipped Lithics Using Fluorine Diffusion Profiles. *Los Alamos Scientific Series*, in press.

Tite, M. S.
1972 *Methods of Physical Examination in Archaeology.* New York: Seminar Press.

Turekian, K. K., and J. L. Bada
1972 The Dating of Fossil Bones. In *Calibration of Hominoid Evolution,* edited by W. W. Bishop and J. A. Miller. Edinburgh: Scottish Academic Press.

de Vries, H.
1958 Variations in Concentrations of Radiocarbon with Time and Location on Earth. Koninklijke Nederlandse Akademie Van Wetenschappen, *Proceedings,* series B, **61:**94–102.

Watson, P. J., S. A. LeBlanc, and C. L. Redman
1971 Explanation in Archaeology: An Explicity Scientific Approach. New York: Columbia University Press.

Wehmiller, J., and P. E. Hare
1971 Racemization of Amino Acids in Marine Sediments. *Science* **173:**907–911.

Weyl, W. A., and E. R. Marboe
1964 *The Constitution of Glasses.* Vol. 2, part 1. New York: Interscience.

Willey, G. R., and J. A. Sabloff
1974 *A History of American Archaeology.* San Francisco: Freeman.

Willis, E. H., H. Tauber, and K. O. Munich
1960 Variations in Atmospheric Radiocarbon Concentration over the Past 1300 Years. *Radiocarbon* **2:**1–4.

Yang, A. I. C., and A. W. Fairhall
1973 Variations of Natural Radiocarbon During the Last 11 Millennia and Geophysical Mechanisms for Producing Them. *Proceedings of the 8th International Conference on Radiocarbon Dating,* edited by T. A. Rafter and T. Grant-Taylor. Wellington, New Zealand: Royal Society.

Western Arctic and Sub-Arctic

DOUGLAS D. ANDERSON

I. INTRODUCTION

The Western Arctic and sub-Arctic regions of North America are the homelands of the Western Eskimos, Aleuts, and Northwestern Athapaskan Indians. Comprising the Upper Yukon and Lower Mackenzie River areas of Canada and nearly all of Alaska, these regions may be divided into four major zones: the Arctic Coast, the Arctic Interior, the sub-Arctic, and the Aleutian–Pacific Coast (Figure 2.1). The Arctic Coast, inhabited by Eskimos, includes all of treeless coastal lands from the mouth of the Mackenzie River to Bristol Bay, Alaska, and the islands in the Bering Sea. The Interior Arctic, inhabited mainly by Eskimos, includes the treeless tundra region of northwestern Alaska and Seward Peninsula, and also the northernmost woodland region in Alaska. The sub-Arctic includes all the interior lands drained by the Yukon, Kuskokwim, and lower part of the Mackenzie, and the numerous other rivers flowing to the Bering, Chukchi, and Beaufort

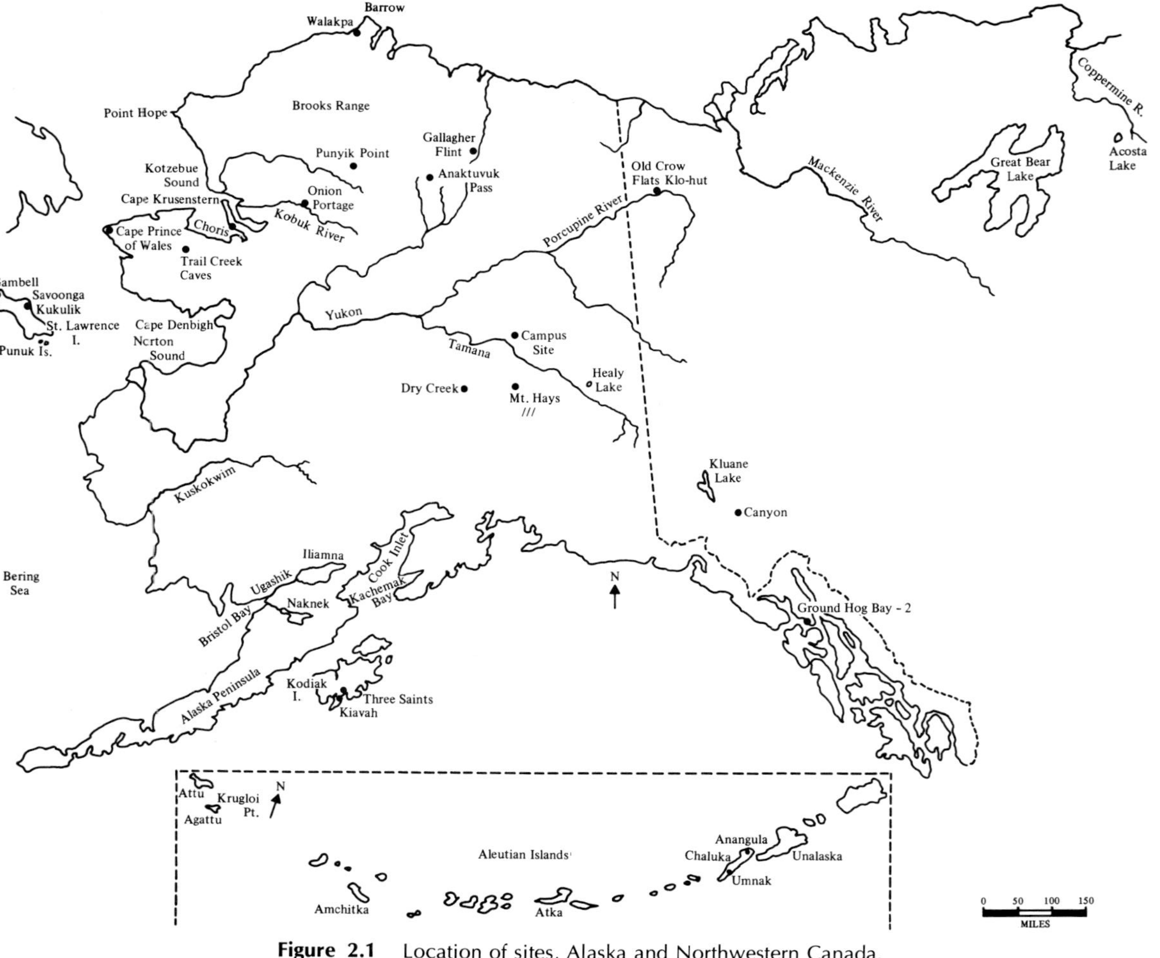

Figure 2.1 Location of sites, Alaska and Northwestern Canada.

seas, a vast area occupied mainly by diverse groups of Athapaskans. The Aleutian–Pacific Coast zone includes the Aleutian Islands, the Alaska Peninsula, and the areas around Cook Inlet, areas inhabited by Aleuts, Eskimos, and Tanaina Athapaskans.

II. DEVELOPMENT OF CHRONOLOGY

Before radiocarbon dating, Northern archaeologists were only rarely able to assign absolute ages to sites. These rare occasions were through the chance finding of decorated objects in styles related to art styles of historic periods in Asia or Europe, and to the development of tree-ring dated sequences. Outside the major pottery-making areas of North America, most of the North could not even anticipate the establishment of sequences by the elsewhere successful methods of pottery seriation. Nevertheless, by 1950 the outline of Arctic prehistory of the last two millennia was relatively complete. The sequences were based primarily on the results of midden excavations along the coasts of mainland Alaska, St. Lawrence, and other Bering Sea islands, and the Aleutian Islands (Figure 2.1). In the Interior Arctic and sub-Arctic, few sites of any sort had been located, and chronologies were not seriously attempted for any of these vast regions.

A. Aleutians and Pacific Coast

Among the earliest chronologies proposed for the Western Arctic or sub-Arctic was that for the Aleutian Islands. Midden excavations on Attu, Atka, Amaknak, Amchitka, and other islands by W. H. Dall evidenced three periods of occupation (1877). According to Dall, the earliest period, the littoral, represented a very primitive sea urchin–shellfish collecting people who populated the islands from the east about 3000 years ago. These people supposedly did not use fire for cooking or heating, wore few clothes except possibly some plaited grass garments, and lived in crude houses made of perishable materials such as grass matting. Dall likened their way of life to that of the nineteenth-century Tierra del Fuegians, who inhabited a similar environment on the southern tip of South America (Dall 1877:50–56). Based on his calculations on the rate of midden accumulation, Dall believed that these people occupied the islands for over 1000 years. Dall's next period, the fishing period, supposedly began about 2000 years ago, when a new group of people entered the island chain from the east. Bringing with them a knowledge of fishing with seine nets, these people subsisted on salmon, cod, and other fish, in addition to molluscs. After several centuries, these people developed skills and a technology that enabled them to hunt sea lions, fur seals, and later, whales. This last period was called the hunting period.

Excavating on Attu, Atka, and Amaknak islands 30 years after Dall, Jochelson found no evidence of a littoral period in any of his midden excavations (1925:101–125). He concluded that Dall may have mistaken natural alluvial accumulations of fragmented water-worn sea urchin spines for midden debris. Jochelson further concluded that a single Aleut population was responsible for all of the cultural remains in the middens and that these Aleuts had been on the islands a very long time. He agreed with Dall that the Aleutian Islands had been populated from the Alaskan mainland.

Hrdlicka's excavations in the 1930s at first supported Jochelson's findings that the cultural changes in the Aleutian sequence were gradual and uninterrupted (1932:44, 1935:50–52), but with more work and analysis, he concluded that there had been in fact two different cultural periods. On the basis of his physical anthropological research, Hrdlicka postulated the succession of two populations in the islands, the earlier an oblong-headed pre-Aleut (Indian) and later a round-headed Aleut population. His view of a population replacement in the Aleutians is now in doubt—the changes in physical type are seen to be due more to an indigenous development, rather than to the introduction of a new population.

The Pacific Coast was one of the most thoroughly studied areas of the Western Arctic and sub-Arctic before the age of radiocarbon dating, owing to the work of de Laguna in Cook Inlet. She discovered that the prehistoric coastal culture, particularly around Kachemak Bay, was a "fairly generalized type of Eskimo culture, which itself included a number of elements common to the Arctic and North Pacific areas (1934:217)," yet it maintained a distinctiveness throughout its development (1934:131). In Kachemak Period I, the culture had a relatively simple cast that shared many features with Eskimo culture to the north. Over time, Kachemak Bay culture (II and III) developed an increasingly specialized and locally suitable complex of tools, particularly by incorporating Indian elements from further south along the coast.

B. Arctic Coast

The first reliable sequence of early Northwestern Eskimo cultures was obtained from midden excavations on St. Lawrence Island and other western Alaskan islands by Geist, Rainey, and Collins in the late 1920s and the 1930s. Spurred particularly by the suggestion of Diamond Jenness (1928:78) that there had once been a distinct and highly developed Eskimo culture along the shores and islands of the Bering Sea, Collins initiated extensive excavations in the several village middens on St. Lawrence Island (1937:26–36). Old Bering Sea culture was finally isolated, after a 2-year search, in the Miyowagh Midden near Gambell village. By correlating art styles and harpoon head types between Miyowagh and several other middens of overlapping ages, Collins was able to document a three-period sequence for the development of Eskimos in the region: Old Bering Sea–Punuk–Recent Eskimos. Collins did not attempt to assign absolute ages to his sequence, but, owing to the presence of Asian-derived art styles and iron in Old Bering Sea, he suggested that cross ties might one day be made with early historic Oriental cultures (Collins 1932).

At the Kukulik middens of St. Lawrence Island, Geist and Rainey found the same general sequence as Collins, but again were unable to suggest absolute dates. They also found evidence of Birnirk, an early Eskimo culture previously isolated but undated at Barrow on mainland Alaska, at slightly below Punuk levels (1936:224–233). Collins later also located Birnirk-style artifacts at Cape Prince of Wales, and from the middens there he found clear evidence of the transition from Birnirk to Thule culture (1937:66). This discovery was particularly important in establishing the coastal chronology of Alaska because it showed that Thule did not simply develop from Old Bering Sea or early Punuk on St. Lawrence Island, but rather from an indigenous mainland Alaskan culture. Although to Collins this simply clarified his postulated developmental sequence of Eskimo culture from Old Bering Sea to Birnirk to Thule (1943:220–221), it suggested to others that a yet earlier mainland Alaskan Eskimo culture—one that could be ancestral to both Birnirk and Thule, yet different from Old Bering Sea—was to be found on the Alaskan mainland. The existence of this "Proto-Thule" culture had been postulated by de Laguna from her work in Cook Inlet, where Kachemak Bay Period I Eskimo-like traits were all rather undeveloped relative to Old Bering Sea and were what might reasonably be expected from an ancestral Eskimo culture (de Laguna 1934:217–220).

The discoveries of Ipiutak and Near Ipiutak cultures in 1939 at Point Hope upset the picture of a unilineal development of Eskimo culture on mainland Alaska. In that year, Helge Larsen, Froelich Rainey, and J. L. Giddings discovered Ipiutak, a highly developed Arctic culture with Oriental-influenced art styles (Larsen and Rainey 1948) that was largely contemporaneous with Old Bering Sea culture, a correlation indicated by the presence of Old Bering Sea style art elements. By correspondences between Ipiutak and Oriental art work, an absolute age of the first and second century A.D. was indicated, a suggestion later confirmed by radiocarbon assays. Ipiutak economy was based on the taking of sea mammals, except whales, and caribou—a pattern that brought to mind a theory of Eskimo origins presented by H. P. Steensby some 30 years earlier. According to Steensby (1916), Eskimo culture had progressed through two stages of development. During the earlier Paleo-Eskimo stage, people (who originally possessed a Northern Indian form of culture) developed an adaptation to hunting sea mammals from the winter ice-covered Arctic Ocean, a development that was seen to take place along the coasts of the Arctic Archipelago and the areas west of Hudson Bay. With the ability to live along the coasts in winter and in the interior in summer, these Paleo-Eskimos spread out across the entire American Arctic. During the second stage—the Neo-Eskimo—those who reached Alaska learned how to live year round on the coast and, from the North Pacific Asians (Ainus, Kamchadals, Coast Koryaks, and Coast Chukchi), how to hunt whales. The realization in the 1940s that Ipiutakers did not hunt whales and had an economy more oriented to land hunting than to sea hunting, in contrast to the St. Lawrence Islanders who did hunt whales and exhibited evidence of influence from Asia (e.g., pottery making), seemed to be a clear archaeological demonstration of Steensby's views—whereas Old Bering Sea was Neo-Eskimo like, Ipiutak was Paleo-Eskimo. Further supporting these conclusions was the presence of Near Ipiutak at Point Hope, a culture that had many Ipiutak, or Paleo-Eskimo features and also many Neo-Eskimo features, such as the use of slate and pottery and techniques for hunting whales. Near Ipiutak fit logically between Ipiutak and Birnirk. Later, however, it was learned that Near Ipiutak actually preceded Ipiutak in time, a fact that eliminated it from consideration as a transitional Neo-Eskimo culture. At the present, the distinction between Paleo-Eskimo and Neo-Eskimo remains useful in describing two different economic orientations of prehistoric Arctic Eskimos, but it no longer holds valid as a description of how Eskimo culture in fact developed.

It was not until Rainey's skillful analysis of Okvik culture from the Punuk Islands in 1940 that a dated sequence was proposed for the entire Eskimo culture area (1941:564–565). The sequence was divided into two major periods of Arctic coastal culture, an early period of local development in the Bering Strait between 100 B.C. and A.D. 1000, and a later period of Eskimo expansion after A.D. 1000. Rainey also listed the three cultures, Ipiutak, Dorset (an early Eastern Arctic culture), and modern Central Eskimo, as different from the basic Arctic coastal cultures. He felt that Ipiutak (and presumably Dorset) represented survivals of an earlier Eskimo form of culture. Although the earliest stage (Okvik–Old Bering Sea I) is now seen to be slightly younger than Rainey concluded, his chronology was remarkably accurate.

The first absolute dates for the Arctic came from Giddings's 970-year-long tree-ring dated sequence along the Kobuk River, Alaska (1944; 1952:3). Giddings provided a chronology spanning five periods of cultural development, the earliest of which dated to A.D. 1250. Through cross ties with harpoon and art styles, this sequence also provided the first reliable dates for early Punuk and Thule culture. Because radiocarbon dating emerged such a short time later, tree-ring dating in the Arctic has since Giddings's pioneering work, had only a limited application (Hickey 1968:63–66; Oswalt 1954:203–214; Van Stone 1955:126–129).

Western Arctic archaeology came to a halt duing the war years, and, except for Larsen and Rainey's analysis of Ipiutak, few new insights were achieved into chronological problems of the region at that time. Then, in 1948, Giddings discovered the stratified Iyatayet Site at Cape Denbigh on Norton Sound. In the lowest layer was a culture, estimated at the time to be between 6000 and 8000 years old, that was old enough to be ancestral to all Eskimo cultures, including Ipiutak (Giddings 1949). Containing microblades, burins, and other flaked implements, it also provided a link with Mesolithic–early Neolithic cultures of Asia (Larsen 1961:9). At present it is widely conceded that Denbigh is the earliest culture in the American Arctic that can be assigned to Eskimos. Above the Denbigh Flint Complex stratum was a thick layer of Near Ipiutak-like culture, called Norton, and on top of this were three layers of Thule culture. Norton culture has now been found over much of coastal Alaska.

C. Interior Arctic and Sub-Arctic

From the interior of Alaska, isolated finds of Paleo-Indian projectile points (Yuma-like) have been reported since the 1930s. Several points had been obtained from gold-dredging operations around Fairbanks (Rainey 1939, 1940; Hibbon 1943), but none from stratigraphic contexts. In the late 1940s even some fluted Clovis- or Folsom-like points were recovered from the Brooks Range (Solecki 1951; Thompson 1948), and although also from undatable contexts, they were viewed as perhaps representing a stopover in the trail of earliest man from Asia into the New World.

More direct links between Asia and America were found at the Campus Site, University of Alaska, where narrow, wedge-shaped microblade cores like those from Central Asia appeared (Nelson 1937). Although regarded as pre-Neolithic or Neolithic age in Asia, this microblade core type in Alaska was also found in apparent association with recent Athapaskan culture (Rainey 1939:388–389). It was not until the discovery of the Denbigh Flint Complex that microblades were demonstrably also very early in the American Arctic.

The archaeology of deep interior Alaska and northwestern Canada developed as a result of building the Alcan Highway during World War II. Investigations along its route from 1944 onward revealed numerous shallow sites representing many different cultures (Johnson 1946; MacNeish 1964). But because the sites were so shallow, there was no opportunity to build any chronological sequences from the scattered finds.

Thus, even before radiocarbon dating, the relative chronology of maritime whale-hunting Eskimo cultures was documented for Alaska (as well as for Canada and Greenland), the long, gradual development of Aleut culture had been noted, and an absolute chronology of 700 years had been developed for the Kobuk River Woodlands. Dates were also suggested for other sites based on ties to Oriental cultures in the west (and to Norse cultures in the east). The presence of Paleo-Indian culture in the Arctic and sub-Arctic was also postulated, and the complexity of the archaeology of the western American sub-Arctic Interior was becoming apparent. By 1971, the time depth had been increased tenfold and the dating was sufficiently detailed to permit archaeologists to consider problems of cross-cultural relations on many different time levels. The focus of the questions shifted from seeking the cultural origins of the major ethnic groups to a study of Arctic man's adjustments to his habitat. This approach was foreshadowed by de Laguna's perceptive conclusions regarding the nature of Eskimo culture:

> I now believe that we must think of Eskimo culture in the same way that we think of Ice-hunting "culture," not as one culture that is or ever was uniform, but rather as a series of more or less similar ways of living that have always exhibited local differences. Furthermore, these local differences must have been greater in earlier times than at present [1947:285].

III. CURRENT VIEWS

The intensive archaeological work in the Western Arctic and sub-Arctic between 1950 and 1975 has produced an abundance of local sequences. Most of these are firmly dated, owing primarily to the interest and cooperation of Froelich G. Rainey and Elisabeth Ralph of the University of Pennsylvania, who have processed the majority of radiocarbon dates available for the Western Arctic (Figure 2.2). The overall impression one gets from these sequences is the exceptional diversity of archaeological cultures in the Western Arctic. Were it not for the chronological framework, meaningful comparisons between the regions would be difficult to make.

A. Aleutians and Pacific Coast

Two sites from the southern Alaskan coast are dated to very early times. The earlier is the Ground Hog Bay-2 Site located in Icy Strait, which although outside the area of direct concern here, is important in showing the existence of man along the North Pacific coast by 10,000 years ago (Ackerman 1968). Dating to 10,000 B.P. (WSU-412) on charcoal from Cultural Layer III, the component overlies two older, yet undated, culture-bearing strata, IV and V. A pebble chopper, several biface point or knife fragments of obsidian, and chipped slate come from the two lowest layers. These same types appear in Level III, associated with microblades, whetstones, and a variety of chopper tools. Ackerman believes that this assemblage has affinities with MacNeish's Kluane Complex from the Kluane Lake region of southwestern Yukon. However, excavations of Kluane-like artifacts from the Aishishik River area by Workman (1974) have yielded a date of 7195 ± 100 B.P. (SI-1117), which places Ground Hog Bay-2 much earlier than Kluane. Insofar as it is less than 600 miles south of Cook Inlet and the Alaska

Peninsula, the layer III assemblage of Ground Hog Bay-2 may also reflect the culture of these areas at about the time of the flooding of the Bering Land Bridge.

The Anangula Site on Umnak Island, Aleutians, dates to between 8500 and 7900 B.P. (Laughlin 1963a:90, 1963b:633). Investigated nearly continuously for 15 years, Anangula documents an early coastal sea mammal hunting adaptation that foreshadows both Aleut and Bering Sea Eskimo ways of life (Laughlin 1967). The site contains a developed uniface stone artifact industry with blades and microblades from oval-platformed cores, and burins, to mention only a few artifact types. It likely reflects a sea mammal hunting economy of a type developed earlier by Bering Sea Mongoloids along the southern coast of Beringia before it began to flood. Laughlin believes that the Anangula people were early Aleuts, who, as descendants of the Bering Land Bridge population, had begun to differentiate physically from other Land Bridge populations, such as ancestral Eskimo. According to Laughlin, the site also plays an important role in the study of northern coastal adaptation in general, inasmuch as the open-water sea mammal hunting techniques developed there were adopted by subsequent Aleuts and Eskimos. Excavations since 1970 have revealed house and faunal remains and artifacts at Anangula that bespeak of a sizable settlement of maritime adapted peoples, occupied perhaps by between 75 and 100 individuals (Aigner 1976:42).

The more than a dozen long radiocarbon dated sequences for the Aleutians and Alaska Peninsula postdating Anangula have established a picture of the cultural development in the area that spans nearly 6000 years.The Sandy Beach Bay Midden and the Chaluka Midden, both on Umnak Island, alone document nearly 4000 years of Aleut prehistory and physical development (Aigner *et al.*, 1976:86). The Aleut peoples responsible for the accumulation of Chaluka midden gradually changed in physical appearance through time, but the change was the kind that "commonly takes place inside populations and does not necessarily reflect a migration from the outside [Laughin 1966:24]." In general, the "basic cultural manifestation" of Eastern Aleuts was conservative throughout the entire sequence (Aigner 1966:67). The many cultural changes, particularly in relative frequencies of ivory and bone weapon types, may have been in response to fluctuations in the number of available fish, seals, and sea otters, and not to outside contacts. Stone tool styles changed over time from primarily small uniface varieties to large biface ones, but owing to a 1200-year gap in the sequence (between 700 B.C. and A.D. 500), it is impossible to determine what might have caused the change (Denniston 1966:111).

In contrast to the indigenous developments seen in the Chaluka sequence, the archaeology of Naknek drainage and the Pacific coast of the Alaska Peninsula shows a history of intermittent outside influence. Takli Alder Phase, the earliest of the known occupations of the Pacific side of Alaska

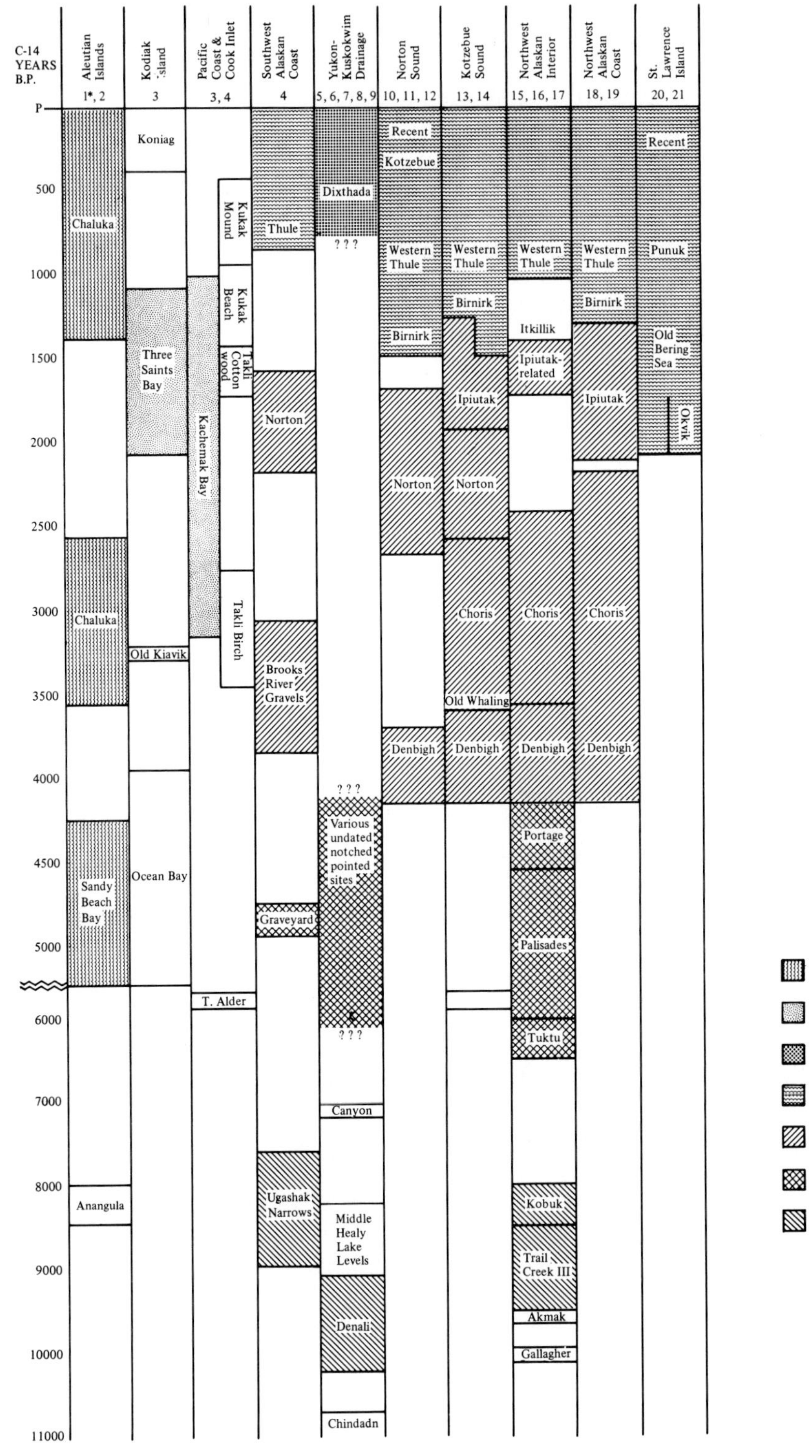

C-14 YEARS B.P.: P, 500, 1000, 1500, 2000, 2500, 3000, 3500, 4000, 4500, 5000, 6000, 7000, 8000, 9000, 10000, 11000

Aleutian Islands	Kodiak Island	Pacific Coast & Cook Inlet	Southwest Alaskan Coast	Yukon-Kuskokwim Drainage	Norton Sound	Kotzebue Sound	Northwest Alaskan Interior	Northwest Alaskan Coast	St. Lawrence Island
1*, 2	3	3, 4	4	5, 6, 7, 8, 9	10, 11, 12	13, 14	15, 16, 17	18, 19	20, 21
Chaluka	Koniag	Kukak Mound	Thule	Dixthada	Recent	Western Thule	Western Thule	Western Thule	Recent
Chaluka	Three Saints Bay	Kukak Beach	Norton	? ? ?	Kotzebue	Birnirk	Itkillik	Birnirk	Punuk
Sandy Beach Bay	Old Kiavik	Takli Cottonwood	Brooks River Gravels	? ? ?	Western Thule	Ipiutak	Ipiutak-related	Ipiutak	Old Bering Sea
Anangula	Ocean Bay	Kachemak Bay	Graveyard	Various undated notched pointed sites	Birnirk	Norton	Choris	Choris	Okvik
		Takli Birch	Ugashak Narrows	? ? ?	Norton	Choris	Denbigh	Denbigh	
		T. Alder		Canyon	Denbigh	Old Whaling	Portage		
				Middle Healy Lake Levels		Denbigh	Palisades		
				Denali			Tuktu		
				Chindadn			Kobuk		
							Trail Creek III		
							Akmak		
							Gallagher		

Peninsula may represent part of a pan-Aleutian–Alaska Peninsula culture that existed 5500 years ago. Dumond's conclusion (1971) is based on similarities in stone artifact styles between Krugloi Point on Agattu Island in the western Aleutians (Spaulding 1962) and Takli Alder Phase, a suggestion with which, however, other experts have disagreed (McCartney 1971:105). The prehistory of Kodiak Island, the region supporting the greatest population density of all Eskimos historically, begins at about the same time as Takli Alder Phase. These early Kodiak Islanders, of Ocean Bay Periods I (5500 B.P.) and II (4000 B.P.), developed a culture that had much in common with Takli Alder Phase (Clark 1971:27). A cultural discontinuity occurred between Ocean Bay II and Old Kiavak (3300 B.P.), the next younger phase on Kodiak Island (Clark 1966:363). Seen as a replacement of one culture by another, the discontinuity may also signify a population replacement.

By at least 2500 B.P., people, perhaps originally from the interior of southwestern Alaska, came into the Naknek drainage hunting caribou and fishing for salmon (Dumond 1971:40). Around 3900 B.P., Eskimos of the Arctic Small Tool Tradition (see below) spread into the Naknek drainage from the north, with a culture similar to that of Denbigh Flint Complex. They continued to live there for at least the next millennium, taking part in such northern cultural developments as pottery making, an invention that spread to southern Alaska during the Norton Period, or as it is locally known, the Brooks River Period. While these early Eskimos lived on the north side of Alaska Peninsula, Aleuts, with an entirely different culture, lived on the south side. These two peoples maintained their distinctness for 1000 years—until A.D. 1, when northern influences such as pottery making and some stone tool manufacturing techniques finally began to infiltrate the Pacific coast of Alaska. These influences steadily increased until a little before A.D. 1000, when Eskimos themselves moved south (Dumond 1971:41–43). Eskimos got to Kodiak Island probably around A.D. 1200,

---

Figure 2–2. Chronological chart for the Western American Arctic (based on radiocarbon dated sequences). Key to the archeological traditions: ▥ Aleut; ▢ Kachemak; ▩ Denetasiro (Athapaskan); ▤ Northern Maritime Eskimo; ▨ Arctic Small Tool; ▩ Northern Archaic; ▧ American Paleo Arctic.

Explanation: The archeological complexes listed on the chronological chart are, with the exception of the middle period Yukon-Kuskokwim drainage sites, derived from radiocarbon dated sequences. For purposes of clarity some well-dated local sequences have been omitted, and where possible regional terms for periods or phases are used in place of local terms. The horizontal lines separating complexes within a tradition indicate major stratigraphic, temporal, or cultural breaks within the local sequence.

References: (1) Laughlin 1967; (2) Aigner *et al.* 1976; (3) Clark 1973; (4) Dumond *et al.* n.d.; (5) MacNeish 1964; (6) Cook and McKennan 1970; (7) Workman 1974; (8) West 1975; (9) Powers and Hamilton n.d.; (10) Giddings 1964; (11) Bockstoce 1972; (12) Lutz 1972; (13) Giddings 1967; (14) Giddings & Anderson unpublished; (15) Giddings 1967; (16) Campbell 1962; (17) Anderson 1968; (18) Ford 1959; (19) Stanford 1970; (20) Collins 1937; (21) Rainey 1941.

when Three Saints Phase artifacts were replaced by Koniaq Eskimo artifacts (Clark 1966:365, 370).

B. Interior Arctic and Sub-Arctic

The treeless portion of the Arctic Interior was much larger in the distant past than it has been in recent times. Until shortly before 10,000 years ago it included nearly all the interior lands of Alaska and western Canada. After that date, spruce spread northward, valley by valley, until about 6000 years ago it reached its present northern limits along the Kobuk, upper Koyukuk, and lower Mackenzie rivers (Schweger 1976). For the discussion here, archaeological remains found in areas that were treeless tundra at the time of occupation will be considered remains of Interior Arctic cultures, whereas later ones located in areas that were wooded at the time of occupation will be considered sub-Arctic.

1. Early Cultures

Among the problems set in the north, that of the arrival and dispersal of the earliest North Americans is still unsolved. We have no evidence of man at a period of time approaching his assumed arrival in the New World. The earliest dated Arctic site, discovered by Harrington and Irving, is in the Crow Flats, northwestern Canada (Irving 1971). In reworked river deposits, a toothed scraper of a fossilized caribou tibia was found associated with extinct fauna, including giant beaver, bison, horse, and mammoth. The faunal remains were dated to between 24,000 and 30,000 years ago (apitite dates). The caribou tibia artifact itself was dated to $27{,}000^{+3000}_{-2000}$ B.P. (GX-1640). Although some experts have questioned either the association of the artifact with the extinct fauna or the age of the artifact, Irving is undoubtedly correct in stating that the artifact could only have been made when the bone was fresh. Numerous other bones of extinct fauna from the site appear to have been worked. These include chopped, carved, and shaped mammoth bone fragments and a horse mandible. The precision of the cuts on the bones indicate that the bones were worked by stone tools of considerable sophistication.

The next oldest Arctic sites are between 15,000 and 10,000 years more recent than the Old Crow Flats finds. They derive from the terminal period of the Bering Land Bridge, between 16,000 and 9500 years ago. At Trail Creek caves on Seward Peninsula, bison bones, presumably cracked by man, were dated to 15,750 ± 350 B.P. (K-1210), and a possible worked horse scapula to 13,670 ± 280 B.P. (K-1327), though without definite artifactual association (Larsen 1968).

The earliest dated Interior Arctic or sub-Arctic sites with stone implements are between 11,000 and 9000 years old. These are the Gallagher Flint

Station in the eastern part of the North Slope (Dixon 1975), the Healy Lake Village Site, the Dry Creek Site (Powers and Hamilton n.d.), the Mt. Hays Site 111 in central Alaska, the Ugashik Narrows east of Bristol Bay and Akmak at Onion Portage on the Kobuk River in northeastern Alaska. At the Healy Lake Site, an age of 11,090 ± 170 B.P. (GX-1341) was obtained from bone fragments in a hearth on Level 8, the third level from the bottom (McKennan and Cook 1968:4). The associated artifacts include thin, small, triangular bifaces, burins, and bladelike flakes, none of which suggest relationships with any other known assemblages outside of central Alaska.

Mt. Hays 111 is one of the Tangle Lake sites on shorelines of proglacial lakes at the headwaters of the Delta River. According to West, the sites may be classified into two groups: The earlier belong to the Amphitheater Mountain Complex and the latter to the Denali Complex, as defined by him in 1967 (West 1973:209–210). The earlier complex contains biface projectile points, pebble choppers, and crude burins, whereas the latter contains narrow, wedge-shaped microblade cores, core tablets, microblades, leaf-shaped biface knives, and notched cobbles. A buried beaver dam on a proglacial lake at about the same level as Denali sites produced dates of 11,800 ± 750 B.P. and 9000 ± 90 B.P., and the Denali Complex site Mt. Hays 111 yielded a radiocarbon date of 10,150 ± 280 B.P. (UGa-572) (West 1975). The artifacts from these two complexes, particulary the Denali, are remarkably like Duktai Tradition artifacts from eastern Siberia (Yakutsko-Chukotskaia region), and undoubtedly mark a historical connection.

The Akmak assemblage from Onion Portage, dated from a caribou scapula to 9570 ± 150 B.P. (K - 1583), is characterized by true blades from large polyhedral cores, core bifaced tools, and numerous large, well-made unifaced and bifaced artifacts (Anderson 1970a). In addition, microblades from narrow, wedge-shaped microblade cores of the type found in Denali Complex, at the Campus Site, and over much of Eurasia and Arctic Alaska, were apparently made for use as antler arrowhead insets. Although bifacially flaked knife blades are present in the Akmak assemblage, stone biface projectile points are absent. Akmak relates to Duktai of the eastern Soberian Upper Paleolithic (Mochanov 1973), to the Denali Complex defined by West (1967) and to Ugashik Narrows (Dumond *et al.* n.d.). The Ugashik Narrows site, dating from 9000 B.P., also contains core bifaces, blades, and microblades, and, in addition, a bifacially flaked point that may have been used to tip a projectile. The four complexes appear to define a large region of interior Arctic and sub-Arctic Asia and America within which several cultural traits were shared at the end of the Pleistocene and the beginning of the Holocene. In North America these can be grouped together as part of the American Paleo-Arctic Tradition (Anderson 1970a; Dumond *et al.* n.d.). On the other hand, the fact that Gallagher, only 340 miles northwest of Akmak, Healy Lake, only 75 miles northeast of the Tangle Lakes sites, and Anangula, 560 miles southwest of Ugashik Narrows, are very different from the four and from each other emphasizes that the picture of Early Holocene prehistoric Alaska is far from clear.

2. Paleo-Indian

Another continuing chronological problem in the Arctic Interior and sub-Arctic has been the nature and duration of influence from the Paleo-Indian cultures from the south. Former attempts to derive fluted point types from Siberia via Alaska have largely been abandoned (although not completely), since no Asian counterparts have ever been located. However, many archaeologists still see the Arctic fluted points as historically related to Clovis fluted points from southwestern United States, and suggest an approximately equal antiquity for them (Alexander 1974:2–3; Clark 1975:33–34). Unfortunately, Arctic fluted points have been obtained from surface sites, for which radiocarbon dating of associated charcoal is impossible. Obsidian fluted points found in the Koyukuk drainage just south of the Brooks Range are potentially datable by the obsidian dating method (Clark 1972:15–16, 1975). The problem, however, is in determining a proper hydration rate for the Koyukuk region. A hydration rate has been established for the obsidian artifacts from the deeply stratified Onion Portage Site 100 miles northwest of the Koyukuk, but the chances are that the Onion Portage rate is not at all applicable to the surface-derived Koyukuk region fluted points. One attempt to date fluted points by correlating their provenience with the glacial sequence in the Sagavanirktok Valley suggests that the points are no older than 11,500 years old, and more likely about 8500 years old (Dixon 1976).

Similar to the type of evidence for early Paleo-Indian influence in the north is the presence in Alaska and northwestern Canada of various lanceolate point types suggestive of Plano (Yuma-like) forms. In many cases the Arctic specimens have been regarded as being considerably old—10,000 to 5000 years old—based on assumed contemporaneity with their southern counterparts. At only one site, the Canyon site in the Southwest Yukon, has a radiocarbon date approached the assumed antiquity of the northern Plano points (Workman 1974:101). At the Canyon site, two convex based points, one with burin blows along one long edge, were found associated with charcoal that dated to 7195 ± 100 (SI 1117). None of the other dated sites containing lanceolate points appear so early. The westernmost Alaskan forms have in fact been dated to between 4400 and 4300 B.P. for short pentagonal forms (Portage Complex, Onion Portage), 3500 B.P. to 2600 B.P. for Plainsview-like and Scottsbluff-like forms (Choris culture, northwestern Alaska), and 100 B.P. for other straight-based lanceolate forms (Itkillik Complex, Onion Portage) (Anderson 1968, Giddings 1965). In the Eastern Arctic, the Coppermine Terrace site near Coronation Gulf, was found to contain Scottsbluff-like, Agate Basin-like, and pentagonal forms. Typologically, they are like the Plano forms that date to between 5000 and 3000 years ago, but their actual radiocarbon dates, on hearth charcoal, are in fact between A.D. 160 and A.D. 570 (McGhee 1970:59–64). On the other hand, lanceolate points have been reliably dated to 7000 B.P. at Acosta Lake just east of the Great Bear Lake. These include Agate Basin-like forms in addition to elongate side notched points (Noble 1971:104–105).

The conclusion seems to be that lanceolate points occur in the Interior Arctic and sub-Arctic over a long time span, and dating any Arctic site by reference to true Plano points can be extremely misleading. Schemes established for the Arctic on the basis of such finds ought to be treated with much skepticism.

3. Archaic Tradition Influences.

The presence of Archaic-like assemblages in the Western Arctic has been noted for several years. In Alaska and western Canada, notched points and other Archaic-like implements, such as large semilunar bifaces, end scrapers, worked slate, notched sinkers, quartzite knives, and cobble choppers are found in assemblages along the northernmost part of the boreal woodlands from 6500 B.P. onward. Although they continue in Interior Alaska and southwestern Yukon into the Christian era (MacNeish 1964:286), they are replaced by Arctic cultures along the northern and western Alaskan rim about 4300 or 4200 B.P. by the Arctic Small Tool Tradition. The Archaic-like assemblages have been grouped variously under the term Northwest Microblade Tradition (MacNeish 1959:12–14) or the Northern Archaic Tradition (Anderson 1968; Dumond *et al.* n.d.:9). Except for the fact that microblades occur in some sites but not in others, most of these assemblages are remarkably similar to one another. As yet we have been unable to determine whether the microblades are restricted to only certain time periods of the tradition or to only certain kinds of sites throughout the tradition.

The nature of the relationship of the Western Arctic and sub-Arctic Archaic-like traditions to the Eastern Archaic Tradition is unknown.

4. Development of Athapaskan Culture

Until the mid-1960s Athapaskan prehistory lagged far behind Eskimo and Aleut prehistory, owing primarily to the paucity of deeply stratified sites and datable remains in the interior. In the major synthesis of western sub-Arctic archaeology, MacNeish has identified an Athapaskan cultural continuum (termed archeologically the Denetasiro Tradition) from as far back perhaps as A.D. 300 (1964:348). An even longer cultural continuity is implied by MacNeish from the presence in Denetasiro of many artifactual forms from yet older traditions (1964:286–287). A more recent analysis of the Athapaskan language has suggested to M. Krause, University of Alaska, that Athapaskans have occupied central Alaska for many millennia, a conclusion that has gained support from the archaeology at the Healy Lake Site.

According to Cook and McKennan, an Athapaskan Tradition has existed at Healy Lake for at least 6500 years (Cook and McKennan 1970:2). Although the site's shallow deposition has precluded the possibility of identifying individual cultural phases, a general outline of cultural change has been possible. The earliest artifacts attributed to the Athapaskan tradition include side-notched points (of the Northern Archaic or Northwest microblade tradition) and microblades, types dated from Anaktuvuk Pass Tuktu Complex to 6510 ± 610 B.P. (Campbell 1962; Long 1965:250). Next higher in the Healy Lake sequence are artifacts related to Denali Complex, as well as to Tuktu. According to the authors, these date from 4500 years ago and more recently. It should be noted that their dates for Denali disagree with West's original early estimates and subsequent radiocarbon date of about 10,000 years ago for the complex in the Tangle Lakes area (West, personal communication). The link between Denali-like and Athapaskan culture is not clear at Healy Lake, where there is a significant temporal break in the sequence between the post-1200 B.P. and pre-4000 B.P. materials. Cook and McKennan feel that the connection is seen at the nearby Dixthada Site, where microblades and other early artifacts are found along with identifiable Athapaskan artifacts. However, the contemporaneity of microblades and Athapaskan culture at Dixthada has yet to be demonstrated by excavation, and in the opinion of some archaeologists the postulated long continuity of Athapaskan culture in central Alaska is not yet proven.

Other attempts to connect the earlier sub-Arctic cultures with Athapaskan culture have also proved unconfirmed. For example, Giddings (1966) and Anderson (1968, 1970b) have attempted to relate the 5500-year-long sub-Arctic Tradition defined at Onion Portage (Northern Archaic Tradition) to historic Athapaskans, but since the latest phase, Itkillik, which is only 600 years old, does not appear to relate to any other interior Alaskan archaeological remains—not even from the Koyukuk River area, which is the Athapaskan area nearest Onion Portage, such connections remain conjectural (Clark 1969). However, as yet no sites contemporaneous with Itkillik Complex at Onion Portage have been found in the Koyukuk drainage, so the question remains open.

Connecting historic Athapaskan culture with indigenous prehistoric cultures has met with most success in the Kutchin area. With a sequence that begins around A.D., 700, Morlan's Klo Kut site in the Porcupine drainage documents Athapaskan material culture that includes both deposits that were laid down within the memory of living Kutchins and deposits of their ancestors (Morlan 1970). Many artifact styles continue throughout the sequence, but some of the earlier ones are surprisingly Eskimo-like. In the Tanaina Athapaskan area of Cook Inlet, archaeologists have likewise found sites that bridge the initial historic contact period. There, however, the problem of identifying the ethnic group from the material culture is compounded, since, for example, artifacts that are usually associated with Eskimos are found in sites that have known historic Tainana Athapaskan affiliation. It is obvious that the material culture distinctions between Indians and Eskimos of that area, at least in the recent prehistoric period, are blurred (Townsend 1970).

C. Arctic Coast

To date, no evidence has been found to indicate that peoples were hunting sea mammals along the Alaskan Arctic Coast prior to about 2500 B.C., when sea level, which had been gradually rising since the end of the last major glaciation, reached its present position. Because of the rising sea level, the Western Arctic Coast did not attain its present configuration until then. Thus, coastal archaeology has its early period defined not so much by when people first settled along the coast but by when sites were no longer washed away. It is likely that people were making some use of the coast, though perhaps very limited use, for millennia before our earliest obtainable evidence for them.

1. Arctic Coastal Traditions

The earliest Arctic sites associated with coastal life belong to the Denbigh Flint Complex (Giddings 1964). Denbigh is the Western Arctic representative of the Arctic Small Tool Tradition, a tradition that spread eastward before the end of the second millennium B.C. as far as Greenland (Irving 1964). The dating of Denbigh Flint Complex was contested for many years. After initially suggesting an age of between 8000 and 6000 years ago for Denbigh Flint Complex, Giddings made further discoveries of Denbigh around Kotzebue Sound that led him to revise the age to between 5000 and 4500 years ago. Subsequent dating of Denbigh at Onion Portage (Anderson 1968; Giddings 1966) and Punyik Point, a site in the central Brooks Range (Irving 1964) have placed the age of Denbigh somewhat even more recent—4300 to 3600 B.P.

The origin of the Arctic Small Tool Tradition is not known. Sites in the Aldan region of Siberia that date to the late fourth millennium or early third millennium B.C. look very Denbigh-like and suggest relationships (Mochanov 1968). Some archaeologists postulate on the basis of the similarities, particularly between the Belkachi Site and Denbigh Flint Complex, that Denbigh was introduced into the American Arctic by a population movement from interior Siberia in the third millennium B.C. (Irving 1968). On the other hand, it is possible that Denbigh developed from earlier microblade cultures in Alaska. There are, in fact, some indications of this from parts of the Brooks Range, Alaska, though none of the suspected ancestral Denbigh sites have been dated yet.

Denbigh peoples inhabited the northwestern Alaskan tundra and taiga and, at least during the summer months, also the coast. The development of the year-round coastal life that characterizes historic Eskimos is still surprisingly unclear, despite the seemingly complete archaeological record for the region. Ironically, the earliest winter sites along the Western Arctic Coast do not belong to the Arctic Small Tool Tradition, but rather to Old Whaling, a complex known only from Cape Krusenstern. Old Whaling is as yet unique, without any relationships to other known cultures (Giddings 1961).

Choris culture (3500 to 2600 B.P.), a derivative of Denbigh Flint Complex, records the first coastal winter occupation by Eskimos in northwestern Alaska (Giddings 1957). Choris is a highly variable complex; in the more northerly sites the traits appear very Denbigh-like, as along the Noatak River, at Walakpa and on the eastern Brooks Range. The most intense winter use of the coast by early Eskimos, comes in the Norton Period, when sizable settlements of large houses emerge along the northern shores of Norton Sound (Bockstoce 1972; Lutz 1972). Except for Choris, winter settlements do not appear along the coast north of Bering Strait until the Ipiutak Period, and even these may have been of a people who are more oriented to a part-time use of the coast (Larsen and Rainey 1948).

Eskimo material culture stylistically related to Eskimo culture of the eighteenth and nineteenth centuries does not appear on the Alaskan mainland until the Birnirk Period, although elements were already present in Old Bering Sea culture on St. Lawrence Island shortly after the beginning of the present era (Collins 1937). Our understanding of the development of Birnirk and its derivative Thule culture and their relation to the historically recorded Eskimo cultures has expanded in details since the early work of Collins, Rainey, and others, but the question of Birnirk's ancestry is yet unsolved.

Thus by 1975 the chronological framework for the Western Arctic and sub-Arctic appeared rather complete, but the gaps that remain in the sequences are crucial links between the early prehistoric traditions and the historically recorded ones.

BIBLIOGRAPHY

Ackerman, R.E.

1968 The Archaeology of the Glacier Bay Region, Southeastern Alaska. *Washington State University, Laboratory of Anthropology, Report of Investigations* No. 44.

Aigner, J.S.

1966 Bone Tools and Decorative Motifs from Chaluka, Umnak Island. *Arctic Anthropology* **3**(2):57–83.

1976 Early Holocene Evidence for the Aleut Maritime Adaptation. *Arctic Anthropology* **13**(2):32–45.

Aigner, J.S., B. Fullem, D. Veltre, and M. Veltre

1976 Preliminary Reports on Remains from Sandy Beach Bay, A 4300–5600 B.P. Aleut Village. *Arctic Anthropology* **13**(2):83–90.

Alexander, Herbert L.
1974 The Association of Aurignacoid Elements with Fluted Point Complexes in North America. Unpublished manuscript, Simon Fraser University.
Anderson, D.D.
1968 A Stone Age Campsite at the Gateway to America. *Scientific American* **218**(6):24–33.
1970a Akmak: An Early Archaeological Assemblage from Onion Portage, Northwest Alaska. *Acta Arctica* **16.**
1970b Athapaskans in the Kobuk Arctic Woodlands, Alaska? *Canadian Archaeological Association Bulletin* **2**:3–12.
1972 An Archaeological Survey of the Noatak Drainage, Alaska. *Arctic Anthropology* **9**(1):66–117.
Bockstoce, J.R.
1972 The Archaeology of Cape Nome. Unpublished manuscript, University Museum, University of Pennsylvania.
Campbell, J.M.
1962 Cultural Succession at Anaktuvuk Pass. In *Prehistoric Cultural Relations between the Arctic and Temperature Zones of North America*, edited by J. M. Campbell. *Arctic Institute of North American Technical Paper* **11**:39–54.
Clark, D.W.
1966 Perspectives in the Prehistory of Kodiak Island, Alaska. *American Antiquity* **31**(3,1):358–371.
1969 Preliminary Report on 1969 Field Work in the Northwest Territories and Alaska. Informal paper, National Museum of Man, Ottawa.
1971 Preliminary Report on 1971 Field Work. Unpublished manuscript, National Museum of Man, Ottawa.
1972 Archaeology of the Batza Tena Obsidian Source, West Central Alaska. *Anthropological Papers of the University of Alaska* **15**(2):1–21.
1973 Technological Continuity and Change Within a Persistent Maritime Adaptation, Kodiak Island, Alaska. Paper prepared for the IX International Congress of Anthropological and Ethnological Sciences, Chicago.
1975 Fluted Points from the Batza Tena Obsidian Source of the Koyukuk River Region, Alaska. *Anthropological Papers of the University of Alaska* **17**(2):31–38.
Collins, H.B., Jr.
1932 Prehistoric Eskimo Culture on St. Lawrence Island. *Geographical Review* **22:**107–119.
1937 Archaeology of St. Lawrence Island, Alaska. *Smithsonian Miscellaneous Collections* **96**(1).
1943 Eskimo Archaeology and Its Bearing on the Problem of Man's Antiquity in America. *American Philosophical Society Proceedings* **86:**220–235.
Cook, J.P., and R.A. McKennan
1970 The Athapaskan Tradition: A View from Healy Lake in the Yukon-Tanana Upland. Paper read at the 10th Annual Meeting of the Northwestern Anthropological Association, Ottawa.
Dall, W.H.
1877 On the Succession in the Shell-Heaps of the Alaskan Islands. *Contributions to North American Ethnology* **1:**41–91.
Denniston, G.B.
1966 Cultural Change at Chaluka, Umnak Island: Stone Artifacts and Features. *Arctic Anthropology* **3**(2):84–124.
Dixon, E.J., Jr.
1975 The Gallagher Flint Station, an Early Man Site on the North Slope, Arctic Alaska, and Its Role in Relation to the Bering Land Bridge. *Arctic Anthropology* **XII**(1):68–75.

1976 The Pleistocene Prehistory of Arctic North America. Paper presented at the XI International Congress of Prehistoric and Protohistoric Sciences, Nice, France.

Dumond, D.E.

1971 A Summary of Archaeology in the Katmai Region, Southwestern Alaska. *University of Oregon Anthropological Papers* No. **2.**

Dumond, D.E., W. Henn, and R. Stuckenrath

n.d. Archaeology and Prehistory on the Alaska Peninsula. Unpublished manuscript, University of Oregon, Eugene.

Ford, James A.

1959 Eskimo Prehistory in the Vicinity of Point Barrow, Alaska. *Anthropological Papers of the American Museum of Natural History* **47**(1).

Geist, O.W., and F.G. Rainey

1936 Archaeological Excavations at Kukulik, St. Lawrence Island, Alaska. *University of Alaska Miscellaneous Publications* No. **2.**

Giddings, J.L.

1944 Dated Eskimo Ruins of an Inland Zone. *American Antiquity* **10**(2):113–135.

1949 Early Flint Horizons on the North Bering Sea Coast. *Journal of the Washington Academy of Sciences* **39**(3):85–90.

1952 The Arctic Woodland Culture of the Kobuk River. *Museum Monographs,* The University Museum.

1961 Cultural Continuities of Eskimos. *American Antiquity* **27**(2):155–173.

1964 *The Archeology of Cape Denbigh*. Providence, Rhode Island: Brown University Press.

1965 A Long Record of Eskimos and Indians at the Forest Edge. In *Context and Meaning in Cultural Anthropology*, edited by M.E. Spiro. New York: The Free Press. Pp. 189–205.

1966 Cross-Dating the Archaeology of Northwestern Alaska. *Science* **153**(3732):127–135.

Hibbon, F.C.

1943 Evidence of Early Man in Alaska. *American Antiquity* **8**(3):254–259.

Hickey, C.G.

1968 The Kayak Site: An Analysis of the Spatial Aspect of Culture as an Aid to Archaeological Inference. Unpublished M.A. thesis, Brown University, Providence, R.I.

Hrdlicka, A.

1932 Anthropological Work in Alaska. In *Explorations and Fieldwork of the Smithsonian Institution in 1929.*

1935 Archaeological Excavations on Kodiak Island, Alaska. In *Explorations and Fieldwork of the Smithsonian Institution in 1943.* Pp. 47–52.

Irving, W.N.

1964 Punyik Point and the Arctic Small Tool Tradition. Unpublished Ph.D. dissertation, University of Wisconsin, Madison.

1968 The Arctic Small Tool Tradition. *Proceedings VIII International Congress of Anthropological and Ethnological Sciences* **3:**340–42. Tokyo and Kyoto

1971 Recent Early Man Research in the North. *Arctic Anthropology* **8**(2):68–82.

Jenness, D.

1928 Archaeological Investigations in Bering Strait. *National Museum of Canada Bulletin* **50:**71–80.

Jochelson, W.

1925 Archaeological Investigations in the Aleutian Islands. *Carnegie Institution Publication* No. **367.**

Johnson, F.

1946 An Archaeological Survey Along the Alaska Highway, 1944. *American Antiquity* **11:**183–186.

de Laguna, F.
1934 *The Archaeology of Cook Inlet, Alaska.* Philadelphia: University of Pennsylvania Press.
1947 The Prehistory of Northern North America as Seen from the Yukon. *Memoirs of the Society for American Archaeology* **3.**

Larsen, H.
1961 Archaeology in the Arctic, 1935–1960. *American Antiquity* **27**(1): 7–15.
1968 Trail Creek: Final Report on the Excavation of Two Caves on Seward Peninsula, Alaska. *Acta Arctica* **15.**

Larsen, H., and F. Rainey
1948 Ipiutak and the Arctic Whale Hunting Culture. *Anthropological Papers of the American Museum of Natural History* **42.**

Laughlin, W.S.
1951 Notes of an Aleutian Core and Blade Industry. *American Antiquity* **17**(1):52.
1963a The Earliest Aleuts. *Anthropological Papers of the University of Alaska* **10**(2):73–91.
1963b Eskimos and Aleuts: Their Origins and Evolution. *Science* **142**(3503):633–645.
1966 Aleutian Studies: Introduction. *Arctic Anthropology* **3**(2):23–27.
1967 Human Migration and Permanent Occupation in the Bering Sea Area. In *The Bering Land Bridge,* edited by D.M. Hopkins. Stanford: Stanford University Press. Pp. 409–450.

Long, A.
1965 Smithsonian Institution Radiocarbon Measurements II. *Radiocarbon* **7:**245–256.

Lutz, B.J.
1972 A Methodology for Determining Regional Intra-Cultural Variation Within Norton, an Alaskan Archaeological Culture. Unpublished Ph.D. dissertation, University of Pennsylvania, Philadelphia.

MacNeish, R.S.
1959 A Speculative Framework of Northern North American Prehistory as of April 1959. *Anthropologica* **1**(1-2):7–23.
1964 Investigations in Southwest Yukon: Archaeological Excavation, Comparisons, and Speculation. *Papers of the Robert S. Peabody Foundation for Archaeology* **6**(2):199–488.

McCartney, A.P.
1971 A Proposed Western Aleutian Phase in the Near Islands, Alaska. *Arctic Anthropology* **8**(2):92–142.

McGhee, R.
1970 Excavations at Bloody Falls, N.W.T., Canada. *Arctic Anthropology* **6**(2):53–72.

McKennan, R.A., and J.P. Cook
1968 Prehistory of Healy Lake, Alaska. Paper read at the 8th International Congress of Anthropological and Ethnological Sciences, Tokyo.

Morlan, R.E.
1970 Toward the Definition of a Prehistoric Athabaskan Culture. *Canadian Archaeological Association Bulletin* **2:**24–33.

Motchanov, Y.A.
1973 The North Eurasia Paleolithic and the First Stages of Men Settling in America. In *Theses of the Reports of All-Union Symposium on the Bering Land Bridge and Its Role for the History of Holarctic Floras and Faunas in the Late Cenozoic.* Khabaroush: Academy of Sciences of U.S.S.R., Far eastern Centre. Pp. 11–13.

Nelson, N.C.
1937 Notes on Cultural Relations between Asia and America. *American Antiquity* **2**(4):267–272.

Noble, W.C.
1971 Archaeological Surveys and Sequences in Central District Mackenzie, N.W.T. *Arctic Anthropology* **8**(1):102–135.

Oswalt, Wendell

1954 Regional Chronologies in Spruce of the Kuskokwim River, Alaska. *Anthropological Papers of the University of Alaska* **2**(2): 203–214.

Powers, W.R., and T.D. Hamilton

n.d. Dry Creek: A Late Paleolithic Human Occupation in Central Alaska. In *Proceedings of the 13th Pacific Science Conference, Vancouver, B.C.*, in press.

Rainey, F.G.

1939 Archaeology in Central Alaska. *American Museum of Natural History Anthropological Papers* **36:**351–405.

1940 Archaeological Investigation in Central Alaska. *American Antiquity* **5**(4):299–308.

1941 Eskimo Prehistory: The Okvik Site on the Punuk Islands. *American Museum of Natural History Anthropological Papers* **37**(4):453–569.

Schweger, C.C.

1976 Late Quaternary Paleoecology of the Onion Portage Region, Northwestern Alaska. Unpublished Ph.D. dissertation, University of Alberta, Edmonton.

Solecki, R.S.

1951 Notes on two Archaeological Discoveries in Northern Alaska, 1950. *American Antiquity* **17**(1):52–57.

Spaulding, A.C.

1962 Archaeological Investigations on Agattu, Aleutian Islands. University of Michigan, *Anthropological Papers of the Museum of Anthropology* **18.**

Stanford, Dennis J.

1970 Interim Summary: Pt. Barrow Research. Unpublished manuscript, University of New Mexico, Albuquerque.

Steensby, H.P.

1916 An Anthropogeographical Study of the Origin of the Eskimo Culture. *Meddelelser om Grønland* **53.**

Thompson, R.M.

1948 Notes on the Archaeology of the Utekek River, Northwestern Alaska. *American Antiquity* **14**(1):62–65.

Townsend, J.B.

1970 Tanaina Archaeology in the Iliamna Lake Region, Alaska. *Canadian Archaeological Association Bulletin* **2:**34–41.

Van Stone, J.W.

1955 Archaeological Excavations at Kotzebue, Alaska. *Anthropological Papers of the University of Alaska* **3**(2):75–155.

West, F.H.

1967 The Donnelly Ridge Site and the Definition of an Early Core and Blade Complex in Central Alaska. *American Antiquity* **32**(3):360–382.

1973 Old World Affinity of Archaeological Complexes from Tangle Lakes, Central Alaska. In *Theses of the Reports of All-Union Symposium on the Bering Land Bridge and Its Role for the History of Holarctic Floras and Faunas in the Late Cenozoic.* Khabarovsk: Academy of Sciences of U.S.S.R., Far Eastern Centre. Pp. 209–211.

1975 Dating the Denali Complex. *Arctic Anthropology* **XII** (1):76–81.

Workman, W.B.

1974 First Dated Traces of Early Holocene Man in the Southwest Yukon Territory, Canada. *Arctic Anthropology* **11,** supplement: 94–103.

Eastern United States

JAMES B. GRIFFIN

I. DEVELOPMENT OF A PREHISTORIC TIME SCALE

A. Nineteenth and Early Twentieth Century

The initial ideas of a prehistoric time scale in the East were based for many years on concepts of an essentially biblical chronology modified or interpolated in stories about the various hypothetical migrations to the New World. Among these might be mentioned the Walam Olum and the Book of Mormon. Despite a considerable amount of archaeological work by competent and incompetent individuals and institutions, there were only a few examples of a stratigraphic sequence in the East by 1925 and no broad areal synthesis in terms of a chronology had resulted.

There were many attempts at association of man with glacial events, or man in deep levels in alluvial deposits, or of man with extinct fauna.

A summary of W. H. Holmes on the "early man" problem does not indicate the closed mind or the very short period of time that, it is said, experts of that time were willing to accept.

> As thus presented, the testimony of racial and cultural phenomena dissociated from geological criteria does not serve to indicate clearly an antiquity for the aboriginal occupancy beyond a few thousand years. Through association with geological formations the age of which can be determined with some degree of accuracy, both cultural and somatic remains combine to extend our vision with remarkable clearness well back toward the close of the last glacial occupation of middle North America, a period whose duration is estimated by some students from eight to twenty thousand years. Some students of the subject are satisfied that authentic evidence of man's presence during the glacial period

> has been obtained, others find sufficient reasons for believing in man's existence in both North and South America far back in Tertiary time [Holmes 1919:58].

A few such finds of glacial man may be mentioned. A burial called Lansing Man at Lansing, Kansas, was assigned to the Iowan glaciation. The Iowan glaciation has disappeared and is now regarded as till deposits of older glaciations covered by Wisconsin loess. Lansing Man skeletal material has been radiocarbon dated at about 4000 B.C. by Geochrom Laboratories (personal communication, W. M. Bass, University of Tennessee) and at the University of Michigan (UM-1890) at 4750 (±250) B.P. on a left tibia and a humerus submitted by W. M. Bass. A controversy raged for years over the age of skeletal and artifactual materials from the Trenton gravels in New Jersey, but claims for high antiquity have been abandoned for many years. Former hearths, implements, and occupation zones along the Ohio River and some of its immediate tributaries were interpreted as evidence of occupation back into the Pleistocene, but none of them have been substantiated (Fowke 1902:6–30).

Cave explorations by competent paleontologists and archaeologists in Pennsylvania, Tennessee, Maryland, Kentucky, Arkansas, and Alabama over the last 50 or more years have failed to find satisfactory evidence of the association of man and the large (or small) extinct fauna of the closing phases of the Wisconsin.

Other finds purporting to substantiate evidence of man with extinct fauna such as at Vero Beach, Florida, the finds by Koch in Missouri, or the Richard locality in Indiana, and at Natchez, Mississippi, have not been subsequently supported to the point where they can be accepted.

One of the major problems of chronology in the Eastern United States in the 1800s was the belief that the "Mound Builders" were a separate and earlier race of people much more civilized than the later and more barbarous Indians who drove out the "Mound Builders" and supplanted them. This concept was supported by theories of multiple migrations into the New World at different time periods and by various routes from widely separated areas of Asia, and from Europe, and even Africa. Archaeological work during the last quarter of the nineteenth century clearly established that the "Mound Builders" were in most instances the ancestors of the historic Indian tribes and in some instances that early historic Indians were building and occupying mounds. By the first half of the twentieth century it was clearly recognized that the wide variety of cultural complexes identified in the East required substantial time differences. This was also implied by the linguistic diversity at the historic period, and by the considerable difference in physical type of the populations of both the historic and the prehistoric periods.

Tree-ring counts in Tennessee stated that at least one of the mounds must be 500 to 600 years old. A portion of the earthworks at Marietta, Ohio, was stated to be 1000 years old as long ago as 1788 by a simple tree count.

Thomas (1898) felt that the American Indians had come into the New World at least 3000 years ago, which would have been long enough, in his opinion, for Iroquoian linguistic stock to have diverged from Algonquian; and that the period of mound construction began about A.D. 500.

Shetrone (1920) thought "Algonquian" people were the first people in Ohio, occupied more territory than any other group, and were the last to leave. Thus, they were contemporary with all groups. Fort Ancient and Hopewell were contemporary—the Stone Grave people were contemporary with Hopewell (hence with Fort Ancient). The Iroquois arrived in late prehistoric times.

One of the rare examples of stratigraphy was the Hawkes and Linton paper describing three distinct artifact-bearing strata at the Crispin Site in New Jersey (Hawkes and Linton 1916). There were a few other examples in New York, Illinois, and a number of other areas. There were, however, no clearly recognized complexes of broad geographic sweep that represented a developing cultural sequence.

University of Chicago work in Fulton County in 1930–1932 had established as a working proposition the sequence back into the past of Spoon River–Maples Mills–Hopewell and then Black Sand and Red Ocher (Cole and Deuel 1937). The relative time position of the latter two was not clear in regard to each other. Langford (1927, 1928) had presented evidence for stratigraphy in Illinois, as did Krogman (1931). In New York, Ritchie (1932) had established the distinctiveness of Lamoka as an early non-pottery-using group. In Louisiana and Mississippi, Henry B. Collins and Winslow M. Walker had recognized the succession of cultures that Ford (1935, 1936) was to document in the 1930s.

One of the distinctive methods in the East of developing a chronology was that of a correlation and comparison of sites having different archaeological complexes with the former stream channels of the Mississippi Alluvial Valley. This approach was suggested by Winslow Walker at the Conference on Southern Prehistory held in Birmingham in 1932. The recent drainage history of the Lower Mississippi Valley was, of course, developed by Harold N. Fisk (1944) of Louisiana State University. This approach was used by Kniffen (1936) to help in establishing a prehistoric cultural chronology in southern Louisiana but was given a much more extensive test in the Memphis area by Phillips *et al.* (1951) and by subsequent archaeological work in the Lower Mississippi Alluvial Valley. Fisk's interpretations are being revised, as the result of continuing studies by Roger T. Saucier.

An early attempt to provide an estimate for the age of Indian cultures in New England was by H. W. Shimer (1918), who investigated the Boylston Street Fish Weir in Boston in 1913, he studied the silt formations and fauna and estimated the age of the weir at 2000 to 3000 years.

Paul B. Sears (1932) in his pollen studies provided a sequence of vegetational succession in Eastern North America and implied that the high cultures of Ohio would have had optimal conditions for maize production during a warm dry continental maximum of roughly 2500 to 4500 years ago, which would correspond to the Subboreal period of the North Sea area.

A recent chronological assessment of the Poverty Point culture has been made by the thermoluminiscent dating of baked clay objects from six sites in Louisiana and Mississippi (Huxtable, Aitken, and Weber 1972). Dates were obtained on 31 specimens from six sites. There is a spread from about 2500 to 120 B.C., but average dates from four sites are between 1100 and 1000 B.C. (±110 to 170 years). The other two sites have average dates of 750 and 650 B.C. These correspond quite well with radiocarbon dates from Poverty Point.

B. WPA Period

The development of the federally supported archaeological programs using "relief" labor had a profound effect upon Eastern United States archaeology. Without one scrap of measurement by weight, or area of earth involved, it is safe to say that X times the amount of earth was moved by relief labor between 1932 and 1942 than had been moved by all archaeological work in the preceding 150 years. A number of areas of work are outstanding: First is the Tennessee Valley, where work in eastern and western Tennessee and northern Alabama produced the best framework for a succession of cultures in the mid-South. Second, Kentucky, where the northern Alabama sequence was tied to work in the then known sequence in Ohio, Indiana, and Illinois and to other northern areas. Third was the work done in Louisiana, which extended the cultural sequence into the Lower Mississippi Valley. Fourth, the work in Bibb County, Georgia, under A. R. Kelley with notable assists from a younger supporting cast in developing a number of distinctive complexes that could be connected with those to the west. Other programs were in operation from the Plains to the Atlantic and contributed their share of information and misinterpretation.

Another attempt at producing a chronology was the study of dendrochronology, first in the Tennessee Valley and subsequently in the Illinois area, which eventually culminated in the Kincaid chronology published by Bell (1951, 1952).

C. Post–World War II

The time framework I prepared for the Eastern United States during the late 1940s appears in *Archaeology of the Eastern United States* on maps and a chronology chart (Griffin 1952: Figs. 199–205). After the maps and chart were prepared, Phillips, Ford, and I fashioned the concluding chapter of the Lower Mississippi Valley report in August 1949. We arrived at the chronology chart for the ceramic periods of the Lower Mississippi Valley included in that report (Phillips *et al.* 1951:454), which pushed back the Mississippian and earlier ceramic complexes to close to the figures of the first radiocarbon dates.

The first radiocarbon dates were announced to a wide audience at the Twenty-ninth International Congress of Americanists by W. F. Libby in September 1949. Since that time, some thousands of dates have been produced bearing on the chronology of the prehistoric Eastern United States. This has altered many of the earlier interpretations of the temporal position of a large number of the cultural complexes recognized by archaeologists. Probably the most important changes have been within the time period attributed to the Archaic cultures, but all other periods have also been affected by the more accurate temporal assessments provided by radiocarbon.

Little or no attempt has been made in this chapter to separate cultural divisions, establish fine temporal divisions between "periods," accurately determine the time span of a "tradition," or prove the point of origin of a culture or the time and place of a major innovation or decline, by radiocarbon dates. While this method of dating has been a boon, there are a significant number of difficulties in applying radiocarbon dates to archaeology. These difficulties may lie in the corrections that may need to be applied to the radiocarbon age determination of a laboratory because the past atmospheric inventory of $^{14}CO_2$ has not been constant (Ralph *et al.* 1973; Suess 1970). There are also a series of problems in working with radiocarbon dates which deal with the relationship of the materials dated and their measurable content to the archaeological event for which a date is desired. These have been admirably outlined by Waterbolk (1971). Another known factor is that some radiocarbon laboratories seem to vary fairly consistently in their results from other laboratories. These problems and others lead me to believe that at present I am not in a position to identify the best radiocarbon ages of specific cultural events in the East within a narrow time range of 50 years, or in many cases of much longer periods of time. I have normally avoided horizontal lines on chronology charts and have done so with this presentation (see chronology chart, Figure 3.1 of Eastern United States culture complexes). If the presentation lacks precision, it does not present a false security.

II. THE PALEO-INDIAN PERIOD

So far in the Eastern United States there is no satisfactory evidence of prehistoric populations before the appearance of the fluted point cultures of sometime before 8000 B.C. Various claims have been made in the past for

		1 Northeast	2 New York	3 Michigan	4 Ohio Valley	5 Upper Mississippi	6 St. Louis Area	7 Northern Alabama–Tennessee	8 Lower Mississippi	9 Yazoo Basin	10 Northwest Florida	11 Northeast Florida	12 Southeast Coastal	
	1500	Fort Shantok	Iroquois Chance	Juntunen	↑		Sand Prairie	McKee Island	Natchezan Lake George	Russell Lake George Mayersville	Ft. Walton Safety Harbor	Spanish Mission St. Johns IIB	Irene Pee Dee Etowah	1500
A.D.	1000	Niantic	Castle Creek Canandaigua Hunter's Home	Bois Blanc Mackinac	Fort Ancient ↓	Oneota Aztalan	Moorehead Sterling Fairmount	Moundsville Hamilton	Plaquemine Coles Creek	Crippen P.	Weeden Island II	St. Johns IIA	Pisgah Macon Plateau	1000
	200	Clearview	Kipp Island	Wayne	Newtown	Black Duck Arvilla Effigy Mound	Patrick Early Bluff Pike	McKelvey	Baytown Issaquena	King's Crossing Aden Bayland Deasonville	Weeden Island I	St. Johns IB	Mandeville	200
	0	North Beach Lagoon Bushkill Pratt	Squawkie Hill Middlesex	Norton Carrigan	Ohio Hopewell Adena	Trempealeau	Bedford Calhoun Peisker Red Ocher	Copena Watts Bar Alexander Kirby	Marksville Tchula Tchefuncte Poverty Point	Issaquena Anderson Landing Tuscola Jaketown	Santa Rosa Swift Creek Deptford	St. Johns IA Deptford	Deptford	0
B.C.	1000 2000	Orient Watertown Perkiomen Lehigh Squibnockett	Meadowood Brewerton	Andrews Glacial Kame Old Copperr Feehely	Glacial Kame Green River	Reigh	Etley Riverton Chrisman	Ledbetter Wheeler Big Sandy Lauderdale	Amitte River	Teoc Creek	Norwood Elliot Point	Orange	Refuge Thom's Creek Savannah River	1000 2000
	3000 4000	Wapanucket #6 Boylston Street Hathaway	Lamoka Vosburg Vergennes		Faulkner		Helton	Three Mile Worley Eva I.		Denton		Tick Island	Rabbit Mount Halifax Morrow Mountain	3000 4000
	6000 8000	Bull Brook Shoop Debert	Reagan Plenge Dutchess	Lake George Hi-Lo Holcomb Barnes	Thebes Henderson Parrish	Brohm Renier Kouba Durst	Hidden Valley	Stanfield Nuckolls Quad Cumberland	Jones Creek San Patrice		Aucilla	Suwannee Aucilla	Hardaway Williamson	6000 8000
	11000		Quarry											11000

such finds, but so far convincing evidence has not been produced for such groups as interstadial man in Ontario (Lee 1957), for a preprojectile point Lively Complex in Alabama or other such examples of wishful thinking.

Occupation of the Eastern United States by fluted point hunters and their descendants has been known for a long time, but we are still unable to put a firm date on the first appearance of these populations or to know in which region they first appeared or when the practice of definitely fluting the points and/or knives was abandoned. One thing is certain, the major features of the lithic complex associated with the Clovis to Folsom complexes in the High Plains to Southwestern areas is distributed over the entire area from the Gulf to the Laurentian Shield in Ontario, and from Nova Scotia to Minnesota and Texas. There were many widely differing environmental areas in which these people were able to survive.

Dates have been obtained from the Debert Site in Nova Scotia (MacDonald 1968) that indicate a temporal position of approximately 8600 B.C. for the complex at the extreme northeastern margin of its distribution, which is rather remarkable. A radiocarbon date of 10,580 B.C. has been attributed to a fluted point dated by caribou bone colagen from a rock shelter in Orange County, New York (Funk *et al.* 1969). Reasonable, if not accurate, temporal associational inferences of Lake Michigan and Huron fossil beaches imply that fluted point hunters occupied this area prior to the drop of the lake waters from the Algonquin level now dated about 9000 B.C. (Mason 1958). Projectile point styles known stratigraphically to follow Folsom in the High Plains are associated with beaches formed during the drop of water levels from Lake Algonquin, so that the association of fluted points with Lake Algonquin or earlier still seems a valid one.

If we have no firm date for a beginning of the fluted point peoples occupations of the East, we are little better off in recognizing the disappearance of this style and the beginning of the Archaic complexes. We have, however, some indications of the approximate time when a separation can be made from Paleo-Indian to Early Archaic. Graham Cave in Missouri has no true fluted points but does have forms that are possibly typologically connected with the Quad points of the Tennessee Valley, Suwannee points of Florida, and perhaps others as well. There is stylistic justification for the belief that Dalton and related points are still later in time, and these date in the time range of 8000 to 6500 B.C. at Research Cave in Missouri, Stanfield-Worley in Alabama, and in North Carolina. The radiocarbon dates for the St. Albans deeply stratified sites in West Virginia have corner- and side-notched projectiles back to ca. 8000 B.C. (Broyles 1971).

The interpretation of these data by me is the same as it has been for many years, namely, that the fluted point or Paleo-Indian occupation took place

Figure 3.1. A chronological alignment of prehistoric Eastern United States culture complexes.

significantly before 8000 B.C., and that, over much of the area, the Early Archaic complexes gradually evolved from them.

III. ARCHAIC PERIOD

Continuities for the Fluted Point complexes have been identified or asserted in several publications by various authors, and firm evidence is provided at such sites as the basal layer of the Stanfield-Worley Shelter (De Jarnette *et al.* 1962) and of Graham Cave (Klippel, 1971). The difficulty in chronologically separating the Fluted Point complexes from what is called Early Archaic is simply that we do not have sound stratigraphic data or dated remains of the presumed earliest Archaic groups. Some archaeologists continue to refer to complexes as Paleo-Indian until 6000 to 5000 B.C. They like the term *paleo*. An arbitrary date of 8000 B.C. has been used by many archaeologists to represent the beginning of Early Archaic, and a date of 1000 B.C. has been used for the beginning of the Early Woodland complexes. There is, then, a span of about 7000 years for the Archaic Period, during which many regional Archaic traditions or sequences develop. There is somewhat less uniformity in archaeologists' attempts to divide this time span into smaller temporal units.

In the time period 8000–6000 B.C., in complexes in the mid-South that are identified by Dalton, Big Sandy, Kirk, Suwannee, Plano, and early LeCroy points, there are no ground or polished stone tools. It is therefore tempting to recognize this period as Early Archaic (Broyles 1971; Chapman 1973; Griffin 1967; Morse 1973; Neil 1958).

A number of sites occupied during *Early Archaic* times are under the Atlantic and the Gulf of Mexico; others are covered up by alluvial deposits of rivers, by aeolian deposits, and, particularly in the Great Lakes, by waters of the present lakes. Besides projectile and knife forms of the varieties already mentioned, lithic artifacts include both hand and slab stones for grinding; hammerstones; large ovoid to triangular blades, scrapers, or knives; a variety of scraper forms including uniface end scrapers, teardrop-shaped scrapers, and side, crescent, and stemmed scrapers; flint drills with expanded or cylindrical bases; blades; gravers; chipped stone adzes or gouges; chipped grubbing tools or hoes; and pebble pendants. Very few bone awls or other tools have been recovered.

Occupation sites are in rock shelters, in caves, in the open, in stream valleys, and along lake beaches; and hunting camps have been identified on mountain ridges and passes. One of the few burials presumably associated with this period, at the Renier Site in Wisconsin (Mason and Irwin, 1960), was cremated. A wide variety of food consumed was both animal and vegetal.

A *Middle Archaic* of 6000 to 4000 B.C. can be recognized in the appearance of such forms as grooved axes, stone pendants, and early bannerstone forms, and such grinding and pounding tools as the bell pestle. A well developed bone industry of awls, projectile points, flakers, and atlatl hooks is assigned to the Morrow Mountain Complex at the Stanfield-Worley Shelter in northern Alabama by DeJarnette *et al.* (1962). A bone industry is also recognized in the Eva Complex of west Tennessee (Lewis and Kneberg 1961) and the first dog burials also appear at this time. At the Koster Site in Jersey County, Illinois, a child's burial was covered with powdered hematite and is probably the earliest such example. It must begin the Red Ocher Tradition.

The *Late Archaic* period, from about 4000 to 1000 B.C. has many excavated open sites and occupations in caves, in shelters, and in deeply stratified open sites. This is a reflection of larger populations, increase in production of tools, and better preservation, particularly where the occupation areas include the deposition of large numbers of marine or fresh water shells. While this period has many clearly distinguishable regional complexes, which gradually change through time, there is also a marked development of the exchange of both raw materials and manufactured items between contiguous regions and over long distances. This period represents the major adaptations of populations to regional environments that became more or less stable in terms of many vegetational, faunal, physiographic, and climatic patterns.

There are Late Archaic complexes along the sea coast from the Maritime Archaic development of Maine to Newfoundland (Tuck 1970) to Louisiana (Gagliano, 1967). In the mid-South, the shell mound sites of Alabama, Tennessee, and Kentucky had extensive occupations, and there is a considerable volume of publications describing and interpreting them. Unfortunately the major excavations during the 1930s, which produced so much data on this period, have not had their materials well dated. In the early days of radiocarbon dating, many of the dates produced by the University of Chicago laboratory were either older or younger than their true radiocarbon age. Material submitted by W. S. Webb from Kentucky shell mounds and some others, such as those for the Perry Site in Northern Alabama, unfortunately fall into this group of dates that cannot be regarded as acceptable until comparable material has been run by more modern methods. While some valid dates from the so-called Shell Mound Archaic may go back a bit beyond 3000 B.C., most of the occupation seems to be between that date and as late as 500 B.C.

The excavations at the Robinson Site by Morse (1967) in Smith County, Tennessee, uncovered a terminal Archaic Complex resembling that called Ledbetter by Lewis and Kneberg (1959) in west Tennessee. It contained items indicating contact with the Glacial Kame Complex north of the Ohio, as well as Adena points—evidence of the development of this form during the Late Archaic. The radiocarbon dates have been published and a series of nine dates run from 1280 to 460 B.C. (Crane and Griffin 1968:93–94).

In the Lower Illinois Valley and St. Louis, the Titterington Complex is now recognized as an archaeologists' combination of a number of successive Late Archaic complexes (Griffin 1968b:133–134). The material from the Etley Site in Calhoun County, Illinois, is also found at the Booth Site in Monroe County, Missouri (Klippel 1969), and is one of the latest Archaic levels at the Koster Site in Jersey County, Illinois (T. Cook, personal communication 1973). A reasonable date for this Etley Phase would be about 1500 to 1000 B.C. In the Lower Wabash Valley, the fine study by Winters (1969) of the Riverton culture places this Late Archaic group between 2000 and 1000 B.C.

In the Northeast, the first complex identified as Archaic is known as Lamoka, after the type site in central New York (Ritchie 1932). It is dated about 2500 B.C. The more widespread and varied phases of what is called Laurentian range from 4000 to about 2000 B.C. From 2000 to about 1000 B.C. the River and Snook Kill phases are identified in the eastern Susquehanna drainage of New York and Pennsylvania, while the Frost Island Phase is identified in western central New York (Ritchie 1969a). These three phases are regarded as part of the Susquehanna Late Archaic Tradition. There are comparable phases in eastern Pennsylvania and New Jersey (Kinsey 1972).

The so-called Old Copper Culture in the Upper Great Lakes and Upper St. Lawrence Valley is instead a series of regional traditions in a somewhat similar environmental zone. Their use of native copper began about 3000 B.C. in the Lake Superior area. As knowledge of copper spread, the movement of copper took place both in the form of raw copper and apparently of formed artifacts. The distinctive complex of tools called Old Copper was most common between 2000 and 1000 B.C., but the use of copper for tools and ornaments continued down to the historic period in the Upper Great Lakes (Griffin 1961).

In the Lower Mississippi Valley and adjacent Gulf Coast, the Late Archaic complexes begin to have baking ovens with clay balls by 2000 B.C. Gagliano (1963, 1971) has recognized several different complexes occupying different areas in southern Louisiana. He has emphasized the evidence of interregional trade before strictly Poverty Point times and it seems clear that the Poverty Point culture of about 1000 B.C. is primarily derived from Late Archaic. Baked clay objects are known along the Gulf Coast to the east and up the South Atlantic Coast into the Carolinas. For a time they were regarded as diagnostic of Poverty Point culture, but they are now best regarded as representing a technique of cooking and are associated with the Late Archaic of about 2500 to 1000 B.C.

One of the most surprising results of radiocarbon dating was the age of the fiber-tempered pottery in the Southeast at the sites in the Savannah River area and in northeastern Florida along the St. Johns River. Apparently in both areas the earliest pottery has a plain outer surface which appears about

2500 B.C. in Georgia and about 2140 B.C. in Florida (Bullen and Stoltman 1972). Decorated exterior surfaces on the flat-bottomed bowls or deep, pan-shaped vessels appear around 2000 B.C. in Georgia, and somewhat later in Florida. The paste features and decorative styles of the two areas are distinctive, do not show much relationship, and are replaced in the two areas with quite different ceramic complexes. At sites with sufficient stratigraphic depth, the appearance of fiber-tempered pottery is not accompanied by any other significant artifactual changes. Instead, it is added to the Stalling's Island Late Archaic Complex and to that of the St. Johns. The origin is obscure. The proposal that southeastern fiber-tempered pottery is an introduction from South America (Ford 1969) is not adopted here.

In the Savannah River area, a gradual shift from fiber tempering to sand tempering takes place around 1500 to 1000 B.C. During the next few hundred years, the stamped pottery of the Deptford Period, with jar-shaped vessels, appears. In eastern Florida the shift from fiber-tempered to the St. Johns ceramic complex is also a gradual one, at about 1000 B.C. or slightly later.

The spread of fiber-tempered pottery to the west took place along the Gulf coastal plain. It spread up the Savannah River, and eventually appeared in the Tennessee Valley in northern Alabama and in northeastern Mississippi. There are no radiocarbon dates in northern Alabama, but a date of 1370 (± 160) B.C. has been attributed to a fiber-tempered occupation in western Tennessee (Peterson 1973:35). There are dates from the Teoc Creek Site in Carrol County, Mississippi (Crane and Griffin 1972:176–177), which indicate that fiber-tempered pottery reached the lower Mississippi Valley from the east by about 1000 B.C. It apparently precedes all other ceramic complexes at Teoc Creek and, I would expect, in most of the rest of the Lower Mississippi Valley including Poverty Point.

The fiber-tempered spread to the west is not accompanied by any other notable associations and appears to have a considerable time slope from east to west.

To the north, we find that the earliest pottery in the Middle Atlantic states is around 1200 to 1000 B.C., in the Ohio Valley perhaps by 1000 B.C. or a little earlier, and in New York by about the same age. In the Upper Mississippi Valley and western Great Lakes, the earliest pottery is about 1000 to 500 B.C.

Radiocarbon dating has effectively helped to eliminate the hypothesis of a Eurasiatic origin of Eastern Woodland pottery. Asiatic pottery arrives too late in Alaska, does not spread into central western or southern Canada and has the wrong ceramic attributes to have been the source of Eastern pottery (Griffin 1968a).

At the present time, students of Eastern United States prehistory, with rare exceptions, do not look outside that area for significant population movements to explain the cultural introductions of new complexes which could afford a base for a significant cultural and chronological break. Even those archaeologists who look to Middle or South America for such introductions cannot identify a clearly distinctive cultural complex that arrived at a particular location at a narrow point in time.

IV. WOODLAND COMPLEXES

For some time, archaeologists in the Eastern United States have recognized a number of cultural developments in the period now known to be from about 1000 B.C. or slightly earlier to around 500 B.C. or slightly later. Among these developments are the appearance of burial mounds from Michigan (Crane and Griffin 1968:78, 1970:167; Prahl 1966) dated at 590 and 540 B.C. in the Muskegon Valley, to 1200–400 B.C. at Mound B at Poverty Point, Louisiana (Ford and Webb 1956:122). Hardly any recognizable cultural evidence was obtained at this latter mound, and very few other early mounds have been reliably dated in the Southeast. It is now recognized that occupation of the Poverty Point Site began about 10,000 to 8000 B.C. and for many millennia thereafter (C. H. Webb, personal communication), so that the story of the construction and function of the several earthworks and associated material in the prehistory of the Southeast is still to be deciphered. A small conical earth mound at Avery Island produced a charcoal sample with a date of 2488 (± 260) B.C. (Gagliano 1963:114), but it is difficult to believe it represents the time when the mound was constructed. It is doubtful if there are any burial mounds in the East much before 1000 B.C. They do not seem to appear in north Florida or Georgia until shortly before the time of Christ.

In the Ohio Valley, the Adena culture with burial mounds probably does not get under way until about 500 B.C., for I have become increasingly skeptical of the Chicago date for the Toepfner Mound near Columbus, Ohio, which goes back beyond that period (Libby 1955:104). This corresponds to some degree with the opinions of Shane and Prufer, who see the Adena Phase as occupying a time period between 500 B.C. and 100 B.C. (Shane 1971:144). Adena may last in southeastern Indiana and northern Kentucky so as to be contemporary with Ohio Hopewell. I cannot, however, see them occupying the same or adjacent territory without more evidence of specific Hopewell items in Adena. I would expect Adena had essentially disappeared.

Other Early Woodland complexes that are in the Great Lakes area are dated between 1000 B.C. and up to the appearance of Hopewell about the beginning of our era; and in New York the Meadowood, Orient, and Middlesex phases fill the same time period. Some of these have Early Woodland pottery associated with them.

We now recognize a distinctive time period in much of the East because of the ease in distinguishing Hopewellian pottery and other patterns of artifact manufacture and behavior found at the Hopewell site in Ohio (Shetrone 1926). In the Illinois Valley, an arbitrary date of about 200 B.C. is reasonable for the Fulton and Calhoun phases (Griffin *et al.* 1970: Table I), which provide the ceramic and lithic basis for the more fully developed Havana–Hopewellian Ogden and Bedford phases some two hundred years later. A separation in the central Ohio Valley between Adena burial or village complexes and Hopewell can be made, even though many of the distinctively Adena characteristics are present in an altered form in Hopewell sites. In terms of dates, there is a clear overlap, with some Hopewell dates running back to 200 B.C. and others running up into the sixth century A.D. or later In the central Ohio Valley an end date of Hopewell of about A.D. 400 can be used, and the same figure is even more suitable for the virtual disappearance of Hopewellian traits in Illinois, Michigan, Wisconsin (Freeman 1969:87), Iowa, Missouri, and Kansas. In the South, the Issaquena Phase of the Lower Mississippi Valley lasts a hundred years or so later (Phillips 1970:955–1961), although the exact temporal position is uncertain.

One of the cultural developments that has been of importance to archaeologists in the Eastern United States is the appearance and gradually increasing importance of agriculture. For years, the absence or presence of agriculture helped differentiate the Archaic from the later Woodland and Mississippian cultural groups. From time to time various people have claimed an "independent invention" of agriculture in the East but so far none of these predate the known introduction of agriculture represented by gourd, squash, and sunflower, which are best dated at Salts Cave, Kentucky (Watson 1969), during the middle third of the first millennium B.C. Squash is reported during this same period from Ohio and Michigan. Since this was written cucurbits have been found in Late Archaic sites in Kentucky and in Missouri dating to the last half of the third millennium B.C. (P. J. Watson, personal communication). It can be assumed that some amount of agriculture was practiced over a fair-sized area in the East during this period. Corn does not make its initial appearance until about the time of Christ, when it is reported from a few Hopewellian sites in Ohio and Illinois, and then only in small amounts. It took from roughly 1000 B.C. to A.D. 700 for agriculture to become a basic subsistence factor, and the populations in the East continued their dependence on hunting and gathering skills developed during the long Archaic Period.

Two radiocarbon dates have recently been obtained that probably date some part of the Copena Complex in northern Alabama long known to have associations with Hopewell. These dates in the fourth century A.D. (Walthall 1972) will not cover the entire time span of Copena but clearly indicate a correspondence with the latter part of Middle Woodland Hopewellian activities.

In the eastern Tennessee–North Carolina area, evidence of Hopewellian contact at a number of sites has been recognized (Keel 1976). Ceramic materials and clearly imported Flint Ridge Ohio blades belong in a time period identified as the Connestee Phase, estimated to be around A.D. 300 to 400. This would seem to be a bit late for evidence of Hopewellian material at the Mandeville Site in southwest Georgia (Kellar *et al.* 1962; Crane and Griffin 1964:9). Its date of A.D. 420 (± 120) is thought to be toward the upper temporal limits of Hopewellian trade. The only dated site in Florida with strong and direct connections to Northern Hopewell is Crystal River in Citrus County, where dates of A.D. 80 (± 130) and A.D. 200 (± 170) are in good conformity with Northern time assessments (Buckley *et al.* 1968:282–283), although it is not clear what the direct association with Hopewell might be.

On the southwestern edge of Hopewellian exchange is the border area of Louisiana and Texas, where, in the Coral Snake Mound, copper earspools, copper beads, a copper gorget fragment, and a very late "Marksville Stamped" bird design on a burial vessel, sherds, projective points, boatstones, and a most unusual quartz figurine, probably of Mexican derivation, is presumably associated with a radiocarbon date of A.D. 300 (Tx-265, 1650 [± 90]). (McClurkan *et al.* 1966). Subsequent excavation produced additional Marksville style pottery, and a radiocarbon date of 20 B.C. is assigned to this material (Jensen 1968).

Along the north-central border of the United States, the Laurel culture of Minnesota, Wisconsin, and Michigan belongs in the Middle Woodland Period for some part of its life span. It shows some ceramic and other connections to Hopewellian sites to the south and more expecially to Point Peninsula sites in Ontario and the New York area. Available radiocarbon dates and a discussion of this complex may be found in Stoltman (1973:87). The complex may be said to begin around A.D. 1, but, like its Point Peninsula relative to the east, lasts longer temporally than do the Hopewellian complexes to the south.

The Point Peninsula Tradition in the east is interpreted as lasting from the second century A.D. to close to A.D. 1000 (Ritchie 1969a:Fig 1). It does not conform in its temporal range to Middle Woodland in the Mississippi Valley, which, with the disappearance of Hopewellian characteristics, is essentially over in the early fifth century A.D. Since the archaeologists in the mid-Atlantic states and New England find their closest comparative material in New York, they also have tended to regard Middle Woodland and Point Peninsula as essentially the same thing in terms of time (Kinsey 1972:364–373; Ritchie 1969b:226).

In the northwest part of the area, the Arvilla culture stratigraphically follows Laurel and precedes the Cambria and Oneota complexes. Arvilla's time period is believed to be from about A.D. 500 to 900 by Johnson (1973:66). He also indicates that Black Duck, a major Late Woodland Complex in Minnesota, may have developed in part from Arvilla. Related Late Woodland groups such as Clam River and Kathio of the Upper Mississippi are believed to belong to the post–A.D. 900 time period.

V. AGRICULTURAL COMPLEXES IN THE MISSISSIPPIAN PERIOD

In much of the central and lower Mississippi Valley between A.D. 500 and 1000, a series of gradual changes took place that served to reorient the cultural structure over much of the Eastern United States. There was a marked increase in the adoption of agriculture as an important subsistence base, the first appearance of earthen platform mounds to support civic and religious structures, the development of ceremonial plazas, and fortified villages, a major increase in the number of ceramic forms and decorative techniques for a variety of functions and an increase in pottery production, the beginning of art styles and ceremonial objects associated with regular annual group ceremonies and observances, the introduction of the bow and arrow, indications of increased intersite and interregional trade, and solid evidence for the rise of class distinctions reflected primarily in certain burial practices at major ceremonial centers.

These changes are not sudden but gradual and do not take place in any one center and radiate from there. The major region in which the developments are seen is roughly from St. Louis to Vicksburg in the Mississippi Alluvial Valley. Comparable developments gradually appear in the rest of the Southeast from Florida to southern Ohio.

One of the major centers in the North was in the American Bottoms from about Alton to Columbia, Illinois. The group of archaeologists concerned with this area have recently issued a short revision of the developmental sequence in this Cahokia area, along with a brief itemization of some developments of the several periods (Fowler and Hall 1972). This underwent some revisions at the Cahokia Conference in July of 1973. The Late Woodland occupation at Cahokia from about A.D. 600 to 800 is named the Patrick Phase. An unnamed phase was suggested for the period A.D. 800–900, which is thought to represent some of the first shifts of vessel forms to the Mississippian shapes and certain other changes in houses, projectiles, and so on. The Fairmount Phase from A.D. 900 to 1050 clearly is in the Mississippian cultural framework in terms of house, ceramic and projectile forms, and the beginning of the construction of Monks Mound. The Sterling Phase from A.D. 1050 to 1150 is the early part of the former term "Old Village" and has the well-developed early shell tempered pottery complex, evidence of strong exchange or influence from the as yet unknown Caddoan centers in southwest Arkansas, and presumably fortifications around a plaza. The succeeding Moorehead Phase is from A.D. 1150 to 1250 and is the last half of "Old Village" and the beginning of the "Trappist Phase." It corresponds to what was called the "Cahokia Climax." Most of the Trappist Phase or late Mississippian material at Cahokia is now called the Sand Prairie Phase from A.D. 1250 to 1500. This occupation corresponds and is analogous to the major Mississippian occupation in the central Illinois Valley and in the Lower Wabash. There was quite a bit of activity at Monks Mound as revealed by additions to the east and south slopes, but evidence for this period had disappeared from the top before the Washington University excavations of a few years ago. There is little solid evidence for occupation in the central area from A.D. 1500 to 1700.

At the other end of the valley, our most recent chronological ordering is in Phillips (1970:955–961), whose emphasis is on the Lower Yazoo Basin. Following the Marksville Period, there is a Baytown Period from about A.D. 300 to 700; Coles Creek from A.D. 700 to 1000, followed by a four-phase division of the Mississippi Period from A.D. 1000 to 1750. This temporal alignment is "arranged" rather than being based on a large, consistent series of radiocarbon dates. Of primary interest is the Coles Creek Period, in which the initial elements of Mississippian Culture (in a broad sense) begin to appear. Coles Creek, however, is a distinctive development in the Deep South and reflects considerable interaction along the coastal area from Florida to northeast Texas. It also has extensive relationships into the Red River area of Louisiana and into southern and eastern Oklahoma, where the early Caddoan complexes are under way by the latter part of the first millennium.

AUTHOR'S NOTE

The manuscript was submitted in October, 1973.

BIBLIOGRAPHY

Bell, R.

1951 Dendrochronology at the Kincaid Site. In *Kincaid: A Prehistoric Illinois Metropolis* edited by Fay Cooper Cole and others. Chicago: University of Chicago Press. Pp. 233–292.

1952 Dendrochronology in the Mississippi Valley. In *Archeology of Eastern United States,* edited by J. B. Griffin. Chicago: University of Chicago Press. Pp. 345–351.

Broyles, B. J.

1971 Second Preliminary Report: The St. Alban's Site, Kanawha County, West Virginia. *Report of Archeological Investigations No. 3*. West Virginia Geological and Economic Survey. *Pp. I–XI, 1–104.*

Buckley, J. D., M. A. Trautman, and E. H. Willis

1968 Isotopes' Radiocarbon Measurement VI, *Radiocarbon* **10**(2):246–294.

Bullen, R. P., and J. B. Stoltman (Editors)

1972 Fiber-Tempered Pottery in Southeastern United States and Northern Columbia: Its

Origins, Context and Significance. *The Florida Anthropologist* **25** (2) pt.2: *Florida Anthropological Society Publication* No. **6.**

Chapman, J.

1973 An Early Archaic LeCroy Site in the Little Tennessee Valley. Paper read at Southeast Archaeological Conference, Memphis, Oct. 5.

Cole, F. C., and T. Deuel

1937 *Rediscovering Illinois: Archaeological Explorations in and around Fulton County. Chicago: The University of Chicago Press.*

Crane, H. R., and J. B. Griffin

1964 University of Michigan Radiocarbon Dates IX. *Radiocarbon* **6:**1–24.

1968 University of Michigan Radiocarbon Dates XII. *Radiocarbon* **10** (1):61–114.

1970 University of Michigan Radiocarbon Dates XIII. *Radiocarbon* **12** (1):161–180.

1972 University of Michigan Radiocarbon Dates XIV. *Radiocarbon* **14** (1):155–194.

DeJarnette, D. I., E. B. Kurjack and J. W. Cambron

1962 Stanfield-Worley Bluff Shelter Excavation. *Journal of Alabama Archaeology* **8** (1–2): 1–119.

Fisk, H. N.

1944 Geological Investigation of the Alluvial Valley of the Lower Mississippi River. War Department, Corps of Engineers, U.S. Army, *Mississippi River Commission Publication* No. **52.**

Ford, J. A.

1935 Ceramic Decoration Sequence at an Old Indian Village Site near Sicily Island. Louisiana. *Louisiana Geological Survey, Anthropological Study* No. **1.**

1936 Analysis of Indian Village Site Collections from Louisiana and Mississippi. *Louisiana Geological Survey, Anthropological Study* No. **2.**

1969 A Comparison of Formative Cultures in the Americas, Diffusion or the Psychic Unity of Man. *Smithsonian Contributions to Anthropology* No. **2.**

Ford, James A., and C. H. Webb

1956 Poverty Point, A Late Archaic Site in Louisiana. Anthropological *Papers of the American Museum of Natural History* **46**(1) 1–136.

Fowke, G.

1902 *Archaeological History of Ohio*. Columbus: Ohio Archaeological and Historical Society.

Fowler, M. L., and R. L. Hall

1972 Archaeological Phases at Cahokia. *Illinois State Museum, Research Papers in Anthropology* No. **1.**

Freeman, J. E.

1969 The Millville Site, a Middle Woodland Village in Grant County, Wisconsin. *The Wisconsin Archaeologist* **50:**37–88.

Funk, R. E., G. Walters, W. F. Ehlers Jr., J. E. Guilday, and G. G. Connally

1969 The Archaeology of Dutchess Quarry Cave, Orange County, New York. *Pennsylvania Archaeologist* **39** (1–4):7–22.

Gagliano, S.

1963 A Survey of Preceramic Occupations in Portions of South Louisiana and South Mississippi. *Coastal Studies Institute Contribution* **63-7.** *United States Gulf Coastal Studies Tech. Report* **16,** Part E.

1967 Late Archaic–Early Formative Relationships in South Louisiana. *Proceedings of the 23rd Southeastern Archaeological Conference, Bulletin* **6:**9–22.

1971 Archaic Poverty Point Transition at the Pearl River Mound. *Southeastern Archaeological Conference Bulletin* **12.**

Griffin, J. B.

1952 Culture Periods in Eastern United States Archeology. In *Archeology of Eastern*

United States, edited by J. B. Griffin. Chicago: University of Chicago Press. Pp. 352–364.

1961 Lake Superior Copper and the Indians; Miscellaneous Studies of Great Lakes Prehistory. *University of Michigan Anthropological Papers* No. **17.**

1967 Eastern North American Archaeology: A Summary. *Science* **156** (3732):175–191.

1968a Northeast Asian and Northwestern American Ceramics. *Proceedings of the VIIIth International Congress of Anthropological and Ethnological Sciences* **3:**327–330.

1968b Observations on Illinois Prehistory in the Late Pleistocene and Early Recent Times in the Quaternary of Illinois. *University of Illinois College of Agriculture Special Publication* No. **14.**

Griffin, J. B., R. E. Flanders, and P. F. Titterington

1970 The Burial Complexes of the Knight and Norton Mounds in Illinois and Michigan. *University of Michigan, Memoirs of the Museum of Anthropology* **2.**

Hawkes, E. W., and R. Linton

1916 A Pre-Lenape Site in New Jersey. *University of Pennsylvania Anthropological Publications* **6,** No. 3:43–80.

Holmes, W. H.

1919 Handbook of Aboriginal American Antiquities. Part 1. Introductory. The Lithic Industries. *Bureau of American Ethnology Bulletin* No. **60.**

Huxtable, J., M. J. Aitken, and J. C. Weber.

1972 Thermoluminescent Dating of Baked Clay Balls of the Poverty Point Culture. *Archaeometry* **14** (2):269–275.

Jensen, H. P., Jr.

1968 Coral Snake Mound. *Bulletin of the Texas Archaeology Society* **39:**9–44.

Johnson, E.

1973 The Arvilla Complex. *Minnesota Historical Society, Minnesota Prehistoric Archaeology Series* No. **9.**

Keel, B. C.

1976 Cherokee Archaeology. A Study of the Appalachian Summit. Knoxville: University of Tennessee Press.

Kellar, J. H., A. R. Kelly, and E. V. McMichael

1962 The Mandeville Site in Southwest Georgia. *American Antiquity* **27** (3):336–355.

Kinsey, W. F.

1972 Archaeology in the Upper Delaware Valley. With contributions by H. C. Kraft, P. Marchiando and D. Werner. *Pennsylvania Historical and Museum Commission, Anthropological Series* No. **2.**

Klippel, W. E.

1969 The Booth Site: A Late Archaic Campsite. *Missouri Archaeological Society Research Series* No. **6.**

1971 Graham Cave Revisited: A Re-Evaluation of Its Cultural Position During the Archaic Period. *Missouri Archaeological Society Memoir* No. **9.**

Kniffen, F. B.

1936 A Preliminary Report of the Mounds and Middens of Plaquemine and St. Bernard Parishes, Lower Mississippi River Delta. *Louisiana Department of Conservation, Geological Bulletin* **8:**407–422.

Krogman, W. M.

1931 Archaeology of the Chicago Area. *Transactions of the Illinois Academy of Science* **23** (3):413–420.

Langford, G.

1927 The Fisher Mound Group. *American Anthropologist* **24** (3):153–206.

1928 Stratified Indian Mounds in Will County. *Transactions of the Illinois Academy of Science* **20:**247–254.

Lee, T. E.
1957 The Antiquity of the Shequiandah Site. *Canadian Field Naturalist* **71** (3):117–137.
Lewis, T. M. N., and M. Kneberg
1959 The Archaic Culture in the Middle South. *American Antiquity* **25** (2):161–183.
1961 *Eva, An Archaic Site*. University of Tennessee Study in Anthropology. Knoxville: Univ. of Tennessee Press.
Libby, W. F.
1955 *Radiocarbon Dating*. 2nd ed. Chicago: University of Chicago Press.
MacDonald, G. F.
1968 Debert: A Paleo-Indian Site in Central Nova Scotia. *National Museum of Canada Anthropological Papers* No. **16.**
Mason, R. J.
1958 Late Pleistocene Geochronology and the Paleo-Indian: Penetration of the Lower Michigan Peninsula. *Museum of Anthropology, University of Michigan, Ann Arbor, Anthropological Papers* No. **11.**
Mason, R. J., and C. Irwin
1960 An Eden-Scottsbluff Burial in Northeastern Wisconsin. *American Antiquity* **26** (1):43–57.
McClurkan, B., W. T. Field, and J. N. Woodall
1966 Excavations in Toledo Bend Reservoir, 1964–65. *Papers of the Texas Archaeological Salvage Project* No. **8.**
Morse, D. F.
1967 The Robinson Site and Shell Mound Archaic Culture in the Middle South. Unpublished Ph.D. dissertation, University of Michigan, Ann Harbor.
1973 Dalton Culture in Northeast Arkansas. *Florida Anthropologist* **26** (1):23–28.
Neill, W. T.
1958 A Stratified Early Site at Silver Springs, Florida. *Florida Anthropologist* **11:**35–52.
Peterson, D. A., Jr.
1973 The Spring Creek Site, Perry County, Tennessee: Report of the 1972–73 Excavations. *Memphis State University Anthropological Research Center Occasional Papers* No. **7.**
Phillips, P., J. A. Ford, and J. B. Griffin
1951 Archaeological Survey in the Lower Mississippi Alluvial Valley, 1946–1947. *Harvard University, Papers of the Peabody Museum of American Archaeology and Ethnology* Vol. **25.**
Phillips, P.
1970 Archaeological Survey in the Lower Yazoo Basin, Mississippi, 1949–1955. *Harvard University, Papers of the Peabody Museum of Archaeology and Ethnology* Vol. **60.**
Prahl, E. J.
1966 The Muskegon River Survey: 1965 and 1966. *The Michigan Archaeologist* **12** (4):183–209.
Ralph, E. K., H. N. Michael, and M. C. Han
1973 Radiocarbon Dates and Reality. *MASCA Newsletter* **9** (1):1–20.
Ritchie, W. A.
1932 The Lamoka Lake Site: The Type Station of the Archaic Algonkin Period in New York. *Researches and Transactions of the New York State Archaeological Association* **7** (4).
1969a *The Archaeology of New York State*. Rev. ed. New York: Natural History Press.
1969b *The Archaeology of Martha's Vineyard.* New York: Natural History Press.
Sears, P. B.
1932 The Archaeology of Environment in Eastern North America. *American Anthropologist* **34** (4):610–622.

Shane, O. C. III

1971 *Adena: The Seeking of an Identity,* edited by B. K. Swartz, Jr. Muncie, Indiana: Ball State University.

Shetrone, H. C.

1920 The Culture Problem in Ohio Archaeology. *American Anthropologist* **22** (2):144–172.

1926 Exploration of the Hopewell Group of Prehistoric Earthworks. *Certain Mounds and Village Sites in Ohio* **4**(4):79–305.

Shimer, H. W.

1918 Post-Glacial History of Boston. *Proceedings of the American Academy of Arts and Sciences* **53:**441–463.

Stoltman, J. B.

1973 The Laurel Culture in Minnesota. *Minnesota Historical Society, Minnesota Prehistoric Archaeology Series* No. **8.**

Suess, H. E.

1970 Bristlecone Pine Calibration Time-Scale 5200 B.C. to the Present. In *Proceedings of the 12th Nobel Symposium, Uppsala*, edited by I. U. Olsson. New York: Wiley. Pp. 303–312.

Thomas, C.

1898 *Introduction to the Study of North American Archaeology*. Cincinnati: The Robert Clarke Company.

Tuck, J. A.

1970 An Archaic Indian Cemetery in Newfoundland. *Scientific American* **222**(6):112–121.

Walthall, J. A.

1972 The Chronological Position of Copena in Eastern States Archaeology. *Journal of Alabama Anthropology* **28** (2):136–151.

Waterbolk, H. W.

1971 Working with Radiocarbon Dates. *Proceedings of the Prehistoric Society for 1971* **38:**15–33.

Watson, P. J.

1969 The Prehistory of Salts Cave, Kentucky. *Illinois State Museum Report of Investigations* No. **16.**

Winters, H. D.

1969 The Riverton Culture. *Illinois State Museum Report of Investigations* No. **13** (Published also as Illinois Archaeological Survey Monograph No. 1).

Diablo Range

EDWARD B. JELKS

I. INTRODUCTION

A. Geographical Characteristics

Hemmed in by the Plains Culture area on the north, the Southeastern United States Culture area on the east, the Southwestern United States Culture area on the west, the Mesoamerican Culture area on the southwest, and the Gulf of Mexico on the southeast is a semiarid region comprising some 230,000 square miles which was the homeland of perhaps the most tenaciously conservative prehistoric population in all of North America. From the Sierra Madre of Coahuila to the rugged canyons of the Lower Pecos River, from the rocky hill country of Central Texas to the sandy shores of the Gulf Coast—virtually everywhere in this vast area the earliest

European explorers discovered seminomadic bands of nonagricultural peoples who subsisted by foraging off the floral and faunal resources of land and sea. Subsequently, archaeological investigations revealed that the forebears of those historic tribes had followed essentially the same mode of existence over the preceding 10,000 years or more. Because of the simple life style of its inhabitants, the eastern part of this region has been referred to by such derogatory appellations as *cultural sink* (Swanton 1924), *cultural sump* (Kroeber 1939), and *ethnographic sink* (Sjoberg 1953:280). Newcomb (1956) has suggested a more appropriate name: *the Western Gulf area.*

The archaeological culture area we are concerned with here, however, comprises considerably more territory than Newcomb included in his Western Gulf area. A singular country of distinctive character, it has long been associated with hellishness, owing no doubt to its overall harshness: its intense heat, aridity, and rocky soils; its rattlesnakes, scorpions, and centipedes; its cacti and relentlessly clutching, thorned vegetation. Testifying to its satanic image are such place names as *Devils River, Satan Canyon, Devil's Backbone, Canyon Diablo,* and the like—names which are common from western Texas to the Sierra de Tamaulipas. Having fallen under the region's Mephistophelean spell, archaeologists have coined such terms as the *Diablo Complex,* the *Infiernillo Complex,* and *Frightful Cave.* This colorful archaeological culture area has long needed a fitting name; therefore I christen it, here and now, the *Diablo Range.*

The indigenous peoples of the Diablo Range constituted part of the so-called Desert Culture (Jennings and Norbeck 1955; Kelley 1959), a hunting–gathering culture that was dispersed broadly across arid and semiarid North America several thousand years ago, but which eventually was superseded in most localities by more sedentary cultures. A Mesoamerican-inspired, agriculturally based culture wedging northward into the Southwestern United States in relatively recent prehistoric times sundered the Desert Culture peoples into two major segments, both of which survived virtually unchanged into historic times. One such Desert Culture island was in the Great Basin area of Nevada and adjoining states; the other occupied the Diablo Range.

Boundaries of the Diablo Range may be described approximately by a line starting at the mouth of the Sabine River near the Texas–Louisiana border, running up the Sabine for some 50 or 60 miles, then curving west-northwest and continuing to the headwaters of the Brazos River; turning southwest at that point, it crosses the Pecos River in its middle course and heads for the confluence of the Conchos and Rio Grande rivers, whence it runs up the Conchos to its headwaters in the mountains of southeastern Chihuahua; there it turns sharply toward the east-southeast, passes near the southern border of Coahuila, crosses southern Nuevo Leon and central Tamaulipas, and returns to the Gulf of Mexico at the mouth of the Rio Soto la Marina (Figure 4.1).

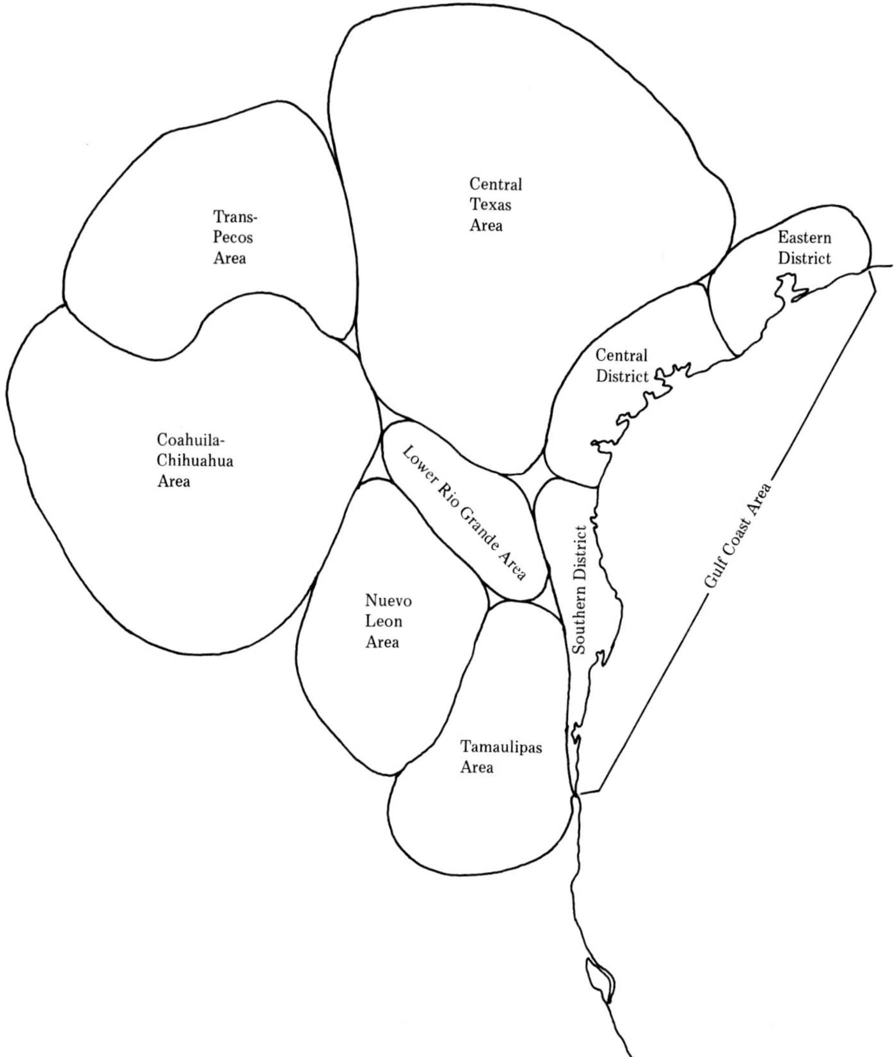

Figure 4.1. Location map of the Diablo Range, its areas, and its districts.

Except for a strip of coastal plain 50 to 150 miles wide, this entire region presents a rugged topography, much of it mountainous. Vegetation over most of the region consists of cactus, desert grasses, and scrubby, thorny shrubs and trees. But oaks, cottonwoods, and other large trees grow along permanent streams, and there are pines and junipers at higher elevations in the mountains, as well as atop the Edwards Plateau of Central and West-Central Texas. Although much of the countryside is rather forbidding and vegetation is anything but lush, there are large quantities of readily available foods that are quite nutritious, if not especially appetizing: sotol and agave plants, which can be baked and eaten like artichokes, mesquite beans, cactus pads and fruits, land snails, river mussels, and various kinds of grass seeds. Fish, deer, and rabbits were utilized as food by the inhabitants all over the region, and bison were numerous at times in many localities on the Edwards Plateau and the Coastal Plain. That these food resources were abundant and dependable is evidenced by the fact that they supported a sizable population of people for hundreds of generations.

B. Chronological Structure

Archaeologists working in the Diablo Range invariably have been struck by the persistence of the basic Desert Culture pattern through the 10 or 12 millennia represented by the archaeological record as currently known. Consequently, the problem of ordering archaeological data chronologically does not turn on a series of major changes in culture patterns; rather, a chronology must be framed largely from subtle changes in styles of artifacts, manufacturing techniques, resource utilization, and the like. However, a uniform chronology for the whole region is not feasible, except at a very general level, as there are significant variations in material culture in the geographical, as well as in the temporal, dimension. The problem of establishing a general chronology has been compounded further by the fact that each of the archaeologists who has worked in the area has specialized in only one or two subareas—a practice that has nurtured fragmentation, instead of synthesis, of knowledge about the region.

Seven geographically and culturally distinct areas traditionally have been recognized within the Diablo Range: the Central Texas, Trans-Pecos, Coahuila–Chihuahua, Nuevo Leon, Tamaulipas, Lower Rio Grande, and Gulf Coast areas.

For each of these seven areas a local chronology has been worked out more or less independently of the other areas. This has resulted in duplicate and even triplicate names for what obviously are the same types of artifacts, in controversies about how two independently formulated local chronologies should be aligned, and in other problems inherent in independently pursued local studies that are not adequately coordinated at the regional level. The major exception is in the Central Texas and Trans-Pecos areas, where most research has been conducted by the same small group of archaeologists (who, however, have had little or no firsthand experience in the other five areas), and consequently the chronologies for those two areas are closely coordinated. There are also vast differences in the quantity and quality of chronological data that are available for the respective areas. For example, no more than half a dozen important sites—if that many—have been excavated in the Coahuila–Chihuahua area, and there are virtually no published descriptions of artifact types, stratigraphy, or other data that can be used for comparison with other areas. In contrast, hundreds of important sites—many of them beautifully stratified—have been excavated in the Central Texas and Trans-Pecos areas combined, and hundreds of detailed descriptive reports about them are in print.

I shall here attempt to synthesize a general chronology for the Diablo Range, using published data almost exclusively. Wherever possible, only those data will be used that are properly supported by controlled stratigraphic excavation or by contextually conjoined radiocarbon dates, but sometimes it is necessary to fall back on surface material as no other data are available. By and large, projectile point morphology has been the most sensitive and effective temporal indicator thus far recognized among the various classes of artifacts present in the region, and projectile point typology has been used as a major criterion for chronological ordering in all the respective areas of the region. Therefore, the regional chronology presented here is oriented around changes in projectile point morphology through time. Specific types of points that have been described in print previously and are generally recognized as valid cultural types constitute the building blocks of the chronology. Morphologically similar types considered to be historically related are combined into groups termed *series,* and series are grouped into larger classes called *styles.* The approach of classing projectile points into series of morphologically similar types has precedence in the Diablo Range, especially in the Trans-Pecos (e.g., Epstein 1963; Johnson 1967; Nunley *et al.* 1965; Ross 1965). Different styles, at a higher level of classification than series, have also commonly been recognized, but a formal classification of styles as such has not heretofore been formulated. The classification of series presented here represents in part a synthesis of the series schemes cited above. Typological and chronological data from Central Texas and the Trans-Pecos constitute the primary foundation of the chronology because the data from those two areas are much more extensive and substantial than data from the other areas.

The respective series and styles are believed to follow the same sequential order over the whole Diablo Range. In some areas, certain types or series may be extremely rare or not present at all; but wherever present, a particular series occupies the same temporal position relative to the other series. However, each series does not necessarily occupy precisely the same time period in terms of calendrical dates throughout the entire region.

II. PROJECTILE POINT CHRONOLOGY

Looking at the Diablo Range as a whole, it is patent that three distinctive, readily recognizable projectile point traditions—or *styles* as they are here termed—are well represented. These are formally designated as follows:

1. *The Paleomorphic Style:* typical dart points of what is widely known as the Paleo-Indian cultural tradition
2. *The Archeomorphic Style:* typical dart points of what might be termed the Western Archaic, or perhaps the Desert, cultural tradition
3. *The Neomorphic Style:* typical arrow points, much smaller and lighter than the dart points of the Paleomorphic and Archeomorphic styles.

Our regional chronology, then, consists fundamentally of these three major styles, each of which has significant internal variations that can be ordered temporally and geographically in terms of types and in groups of related types that will be designated *series*. Figure 4.2 outlines the chronol-

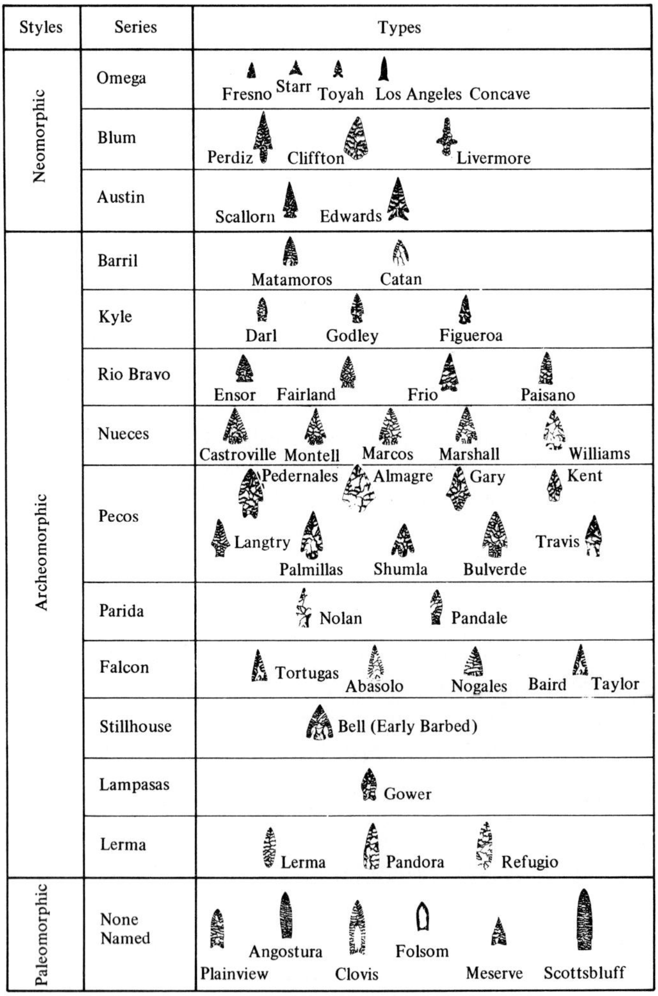

Styles	Series	Types
Neomorphic	Omega	Fresno, Starr, Toyah, Los Angeles Concave
	Blum	Perdiz, Cliffton, Livermore
	Austin	Scallorn, Edwards
Archeomorphic	Barril	Matamoros, Catan
	Kyle	Darl, Godley, Figueroa
	Rio Bravo	Ensor, Fairland, Frio, Paisano
	Nueces	Castroville, Montell, Marcos, Marshall, Williams
	Pecos	Pedernales, Almagre, Gary, Kent, Langtry, Palmillas, Shumla, Bulverde, Travis
	Parida	Nolan, Pandale
	Falcon	Tortugas, Abasolo, Nogales, Baird, Taylor
	Stillhouse	Bell (Early Barbed)
	Lampasas	Gower
	Lerma	Lerma, Pandora, Refugio
Paleomorphic	None Named	Plainview, Angostura, Clovis, Folsom, Meserve, Scottsbluff

Figure 4.2. Chronological classification of projectile points for the Diablo Range.

ogy. The reader who wants to comprehend the whole chronology is advised first to go over Figure 4.2 thoroughly and thereafter to consult it from time to time while reading the comments about each of the respective styles, series, and types that follow.

A. Paleomorphic Style

Dart points of widely recognized Paleomorphic types (i.e., types generally associated with the so-called Paleo-Indian cultural tradition) have been reported in relatively small numbers from all seven areas of the Diablo Range. The heaviest occurrence, however, appears to be in Central Texas and the Trans-Pecos.

More *Plainview* type points have been found than any other Paleomorphic type, the *golondrina* variety of *Plainview* (Johnson 1964:46–52) being especially characteristic. Other reported types include *Angostura* (second most frequent), *Clovis, Folsom, Meserve,* and *Scottsbluff.* When found in clear stratigraphic context, the Paleomorphic points usually occur in the deepest strata of a site: at the Levi Site in Central Texas (Alexander 1963) and at Devil's Mouth (Johnson 1964; Sorrow 1968a) and Bonfire Cave (Dibble and Lorrain 1968) in the Trans-Pecos, to cite examples. It is not uncommon, however, to find a Paleomorphic point or two in an Archaic component anywhere in the Diablo Range. These may have been picked up and brought home by Archaic people as curiosities or for reworking (as is evidenced by patinated specimens that were subsequently reflaked through the patina); or it is possible that early Archeomorphic and late Paleomorphic types sometimes were made and used by the same people.

While the Paleomorphic types validly might be put into series (e.g., *Fluted Series*), the total sample is so small—and evidence for ordering the types in the Diablo Range is so sparse—that it would not be appropriate to do so at this point. Paleomorphic style points date generally earlier than about 6000 B.C. in the Diablo Range.

B. Archeomorphic Style

Most Archeomorphic dart points are different from classic Paleomorphic points in having separate and distinct stem and blade areas, and in having shoulders at the corners of the blade. There are some bipointed, leaf-shaped, triangular, and other Archeomorphic forms that are not shouldered; but these almost always can be readily distinguished from Paleomorphic points because they do not have the precise, delicate workmanship, smoothed basal edges, concave base, or overall shape of the latter.

Archeomorphic points of the Diablo Range exhibit, as a group, what appears on first examination to be a hopelessly bewildering array of forms. Yet, on close analysis, there are certain morphological themes that can be related, respectively, to particular time periods and/or to particular geographical localities. These themes constitute the basis for the Archeomorphic projectile point sequence presented here.

The Archeomorphic sequence is organized into nine separate, chronologically ordered series, each series normally consisting of several established types, together with specimens that fit generically into the series even though they cannot be assigned to specific types at the present time. The Archeomorphic sequence correlates approximately with the Archaic Stage or cultural tradition as defined for Texas by Suhm *et al.* (1954:18–20). Thus it roughly spans the period 7000 B.C. to A.D. 500–1000 for the Diablo Range as a whole, not taking local variations into account. The Archaic Stage is further divided into six substages: Incipient Archaic, Early Archaic, Middle Archaic, Late Archaic, Terminal Archaic, and Transitional Archaic. Correlation of the Archeomorphic series and types with the Archaic substages and with calendrical dates is shown in Figures 4.1 and 4.2. Each of the Archeomorphic series is now described separately.

LERMA SERIES

Morphological Description: Unstemmed, double-pointed dart points, relatively large and crudely chipped.

Included Types: *Lerma* principal type; possibly also *Refugio* and *Pandora*. The concept of the *Lerma* type has not been applied consistently throughout the Diablo Range. Here are included not only those specimens identified as *Lerma* in various published reports but also what has been termed *Form 8* knives by Johnson (1964: 62, Fig. 19 E, F) and by Sorrow (1968a:32–35, Fig. 24 f, g), and *Fragua* points by Taylor (1966: Fig. 3).

Descriptive References: Bell 1958:40, Pl. 20; Epstein 1963:43, Fig. 9 F–I; MacNeish 1958:62, Fig. 23, Specimens 22–27; Nunley *et al.* 1965:55–56, Fig. 17 H–J; Suhm *et al.* 1954:440, Pl. 99.

Sequential Level: Incipient Archaic.

Estimated Dates: MacNeish (1958: 199) 8000–6800 B.C. for Lerma Phase in the Sierra de Tamaulipas; Epstein (1963: 116) 7000–4000 B.C. for Amistad Reservoir area; Johnson (1964: Fig. 25) earlier than 5000 B.C. for Area C at Devil's Mouth Site; Story (1966: Table 1) earlier than 7000 B.C. for Time Period I at Amistad Reservoir area. *Present estimate for Diablo Range:* 8000–5000 B.C.

Geographic Distribution: Has been reported from all areas of the Diablo Range, most frequently from the Sierra de Tamaulipas and the Trans-Pecos.

LAMPASAS SERIES

Morphological Description: Small, stemmed points with concave bases and weak shoulders.

Included Types: *Gower* (including Kelly's [1961a] *Crumley* points).

Descriptive References: *Gower:* Shafer 1963:64–65, Fig. 7 A–K; Prewitt 1966:223; Sorrow *et al.* 1967:80, Fig. 47 n–p. *No type name given:* Johnson 1964:55, Fig. 17 J; Sorrow 1968a:21, Fig. 18 a–b.

Sequential Level: Incipient Archaic.

Estimated Dates: Sorrow *et al.* (1967: 143, Fig. 72) 6000–4500 B.C. for Central Texas; Story (1966: Table 1) 7000–4000 B.C. for Time Period II at Amistad Reservoir area. *Present estimate for Diablo Range:* 7000–4500 B.C.

Geographical Distribution: Well established for Central Texas and the eastern Trans-Pecos; probably present in Coahuila–Chihuahua, Nuevo Leon, and Central Coast; apparently absent in Lower Rio Grande, Tamaulipas, Southern Coast, and Eastern Coast.

STILLHOUSE SERIES

Morphological Description: Varied group having conspicuously barbed shoulders, and stems with approximately parallel lateral edges; bases range from mildly convex to deeply concave.

Included Types: *Bell;* also what has become commonly known as "Early Barbed."

Descriptive References: *Bell:* Sorrow *et al.* 1967:12–14, Fig. 10 a–j. *Early Barbed:* Johnson 1964:33–34, Fig. 11 J–S; Ross 1965:52–53, Fig. 12 G–O; Sorrow 1968a:26–28, Fig. 18 p–q.

Sequential Level: Early Archaic.

Estimated Dates: Johnson (1964:98) 4500–4000 B.C. for Amistad Reservoir area; Ross (1965:139) ca. 6700–4000 B.C. for Eagle Cave in Trans-Pecos; Story (1966: Table 1) 7000–4000 B.C. for Amistad area; Sorrow *et al.* (1967: Fig. 72) 4500–3500 B.C. for Central Texas. *Present estimate for Diablo Range:* 6500–4000 B.C.

Geographical Distribution: A common Early Archaic form in Central Texas and in the eastern part of the Trans-Pecos; not reported from other areas, but could be present elsewhere, especially in the Coahuila–Chihuahua and central Gulf Coast areas.

FALCON SERIES

Morphological Description: Unstemmed, large, triangular or subtriangular dart points.

Included Types: *Tortugas, Baird, Taylor, Abasolo, Nogales.* (*Note:* Suhm *et al.* [1954:482, Pl. 120] lumped the *Baird* and *Taylor* types together with other triangular forms under the single type name *Tortugas.* A typological distinction between *Tortugas, Baird,* and *Taylor* recently has been recognized by Sorrow [1969:19], a reversion to a distinction made earlier by Kelley [1947a:99; 1959:285].)

Descriptive References: *Tortugas:* Suhm *et al.* 1954:482, Pl. 120; MacNeish 1958:64–65, Fig. 23, Specimens 1–7. *Baird* and *Taylor:* Kelley 1959:285, Fig. 2; Sorrow 1969:19, Fig. 16. *Abasolo:* Suhm *et al.* 1954:400, Pl. 79; MacNeish 1959:62–64, Fig. 23, Specimens 15–21. *Nogales:* MacNeish 1959: 64, Fig. 23, Specimens 8–14.

Sequential Level: Early Archaic, surviving into Middle or Late Archaic in Lower Rio Grande and Tamaulipas.

Estimated Dates: Kelley (1947a) from 4000 or 2000 B.C. to A.D. 1500; Suhm *et al.* (1954:482) from possibly 4000 B.C. to A.D. 1000; Sorrow (1969:44) possibly 4500–3500 B.C. in Central Texas. *Present estimate for Diablo Range:* 5000 B.C. to A.D. 500.

Geographical Distribution: Very common in Lower Rio Grande and Tamaulipas; occurs occasionally in Central Texas and the Trans-Pecos, rarely in other areas.

PARIDA SERIES

Morphological Description: Dart points with expanding or rectangular, alternately beveled stems.

Included Types: *Nolan, Pandale.*

Descriptive References: *Nolan:* Suhm *et al.* 1954: 458, Pl. 108; Bell 1958:66, Pl. 33; Suhm 1962:63; Nunley *et al.* 1965:34, Fig. 18 F–G. *Pandale:* Suhm *et al.* 1954:464, Pl. 111; Bell 1958:70, Pl. 35; Johnson 1964: 40, Pl. 41; Nunley *et al.* 1965:33, Fig. 18 H–J.

Sequential Level: Early Archaic.

Estimated Dates: Sorrow *et al.* (1967: Fig. 72) 3500–2000 B.C. for *Nolan* in Central Texas; Story (1966:Table 1) 4000–2500 B.C. for *Nolan* and *Pandale* in the Amistad Reservoir area; Johnson (1964: Fig. 25) ca. 4000–2600 B.C. for *Pandale* in Amistad area.

Geographical Distribution: Common over most of Central Texas and Trans-Pecos; rare elsewhere.

PECOS SERIES

Morphological Description: Dart points with contracting to approximately rectangular stems and concave or straight bases.

Included Types: *Pedernales, Almagre, Gary, Kent, Langtry, Palmillas, Shumla, Bulverde, Travis.*

Descriptive References: *Pedernales:* Suhm *et al.* 1954:468, Pls. 113–115; Bell 1958:72, Pl. 36; Johnson 1962a:25–27, Figs. 4, 5 A–B; Sorrow *et al.* 1967:70–73, Figs. 41 h–k, 42, 43 a–f. *Almagre:* Suhm *et al.* 1954:396, Pl. 77; MacNeish 1958:65, Fig. 24, Specimens 45–48; Nunley *et al.* 1965:39–40, Fig. 15 J–N. *Gary:* Suhm *et al.* 1954:430, Pl. 94; MacNeish 1958:65, Fig. 24, Specimens 24–27; Bell 1958:28, Pl. 14. *Kent:* Campbell 1952:66, Pl. 9 A–P; Suhm *et al.* 1954:432, Pl. 95; MacNeish 1958:67, Fig. 24, Specimens 41–44; Bell 1960:60, Pl. 30. *Langtry:* Suhm *et al.* 1954:438, Pl. 98; Bell 1958:38, Pl. 19; Johnson 1962a:23, Fig. 6 F–I; Epstein 1963:36–38, Fig. 8 A–N; Johnson 1964: 38–39, Fig. 12 Q–Y; Nunley *et al.* 1965:36–39, Fig. 17 A–G. *Palmillas:* Suhm *et al.* 1954:462, Pl. 110; MacNeish 1958:67, Fig. 24, Specimens 24–27; Bell 1960:74, Pl. 37. *Shumla:* Suhm *et al.* 1954:480, Pl. 119; Bell 1960:86, Pl. 43; Johnson 1964:42, Fig. 13 E–L; Nunley *et al.* 1965:45–46, Fig. 20 L–N. *Bulverde:* Suhm *et al.* 1954:404, Pl. 81; Bell 1960:12, Pl. 6; Johnson 1962a:19–20, Fig. 6A–E; Sorrow *et al.* 1967:73–77, Figs. 43i–1, 44, 45. *Travis:* Suhm *et al.* 1954:484, Pl. 121; Johnson 1964:43–44, Fig. 3 M–O.

Sequential Level: Middle Archaic.

Estimated Dates: MacNeish (1958:156–157, 178–179, Table 30) ca. 2300–1500 B.C. for the Almagre Phase in the Sierra de Tamaulipas, ca. 3000–1800 B.C. for Repelo Phase in northern Tamaulipas; Kelley (1959:282) from ca. 2500 B.C. to not much earlier than A.D. 1200; Epstein (1963:116) 4000–1000 B.C. for Trans-Pecos; Johnson (1964: Fig. 25) ca. 3000–1700 B.C. for the Middle Archaic in Trans-Pecos; Story (1966: Table 1) 2500–1000 B.C. for Time Period IV in Amistad Reservoir area; Sorrow *et al.* (1967: Fig. 72) ca. 3500–1000 B.C. for local phases V and VI in Central Texas. *Present estimate for Diablo Range:* 3500–1000 B.C.

Geographical Distribution: Very common in middle part of the Archaic in all areas, with the possible exception of the Southern Coastal District, where no Archaic materials have been reported as yet.

NUECES SERIES

Morphological Description: Broad, short, expanding stem with convex or, less commonly, straight or concave base; blade relatively broad; base sometimes notched centrally.

Included Types: *Castroville, Montell, Marcos, Marshall, Williams.*

Descriptive References: *Castroville:* Suhm *et al.* 1954:408, Pl. 83; Bell 1960:14, Pl. 7; Sorrow *et al.* 1967:67, Fig. 40 a–g. *Montell:* Suhm *et al.* 1954:452, Pl. 105; Bell 1958:56, Pl. 28; Tunnell 1962:92, Fig. 34 J–L; Johnson 1964:39–40, Fig. 12 BB–DD; Sorrow *et al.* 1967:67, Fig. 39 e–m; Dibble 1967:35, Figs. 18, 19. *Marcos:* Suhm *et al.* 1954:442, Pl. 100; Bell 1958:42, Pl. 21; Tunnell 1962:92, Fig. 36 G–I; Sorrow *et al.* 1967:65, Fig. 39 a–d; Dibble 1967:34–35, Fig. 16. *Marshall:* Suhm *et al.* 1954:444, Pl. 101; Bell 1958:44, Pl. 22; Johnson 1964:39, Fig. 12 Z–AA; Sorrow *et al.* 1967:67–70, Figs. 40 h–k, 41 a. *Williams:* Suhm *et al.* 1954:490, Pl. 124; Bell 1960:96, Pl. 48; Johnson 1964:45, Fig. 13 X–Y. *General:* Dibble and Lorrain 1968:51–54, Figs. 23, 24 a–e.

Sequential Level: Late Archaic.

Estimated Dates: Johnson (1964: Fig. 25) 1700–1 B.C. for Amistad Reservoir area; Story (1966: Table 1) 1000–200 B.C. for Amistad area; Johnson *et al.* (1962:121, Fig. 45) Late Archaic for Central Texas (no year dates given); Prewitt (1970: Fig. 11) 1200–1 B.C. for the Amistad area. *Present estimate for Diablo Range:* 1200–1 B.C.

Geographical Distribution: Very common in Central Texas and the eastern part of the Trans-Pecos; less common in Central Coast; rare or absent in other areas.

RIO BRAVO SERIES

Morphological Description: Short stem; side-notched to strongly expanding stem; base straight, concave, or slightly convex.

Included Types: *Ensor, Fairland, Frio, Paisano.*

Descriptive References: *Ensor:* Suhm *et al.* 1954:422, Pl. 90; MacNeish 1958:67, Fig. 24, Specimens 14–17; Bell 1960:34, Pl. 17; Tunnell 1962:88–90, Fig. 33; Epstein 1963:45–46, Fig. 11 A–K; Johnson 1964:34–36, Figs. 11 V–Y, 12 A–B; Shafer *et al.* 1964:15–17, Figs 3 E–L, 4 A–E; Nunley *et al.* 1965:47–48, Fig. 16 H–J; McClurkan 1966:30–31, Fig. 8 a–q; Sorrow *et al.* 1967:65, Fig. 38 L–U. *Fairland:* Suhm *et al.* 1954:424, Pl. 91; Bell 1960:38, Pl. 19; Tunnell 1962:90, Fig. 34 G–I; Nunley *et al.* 1965:49–50, Fig. 16 O–P; Sorrow *et al.* 1967:61, Fig. 38 f–k. *Frio:* Suhm *et al.* 1954:428, Pl. 93; Bell 1960:48, Pl. 24; Tunnell 1962:90–92, Fig. 34 A–F; Epstein 1963:46, Fig. 11 L–Q; Johnson 1964:37, Fig. 12 M–N. *Paisano:* Suhm *et al.* 1954:460, Pl. 109 A–L; Ross 1965:46, Fig. 11 A–D.

Sequential Level: Terminal Archaic.

Estimated Dates: MacNeish (1958:157–158, 179, Table 31) 500 B.C. to A.D. 1000 in Sierra de Tamaulipas, 3000–1 B.C. for northern Tamaulipas; Epstein (1963:116) 100 B.C. to A.D. 1000 for Trans-Pecos; Johnson (1964: Fig. 25) ca. 600 B.C. to A.D. 1000 for the Amistad Reservoir area; Story (1966: Table 1) A.D. 200–1000 for the Amistad area; Sorrow *et al.* (1967: Fig. 72) A.D. 1–500 for Central Texas. *Present estimate for Diablo Range:* 200 B.C. to A.D. 800.

Geographical Distribution: Very common in Central Texas and Trans-Pecos; less common in Tamaulipas, the Lower Rio Grande, and the Central and Eastern Coastal districts.

KYLE SERIES

Morphological Description: Small dart points with expanding or rectangular stems; bases convex, straight, or concave.

Included Types: *Darl, Godley, Figueroa.*

Descriptive References: *Darl:* Miller and Jelks 1952:175, Pl. 23; Suhm *et al.* 1954:414, Pl. 86; Suhm 1957:38, Fig. 5 A–E; Shafer *et al.* 1964:11–13, Fig. 2; Sorrow *et al.* 1967:61–64, Fig. 37 a–p; Flinn and Flinn 1968:97, Figs. 2, 3 a–j. *Godley:* Jelks 1962:40, Fig. 16 A–E. *Figueroa:*

Johnson 1964:36–37, Fig. 12 E–L; Shafer *et al.* 1964:18–19, Fig. 4 I–J; McClurkan 1966:31, Fig. 7 a–b; Sorrow *et al.* 1967:64–65, Fig. 37 t–v.

Sequential Level: Transitional Archaic.

Estimated Dates: Johnson (1964:Fig. 25) ca. 400–200 B.C. to A.D. 1200 for *Figueroa* in Amistad Reservoir area; Story (1966: Table 1) between 200 B.C. and A.D. 1000 for *Figueroa* in the Amistad area; Sorrow *et al.* (1967:Fig. 72) between A.D. 1 and 500 for Central Texas. *Present estimate for Diablo Range:* 200 B.C. to A.D. 1000.

Geographical Distribution: Widespread over Central Texas and Trans-Pecos; apparently absent in Coastal and Lower Rio Grande areas; possibly present but unidentified in Coahuila–Chihuahua, Nuevo Leon, and Tamaulipas.

BARRIL SERIES

Morphological Description: Small triangular or subtriangular, unstemmed dart points.

Included Types: *Matamoros, Catan.*

Descriptive References: *Matamoros:* Suhm *et al.* 1954:448, Pl. 103; MacNeish 1958:68, Fig. 24, Specimens 18–20; McClurkan 1966:34–35, Fig. 11, n–s. *Catan:* Suhm *et al.* 1954:410, Pl. 84; MacNeish 1958:68, Fig. 24, Specimens 21–23; McClurkan 1966:27–28, Fig. 6 k–m.

Sequential Level: Terminal–Transitional Archaic.

Estimated Dates: Suhm *et al.* (1954:410, 448) A.D. 500 to eighteenth century; MacNeish (1958:68, 168, 189, Table 30) from ca. 1800 in Guerro Complex of southwestern Tamaulipas to eighteenth century in Los Angeles Phase of the Sierra de Tamaulipas and the Brownsville Complex of the Southern Coastal District; McClurkan (Fig. 40) ca. 500 B.C. to A.D. 1500 for Cueva de la Zona, Nuevo Leon. *Present estimate for Diablo Range:* 1500 B.C. to A.D. 1500.

Geographical Distribution: Broadly distributed in Tamaulipas, Lower Rio Grande, Nuevo Leon, and Southern Coastal District; absent or rare in other areas.

C. Neomorphic Style

The bow and arrow evidently diffused across the Diablo Range in late prehistoric times, as is evidenced by the appearance of small, light arrow points—that is, Neomorphic Style points—which are easily distinguishable from the heavier dart points. These occur in deposits dating after about A.D. 500 in all areas, but their earliest appearance probably differs from area to area. At present there are not enough controlled data to trace the direction of diffusion. Three series of Neomorphic points are currently recognized: the *Austin, Blum,* and *Omega* series.

In some areas, all Neomorphic points are unstemmed; in other areas both stemmed and unstemmed forms are present. Considering the relatively short time span they were in use, there is a lot of morphological variation in both the stemmed and unstemmed groups. In Central Texas, expanding stem points of the Austin Series clearly are generally earlier than contracting stem points of the Blum Series. There is some evidence that triangular arrow points of the Omega Series are the latest series in Central Texas, but some triangular forms may be contemporaneous with stemmed forms. A similar sequence probably obtains in the Central and Eastern Coastal districts, but it is not as clear-cut as in Central Texas. No arrow point sequence has been reported from any of the other areas, though there are several different types in each area. Probably stratified sites will be located in those areas in the future, which will provide a basis for at least some chronology within the Neomorphic Style. It was only in relatively recent times that such sites were found in Central Texas.

AUSTIN SERIES

Morphological Description: Arrow points with strongly to mildly expanding stems; bases vary from convex to concave.

Included Types: *Scallorn, Edwards.*

Descriptive References: *Scallorn:* Krieger 1946:97, 115, Fig. 7 T–U; Wheat 1953:201–202, Pl. 34 o–x (*Scallorn* spelled *Scalhorn;* Wheat's *Eddy* type included here with *Scallorn*); Suhm 1955:20, Pl. 2 A–H; Bell 1960:84, Pl. 42; Tunnell 1962:98, Fig. 37 I–P; Jelks 1962:27–31, Fig. 13; Shafer *et al.* Scurlock 1964:35–38, Fig. 10; Sorrow *et al.* 1967:59, Fig. 36 p–w; Hester 1971:69, Pl. 8 t–b′. *Edwards:* Sollberger 1967:12–22; Hester 1971:67, Fig. 8 c–j.

Sequential Level: Early Neo-American.

Estimated Dates: Jelks (1962:98) from sixth century A.D. until some time before the thirteenth century for Central Texas; Suhm and Jelks (1962:285) some part of the span A.D. 500–1200 for Central Texas; Sorrow *et al.* (1967: Fig. 72) A.D. 500–1200 for Stillhouse Hollow Reservoir in Central Texas. *Present estimate for Diablo Range:* A.D. 500–1200.

Geographical Distribution: Common in Central Texas and the Eastern and Central Coastal districts; absent or rare in other Diablo Range areas.

BLUM SERIES

Morphological Description: Arrow points with contracting, often sharply pointed stems.

Included Types: *Perdiz, Cliffton, Livermore.*

Descriptive References: *Perdiz:* Wheat 1953:201, Pl. 34 a–n; Suhm *et al.* 1954:504, Pl. 131 C–E; Campbell 1956:24, Pl. 3 A–P; Suhm 1957:35, Fig. 4 G–SS; Bell 1960:78, Pl. 39; Jelks 1962:24–26, Fig. 12 A–L; Tunnell 1962:96, Fig. 37 A–H; Shafer *et al.* 1964:32–35, Fig. 9 A–N; Johnson 1964:58, Fig. 14 G–H; Ross 1965:65, Fig. 14 A–B; Hester 1971:67–69, Fig. 8 k–s; Aten 1971:33, Fig. 8 B–E. *Cliffton:* Suhm *et al.* 1954:496, Pl. 127 D–E; Campbell 1956:27, Pl. 3 Q–S; Suhm 1957:35, Fig. 4 TT–VV; Bell 1960:18, Pl. 9; Jelks 1962:26, Fig. 12 M–Q; Tunnell 1962:94–96, Fig. 36 C–D; Epstein 1963:51, Fig. 13 F–I; Ross 1965:65, Fig. 14 D–E. *Livermore:* Kelley *et al.* 1940:30, 163, Fig. 3, Pls. 8, 20; Suhm *et al.* 1954:502, Pl. 130 D–E; Bell 1960:68, Pl. 34.

Sequential Level: Middle to late Neo-American in Central Texas and Gulf Coast; early to late Neo-American in Trans-Pecos.

Estimated Dates: Suhm and Jelks (1962:269, 283) A.D. 1000–1500 for *Perdiz* and *Cliffton;* Jelks (1962:98–99) thirteenth century A.D. until late prehistoric or protohistoric times for *Perdiz* and *Cliffton* in Central Texas; Sorrow *et al.* (1967: Fig. 72) A.D. 1200–1500 for *Perdiz* and

Cliffton in Central Texas; Suhm and Jelks (1962:279) A.D. 800–1200 for *Livermore* in the Trans-Pecos.

Geographical Distribution: Very common in Eastern and Central Coastal districts and in Central Texas; less common in Trans-Pecos, Coahuila–Chihuahua, and Lower Rio Grande; rare in Nuevo Leon and Tamaulipas.

OMEGA SERIES

Morphological Description: Triangular, unstemmed arrow points, some with side and/or base notches.

Included Types: *Fresno, Starr, Toyah, Los Angeles Concave.*

Descriptive References: *Fresno:* Suhm *et al.* 1954:498, Pl. 128; MacNeish 1958:69–70, Fig. 24, Specimens 8–9; Campbell 1958:429, Fig. 3 a–b; Bell 1960: 44, Pl. 22; McClurkan 1966:20, Fig. 3 i–p. *Starr:* Suhm *et al.* 1954:506, Pl. 132 D–E; MacNeish 1958:70, Fig. 24, Specimens 10–11; McClurkan 1966:21–22, Fig. 3 q–u. *Toyah:* Suhm *et al.* 1954:508, Pl. 133 D–E; Bell 1960:88, Pl. 44; Johnson 1964:58, Fig. 14 K–L; Nunley *et al.* 1965:30, Fig. 15 D–E; McClurkan 1966:22–23, Figs. 3 a–h, 5. *Los Angeles Concave:* MacNeish 1958:70, Fig. 24, Specimens 12–13; McClurkan 1966:21, Fig. 4 a–c.

Estimated Dates: MacNeish (1958:69, 70) ca. A.D. 900–1800 for Tamaulipas and Southern Coastal District; Suhm and Jelks (1962:273, 287, 291) A.D. 800–1800; Johnson (1964:98) A.D. 600–1500 for Amistad Reservoir area; McClurkan (1966:99–100) A.D. 800–? for Cueva de la Zona de Derrumbes in Nuevo Leon. *Present estimate for Diablo Range:* A.D. 800–1800.

Geographical Distribution: One or more types of the series occur in each area of the Diablo Range: *Fresno* in all areas; *Starr* in Nuevo Leon, Tamaulipas, Southern Coastal District, and Lower Rio Grande; *Toyah* in Trans-Pecos, Nuevo Leon, and Coahuila–Chihuahua; *Los Angeles Concave* in Tamaulipas and Nuevo Leon.

III. AREA CHRONOLOGIES

A. Central Texas

The land drained by the middle and upper stretches of the Brazos and Colorado rivers and by the upper reaches of the Guadalupe, San Antonio, and Nueces rivers (Figure 4.1) traditionally has been recognized as a distinctive archaeological area (Kelley 1947a; Pearce 1932; Sayles 1935; Stephenson 1950; Suhm 1960; Suhm, Krieger, and Jelks 1954; Willey 1966). The western three-fourths of this area occupies the eastern part of the Edwards Plateau, an uplifted region characterized by rugged, rocky hills; the eastern one-fourth consists of rolling grassland prairie of the coastal plain. There is considerable diversity in flora and fauna as one travels across Central Texas, from the well-watered prairies in the east (average annual rainfall over 30 inches) to the semiarid hills in the west (average annual rainfall less than 20 inches).

Over most of the Edwards Plateau, the bedrock is composed of limestone which, in many localities, weathers to form overhanging ledges, or rockshelters, which were utilized extensively as habitation sites by the prehistoric populations. Limestone slabs were commonly used for pit cooking, a practice that often resulted in the accumulation of massive heaps of discarded, fire-cracked fragments of limestone (so-called burned rock middens), both in rockshelters and in open sites.

The first major efforts at chronological ordering of Central Texas archaeological materials were in the late 1920s and early 1930s by two investigators: Cyrus N. Ray, working in the Brazos River region near Abilene, and James E. Pearce, working in the Colorado River region above Austin. Ray (1929, 1938) recognized an *Abilene Culture* to which he imputed great antiquity (50,000 years or more) and a later sequence of, from early to late, a *Clear Fork Culture,* a *Sand Dune Culture,* a *Large Scraper Culture,* a *Small Scraper Culture,* and a *Valley Creek Culture.* Criteria for defining these cultures included distinctive styles of chipped-stone projectile points, "gouges," scrapers, and other classes of artifacts that Ray had found buried in stratified alluvial deposits of the Brazos and its tributaries.

Pearce (1932) defined briefly three cultural levels that he had recognized at stratified burned rock middens. He referred to these respectively as *Lower, Middle,* and *Upper Kitchen Midden* complexes, distinguishing them from one another on the basis of the chipped-stone projectile point forms which he found in stratified sequence. He gave no date estimates—only a relative temporal sequence.

Sayles (1935) proposed a rather complex chronological scheme for Central Texas, which was articulated with schemes for adjacent areas. The roots, branches, stems, cultures, and phases of Sayles's classification were ordered primarily around stylistic variations in projectile points and other chipped-stone artifacts.

In the 1940s J. Charles Kelley (1947a, 1959) devised a general chronology for Central Texas. Following the Midwestern taxonomic system, he defined two aspects for Central Texas: an earlier *Edwards Plateau Aspect* (part of the *Balcones Phase,* which extended westward and southward beyond Central Texas) and a later *Central Texas Aspect.* Kelley identified three foci within the Edwards Plateau Aspect (*Round Rock, Clear Fork,* and *Uvalde*), which he considered mutually contemporaneous, except that the Uvalde was thought to have survived later than the other two. Within the Central Texas Aspect, two foci were defined: the Austin Focus and the Toyah Focus. Diagnostic traits differentiating the aspects and foci from one another were, for the most part, distinctive types of projectile points. Certain forms of scrapers, knives, and other artifacts were also ascribed to some of the foci.

The next chronological classification for Central Texas was that of Suhm *et al.* (1954) in their *Introductory Handbook of Texas Archeology,* a work that organized all of Texas archaeology within a framework of four stages: *Paleo-American, Archaic, Neo-American,* and *Historic.* Following Kelley's scheme for Central Texas, they assigned the Edwards Plateau Aspect with its three foci to the Archaic Stage, while the Central Texas Aspect was identified with the Neo-American stage. No specific aspects or foci were proposed for the Paleo-Indian or Historic stages in Central Texas. The foci of the Edwards Plateau Aspect were still considered more or less contemporaneous; but in the subsequent Central Texas Aspect it was recognized that the Austin Focus was earlier than the Toyah Focus on the basis of evidence from stratified sites on the Brazos (Jelks 1953, 1962) and on the Colorado (Suhm 1957).

The taxonomic and chronological model of Suhm, Krieger, and Jelks for Central Texas remained standard until the mid-1960s, and parts of the model are still (1973) accepted by most authorities.

In summary, five major schemes of Central Texas cultural classification and chronology were formulated between 1929 and 1954: Ray's, Pearce's, Sayles's, Kelley's, and Suhm, Krieger, and Jelks's. Although there has been a good deal of controversy—some of it quite acrimonious—between some of the principals (especially about dates of some artifact types), the similarities of the schemes are more striking, in retrospect, than their discrepancies. Intensive field work over the past 20 years has produced a vast quantity of data that have resolved most of the earlier chronological arguments. With this solid foundation of carefully collected data, it is now possible to outline a basic chronological framework for Central Texas, the essential accuracy of which can be accepted with great confidence.

Since the mid-1960s, conceptual reorientation among most archaeologists working in Texas has trended away from the use of the Midwestern taxonomic system (aspects, foci, etc.) in favor of simple chronological ordering of artifact classes. Thus in Central Texas the entire Archaic Period is now usually thought of as a more or less integral unit without any clearly delineated foci or other such cultural classes. Chronological ordering within the Archaic is achieved primarily through sequential arrangement of artifact forms (especially projectile point types), chipping techniques, and settlement patterns. Abundant stratigraphic evidence and numerous radiocarbon dates have supplied a firm foundation for an Archaic point-type sequence.

However, for the post-Archaic Period, or Neo-American Stage, the concept of a Central Texas Aspect consisting of an earlier Austin Focus and a later Toyah Focus has been retained by most researchers. This undoubtedly is because there is ample evidence for clearly defining two separate and distinctive cultural patterns representing, respectively, earlier (Austin Focus) and later (Toyah Focus) segments of the late prehistoric populations of Central Texas. Also, since 1954, a focus ascribed to historic Wichita tribes—the Norteño Focus—has been defined which occupies, in part, the northern part of Central Texas from the mid-eighteenth to the mid-nineteenth century (Duffield and Jelks 1961; Jelks 1967).

A basic chronological outline for Central Texas is presented in Figure 4.3.

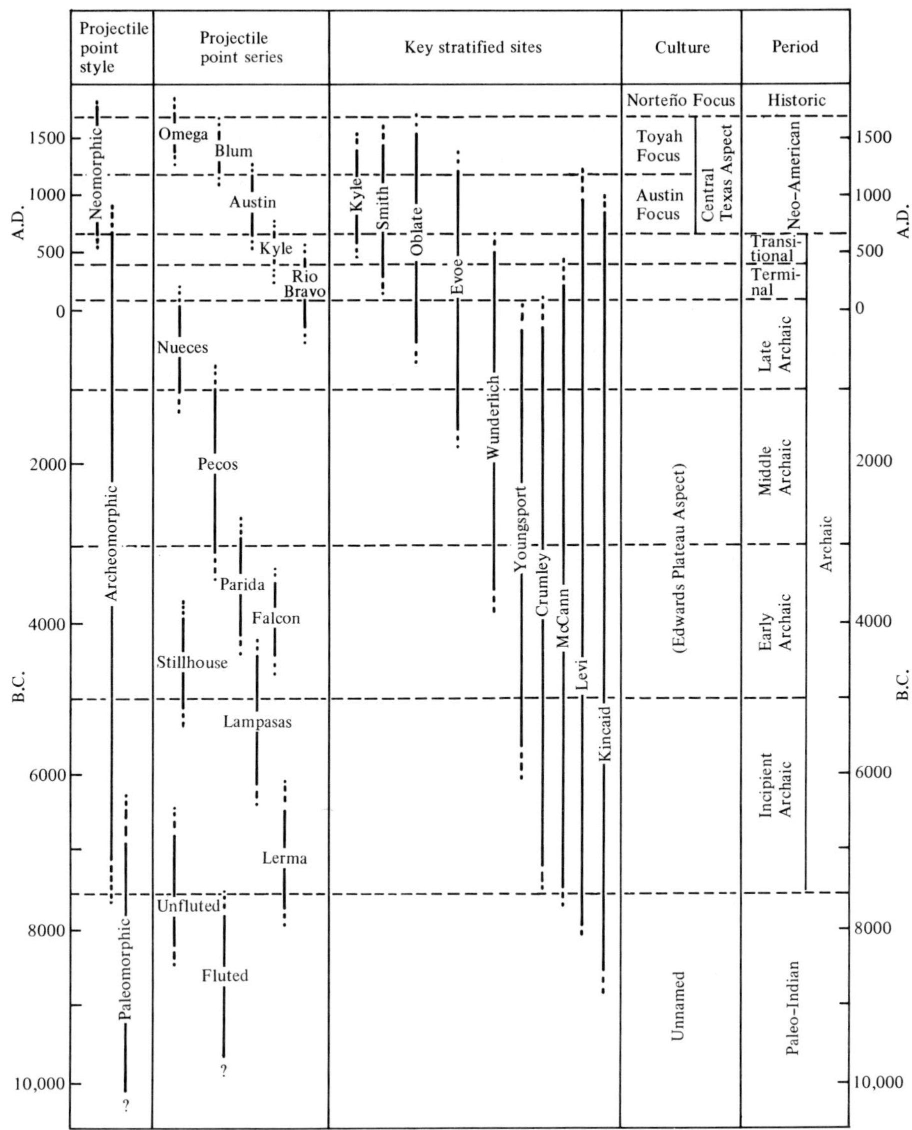

Figure 4.3. Chronology chart for the Central Texas area.

Reflecting the consensus of currently active researchers in the area, the chronology chart for the Central Texas area is structured around changes in certain projectile point types through time. In the interests of simplicity and accuracy, only the most diagnostic and most distinctive types are shown. Many other kinds of artifacts, including additional point types, occur in large quantities in both the Archaic and the Neo-American sites of Central Texas;

however, their typological and chronological significance stands on relatively insecure grounds in comparison to the point types selected here for the chronology.

Frank Weir (1976) recently divided the Central Texas Archaic into five named phases. These are, in chronological order, San Geronimo, Clear Fork, Round Rock, San Marcos, and Twin Sisters. They correlate respectively with the Incipient, Early, Middle, Late, and Terminal Archaic periods, but Weir's estimated dates tend to be slightly later than the dates shown in Figure 4.3.

B. Trans-Pecos

As defined here, the Trans-Pecos area comprises the valley of the Rio Grande between the towns of Candelaria, Texas, and Del Rio, Texas, the valley of the Pecos between its mouth and the town of Pecos, Texas, the entire valley of the Devils, and all the territory lying between those streams (Figure 4.1). It was decided to exclude from the area the extreme western tip of Texas because the cultural affinities there lie largely with the Mogollon and earlier cultures of New Mexico. Traditionally the Trans-Pecos Area has been divided into two archaeological subareas: (*a*) the La Junta District around the mouth of the Conchos River and (*b*) the rest of the area, comprising some 80% of the whole. In the present classification, the area will be divided into three districts: (*a*) the La Junta District; (*b*) an Eastern District that includes the Devils and lower Pecos drainages and the Rio Grande valley between Del Rio and a point a few miles above the town of Langtry; and (*c*) a Western District encompassing the Davis Mountains, the Chisos Mountains, and the Rio Grande valley from Elena Canyon downstream to the border of the Eastern District (Figure 4.1).

The Trans-Pecos area is one of varied topography, with mountains in much of the Western District, and the Stockton Plateau occupying most of the Eastern District. In some places the streams have cut deep, narrow canyons into the limestone bedrock; in others the streams flow through wide valleys. There are caves and rockshelters in many of the cliffs, which were favored habitation spots of the prehistoric peoples who occupied the area. There are open archaeological sites too, including burned rock middens and stratified alluvial terrace sites. The deposits in most caves and rockshelters are dry enough that basketry, cordage, wood, seeds, and other perishable materials have survived intact.

The first serious effort at formulating a prehistoric culture classification for the Trans-Pecos was by Sayles (1935). Working largely with local private collections and with surface collections that he made himself, Sayles recognized a *Pecos River Cave Dweller* culture in the Eastern District and a *Big*

Bend Cave Dweller culture in the Western District. The late prehistoric village sites of the La Junta District he labeled the *Jumano Phase*.

A few years later Albritton and Bryan (1939) conducted a geological survey of alluvial valley fills in the Western and La Junta districts. They defined a widespread sequence of three alluvial depositions: *Neville, Calamity Creek,* and *Kokernot* (from early to late), which are separated from one another at many stations by sharp erosional unconformities. Kelley *et al.* (1940), working with Albritton and Bryan, gathered archaeological materials from the respective alluvial deposits and erosional interfaces, and they classed them into three complexes: the *Maravillas Complex,* the *Santiago Complex* (both Archaic), and the *Livermore Focus* (post-Archaic, with Neomorphic points but no pottery).

Kelley (1959) subsequently set up a chronology comprising two aspects (*Big Bend* and *Bravo Valley*), two complexes (*Maravillas* and *Santiago*), and one independent focus (*Livermore*). The Big Bend Aspect included a *Pecos River Focus,* which was dispersed over the entire Trans-Pecos area as here defined, and a *Chisos Focus,* which followed the Pecos River Focus in the Western District. The Bravo Valley Aspect comprised three foci—*La Junta, Conchos,* and *Concepción* (from early to late)—which were identified with the agricultural villages of the La Junta District, the only sedentary farmers in the Trans-Pecos. There has been no major field work in the La Junta District since the 1940s, and no major excavations in the Western District; consequently, knowledge of those two districts is much as it was 30 years ago. A surface survey of the Big Bend National Park conducted by T. N. Campbell in the mid-1960s resulted in the location of numerous sites, but none have been extensively excavated as yet.

Construction of the Amistad Reservoir on the Rio Grande, Pecos, and Devils rivers in the 1950s and 1960s occasioned a flurry of salvage archaeology in the reservoir area, the heartland of the Eastern District. Following a preliminary survey by John Graham and W. A. Davis (1958), dozens of sites were excavated before the reservoir was filled. Several sites yielded excellent chronological data, the most notable being the Devils Mouth Site (Johnson 1964; Sorrow 1968a), the Arenosa Rockshelter (Dibble 1967), Bonfire Cave (Dibble and Lorrain 1968), Centipede Cave (Epstein 1963), Damp Cave (Epstein 1963), Coontail Spin (Nunley *et al.* 1965), Mosquito Cave (Nunley *et al.* 1965), the Nopal Terrace Site (Sorrow 1968b), Fate Bell Rockshelter (Parsons 1965), Eagle Cave (Ross 1965), Parida Cave (Alexander 1970), and the Piedra del Diablo Site (Prewitt 1970).

Several of the investigators at Amistad Reservoir proposed projectile point chronologies: Epstein (1963), Johnson (1964), Nunley *et al.* (1965), Prewitt (1970). In addition, Story (1966) and Alexander (1970) have published areal chronologies synthesized from the chronologies listed above.

In keeping with the recent trend in Texas archaeology to abandon the

Midwestern classification system, the entire span of prehistory in the Trans-Pecos (excluding the agricultural villages of the La Junta District) is now generally regarded as a single basic culture that did not change significantly in its essential configuration for 10,000 years or so. Consequently, recent chronological ordering has taken the form of either (*a*) sequential numbered periods or (*b*) sequential subdivisions within the Archaic, preceded by late Paleo-Indian at the bottom of the sequence and with the arrow point period on top. Markers for these periods, or interstadial subdivisions, are primarily projectile point forms, although there are other indicators too. The principal chronological schemes—those of Kelley, Epstein, Johnson, Story, and Nunley, Duffield and Jelks—are synthesized in Figure 4.4.

C. Coahuila–Chihuahua

This area comprises the Mexican state of Coahuila and that portion of Chihuahua lying east of the Rio Conchos (Fig. 4.1). Save for the northeastern section, which is an extension of the Coastal Plain, the entire area is mountainous. It is an arid region, the annual rainfall averaging well under 20 inches.

The only significant chronological studies made to date in the Coahuila–Chihuahua area are those of W. W. Taylor, who worked in Coahuila intermittently from the late 1930s to the late 1950s (Taylor 1948, 1956, 1966; Taylor and Gonzáles Rul 1961). Unfortunately, no reports of Taylor's extensive investigations are in print except the brief, preliminary accounts cited above. The only other fieldwork of note in the area was at Candelaria Cave, a late prehistoric burial cave, excavated by Pablo Martinez del Rio in 1953 (Martinez del Rio 1953; Aveleyra Arroyo de Anda *et al.* 1956).

W. W. Taylor (1966) classified the prehistoric cultures of Coahuila into four complexes:

1. The *Cienegas Complex* (estimated age 10,000–5000/4000 B.C.), based primarily on excavations at Frightful and Fat Burro caves in the Cuatro Cienegas locality.
2. The *Coahuila Complex* (estimated age 8000 B.C. to sixteenth century A.D.), based primarily on excavations at Frightful, Fat Burro, and Nopal caves, plus isolated mortuary sites.
3. The *Jora Complex* (estimated age possibly from about A.D. 1 to an unknown termination date), based primarily on excavations at Fat Burro and Nopal caves, and on surface materials from various sites.
4. The *Mayran Burial Complex* (estimated age possibly from about A.D. 1 to the early seventeenth century), based primarily on excavations at Candelaria Cave by Pablo Martinez del Rio.

Distinctive traits of the Cienegas Complex are wads of human hair, rattlesnake rattles, agave scuffer-sandals, twill-pad sandals, narrow plaited

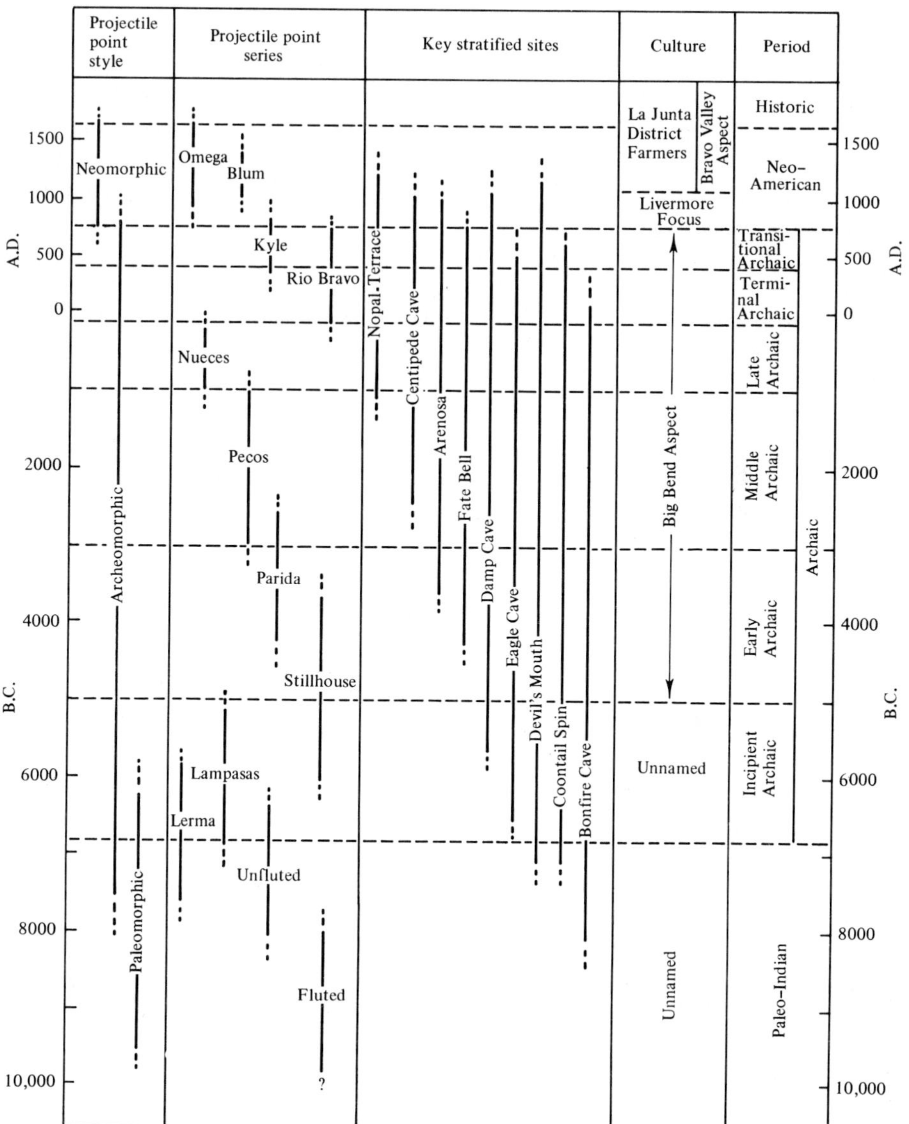

Figure 4.4. Chronology chart for the Trans-Pecos area.

bands, and shells of *Humboldtiana montezuma Pilsbry* (Taylor 1966: 62).

The Coahuila Complex represents the major corpus of prehistoric cultural materials in Coahuila, according to the Taylor scheme. Estimated to have lasted for some 9000 years, this complex experienced material changes during its tenure, including an increase through time in the use of fibrous vegetal foods in comparison to animal foods, an increase in the influx of material imports from other areas, an increased heterogeneity in artifact forms, and a degeneration in craftsmanship (W. W. Taylor 1966:63–65). Wooden and fiber artifacts of Coahuila Complex provenience were found in large quantities and in great variety in the Cuatro Cienegas caves. Included are atlatls, dart foreshafts, shaft wrenches, grooved clubs, fire tongs, digging sticks, fiber cordage, fiber sandals, coiled basketry, and many other things. Taylor, however, does not organize these artifacts into any particular temporal order within the complex.

Marker traits of the Jora Complex—which Taylor (1966:81–82) somewhat confusingly includes within the body of the Coahuila Complex at a relatively late period—are arrow points, self-pointed wooden arrow foreshafts, split-twig loops, *El Paso Brown* pottery, and others (Taylor 1966:82). Burials placed in isolated niches or small shelters on the mountainsides are thought to be of Coahuila Complex origin.

The Mayran Complex burial caves have yielded textiles, triangular stone knives, arrow points of Jora Complex forms, notched and stemmed dart points, elaborate bone and shell ornaments, bows, arrows, and other objects (Taylor 1966:83–84).

Taylor's preliminary reports give little information that is useful for the projectile point chronology being pursued here. He mentions no projectile points at all in his brief description of the Cienegas Complex (1966:62–63). In his discussion of the Coahuila Complex, he refers to points several times, stating that forms similar to the *Lerma, Refugio,* and *Abasolo* types are earliest in the complex and that *Jora* type points occupy a somewhat later position; after *Jora* come "a heterogeneous lot of notched and stemmed points, only a few of which are enough alike to warrant being placed in types (1966: 67)."

Taylor does illustrate a series of dart point forms of the early and middle Coahuila Complex (1966: Figs. 3, 4) and the middle and late forms of the complex (1966: Fig. 5). Judging from the illustrations, our Lerma and Pecos series are well represented among the early and middle Coahuila Complex forms; our Pecos, Rio Bravo, and possibly Kyle series among the middle and late forms. Among the illustrated Neomorphic points of the Jora Complex (Taylor 1966: Fig. 27) are specimens clearly recognizable as *Perdiz, Cliffton, Toyah,* and *Fresno.* Taylor uses his own names for these but adds the Texas names parenthetically for each type.

As there has been no work in the area since Taylor's, his views (presented in Figure 4.5) are the current ones. Because of a possible parallel in Central Texas and the Trans-Pecos—where cleanly stratified deposits are rare and dozens of sites were excavated in each area before clear typological sequences began to emerge—I think it quite likely that much of the present type mixture will resolve into a demonstrable chronology for the Coahuila–Chihuahua area when more cleanly stratified sites have been excavated.

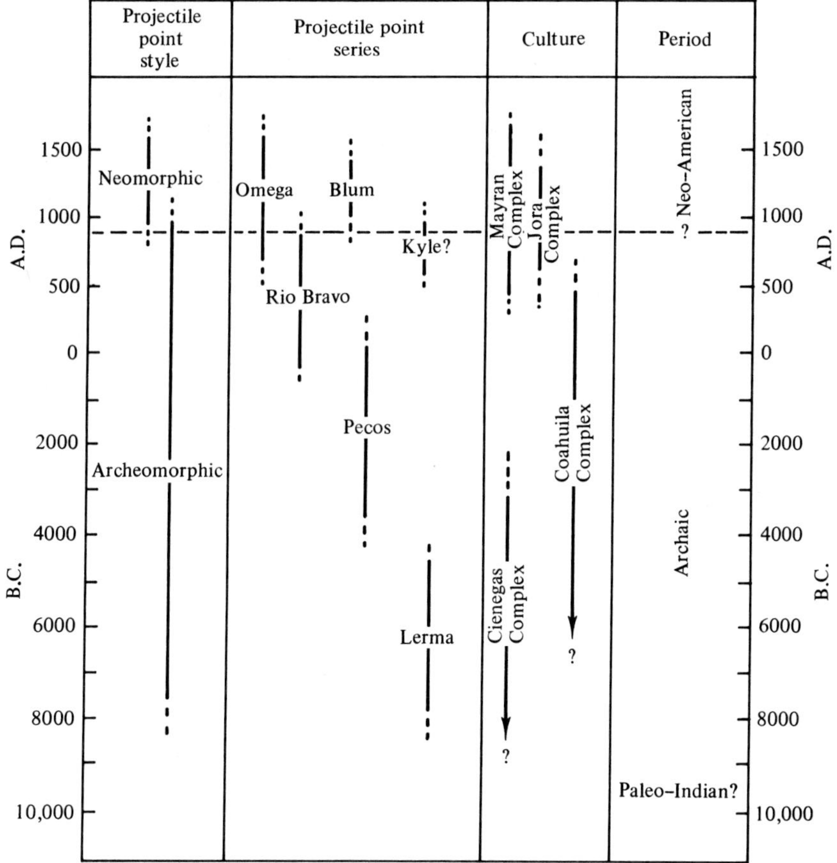

Figure 4.5. Chronology chart for the Coahuila–Chihuahua area.

D. Nuevo Leon

This area (Figure 4.1) consists of that part of the state of Nuevo Leon which lies north of 26° latitude. The southwestern section of the area encompasses part of the Sierra Madre; the northern and eastern sections lie in the Coastal Plain.

The first archaeological work of any consequence in the Nuevo Leon area was a surface survey by J. F. Epstein in 1960, followed by excavation of the San Isidro Site (Epstein 1969) and the Cueva de la Zona de Derrumbes (McClurkan 1966) several years later. Subsequently C. R. Nance excavated a stratified cave, La Calzada (Nance 1971).

The San Isidro Site was an area several acres in extent located approximately 40 miles east of Monterrey, where a number of hearths (piles of fire-cracked limestone) were visible on the surface of the ground, along with a scattering of chipped-stone artifacts and debitage. Epstein postulated three different occupational periods for the site, grounding his interpretation on the differential surface distribution of several artifact classes and types (Epstein 1969). His earliest hypothetical period is characterized by heavy bifaces, pebble tools, and crudely worked flakes, all produced by rather coarse hammerstone percussion. Some soft-hammer thinning flakes came from the same surface locations as the cruder implements, but what kinds of tools were being thinned in uncertain. The second posited period is typified by *Plainview, Lerma,* and *Pandora* type dart points, by Clear Fork gouges, and, probably, by crude percussion-flaked tools like those of the earlier period. The third period, most likely representing sporadic campers, is identified with dart point types *Nogales, Tortugas, Desmuke, Gary, Almagre, Matamoros,* and *Catan.* Epstein (1969:122) suggests an early post-Pleistocene date for the first two periods, but he gives no estimated year dates for any of the three periods.

Cueva de la Zona de Derrumbes, located in southeastern Nuevo Leon, yielded excellent chronological data for the period from ca. 3000 B.C. to A.D. 1500 (McClurkan 1966). Principal Archeomorphic forms include types of the Parida, Pecos, Rio Bravo, Kyle, and Barril series. A large sample of Neomorphic points were almost all of the Omega Series. Falcon and Pecos series points (primarily of the *Tortugas, Abasolo,* and *Shumla* types) were apparently contemporaneous from about 3000 B.C. to perhaps A.D. 300 or 400. They were replaced by types of the Barril and Rio Bravo series, both of which continued until the end of occupation at perhaps A.D. 1500. Neomorphic points of the Omega Series are present in large quantities after about A.D. 900.

At the La Calzada Site, about 20 miles west of Montemorelos, Nance (1971) reports a lengthy occupation, from about 8000 B.C. to about A.D. 1500. A sequence of Archeomorphic types was (from early to late): *Lerma, Stillhouse, Parida,* and *Barril.* After about A.D. 600, Neomorphic points of the Omega Series predominated. There were no Paleomorphic points, but a kind of diamond-shaped point underlay the Lerma Series.

Good series of radiocarbon dates have been run for both Cueva de la Zona de Derrumbes and La Calzada.

There has been no fieldwork of consequence in Nuevo Leon since that reported above; therefore the interpretations of Epstein, McClurkan, and Nance are still current. Their chronology of the area is presented in Figure 4.6.

E. Tamaulipas

The topography of Tamaulipas is varied. Bordering its coastline is a narrow band of Coastal Flats, which is bounded on the inland side by the

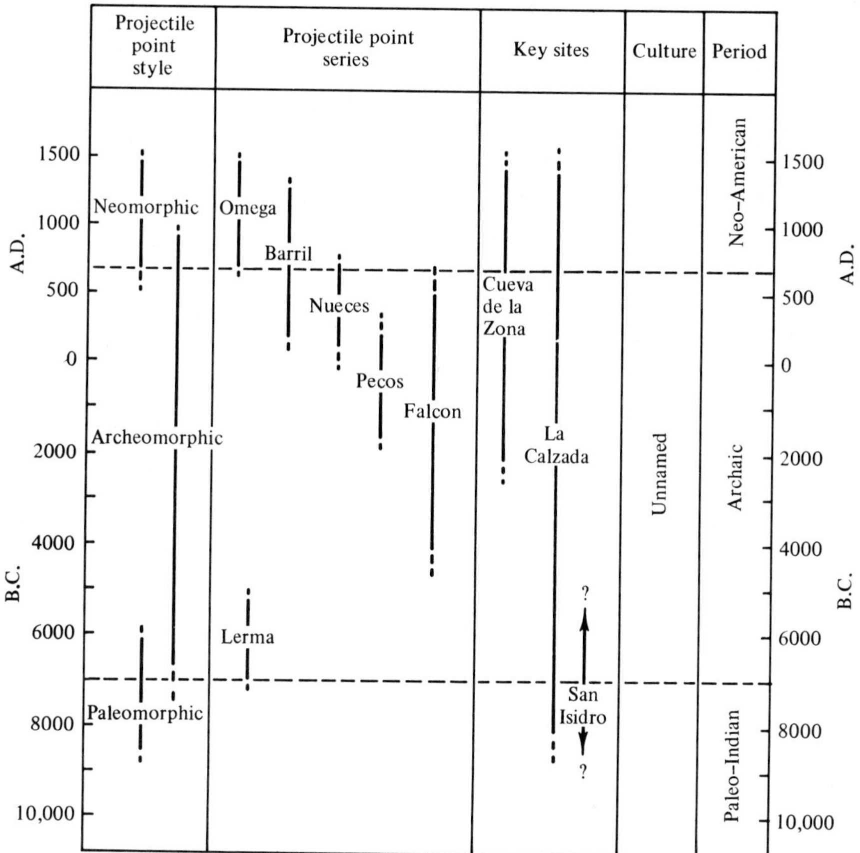

Figure 4.6. Chronology chart for the Nuevo Leon area.

Coastal Plain. Both coastal zones are quite narrow in their southern two thirds, but they widen out markedly to the north. The inland part of the state consists of mountains (the Sierra Madre Oriental to the southwest, the Sierra de Tamaulipas in the south-central region, the San Carlos Mountains in the northwest-central region) and the Dissected Peneplain, a high, rugged land that occupies the central part of the state between the mountains and the coastal zones. Only the Sierra de Tamaulipas, the northern part of the Coastal Plain, and the Sierra Madre in the southwestern part of the state concern us here. The extreme southern parts of Tamaulipas are affiliated culturally with the Mesoamerican culture area, and the coastal zones will be discussed later, in the section on the Gulf Coast area.

The only significant archaeological investigation to date of the Diablo Range in Tamaulipas was an extensive survey, including excavation of several key sites, by Richard S. MacNeish between 1945 and 1954. Mac-

Neish's work has produced the sole chronology we have for the area (MacNeish 1958).

For the Sierra de Tamaulipas District (including not only the mountains themselves but also adjacent portions of the Dissected Peneplain) MacNeish (1958) proposed a sequence of nine cultural phases and complexes, beginning with the *Diablo Complex* (estimated to be older than 10,000 B.C.) and terminating with the *Los Angeles Phase* (dated A.D. 1200–1780). In the same report, MacNeish formulated a somewhat different cultural sequence for the Coastal Plain of northern Tamaulipas, which he believed to correlate temporally with the latter part of his Sierra de Tamaulipas sequence, plus a separate local sequence for the Sierra Madre area of southwestern Tamaulipas. MacNeish's chronologies for the three districts are summarized in Figure 4.7.

Since there have been no major excavations in the Diablo Range region of Tamaulipas since those of MacNeish in the 1940s and 1950s, the only interpretative changes since then have been vicarious criticisms of MacNeish's chronologies, mainly by W. W. Taylor (1960, 1966) and Epstein (1969). Although neither Taylor nor Epstein has worked extensively in Tamaulipas, both suggest that MacNeish's sequences of phases and complexes are oversimplified and at least partially inaccurate. These criticisms are founded in large measure on comparison of MacNeish's Tamaulipas chronologies with a general overview of northeastern Mexico and southern Texas, together with certain internal inconsistencies in MacNeish's published reports.

In terms of the present synthesis, the projectile points described by MacNeish show clear typological relationships to other areas of the Diablo Range. The Parida, Pecos, Rio Bravo, Barril, and Omega series are especially well represented in Tamaulipas. MacNeish's chronological arrangement of the series corresponds reasonably well, in a general way, with chronologies of the other areas. However, I think it probable that a more precise chronology will be forthcoming after additional intensive research has been carried out in Tamaulipas.

F. Lower Rio Grande

This area comprises the lower valley of the Rio Grande south of latitude 28 degrees, exclusive of the Gulf Coast archaeological area (Fig. 4.1). Known locally as the "monte," this is a section of the coastal plain characterized by undulating topography, prickly pear cactus, thorny bushes, mesquite trees, and grasses. Average annual rainfall is in the 20- to 30-inch range.

In his survey of Texas archaeology, Sayles (1935:41) referred briefly to a *Coahuiltecan Branch* that occupied the Rio Grande Valley between McAllen and Eagle Pass. Later, J. Charles Kelley (1947a: 104; 1959: 285) alluded to a

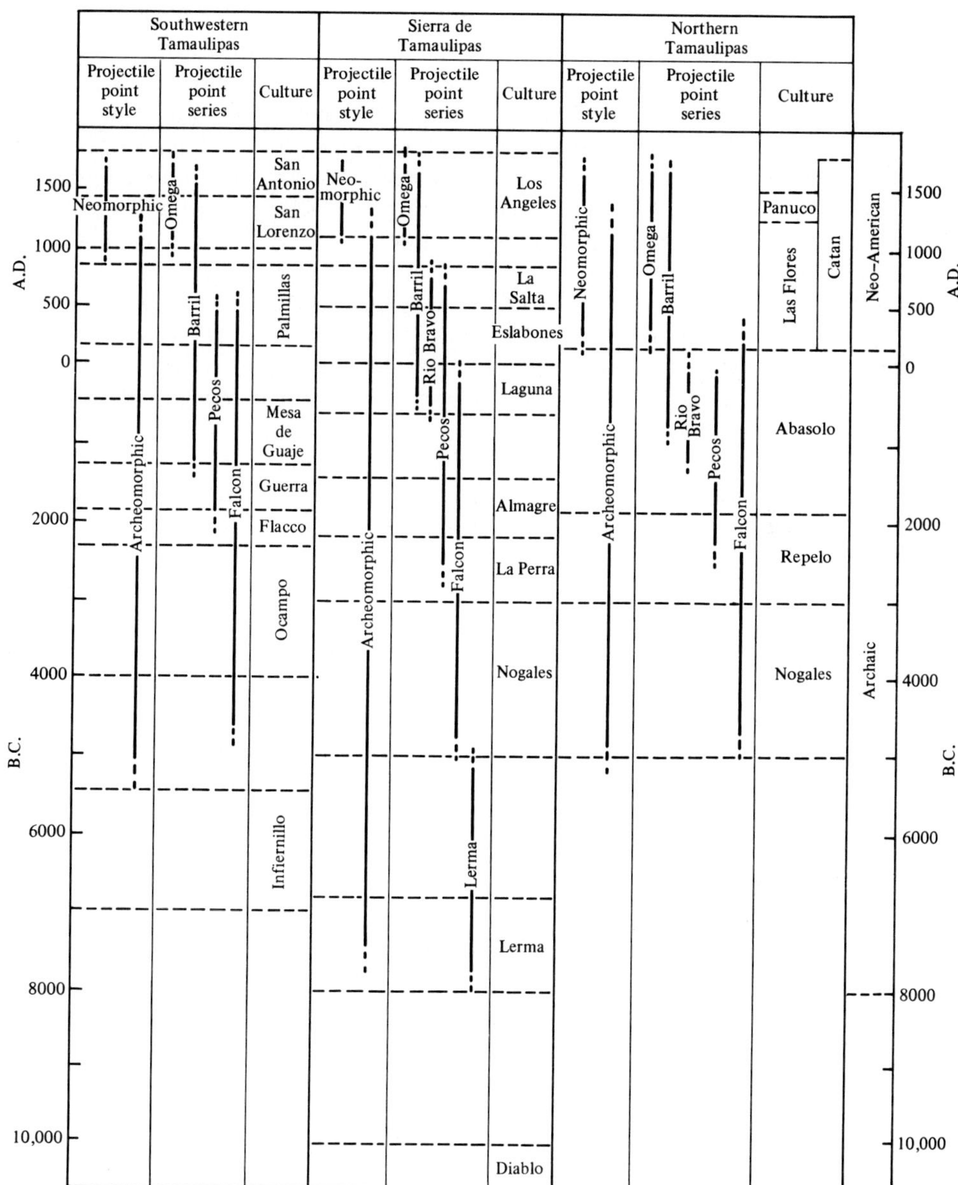

Figure 4.7. Chronology chart for the Tamaulipas area.

Monte Aspect which apparently was intended to include the Archaic cultures of the Lower Rio Grande, but Kelley never defined his aspect. MacNeish (1947:1–3) described an *Abasolo Complex* that was based largely on his investigation of the inland coastal plain of Tamaulipas, which he extended to include southern Texas.

The only intensive excavations in the area were salvage operations in the Falcon Reservoir area below Laredo in the early 1950s. Participants included Alex D. Kreiger, Jack T. Hughes, Donald Hartle, Joe F. Cason, and Edward B. Jelks. Unfortunately for our purposes, only cursory reports of their work have been published (Cason 1952; Hartle 1951; Krieger and Hughes 1950; Suhm *et al.* 1954:135–143). Frank A. Weir (1956) reported finding a number of Paleomorphic points on the surface of the La Perdida Site in Starr County, and Hester (1968) also reported surface finds of Paleomorphic points from sites near the town of Pearsall, Texas.

The first and only serious attempt at establishing a local chronology for the Lower Rio Grande Area grew out of the salvage work at Falcon Reservoir. Two foci were briefly defined by Suhm *et al.* (1954:138–142): the *Falcon Focus,* estimated to have begun possibly about 5000 B.C. and to have lasted until perhaps A.D. 500 to 1000, and the *Mier Focus* which followed the Falcon Focus. The primary evidence for the temporal positions of the two foci was their correlation with a system of alluvial terraces of the Rio Grande (Evans 1962). *Tortugas* was specified as the principal dart point type of the Falcon Focus, with *Abasolo* and *Refugio* occurring in lesser numbers. Marker traits for the Mier Focus included *Matamoros* and *Catan* dart points together with *Perdiz, Fresno,* and *Starr* types of Neomorphic style. *Tortugas, Abasolo,* and *Refugio* were reported to occur in Mier Focus contexts as well as in the Falcon Focus. Pecos Series types *Langtry, Shumla,* and *Almagre* were found in many of the Falcon Reservoir sites, but their chronological positions were not determined.

Since no major studies have been conducted in the area since the early 1950s, there has been no modification of the Falcon–Mier scheme proposed by Suhm *et al.* in 1954 (see Figure 4.8). However, researchers working in related areas (Kelley 1959:268; Epstein 1969:106–107) have been reluctant to adopt this scheme completely on the evidence presented, as the foci were never fully defined nor were they adequately documented by primary data.

G. Gulf Coast

The Gulf Coast Area occupies the Coastal Lowland, a strip varying in width from a maximum of 75 miles in Texas to a minimum of only a mile or so in Tamaulipas. It rises from sea level to an altitude of 100 to 175 feet along its inland edge. This is a land of savannas, marshes, ponds, sand dunes, and clay dunes. In many places on the mainland the topography is flat and monotonous. Long, narrow offshore islands such as Padre Island parallel the

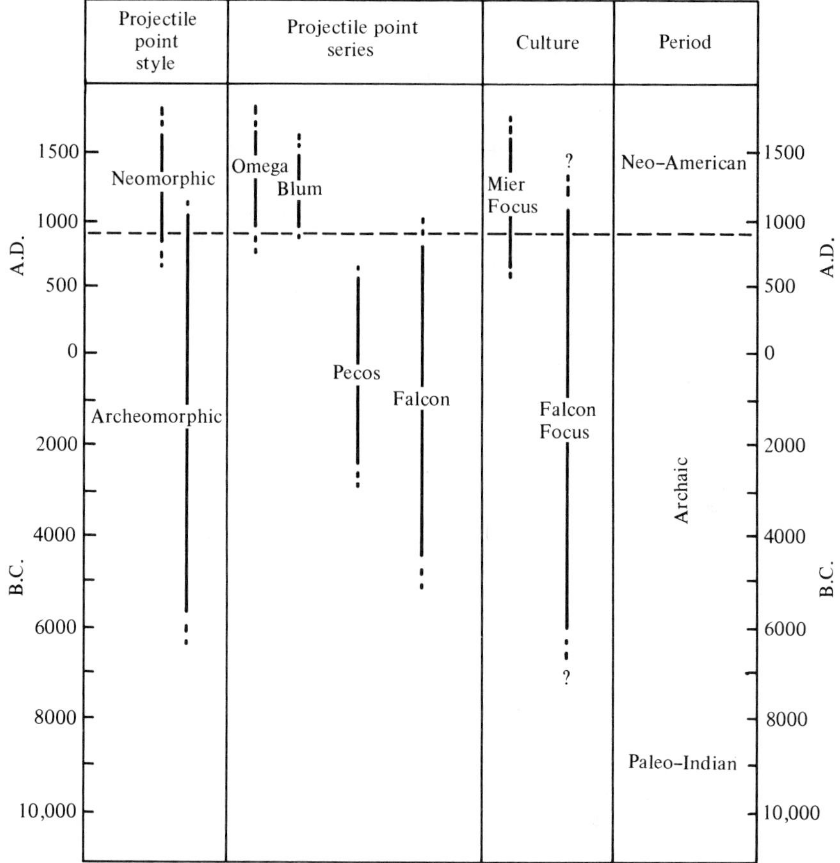

Figure 4.8. Chronology chart for the Lower Rio Grande area.

mainland coastline in most localities between the Texas–Louisiana border and the Rio Soto la Marina in Tamaulipas. Tall grasses are typical ground cover along much of the Texas coast, but pine and oak forests grow along the shores east of Galveston Bay; thorny bushes are characteristic in Tamaulipas. Average annual rainfall ranges between 20 and 40 inches, the Tamaulipas coast being more arid than the coast of Texas.

Three archaeological districts have generally been recognized in the area: (1) an Eastern District between the Sabine and Brazos rivers, (2) a Central District between the Brazos and Baffin Bay, and (3) a Southern District stretching from Baffin Bay to the Rio Soto la Marina (Figure 4.1). Shell middens are common in the Central and Eastern districts but are rare in the Southern District. The chronology for the three districts is shown in Figure 4.9.

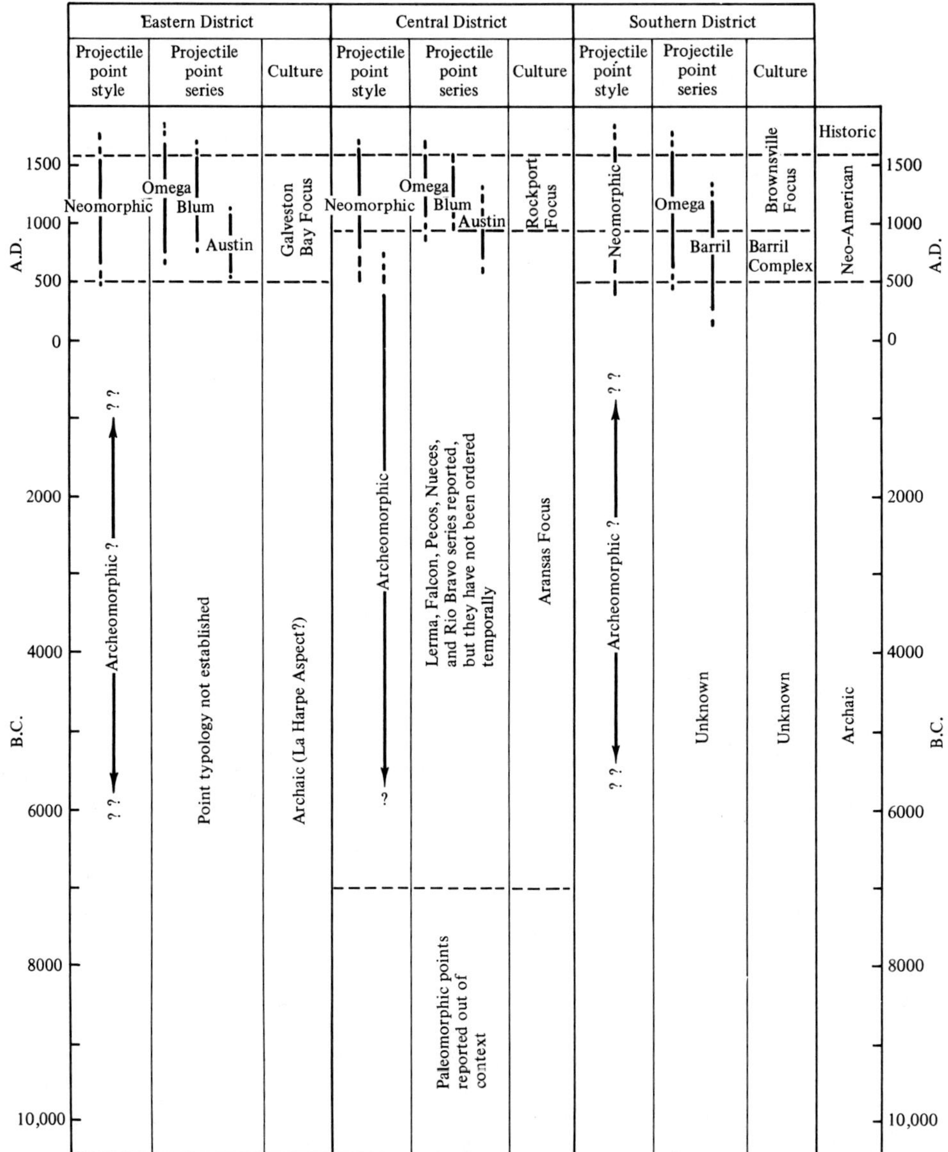

Figure 4.9. Chronology chart for the Gulf Coast area.

1. Eastern District

The first significant work in this district was in 1947 at the Addicks Reservoir just west of Houston, where Joe Ben Wheat (1953) partially excavated four sites and found zones containing pottery and arrow points overlying preceramic Archaic zones.

Basing their classification on Wheat's data, Suhm, Krieger, and Jelks (1954:128–130) described a *Galveston Bay Focus* having arrow points and pottery, and an earlier unnamed Archaic manifestation that was thought to be closely related to the East Texas Aspect, a widely distributed archaeological culture to the north. In 1962, LeRoy Johnson, Jr., included the Archaic of this district in his La Harpe Aspect (1962b).

There has been no further refinement of the Archaic since 1962, but important studies have been made of Neo-American materials—especially ceramics—from the Wright Site (Ambler 1967), the Presidio San Agustín de Ahumada Site (Tunnell and Ambler 1967), the Fullen Site (O'Brien 1971), and the Dow-Cleaver Site (Aten 1971). Also, Aten and Bollich (1969) have contributed a ceramics chronology for the Sabine Lake locality.

The evidence is clear that both Archeomorphic and Neomorphic styles are well represented in the district, but only three Paleomorphic points have been thus far reported: a possible *Clovis* point (Wheat 1953: Pl. 38 l), a *Plainview* point (Wheat 1953: Pl. 39 f). and an *Angostura* point (Ambler 1967: 61, Fig. 23). Making identifications from Wheat's 1953 illustrations for types that had not then been defined, we can enumerate the most common Archeomorphic forms: Falcon Series, types *Tortugas* and *Abasolo;* Pecos Series, types *Bulverde, Gary, Kent,* and *Pedernales;* Rio Bravo Series, type *Ensor;* Kyle Series, type *Darl.* Neomorphic types *Scallorn* (Austin Series), *Perdiz* and *Cliffton* (Blum Series), and *Fresno* (Omega Series) occur consistently, albeit usually in small numbers, in sites attributed to the Galveston Bay Focus. Stratigraphic evidence for placing the Archeomorphic style earlier than the Neomorphic style has been reported from the Wright, Fullen, and Dow-Cleaver sites; however, no clear stratigraphic separation of the respective series or types within either style has yet been observed.

Save for the temporal distinction between the Archeomorphic and Neomorphic styles, the only chronological ordering in the district has been of ceramic types. Beginning with plain sandy paste and clayey paste pottery (type *Goose Creek Plain*) some time before A.D. 150, there was a subsequent shift toward incised decoration (type *Goose Creek Incised*) and grog tempering, followed by a late appearance of bone tempering (Ambler 1967; Aten and Bollich 1969; Aten 1971; O'Brien 1971). Calendrical dates for the appearance of Archeomorphic points and for Neomorphic points are not yet firm, nor can accurate date estimates be given for shifts in ceramics types.

2. Central District

The first serious investigation of the Central Coastal District was by George C. Martin and Wendell H. Potter, who made a rather thorough surface survey of the coast between Matagorda and Baffin bays in the late 1920s (Martin 1929, 1930, 1931; Potter 1930). In his statewide survey, Sayles (1935) recognized a Karankawan culture in the Central Coastal District, which he divided into two phases: a preceramic *Oso Phase* and a later *Rockport Phase* with pottery. In 1940, E. H. Sellards reported on his excavations at the Buckner Ranch Site in Bee County, where he found projectile points that would now be classified as *Clovis, Scottsbluff, Midland,* and *Angostura,* along with other chipped-stone implements, in an alluvial terrace that also contained Late Pleistocene fossils. J. Charles Kelley (1947a:104) alluded to a *Morhiss Focus* in the district, but he has never described it.

The Aransas Focus (Archaic) and the Rockport Focus (Neo-American) were defined in the 1940s and 1950s by T. N. Campbell (1947, 1952, 1956, 1958). Suhm *et al.* (1954:121–128) summarized the Aransas and Rockport foci in their classification of Texas archaeology.

Campbell's work has clearly demonstrated the presence of an Archaic culture, the Aransas Focus, and a subsequent Neo-American culture, the Rockport Focus, in the Central Coastal District. Most Aransas Focus dart points have more or less rectangular stems: Types *Kent, Ellis, Palmillas,* and *Morhiss* are typical, most fitting into the Pecos Series. The *Lerma* and *Refugio* types of the Lerma Series are present, as are type *Abasolo* of the Falcon Series, types *Castroville, Marcos,* and *Marshall* of the Nueces Series, and type *Ensor* of the Rio Bravo Series. Other artifacts attributed to the Aransas Focus include perforated oyster shells and conch-shell adzes, hammers, scrapers, columella awls, and columella gouges (Campbell 1947, 1952, 1956, 1958; Suhm *et al.* 1954:122–125). No temporal sequence *within* the Aransas Focus has yet been demonstrated.

Neomorphic points have been reported from several sites in the district, the Webb Island Site being the most productive one found so far. *Perdiz, Cliffton, Fresno,* and *Starr* are the most common types, but *Scallorn* points occur also. All are affiliated with the Rockport Focus. An occasional *Fresno* point is made of bottle glass, attesting to the survival of the type into historic times. In addition to the Neomorphic points, a distinctive marker of the Rockport Focus is pottery of the *Rockport Black-on-Gray, Rockport Plain,* and *Rockport Incised* types (Campbell 1956, 1958; Suhm *et al.* 1954:125–128).

Campbell has not been specific about estimated dates for the Aransas and Rockport foci. Stephenson (1950:154) estimated that the Aransas Focus began about A.D. 800 and ended about A.D. 1500, and that the Rockport Focus dates entirely after A.D. 1500. Suhm *et al.* (1954:127) give no date for the Aransas Focus but estimate that the Rockport Focus began sometime after A.D. 1000 and lasted until 1800 or 1850. No temporal ordering of Neomorphic types or series within the Rockport Focus has been achieved.

3. Southern District

Of the little fieldwork done in the Southern Coastal District, most has been surface collecting. A. E. Anderson collected from sites near the mouth of the Rio Grande for many years, beginning in 1908 (Anderson 1932; Campbell 1958:163). Sayles (1935) later defined a Brownsville Phase for the general area. MacNeish (1947, 1958:173–174, 186–192) described several types and classes of artifacts for a late prehistoric Brownsville Complex (north of the Rio Grande) and for a Barril Complex (south of the Rio Grande), *Matamoros* and *Catan* points being the most distinctive and diagnostic artifact types for both complexes. He estimated that the Barril Complex began about A.D. 1000 and lasted until about A.D. 1300, and that the Brownsville Complex was later than the Barril (MacNeish 1958: Table 30). MacNeish's study was based almost entirely on surface collections. Suhm *et al.* (1954:130–133) described a Brownsville Focus based on MacNeish's work.

No Archaic assemblage or complex has yet been defined for the Southern Coastal District.

There has been no work in the district that bears significantly on chronology since that of MacNeish in the early 1950s. Such references as there are (Suhm *et al.* 1954:130–133; Campbell 1958:162–165) have been brief and general.

BIBLIOGRAPHY

Albritton, C. C., Jr., and K. Bryan
1939 Quaternary Stratigraphy in the Davis Mountains, Trans-Pecos Texas. *Bulletin of the Geological Society of America* **50:**1423–1474.

Alexander, H. L., Jr.
1963 The Levi Site: A Paleo-Indian Campsite in Central Texas. *American Antiquity* **28**(4):510–528.

Alexander, R. K.
1970 Archaeological Investigations at Parida Cave, Val Verde County, Texas. *Papers of the Texas Archaeological Salvage Project* No. **19.**

Ambler, R. J.
1967 Three Prehistoric Sites Near Cedar Bayou, Galveston Bay Area. *Texas State Building Commission, Archaeology Program* No. **8.**

Anderson, A. E.
1932 Artifacts of the Rio Grande Delta Region. *Bulletin of the Texas Archaeological and Paleontological Society* **4:**29–31.

Aten, L. E.
1967 Excavations at the Jamison Site (41 LB 2), Liberty County, Texas. *Houston Archaeological Society Reports* No. **1.**

1971 Archaeological Excavations at the Dow-Cleaver Site, Brazoria County, Texas. *Technical Bulletin of the Texas Archaeological Salvage Project* No. **1.**

Aten, L. E., and C. N. Bollich

1969 A Preliminary Report on the Development of a Ceramic Sequence for the Sabine Lake Area of Texas and Louisiana. *Bulletin of the Texas Archaeological Society* **40:**241–258.

Aveleyra Arroyo de Anda, L.

1951 Reconocimiento Arqueologico en la Zona de la Presa Internacional Falcon, Tamaulipas y Texas. *Revista Mexicana de Estudios Antropologicos* **12:**31–59.

Aveleyra Arroyo de Anda, L., M. Maldonado-Koerdell, and P. Martinez del Rio

1956 Cueva de la Candelaria. *Memorias del Instituto Nacional de Antropologia e Historia* **I.**

Bell, R. E.

1958 Guide to the Identification of Certain American Indian Projectile Points. *Special Bulletin of the Oklahoma Anthropological Society* No. **1.**

1960 Guide to the Identification of Certain American Indian Projectile Points. *Special Bulletin of the Oklahoma Anthropological Society* No. **2.**

Blaine, J. C., R. K. Harris, W. W. Crook, and J. L. Shiner

1968 The Acton Site: Hood County, Texas. *Bulletin of the Texas Archaeological Society* **39:**45–94.

Campbell, T. N.

1947 The Johnson Site: Type Site of the Aransas Focus of the Texas Coast. *Bulletin of the Texas Archaeological and Paleontological Society* **18:**40–75.

1948 The Merrell Site: Archaeological Remains Associated with Alluvial Terrace Deposits in Central Texas. *Bulletin of the Texas Archaeological and Paleontological Society* **19:**7–35.

1952 The Kent–Crane Site: A Shell Midden on the Texas Coast. *Bulletin of the Texas Archaeological Society* **23:**39–77.

1956 Archaeological Materials from Five Islands in the Laguna Madre, Texas Coast. *Bulletin of the Texas Archaeological Society* **27:**7–46.

1957a The Fields Shelter: An Archaeological Site in Edwards County, Texas. *The Texas Journal of Science* **9**(1):7–25.

1957b Archaeological Investigations at the Caplen Site, Galveston County, Texas. *Texas Journal of Science* **9**(4):448–471.

1958 Archaeological Remains from the Live Oak Point Site, Aransas County, Texas. *Texas Journal of Science* **10**(4):423–442.

1960a Archaeology of the Central and Southern Sections of the Texas Coast. *Bulletin of the Texas Archaeological Society* **29:**145–175.

1960b Texas Archaeology: A Guide to the Literature. *Bulletin of the Texas Archaeological Society* **29:**177–254.

1961 A List of Radiocarbon Dates from Archaeological Sites in Texas. *Bulletin of the Texas Archaeological Society* **30:**311–320.

Campbell, T. N., and J. Q. Frizzell

1949 Notes on the Ayala Site, Lower Rio Grande Valley, Texas. *Bulletin of the Texas Archaeological Society* **20:**63–72.

Cason, J. F.

1952 Report on Archaeological Salvage in Falcon Reservoir, Season of 1952. *Bulletin of the Texas Archaeological Society* **23:**218–259.

Collins, M. B.

1969 Test Excavations at Amistad International Reservoir, Fall, 1967. *Papers of the Texas Archaeological Salvage Project* No. **16.**

Corbin, J. E.

1963 Archaeological Materials from the Northern Shore of Corpus Christi Bay, Texas.

Bulletin of the Texas Archaeological Society **34:**5–30.

Crook, W. W., Jr.

1955 Reconsideration and Geologic Reevaluation of the Famous Abilene, Texas, Sites. *Panhandle–Plains Historical Review* **28:**38–62.

Dibble, D. S.

1967 Excavations at Arenosa Shelter, 1965–66. Report submitted to the National Park Service by the Texas Archaeological Salvage Project, University of Texas.

Dibble, D. S., and D. Lorrain

1968 Bonfire Shelter: A Stratified Bison Kill Site, Val Verde County, Texas. *Miscellaneous Papers of the Texas Memorial Museum* No. **1.**

Dibble, D. S., and E. R. Prewitt

1967 Survey and Test Excavations at Amistad Reservoir, 1964–65. *Survey Reports of the Texas Archaeological Salvage Project* No. **3.**

Duffield, L. F., and E. B. Jelks

1961 The Pearson Site: A Historic Indian Site in Iron Bridge Reservoir, Rains County, Texas. *University of Texas, Department of Anthropology, Archaeology Series* No. **4.**

Epstein, J. F.

1963 Centipede and Damp Caves: Excavations in Val Verde County, Texas, 1958. *Bulletin of the Texas Archaeological Society* **33:**2–129.

1966 Terminal Pleistocene Cultures in Texas and Northeast Mexico. *Quarternaria* **8:**115–123.

1969 The San Isidro Site: An Early Man Campsite in Nuevo Leon, Mexico. *University of Texas, Department of Anthropology, Anthropology Series* No. **7.**

1972 Some Implications of Recent Excavations and Surveys in Nuevo Leon and Coahuila. *Texas Journal of Science* **24**(1):45–56.

Evans, G. L.

1962 Notes on Terraces of the Rio Grande, Falcon–Zapata Area, Texas. *Bulletin of the Texas Archaeological Society* **32:**33–45.

Flinn, R., and J. Flinn

1968 The High Bluff Site on the Clear Fork of the Brazos River. *Bulletin of the Texas Archaeological Society* **38:**93–125.

Fleming, C. B.

1961 A Radiocarbon Date from Goebel Midden, Austin County, Texas. *Bulletin of the Texas Archaeological Society* **31:**330.

Gonzáles Rul, F.

1959 Una Punta Acanalada del Ranco ''La Chuparrosa.'' *Dirección de Prehistoria, Instituto Nacional de Antropologia e Historia.*

Graham, J. A., and W. A. Davis

1958 Appraisal of the Archaeological Resources of Diablo Reservoir, Val Verde County, Texas. Report prepared by the Archaeological Salvage Office, Austin, Texas. U.S. National Park Service.

Greer, J. W.

1968 Notes on Excavated Ring Midden Sites, 1963–1968. *Bulletin of the Texas Archaeological Society* **38:**39–44.

Hartle, D. D.

1951 Archaeological Excavations at the Falcon Reservoir, Starr County, Texas. *Smithsonian Institution, River Basin Surveys.*

Hasskari, R. A., Jr.

1961 The Boggy Creek Sites of Washington County, Texas. *Bulletin of the Texas Archaeological Society* **30:**287–300.

Hester, T. R.

1968 Paleo-Indian Artifacts from Sites Along San Miguel Creek: Frio, Atascosa, and McMullen Counties, Texas. *Bulletin of the Texas Archaeological Society* **39:**146–161.

1971 Archaeological Investigations at the La Jita Site, Uvalde County, Texas. *Bulletin of the Texas Archaeological Society* **42:**51–148.

Hester, T. R., and R. C. Parker
1970 The Berclair Site: A Late Prehistoric Component in Goliad County, Southern Texas. *Bulletin of the Texas Archaeological Society* **41:**1–23.

Holden, W. C.
1937 Excavation of Murrah Cave. *Bulletin of the Texas Archaeological and Paleontological Society* **9:**48–73.

Huskey, V.
1935 An Archaeological Survey of the Nueces Canyon. *Bulletin of the Texas Archaeological and Paleontological Society* **7:**105–114.

Jackson, A. T.
1938 The Fall Creek Sites. *University of Texas Publications* No. **3802.**
1939 A Deep Archaeological Site in Travis County, Texas. *Bulletin of the Texas Archaeological and Paleontological Society* **11:**203–225.

Jelks, E. B.
1953 Excavations at the Blum Rockshelter. *Bulletin of the Texas Archaeological Society* **24:**189–207.
1962 The Kyle Site: A Stratified Central Texas Aspect Site in Hill County, Texas. *University of Texas, Department of Anthropology, Archaeology Series* No. **5.**
1964 The Archaeology of McGee Bend Reservoir, Texas. Unpublished Ph.D. dissertation. University of Texas, Austin.
1967 (Editor) The Gilbert Site: A Norteño Focus Site in Northeastern Texas. *Bulletin of the Texas Archaeological Society* **37.**

Jennings, J. D., and E. Norbeck
1955 Great Basin Prehistory: A Review. *American Antiquity* **21**(1):1–11.

Johnson, L., Jr.
1962a Wunderlich: A Burned-Rock Midden Site. In Salvage Archaeology of Canyon Reservoir: The Wunderlich, Footbridge, and Oblate Sites, edited by LeRoy Johnson, Jr., Dee Ann Suhm, and Curtis D. Tunnell. *Bulletin of the Texas Memorial Museum* **5:**13–48.
1962b The Yarbrough and Miller Sites of Northeastern Texas, with a Preliminary Definition of the La Harpe Aspect. *Bulletin of the Texas Archaeological Society* **32:**141–284.
1963 Pollen Analysis of Two Archaeological Sites at Amistad Reservoir, Texas. *Texas Journal of Science* **15**(2):225–230.
1964 The Devil's Mouth Site: A Stratified Campsite at Amistad Reservoir, Val Verde County, Texas. *University of Texas, Department of Anthropology, Archaeology Series* No. **6.**
1967 Toward a Statistical Overview of the Archaic Cultures of Central and Southwestern Texas. *Bulletin of the Texas Memorial Museum* No. **12.**

Johnson, L., Jr., D. A. Suhm, and C. D. Tunnell
1962 Salvage Archaeology of Canyon Reservoir: The Wunderlich, Footbridge, and Oblate Sites. *Bulletin of the Texas Memorial Museum* No. **5.**

Kelley, J. C.
1947a The Cultural Affiliations and Chronological Position of the Clear Fork Focus. *American Antiquity* **13**(2):97–109.
1947b The Lehmann Rock Shelter: A Stratified Site of the Toyah, Uvalde, and Round Rock Foci. *Bulletin of the Texas Archaeological and Paleontological Society* **18:**115–128.
1949 Archaeological Notes on Two Excavated House Structures in Western Texas. *Bulletin of the Texas Archaeological and Paleontological Society* **20:**89–114.
1957 The Livermore Focus: A Clarification. *El Palacio* **64**(1–2):42–52.
1959 The Desert Culture and the Balcones Phase: Archaic Manifestations in the Southwest and Texas. *American Antiquity* **24**(3):276–288.

Kelley, J. C., and T. N. Campbell

1942 What Are the Burnt Rock Middens of Texas? *American Antiquity* **7**(3):319–322.

Kelley, J. C., T. N. Campbell, and D. J. Lehmer

1940 The Association of Archaeological Materials with Geological Deposits in the Big Bend Region of Texas. *West Texas Historical and Scientific Society Publications* **10**:9–173.

Kelly, T. C.

1961a The Crumley Site: A Stratified Burnt Rock Midden, Travis County, Texas. *Bulletin of the Texas Archaeological Society* **31**:239–272.

1961b A Radiocarbon Date from Central Texas. *Bulletin of the Texas Archaeological Society* **31**:329–330.

1963 Archaeological Investigations at Roark Cave, Brewster County, Texas. *Bulletin of the Texas Archaeological Society* **33**:191–227.

Kelly, T. C., and H. P. Smith, Jr.

1963 An Investigation of Archaeological Sites in Reagan Canyon, Brewster County, Texas. *Bulletin of the Texas Archaeological Society* **33**:167–190.

Krieger, A. D.

1946 Culture Complexes and Chronology in Northern Texas. *University of Texas Publications* No. **4640.**

Krieger, A. D., and J. T. Hughes

1950 Archaeological Salvage in the Falcon Reservoir Area: Progress Report No. 1. (mimeographed) University of Texas, Austin.

Kroeber, A. L.

1939 *Cultural and Natural Areas of Native North America*. University of California Publications in American Archaeology and Ethnology 38.

Lehmer, D. J.

1960 A Review of Trans-Pecos Texas Archaeology. *Bulletin of the Texas Archaeological Society* **29**:109–144.

Long, J. K., III

1961 Three Central Texas Aspect Sites in Hill County, Texas. *Bulletin of the Texas Archaeological Society* **30**:223–252.

MacNeish, R. S.

1947 A Preliminary Report on Coastal Tamaulipas, Mexico. *American Antiquity* **13**(1):1–15.

1958 Preliminary Archaeological Investigations in the Sierra de Tamaulipas, Mexico. *Transactions of the American Philosophical Society* **48:** pt. 6.

1961 Recent Finds Concerned with the Incipient Agriculture Stage in Prehistoric Mesoamerica. In *Homenaje a Pablo Martinez del Rio*, edited by Ignacio Bernal, Jorge Gurría, Santiago Genovés, and Luis Aveleyra. Mexico City: Instituto Nacional de Antropología e Historia, Pp. 91–101.

Martin, G. C.

1929 Notes on Some Texas Coast Campsites and Other Remains. *Bulletin of the Texas Archaeological and Paleontological Society* **1**:50–57.

1930 Two Sites on the Callo del Oso, Nueces County, Texas. *Bulletin of the Texas Archaeological and Paleontological Society* **2**:7–17.

1931 Texas Coastal Pottery. *Bulletin of the Texas Archaeological and Paleontological Society* **3**:53–56.

Martinez del Rio, P.

1953 A Preliminary Report on the Mortuary Cave of Candelaria, Coahuila, Mexico. *Bulletin of the Texas Archaeological Society* **24**:208–255.

McClurkan, B. B.

1966 The Archaeology of Cueva de la Zona de Derrumbes, a Rockshelter in Nuevo Leon, Mexico. Unpublished M.A. thesis. University of Texas, Austin.

Miller, E. O., and E. B. Jelks
1952 Archaeological Excavations at the Belton Reservoir, Coryell County, Texas. *Bulletin of the Texas Archaeological and Paleontological Society* **23:**168–217.

Nance, C. R.
1971 The Archaeology of La Calsada: A Stratified Rock Shelter Site, Sierra Madre Oriental, Nuevo Leon, Mexico. Unpublished Ph.D. dissertation, University of Texas, Austin.

Newcomb, W. W., Jr.
1956 A Reappraisal of the "Cultural Sink" of Texas. *Southwestern Journal of Anthropology* **12**(2):145–153.

Newton, M. B., Jr.
1968 The Distribution and Character of Sites, Arroyo Los Olmos, Starr County, Texas. *Bulletin of the Texas Archaeological Society* **38:**18–24.

Nunley, J. P., L. F. Duffield, and E. B. Jelks
1965 Excavations at Amistad Reservoir, 1962 Season. *Miscellaneous Papers of the Texas Archaeological Salvage Project* No. **3.**

O'Brien, M.
1971 The Fullen Site, 41 HR 82. *Bulletin of the Texas Archaeological Society* **42:**355–361.

Parsons, M. L.
1965 1963 Text Excavations at Fate Bell Shelter, Amistad Reservoir, Val Verde County, Texas. *Miscellaneous Papers of the Texas Archaeological Salvage Project* No. **4.**

Pearce, J. E.
1932 The Present Status of Texas Archaeology, *Bulletin of the Texas Archaeological and Paleontological Society* **4:**44–54.

Pearce, J. E., and A. T. Jackson
1933 A Prehistoric Rock Shelter in Val Verde County, Texas. *University of Texas Bulletin* No. **3327.**

Pollard, J. C., J. W. Greer, and H. F. Sturgis
1963 Archaeological Excavations at the Boy Scout Rockshelter (41 TV 69), Travis County, Texas. *Bulletin of the Texas Archaeological Society* **34:**31–56.

Potter, W. H.
1930 Ornamentation on Pottery of the Texas Coastal Tribes. *Bulletin of the Texas Archaeological and Paleontological Society* **2:**41–44.

Preston, N. E.
1969 The McCann Site. *Bulletin of the Texas Archaeological Society* **40:**167–192.

Prewitt, E. R.
1966 A Preliminary Report on the Devils Rockshelter Site, Val Verde County, Texas. *Texas Journal of Science* **18**(2):206–224.
1970 The Piedra del Diablo Site, Val Verde County, Texas, and Notes on Some Trans-Pecos, Texas, Archaeological Material in the Smithsonian Institution, Washington, D.C. *Texas Historical Survey Commission, Archaeology Series* No. **18.**

Ray, C. N.
1929 A Differentiation of the Prehistoric Cultures of the Abilene Region. *Bulletin of the Texas Archaeological and Paleontological Society* **1:**7–22.
1938 The Clear Fork Complex. *Bulletin of the Texas Archaeological and Paleontological Society* **10:**193–207.
1941 The Various Types of the Clear Fork Gouge. *Bulletin of the Texas Archaeological and Paleontological Society* **13:**152–162.
1948 The Facts Concerning the Clear Fork Culture. *American Antiquity* **13**(4):320–322.

Ring, E. R., Jr.
1961a An Evaluation of Radiocarbon Dates from the Galena Site, Southeastern Texas. *Bulletin of the Texas Archaeological Society* **31:**317–325.

1961b Two Radiocarbon Dates from the Galena Site of Southeastern Texas. *Bulletin of the Texas Archaeological Society* **31:**329.

Ross, R. E.
1965 The Archaeology of Eagle Cave. *Papers of the Texas Archaeological Salvage Project* No. **7.**

Sayles, E. B.
1935 An Archaeological Survey of Texas. *Medallion Papers* No. **17.**

Schuetz, M. K.
1956 An Analysis of Val Verde County Cave Material. *Bulletin of the Texas Archaeological Society* **27:**129–160.
1957a A Carbon-14 Date from Trans-Pecos Texas. *Bulletin of the Texas Archaeological Society* **28:**288–289.
1957b A Report on Williamson County Mound Material. *Bulletin of the Texas Archaeological Society* **28:**135–168.
1961 An Analysis of Val Verde County Cave Material: Part II. *Bulletin of the Texas Archaeological Society* **31:**167–205.
1963 An Analysis of Val Verde County Cave Material: Part III. *Bulletin of the Texas Archaeological Society* **33:**131–165.

Sellards, E. H.
1940 Pleistocene Artifacts and Associated Fossils from Bee County, Texas, with Notes on Artifacts by T. N. Campbell and Notes on Terrace Deposits by G. L. Evans. *Bulletin of the Geological Society of America* **51:**1627–1658.
1952 *Early Man in America: A Study in Prehistory.* Austin: University of Texas Press.

Setzler, F. M.
1935 A Prehistoric Cave Culture in Southwestern Texas. *American Anthropologist* **37**(1):104–110.

Shafer, H. J.
1963 Test Excavations at the Youngsport Site: A Stratified Terrace Site in Bell County, Texas. *Bulletin of the Texas Archaeological Society* **34:**57–81.
1968 Archaeological Investigations in the San Jacinto River Basin, Montgomery County, Texas. *Papers of the Texas Archaeological Salvage Project* No. **13.**

Shafer, H. J., D. A. Suhm, and J. D. Scurlock
1964 An Investigation and Appraisal of the Archaeological Resources of Belton Reservoir, Bell and Coryell Counties, Texas: 1962. *Miscellaneous Papers of the Texas Archaeological Salvage Project* No. **1.**

Sjoberg, A. F.
1953 The Culture of the Tonkawa, a Texas Indian Tribe. *Texas Journal of Science* **5**(3):280–304.

Skinner, S. A.
1971 Prehistoric Settlement of the DeCordova Bend Reservoir, Central Texas. *Bulletin of the Texas Archaeological Society* **42:**149–269.

Skinner, S. A., and R. Rash
1969 A Clovis Fluted Point from Hood County, Texas. *Bulletin of the Texas Archaeological Society* **40:**1–2.

Smith, V. J.
1941 Some Unusual Basketry and Bags from the Big Bend Caves. *Bulletin of the Texas Archaeological and Paleontological Society* **13:**133–151.

Sollberger, J. B.
1967 A New Type of Arrow Point with Speculations as to Its Origins. *The Record* **23**(3):16–22.

Sorrow, W. M.
1968a The Devil's Mouth Site: The Third Season—1967. *Papers of the Texas Archaeological Salvage Project* No. **14.**

1968b Test Excavations at the Nopal Terrace Site: Val Verde County, Texas. *Papers of the Texas Archaeological Salvage Project* No. **15.**

1969 Archaeological Investigations at the John Ischy Site: A Burnt Rock Midden in Williamson County, Texas. *Papers of the Texas Archaeological Salvage Project* No. **18.**

Sorrow, W. M., H. J. Shafer, and R. E. Ross

1967 Excavations at Stillhouse Hollow Reservoir. *Papers of the Texas Archaeological Salvage Project* No. **11.**

Stephenson, R. L.

1950 Culture Chronology in Texas. *American Antiquity* **16**(2):151–157.

1970 Archaeological Investigations in the Whitney Reservoir Area, Central Texas. *Bulletin of the Texas Archaeological Society* **41:**37–277.

Story, D. A.

1966 Archaeological Background. In A Preliminary Study of the Paleocology of the Amistad Reservoir Area. Final report of research under the auspices of the National Science Foundation (GS-667), assembled by D. A. Story and V. M. Bryant, Jr.

1968 Archaeological Investigations at Two Central Texas Gulf Coast Sites. *Texas State Building Commission, Archaeology Program* No. **13.**

Story, D. E., and V. M. Bryant, Jr. (Assemblers)

1966 A Preliminary Study of the Paleoecology of the Amistad Reservoir Area. Final report of research under the auspices of the National Science Foundation (GS-667).

Suhm, D. A.

1955 Excavations at the Collins Site, Travis County, Texas. *Bulletin of the Texas Archaeology Society* **26:**7–54.

1957 Excavations at the Smith Rockshelter, Travis County, Texas. *Texas Journal of Science* **9**(1):26–58.

1959 The Williams Site and Central Texas Archaeology. *Texas Journal of Science* **11**(2):218–250.

1960 A Review of Central Texas Archaeology. *Bulletin of the Texas Archaeological Society* **29:**63–107.

1962 Footbridge: A Terrace Site. In *Salvage Archaeology of Canyon Reservoir: The Wunderlich, Footbridge, and Oblate Sites,* edited by L. Johnson, Jr., D. A. Suhm, and C. D. Tunnell. *Bulletin of the Texas Memorial Museum* **5:**49–75.

Suhm, D. A., and E. B. Jelks

1962 Handbook of Texas Archaeology: Type Descriptions. *Texas Archaeological Society Special Bulletin* **1** (also *Bulletin of the Texas Memorial Museum* No. **4**).

Suhm, D. A., A. D. Krieger, and E. B. Jelks

1954 An Introductory Handbook of Texas Archaeology. *Bulletin of the Texas Archaeological Society* No. **25.**

Swanton, J. R.

1924 Southern Contacts of the Indians North of the Gulf of Mexico. *Annaes, XX Congreso Internacional de Americanistas,* 53–59.

Taylor, H. C., Jr.

1949 A Tentative Cultural Sequence for the Area about the Mouth of the Pecos. *Bulletin of the Texas Archaeological and Paleontological Society* **20:**73–88.

Taylor, W. W.

1948 A Study of Archaeology. *Memoirs of the American Anthropological Society* No. **69.**

1956 Some Implications of the Carbon-14 Dates from a Cave in Coahuila, Mexico. *Bulletin of the Texas Archaeological Society* **27:**215–234.

1960 Review of "Preliminary Archaeological Investigations in the Sierra de Tamaulipas, Mexico," by R. S. MacNeish. *American Antiquity* **25**(3):434–436.

1964 Tethered Nomadism and Water Territoriality: An Hypothesis. *Acts, 35th International Congress of Americanists* 197–203.

1966 Archaic Cultures Adjacent to the Northeastern Frontiers of Mesoamerica. In *Handbook of Middle American Indians,* edited by R. Wauchope, G. F. Ekholm, and G. R. Willey. Vol. 4. Austin: University of Texas Press. Pp. 59–94.

Taylor, W. W., and F. González Rul

1961 Archaeological Reconnaissance Behind the Diablo Dam, Coahuila, Mexico. *Bulletin of the Texas Archaeological Society* **31:**153–165.

Tunnell, C. D.

1962 Oblate: A Rockshelter Site. In *Salvage Archaeology of Canyon Reservoir: The Wunderlich, Footbridge, and Oblate Sites,* edited by L. Johnson, Jr., D. A. Suhm, and C. D. Tunnell. *Bulletin of the Texas Memorial Museum* **5:**77–116.

Tunnell, C. D., and J. R. Ambler

1967 Archaeological Excavations at Presdio San Agustin de Ahumada. *Texas State Building Commission, Archaeology Program* No. **6.**

Wakefield, W.

1968 Archaeological Survey of Palmetto Bend and Choke Canyon Reservoirs, Texas. *Survey Reports of the Texas Archaeological Salvage Project* No. **5.**

Walley, R.

1955 A Preliminary Report on the Albert George Site in Fort Bend County. *Bulletin of the Texas Archaeological Society* **26:**218–234.

Watt, F. H.

1961 Two Radiocarbon Dates from the Central Brazos Valley. *Bulletin of the Texas Archaeological Society* **31:**327–328.

Weir, F. A.

1956 Surface Artifacts from La Perdida, Starr County, Texas. *Bulletin of the Texas Archaeological Society* **27:**59–78.

1976 The Central Texas Archaic Reconsidered. In The Texas Archaic: A Symposium, edited by T. R. Hester. Center for Archaeological Research, University of Texas at San Antonio, *Special Report,* No. **2:** 60–66.

Wheat, J. B.

1953 An Archaeological Survey of the Addicks Dam Basin, Southeast Texas. *Bureau of American Ethnology Bulletin 154 River Basin Papers* No. 4:143–252, Pls. 1–47.

Willey, G. R.

1966 *An Introduction to American Archaeology.* Vol. 1. *North America.* Englewood Cliffs, New Jersey: Prentice-Hall.

Word, J. H.

1971 The Dunlap Complex in Western Central Crockett County, Texas. *Bulletin of the Texas Archaeological Society* **42:**271–318.

North American Plains

WARREN W. CALDWELL AND DALE R. HENNING

I. DEVELOPMENT OF PLAINS CHRONOLOGY

Over many millennia, this broad expanse of land, the North American Plains, has been the home of peoples who developed surprisingly varied means for dealing with a changing, often capricious environment. Despite heterogeneous origins, the stresses of life on the Plains and the ease of cultural interaction have brought about a surficial similarity. It is possible then to speak of "Plains cultures" yet recognizing that they have come from or received strong influence from elsewhere.

The many schemes whereby these disparate complexes have been ordered are complex, sometimes disconcerting, and always consistent in their inconsistency. Seemingly, much past research was not undertaken within a clear-cut theoretical paradigm, or, perhaps at best, a consistent approach was articulated only after the fact as a gesture toward respectability. This is not offered as an indictment. As recently as a decade ago in many parts of the Plains, we had only the broadest sorts of leads, and "problem" archaeology in its present sense was scarcely an issue. The result has been an eclecticism that threatens to remain with us for some time to come. As recently as 1965 the archaism of a Birdwood "culture" was described, based upon sites in central Nebraska (Garrett 1965), despite the availability of more current paradigms. Thus our position is difficult; we cannot phrase our review in terms of a consistent, durable scheme short of a vast reworking of the material, a project beyond our reach. As a result, our approach will be as eclectic as that of our colleagues both past and present.

During the early years of this century, the bulk of archaeological investigation was concentrated within the area now called the Central Plains, particularly Nebraska. As a natural result, much has been written about Nebraska prehistory. Almost from the beginning, investigations were both intensive and systematic. Much of the conceptual framework presently explicit in the Plains was first explored here and the area continues to serve as a laboratory for the development of new approaches (cf. Krause 1969). David M. Gradwohl (1969: Chapter V) has provided a perceptive review of the situation vis-à-vis eastern Nebraska.

A staff archaeologist, E. E. Blackman, was appointed by the Nebraska State Historical Society as early as 1901. In the following 15 years, Blackman, Robert F. Gilder, an energetic journalist and later archaeologist for the University of Nebraska State Museum, and, particularly, F. H. Sterns, accumulated a corpus of data that still constitutes an important resource. Perhaps Sterns, who worked in Iowa and Kansas as well as in Nebraska, was the most influential of this group. Much of Sterns' work is embodied in his Ph.D. dissertation (Harvard 1915) that remains unpublished, but it has been important to all later archaeologists concerned with the area (Gradwohl 1969:20–21, 23).

The pioneering archaeologists, not surprisingly, were concerned with the identification of cultural complexes and their definition in time and space. An explicit conceptual framework was lacking (Blakeslee and Caldwell 1972:12), and no precise classificatory terminology was employed (Gradwohl 1969:36). However, in discussing the dominant Prehistoric Sedentary Villager Complex of eastern Nebraska, "[Gilder] did use the term "culture," referring to his discoveries as "a new culture" and "an unexploited culture (Gilder 1911:249)." While Gilder did not explicitly state how he was using the term "culture," it is apparent that he was considering spatial as well as formal factors (Gradwohl 1972:36). By 1926, the term *Nebraska culture* had evolved (Gradwohl 1972:37), a name and concept that survive in present usage (cf. Garrett 1965).

In a now classic paper, *The Plains Culture Area in the Light of Archeology,* W. D. Strong (1933) used the Gilder terminology, but in the context of an expanded, systematic ordering of archaeological complexes over a broad area. Each "culture" had a specific milieu of time, space, and form that segregated it from others. Thus the Nebraska culture is distinguished from the coeval Upper Republican culture of the Loess Plains to the west and from the precedent Sterns Creek culture of eastern Nebraska (Gradwohl 1969:38; Strong 1933:274). The approach is clear enough even though the conceptual elements were never plainly articulated (Gradwohl 1969:38–39).

It is current in the sense that it was conscious of time, space, and morphology. Within a short time, however, the constituent complexes were transmuted into elements of the Midwestern Taxonomic System (MTS), which is both timeless and spaceless, without regard to the conceptual dissonance. The system and order inherent in the new scheme were so advantageous that the debits could be accepted with equanimity. Waldo R. Wedel (1935), in considering archaeological units in both Kansas and Nebraska, relabeled the Nebraska culture as the *Nebraska Aspect* and assigned it to an Upper Mississippi Phase. The Upper Republican culture became an aspect within a Central Plains Phase. Strong and Wedel apparently worked in close association (Gradwohl 1969:39; Blakeslee and Caldwell 1972:13) and in *An Introduction to Nebraska Archeology* (Strong 1935) Wedel's systematization was accepted with only scant alteration.

The MTS, or more correctly, a bastardized version thereof, rapidly became the usual framework for considering archaeological complexes within the Central Plains. New foci were added and realignments were proposed as fieldwork progressed (Gradwohl 1969:40,42). Wedel (1940) was then able to outline a broad scheme that remained current for a number of years to come.

The growth of the Interagency Archeological and Paleontological Salvage Program following World War II brought a surge of new data and a broadened view of Central Plains relationships. Inevitably the MTS in its ad hoc "Plains" character was subject to a reexamination (Champe 1961). Revisions stemmed from the "Accidental (or Tenth and a half) Plains Conference" in the summer of 1953, during which current taxonomic units were reassessed. The results were formalized and presented to the Eleventh Plains Conference in November 1953 (Gradwohl 1969:42). For the first time, Plains specialists as a group came to grips with the canon of the MTS, "reclassifying" entities by morphology alone and only subsequently considering factors of time and space (Stephenson 1954: Tables I and II). The result was a taxonomy by consensus, a communal effort to achieve an understanding of relationships over a wide area of the Central Plains and Middle Missouri. In retrospect, we can only view the effort as inordinately successful. Indeed, "Stephenson 1954" is still cited, still serves as an important baseline and, although modified and expanded, still retains a considerable degree of utility. The group approach could well have immured the consensus as *the* paradigm suitable for Plains archaeology, but already in 1954 there were portents of change. Stephenson suggested that the concepts specified by Phillips and Willey (1953) "deserve serious consideration for future revision of the presently prepared framework [Stephenson 1954:16]." (See also Gradwohl 1969:42.) Although Stephenson's comment was no more than an *obiter dictum,* changes were already under way.

By the 1950s, the focus of fieldwork had shifted to the Missouri River Trench in the Dakotas. Excavations in the Oahe, Fort Randall, Garrison, and Big Bend Reservoirs added vastly to the corpus of data and stimulated the reexamination of taxonomic issues. Donald J. Lehmer, who had worked in the Oahe area of central South Dakota, espoused a new approach permitting widely ranging relationships to be dealt with in both space and time (Lehmer 1952, 1954a, 1954b). Sites and components were phrased within the MTS, but evident continuities were recognized through the concept of *branch*, which was transferred from the Southwest where it connoted "cultural development through time within a limited geographic area." [Lehmer 1954a:117]. Moreover, the Fort Pierre Branch, encompassing the principal sites within Lehmer's purview, was placed within the context of three traditions, *Central Plains, Middle Missouri,* and *Coalescent*, units of the Plains Village Pattern that were applicable over much of the Plains. Immediately, an effort was made to recast the traditions into the MTS framework (Hurt 1953:54) regardless of the conceptual inconsistency. Despite such tribulations, the traditions, as defined by Lehmer, have been accepted as useful tools by most Plains specialists. The idea of the branch, as proposed, is no longer current and, as far as we are aware, has never been applied in the Plains outside of the Pierre region.

Lehmer's scheme has been remarkably effective and has had a long life. The idea of the tradition has been quite adaptable. Wedel (1961) has used it interchangeably with that of the MTS phase. They are, after all, hierarchical equivalents even though they are conceptually different sorts of devices. Despite its durability, Lehmer's approach has not remained unchanged. As early as 1961, the concepts embodied in the Willey and Phillips volume *Method and Theory in American Archaeology* (1958) were used to organize archaeological data from southwestern Iowa (Anderson 1961). Shortly thereafter, the Willey and Phillips scheme, modified by inclusion of additional spatial and integrative units (Lehmer and Caldwell 1966), was proposed for use in the Middle Missouri area. Subsequent modifications argued by Krause (1969) and Lehmer (1971) will be considered in the next section.

II. CHRONOLOGICAL REVIEW (See Figure 5.1)

A. Paleo-Indian

In discussing the earliest occupations of the Plains, one is faced with myriad hypotheses but a distressing dearth of hard data. The problem is linked directly with the peopling of the New World and, of course, with the environmental conditions that then prevailed. As recently as 1971, Wormington stressed that "no one really knows when man first came into North America [1971:84]." However, if we are correct in assuming, as many do, that the principal entrants came via the Bering Strait and ultimately southward along the Mackenzie River Valley, the Northern Plains should have

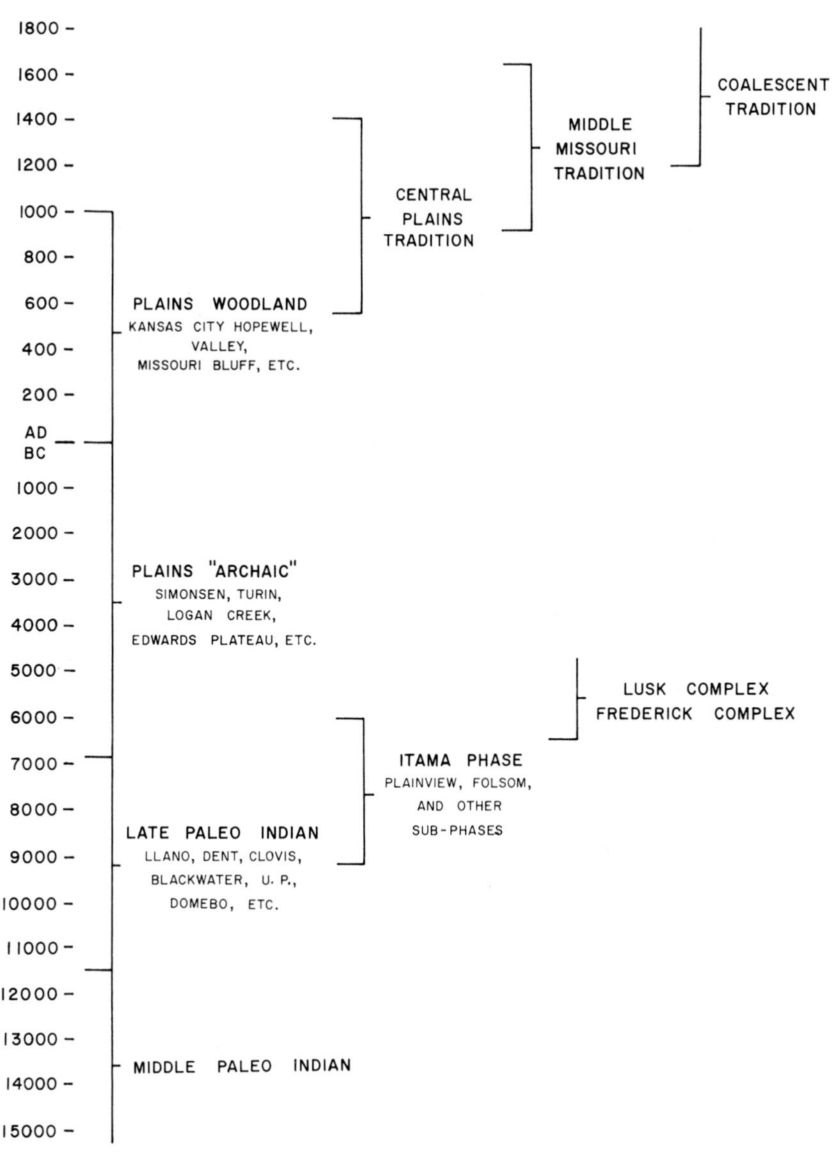

Figure 5.1. Chronology of archaeological complexes in the Plains.

been crossed by the earliest entrants whoever they were and whenever they arrived.

The earliest populations in North America have been named variously Early Man (Hrdlicka 1907), Paleo-Indian (Roberts 1940), and Early Big-Game Hunters (Sauer 1944)—all of which are applied, often synonymously, today. For reasons that need not be developed here, we prefer the Roberts terminology, just as we opt to follow Haynes's (1971) suggestion of subdividing the Paleo-Indian into Early, Middle, and Late periods. The *Early* Period, dating at pre-27,000 B.P., is defended on the basis of flints of questionable human workmanship (Haynes 1971:4), including such remains as those found at the Calico Mountains Site in California. Comparable remains have not been found *in situ* on the Plains. Haynes's *Middle* Paleo-Indian period dates from 27,000 to 11,500 B.P. (Haynes 1971:4) and includes data from sites in both North and South America. These sites support no single technological tradition, but all suggest that man was occupying portions of the New World from at least 27,000 B.P., with evidence for occupations increasing through time. The Cooperton Site in Oklahoma (Anderson 1962) is an important site from this time period, dating by radiocarbon at about 20,000 B.P. Although no identifiable stone tools were found in association, the bones appear to have been intentionally broken while green, apparently by man (Bonfield and Li 1966).

Haynes's *Late* Paleo-Indian period begins at ca. 11,500 B.P. and terminates at ca. 7000 B.P. The beginning date is acceptable to us, although some tend to push the same "Llano" cultural pattern back to 13,000 B.P. (Wheat 1971:22). Haynes's extension of the Late Paleo-Indian period to as recently as 7000 B.P. could be confusing, however. While in some regions, an attenuated Late Paleo-Indian pattern does persist to that time, elsewhere we find regionalized specializations that "fit" far more comfortably into the "Archaic." Haynes refers to the earliest cultural configuration of the Late Period as "Clovis," which ties it to, and by inference limits it to, a specific projectile point technology. For our purposes, we prefer to use the term *Llano,* which is commonly applied to the *culture* of peoples who made the distinctive Clovis-type projectile points. Important Llano sites on the Plains include Dent (Figgans 1933), the Clovis Lake Beds (Sellards 1952; Warnica 1966), Blackwater Draw (Haynes, Agogino, and Rovner 1969), the U.P. Site (Irwin-Williams, Irwin and Agognino 1962; Irwin 1968) and Domebo (Leonhardy 1966).

Judging from evidence derived from these sites, as well as from locations outside the Plains, one of the principal attractions for Llano peoples was water. At such loci, single elephants could be attacked and killed, perhaps following some form of containment (Wheat 1971:24). For obvious reasons, the kill site was also used for butchering. Other large animals taken by Llano peoples include tapir, horse, and bison. Only one bison kill in which Clovis-type points were used has been reported (Agogino 1968); more such kills will probably be forthcoming in the future.

The Llano Complex is characterized by very typical lanceolate, bifacially flaked projectile points with basal and edge grinding and short, single or multiple thinning or fluting flakes struck on both sides of the center of the base. Llano sites also yield beaks, burins, side and end scrapers, some "spokeshaves," bifacially flaked knives, and gravers and flakes with abrupt marginal retouch. In addition to the chipped stone, other Clovis sites (but not on the Plains), have yielded a cylindrical bevel-based bone or ivory point and a mammoth bone shaft wrench (Haynes and Hemmings 1968).

Llano settlement patterns are not well known. The bulk of the Plains Llano components are kill sites. The few known campsites suggest a migratory pattern, the movements being dependent upon climatic conditions and available floral and faunal resources. The lack of sites other than temporary hunting–butchering campsites is probably due to the fact that we do not yet fully understand the Llano cultural system: Such insights would allow greater predictive capability as regards site location.

The "Plano" Complex, characterized by the Folsom fluted and a host of other projectile points with parallel, collateral, and/or oblique flaking, follows the Llano. These projectile points, when found *in situ,* have generally been associated with the remains of extinct species of bison.

We see great utility in considering the succeeding period of time (ca. 3000 years) as a single cultural unit. There are variations and changes in basic tool kits, but the constituent complexes are basically similar. The associated faunal remains are invariably extinct forms of bison. H. T. Irwin, utilizing evidence from the deeply stratified Hell Gap Site in Wyoming, has termed these basically similar complexes the "Itama culture."

We are willing to accept the idea of basic cultural similarity during the 3000 years of the Itama culture. However, detailed analyses and comparison of data from sites assigned to the subphases will undoubtedly demonstrate substantive differences. Knudson's detailed comparison of the Plainview and MacHaffie II assemblages (Knudson 1973) suggests the possibilities for such detailed analyses.

The Itama culture includes seven subphases followed by two "complexes"; each of these is to be found at the Hell Gap Site as well as elsewhere. In each instance, the "index fossil," which serves as the identifying feature for each, is a "type" projectile point or knife. The subphases suggested by Irwin are, in order from the earliest, the Plainview, Folsom, Midland, Agate Basin, Hell Gap, Alberta, and Cody. The Cody Subphase is followed by the Frederick and Lusk complexes. The distributions of these (Irwin 1971: Figs. 5, 6) include portions of the Plains in all instances.

Itama culture peoples were bison hunters, generally employing "drives" in order to kill large numbers of the animals during the autumn months. Kill and butchering sites of the Itama culture are not uncommon on the Plains. These locations, the sites of drives or traps for bison, yield projectile points, knives, scrapers, and battering tools used for killing, butchering, and hide processing. A distinctive class of tools used in butchering are the patterned items made of roughly shaped bison bone. Obviously, throughout Itama culture times, fairly large groups banded together for communal drives, some of which were very complex. The Casper Site (Frison 1971; 1972), located in Casper, Wyoming, is a good example of a communal drive. It employed a large, parabolic sand dune as a trap. At least 100 bison were herded through the open end of the dune and dispatched at one time. The most common projectile point type recovered was the Hell Gap; many of the points had been resharpened and used as knives. The site probably dates between 9500 and 10,000 years ago.

Other later sites, which Irwin places in the Cody subphase, include kill, butchering, and campsites that suggest, by the variations in projectile point types, increasing cultural complexity and a range of techniques for stone tool manufacture. The number of people on the Plains appears to have increased; very likely, the herds of bison swelled during this period (8500–9000 B.P.) as well. The Olsen–Chubbuck Site, for instance, is a good example of a single-kill site in which animals were dispatched, butchered, eaten, and processed. Wheat has suggested that no less than 100 persons could have been involved in this effort (Wheat 1971).

Such communal efforts required much more than just available animals and a large number of people. A thorough knowledge of the habits of the bison was essential; such knowledge was coupled with the capability to dispatch the animals in comparative safety, to butcher efficiently, removing the hides, and to prepare the meat for storage and use through the winter months. We know from ethnographic literature that well-developed patterns of leadership, both secular and religious, were required to ensure the success of large-scale bison procurement endeavors.

B. Archaic

The concept of a "Plains Archaic" has been used in cavalier fashion for years. "Middle Prehistoric," or "Forager" has been preferred by some, but often, we believe, with little sense of meaning. Following Willey and Phillips (1958), we regard the Archaic as a cultural "stage" representative of a fairly specific way of life, tool complex, subsistence orientation, and level of social organization. The stage in this sense has neither temporal nor spatial parameters; the Archaic is identified by culture content wherever it is found and at whatever time. Used in this way, the concept of Archaic has a degree of utility in the Plains. However, the Archaic, as we visualize it, is a complex oriented to a woodland environment and seems anomalous in a grasslands ecotone.

Archaic peoples on the Plains were hunters and gatherers dependent on smaller and more varied fauna than were the Paleo-Indian groups. Their tool inventory included chipped stone projectile points, knives, and scrapers—all lacking the craftsmanship exhibited by Paleo-Indian flintknappers. Their tool complex also included pecked and ground tools such as axes, milling stones, handstones, and (rarely) bannerstones and/or atlatl weights. In addition, there were bone awls, needles and tubes, and, occasionally, harpoons and fishhooks. Shell beads are also found. Archaic peoples on the Plains comprised groups with a distinct woodland orientation who made seasonal use of the Plains. Such Archaic peoples did not necessarily succeed the Paleo-Indian hunters in time; in some instances they were contemporaneous with those groups.

The Turin, Simonsen, and Logan Creek sites are among the earliest exhibiting use of the plains–prairie ecotone by peoples with an eastern woodland cultural orientation. The Turin Site in western Iowa was a burial of several individuals, each flexed and placed in an individual pit. Some were sprinkled with red ochre (Wormington 1957:247–248). Associated with one adolescent was a large corner- or side-notched projectile point of Knife River flint and a number of freshwater shell beads of *Anculosa* (sp), presumably constituting the remains of a necklace. One radiocarbon assay on skeletal materials produced a date of 270 B.C.; probably it is far too recent.

The Simonsen Site is a bison kill and butchering component located in terrace fill along the Little Sioux River, near Quimby, Iowa. Frankforter and Agogino (1960) suggest that bison *(Bison occidentalis)* were driven over a bank, then butchered where they fell near the stream. The use of a drive, the apparent butchering techniques, and the tools utilized are, with some important exceptions, similar to contemporary sites further to the west, which are ascribed to Paleo-Indian groups. The Simonsen points are—contrary to those from most coeval sites on the High Plains—small, concave or straight-based, and side-notched. They are smaller than, but similar in outline to, the Turin projectile point briefly discussed earlier. A large, full-grooved ax head, recovered following formal excavations, offers further evidence for a woodland orientation. Charcoal from a hearth associated with the kill dates at 6480 (± 520) B.C.

The Logan Creek Site (Kivett 1958) in Burt County, Nebraska, is a stratified site with four occupation levels; each is thought to represent a single component. Hearths, both stone-filled and plain, are reported, and artifacts include projectile points with side or corner notches, side-notched and stemmed scrapers, milling stones, bone awls, a bone fishhook, and tubular beads. Bison bone was commonly found; freshwater mussel shell was also recovered. Radiocarbon dates from the site are comparable to those from the Simonsen Site.

In the summer of 1973, a site was discovered through removal of earth from a barrow pit adjacent to a new sewage lagoon being constructed along the Little Sioux River on the south edge of Cherokee, Iowa. Here, three separate cultural levels, ranging between 8 and 21 feet below the surface, were identified through trench testing. In each, faunal and floral remains were recovered and (from the two upper levels) there were small side-notched projectile points resembling closely the Hill (Frankforter 1959) and Simonsen specimens. The single projectile point from the lowest level is a lanceolate form. *Bison* (sp) bone is found in each layer; some layers have produced the remains of smaller mammals as well. Judging from the evidence at hand, the Sewer site suggests stratified complexes ranging from the Paleo-Indian into the Archaic stage.

The Nebo Hill Complex (Shippee 1948, 1954, 1957, 1962) localized in the vicinity of Kansas City, Missouri, is characterized by long, narrow lanceolate projectile points with a diamond-shaped cross-section. Also associated are chipped stone drills or perforators, "blanks" or preforms, adzes, axes, digging tools, and chert hammers. Pecked and ground tools include: hematite celts; flat, oval quartzite manos; three-quarter grooved axes; and deep, bowl-shaped mortars of quartzite. Excavations on several Nebo Hill components in Kansas City and its environs have been undertaken under Shippee's direction, with one aim to collect samples for radiocarbon assay. To date, no sufficient samples have been obtained, and the Nebo Hill Complex must, perforce, "float" in time.

Further south, the Grove Focus (Bell and Baerreis 1951) includes numerous small, deep sites located in shelters and along streams in northeastern Oklahoma. Some of these have been excavated to a depth of as much as 12 feet, yielding stemmed and notched points, drills, scrapers, knives, and choppers. Grooved axes, grinding stones, anvils, and small mortars constitute the pecked and ground categories; such tools imply a degree of permanence of occupation. These sites were occupied by peoples who hunted and gathered, subsisting upon game, principally deer, and upon the abundant floral materials of this westward extension of the Ozark Highlands.

Other, probably later, stratified midden sites of the Archaic stage are found in east central Oklahoma; these constitute the remains of the Fourche Maline peoples. Here again, the cultural inventory (Bell and Baerreis 1951) suggests an eastern Archaic orientation with a woodland exploitative pattern. Some of the sites are transitional into Woodland. Pottery is found in the upper levels, suggesting that ceramic technology was absorbed by the local populace without significant loss or alteration of traditional elements.

Further to the south, in central Texas, is a generalized complex referred to as the Edwards Plateau Aspect (Suhm, Krieger, and Jelks 1954). The sites are characterized as middens, composed primarily of burned rock, which are located in rock shelters and open terraces near water. The middens often reach depths of 5 to 6 feet. Within the middens are dart points, scrapers, knives, axes, choppers, and pecked and ground milling stones and manos. Polished stone pendants, boat-shaped atlatl weights, bone awls, antler flaking tools, and perforated shell hoes are also found. There is no evidence of horticulture. The data available suggest fairly permanent settlements of deer hunters and collectors of wild floral materials. A woodland orientation is suggested. The Edwards Plateau Aspect must have begun as early as 5000 B.C. and may have persisted past the time of Christ.

Following our definition, there are complexes that must be considered as Archaic in the Northwestern Plains as well. The Oxbow Dam Site produced side-notched points of the Saskatchewan "Prairie Archaic" (Kehoe and Kehoe 1968:23); these points are morphologically similar to those recovered from Simonsen, Turin, and Logan Creek. A series of kill and campsites dating from ca. 3250 B.C., found in the Northwestern Plains, suggest extensive bison hunting and collecting by diverse groups of people. Projectile point types include Long Creek, Duncan, McKean, Hanna, and Pelican Lake, to name a few. Precisely what relationships there are, if any, between the Saskatchewan "Prairie Archaic" Complex and the side-notched tradition characterized by the Simonsen point, we cannot determine at this time.

C. Woodland

Woodland materials are scattered over the Plains, left in the form of small temporary villages or campsites and mounds. Woodland, as the name implies, is generally assumed to refer to peoples whose culture was best adapted to a woodland environment. Woodland camp and village sites are often found along river and stream valley margins, where a woodland environment extended into the plains proper. From these locations, both the plains and the extended woodland environments could be exploited with relative ease. In addition, some expeditions onto the plains were undertaken by Woodland peoples for the purpose of procuring bison meat and hides. Sites that can most easily be identified as Woodland are those yielding pottery; indeed, for the most part, the Woodland stage or stages are the first pottery-using cultures on the Plains. In time, we feel certain that archaeologists will become sufficiently sophisticated so that other aspects of Woodland technology will be recognized. Undoubtedly there will be evidence for bison procurement and butchering by Woodland peoples, probably to a degree not suspected at this time.

Probably the best-known Woodland remains are those recovered from along the eastern borderland of the Central Plains. A series of sites in the Kansas City region (Wedel 1943, 1959; Shippee 1967; Chapman and Chapman 1964; Johnson 1969) range in time from A.D. 100 to 400 and are generally assigned to the Middle Woodland Stage. The Kansas City materials are generally believed to be closely related to Middle Woodland Hopewellian materials in the Lower Illinois Valley and around the mouth of the Missouri. It is interesting to note that Middle Woodland sites are rare to absent from the Missouri to about midway between St. Louis and Kansas City. Here, near the mouth of the Lamine River, the Missouri floodplain becomes very wide—a geographic factor that persists to Kansas City and further upstream. Middle Woodland sites are found along the Missouri as far upstream as St. Joseph, Missouri, and along the lower Lamine. Some gardening was probably practiced on the floodplain, providing an important contribution to the subsistence pattern of these people.

Middle Woodland sites in this region exhibit definite relationships to those in the Illinois Valley in subsistence pattern, ceramic and stone tool technology, and, probably, social organization. Much of the religious behavior exhibited in Illinois Valley mortuary customs is lacking in the Kansas City area, however. Precisely why Middle Woodland sites are found in the Kansas City region cannot be stated definitely at this time. However, it seems logical that Middle Woodland settlement or the diffusion of Middle Woodland technology to resident receptors was possible because of complementary environments. In addition, the potential availability of bison near Kansas City was probably an important attraction.

Middle Woodland culture persisted in and around Kansas City over a number of generations; ceramics suggest a transition in popularity from the Havana to Weaver wares, probably reflective of similar changes in the Illinois River Valley. Attenuated Middle Woodland site remains are found in east and central Kansas and extend at least as far west as Chase County (Wedel 1959:495).

Middle and Late Woodland remains occur in southeastern Kansas (Marshall 1972) and northeastern Oklahoma (Baerreis 1953). Marshall refers to his Middle Woodland materials as belonging to the Cuesta and Hopewell "phases." We prefer to visualize "Hopewell" as it is defined in terms of a fairly specific subsistence pattern, a number of technological indices, a settlement pattern, religious practices, and related social organization. "Hopewell" should be carefully defined in terms of the Illinois River Valley. The Middle Woodland materials from southeastern Kansas appear to be attenuated. They must have passed through a fine-mesh Kansas City "Hopewellian" filter.

Woodland materials outside the Kansas City region are less well known. The sites are often deeply buried; they are smaller or even ignored because other remains were more visible and readily dug. Kivett's work in Nebraska (Kivett 1952) has resulted in definition of the Valley, Keith, and Loseke Creek foci. In western Iowa and eastern Nebraska, "Missouri Bluff" remains have been found (Keyes 1949), but no extensive excavations have yet been carried out on a Missouri Bluff site to date. The Sterns Creek materials in eastern Nebraska (Strong 1935) and western Iowa have been discussed as taxonomically tied to the Late Woodland stage but they lack a full published report.

The stratified Beals Site in Cherokee County, Iowa, yields Great Oasis remains above Late Woodland. Late Woodland pits at the site suggest some permanence of occupation, and subsistence on deer, smaller mammals, and fish and mussels from nearby Mill Creek. There is one date from the Woodland component, A.D. 690 (± 110).

Woodland materials likely emanating from western Minnesota are fairly common along the Middle Missouri River Trench. They occur in the form of low circular and linear mounds (Wood 1960, Neuman 1961), mixed with the remains of other peoples in village sites (Johnston 1967), stratigraphically below the Plains villagers' deposits or in separate single component villages (Wedel 1961:165). Several Woodland sites suggesting some permanence of use through repeated occupations have been investigated in South Dakota. The Scalp Creek, Ellis Creek (Hurt 1952), and Arp Sites yielded hearths, pits, and scattered post molds. The Scalp Creek component may have been associated with a nearby low mound.

The dating of Woodland in the Plains from ca. A.D. 400 to at least A.D. 1000 is generally accepted. We must remember, too, that a Woodland pattern persisted in Northern Minnesota until much later (Johnson 1969:20); undoubtedly, these peoples made occasional forays onto the Plains to hunt and trade.

D. Plains Village Pattern

Much of the recent prehistory of the northern and central portions of the Plains can be encompassed within the *Plains Village Pattern*. The constituent traditions, first described in detail by Lehmer (1954) continue to serve as prime integrating devices over much of the area. On an operational level, the tripartite traditions have been unusually fruitful (cf. Caldwell and Jensen 1969:83), yet the situation is paradoxical. The material distinctions are often not sharp nor are the spatial flows and temporal relationships as clear-cut as the conceptual framework implies. By definition, the traditions deal with cultural continuities through time and space but they do not exist necessarily *en seriatum* or in congruent space. The Central Plains tradition and the Middle Missouri tradition are roughly coeval in time, although the latter seems to be longer lived, extending in its terminal "variant" into the late years of the seventeenth century (Lehmer 1971:124). The Middle Missouri tradition, too, was coeval (for several centuries) with the Coalescent tradition, of which it was a parent. The Coalescent Tradition outlived both the Middle Missouri Tradition and its extralocal parent, the Central Plains Tradition. Moreover, the Coalescent Tradition came to occupy much of the area of both its parents as it alloyed and refactored the contribution of each.

The Central Plains Tradition includes a number of subdivisions conceived variously within the MTS and the Willey and Phillips units or modifications thereof. Wedel, in his monumental study of Kansas prehistory (1959), discusses a Central Plains Phase, which in large part we take to be equivalent to the tradition. Included are three major units: the Nebraska Aspect, The

Upper Republican Aspect and the Smoky Hill Aspect (Wedel 1959:566, 567). The latter, found in the Smoky Hill, Blue, and Kansas River drainages of Kansas, was viewed as ancestral to the other Aspects, both of which are best known from Nebraska. Champe (1961), applying the MTS canons with a renewed rigor, reassigned the taxonomic units within an *Aksarben Aspect*. The four constituent foci—Nebraska, Upper Republican, St. Helena, and Sweetwater—are not conceptually equal to the units proposed by Wedel. Anderson (1961), Brown (1967), Gradwohl (1969), and Blakeslee and Caldwell (1972) have treated specific manifestations of the Central Plains Tradition within the Willey and Phillips concepts. The most recent synthetic model (Krause 1969) seems to have evolved in reaction to that proposed by Lehmer and Caldwell (1966) for the Middle Missouri *region* of the Northern Plains *subarea*. Krause saw fit to replace the latter with three *subareas*, one of which is the Central Plains as defined by Wedel. Within the Central Plains, Krause specifies *regions* that follow substantially the physiographic units defined by Fenneman (1931) (see Steinacher and Ludwickson 1972). Furthermore, he argues for a new integrative unit, the regional–temporal *variant* as a replacement for the *horizon* as a means of distinguishing and at the same time relating constituent phases.

As with previous efforts of the recent past, Krause's approach has not achieved complete acceptance. Perhaps revisions or extensions are warranted. The Loup drainage, eastern Kansas, and the High Plains, are not considered by Krause, and the integrative units as propounded, are open to dispute. Under the circumstances one might argue for reliance on the Willey and Phillips approach in its "pure" form, at least for the present, because it is economical, flexible, and indeed will serve to order the cultural units of the Central Plains. For these reasons, Steinacher and Ludwickson have cast their intensive analysis within the framework of Willey and Phillips. They outline a number of new phases, which may or may not be valid; but for our purposes their principal contribution lies in the emphasis upon chronology and chronological relationships among the several components and phases. They have built logically, within localities where possible, and in terms of a reasonably secure time scale.

Presently, the Solomon River Phase in the Glen Elder locality of north-central Kansas is the earliest dated manifestation of the Central Plains Tradition (Carlson 1971; Steinacher and Ludwickson 1972:51). Rectangular houses with four-post central supports, and ceramics with unsmoothed, cord-roughened bodies of globular or subconoidal shape and collared and plain rims with incised decoration are typical and can be taken as symptomatic of the tradition as a whole.

If the data have been properly interpreted, components of the Solomon River Phase range from the last quarter of the sixth century A.D. to the middle of the ninth century. Steinacher and Ludwickson speculate that "it [the Solomon Phase] originated from some indigenous Woodland pattern, probably to be found in southern Kansas or northern Oklahoma, spreading north displacing or absorbing other Woodland peoples such as Loeske Creek, Sterns Creek, and other complexes [1972:52]."

A component of the Sumpter Site (140B27) (Carlson 1967) dated in the seventh century A.D., contained ceramic traits reminiscent of those from such Woodland sites as well as eight-rowed maize, a newly introduced (Galinat and Gunnerson 1963; Cutler and Blake 1969:62) and perhaps dynamic element in the emergence of the Central Plains Tradition (Steinacher and Ludwickson 1972:52–58). Even in the absence of dates, the character of the site would warrant that it be viewed as early in the development of the tradition.

Subsequent to the Solomon River Phase, and developing out of it, were (*a*) the Upper Republican Phase in its "classic" form and (*b*) the Smoky Hill Phase. The former is manifest in the Solomon locality (Carlson 1971:93–94) and the Upper Smoky Hill and Republican River localities (Steinacher and Ludwickson 1972:53). The Smoky Hill Phase, developing along the river that has provided its "type" name, seems to have diverged from the parent stem because of its easterly position, where it was exposed to pressures from 'Mississippian' peoples filtering up the rivers, perhaps from the Steed–Kisker sites in the Kansas City area. Sites in the Milford locality, the Tuttle Creek locality, and elsewhere in northeastern Kansas document such a northwestward drift of 'Mississippian' traits.

Within the Central Plains Tradition, one can document a trend through time toward increasingly greater frequencies of collared rims. At the Miller Site (14GB21), a Steed–Kisker-like manifestation in the Milford locality dated as early as A.D. 1060, there are no collared rims. At Miller, shell tempering, smoothing of surfaces, and shoulder incising—all acceptable Mississippian traits—appear in the area for the first time. The early appearance of such eastern influences within this locality may well account for the long-standing conviction among some that the origin of the Central Plains Tradition is to be found in a Mississippian context.

The Upper Republican Phase is identifiable in the Lost Creek (Strong 1935:69ff), Harlan County (Roll 1968), and Medicine Creek (Wedel 1948, 1953; Kivett 1949) localities of south–central Nebraska. There may be differences in content and time within the phase in the three localities; however, much of the data are unpublished, and distinctions cannot be made at present. There is a major suite of radiocarbon dates for the Medicine Creek locality that can be applied to the group of manifestations as a whole. Most dates fall within the twelfth and thirteenth centuries A.D., although a few are in the eleventh and fourteenth centuries. The period 1100–1300 might well be taken as the florescence of the "classic" Upper Republican.

A putative phase (or phases) in The High Plains of western Nebraska and adjacent parts of Colorado and Wyoming seems to be related directly to the Upper Republican Phase.

It has been variously hypothesized that the constituent sites are evidence of (*a*) hunting camps, (*b*) agricultural frontiersman, (*c*) Woodland groups with an overlay of Upper Republican Phase material but continuing a hunting–gathering economy, or (*d*) splinter Upper Republican peoples who adopted a nomadic economy while retaining contacts with their eastern relatives. The sites are not abundant, and in some cases the data are so scanty that assessment of the radiocarbon dates is difficult. Representative ceramics (Wood 1971:64, 68; Bell and Cape 1936; Irwin and Irwin 1957) have many similarities in decorative motif with the western Upper Republican localities (Medicine Creek, Red Willow) and suggest that those dates falling in the thirteenth century is a reasonable possibility, although there is evidence of eastern influences as early as the Solomon River Phase.

Apparently, climatic changes during the late thirteenth century made the continued existence of the Upper Republican Phase in the western localities hopelessly precarious. Some Upper Republican peoples may have moved southward into Oklahoma and Texas, where, according to one view, they emerge as the Panhandle Aspect. It is more probable that Upper Republican Phase peoples moved northward across the Platte River and into the Loup River Valley fringing the Sand Hills (Steinacher and Ludwickson 1972:55). Here, the sites of the Davis Creek locality are probably representative of a new phase. The Davis Creek sites are known, in spite of limited published data, to have higher frequencies of unthickened rims, as well as other differences. Settlements are larger and, contrary to the usual pattern, contain numbers of circular and subcircular houses. At the Coufal Site (25HW6) at least one rectangular house floor lay beneath a circular lodge (Steinacher and Ludwickson 1972:34–35). The situation suggests a relationship to the Arzberger, Black Partizan, and other sites of the Initial Coalescent (see p. 133). The early Coalescent houses are subrectangular to circular. Unthickened rims are most abundant and collared or "S" rims relatively few. Thus the putative Davis Creek Phase may be culturally and temporally intermediate between Upper Republican and Initial Coalescent, just as it is spatially.

The Sweetwater Site (25SM4; 25BF1) on Muddy Creek, a tributary of the South Loup (Champe 1936) may reflect the same sort of movement by Upper Republican peoples from the south. Brown (1966) has proposed a Muddy Creek locality and Krause (1969) a Loup River Phase based on Champe's site description. Similar architectural features argue for a close relationship with Davis Creek, but differences in ceramics are significant. Collared rims are numerous, and a high percentage of them are decorated with single-line cord impressions, a decorative technique anomalous to the Upper Republican pattern.

The Pomona Phase, localized along the Kansas–Missouri border south of the Kansas River, is equally ambiguous. It may be a transitional complex linking the Woodland and Central Plains traditions, but radiocarbon dates range from A.D. 1055 to 1438. Moreover, Witty (1967) indicates that the ceramic forms owe much to Mississippian influences. Perhaps the Pomona Phase is best viewed in the same manner as the sites in the Milford locality (see p. 127), the Tuttle Creek reservoir, and adjacent areas, that is, as essentially Central Plains Tradition but with continuing interaction with 'Mississippian' people.

Much the same model can be used to understand the Nebraska Phase. The Nebraska Phase is found in several localities on both banks of the Missouri River, from northwestern Missouri northwest to Dixon County, Nebraska. The complex has been studied intensively, most recently by Blakeslee and Caldwell (1972). The relationship to the Upper Republican Phase is quite close. Indeed, usually the Nebraska Phase has been viewed in the context of similarities and differences vis-à-vis Upper Republican and those sites putatively "transitional" between. Surely they have a similar origin, although the immediate progenitor of the Nebraska Phase may have been Smoky Hill or one of those related sites suggesting Mississippian interaction. The Nebraska Phase shows a number of changes through time; perhaps most impressive is a possible northern drift of population.

The earliest sites are at the south of the range, with the period A.D. 1000 to post-1300 the probable span. One date in the eighth century (SI-618 from Site 25RH1) is perhaps anomalous even though it derives from the southerly end of the range. The situation seems to parallel that of the Upper Republican Phase; a northward drift of population, with the northernmost sites, like those of Davis Creek, among the penultimate occupations of the Central Plains Tradition.

Perhaps the St. Helena Phase (Cooper and Bell 1936) in the localities just northwest of the northernmost locality of the Nebraska Phase is the most recent complex within the Central Plains Tradition. The phase is not firmly dated, but artifact similarities (perhaps trade objects) with northern Nebraska Phase sites suggest that they will fall within the fourteenth century. At various times, St. Helena has been regarded as late Nebraska Phase, Late Upper Republican, or a fusion of the two (Steinacher and Ludwickson 1972:49). Probably the first view is closest to the mark. Presently, the St. Helena Phase seems to relate to the Nebraska Phase rather as the Davis Creek sites relate to Upper Republican, although perhaps with less sense of continuity. The St. Helena Phase may have been a dead end, although it contains "echoes" of the Coalescent Tradition and may have made some contribution to its formation or vice versa.

The literature concerned with both the Middle Missouri and Coalescent traditions is more abundant than that of the Central Plains, largely because of the impetus of the federal salvage program in the Dakotas. However, the situation is no less confusing, and taxonomic approaches have experienced no fewer vagaries and convolutions (Lehmer 1971). Chronological and spatial orderings are still in flux and remain matters of contention.

Most recently, a modified form of the Willey and Phillips scheme has been used (see p. 126), just as in the Central Plains. Lehmer and Caldwell (1966; Caldwell 1966b), considering archaeological problems within the Missouri River Trench of the Dakotas, proposed an additional spatial unit, the *district* and a broad temporal division, the *horizon*. Both were ad hoc and particularly applicable to the special needs of the area. Subsequently Lehmer, in what we assume to have been a search for greater spatial control, has substituted the term *region* for *district*, "reserving the latter concept for future use in recognizing the major subdivisions which are beginning to become apparent (Lehmer 1971:29)."

At the same time, the term *variant* has been substituted for the concept of *horizon* (Lehmer 1971:33). Krause contends that such divisions as the latter, as manifest within the Central Plains Tradition, seem to be "contemporaneous regional variations of the basic Central Plains configuration rather than sequent stages" (Lehmer 1971:33; also in Krause 1969:94–96)." However, in view of our discussion of the Central Plains (see pp. 125–129) and the increasing evidence for sequence, the institution of the "variant" concept seems to have been premature and, perhaps, even precipitate. It was probably equally unnecessary within the Middle Missouri and Coalescent traditions, but, taken as little more than a change in terminology, *variant* will be used here because it has already achieved some currency (Calabrese 1972).

Originally, the Middle Missouri Tradition was assumed to be limited largely to the Missouri River Trench in North and South Dakota. More recently, Great Oasis and Mill Creek, sites on the upper Des Moines, (Great Oasis), Big Sioux, Little Sioux (Great Oasis, Mill Creek, and Over) and James Rivers (Over) have been included.

The tradition consists of three units, in Lehmer's 1971 terminology, the *Initial Middle Missouri Variant, Extended Middle Missouri Variant,* and *Terminal Middle Missouri Variant*. The first is southerly in distribution, in that it is limited to the Missouri Trench south of the Cheyenne River, to the lower James and Big Sioux valleys, and to adjacent localities in northwestern Iowa. The published sites and components are most numerous in the Pierre–Chamberlain area of south-central South Dakota (the Bad–Cheyenne and Big Bend regions). The Extended Variant is more northerly, ranging northward and westward along the Missouri almost to the mouth of the Little Missouri in west-central North Dakota. In the Bad–Cheyenne region, and to a lesser extent in the Big Bend region, there is a degree of spatial overlap. There is a discernible pattern: components of the Initial Variant are restricted to the right (west) bank of the Missouri in the Bad–Cheyenne and Upper Big Bend region; components of the Extended Variant occur throughout the former region but, with a few exceptions, are not present in the latter. The Terminal Middle Missouri Variant has a relatively limited distribution, at least when compared to its antecedents. Terminal sites and components are found in the Cannonball and Knife–Heart regions, essentially that stretch of the Missouri between the Grand River in northern South Dakota and the Knife River in west-central North Dakota. Both of the regions contain sites of the Extended Variant as well. Indeed, these are far more numerous (cf. Lehmer 1971; Figs. 39, 79).

The characteristic house type—an elongate, rectangular, semisubterranean structure—differs only slightly with time and place; however, settlement pattern, or, more accurately, size and density of settlements, is much more variable. Villages of the Initial and Extended Variants may have as many as 20 to 30 houses, but many are substantially smaller (Lehmer 1971:69). Settlements of the Terminal Variant are much larger; one at least has in excess of 100 houses. A concentration and "compression" of population through time is indicated, reaching a maximum at the end of the tradition. In addition, houses tend to be aligned in regular, streetlike rows, and frequently villages are fortified. Defensive measures vary from simple ditches to elaborate, bastioned moats and curtain walls (Lehmer 1971: Fig. 42).

Ceramics are essentially similar throughout the components of the tradition. They share a coarse, friable, grit-tempered paste and a relatively narrow range of forms, decorative motifs, and surface finishes. Surface finish provides an important marker. Vessels associated with the Initial Variant are usually textured by means of a cord-wrapped paddle. Subsequently, most vessels were smoothed or, occasionally, simple stamped. Other traits—rim form, decorative motif, and so on—persist through time and space, varying only in detail and frequency. Nonceramic artifacts have a similar pattern of persistence and variation in detail. It is apparent, however, that there were emphases characteristic of time and place. Thus objects made from marine shell are most numerous and elaborate in the Initial Variant and artifacts of bone become more frequent, complex, and even flamboyant in the Terminal Variant.

It might be argued that more of the constituent complexes are securely defined and dated than is the case with the Central Plains Tradition. Yet, despite an impressively large suite of dates from components of the Middle Missouri Tradition, the chronology and chronological relationships of many elements remain at issue. The preponderance of radiocarbon dates applicable to the Initial Middle Missouri Variant fall between A.D. 900 and 1300 (Lehmer 1971, Fig. 34). The earliest components are those assigned to the Great Oasis Phase, which seems to have developed out of a Late Woodland Tradition. Following Great Oasis, and in part deriving from it, are the Mill Creek and Over phases. Great Oasis has a wide distribution, extending from Iowa, north and west at least into the Big Bend region of the Missouri Trench. Mill Creek sites are localized in northwestern Iowa, and the Over Phase is found on the Lower James and the Big Bend region.

Mill Creek and Over components are so similar that they might well have been considered as a single phase. There are some differences; these are due to geographic distance rather than to cultural–traditional factors. Both Mill Creek and Over sites yield ceramic materials and trade items indicative of contact with peoples to the south and east, particularly, to all appearances, with Middle Mississippian groups. Such contact appears to have been very important from ca. A.D. 1150 and to have persisted until ca. 1350, when most Mill Creek and Over sites were no longer occupied.

Radiocarbon dates for the Extended Middle Missouri Variant derive from two widely separate areas (*a*) the Bad–Cheyenne region and (*b*) the Knife–Heart and Cannonball regions. For the former, most of the dates fall in the twelfth and thirteenth centuries, but there is some suggestion of an occupation in the fifteenth century as well (Lehmer 1971:97). A discordant series from the Ben Standing Soldier Site (32517) in the Cannonball region extends from A.D. 342 to 1501. A small group of tentative tree-ring dates (Missouri Basin Chronology Program, Statement 3) supports such a late continuation (or resurgence) of the variant. In the Knife–Heart and Cannonball regions, radiocarbon dates range from the twelfth century through the fifteenth century A.D., but most are in the thirteenth century (Lehmer 1966: Calabrese 1972:35–36), confirming the earlier major occupation of the Bad–Cheyenne region. Dates derived from the Terminal Middle Missouri Variant are few and relatively inconclusive. A suite of radiocarbon dates from the Huff Site (32MO11) in south-central North Dakota ranges from A.D. 1220 to 1719. Neither of the extremes fits the pattern of evidence. Wood (1967:115–116) suggests that the occupation fell in the fifteenth and sixteenth centuries, a dating supported by a series of unverified tree-ring dates (Will 1946:15–16). Lehmer assigns the variant to the period A.D. 1550–1675.

The Initial Middle Missouri Variant is surely the earliest manifestation of the tradition. Most agree that the origins lie in southwestern Minnesota and northwestern Iowa; perhaps village peoples followed an expanding agriculture into the Northern Plains during the climatic amelioration of the eighth and ninth centuries A.D. (the neo-Atlantic episode) (Baerreis and Bryson 1965; Lehmer 1971:105; Caldwell and Jensen 1969:80–81; Caldwell 1968a:109,111). The radiocarbon dates suggest that the Initial Variant was the sole sedentary village complex in the region for perhaps as much as two centuries (Lehmer 1971:98). Majority opinion assumes that the Extended Middle Missouri Variant developed out of the Initial Variant. The possibility remains of course, but an alternative view that they were, in part, interacting, parallel regional developments (Hurt 1953: Chart V) receives support from the present chronology.

The Terminal Middle Missouri Variant is surely a lineal descendent of the Extended Variant. The Terminal Variant villages are few but large and in the southern part of their range; they are strongly fortified as well. There is no reason to doubt that they were under pressure from the Coalescent Tradition, which ultimately came to dominate the Dakotas.

The Coalescent Tradition, as the name suggests, is a coalescing, merging, and refactoring of preexisting complexes. The Initial Coalescent Variant is closely related to the Central Plains Tradition and, as Lehmer (1971:111) suggests, might well be considered as a modification thereof. It does differ, however, and those differences (e.g., fortification) are all attributable to contributions from the Middle Missouri Tradition. The extended Coalescent Variant emerged directly from the Initial Variant, largely as a result of internal dynamics. By this time (mid-sixteenth century) the impetus from parent stock was drastically weakened or absent. The Post-Contact Coalescent Variant and a weak appendage, the Disorganized Coalescent Variant, are rooted in the Extended Variant but with new ingredients and new dynamics brought by Europeans. The first saw a florescence stimulated by the fur trade. The second saw virtual destruction from disease, population displacement, and other external pressures.

The Initial Coalescent Variant is known from a small number of sites in the Big Bend region and perhaps a site or two in northern Nebraska. At most, only four or five villages of the Initial Coalescent Variant have been excavated (Spaulding 1956: Caldwell 1966a). Although there is considerable variability, houses are reminiscent of the Central Plains rather than the Middle Missouri. They tend to be variable but often are "square" or subrectangular, with a structure based on four center posts. Within the village area, houses are widely spaced and seemingly randomly distributed. The Arzberger (Spaulding 1956) and Black Partizan sites (Caldwell 1966) were fortified by bastioned ditches and palisades. The defended perimeters are in sharp contrast with the usual unfortified communities in the Central Plains. Lehmer (1971:113) suggests that possibly the Initial Coalescent villages were of the typical scattered Central Plains type but that subsequent pressures required the construction of defenses.

The artifact assemblages from Initial Coalescent components suggest a blending of Central Plains and Middle Missouri attributes. Ceramic relationships are particularly apparent; plain, cord-roughened, and simple stamped surface treatments are all present. The last of these is most frequent and becomes one of the "hallmarks" of coalescence in the Dakotas (Lehmer 1971:114).

The chronology of the Initial Coalescent is insecure because dates are so few. Two radiocarbon determinations, from the unreported Crow Creek Site (39BF11) and the Arzberger Site (39HU6), fall in the late years of the fourteenth century. Unverified tree-ring dates from Crow Creek (1441) and the Black Partizan Site (1468) (Missouri Basin Chronology Program, Statement #3), and another more secure suite from Crow Creek (Weakly 1971: Table 11), generally are in agreement with the radiocarbon series.

The Extended Coalescent Variant is marked by an increase in the number of sites or components, perhaps by a factor of ten. Moreover, the variant is much more widely distributed, extending at least from the White River in south-central South Dakota, northward to the North Dakota border. The area encompasses the Big Bend, Bad–Cheyenne, Grand Moreau, and lowermost Cannonball regions.

"The ideal house was a circular structure having a central firepit, four primary superstructure support posts . . . and an enclosed entrance passage (Lehmer 1971:115)," but many were not significantly different from those of the Initial Coalescent. Houses of the latter sort seem to have been little more than ephemeral or, at most, intended for short-term use. Settlement patterns are equally variable. Most are irregular groupings of houses; the "village" may be scattered for hundreds of yards along the river edge. In a putative frontier zone of the Cheyenne River, a number of villages are fortified, either with houses clustered tightly within a small encircling ditch—with a moat detaching a terrace spur—or by means of a small defensive center.

There remains a sense of continuity with precedent complexes, yet the ceramics of the Extended Coalescent are rather distinctive. Instead of the usual gritty, friable paste, here it is hard, compact, and capable of being formed into vessels with remarkably thin walls. Cord-roughened exteriors are an anachronism. Instead, most are plain or, more frequently, strongly simple stamped. Rim forms are not unlike those of the past, but a new type, high shallow "S" appears, and lips on many specimens are thickened, sometimes to sharply angular "L" and "T" forms. Bold incisions and stamps on lips are usual. Other artifacts are close counterparts of those present in the Initial Coalescent. However, at least two new types, the "L"-shaped antler fleshing adze and bone ice gliders, are distinctive additions (Lehmer 1971:119, Fig. 78).

By now a considerable number of radiocarbon and tree-ring dates have accumulated for components of the Extended Coalescent Variant. A suite of radiocarbon determinations from the Molstad Village (39DW234), a fortified site not far south of the Grand River, ranges from the mid-fourteenth to the mid-sixteenth century A.D. Another, from the Lower Grande Site, averages 1354 (±133). The LaRoche Site (395T9), a large, unfortified village in the Big Bend region (Hoffman 1968) produced dates from 1340 to 1562. Site 39SL4, in the Bad–Cheyenne region, has been dated as late as 1627, probably far too late for the complex (Lehmer 1971:119), and a date of 1278 for the McClure site, near the mouth of the Bad River, is far too early. An unverified tree-ring date of 1566 derives from the No Heart Creek Site (39AR2), a small, fortified village just above the mouth of the Cheyenne River, and a specimen from the Medicine Creek Site (39LM222) in the Big Bend region is thought to date from later than 1650 (Missouri Basin Chronology Program, Statement #3). Weakly has reported a series of tree-ring dates for the latter site ranging from 1574 to 1593. Lehmer, on the basis of available evidence, estimates that the life of the variant extended from 1550 to 1675.

The Coalescent Tradition is not restricted to the Dakotas. Several complexes in Nebraska are close counterparts, particularly of the Extended Variant. Differences exist in house type, village plan, and artifact assemblage, yet the similarities are close. The Red Bird (Wood 1965), Birdwood (Garrett 1965), and perhaps Lower Loup (Grange 1968) complexes may well be considered as putative phases within the variant. Probably they were functional over a fair span of years, but useful dates are not numerous. A radiocarbon date of A.D. 1551 from the Burkett site suggests that all of these sites are relatively late. The Lower Loup "phase" has been considered to be proto-Pawnee and to lack immediate progenitors within Nebraska. It is only reasonable to seek Pawnee origins in South Dakota among those complexes or phases of the Extended Variant that also must have given rise to their close relatives, the Arikara.

The Post-Contact Coalescent variant, encompassing the late seventeenth and eighteenth centuries, is largely protohistoric. Conventional literary documentation is scarce, but even so one can grasp the continuities that lead to the Arikara, Mandan, and Hidatsa—the historic village peoples of the area. Sites "varied considerably through time, with a marked reduction in both the total extent and in the number of villages during the later years of the variant (Lehmer 1971:136)." Settlements group into two areas: (*a*) the White River to just above the Grand River and (*b*) the Knife–Heart region. The latter are surely ancestral Mandan and Hidatsa. The former include the Arikara, but other peoples probably are also included (e.g., Cheyenne).

Although there is a degree of variability, the basic house type is the circular earth lodge based on a foundation of four center posts. Villages differ considerably in pattern and size. "Some of the South Dakota sites, apparently dating from the first half of the 18th century, contain only a dozen or so houses, but the Sully Site (39SL4), occupied into Post-Contact Coalescent times, is the largest village in the Middle Missouri Valley, and the Double Ditch Site (32BL8), north of Bismarck, is shown on early maps . . . as having over 150 houses (Lehmer 1971:141)." Within villages, houses seem to have been scattered without plan, although there is often evidence of an open plaza in sites attributed to the Mandan. Many villages were fortified, but the defensive schemes are much less elaborate than those of earlier variants.

The characteristic ceramics have a coarsely tempered fabric with a smooth or simple stamped finish. In many cases, the neck of the vessel is marked by vertical striae, perhaps from brushing with stiff fibers. A few rims are collared and others have a shallow "S" profile, but most frequently rims are vertical and rise abruptly from a curved shoulder. A particularly distinctive feature is a thickening fillet or "brace" welded to the rim just below the lip. Other artifacts continue from the past, but tempered by the impact of Euro-American trade.

The early and middle years of the eighteenth century might be viewed as a kind of florescence, but by A.D. 1800 there was decay and contraction. The Arikara were living in three villages just above the mouth of the Grand River, and the Mandan and Hidatsa occupied a handful of communities in the vicinity of the Knife River. Elsewhere, the area was held by nomadic hunters who accelerated the focus and decline of population until the 1860s, when all of these groups were concentrated in a single village.

It has been customary to see the Plains in terms of its heartland (or heartlands) and its peripheries. The latter have been viewed as reflective and derivative of the more significant events in the central areas. Only recently has it been possible to see that occupants of some of the peripheral regions had distinctive patterns of their own. They have been long emerging, and they remain difficult to characterize and to date with confidence.

The Northwestern Plains offers a case in point. As recently as 1968 it was asserted that the prehistory of the area suffered from "a notable lack of synthesis (Caldwell 1968b:7)." The situation is scarcely different today, in part because the region has been innocent of those taxonomic concerns (and strains) that have been apparent elsewhere. Although there are exceptions, most of those who have worked in the Northern and Northwestern Plains have chosen to deal only in major units, such as Early Prehistoric, Middle Prehistoric, and Late Prehistoric, or in temporal subdivisions thereof. These are useful devices, but we are convinced they have not encouraged assessment of detailed relationships in time and space. Time within the Middle Prehistoric Period has been provided for through recognition of early, middle and late segments (Mulloy 1958:161, 162). Perhaps these major divisions might be viewed most effectively as sequent traditions that include a number of economic, technological and perhaps social subtraditions. The subtraditions, whether focusing upon widely distributed projectile point types or other artifacts, might well serve as index fossils for recognition of regional horizons or "variants."

It is difficult to come to grips with the archaeology in much of the area, in large part because there has been little concern with cultural complexes of the sort that are amenable to taxonomic manipulation or that have enough substance to provide a well-fleshed picture. Instead, we are faced with cultural units that are no more than projectile point types or, in the case of bison kills, important but one-sided aspects of regional economics. Among the latter, Kehoe (1967) and Frison (1971 and others) have provided leads of major ecological, technological, and cultural significance.

Much of the data relevant to the Early Prehistoric and Middle Prehistoric periods have already been reviewed. It should be stressed however, that the economic base, focusing upon large game, that was established at this time persisted until the Historic Period. A distinctive feature of the later portion of the Middle Prehistoric is the introduction, or perhaps elaboration (Forbis 1968:17), of the buffalo jump as a hunting–killing technique (cf. Forbis 1962; Kehoe 1966). The method was undoubtedly present by the third or fourth century B.C. (the Lance Creek Bison Fall in Wyoming dates at 500 B.C.). Kehoe and Kehoe are convinced that the earliest "complex, ritualized, planned" bison drives, at least in Saskatchewan, are found at the Avonlea sites, which are approximately coeval with the Besant Complex of about A.D. 350 (1968:28). The latter, as represented at the Walter Felt Site contains the earliest evidence of pottery in the area (Kehoe 1964:52,53). The Avonlea sites in Canada and Montana are characterized by small, triangular, side-notched projectile points (Kehoe and McCorquodale 1961:186) that may mark the initial appearance of the bow. Avonlea specimens from components in Montana have been dated by obsidian hydration at A.D. 350, and A.D. 450 (±200) [Davis 1966:106]. The last date is a close approximation of the radiocarbon date reported for the type site (Kehoe and McCorquodale 1961). The appearance of the small, side-notched point tradition (Kehoe 1966) seems to be the watershed marking the end of the Middle Prehistoric Period and the beginning of the Late Prehistoric Period. The terminal date for the former has been estimated to fall in the period A.D. 450–600 (Mulloy 1958:222; Kehoe and McCorquodale 1961:186; Forbis 1962:82; Wormington and Forbis 1965:88). The subsequent period is characterized by the continuation, and to some degree an intensification, of the pattern. Dependence on bison for subsistence grew, and if inferences from drive sites are valid, there were increasingly greater numbers of bison available. Tipi rings in abundance (Kehoe 1960; Mulloy 1965), several ceramic traditions (Kehoe 1959; Griffin 1965), and a variety of other traits document the emergence of the ethnographic present.

The later archaeological complexes in the Southern Plains are surprisingly similar to those that dominated the Central Plains during the centuries following A.D. 900. The population was basically sedentary and, like that of the Central Plains, lived in villages strung along the wooded stream valleys that dissect the grasslands.

Village sites assigned to the Washita River Focus, in Garvin and Grady counties, Oklahoma (Bell and Baerreis 1951:75–81), consist of square, heavily constructed houses with cache pits and a central fire basin (Wedel 1961:139–140). The people were hunters of bison, deer, antelope, turkey, rabbit, and smaller mammals. Riverine resources and cultigens, including corn and beans, complemented the meat diet.

Further upstream, in the Washita River Valley, there are a number of sites that have been assigned to the Custer Focus (Bell and Baerreis 1951:81–83). The Custer and Washita River foci are closely related and may be contemporaneous, dating at ca. A.D. 1250.

In northern Texas, on the upper Brazos and Red rivers, are the numerous sites of the Henrietta Focus. The sites are fairly large, ranging from 1 to 5 acres, with deep refuse deposits. Bison and smaller mammals were hunted, fish were taken from the streams, and maize was apparently imported as well. Wedel (1961:141) suggests that the Henrietta Focus may ultimately be proven to be remains of a Caddoan people, perhaps the ancestral Wichita.

Sites of the Wylie Focus (Stephenson 1952) are found in north-central Texas in the Upper Trinity drainage. The Wylie people constructed small, fairly permanent houses and lived by hunting, gathering, fishing, and corn gardening. Wedel (1961:142) suggests that they shared material traits with the Henrietta focus and Caddoan peoples.

Along the Canadian River are a number of village sites referred to as the Antelope Creek Focus in the Texas panhandle and as the Optima Focus in Oklahoma. Sometimes they are grouped together in the Panhandle Aspect (Wedel 1961:142). The house style, featuring adjoining rooms and associated storage cubicles, and the stone construction strongly suggest southwestern puebloan influence, probably acting upon resident populations similar to peoples of the Central Plains Tradition (cf. Wedel 1961:144). The sites of the Panhandle Aspect are quite late, dating ca. A.D. 1330–1450.

While not in the Plains, per se, a few words regarding Caddoan sites in the Southeastern Plains border are in order. Caddoan peoples obviously influenced those groups located to the east and west and may have been more influential to the north than has been credited in the literature. Most recently, a sequence including five divisions, from Caddo I through Caddo V, has been proposed (Davis 1970) to replace the old Gibson–Fulton chronological framework. The Caddo sites found along the Plains border consist of mortuary and burial centers coupled with numerous small village sites. Dates for the Caddo sites (Davis 1970:142–155) are not included specifically because of geographical factors, but are summarized as: Caddo I (just prior to A.D. 1000 to ca. 1200); Caddo II (1200–1400); Caddo III (fifteenth century), Caddo IV (sixteenth century), and Caddo V (post-1600).

Oneota remains are generally restricted to the prairie peninsula (Wedel 1957; Henning 1970) but several important sites are located in the Eastern Central Plains margin or plains–prairie ecotone. Oneota remains dating from as early as A.D. 1100 at the Dixon Site in northwestern Iowa and at ca. A.D. 1250 in one component at the Leary Site in southeastern Nebraska argue for Oneota occupation contemporaneous to Mill Creek, Nebraska, St. Helena, and Upper Republican. Oneota sites such as Blood Run, Gillett Grove, and other sites in northwestern Iowa were occupied by groups with at least attenuated contact with Europeans. Oneota was at one time believed to have been protohistoric, extending into the Historic Period. Now, with chronometric dates suggesting earlier beginnings and possible interaction with Central Plains and Initial Middle Missouri peoples, Oneota peoples must assume a different kind of importance in Eastern Plains prehistory.

The Dismal River Aspect, an extra-areal complex quite foreign to the Central Plains Tradition, has been found in western Nebraska, western Kansas, eastern Colorado, and southeastern Wyoming. In its emphasis upon hunting and gathering, the Dismal River Aspect stands closer to the complexes of the Northwestern Plains than to those of the Central Plains. Dismal River sites are distributed in much the same area as those of the Upper Republican Phase or its cognates (Gunnerson 1960:236). Moreover, despite a temporal hiatus, it succeeds the Upper Republican Phase, although in no sense is it a descendent of the earlier complex. There is no reason to doubt the exotic origins of Dismal River. It is true that many artifacts (bison scapula hoe, metapodial scrapers, simple stamped ceramics, etc.) are typically "plains"; but the characteristic house type, with five center posts and distinctive baking pits, has no regional counterparts (Gunnerson 1960:241). The Dismal River Aspect has been identified with the Plains Apache of the late seventeenth and early eighteenth centuries (Champe 1949). An unverified series of tree-ring dates places certain of the Nebraska sites in, at least, the first three decades of the eighteenth century (Gunnerson 1960:177, 216, 221; see also Hill and Metcalf 1942:205).

III. PROSPECT AND RETROSPECT

If Plains archaeology has suffered one significant debit, it has been a lack of problem-directed research. Of course there have been exceptions, but in general the lively, productive years of the 1930s were followed by several decades of intensive salvage archaeology in which little could be done except react to the insistent pressures of public works. Yet, despite the patent limitations of the situation, a great deal was accomplished.

We are confident that within the Middle Missouri and the Central and Southern Plains, the basic archaeological complexes are blocked out, and, by now, most have been reduced to a fair degree of temporal control. At the same time, we have an understanding of process and relationship that belies the reactive needs of salvage.

In the heartland of the Plains, *definition* is largely at an end. Indeed, in the case of the Middle Missouri River Trench, only limited new data can come available because the majority of sites have been destroyed or covered by reservoir impoundments. Parenthetically we might add that elsewhere, particularly in peripheral areas, there is still a sense of groping—a need for new data and a new ordering to give the indigenous complexes a substance that they now lack.

During the recent past, knowledgeable amateurs have played a remarkably important role (Caldwell 1968; Conner 1968). Trained archaeologists were few and could not hope to cover the area, even to meet emergencies. Thus in the Northwestern Plains, for instance, the nonprofessionals filled a vacuum and provided much of the data and a large share of the literature (Stallcop 1966). The growth of university-based anthropology during the 1960s brought a new professionalism to the Plains, so that the contribution of the amateur may henceforth decline; yet we are confident that nonprofessionals will continue to have a function.

Coupled with the concern for additional data of a conventional sort is a new concern with the ecology of Plains cultures. The goal here as elsewhere is a vast enlargement of our view of the Prehistoric world and its human, and natural relationships. The analyses and syntheses reported in *Two House Sites in the Central Plains: An Experiment in Archaeology* (Wood 1969), with all their debits (Wedel 1970), can be taken as representative of the new approach, an approach that we see as the "wave of the future" on the Plains.

BIBLIOGRAPHY

Agogino, G. A.
1968 Archaeological excavations at Blackwater Draw locality no. 1, New Mexico, 1963–64. *National Geographic Society Research Reports, 1963 Projects,* pp. 1–8.

Agogino, G. A. and W. D. Frankforter
1970 A Paleo-Indian bison kill in northwestern Iowa. *American Antiquity 25:*414–415.

Agogino, G. A. and I. Rovner
1969 Preliminary report of a stratified post-Folsom sequence at Blackwater Draw locality no. 1. *American Antiquity 4*(28):510–528.

Anderson, A. D.
1961 The Glenwood sequence. *Journal of the Iowa Archaeological Society 10:*3.
1962 The Cooperton mammoth: A preliminary report. *Plains Anthropologist 7:*110.

Baerreis, D. A.
1953 Woodland pottery of northeastern Oklahoma. In *Pottery of Eastern United States.* Ann Arbor, Mich.: Museum of Anthropology, University of Michigan.

Baerreis, D. A. and R. A. Bryson
1965 Climatic episodes and the dating of Mississippian cultures. *Wisconsin Archaeologist 4*(46):203–220.

Bell, E. H. and R. E. Cape
1936 The rock shelters of western Nebraska in the vicinity of Dalton, Nebraska. *Chapters in Nebraska Archaeology 1:*1.

Bell, E. H. and P. Cooper
1936 The archaeology of certain sites in Cedar County, Nebraska. *Chapters in Nebraska Archaeology 1*:1.

Bell, R. E. and D. A. Baerreis
1951 A survey of Oklahoma archaeology. *Bulletin of the Texas Archaeological and Paleontological Society 22:*7–100.

Blakeslee, D. and W. W. Caldwell
1972 The Nebraska phase: An archaeological assessment. Typescript, University of Nebraska, Lincoln.

Brown, L. A.
1966 Temporal and spatial order in the cultural plains. *Plains Anthropologist 11*(34):294–301
1967 Pony Creek archaeology. *Smithsonian Institution, River Basin Surveys, Publications in Salvage Archaeology 5.*

Calabrese, F. A.
1972 Cross Ranch: A study of variability in a stable cultural tradition. *Plains Anthropologist Memoir 9:*17–58.

Caldwell, W. W.
1966a The Black Partizan site. *Smithsonian Institution, River Basin Surveys, Publications in Salvage Archaeology 2.*

1966b The Middle Missouri tradition reappraised. *Plains Anthropologist 11*(32):152–157.

1968a Archaeological sites in Loess regions of the Missouri Drainage Basin. Part II. In Loess and related eolian deposits of the world. *VII Congress of the International Association for Quaternary Research, 1965, Proceedings,* Vol. *12.*

1968b The northwestern Plains: A symposium. *Rocky Mountain College, Center for Indian Studies, Occasional Papers* No. *1.*

Caldwell, W. W. and R. E. Jensen

1969 The Grand Detour phase. *Smithsonian Institution, River Basin Surveys, Publications in Salvage Archaeology 13.*

Carlson, G. F.

1967 Excavations at the Sumpter site (140B27) in the Glen Elder Reservoir, north central Kansas. *Plains Anthropologist 12:*36.

1971 A local sequence for upper Republican sites in the Glen Elder Reservoir locality, Kansas. Unpublished M.A. thesis. University of Nebraska, Lincoln.

Champe, J. L.

1936 The Sweetwater culture-complex. *Chapters in Nebraska Archaeology 1:*3.

1946 Ash Hollow cave. *University of Nebraska Studies* No. *1.*

1949 White Cat village. *American Antiquity 14:*285–292.

1961 Aksarben. *Plains Anthropologist 6*(12):103–107.

Chapman, C. H. and E. F. Chapman

1964 Indians and archaeology of Missouri. *Missouri Handbook* No. *6.* Columbia, Mo. Univ. of Missouri Press.

Conner, S. W.

1968 An introduction. In The northwestern Plains: A symposium, edited by W. W. Caldwell. *Rocky Mountain College Center for Indian Studies, Occasional Papers* No. *1.*

Cutler, H. C., and L. W. Blake

1969 Corn. In Two house sites on the cultural Plains: An experiment in archaeology, edited by W. R. Wood. *Plains Anthropologist 14*(44), Part. 2, *Memoir* No. *6.*

Davis, H. A. (Editor)

1970 Archaeological and historical resources of the Red River basin. *Arkansas Archaeological Survey Research Series* No. *1.*

Davis, L. B.

1966 Avonlea point occurrence in northern Montana and Canada. *Plains Anthropologist 11:*32.

Fenneman, N. M.

1931 *Physiography of western United States.* New York: McGraw-Hill.

Figgins, J. D.

1933 A further contribution to the antiquity of man in America. *Colorado Museum of Natural History Proceedings, 10*(2).

Forbis, R. G.

1962 The old women's buffalo jump. *Contributions to Anthropology 1960*, Part 1. *National Museum of Canada Bulletin 180.*

Frankforter, W. D.

1959 The Hill site. *Journal of the Iowa Archaeological Society 8:*47–72.

Frison, G. C.

1971 Shoshonean antelope procurement in the upper Green River basin, Wyoming. *Plains Anthropologist 16*(54) Part 1: 258–284.

Galinat, W. C. and J. H. Gunnerson

1963 The spread of eight-rowed maize from the prehistoric southwest. *Harvard University Botanical Museum Leaflets 20*(5):117–160.

Garrett, J. W.

1965 The Birdwood culture of the west-central Plains. *American Antiquity 31*(1):74–80.

Gilder, R. F.
1911 Discoveries indicating an unexploited culture in eastern Nebraska. *Records of the Past 10*(5):249–259.

Gradwohl, D. M.
1969 Prehistoric villages in eastern Nebraska. *Nebraska State Historical Society, Publications in Anthropology* No. *4*.

Grange, R. T.
1968 Pawnee and Lower Loup pottery. *Nebraska State Historical Society, Publications in Anthropology* No. *3*.

Griffin, J. B.
1965 Prehistoric pottery from southeastern Alberta. Appendix to An introduction to the archaeology of Alberta. *Denver Museum of Natural History Proceedings 11*.

Gunnerson, J. H.
1960 An introduction to Plains Apache archaeology—the Dismal River aspect. *Bureau of American Ethnology Bulletin 173 (Anthropological Paper* No. *58)*.

Haynes, C. V.
1971 Time, environment, and early man. *Arctic Anthropology 8*(2):3–14.

Haynes, C. F. and G. Agogino
1966 Prehistoric springs and geochronology of the Clovis Site, New Mexico. *American Antiquity 31*(6):812–821.

Haynes, C. V. and E. T. Hemmings
1968 Mammoth bone shaft wrench from Murray Springs, Arizona. *Science 159*(3811):186–187.

Henning, D. R.
1970 Development and inter-relationships of Oneota culture in the lower Missouri River valley. *The Missouri Archaeologist 32*.

Hill, A. T. and G. Metcalf
1942 A site of the Dismal River aspect in Chase county, Nebraska. *Nebraska History Magazine 22*(2):158–226.

Hoffman, J. J.
1968 The LaRoche site. *Smithsonian Institution, River Basin Surveys, Publications in Salvage Archaeology* No. *11*.

Hrdlicka, A.
1907 Skeletal remains suggesting or attributed to early man in North America. *Bureau of American Ethnology Bulletin 33*.

Hurt, W. R.
1952 Report of the investigation of the Scalp Creek site 39GR1 and the Ellis Creek site 39GR2, Gregory County, South Dakota. *South Dakota Archaeological Commission, Archaeological Studies Circular* No. *4*.
1953 Report of the investigations of the Thomas Riggs site 39HU1, Hughes County, South Dakota, 1952. *South Dakota Archaeological Commission, Archaeological Studies Circular* No. 5.

Irwin, C. and H. Irwin
1957 The archaeology of the Agate Bluff area, Colorado. *Plains Anthropologist 8*:15–38.

Irwin-Williams, C., H. Irwin and G. Agogino
1962 Ice Age man vs. mammoth in Wyoming. *National Geographic Magazine 121*(6):828–837.

Irwin, H. T.
1968 The Itama: Late Pleistocene inhabitants of the Plains of the United States and Canada and the American southwest. Unpublished Ph.D. dissertation. Harvard University.

Johnson, E.
1969 The prehistoric peoples of Minnesota. *Minnesota Historical Society*.

Johnston, R. B.
1967 The Hitchell Site. *Smithsonian Institution, River Basin Surveys, Publications in Salvage Archaeology* No. *3*.

Kehoe, A. B.
1959 Ceramic affiliations in the northwestern Plains. *American Antiquity 25*, No. 2.
1964 Middle woodland pottery from Saskatchewan. *Plains Anthropologist* 9(23):51–53.
1966 The small side-notched point system of the northern Plains. *American Antiquity 31*(6).

Kehoe, T. F. and A. B. Kehoe
1968 Saskatchewan. In *The northwestern Plains; A symposium*, edited by W. W. Caldwell. Billings, Montana: The Center for Indian Studies. Pp. 21–36.

Kehoe, T. F. and B. A. McCorquodale
1961 The Avonlea point. *American Antiquity* 6(13).

Kivett, M. F.
1949 Archaeological investigations in Medicine Creek Reservoir, Nebraska. *American Antiquity 14*(4), Part 1:278–284.
1952 Woodland sites in Nebraska. *Nebraska State Historical Society Publications in Anthropology* No. *1*.

Knudson, R.
1973 Organizational variability in late Paleo-Indian assemblages. Unpublished Ph.D. dissertation, Department of Anthropology, Washington State University.

Krause, R. A.
1969 Correlation of phases in central Plains prehistory In Two house sites on the central Plains: An experiment in archaeology, edited by W. R. Wood. *Plains Anthropologist 14*(44), Part 2, *Memoir* No. *6*.

Lehmer, D. J.
1952 The Fort Pierre branch, central South Dakota. *American Antiquity 17*(4):329–336.

Lehmer, D. J.
1954a Archaeological investigations in the Oahe Dam area, South Dakota, 1950–51. *Smithsonian Institution, River Basin Surveys, Anthropological Papers* No. *7*. *(Bureau of American Ethnology (Bulletin 158)*.
1954b The sedentary horizon of the northern Plains. *Southwestern Journal of Anthropology 10*(2):139–159.
1966 The Fire Heart Creek site. *Smithsonian Institution, River Basin Surveys, Publications in Salvage Anthropology* No. *1*.
1971 Introduction to middle Missouri archaeology. *National Park Service Anthropological Papers* No. *1*.

Lehmer, D. J. and W. W. Caldwell
1966 Horizon and tradition in the northern Plains. *American Antiquity 31*(4):511–516.

Leonhardy, F. C.
1966 Domebo: A Paleo-Indian mammoth kill in the Prairie-Plains. *Contributions of the Museum of the Great Plains* No. *1*.

Marshall, J. O.
1972 The archaeology of the Elk City Reservoir—a local archaeological sequence in southeast Kansas. *Kansas State Historical Society Anthropological Series* No. *6*.

Missouri Basin Chronology Program
1962 Statement 3. *Smithsonian Institution Missouri Basin Project*.

Mulloy, W.
1958 A preliminary historical outline for the northwestern Plains. *University of Wyoming Publications 22* (1–2).
1965 Archaeological investigation along the north Platte River in eastern Wyoming. *University of Wyoming Publications 13* (1–3).

Neuman, R. W.
1961 Salvage archaeology at a site near Fort Thompson, South Dakota. *Plains Anthropologist 6*(13):189–200.

Phillips, P. and G. R. Willey
1953 Method and theory in American archaeology: An operational basis for culture-historical integration. *American Anthropologist 55*:615–6531.

Roll, T. E.
1968 Upper Republican cultural relationships. Unpublished M.A. thesis. Department of Anthropology, University of Nebraska Lincoln.

Roberts, F. H. H., Jr.
1940 Developments in the problem of the North American Paleo-Indian. *Smithsonian Miscellaneous Collections 100*:51–116.

Sauer, C. O.
1948 Environment and culture during the last glaciation. *American Philosophical Society Proceedings 92*(1):65–77.

Sellands, E. H.
1952 *Early man in America: A study in prehistory*. Austin: University of Texas Press.

Shippee, J. M.
1948 Nebo Hill, a lithic complex in western Missouri. *American Antiquity 14*(1):29–32.
1957 The diagnostic point type of the Nebo Hill complex. *The Missouri Archaeologist 19*(3):43–47.
1962 Transriver variations in artifacts of Nebo Hill complex sites. *Missouri Archaeological Society Newsletter 162*:3–9.
1967 Archaeological remains in the area of Kansas City: The Woodland period-early, middle and late. *Missouri Archaeological Society Research Series* No. *5*.

Spaulding, A. C.
1956 The Arzberger site, Hughes County, South Dakota. *Occasional Contributions from the Museum of Anthropology of the University of Michigan* No. *16*.

Stallicop, E.
1966 The distribution in north-central Montana of variant basally indented projectile points. *Montana Archaeological Society, Archaeology in Montana 7*:2.

Steinacher, T. L. and J. Ludwickson
1972 *The central Plains tradition reappraised*. Lincoln: Department of Anthropology, University of Nebraska.

Stephenson, R. L.
1952 The Hogge Bridge site and the Wylie focus. *American Antiquity 17*(4):299–312.
1954 Taxonomy and chronology in the central Plains—middle Missouri River area. *Plains Anthropologist 1*:15–21.

Strong, W. D.
1933 The Plains culture area in the light of archeology. *American Anthropologist, 35*(2):271–287.
1935 An introduction to Nebraska archeology. *Smithsonian Institution Miscellaneous Collections 93,* No. 10.

Suhm, D. A., A. D. Krieger and E. B. Jalks
1954 An introductory handbook of Texas archaeology. *Bulletin of the Texas Archaeological Society 25*.

Warnicka, J. M.
1966 New discoveries at the Clovis site. *American Antiquity 31*:345–357.

Weakly, W. F.
1971 Tree-ring dating and archaeology in South Dakota. *Plains Anthropologist 16*(54):2, *Memoir* No. *8*.

Wedel, M. M.
1959 Oneota sites on the upper Iowa River. *The Missouri Archaeologist 21*(2–4).

Wedel, W. R.
1935 Preliminary classification for Nebraska and Kansas cultures. *Nebraska History Magazine 15:*251–255.
1940 Cultural sequence in the central Great Plains. In Essays in historical anthropology of North America. Smithsonian Institution Miscellaneous Collections 100:291–352.
1943 Archaeological investigations in Platte and Clay counties, Missouri. *United States National Museum Bulletin 183.*
1948 Prehistory and the Missouri Valley development program in 1947. *Smithsonian Institution Miscellaneous Collections 111:*2.
1953 Prehistory and the Missouri Valley development program in 1948. *Smithsonian Institution, River Basin Survey Paper* No. *1. Bureau of American Ethnology Bulletin 154.*
1959 An introduction to Kansas archaeology. *Smithsonian Institution, Bureau of American Ethnology Bulletin 174.*
1961 *Prehistoric man on the Great Plains.* University of Oklahoma Press.
1970 Some observations on "Two house sites in the central Plains." *Nebraska History 51:*225–252.

Wheat, J. B.
1971 Lifeways of early man in North America. *Arctic Anthropology 8*(2):22–31.

Will, G. F.
1946 Tree ring studies in North Dakota. *Agricultural Experiment Station, North Dakota Agricultural College Bulletin 338.*

Willey, G. R. and P. Phillips
1958 *Method and theory in American archaeology.* Chicago: Univ. of Chicago Press.

Witty, T.
1967 The Pomona focus. *Kansas Archaeological Association Newsletter 12:*9.

Wood, W. R.
1960 The Boundary Mound group (32S11). *Plains Anthropologist 5*(10):71–78.
1965 The Redbird focus and the problem of Ponca prehistory. *Plains Anthropologist 10:*28, *Memoir* No. *2.*
1967 An interpretation of Mandan culture history. *Smithsonian Institution, River Basin Survey Paper* No. *39. Bureau of American Ethnology (Bulletin 198).*

Wood, W. R. (Editor)
1969 Two house sites in the central Plains: An experiment in archaeology. *Plains Anthropologist 14*(44), pt. 2, *Memoir* No. *6.*

Wormington, H. M.
1957 Ancient man in North America, 4th edition. *Denver Museum of Natural History, Popular Series* No. *4.*
1971 Comments on early man in North America, 1960–1970. *Arctic Anthropology 8*(2):83–91.

Wormington, H. M. and R. G. Forbis
1965 An introduction to the archaeology of Alberta, Canada. *Denver Museum of Natural History Proceedings 11.*

Great Basin

ROBERT F. HEIZER AND THOMAS R. HESTER

I. DEVELOPMENT OF GREAT BASIN CHRONOLOGY

The first significant archaeological excavation carried out in the Great Basin was by L. L. Loud at Lovelock Cave, Churchill County, Nevada, in 1912. Loud was wholly lacking in training, and his work was nothing more than careful collecting. Kroeber, under whom Loud worked as a museum guard, gave Loud no specific instructions on how to excavate or what information to record, probably for the reason that 60 years ago in the United States archaeology was essentially a methodless exercise in collecting prehistoric materials. The closest Loud came to following any technique was in mapping the cave floor and delimiting small areas which he called "lots," the material from each numbered lot being kept together. No depth record of finds was made. Loud simply dug with the aim of finding as much as he could. In 1924, M. R. Harrington, for the Heye Foundation, and Loud, for the University of California, jointly carried out additional excavations, this time with considerably improved technique. N. C. Nelson in 1916 published his important paper, "Chronology of the Tano Ruins, New Mexico," in which he demonstrated that digging a thick refuse deposit by arbitrary 1-foot levels would yield a culture sequence—in this instance of ceramics. Archaeologists all over the United States were quick to adopt this means of determining sequence and relative chronology, among them Harrington, who employed this method in 1922–1923 in digging the Ozark shelters and in the 1924 Lovelock Cave investigations.

We have chosen to introduce this chapter by referring to Lovelock Cave because this site serves as a useful reference point to trace the changing emphases of archaeological technique and interpretation in Great Basin archaeology over the last 60 years.

For convenience in discussion we have identified four "paradigms" [using the term in T. S. Kuhn's (1970) sense of problem-solving models] in the historiography of Great Basin prehistory. Others would make a different list, but this one (sections A–D following) seems suited to our present aim of tracing how our information and insight have become progressively enlarged and sharpened since 1912. These four paradigms are not exclusive as regards time, but overlap to some degree. They do, however, form a kind of structural pyramid where A is the base, B rests on A, C rests on B, and D rests on C. The sequence is not inevitable except insofar as A is basic to all archaeology.

A. Artifact Collecting and the Definition of Variations in Prehistoric Evidence: 1912–1938

Loud's collecting trip to Lovelock Cave produced a remarkable batch of cultural material. Being untrained in writing and employed full time as a museum guard, a report was squeezed out of him after 15 years (in 1927) only with the most strenuous effort by Kroeber (Heizer and Napton 1970b:131–162). Loud's report is purely descriptive, and it was published jointly with that of Harrington in 1929. In addition to the cave material, Loud made collections from surface sites in the neighborhood of the cave, and these are described by him in a separate section of the Lovelock Cave monograph. Loud's surface-collecting technique was good, and this is perhaps the most useful section of the report (Loud and Harrington 1929:124–151).

The 1924 excavations at Lovelock and Ocala caves were followed by Harrington's exploration in 1927 of Thea Heye Cave at Pyramid Lake. This excavation was never published. Harrington next moved his attention south, to extreme southern Nevada, exploring the site called Pueblo Grande, or Lost City, and Mesa House near Overton, where he defined an outpost of the Southwestern or Puebloan culture, dug in the prehistoric salt mines near St. Thomas [the first archaeological sites to be noted in Nevada—by Jedediah Smith in 1826 (see Merriam 1923)] and in several dry caves in the same vicinity. In 1930, Harrington excavated Gypsum Cave, and he and others spent time scouting cave sites in Nevada just west of the Utah border. By 1928, Harrington could draw a boundary line for the western limits of Puebloan pottery in Nevada (Harrington 1928; Grosscup 1957: map). Still further west, in the basin-and-range area of southeastern California, Mr. and Mrs. W. Campbell were studying the archaeological situation at Lake Mohave—initiating research on a problem that is not yet satisfactorily solved. Far to the north, in southern Oregon, L. S. Cressman in 1936 began to investigate this portion of the Great Basin, and from his efforts another variation of regional culture came into view. In the eastern Great Basin, work by N. M. Judd (1917a, 1917b, 1919) and Neil Morss (1931) were important in initial definitions of the Puebloan and Fremont culture manifestations.

It can be said that, by 1938, the prehistoric archaeology of the Great Basin had been sufficiently sampled through reconnaissance and excavation that its regional variations were known. The extent of sampling and amount of analysis varied from one subarea to another, but the important point is that the main Great Basin sections had at least been looked at by archaeologists. This process of overall sampling was vitally necessary for work that was to follow.

This exploration phase has, of course, never stopped. Any survey and digging today in a part of the Great Basin that has not yet been investigated brings to light something new, but at the same time nothing really surprising. For about the last 40 years, private collectors have been increasing both in number and efficiency, if this word can be used to describe their energy and destructiveness. Newspaper articles are common in which there is described another cave that has been looted, or a new area is advertised as accessible for "good arrowhead hunting" by four-wheel-drive vehicles. State and federal laws are, for some reason, not invoked against known violators of antiquities protection acts. Anyone wishing to estimate the Stone Age level of public regard for Great Basin archaeology should look at Emory Strong's *Stone Age in the Great Basin* (Portland 1969). Some very important caves and open sites have been plundered by collectors, and these will always constitute lacunae in the data on Great Basin prehistory. Cougar Mountain Cave in Oregon is a prime example of illegal site looting (Cowles 1960), and the Black Rock Desert area is another.

B. Fitting Great Basin Prehistory into a Wider Perspective: 1929–1940

As the Great Basin became known archaeologically on a piece-by-piece basis, each worker tried to see wider relationships and ties with the prehistory of one or more of the culture areas, such as California, the Plateau, the Plains, and the Southwest, that lie in the penumbra of the Basin. In some ways this was a case of the blind leading the blind. The Southwestern sequence was pretty well defined by 1927 through Kidder's Pecos Conference, but time estimates were in error. California was a terra incognita, as was the Plateau. Actually nothing very substantial, we now see, could come from such comparisons as far as exact time relations went.

The first such attempt at seeing outside relationships was by Harrington, who concluded on the basis of comparing materials from Lovelock Cave with those from Basket Maker sites in the Southwest that "the Early Period of our cave belongs to the Basket-Maker horizon, and therefore if Kidder is right an estimate of 1000 B.C. would be a conservative guess of first occupation of Lovelock Cave [Loud and Harrington 1929:119–123]." Harrington entertained, but did not press, the idea that the Lovelock Cave materials might be the "basic culture" from which Basket Maker culture with agriculture developed (cf. Zingg 1939). The Late Period materials of Lovelock Cave were seen by Harrington to be very similar to their counterparts among the historic Northern Paiute. Kroeber agreed on the Southwestern (i.e., Basket Maker) similarities (woven bags, atlatl, curved rabbit clubs, sandals, sheephorn sickles, rabbit nets), and also saw in the later Lovelock material "strong relations with the native culture of California in historic times [Loud and Harrington 1929:vii]" (cf. Kroeber 1939:50–51).

In southern Nevada, Harrington rightly identified the transplanted Southwestern culture that had briefly occupied the Virgin–Muddy–Moapa river bottomlands—a manifestation now labeled Patayan or Virgin Branch (Shutler 1961a:65). But this western extension of Pueblo culture was localized, and in order to delimit it Harrington conducted a surface survey of Nevada that resulted in his being able to show a line marking the western limits of Puebloan pottery, though Southwestern masonry houses and agriculture were not observed. Shutler (1961:5–12) supports and amplifies to some degree this earlier work of Harrington. In Gypsum Cave, Harrington noted what he believed were materials indicative of the presence of Basket Maker and Pueblo peoples, as well as an earlier human occupation that he thought (wrongly we now know) was contemporaneous with the extinct ground sloth (*Nothrotherium*).

In 1940, J. H. Steward published a detailed review and historical reconstruction of Great Basin ethnography and archaeology. He was of the opinion that Great Basin culture was not "the surviving substratum of an ultramontane, a Basket Maker, or any other early and widespread culture," and that "the total Intermontane culture was the product of diverse borrowing from different sources at different periods and of a certain measure of internal development [Steward 1940:450]."

C. The Development of Exact Chronologies: 1949–1972

In 1951 when the Society for American Archaeology published *Radiocarbon Dating* as its Memoir No. 8, Great Basin archaeology was represented with thirteen dates for Nevada sites (Gypsum Cave, Leonard Rockshelter, Lovelock Cave—C-221, C-222, C-276/278, C-281, C-298, C-554), Oregon caves, and the Mt. Mazama eruption (Fort Rock Cave, Catlow Cave—C-427, C-428, C-430), and one Utah site (Danger Cave—C-609/610). For the first time Great Basin archaeologists had something objective (if not precisely accurate) in the way of dating their cultures. Geologists and climatologists had often tried to estimate the ages of the Lake Lahontan and Bonneville stages or the eruption of Mt. Mazama or the extinction of megafauna, but these were, before 1949, only guesses. Some of these were pretty close to the mark, but they are for the most part now useless in the presence of ^{14}C dates.

Since 1950, a large number of radiocarbon dates for Great Basin archaeological and geological sites have been secured and they are listed in Tables 6.7–6.11.[1] A discussion of radiocarbon dates from the Great Basin is presented in a later section of this chapter.

Harrington was especially interested in Early Man and believed that he had found proof of the contemporaneity of man and the extinct ground sloth at Gypsum Cave in 1930. Sloth dung from Gypsum Cave was ^{14}C dated by Libby in 1950 (C-221, C-222) at 10,902 (± 440) and 10,075 (± 550)—average 10,455 (± 340)—and 8692 (± 500), 8051 (± 450), and 8838 (± 430)—average 8527 (± 250) years B.P.—thus demonstrating the antiquity of the sloth in the cave. In 1951 one of us pointed out that artifacts should be similarly dated since the association of sloth and man might not be contemporaneous (Heizer 1951a:24). This check was not made until 1966 when two wooden artifacts were dated by Rainer Berger (UCLA-1069, UCLA-1223) at 2400 (± 60) and 2900 (± 80) years B.P. (Heizer and Berger 1970). Gypsum Cave as an Early Man site can now be eliminated. As Lanning (1963:293, 295) pointed out before the Gypsum Cave artifacts were dated, the distinctive Gypsum Cave type of projectile points were in vogue between about 1500 B.C. and A.D. 600 (Clewlow 1967:144).

[1]Many of these are not published in archaeological reports or *Radiocarbon* date lists. We thank the following persons who generously provided dates, sample numbers, and background information: Robert Elston, Don Fowler, Jesse Jennings, Donald Tuohy, Gardiner Dalley, and David H. Thomas. A number of radiocarbon dates obtained since the compilation found in Tables 6.7–6.11 have been published by J. O. Davis in the 1977 issues. Nevada Archeological Survey *Reporter*.

Early Man (sometimes called Big Game Hunters or Paleo-Indians) was present in the Great Basin. The widespread occurrence in Nevada of fluted points made in the Clovis tradition (Campbell and Campbell 1940; Clewlow 1968; Davis and Shutler 1969; Shutler and Shutler 1959; Tuohy 1968, 1969) make it undeniable that this is true. But whether an actual big game hunting mode of life was carried out around 10,000–8000 B.C. in the Great Basin is another matter. The *presumed* hunting of megafauna (sloth, elephant, camel, horse) in the Great Basin (Cressman 1966; Meighan 1959:51–53; Tuohy 1968) rests at this time upon no concrete evidence at all as Heizer and Baumhoff (1970) pointed out after a hard second look at the archaeological–paleontological data. All of the fluted points from Nevada are surface finds and cannot be dated. Ages of 7000 to 10,000 years have been suggested, and this can be accepted for working purposes. We can only hope that future work will lead to discovery of camp, occupation, or kill sites in which these important projectile points occur. It is possible that the big game animals were already extinct when man first occupied the Great Basin (Heizer and Baumhoff 1970; Jennings and Norbeck 1955:2).

D. The Ecological Interpretation Model: 1938 to the Present

Although all ethnographers who worked in the Great Basin were fully aware of the special nature of the environment and saw that the culture of the Shoshonean tribes was closely attuned to the environment, it was not until Julian Steward published his important *Basin-Plateau Aboriginal Sociopolitical Groups* in 1938 that the ecological model was fully appreciated. The ecological model for archaeological interpretation was first proposed by Jennings (1953:207) by the term "Desert Culture." He shortly afterward elaborated the idea (Jennings and Norbeck 1955) and tested it specifically with the data from Danger Cave Site (Jennings 1957) where, in the section entitled "Comparisons" (Jennings 1957:265–275), he ranged widely over the continent pointing out similarities. The Desert Culture (a dry land adapted lifeway) model has been an important one for the last 15 years, and it has attracted both adherents and objectors. The term *Desert Culture* is now less frequently used than *Desert Archaic* (Jennings 1964:152). There are at least two main Desert Archaic aspects, one the dry desert adaptation and the other the lake margin accommodation. Both are ancient, perhaps going back to 9000 or 10,000 B.C. The lake margin ecology was noted specifically by Heizer and Krieger (1956) in their report on the archaeology of Humboldt Cave and has been, since then, often commented on (Bedwell 1970; Cowan 1967; Heizer and Napton 1970a; Napton 1969; Rozaire 1963). Other human ecology oriented studies centering on specific problems have been done. Included among these are detailed analyses of human coprolites (Fry 1970; Heizer and Napton 1969, 1970a; Napton 1969); identification of faunal remains from caves (Thomas 1969, 1971a); seasonal settlement–economic exploitation patterns (Thomas 1971b); and petroglyphs as a reflection of hunting magic on game migration routes (Heizer and Baumhoff 1959, 1962; von Werlhof 1965).

II. GREAT BASIN PROJECTILE POINTS AS CHRONOLOGICAL INDICATOR CHARACTERISTICS

A. General

In the space allowed by the editors of the present volume we cannot adequately review and evaluate the data from the scores of excavated or surface sites in the Great Basin. Such summaries, each adequate for the time at which they were written, have been published by Jennings (1957, 1964), Bennyhoff (1958), and Willey (1966). A more detailed review of Great Basin chronology has recently been prepared by Hester (1973).

Out of the welter of reported data, we have selected flaked projectile points as a demonstration element of the continuum of prehistoric cultures in the Great Basin (see Figure 6.1). There are several other kinds of artifacts that might be equally useful for chronological ordering, and these include basketry, ceramics, and shell beads. With more data (by which we mean more and better publication) one might also consider the chronological placement of such items as the L-shaped awl, atlatl, grooved rabbit stick, horn sickle (cf. Heizer 1951b), and hafted knife (cf. Hester 1970). However, we have chosen to emphasize projectile points since, in most cases, they are associated with a number of radiocarbon dates and seem at present to offer the best potential for precise cross-dating between Great Basin sites.

The use of projectile points as chronological indicators is, of course, quite firmly established in New World archaeology (see the useful discussion in Kreiger 1960:145). In many areas of North America, stratigraphic excavations have provided evidence that projectile points are subject to distinctive morphological variation through time, and these changes have made them extremely important as "time markers" (the "historical-index" types of Steward 1954) in archaeological research. The value of projectile points in chronological ordering has in the past led to too great emphasis at times on the importance of the development of local point sequences. However, no one can deny the value of projectile point types as guides to the chronological ordering of prehistoric cultural development. As W. A. Davis has stated: "The archaeological record provides a succession of specialized lithic artifacts, the projectile points, which substantially support theories of culture change by providing a chronological framework based upon index forms [1966:151]." Projectile points are found in abundance in the Great Basin, and at many sites, such as those at which there is no preserved organic material, they often provide the sole means of establishing temporal control. Thus, we

AD/BC	Southwestern	Northern	Western	Eastern
	Late Prehistoric	Late Prehistoric	Late Prehistoric	Late Prehistoric
1000	Rose Spring/ Eastgate	Rose Spring/ Eastgate ?	Rose Spring/ Eastgate	Fremont/ Virgin Branch
0				
			Great Basin Archaic	Great Basin Archaic
1000				
	Great Basin Archaic	Great Basin Archaic	Martis Complex	Hogup II
2000				
				Danger V
3000	(Pinto Basin, Death Valley II, Pre-Yuman)		Lovelock culture	Danger IV
			Leonard culture	Hogup I
4000				
5000	Occupational hiatus?	Altithermal?	Altithermal?	Danger III
		Mazama	Humboldt culture	
6000				
	Western Pluvial Lakes Tradition	Western Pluvial Lakes Tradition	Western Pluvial Lakes Tradition	
7000				
				Danger II; Escalante Valley
8000	(San Dieguito; Death Valley I; Lake Mohave)	(Connley Caves, Cougar Mtn. Caves, Coyote Flat, Guano Valley)	(Sadmat; Tonopah; Black Rock, Coleman)	
9000				Deer Creek Cave Danger I
	Fluted Point Tradition?	Fluted Point Tradition?	Fluted Point Tradition?	
10,000				
		Fort Rock Cave	Fishbone Cave?	
11,000				
		Paisley and Catlow Caves?		Tule Springs
12,000				
		Wilson Butte Cave		
13,000				

Figure 6.1. Chronological framework for the Great Basin.

are fortunate that a number of projectile point types, with restricted temporal and geographic distribution, have been defined. Because most of these types have been placed in their appropriate time context, through stratigraphy and radiocarbon dates, they can be satisfactorily employed as *fossil directeurs* by archaeologists working in the Great Basin.

Projectile point types in the Great Basin are generally designated by a binomial descriptive system (earlier research, such as that reported by the Campbells (Campbell and Campbell 1935; Campbell *et al.* 1937), used a monomial system in naming point types). The first term in the binomial system generally refers to the site at which the stratigraphic position of the types was first established; the second designator is descriptive of some aspect of the point's form. We have followed the lead of Lanning (1963) by grouping, where possible, several associated point types into a series.

In the section that follows, the dating of the major Great Basin projectile point types is reviewed, and some new data are added (cf. Hester and Heizer 1973). There has been considerable previous research into the chronological ordering of point types in this region (Baumhoff and Byrne 1959; Clewlow 1967; Heizer and Baumhoff 1961; O'Connell 1967). This earlier work has established a "Medithermal" point sequence, and while some new information is provided in the following pages, the basic structure of this sequence remains unaltered (cf. Fowler 1968a:13). Some comments are also provided here on the weaknesses inherent in the definition of certain types. Along similar lines, Thomas (1970) has suggested "Key 1," a technique for the objective quantification of regional point type attributes. Aside from recognizing some problems in the Rose Spring and Pinto series, Thomas' technique thus far offers little that is new since, in his words, it "reproduces the accepted Great Basin types [1970:48]."

B. Humboldt Series

The Humboldt Series (see Figure 6.2) was first defined by Heizer and Clewlow (1968), based on materials from site Nv-Ch-15, the Humboldt Lake Bed Site. The points are lanceolate to triangular in outline, and three varieties have been named: Concave Base A, Concave Base B, and Basal Notched. Of these, Humboldt Concave Base A seems to be the most common in Great Basin sites. Several radiocarbon dates are available, and most are primarily applicable to Humboldt Concave Base A (LJ-212, UCLA-295 and 296, and WSU-944 can also be related to the Basal Notched variant). These dates are listed in Table 6.1.

The date of 1100 B.C. from Hidden Cave represents the termination of the Humboldt Series at that site. Roust and Clewlow (1968:108) believe that the series does continue throughout the Great Basin projectile point sequence, becoming smaller in size through time. The series may have earlier origins than indicated by the ca. 4000 B.C. date from Newark Cave. For example, four specimens of Humboldt Concave Base A occur in the Mud Flow gravels at Hidden Cave attributed to the Anathermal climatic episode (Roust and Grosscup 1957). Similarly, Humboldt points are found in Danger Cave II and Danger Cave III, and in Strata 5–10 (ca. 5300 to 650 B.C.) at Hogup Cave (Aikens 1970; Fry and Adovasio 1970). Thomas (1971a:91) believes that Humboldt Concave Base A is equivalent in age to the Pinto Series. Layton

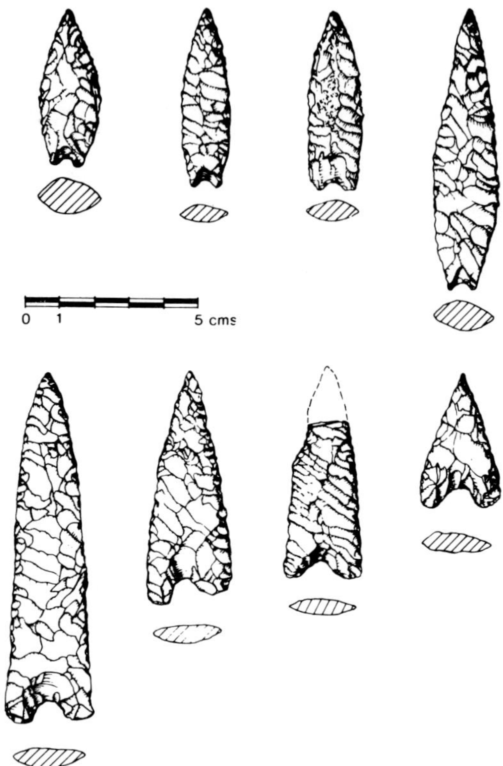

Figure 6.2. Humboldt Series.

TABLE 6.1

Radiocarbon Dates of Humboldt Series Samples

Date[a]	Sample number	Site
1100 B.C.	LJ–289BB	Hidden Cave (Roust and Clewlow 1968)
1370 B.C.	LJ–212	South Fork Shelter (Heizer *et al.* 1968)
2360 B.C.	UCLA–295	South Fork Shelter (Heizer *et al.* 1968)
2410 B.C.	UCLA–296	South Fork Shelter (Heizer *et al.* 1968)
3350 B.C.	WSU–994	Hanging Rock Shelter (Layton 1970)
3920 B.C.	WSU–511	Newark Cave (Fowler 1968)

[a] B.P. dates are available, along with indicated range of error, in Tables 6.8 and 6.9.

(1970:249) has excavated Humboldt Series points at Hanging Rock Shelter. He divides his specimens into six numbered varieties (Nos. 1–6). Humboldt No. 1 is equivalent to Humboldt Concave Base A and B and is believed by him to postdate the local Parman Phase of the early Anathermal (ca. 6000 B.C. ?). Humboldt No. 2 points are the same as Humboldt Basal Notched and are dated at their maximum popularity between the Altithermal maximum and 3350 B.C. (WSU-994).

C. Pinto Series

Pinto points (Figure 6.3) were originally defined by Amsden (Campbell and Campbell 1935:43–44) based on the analysis of specimens from the Pinto

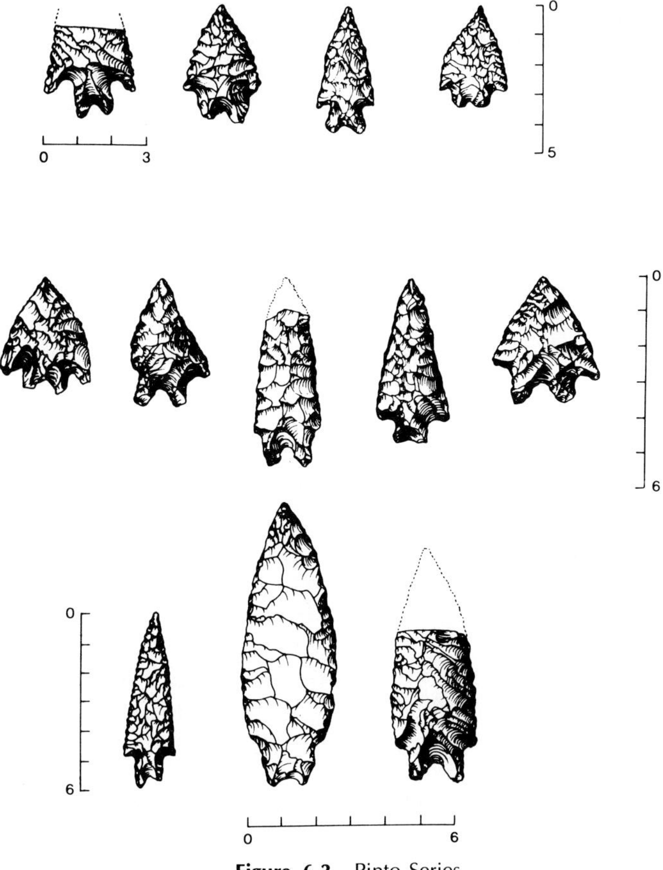

Figure 6.3. Pinto Series.

Basin Site in the southwestern part of the Great Basin. More recent evaluations and discussions of Pinto Series points have appeared in Harrington (1957) and Lanning (1963). Harrington's specimens were excavated from the Stahl Site near Little Lake. Using the 497 specimens from the site, he set up five varieties ("subtypes") which he called Shoulderless, Sloping Shoulder, Square Shoulders, Barbed Shoulders, and One-Shoulder. Reference to these varieties is still made in the typological analysis of Pinto points in the Great Basin (cf. Heizer and Clewlow 1968). In his paper on the Rose Spring Site, Lanning (1963:250–251) refers to Pinto points as the Little Lake Series, in which he includes only those specimens from the Stahl Site and Rose Spring.

Some investigators, notably Layton (1970) and O'Connell (1971), have observed that the Pinto Series is very broadly defined and loosely applied. Thus, in their particular areas, they have set up new types which include forms originally included in the Pinto Series. In Surprise Valley, O'Connell (1971:68) has defined the Bare Creek Series, with Sloping Shoulder, Square Shoulder, and barbed variants. Layton (1970) working in the High Rock area of northwestern Nevada, has proposed the Silent Snake Bifurcate Base (Pinto Barbed) type. Layton believes the continued use of the type is "naive," and he suggests that there are important differences between Pinto points as illustrated by Campbell and Campbell (1935: Plate 13) and those shown by Harrington (1957:Fig. 39). Layton is, of course, entitled to his own evaluation, but as we compare the two illustrated series, we can see nothing but similarities, especially if we delete specimens *a, d,* and *m* from the Campbells' series (*a* and *d* are reminiscent of the Silver Lake type). However, we agree with Layton, O'Connell, and others that the Pinto Series is in great need of further analysis and refinement. Until this is done, we prefer to retain the original designation (cf. Thomas 1971a:89) as we believe that it still has cultural–historical significance.

The age of the Pinto Series has been the subject of many estimates. It was once thought to represent an "early" form (cf. Wormington 1957:168–169), although some, like Rogers (1939) guessed that it was much later. There are now several radiocarbon dates which can be applied to the problem (see Table 6.2).

Thus, it seems that the Pinto Series may have been in use during the time between ca. 3000 and 700 B.C. It is possible that the type began somewhat earlier, given the occurrence of Pinto-like points in the Aeolian Silts at Hidden Cave, believed to be of Altithermal age by Roust and Grosscup (1957) and Roust and Clewlow (1968). Pinto Series points are present at Hogup Cave in Strata 3–9 (Aikens 1970), although they are most common in Strata 7–9, roughly 1000 B.C. (cf. GaK-1564). We do not think that an isolated "Pinto" from Stratum 1 at Hogup (ca. 6400 B.C.) can be truly assigned to this type (cf. Aikens 1970:40). At Weston Canyon Rockshelter, Idaho, barbed or square-shouldered Pinto points are said to appear prior to 5200 B.C. (S. Miller, in Green 1972:14).

TABLE 6.2

Radiocarbon Dates of Pinto Series Samples

Date[a]	Sample number	Site
670 B.C.[b]	UCLA–1222	Rodriguez Site (O'Connell 1971)
680 B.C.	RL–109	Swallow Shelter (G. Dalley, Letter to R. F. Heizer 1972)
1880 B.C.[c]	GaK–2387	Kramer Cave (D. Tuohy, letter to R. F. Heizer 1971)
1920 B.C.	M–377	Stuart Rockshelter (Shutler *et al.* 1960)
2100 B.C.	M–376	Stuart Rockshelter (Shutler *et al.* 1960)
2360 B.C.	UCLA–296	South Fork Shelter (Heizer, Baumhoff, and Clewlow 1968)
3350 B.C.	WSU–994	Hanging Rock Shelter (Layton 1970)

[a] B.P. dates, along with possible range of error, are given in Tables 6.8 and 6.9.

[b] O'Connell has told Thomas (1971a:89) that he believes this date to be ca. 300 years too late.

[c] This is a very significant date in that the Pinto specimen ("Bare Creek Eared") was attached to the atlatl dart shaft which was dated.

D. Elko Series

The Elko type (Figure 6.4) was originally defined by Heizer and Baumhoff (1961; see also Heizer *et al.* 1968 for specimens from the type site, South Fork Shelter). There are several varieties, including Side-Notched, Eared, Corner-Notched, and Contracting Stem. The series is found throughout the Great Basin (including the Lake Bonneville area) and is particularly abundant in central and western Nevada. A study of the significance of this type (particularly the Eared and Corner-Notched varieties) as a time marker was made by O'Connell (1967). On the basis of data available at that time, O'Connell (1967:134–135) postulated that the type appeared in the Eastern Basin after 1300 B.C., and in the Central and Western Basin, between 1500 and 500 B.C.; the type declined in popularity in the early Christian era, terminating around A.D. 500–600. There is some evidence, suggested on stratigraphic evidence reported by Bedwell (1970), that Elko Series points occur in the Fort Rock area of Oregon at a much earlier date.

Listed in Table 6.3 are 16 radiocarbon dates currently available for the Elko Series.

Summarizing, the available radiocarbon dates suggests a time span for the Elko Series of ca. 2000 B.C. to A.D. 1080. However, it is possible that the two most recent dates (both from O'Malley Shelter) may be aberrant, although at Hogup Cave, Aikens (1970) presents data that suggest the survival of the Elko Corner-Notched variant to ca. A.D. 1350. In fact, the data from Hogup suggest that Elko Corner-Notched may be useless as a strict time maker (cf. Aikens 1970:51), as it begins in Stratum 3 (ca. 6000 B.C.) and persists through Stratum 14 (ca. A.D. 1350). Elko Eared points at Hogup first appear in

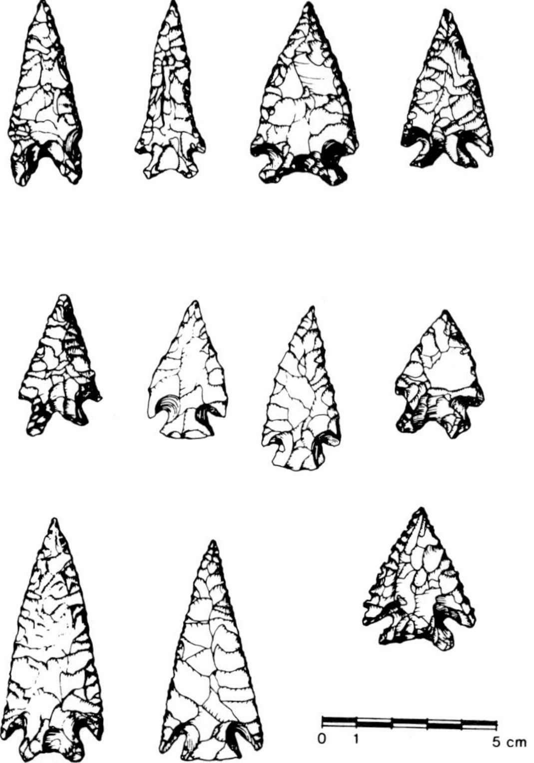

Figure 6.4. Elko Series.

Stratum 1 at ca. 6400 B.C. and terminate in Stratum 8 (ca. 1250 B.C.); the type is most common in Stratum 5. These data, and similar data from Danger Cave (Aikens 1970; Fry and Adovasio 1970), suggest an early origin for the Elko Series in the Eastern Great Basin.

E. Rose Spring and Eastgate Series

The Rose Spring and Eastgate types (Figures 6.5 and 6.6) were originally defined as separate types, Rose Spring by Lanning (1963) and Eastgate by Heizer and Baumhoff (1961). Rose Spring has three varieties, Side-Notched, Corner-Notched (the most common), and Contracting Stem. In the Eastgate Series, there are Expanding Stem and Split-Stem subtypes. In general, both series are small arrow points with triangular bodies, and stems that show quite similar treatment (cf. Heizer and Baumhoff 1961: Fig. 2). In the past few years, many archaeologists working in the Great Basin have come to suspect that both series, since they usually occur together, represent in fact

TABLE 6.3

Radiocarbon Dates of Elko Series Samples

Date[a]	Sample number	Site
A.D. 1080	RL–43	O'Malley Shelter (Madsen 1971)
A.D. 1060	RL–42	O'Malley Shelter (Madsen 1971)
A.D. 370	GaK–3610	Gatecliff Shelter (D. Thomas, letter to R. F. Heizer 1972)
A.D. 280	GaK–3609	Gatecliff Shelter (D. Thomas, letter to R. F. Heizer 1972)
A.D. 130	I–2846	Shaman's burial near Pyramid Lake (Tuohy and Stein 1969)
30 B.C.	RL–41	Conaway Shelter (D. Fowler, letter to R. F. Heizer 1971)
100 B.C.	RL–39	Conaway Shelter (D. Fowler, letter to R. F. Heizer 1971)
140 B.C.	RL–40	Conaway Shelter (D. Fowler, letter to R. F. Heizer 1971)
200 B.C.	I–3209	Rodriguez (O'Connell 1971)
290 B.C.	UCLA–1093A	Rose Spring (Clewlow *et al.* 1970)
330 B.C.	GaK–3617	Gatecliff Shelter (D. Thomas, letter to R. F. Heizer 1972)
400 B.C.	LJ–76	Karlo (Riddell 1960)
680 B.C.	RL–109	Swallow Shelter (G. Dalley, letter to R. F. Heizer 1971)
950 B.C.	UCLA–1093B	Rose Spring (Clewlow *et al.* 1970)
980 B.C.	LJ–203	Wagon Jack Shelter (Clewlow *et al.* 1970)
1020 B.C.	RL–44	O'Malley Shelter (Madsen 1971)
1100 B.C.	LJ–289BB	Hidden Cave (Roust and Clewlow 1968)
1190 B.C.	GaK–3615	Gatecliff Shelter (D. Thomas, letter to R. F. Heizer 1972)
1370 B.C.	LJ–212	South Fork Shelter (Heizer *et al.* 1968)
1740 B.C.	GaK–3618	Gatecliff Shelter (D. Thomas, letter to R. F. Heizer 1972)
1990 B.C.	RL–45	O'Malley Shelter (Madsen 1971)

[a] B.P. dates, along with possible range of error, are given in Tables 6.9 and 6.10.

Figure 6.5. Rose Spring Series.

Figure 6.6. Eastgate Series.

a single continuum, with only subtle morphological differences. One of these differences, and one which has been used to separate the two series, is that on Eastgate points, the barbs are usually squared (Heizer and Clewlow 1968; Heizer and Baumhoff 1961: Fig. 2, o, q, and s). On the other hand, Eastgate points seem to have a distribution restricted to central and western Nevada, whereas Rose Spring points are found in most parts of the Basin. Perhaps this is sufficient basis to warrant a distinction between the two types; or perhaps Eastgate should be designated as another variety in the Rose Spring Series.

There has recently come to light some new evidence bearing directly on the Rose Spring–Eastgate problem. An animal skin pouch dug from a cave on the south shore of Lake Winnemucca was found to contain a variety of materials, the most important of which were a pressure-flaking tool and 98 projectile points, both finished specimens and blanks. A discovery such as this one, as in the finding of a cache of projectile points or a number of points associated with a burial, provides the ideal method of testing the validity of a typological construct. The materials in the pouch from the Winnemucca lake have been published by Hester (1974). There are 98 projectile points (29 of these are triangular blanks) from the pouch. Based on comparisons with illustrated specimens of both series (Heizer and Baumhoff 1961; Heizer and Clewlow 1968; Lanning 1963), it is our opinion that the specimens fit well with the Eastgate Series. Most of the specimens have the distinctive squared barbs, and there are at least two Eastgate Split-Stem points. Those specimens without squared barbs have the broad bodies (with convex lateral edges) and workmanship characteristic of Eastgate points from other sites. Only one small basalt specimen shows a resemblance to the Rose Spring type. We believe that these data support the hypothesis that the Eastgate type is a discrete entity, and that the series represents a typological development concentrated in western and central Nevada.

Assembled in Table 6.4 are radiocarbon dates for the Rose Spring and Eastgate series. Since the dates for both series overlap, it seems only sensible to present them in this manner.

On the basis of the date list in Table 6.4, it would appear that both series experienced a floruit between A.D. 600–700 and A.D. 1100, with specimens continuing to be used into Historic times. The date from Swallow Shelter is for Eastgate specimens found at that site, and we suspect that it is in error. However, obsidian hydration measurements of Rose Spring and Eastgate specimens from the High Rock area (Layton 1970) suggest that the types began by 300 B.C. or earlier. More dates will be needed before this question is satisfactorily resolved. Similarly, Aikens (1970) presents stratigraphic data that would indicate the appearance of Rose Spring and Eastgate points in the Eastern Great Basin at ca. 2500 B.C.

Two localized types that probably fit within the Rose Spring Series have been defined for Surprise Valley, northeastern California (O'Connell 1971:64

TABLE 6.4

Radiocarbon Dates of Rose Spring and Eastgate Series Samples

Date[a]	Sample number	Site
A.D. 1720	RL–36	Conaway Shelter (D. Fowler, letter, 1971)
A.D. 1110	WSU–463	Newark Cave (Fowler 1968)
A.D. 1080	RL–43	O'Malley Shelter (Madsen 1971)
A.D. 1060	RL–42	O'Malley Shelter (Fowler 1968)
A.D. 1010	RL–38	Conaway Shelter (D. Fowler, letter to R. F. Heizer 1971)
A.D. 950	GaK–3608	Gatecliff Shelter (D. Thomas, letter to R. F. Heizer 1972)
A.D. 980	RL–47	Scott Site (D. Fowler, letter to R. F. Heizer 1971)
A.D. 900	I–3208	Rodriguez Site (O'Connell and Ambro 1968)
A.D. 740	UCLA–1071F	Lovelock Cave (Heizer and Napton 1970a)
A.D. 620	GaK–2580	King's Dog Site (O'Connell 1971)
680 B.C.	RL–109	Swallow Shelter, Utah (G. Dalley, letter to R. F. Heizer 1972)

[a] B.P. dates, with possible range of error, are given in Tables 6.9 and 6.10.

ff). These are named Surprise Valley Split Stem and Alkali Stemmed. They occur together in the Alkali Phase. Both types appear to resemble closely Rose Spring Series points, with Alkali Stemmed showing strong similarities to Rose Spring Corner-Notched.

It is possible, in fact highly likely, that the introduction of Rose Spring and Eastgate points can be equated with the introduction of the bow and arrow. There have been various guesses as to the date of the appearance of the bow and arrow in the Great Basin, ranging from 1250 B.C. to A.D. 1 (Grosscup 1957:380; W. A. Davis 1966:151; Grant *et al.* 1968:51; Aikens 1970:200). The Rose Spring and Eastgate series represent a "break" in the projectile point sequence—the appearance of smaller and lighter points of the sort that were commonly used with the bow and arrow. In fact, Heizer and Baumhoff (1961) and O'Connell (1971:67) have suggested that these two series may have developed out of the Elko series in response to the need for smaller points when the bow and arrow was introduced. If both series are indeed arrow points, then it seems that the date for the appearance of the bow and arrow might be closer to A.D. 500 or shortly thereafter.

F. Desert Side-Notched Series

Triangular, side-notched points are a common form in Late Prehistoric times in the Great Basin, and are characteristic of late phases from Mexico to the Northern Plains (cf. Kehoe 1966). In the Great Basin, these points (see Figure 6.7) are called Desert Side-Notched by Baumhoff and Byrne (1959),

Figure 6.7. Desert Side-Notched Series.

who recognize four major varieties or "subtypes," General, Sierra, Redding, and Delta (the latter two being confined primarily to California). Baumhoff and Byrne (1959) postulated a date of A.D. 1500 for the introduction of Desert Side-Notched points. Radiocarbon dates for the series are listed in Table 6.5.

The radiocarbon dates indicate that the Desert Side-Notched type appeared sometime after A.D. 1100–1200 and persisted into the Historic era. The date of A.D. 440 from Deer Creek Cave has been discounted as much too

TABLE 6.5

Radiocarbon Dates of Desert Side-Notched Series Samples

Date[a]	Sample number	Site
A.D. 1720	RL–36	Conaway Shelter (Madsen 1971)
A.D. 1710[b]	GaK–2389	NV-Wa-355 (Pyramid Lake: D. Tuohy, letter to R. F. Heizer 1971)
A.D. 1630	UCLA–1071D	Hesterlee Site (Clewlow *et al.* 1970)
A.D. 1620	Tx–1390	Thompson Site (Elston and Davis 1972)
A.D. 1480	GaK–3613	Gatecliff Shelter (D. Thomas, letter 1972)
A.D. 1400	GaK–3614	Gatecliff Shelter (D. Thomas, letter to R. F. Heizer 1972)
A.D. 1360	GaK–3607	Gatecliff Shelter (D. Thomas, letter to R. F. Heizer 1972)
A.D. 1200	GaK–3606	Gatecliff Shelter (D. Thomas, letter to R. F. Heizer 1972)
A.D. 1110	WSU–463	Newark Cave (Fowler 1968)
A.D. 440	WSU–245	Deer Creek Cave (Shutler and Shutler 1963)

[a] B.P. dates, with range of error indicated, can be found in Table 6.10.

[b] This radiocarbon assay is on an arrowshaft to which a Desert Side-Notched point remains attached.

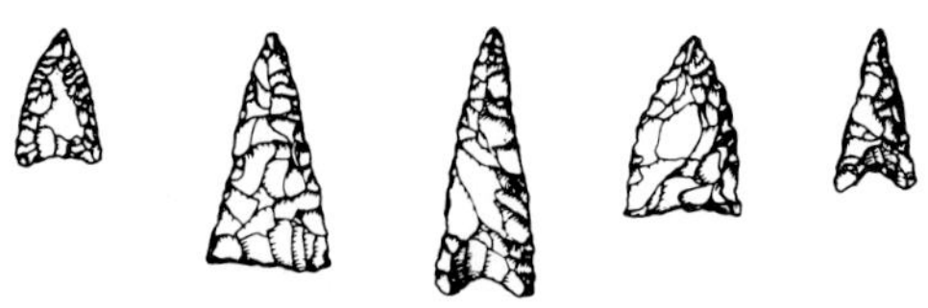

Figure 6.8. Cottonwood Series.

early by Shutler and Shutler (1963:51). However, there is a date of A.D. 20 (C-635) attributed to the type at Danger Cave (discounted by Aikens 1970), and there are indications of a similar early origin for Desert Side-Notched points at Hogup Cave (Aikens 1970).

Desert Side-Notched points continued to be used well into the eighteenth century, and were, of course, being used by known ethnographic peoples. Layton (1970:225) found a Desert Side-Notched specimen in association with the charred bones of a domestic cow at Hanging Rock Shelter, northwestern Nevada; he infers from this find the use of the type by Historic Northern Paiute. For the persistence of Desert Side-Notched points among the Washo of historic times see Heizer and Elsasser (1953).

G. Cottonwood Series

The Cottonwood Series (Figure 6.8) was originally named by Lanning (1963) in his analysis of projectile points from the Rose Spring Site. He recognized two varieties, Cottonwood Triangular and Cottonwood Leaf-Shaped. A third variety, Cottonwood Bipointed, was later added by Heizer and Clewlow (1968). These small arrow points are common in Late Prehistoric and Historic times in the Great Basin (for an example of the series in a Historic context, see H. S. Riddell 1951). In many instances, Cottonwood points co-occur with specimens of the Desert Side-Notched Series. There are five radiocarbon dates that refer to the Cottonwood Series, as shown in Table 6.6.

TABLE 6.6

Radiocarbon Dates of Cottonwood Series Samples

Date[a]	Sample number	Site
A.D. 1630	UCLA–1071D	Hesterlee Site (Clewlow *et al.* 1970)
A.D. 1110	WSU–463	Newark Cave (Fowler 1968)
A.D. 1010	RL–38	Conaway Shelter (D. Fowler, letter to R. F. Heizer 1971)
A.D. 980	RL–47	Scott Site (D. Fowler, letter to R. F. Heizer 1971)
A.D. 900	RL–37	Conaway Shelter (D. Fowler, letter to R. F. Heizer 1971)

[a] B.P. dates, with range of error indicated, can be found in Table 6.10.

These dates suggest that the series may have begun prior to ca. A.D. 1300, which is earlier than the date proposed by Lanning (1963) for its origin.

H. Martis Series

The Martis type (Figure 6.9) was originally defined by Heizer and Elsasser (1953) during their work in the Central Sierra Nevada of California. Recently, Elston (1971) has revised the classification to include three separate types, Martis Triangular, Martis Stemmed-Leaf, and Martis Corner-Notched. This series appears to be confined to the westernmost Great Basin, particularly that area around and to the east of Lake Tahoe, occupied in ethnographic times by the Washo. Elston (1971:35) agrees with Heizer and Elsasser (1953) that the series is a time marker for the Martis Complex, and, based on radiocarbon dates from the Spooner Lake Site (see Table 6.9), he places their age at 1000 B.C. to A.D. 500.

I. Sierra Stemmed Triangular Type

The Sierra Stemmed Triangular is another type defined by Elston (1971:35). It is found in the ethnographic Washo area and possibly in parts of California just outside the Great Basin. Elston notes some similarities between this type and the Gypsum point. Sierra Stemmed Triangular points were popular during the early phase of the Martis Complex (Elston 1971), sometime between 1000 B.C. and A.D. 1.

J. Lake Mohave Type

Lake Mohave points (Figure 6.10) were defined by Amsden (in Campbell *et al.* 1937:80 ff), based on collections from high terraces bordering pluvial

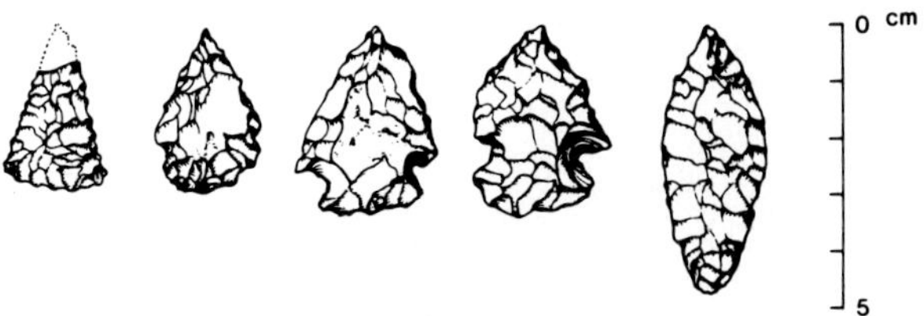

Figure 6.9. Martis Series.

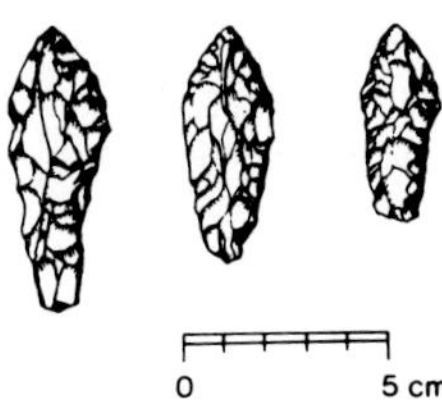

Figure 6.10. Lake Mohave points.

Lake Mohave. The specimens are often lozenge-shaped, with long, contracting stems and rounded bases. The type is a major element in the San Dieguito Complex, and a specimen reminiscent of the type was found in the San Dieguito component at the C. W. Harris Site (radiocarbon dated at between 6500 and 7100 B.C.; see Table 6.7). A Lake Mohave point was also found in deep deposits at Fort Rock Cave, Oregon (Bedwell 1970), associated with a radiocarbon date of 11,250 B.C. (see Table 6.7).

K. Silver Lake Type

The Silver Lake Type is comprised of stemmed points first recognized during the investigations at pluvial Lake Mohave (Amdsden, in Campbell *et al*. 1937:84). They have often been collected from sites in apparent association with Lake Mohave points. However, if they were indeed coeval with the Lake Mohave type (there is, in fact, considerable morphological intergrading between the two types), they appear to have survived later in time. E. L. Davis (1970) believes that Silver Lake points begin sometime after 4000 B.C. in the Panamint Basin. There are also numerous Silver Lake points at the Stahl Site (Harrington 1957). In the Northern Great Basin, Layton (1970) has combined Silver Lake and Lake Mohave points into his Lake Parman Series, which he attributes to a long time span predating the onset of the Altithermal.

L. The Black Rock Concave Base and Great Basin Transverse Types

In his research in the Black Rock Desert, Clewlow (1968) recorded a number of probable Paleo-Indian and other "early" projectile point forms. Among these is a locally defined type named Black Rock Concave Base by Clewlow (1968:13–14) (see Figure 6.11). In many respects, these are similar to the Plainview type of the Plains area, although the Black Rock Concave

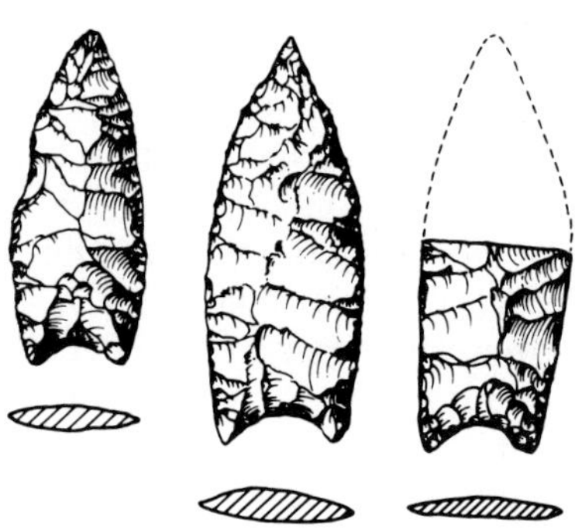

Figure 6.11. Black Rock Concave Base points.

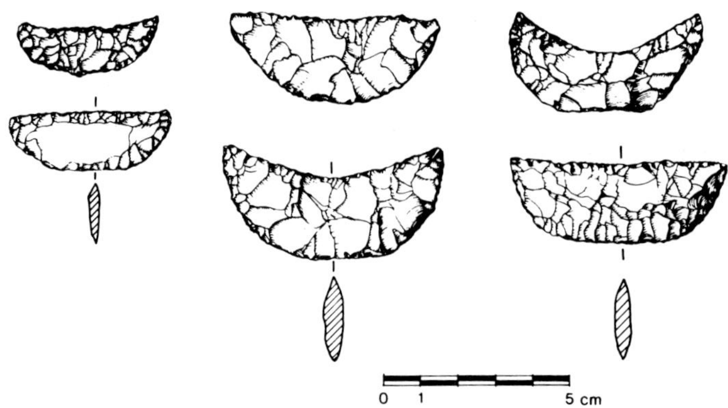

Figure 6.12. Great Basin Transverse points.

Base points tend to be considerably thinner than Plainview. The type exhibits parallel flaking and has light smoothing on the lower lateral edges.

Specimens known as "crescents" in the Great Basin literature (cf. Tadlock 1966) are found in numbers in the Black Rock Desert. Since these crescentic chipped stone objects are thought to have been used as transversely mounted projectile points (used in hunting waterfowl), Clewlow has designated them the Great Basin Transverse type (Figure 6.12). Additional descriptive and statistical data on this type can be found in Hester (1977) and Mitchell *et al.* (1977).

Both of these point types are assumed to be Anathermal in age (cf. Clewlow 1968) and are considered to be traits of the Western Pluvial Lakes Tradition. An anomalous situation apparently exists at Hogup Cave, where the Black Rock Concave Base type begins around 5850 B.C., yet survives to Stratum 9, dated at between 1250 and 650 B.C. Black Rock Concave Base specimens were the earliest points excavated at Hanging Rock Shelter (Layton 1970). Layton (1970) reports obsidian hydration measurements indicating great antiquity for the type.

Clewlow (1968) indicates that the Black Rock Concave Base type is a tentative one. It is clear that morphologically similar points occur prior to 5000 B.C. in the Great Basin and constitute an element in the Western Pluvial Lakes Tradition. However, the data from Hogup Cave suggest that the typological criteria for Black Rock Concave Base need to be more clearly defined.

An "eccentric" crescent was found in the San Dieguito component at the C. W. Harris Site, southern California (Warren 1967: Fig. 2, d). Dates for the San Dieguito materials at that site range from 6540 to 7080 B.C. Crescents (in the typical form of the Great Basin Transverse point) have been excavated at the Connley Caves, Oregon (Bedwell 1970), and are attributed to his Period III, which has a time span of 9000–6000 B.C. (the Western Pluvial Lakes Tradition).

A different view of the function of Great Basin Transverse points has been offered by Butler (1970:39). Butler's laboratory assistant examined 84 of these specimens (from Coyote Flat, southeastern Oregon) under low-power magnification. According to Butler, the results point to the use of these artifacts "as scrapers, as knives and as gravers" [1970:39]. "Unfortunately, Butler does not describe the types of wear observed on the specimens that enable him to make this broad statement about their function. If his specimens are like those from the Black Rock Desert, they have undergone considerable weathering, and we would suspect that most meaningful wear patterns (if present) might be badly obscured. In addition, extensive smoothing of artifact edges, a feature that usually indicates use, could have been caused on these specimens through weathering processes while they were exposed on the surface (cf. Hester 1970:48; Hester and Green 1972). Thus, we believe that Butler's hypotheses as to the use of these specimens require further test; we would urge that when such tests are made, the results be more fully described.

The hypothesis advanced by Tadlock (1966) and by Clewlow (1967), that Great Basin Transverse specimens served as projectile points, has been partially tested in experiments at the University of California, Berkeley. Though these experiments were inconclusive, they did show that such specimens, hafted as transverse points, did not affect the trajectory of a shaft while in flight and thus could have served as projectile tips.

M. Gypsum Type

Projectile points with triangular bodies and short, contracting stems were found by Harrington (1933) at Gypsum Cave, Nevada. He referred to the points as the Gypsum Cave type (Figure 6.13), and because of their apparent association with extinct fauna at the site, they have long been considered by many archaeologists as dating from Paleo-Indian times (Wormington 1957:157). However, radiocarbon analyses published by Heizer and Berger (1970) have established that the site of Gypsum Cave is much more recent in time. It is likely that the Gypsum points date from sometime around 950–450

Figure 6.13. Gypsum points.

B.C. (UCLA-1069; UCLA-1223) or earlier, since D. Fowler (letter, 1971) has found 50 Gypsum points in Unit III at O'Malley Shelter, radiocarbon dated at 1790 B.C.

N. McKean Type

In a paper delivered at the 1972 Northwest Anthropological Conference, J. P. Green (1972) discussed the occurrence of McKean points (Wheeler 1952) in the Great Basin. His studies have revealed that true McKean points are found at Wilson Butte Cave (in the Wilson Butte V assemblage, dated at 2000–500 B.C.) and in collections from Coyote Flat, southeastern Oregon (Butler 1970). Butler (1970) included McKean points in a McKean–Humboldt Concave Base A–Pinto Series, a most confusing congeries. Green (1972:10) points out that McKean is technologically distinct from both the Humboldt and the Pinto series. He believes that specimens classified as McKean at Danger Cave are definitely not of that type.

O. Northern Side-Notched Type

Gruhn (1961) used this term to refer to a series of large side-notched points (with several variants—cf. Green 1972:34), one of the traits of the Bitterroot culture, an early culture defined by Swanson (1966). In Idaho, Northern Side-Notched points are thought to date ca. 7000–1000 B.C. (Fig. 6.14)

However, specimens of this type are found in the Great Basin, particularly in the northern fringes, such as the High Rock country (Layton 1970) and in the Black Rock Desert (Clewlow 1968; Hester 1977). In northern Nevada, Layton (1970) believes that the types occur earlier than the introduction of what he calls "Silent Snake" points (resembling the Pinto Series). Northern Side-Notched points were recovered by Riddell (1960) at the Karlo site (he referred to them as "Madeline Dunes" points). In Surprise Valley, O'Connell (1971) reports that Northern Side-Notched points are a key trait of the Menlo phase, dated at ca. 5000–2000 B.C. Several radiocarbon dates are available for this phase, and one of them (I–4782; 3300 ± 120 B.C.) appears to be directly linked to the Northern-Side-Notched type. In the eastern Basin,

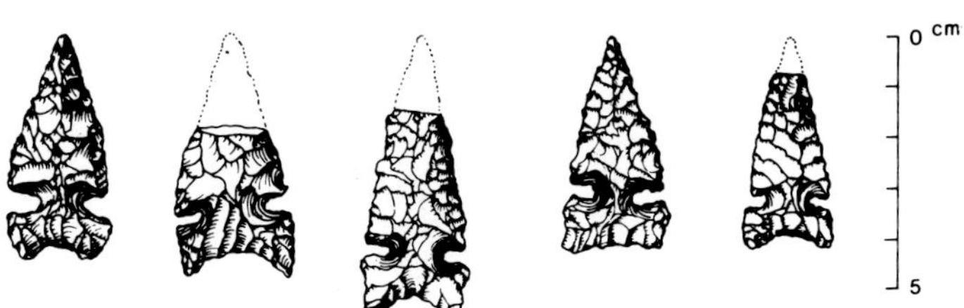

Figure 6.14. Northern Side-Notched.

Northern Side-Notched points are a part of the "Early Complex" found by Delisio (1971:51) at Weston Canyon Rockshelter, dating ca. 5250–1300 B.C.

P. Miscellaneous Early Man Points

There are a variety of projectile points found at Great Basin sites that can be attributed, on typological grounds, to Paleo-Indian times. These include the Haskett type (defined by Butler, 1965, 1967), one of the traits (along with "Haskett-like" points; cf. Hester and Jameson 1977) of the Hascomat Complex defined by Warren and Ranere (1968). The type is thought to date around 6000–5000 B.C. (there are radiocarbon dates applicable to the type from the Veratic Rockshelter, Idaho; see Butler 1965). Another similar form is the so-called Cougar Mountain point, described by Layton (1970) as large, edge-ground points with tongue-shaped stems (similar to his Lake Parman Series points; see discussion of the Silver Lake type). These points, originally found at Cougar Mountain Cave, Oregon (Cowles 1960), may have been present in the Great Basin around 6500 B.C., if the date from Level 1 of Cougar Mountain Cave is considered to be applicable (UCLA-112). Specimens resembling the projectile points found at Lind Coulee (Daugherty 1956) have been reported by Clewlow (1968) from the Black Rock Desert; their temporal span in the Great Basin is not known. Cascade points, characteristic of Butler's hypothetical Old Cordilleran culture (see Butler 1961), are found in some sites in the Northern Great Basin; for example, Weide (1968) places them in her "early" period in the Warner Valley, Oregon. Finally, there are a variety of fluted points (see Figure 6.15), many of which can be typologically linked to the Folsom and Clovis types, and some resemble specimens found at the Borax Lake Site, California (cf. Clewlow 1968 for such specimens in collections from the Black Rock Desert).

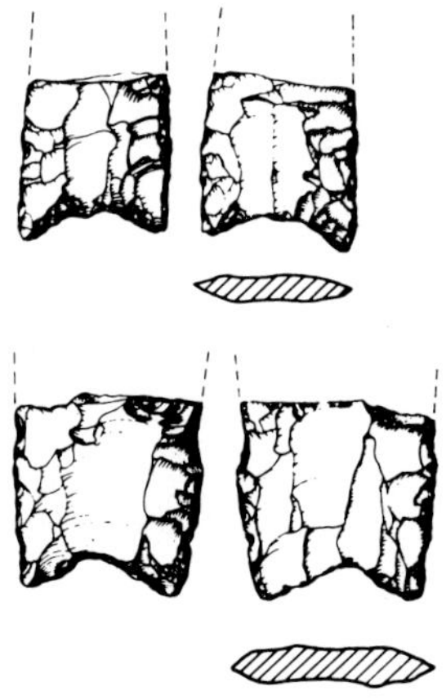

Figure 6.15. Fluted points.

III. SUMMARY OF GREAT BASIN CHRONOLOGY

In Tables 6.7–6.10, we have listed Great Basin archaeological radiocarbon dates available to us. Although there are no doubt some dates missing from these tables, we feel that the list is reasonably complete. To facilitate use of the radiocarbon lists we have divided the dates into four time periods. While we attach no particular importance to these arbitrary divisions, we feel that we should offer a few comments on some of the dates contained in these tables.

Our time divisions, according to which Tables 6.7–6.10 are organized, are:

Period I	+ 10,000–5000 B.C.
Period II	5000–2000 B.C.
Period III	2000–1 B.C.
Period IV	1 A.D.–present

The radiocarbon assays in Table 6.7 span the period between 11,250 B.C. (GaK-1738) and 5090 B.C. (RL-55). It is during this time span that the

TABLE 6.7

Period I (10,000–5,000 B.C.)

Site	Sample number	Date	Reference
Oregon			
Fort Rock Cave	GaK–1738	13,200 ± 720 (11,250 B.C.)	Bedwell 1970
Fort Rock Cave	GaK–2146	8,550 ± 150 (6,600 B.C.)	Bedwell 1970
Fort Rock Cave	GaK–2147	10,200 ± 230 (8,250 B.C.)	Bedwell 1970
Fort Rock Cave	C–428	9,053 ± 350 (7,103 B.C.)	Libby 1955
Paisley Five Mile Point Cave No. 3	Y–109	7,619 ± 120 (5,669 B.C.)	*Science* 122:958
Connley Cave No. 3	GaK–1739	8,290 ± 310 (6,340 B.C.)	Bedwell 1970
Connley Cave No. 4A	GaK–1741	7,900 ± 170 (5,950 B.C.)	Bedwell 1970
Connley Cave No. 4A	GaK–1742	10,100 ± 400 (8,150 B.C.)	Bedwell 1970
Connley Cave No. 4A	GaK–2136	9,150 ± 150 (7,200 B.C.)	Bedwell 1970
Connley Cave No. 4B	GaK–2140	7,240 ± 150 (5,290 B.C.)	Bedwell 1970
Connley Cave No. 4B	GaK–2141	11,200 ± 20 (9,250 B.C.)	Bedwell 1970

TABLE 6.7 (Continued)

Site	Sample number	Date	Reference
Connley Cave No. 4B	GaK–2142	9,670 ± 180 (7,720 B.C.)	Bedwell 1970
Connley Cave No. 4B	GaK–2143	10,600 ± 190 (8,650 B.C.)	Bedwell 1970
Connley Cave No. 5A	GaK–1743	9,800 ± 250 (7,850 B.C.)	Bedwell 1970
Connley Cave No. 5B	GaK–1744	9,540 ± 260 (7,590 B.C.)	Bedwell 1970
Connley Cave No. 5B	GaK–2135	7,430 ± 140 (5,480 B.C.)	Bedwell 1970
Connley Cave No. 6	GaK–1745	9,710 ± 880 (7,760 B.C.)	Bedwell 1970
Cougar Mountain Cave No. 1	UCLA–112	8,510 ± 250 (6,560 B.C.)	*Radiocarbon* 1962:111
Cougar Mountain Cave No. 2	GaK–1751	11,950 ± 350 (10,000 B.C.)	Bedwell 1970
Idaho			
Wilson Butte Cave (Stratum C)	M–1409	14,500 ± 500 (12,550 B.C.)	Gruhn 1965:57
Wilson Butte Cave (Stratum E)	M–1410	15,000 ± 800 (13,050 B.C.)	Gruhn 1965:57
California			
Bench Mark Bay (Lake Mohave)	Y–2406	10,270 ± 160 (8,320 B.C.)	*Radiocarbon* 1969:583
C. W. Harris (San Dieguito component)	A–724	8,490 ± 400 (6,540 B.C.)	Warren 1967:179
C. W. Harris (San Dieguito component)	A–725	8,490 ± 400 (6,540 B.C.)	Warren 1967:179
C. W. Harris (San Dieguito component)	A–722A	9,030 ± 400 (7,080 B.C.)	Warren 1967:179
Menlo Baths[a]	I–4604	13,750 ± 250 (11,800 B.C.)	O'Connell 1971
King's Dog	GaK–2876	7,430 ± 150 (5,480 B.C.)	O'Connell and Ericson n.d.
Nevada			
Gypsum Cave (sloth dung)	C–222	av. 8,527 ± 250 (6,577 B.C.)	Libby 1955:118
Gypsum Cave (sloth dung)	C–221	av. 10,455 ± 340 (8,505 B.C.)	Libby 1955:117
Gypsum Cave (sloth dung)	LJ–452	11,690 ± 250 (9,740 B.C.)	Hubbs *et al.* 1963:259
Tule Springs	UCLA–552[b]	13,100 ± 200 (11,150 B.C.)	Haynes 1968:616; 622; 626
Tule Springs	UCLA–636	11,500 ± 500 (9,550 B.C.)	Haynes 1968:616; 622; 626
Tule Springs (Deposition B2)	UCLA–519	7,480 ± 120 (5,530 B.C.)	Haynes 1968:616; 622; 626

TABLE 6.7 (Continued)

Site	Sample number	Date	Reference
Tule Springs (Deposition B2)	A–463a	8,540 ± 340 (6,590 B.C.)	Haynes 1968:616; 622; 626
Tule Springs (Deposition B2)	I–991	9,670 ± 200 (7,720 B.C.)	Haynes 1968:616; 622; 626
Tule Springs (Deposition B2)	UCLA–505	10,000 ± 200 (8,050 B.C.)	Haynes 1968:616; 622; 626
Leonard Rockshelter (NV-Pe-14)	C–281	8,660 ± 300 (6,710 B.C.)	Grosscup 1958
Leonard Rockshelter (NV-Pe-14)	C–298	7,038 ± 350 (5,088 B.C.)	Grosscup 1958
Deer Creek Cave	I–1028	10,085 ± 400 (8,135 B.C.)	Shutler and Shutler 1963
Deer Creek Cave	I–1029	9,670 ± 300 (7,720 B.C.)	Shutler and Shutler 1963
O'Malley Shelter	RL–92	7,100 ± 190 (5,150 B.C.)	Fowler letter
Spooner Lake	I–2001	7,100 ± 140 (5,140 B.C.)	Elston 1971
Fishbone Cave	L–245	11,200 ± 250 (9,245 B.C.)	*Science* 124:163
Fishbone Cave	L–289K	7,830 ± 350 (5,880 B.C.)	*Science* 126:1332
Fishbone Cave	RL–49	7,240 ± 180 (5,290 B.C.)	Adovasio 1970:Table 3
Utah			
Danger Cave I	TX–85	10,600 ± 20 (8,650 B.C.)	*Radiocarbon* 1964:156; 157
Danger Cave I	TX–86	8,970 ± 150 (7,020 B.C.)	*Radiocarbon* 1964:156; 157
Danger Cave I	TX–87	10,150 ± 170 (8,200 B.C.)	*Radiocarbon* 1964:156; 157
Danger Cave I	TX–88	9,050 ± 180 (7,100 B.C.)	*Radiocarbon* 1964:156;157
Danger Cave I	TX–89	9,740 ± 210 (7,790 B.C.)	*Radiocarbon* 1964:156; 157
Danger Cave I	C–610	11,151 ± 570 (9,201 B.C.)	Libby 1955:119
Danger Cave I	C–609	11,453 ± 600 (9,503 B.C.)	Libby 1955:119
Danger Cave I	C–640	8,960 ± 340 (7,010 B.C.)	Libby 1955:119
Danger Cave I	M–204	10,270 ± 650 (8,320 B.C.)	*Science* 124:670
Danger Cave I	M–202	10,270 ± 650 (8,320 B.C.)	*Science* 124:670

TABLE 6.7 (Continued)

Site	Sample number	Date	Reference
Danger Cave I	M–119	10,400 ± 700 (8,450 B.C.)	Dalley letter
Danger Cave I	M–118	11,000 ± 700 (9,050 B.C.)	*Science* 124:670
Danger Cave II	GaK–1900	10,900 ± 200 (7,950 B.C.)	Dalley letter
Danger Cave II	GaK–1899	10,130 ± 250 (8,180 B.C.)	Dalley letter
Danger Cave II	GaK–1896	9,590 ± 160 (7,640 B.C.)	Dalley letter
Danger Cave II	GaK–1895	6,960 ± 210 (5,010 B.C.)	Dalley letter
Danger Cave II	C–611	9,789 ± 630 (7,837 B.C.)	Libby 1955:119
Danger Cave III	GaK–1897	7,100 ± 150, (5,150 B.C.)	Libby 1955:119
Hogup Cave	GaK–2086	7,860 ± 160 (5,910 B.C.)	Dalley letter
Hogup Cave	GaK–1569	8,350 ± 160 (6,400 B.C.)	Dalley letter
Hogup Cave	GaK–2083	8,880 ± 200 (6,850 B.C.)	Dalley letter
Hogup Cave	GX–1287	7,815 ± 350 (5,865 B.C.)	Dalley letter
Hogup Cave	GaK–2082	7,250 ± 100 (5,300 B.C.)	Dalley letter
Sandwich Shelter	RL–55	7,040 ± 280 (5,090 B.C.)	Marwitt *et al.* 1971

[a] O'Connell (1971) dismisses this date as aberrant.

[b] UCLA–552 and UCLA–636 (Tule Springs) are the earliest and latest of 11 radiocarbon dates obtained on the oldest occupation at the site.

earliest, definitely recognized human occupation of the Great Basin took place. From the Fort Rock Valley of southeastern Oregon come the earliest dates. At the base of Fort Rock Cave, Bedwell (1970) obtained a date of 11,250 B.C. for a small lithic assemblage, including what he described as a fluted point (Fagan 1975:356–357 has reanalyzed this specimen, producing evidence that it is *not* a fluted point). A date of 10,000 B.C. (GaK-1751) is reported for Cougar Mountain Cave #2. Another series of dates averaging ca. 11,000 B.C. has been obtained at Tule Springs (Haynes 1968). Eleven radiocarbon assays were run on the earliest occupation at this site; the youngest of this series was 9,550 B.C. (UCLA-636) and the oldest, 11,150 B.C. (UCLA-552). Estimates of much greater age for this site (Harrington and Simpson 1961) are thus shown to be in error.

As of the present, we are unable to define the temporal parameters of the Fluted Point Tradition in the Great Basin. The widespread occurrence of fluted forms, many resembling the Folsom and Clovis types, has been well documented (Davis and Shutler 1969; Tuohy 1968). However, the radiocarbon assay from Fort Rock Cave, of 11,250 B.C., is the only date that can be directly linked to the Fluted Point Tradition; it should be noted that the fluted specimen at Fort Rock Cave is not typical of Great Basin fluted points in general.

From the Connley Caves in southeastern Oregon (Bedwell 1970), there is a long series of radiocarbon dates. These are important primarily because of their relevance to the dating of a widespread Early Lacustrine Tradition in the Great Basin. The occurrence of this early adaptation has long been hypothesized (Heizer and Krieger 1956; Rozaire 1963), and its characteristic lithic traits (such as the Great Basin Transverse points or "crescents") are well known. The data from the Connley Caves enabled Bedwell (1970) to place the temporal span of this tradition at between 9000 and 6000 B.C. He has grouped the various manifestations of the Early Lacustrine Phase (including the San Dieguito, Lake Mohave, and Hascomat complexes) in the Western Pluvial Lakes Tradition (a more detailed discussion and review of the Western Pluvial Lakes Tradition can be found in Hester, 1973). Dates supporting Bedwell's postulated time span for the Western Pluvial Lakes Tradition come from the C. W. Harris Site (A-724, 725, 722A) and the Bench Mark Bay Site on Lake Mohave (Y-2406).

There are, of course, a number of rather early sites in the Great Basin that fit into neither the Fluted Point Tradition nor the lacustrine-oriented lifeway. Typical of these sites are Danger Cave (I and II), Hogup Cave, Leonard Rockshelter, and Deer Creek Cave. At Danger and Hogup caves, the earliest materials form part of Jennings' Desert Culture, or Desert Archaic.

In Table 6.7, we list three dates obtained on sloth dung at Gypsum Cave (C-221, 222, and LJ-452). These dates do not, as Harrington (1933) supposed, date the earliest human occupation of this southern Nevada site. Recent radiocarbon determinations of artifacts that Harrington attributed definitely to the same age as the sloth (Heizer and Berger 1970) indicate that the cultural materials date from much later in time, between 950 and 450 B.C. (see Table 6.9).

It is probable that somewhat earlier dates may eventually be obtained at Great Basin sites, given the early cultural remains found on the northern fringe of the Basin. For example, at Wilson Butte Cave, Idaho (Gruhn 1965:57), the basal cultural deposits (Strata C and E) date to 12,550 B.C. (M-1409) and 13,050 B.C. (M-1410). There is also a date of 9600 B.C. at Jaguar

TABLE 6.8

Period II (5,000–2,000 B.C.)

Site	Sample number	Date	Reference
Oregon			
Fort Rock Cave	GaK–2145	4,450 ± 100 (2,500 B.C.)	Bedwell 1970
Connley Cave No. 5A	GaK–2134	4,320 ± 100 (2,370 B.C.)	Bedwell 1970
Connley Cave No. 6	GaK–2131	4,350 ± 100 (2,400 B.C.)	Bedwell 1970
Connley Cave No. 6	GaK–2132	4,720 ± 200 (2,770 B.C.)	Bedwell 1970
Table Rock Cave No. 1	GaK–1748	5,520 ± 210 (3,270 B.C.)	Bedwell 1970
Idaho			
Wilson Butte Cave (Upper Stratum C)	M–1087	6,850 ± 300 (4,900 B.C.)	Gruhn 1961:27
California			
Menlo Baths	I–4782	5,250 ± 120 (3,300 B.C.)	O'Connell 1971
King's Dog	UCLA–1770	5,640 ± 155 (3,690 B.C.)	O'Connell and Ericson n.d.
Nevada			
Stuart Rockshelter	M–376	4,050 ± 300 (2,100) B.C.)	Shutler *et al.* 1960:Plate 3
Tule Springs (preceramic hearth)	A–465	4,190 ± 170 (2,240 B.C.)	Haynes 1968:621
Corn Creek Dunes	UCLA–526	5,200 ± 100 (3,250 B.C.)	Williams and Orlins 1963
Corn Creek Dunes	UCLA–525	4,440 ± 100 (2,490 B.C.)	Williams and Orlins 1963
Corn Creek Dunes	UCLA–531	4,580 ± 100 (2,630 B.C.)	Williams and Orlins 1963
Corn Creek Dunes	UCLA–532	4,610 ± 100 (2,660 B.C.)	Williams and Orlins 1963
Corn Creek Dunes	UCLA–533	4,900 ± 100 (2,950 B.C.)	Williams and Orlins 1963
Corn Creek Dunes	UCLA–534	4,380 ± 100 (2,430 B.C.)	Williams and Orlins 1963
Corn Creek Dunes	UCLA–535	4,030 ± 100 (2,080 B.C.)	Williams and Orlins 1963
Deer Creek Cave	I–1031	4,170 ± 150 (2,220 B.C.)	Shutler and Shutler 1963
South Fork Rockshelter	UCLA–295	4,360 ± 300 (2,410 B.C.)	*Radiocarbon* 1964:328
South Fork Rockshelter	UCLA–296	4,310 ± 40 (2,360 B.C.)	*Radiocarbon* 1964:328

TABLE 6.8 (Continued)

Site	Sample number	Date	Reference
O'Malley Shelter	RL–91	4,630 ± 170 (2,680 B.C.)	Fowler letter
O'Malley Shelter	RL–46	6,700 ± 140 (4,750 B.C.)	Fowler letter
Lovelock Cave	I–4631	3,980 ± 20 (2,030 B.C.)	Heizer and Napton 1970a: Table 4
Lovelock Cave	I–4632	4,720 ± 110 (2,320 B.C.)	Heizer and Napton 1970a: Table 4
Lovelock Cave	I–4634	4,430 ± 130 (2,480 B.C.)	Heizer and Napton 1970a: Table 4
Lovelock Cave	I–4633	4,520 ± 110 (2,570 B.C.)	Heizer and Napton 1970a: Table 4
Lovelock Cave	I–4673	4,580 ± 120 (2,630 B.C.)	Heizer and Napton 1970a: Table 4
Lovelock Cave	I–3692	4,690 ± 110 (2,740 B.C.)	Heizer and Napton 1970a: Table 4
Silent Snake Springs	WSU–994	5,300 ± 380 (3,350 B.C.)	Layton 1970
Leonard Rockshelter (NV-Pe-14)	C–544	5,737 ± 250 (3,787 B.C.)	Grosscup 1958
NV-Wa-200	UCLA–978	4,030 ± 85 (2,080 B.C.)	*Radiocarbon* 1966:473
NV-Wa-525	GaK–2808	4,470 ± 110 (2,520 B.C.)	Tuohy letter
Newark Cave	WSU–511	5,470 ± 400 (3,920 B.C.)	Fowler 1968b
Spooner Lake	I–2000	4,920 ± 120 (2,970 B.C.)	Elston 1971
Cow Bone Cave	L–289FF	5,970 ± 150 (4,020 B.C.)	Grosscup 1958
Utah			
Danger Cave III	GaK–1901	6,570 ± 110 (4,620 B.C.)	Dalley letter
Danger Cave III	GaK–1898	6,560 ± 120 (4,610 B.C.)	Dalley letter
Danger Cave IV (or late D–III)	GX–1465	6,825 ± 160 (4,875 B.C.)	Dalley letter
Danger Cave IV	GaK–1902	5,050 ± 120 (3,100 B.C.)	Dalley letter
Danger Cave V	M–203	4,000 ± 300 (2,050 B.C.)	*Science* 124:670
Danger Cave V	M–205	4,900 ± 350 (2,850 B.C.)	*Science* 124:6670
Hogup Cave	GaK–1570	3,970 ± 100 (2,020 B.C.)	Dalley letter
Hogup Cave	GX–1286	6,020 ± 380 (4,070 B.C.)	Dalley letter

TABLE 6.8 (Continued)

Site	Sample number	Date	Reference
Hogup Cave	GX–1288	5,795 ± 160 (3,845 B.C.)	Dalley letter
Hogup Cave	GaK–1567	5,960 ± 100 (4,010 B.C.)	Dalley letter
Hogup Cave	GaK–1563	6,400 (4,450 B.C.)	Dalley letter
Hogup Cave	GaK–2048	6,190 ± 110 (4,240 B.C.)	Dalley letter
Hogup Cave	GaK–1568	4,610 ± 100 (2,660 B.C.)	Dalley letter
Hogup Cave	GaK–2076	4,490 ± 100 (2,540 B.C.)	Dalley letter
Thorne Cave	M–783	4,230 ± 250 (2,280 B.C.)	Dalley letter
Thorne Cave	W–1395	4,170 ± 250 (2,220 B.C.)	Dalley letter
Spotten Cave	I–3363	4,200 ± 120 (2,250 B.C.)	Dalley letter
Spotten Cave	I–3362	4,640 ± 120 (2,690 B.C.)	Dalley letter
Spotten Cave	I–4484	5,580 ± 120 (3,630 B.C.)	Dalley letter

Cave in Idaho (Sadek-Kooros 1972), although no data on associated cultural materials have yet been published.

Period II (Table 6.8) lists radiocarbon dates ranging in age from 5000 to 2000 B.C. This period roughly approximates the span of the hypothesized Altithermal, and encompasses much of the "Desert Archaic" or "Great Basin Archaic" (Shutler 1968). There are fewer dates for this period from southeastern Oregon caves than in Period I; the Mazama eruption occurred in this region during the early part of Period II, and probably caused some alteration in the settlement pattern. These alterations may have been further aggravated by climatic changes associated with the Altithermal temperature age. Bedwell (1970) believes that there was no water near the cave sites during this time, and that settlement shifted to lake or marsh margin sites. Later in Period II, around 3000 B.C., occupation at these southeastern Oregon caves was resumed.

There are abundant Period II dates from Nevada sites and from several sites in western Utah. Lovelock Cave was first occupied during the latter part of Period II (I-3692, I-4673, and I-4633, for example), while the last series of occupations at Danger Cave (D III-V) also take place during this period.

TABLE 6.9

Period III (2,000–1 B.C.)

Site	Sample number	Date	Reference
Oregon			
7-Mile Ridge	GaK–1747	2,250 ± 100 (300 B.C.)	Bedwell 1970
Connley Cave No. 3	GaK–2144	3,080 ± 140 (1,130 B.C.)	Bedwell 1970
Connley Cave No. 4	GaK–1740	3,420 ± 140 (1,470 B.C.)	Bedwell 1970
Connley Cave No. 4A	GaK–2137	3,140 ± 80 (1,190 B.C.)	Bedwell 1970
Connley Cave No. 4A	GaK–2138	3,730 ± 90 (1,780 B.C.)	Bedwell 1970
Connley Cave No. 5A	GaK–2133	3,330 ± 110 (1,380 B.C.)	Bedwell 1970
Connley Cave No. 6	GaK–2130	3,720 ± 270 (1,770 B.C.)	Bedwell 1970
Table Rock Cave No. 2	GaK–1750	3,068 ± 420 (1,118 B.C.)	Bedwell 1970
California			
Rose Spring	UCLA–1093A	2,240 ± 145 (290 B.C.)	Clewlow *et al.* 1970
Rose Spring	UCLA–1093B	2,900 ± 80 (950 B.C.)	Clewlow *et al.* 1970
Rose Spring	UCLA–1093C	3,520 ± 80 (1,570 B.C.)	Clewlow *et al.* 1970
Rose Spring	UCLA–1093D	3,580 ± 80 (1,630 B.C.)	Clewlow *et al.* 1970
Rose Spring	UCLA–1093E	3,900 ± 180 (1,950 B.C.)	Clewlow *et al.* 1970
Crane Flat	UCLA–278	2,040 ± 100 (90 B.C.)	E. Davis 1964:257
Bare Creek Ranch	I–2007	2,130 ± 105 (180 B.C.)	*Radiocarbon* 1968:278
Rodriguez	I–3209	2,150 ± 100 (200 B.C.)	*Radiocarbon* 1969:76–77
Rodriguez	UCLA–1222	2,620 ± 80 (670 B.C.)	O'Connell and Ambro 1968
King's Dog	UCLA–1732	3,000 ± 80 (1,050 B.C.)	O'Connell and Ericson n.d.
Karlo	LJ–76	2,350 ± 150 (400 B.C.)	Riddell 1960:91
Nevada			
Stuart Rockshelter	M–377	3,870 ± 250 (1,920 B.C.)	Shutler *et al.* 1960
Gypsum Cave (sticks)	UCLA–1069	2,400 ± 60 (450 B.C.)	Berger and Libby 1967:479–480

TABLE 6.9 (Continued)

Site	Sample number	Date	Reference
Gypsum Cave (atlatl dart shaft)	UCLA–1223	2,900 ± 80 (950 B.C.)	Berger and Libby 1967:479–480
Deer Creek Cave	I–1030	2,640 ± 140 (690 B.C.)	Shutler and Shutler 1963
Deer Creek Cave	I–1032	2,585 ± 150 (635 B.C.)	Shutler and Shutler 1963
Conaway Shelter	RL–39	2,050 ± 110 (100 B.C.)	Fowler letter (see also *Radiocarbon* 1971:75)
Conaway Shelter	RL–40	2,090 ± 100 (140 B.C.)	Fowler letter (see also *Radiocarbon* 1971:75)
Conaway Shelter	RL–41	1,980 ± 110 (30 B.C.)	Fowler letter (see also *Radiocarbon* 1971:75)
O'Malley Shelter	RL–44	2,970 ± 100 (1,020 B.C.)	Fowler letter (see also *Radiocarbon* 1971:75)
O'Malley Shelter	RL–93	3,740 ± 170 (1,790 B.C.)	Fowler letter (see also *Radiocarbon* 1971:75)
O'Malley Shelter	RL–45	3,940 ± 120 (1,990 B.C.)	Fowler letter (see also *Radiocarbon* 1971:75)
O'Malley Shelter	RL–106	3,290 ± 170 (1,970 B.C.)	Fowler letter (see also *Radiocarbon* 1971:75)
Thompson Site (Steamboat Springs)	TX–1391	3,480 ± 110 (1,530 B.C.)	Elston and Davis 1972
Hidden Cave	L–289BB	3,050 ± 200 (1,100 B.C.)	*Radiocarbon* 1967:478
Humboldt Cave	C–587	1,953 ± 175 (3 B.C.)	Grosscup 1958
Crypt Cave	L–289II	2,400 ± 200 (450 B.C.)	Grosscup 1958
Guano Cave	L–356B	3,200 ± 130 (1,250 B.C.)	Grosscup 1958
NV-Ch 15	M–649	2,690 ± 250 (740 B.C.)	Grosscup 1958
Lovelock Cave	C–276	2,481 ± 260 (531 B.C.)	Heizer and Napton 1970a:Table 4
Lovelock Cave	I–4630	2,610 ± 120 (660 B.C.)	Heizer and Napton 1970a:Table 4
Lovelock Cave	C–735	3,168 ± 260 (1,218 B.C.)	Heizer and Napton 1970a:Table 4
Lovelock Cave	I–4758	3,370 ± 100 (1,420 B.C.)	Heizer and Napton 1970a: Table 4

TABLE 6.9 (Continued)

Site	Sample number	Date	Reference
Lovelock Cave	UCLA–1459C	3,400 ± 80 (1,450 B.C.)	Heizer and Napton 1970a:Table 4
NV Do 1	GaK–3358	3,720 ± 100 (1,770 B.C.)	Tuohy letter
Kramer Cave	UCLA–122	3,720 ± 100 (1,770 B.C.)	*Radiocarbon* 1962:114
Spooner Lake	I–1999	2,960 ± 195 (1,010 B.C.)	Elston 1971
Spooner Lake	I–1998	3,050 ± 105 (1,110 B.C.)	Elston 1971
Wagon Jack Shelter	LJ–203	2,930 ± 200 (980 B.C.)	Clewlow *et al.* 1970 (and *Radiocarbon* 1967:478)
South Fork Rockshelter	LJ–212	3,320 ± 200 (1,370 B.C.)	Heizer *et al.* 1968
Newark Cave	WSU–538	2,035 ± 315 (85 B.C.)	Fowler 1968
Chimney Cave (dessicated human burial)	UCLA–689	2,500 ± 80 (550 B.C.)	*Radiocarbon* 1965:337
Chimney Cave (dessicated human burial)	UCLA–690	2,510 ± 80 (560 B.C.)	*Radiocarbon* 1965:337
Chimney Cave (dessicated human burial)	UCLA–692	2,590 ± 80 (640 B.C.)	*Radiocarbon* 1965:337
Chimney Cave (matting with burial)	M–437	2,040 ± 250 (90 B.C.)	*Radiocarbon* 1965:337
Pintwater Cave	UCLA–752	3,255 ± 80 (1,305 B.C.)	*Radiocarbon* 1965:342
NV Wa 198 (Falcon Hill)	UCLA–904	2,175 ± 80 (225 B.C.)	*Radiocarbon* 1966:472
NV Wa 196	UCLA–905	3,660 ± 80 (1,710 B.C.)	*Radiocarbon* 1966:472
NV Wa 202	UCLA–931	3,325 ± 90 (1,375 B.C.)	*Radiocarbon* 1966:472
NV Wa 196	UCLA–932	3,745 ± 90 (1,795 B.C.)	*Radiocarbon* 1966:472
NV Wa 196	UCLA–976	3,620 ± 80 (1,670 B.C.)	*Radiocarbon* 1966:473
NV Wa 196	UCLA–979	3,660 ± 100 (1,710 B.C.)	*Radiocarbon* 1966:473
NV Wa 196	UCLA–980	3,760 ± 80 (1,180 B.C.)	*Radiocarbon* 1966:473
NV Wa 196	UCLA–983	3,850 ± 100 (1,900 B.C.)	*Radiocarbon* 1966:473
NV Wa 196	UCLA–984	3,700 ± 80 (1,750 B.C.)	*Radiocarbon* 1966:473
NV Wa 315	GaK–2805	3,270 ± 180 (1,320 B.C.)	Tuohy letter

TABLE 6.9 (Continued)

Site	Sample number	Date	Reference
NV Wa 404	GaK–2386	2,480 ± 120 (530 B.C.)	Tuohy letter
NV Wa 196	GaK–2387	3,830 ± 110 (1,880 B.C.)	Tuohy letter
NV Wa 275	GaK–2388	2,430 ± 100 (480 B.C.)	Tuohy letter
NV Wa 275	GaK–2390	2,140 ± 110 (190 B.C.)	Tuohy letter
NV Wa 525	GaK–3361	2,410 ± 90 (460 B.C.)	Tuohy letter
Gatecliff Cave	GaK–3618	3,690 ± 100 (1,740 B.C.)	D. Thomas letter
Gatecliff Cave	GaK–3615	3,140 ± 120 (1,190 B.C.)	D. Thomas letter
Gatecliff Cave	GaK–3617	2,280 ± 90 (330 B.C.)	D. Thomas letter
Utah			
Danger Cave IV	C–636	3,819 ± 160 (1,869 B.C.)	Libby 1955:120
Hogup Cave	GaK–1564	3,200 ± 140 (1,250 B.C.)	Dalley letter
Hogup Cave	GaK–2081	2,600 ± 100 (650 B.C.)	Dalley letter
Hogup Cave	GaK–2079	2,550 ± 70 (600 B.C.)	Dalley letter
Hogup Cave	GaK–1560	2,920 ± 80 (970 B.C.)	Dalley letter
Deluge Shelter	GX–0898	3,840 ± 210 (1,890 B.C.)	Dalley letter
Deluge Shelter	GX–0899	3,630 ± 85 (1,680 B.C.)	Dalley letter
Deluge Shelter	GX–0897	3,260 ± 120 (1,310 B.C.)	Dalley letter
Spotten Cave	I–3364	2,110 ± 100 (160 B.C.)	Dalley letter
Spotten Cave	I–3361	3,660 ± 110 (1,710 B.C.)	Dalley letter
Swallow Shelter	RL–109	2,630 ± 110 (680 B.C.)	Dalley letter
Swallow Shelter	RL–87	2,850 ± 100 (900 B.C.)	Dalley letter
Swallow Shelter	RL–110	3,500 ± 120 (1,550 B.C.)	Dalley letter
Rockshelter near Ferron, Utah	RL–131	3,070 ± 170 (1,120 B.C.)	Dalley letter

The Nevada dates cluster at two extremes—around 4700–4000 B.C. and 2700–2000 B.C.—leaving a hiatus of approximately 1200 years where there is no chronometrically documented human occupation. At Danger and Hogup caves, there is again a bimodal distribution of dates, with one series between 4875 and 4000 B.C. and a second between 3100 and 2000 B.C., a gap of almost 1000 years, roughly similar to that mentioned for Nevada. At Spotten Cave, there is a radiocarbon date of 3630 B.C. (I-4484), which falls in the middle of this apparent hiatus, though the other dates at this site and at Thorne Cave, Utah, cluster between 2300 and 2700 B.C. We do not venture a cultural or environmental explanation for the paucity of dates in the period between 4000 and 3000 B.C. in both Nevada and Utah, as we suspect that this apparent lacuna may be due merely to gaps in the radiocarbon sampling.

Period III covers the last two millennia of the pre-Christian era and roughly equates with the beginning of Antevs' Medithermal climatic episode. This is a period that saw new emphasis placed on lacustrine resources of the remnants of the pluvial lakes (for example, in the Humboldt Basin, and at Winnemucca Lake). In southeastern Oregon, there is a short suite of dates clustering around 1700–1100 B.C. All of these dates result from Bedwell's (1970) investigations in the Fort Rock Valley. In his research in this area, he did not deal extensively with cultural manifestations dating after 1000 B.C. (Bedwell 1970:217).

However, in southeastern and northeastern California (at sites like Rose Spring and Rodriguez), in Nevada, and in western Utah, there are a great number of radiocarbon dates for Period III. In western Nevada and northeastern California, most of these dates are attributable to occupations grouped in the Transitional and Late Lovelock phases. Key sites include Lovelock Cave (and the related open occupation site NV-Ch-15), Humboldt Cave, and a plethora of sites on Winnemucca Lake. The earliest dated occupation in central Nevada is recorded at Gatecliff Cave (GaK-3613).

It is during this period that some Great Basin specialists believe that the bow and arrow was introduced (cf. Davis 1966; Grosscup 1960). Grosscup's estimates were merely guess dates based on the stratigraphic sequence at Lovelock Cave as known at the time of his study. However, Aikens (1970) has radiocarbon dates from Hogup Cave, Utah, which seem to indicate a much earlier introduction of the bow and arrow, at sometime around 1250 B.C. This hypothesis is based on the appearance of Rose Spring and Eastgate points at this time. These data are in conflict with a sizable group of radiocarbon dates from the Western Great Basin linked to the Eastgate and Rose Spring series, and indicating their introduction after A.D. 500 (Hester 1973). Thus, we are of the opinion that the bow and arrow was probably not introduced into the Basin until sometime in the early centuries of the Christian era. Aikens (1976) has provided a detailed discussion of this problem, particularly as it relates to the Eastern Basin.

In Table 6.10 we have listed radiocarbon dates for the period between A.D.

TABLE 6.10

Period IV (1 A.D.–present)

Site	Sample number	Date	Reference
Oregon			
Catlow Cave No. 1	C–430	959 ± 150 (A.D. 991)	Heizer 1951b
7-Mile Ridge	GaK–1746	1,060 ± 80 (A.D. 890)	Bedwell 1970
Idaho			
Wilson Butte Cave	M–1088	425 ± 150 (A.D. 1535)	Gruhn 1961:37
California			
"Moon Mountain Phase" (Lowland Patayan)	?	450 ± 200 (A.D. 1,500)	Harner 1958
"Moon Mountain Phase" (Lowland Patayan)	?	130 ± 200 (A.D. 1,820)	Harner 1958
"Moon Mountain Phase" (Lowland Patayan)	?	120 ± 200 (A.D. 1,830)	Harner 1958
Crane Flat	UCLA–276	950 ± 70 (A.D. 1,000)	E. Davis 1964:257
Crane Flat	UCLA–277	1,580 ± 80 (A.D. 370)	E. Davis 1964:257
Rodriguez	I–3208	1,050 ± 100 (A.D. 900)	O'Connell and Ambro 1968
King's Dog	GaK–2580	1,330 ± 90 (A.D. 620)	O'Connell 1971
Nevada			
Tule Springs (ceramic occupation)	UCLA–640	200 ± 80 (A.D. 1,750)	Haynes 1968:616
Tule Springs (ceramic occupation)	UCLA–635	570 ± 80 (A.D. 1,380)	Haynes 1968:616
Tule Springs (ceramic occupation)	UCLA–515	360 ± 120 (A.D. 1,590)	Haynes 1968:616
Tule Springs (ceramic occupation)	UCLA–516	725 ± 80 (A.D. 1,215)	Haynes 1968:616
Spooner Lake	I–2003	1,720 ± 100 (A.D. 230)	Elston 1971
Spooner Lake	I–1996	1,800 ± 100 (A.D. 150)	Elston 1971
Spooner Lake	I–1997	1,890 ± 100 (A.D. 60)	Elston 1971
Spooner Lake	I–1995	565 ± 120 (A.D. 1,385)	Elston 1971
Spooner Lake	I–2004	380 ± 0 (A.D. 1,570)	Elston 1971
Spooner Lake	I–2002	410 ± 95 (A.D. 1,540)	Elston 1971

TABLE 6.10 (Continued)

Site	Sample number	Date	Reference
Daphne Creek (Jack's Valley)	I–2006	460 ± 0 (A.D. 1,490)	*Radiocarbon* 1968:280
Daphne Creek (Jack's Valley)	UCLA–1072	365 ± 135 (A.D. 1,585)	Elston 1971
Thompson (Steamboat Springs)	TX–1390	330 ± 60) (A.D. 1,620)	Elston and Davis 1972
Hesterlee (NV-Pe-67)	UCLA–1071D	320 ± 50 (A.D. 1,630)	Clewlow *et al.* 1970
Lovelock Cave	UCLA–1071E	145 ± 80 (A.D. 1,805)	Heizer and Napton 1970a:Table 4 (see also *Radiocarbon* 1967:479)
Lovelock Cave	I–4672	520 ± 95 (A.D. 1,430)	Heizer and Napton 1970a:Table 4 (see also *Radiocarbon* 1967:479)
Lovelock Cave	UCLA–1071F	1,210 ± 60 (A.D. 756)	Heizer and Napton 1970a:Table 4 (see also *Radiocarbon* 1967:479)
Lovelock Cave	I–3963	1,470 ± 90 (A.D. 480)	Heizer and Napton 1970a:Table 4 (see also *Radiocarbon* 1967:479)
Lovelock Cave	I–4629	1,510 ± 90 (A.D. 440)	Heizer and Napton 1970a:Table 4 (see also *Radiocarbon* 1967:479)
Lovelock Cave	UCLA–1418	1,600 ± 50 (A.D. 350)	Heizer and Napton 1970a:Table 4 (see also *Radiocarbon* 1967:479)
Lovelock Cave	UCLA–1459B	1,650 ± 60 (A.D. 300)	Heizer and Napton 1970a:Table 4 (see also *Radiocarbon* 1967:479)
Lovelock Cave	C–728, C–729 and C–730	1,672 ± 220 (A.D. 268)	Heizer and Napton 1970a:Table 4 (see also *Radiocarbon* 1967:479)
Lovelock Cave	UCLA–1459A	1,830 ± 60 (A.D. 120)	Heizer and Napton 1970a:Table 4 (see also *Radiocarbon* 1967:479)
Lovelock Cave	UCLA–1417	1,900 ± 60 (A.D. 50)	Heizer and Napton 1970a:Table 4 (see also *Radiocarbon* 1967:479)

TABLE 6.10 (Continued)

Site	Sample number	Date	Reference
Lovelock Cave	RL–48	1,440 ± 110 (A.D. 510)	Adovasio 1970:Table 3
NV Ch 15	UCLA–1071A	550 ± 60 (A.D. 1,400)	Clewlow *et al.* 1970
NV Wa 200 Falcon Hill	UCLA–124	1,860 ± 70 (A.D. 90)	*Radiocarbon* 1963:7
Falcon Hill	UCLA–677	580 ± 80 (A.D. 1,370)	Rozaire 1969
Falcon Hill	UCLA–906	1,240 ± 80 (A.D. 710)	*Radiocarbon* 1966:472
NV Wa 198	UCLA–933	1,725 ± 20 (A.D. 225)	*Radiocarbon* 1966:473
NV Wa 205	UCLA–982	390 ± 80 (A.D. 1,560)	*Radiocarbon* 1966:473
NV Wa 205	UCLA–985	400 ± 80 (A.D. 1,550)	*Radiocarbon* 1966:474
NV Wa 198	UCLA–986	595 ± 80 (A.D. 1,395)	*Radiocarbon* 1966:474
NV Wa 385	GaK–2806	1,830 ± 90 (A.D. 120)	Tuohy letter
NV Wa 528	GaK–2809	1,340 ± 100 (A.D. 610)	Tuohy letter
NV Wa 729T	GaK–2810	620 ± 80 (A.D. 1,330)	Tuohy letter
NV Wa 1016	I–2846	1,820 ± 180 (A.D. 130)	Tuohy and Stein 1969
NV Wa 291	GaK–2804	1,950 ± 100 (A.D. 0)	Tuohy letter
NV Wa 372C	GaK–2385	380 ± 100 (A.D. 1,570)	Tuohy letter
NV Wa 355	GaK–2389	240 ± 100 (A.D. 1,710)	Tuohy letter
NV Ch 162 (Hanging Rock Cave)	GaK–2391	1,730 ± 90 (A.D. 220)	Tuohy letter
NV Nye 251	GaK–3359	80 ± 0 (A.D. 1,870)	Tuohy letter
NV Pe 00	GaK–3360	910 ± 80 (A.D. 1,040)	Tuohy letter
NV Do 37	UCLA–1072	365 ± 135 (A.D. 1,585)	*Radiocarbon* 1967:480
Newark Cave	WSU–464	1,760 ± 100 (A.D. 190)	Fowler 1968
Newark Cave	WSU–463	840 ± 340 (A.D. 1,110)	Fowler 1968
Deer Creek Cave	WSU–244	715 ± 140 (A.D. 1,235)	Shutler and Shutler 1963
Deer Creek Cave	WSU–245	1,150 ± 110 (A.D. 440)	Shutler and Shutler 1963

TABLE 6.10 (Continued)

Site	Sample number	Date	Reference
Scott	RL–47	970 ± 120 (A.D. 980)	Fowler letter (see also *Radiocarbon* 1971:74)
Conaway Shelter	RL–36	230 ± 100 (A.D. 1,720)	Fowler letter (see also *Radiocarbon* 1971:74)
Conaway Shelter	RL–37	1,050 ± 100 (A.D. 900)	Fowler letter (see also *Radiocarbon* 1971:74)
Conaway Shelter	RL–38	940 ± 100 (A.D. 1,010)	Fowler letter (see also *Radiocarbon* 1971:74)
O'Malley Shelter	RL–42	890 ± 100 (A.D. 1,060)	Fowler letter (see also *Radiocarbon* 1971:74)
O'Malley Shelter	RL–43	870 ± 100 (A.D. 1,080)	Fowler letter (see also *Radiocarbon* 1971:74)
Gatecliff Cave (Reveille Phase)	GaK–3609	2,020 ± 80 (A.D. 280)	D. Thomas letter
Gatecliff Cave (Reveille Phase)	GaK–3610	1,580 ± 90 (A.D. 370)	D. Thomas letter
Gatecliff Cave (Underdown Phase)	GaK–3608	1,000 ± 90 (A.D. 950)	D. Thomas letter
Gatecliff Cave (Yankee Blade Phase)	GaK–3606	750 ± 90 (A.D. 1,200)	D. Thomas letter
Gatecliff Cave (Yankee Blade Phase)	GaK–3607	590 ± 90 (A.D. 1,360)	D. Thomas letter
Gatecliff Cave (Yankee Blade Phase)	GaK–3614	550 ± 90 (A.D. 1,400)	D. Thomas letter
Gatecliff Cave (Yankee Blade Phase)	GaK–3613	470 ± 90 (A.D. 1,480)	D. Thomas letter
Utah			
Danger Cave V	C–635	1,930 ± 240 (A.D. 20)	Libby 1955:120
Deluge Shelter	GX–0896	1,625 ± 95 (A.D. 325)	Dalley letter
Deluge Shelter	GX–0895	1,215 ± 85 (A.D. 735)	Dalley letter
Deluge Shelter	GX–0894	1,030 ± 85 (A.D. 920)	Dalley letter
Hogup Cave	GaK–1561	1,530 ± 80 (A.D. 420)	Dalley letter
Hogup Cave	GaK–2078	1,210 ± 100 (A.D. 740)	Dalley letter
Hogup Cave	GaK–2080	620 ± 100 (A.D. 1,330)	Dalley letter

TABLE 6.10 (Continued)

Site	Sample number	Date	Reference
Promontory Cave	GaK–1579	1,310 ± 70 (A.D. 640)	Dalley letter
Promontory Cave	GaK–1578	320 ± 80 (A.D. 1,630)	Dalley letter
Promontory Cave	GX–0551	850 ± 75 (A.D. 1,110)	Dalley letter
Spotten Cave	I–3359	730 ± 90 (A.D. 1,220)	Dalley letter
Spotten Cave	I–3358	1,310 ± 90 (A.D. 640)	Dalley letter
Swallow Shelter	RL–108	1,120 ± 100 (A.D. 830)	Dalley letter

1 and the present. During this period, Desert Archaic and, presumably, lacustrine adaptations continued; however, in parts of the Eastern Great Basin, new cultural elements were introduced. In southern Nevada, Puebloan or Anasazi architecture and ceramics appear and are cross-dated with similar Southwestern materials at between A.D. 500 and 1140 (the Virgin Branch of Shutler 1961a). These remains apparently represent an intrusion by Southwestern horticulturalists. Sometime after A.D. 1000, Southern Paiute peoples entered southern Nevada, probably represented by the series of dates at Tule Springs (UCLA-640, 635, 515, 516). In western Utah (and parts of bordering easternmost Nevada) we find evidence of the Fremont culture beginning roughly A.D. 700–1000.

We have been informed (G. Dalley, personal communication, 1972) that a full list of Fremont radiocarbon dates is to be published by J. P. Marwitt and G. Fry in a future issue of the journal *Southwestern Lore*. Other Fremont dates can be found in Madsen and Berry (1975).

Period IV also contains additional dates relevant to Late Lovelock culture occupations, particularly in the Humboldt Sink area, and there is a long series of dates from Winnemucca Lake. Many of the Winnemucca dates are quite late (ca. A.D. 1500) and undoubtedly represent protohistoric Northern Paiute occupations. Along the eastern fringes of the Sierra Nevada (at sites like Spooner Lake and Daphne Creek), we find Late Martis occupations early in Period IV (Elston 1971) subsequently replaced by the King's Beach Complex and finally by ethnographic Washo groups, perhaps represented by the late date of A.D. 1630 at the Thompson Site (Elston and Davis 1972).

Lexicostatistical data indicate that Numic speakers entered the Great Basin during this period, probably after A.D. 1000 (Miller, Tanner, and Foley 1971; see also Madsen 1975). In eastern and central Nevada, the advent of

TABLE 6.11

Geological Radiocarbon Dates from the Great Basin[a]

Site	Sample number	Date	Reference
Oregon			
Christmas Valley; shell sample; old beach line	GaK–1752	13,380 ± 230 (11,430 B.C.)	Bedwell 1970
Christmas Valley; caliche sample; overlies GaK–1752	GaK–1753	9,780 ± 220 (7,830 B.C.)	Bedwell 1970
Fort Rock Valley; caliche sample; late terrace	GaK–1754	2,840 ± 140 (890 B.C.)	Bedwell 1970
Near Crater Lake; Mazama ash	GaK–1124	7,010 ± 120 (5,050 B.C.)	Bedwell and Cressman 1971:10
Near Crater Lake; Mazama ash	TX–487	6,940 ± 120 (4,990 B.C.)	Bedwell and Cressman 1971:10
Mt. Mazama ash	C–247	6,453 ± 250 (4,503 B.C.)	Bedwell 1970
Mt. Mazama ash	W–858	6,650 ± 250 (4,700 B.C.)	Bedwell 1970
California			
Lake Mohave; on *Anodonta* shells between 925 and 930 foot level	LJ–200	9,640 ± 240 (7,690 B.C.)	Warren and DeCosta 1964
Lake Mohave; antedates "Lake Mohave complex"	Y–1585	13,620 ± 160 (11,670 B.C.)	*Radiocarbon* 1969:582–584
Lake Mohave; period of overflow	Y–1586	14,550 ± 140 (12,600 B.C.)	*Radiocarbon* 1969:582–584
Lake Mohave; period of overflow	Y–1587	15,350 ± 240 (13,400 B.C.)	*Radiocarbon* 1969:582–584
Lake Mohave; period of overflow	Y–1588	13,040 ± 120 (11,090 B.C.)	*Radiocarbon* 1969:582–584
Lake Mohave; early high level	Y–1589	13,290 ± 240 (11,340 B.C.)	*Radiocarbon* 1969:582–584
Lake Mohave; early high level	Y–1590	11,320 ± 120 (9,370 B.C.)	*Radiocarbon* 1969:582–584
Lake Mohave; late high stand	Y–1591	10,700 ± 100 (8,750 B.C.)	*Radiocarbon* 1969:582–584
Lake Mohave; late high stand	Y–1592	9,900 ± 100 (7,950 B.C.)	*Radiocarbon* 1969:582–584
Lake Mohave; late high stand	Y–1593	10,580 ± 100 (8,630 B.C.)	*Radiocarbon* 1969:582–584
Panamint Dry Lake; organic mat	UCLA–990	10,520 ± 140 (8,570 B.C.)	E. Davis 1967:345
Panamint Dry Lake; "environment date"	UCLA–989	10,020 ± 120 (8,070 B.C.)	E. Davis 1967:345
Pluvial Manix Lake; on tufa below the high stand shoreline	LJ–269	17,540 ± 400 (15,590 B.C.)	*Radiocarbon* 1962:227

TABLE 6.11 (Continued)

Site	Sample number	Date	Reference
Pluvial Manix Lake; on tufa below the high stand shoreline	UCLA–121	17,340 ± 400 (15,390 B.C.)	*Radiocarbon* 1962:113
Nevada			
Leonard Rockshelter; on shell; high stand of Lake Lahontan	UCLA–298	13,100 ± 100 (11,050 B.C.)	*Radiocarbon* 1964:328
Leonard Rockshelter; on bat guano at base of deposits	C–599	11,199 ± 570 (9,248 B.C.)	Libby 1955
Hidden Cave (tufa)	L–289AA	15,130 ± 400 (13,180 B.C.)	*Science* 126:1332
Dixie Valley; on tufa; last high stand of Dixie Lake	I–3269	11,560 ± 180 (9,610 B.C.)	*Radiocarbon* 1970:90
Dixie Valley; on tufa; last high stand of Dixie Lake	I–3270	11,560 ± 180 (9,750 B.C.)	*Radiocarbon* 1970:90
Boot Hill (Humboldt Sink); on tufa; near 4300′ elevation	L–364AA	9,500 ± 200 (7,550 B.C.)	Shutler 1961b
Boot Hill (Humboldt Sink); on tufa; near 4300′ elevation	L–289G	9,700 ± 200 (7,750 B.C.)	Shutler 1961b
Lovelock Cave; bat guano at base of occupation	C–278	6,004 ± 250 (4,054 B.C.)	Heizer and Napton 1970a:Table 4
Lovelock Cave (bat guano)	C–277	4,448 ± 250 (2,498 B.C.)	Heizer and Napton 1970a:Table 4

[a] We have listed in this table a select group of geological radiocarbon dates. There are many geological radiocarbon assays from the Great Basin region, but only a small percentage are directly applicable to archaeological problems, and it is these pertinent dates which are given here. For more extensive listings of geological radiocarbon dates from this region, see Broecker and Orr (1958) and Broecker and Kaufmann (1965).

these peoples may be represented by radiocarbon dates at Deer Creek Cave, Newark Cave, the Scott Site, Conaway Shelter, O'Malley Shelter, and Gatecliff Cave. These sites, as well as those like the Hesterlee Site in western Nevada (Cowan and Clewlow 1968) contain arrow points (Cottonwood and Desert Side-Notched series) and brownware ceramics attributable to Shoshone and Paiute groups.

In Table 6.11 we have provided a short list of geological radiocarbon dates for the Great Basin. There are many such dates for the Great Basin (cf. Broecker and Orr 1958; Broecker and Kaufman 1965), but few of these are directly applicable to archaeological problems. Of importance in Table 6.11 are dates indicating the time of the Mazama ash fall in Oregon (C-247;

W-858), dates purportedly linked to former high levels of Lake Mohave, and several dates, such as those at Leonard Rockshelter, Hidden Cave, and Lovelock Cave, that indicate basal dates for human occupation at these sites.

BIBLIOGRAPHY

Adovasio, J. M.
1970 The Origin, Development and Distribution of Western Archaic Textiles. *Tebiwa* **13**(2):1–40.

Aikens, C. M.
1970 Hogup Cave. *University of Utah Anthropological Papers* No. **93.**
1976 Cultural Hiatus in the Great Basin? *American Antiquity* **41**(4):543–550.

Baumhoff, M. A., and J. S. Byrne
1959 Desert Side-Notched Points as a Time Marker in California. *University of California Archaeological Survey Reports* **48:**32–65.

Bedwell, S. F.
1970 Prehistory and Environment of the Pluvial Fort Rock Lake Area of South Central Oregon. Unpublished Ph.D. dissertation, University of Oregon, Eugene.

Bedwell, S. F., and L. S. Cressman
1971 Fort Rock Report: Prehistory and Environment of the Pluvial Fort Rock Lake Area of South-Central Oregon. In Great Basin Anthropological Conference 1970, Selected Papers, edited by C. M. Aikens. *University of Oregon Anthropological Papers* **1:**1–26.

Bennyhoff, J. A.
1958 The Desert West: A Trial Correlation of Culture and Chronology. *University of California Archaeological Survey Reports* No. **42.**

Berger, R., and W. F. Libby
1967 UCLA Radiocarbon Dates VI. *Radiocarbon* **9:**479–480.

Broecker, W. S., and A. Kaufman
1965 Radiocarbon Chronology of Lake Lahontan and Lake Bonneville II, Great Basin. *Bulletin of the Geological Society of America* **76**(5):537–566.

Broecker, W. S., and P. C. Orr
1958 Radiocarbon Chronology of Lake Lahontan and Lake Bonneville. *Bulletin of the Geological Society of America* **69:**1009–1032.

Butler, B. R.
1961 The Old Cordilleran Culture in the Pacific Northwest. *Occasional Papers of the Idaho State University Museum* No. **5.**
1965 A Report on Investigations of an Early Man Site Near Lake Channel, Southern Idaho. *Tebiwa* **8:**1–21.
1970 A Surface Collection from Coyote Flat, Southeastern Oregon. *Tebiwa* **13**(1):34–58.

Campbell, E. W. C., and W. H. Campbell
1935 The Pinto Basin Site. *Southwest Museum Papers* No. **9.**
1940 A Folsom Complex in the Great Basin. *Masterkey* **14:**7–11.

Campbell, E. W. C., W. H. Campbell, E. Antevs, C. A. Amsden, J. A. Barbieri and F. D. Bode
1937 The Archaeology of Pleistocene Lake Mohave. *Southwest Museum Papers* No. **11.**

Clewlow, C. W., Jr.
1967 Time and Space Relations of Some Great Basin Projectile Point Types. *University of California Archaeological Survey Reports* **7:**19–27.
1968 Surface Archaeology of the Black Rock Desert, Nevada. *University of California Archaeological Survey Reports* **73:**1–94.

Clewlow, C. W. Jr., R. F. Heizer, and R. Berger
1970 An Assessment of Radiocarbon Dates for the Rose Spring Site (CA-Iny-372), Inyo County, California. *University of California Archaeological Research Facility Contributions* **7:**19–27.
Cowan, R. A.
1967 Lake-Margin Ecological Exploitation in the Great Basin as Demonstrated by an Analysis of Coprolites from Lovelock Cave, Nevada. *University of California Archaeological Survey Reports* **70:**21–35.
Cowan, R. A., and C. W. Clewlow, Jr.
1968 The Archaeology of Site NV-Pe-67. *University of California Archaeological Survey Reports* **73:**195–236.
Cowles, J.
1960 Cougar Mountain Cave in South Central Oregon. Privately printed, Rainer, Oregon.
Cressman, L. S.
1966 Man in Association with Extinct Fauna in the Great Basin. *American Antiquity* **31**(6):866–867.
Daugherty, R. D.
1956 Archaeology of the Lind Coulee Site, Washington. *Proceedings of the American Philosophical Society* **199**(3):223–278.
Davis, E. L.
1964 An Archaeological Survey of the Mono Lake Basin and Excavation of Two Rockshelters, Mono County, California. *University of California, Los Angeles, Archaeological Survey Annual Report for 1963–1964,* 251–392.
1967 Man and Water at Pleistocene Lake Mohave. *American Antiquity* **32**(3):345–353.
1970 Archaeology of the North Basin of Panamint Valley, Inyo County, California. *Nevada State Museum Anthropological Papers* **15:**83–142.
Davis, E. L., and R. Shutler, Jr.
1969 Recent Discoveries of Fluted Points in California and Nevada. *Nevada State Museum Anthropological Papers* **14:**154–178 (with an appendix by D. R. Tuohy).
Davis, W. A.
1966 Theoretical Problems in Western Prehistory. Current Status of Anthropological Research in the Great Basin: 1964. *Desert Research Institute Technical Report* Series S-H:147–165.
Delisio, M. P.
1971 Preliminary Report on the Weston Canyon Rockshelter, Southeastern Idaho: A Big Game Hunting Site in the Northern Great Basin. In Great Basin Anthropological Conference 1970, Selected Papers, edited by C. M. Aikens. *University of Oregon Anthropological Papers* **1:**43–57.
Elston, R. G.
1971 A Contribution to Washo Archaeology. *Nevada Archaeological Survey Research Paper* No. **2.**
Elston, R., and J. Davis
1972 An Archaeological Investigation of the Steamboat Springs Locality, Washoe County, Nevada. *Nevada Archaeological Survey Reporter* **6**(1):9–14.
Fagan, J. L.
1975 A Supposed Fluted Point from Fort Rock Cave, an Error of Identification, and Its Consequences. *American Antiquity* **40**(3):356–357.
Fowler, D. D.
1968 The Archaeology of Newark Cave, White Pine County, Nevada. *Desert Research Institute Technical Report* Series S-H, *Publication* No. **3.**
Fry, G. F.
1970 Preliminary Analysis of the Hogup Cave Coprolites. In *Hogup Cave,* edited by C. M. Aikens. *University of Utah Anthropological Papers* **93:**247–250.

Fry, G. F., and J. M. Adovasio

1970 Population Differentiation in Hogup and Danger Caves, Two Archaic Sites in the Eastern Great Basin. *Nevada State Museum Anthropological Papers* **15:**207–215.

Grant, C., J. W. Baird, and J. K. Pringle

1968 *Rock Drawings of the Coso Range*. China Lake, California: Maturango Press.

Green, J. P.

1972 McKean in the Northern Great Basin. Paper presented at the 25th Northwest Anthropological Conference, Portland, Oregon.

Grosscup, G. L.

1957 A Bibliography of Nevada Archaeology. *University of California Archeological Survey Reports* No. **36.**

1958 Radiocarbon Dates from Nevada of Archaeological Interest. *University of California Archaeological Survey Reports* **44:**17–31.

1960 The Culture History of Lovelock Cave, Nevada. *University of California Archaeological Survey Reports* No. **52.**

Gruhn, R.

1961 The Archaeology of Wilson Butte Cave, South-Central Idaho. *Occasional Papers, Idaho State College,* No. **6.**

1965 Two Early Radiocarbon Dates from the Lower Levels of Wilson Butte Cave, South-Central Idaho. *Tebiwa* **8**(2):57.

Harner, M. J.

1958 Lowland Patayan Phases in the Lower Colorado River Valley and Colorado Desert. *University of California Archaeological Survey Reports* **42:**93–97.

Harrington, M. R.

1928 Tracing the Pueblo Boundary in Nevada. *Indian Notes, Museum of the American Indian, Heye Foundation* **5**(2):235–240.

1933 Gypsum Cave, Nevada. *Southwest Museum Papers* No. **8.**

1957 A Pinto Site at Little Lake, California. *Southwest Museum Papers* No. **17.**

Harrington, M. R., and R. D. Simpson

1961 Tule Springs, Nevada, with Other Evidence of Pleistocene Man in North America. *Southwest Museum Papers* No. **18.**

Haynes, C. V., Jr.

1968 Geochronology of Late-Quarternary Alluvium. In Means of Correlation of Quarternary Successions. *Congress of the International Association for Quarternary Research* 8, *Proceedings* **7:**591–631.

Heizer, R. F.

1951a An Assessment of Certain Nevada, California and Oregon Radiocarbon Dates. *Society for American Archaeology Memoirs* **8:**23–25.

1951b The Sickle in Aboriginal Western North America. *American Antiquity* **16**(3):247–252.

Heizer, R. F., and M. A. Baumhoff

1959 Great Basin Petroglyphs and Prehistoric Game Trails. *Science* **129**(3353):904–905.

1961 The Archaeology of Two Sites at Eastgate, Churchill County, Nevada. I. Wagon Jack Shelter. *University of California Anthropological Records* No. **20**(4).

1962 *Prehistoric Rock Art of Nevada and Eastern California*. Berkeley: University of California Press.

1970 Big Game Hunters in the Great Basin: A Critical Review of the Evidence. *University of California Archaeological Research Facility Contributions* **7:**1–12.

Heizer, R. F., M. A. Baumhoff, and C. W. Clewlow, Jr.

1968 Archaeology of South Fork Shelter (NV-E1-11), Elko County, Nevada. *University of California Archaeological Survey Reports* **71:**1–58.

Heizer, R. F., and R. Berger

1970 Radiocarbon Age of the Gypsum Culture. *University of California Archaeological Research Facility Contributions* **7:**13–18.

Heizer, R. F., and C. W. Clewlow, Jr.
1968 Projectile Points from Site NV-Ch-15, Churchill County, Nevada. *University of California Archaeological Survey Reports* **71**:59–101.

Heizer, R. F., and A. B. Elsasser
1953 Some Archaeological Sites and Cultures of the Central Sierra Nevada. *University of California Archaeological Survey Report* No. **21**.

Heizer, R. F., and A. D. Krieger
1956 The Archaeology of Humboldt Cave, Churchill County, Nevada. *University of California Publications in American Archaeology and Ethnology* No. **48**(1).

Heizer, R. F., and L. K. Napton
1969 Biological and Cultural Evidence from Prehistoric Human Coprolites. *Science* **165**:563–568.
1970a Archaeological Investigations in Lovelock Cave, Nevada. In Archaeology and the Prehistoric Great Basin Lacustrine Subsistence Regime as Seen from Lovelock Cave, Nevada. *University of California Archaeological Research Facility Contributions* **10**:1–86.
1970b Correspondence Concerning the Lovelock Cave Investigations by the University of California in 1912 and 1924, and Preparation of L. L. Loud's Final Report. In Archaeology and the Prehistoric Great Basin Lacustrine Subsistence Regime as Seen from Lovelock Cave, Nevada. *University of California Archaeological Research Facility Contributions* **10**:131–162.

Hester, T. R.
1970 Study of Wear Patterns on Hafted and Unhafted Knives from Two Nevada Caves. *University of California Archaeological Research Facility Contributions* **7**:44–54.
1973 Chronological Ordering of Great Basin Prehistory. *University of California Archaeological Research Facility Contributions* No. **17**.
1974 Archaeological Materials from Site NV-Wa-197, Western Nevada: Atlatl and Animal Skin Pouches. *University of California Archaeological Research Facility Contributions* **21**:1–36.
1977 Archaeological Materials from a Site in the Black Rock Desert of Northern Nevada. *University of California Archaeological Research Facility Contributions* **35**:1–16.

Hester, T. R., and L. M. Green
1972 A Functional Analysis of Large Stemmed Bifaces from San Saba County, Texas. *Texas Journal of Science* **24**:343–350.

Hester, T. R., and R. F. Heizer
1973 *Review and Discussion of Great Basin Projectile Points: Forms and Chronology*. Archaeological Research Facility, University of California, Berkeley.

Hester, T. R., and L. R. Jameson
1977 Evidence for the Early Occupation of the Washoe Lake Basin. *University of California Archaeological Research Facility Contributions* **35**:17–22.

Hubbs, C., G. S. Bien, and H. E. Suess
1963 La Jolla Natural Radiocarbon Dates III. *Radiocarbon* **5**:254–272.

Jennings, J. D.
1953 Danger Cave: A Progress Summary. *El Palacio* **60**:179–213.
1957 Danger Cave. *Society for American Archaeology Memoirs* **14** (also published as *University of Utah Anthropological Papers* No. **27**).
1964 The Desert West. In *Prehistoric Man in the New World,* edited by J. D. Jennings and E. Norbeck. Chicago: University of Chicago Press. Pp. 149–174.

Jennings, J. D., and E. Norbeck
1955 Great Basin Prehistory: A Review. *American Antiquity* **21**:1–11.

Judd, N. M.
1917a Evidence of Circular Kivas in Western Utah Ruins. *American Anthropologist* **19**(1):34–40.

1917b Notes on Certain Prehistoric Habitations in Western Utah. *Proceedings of the 19th International Congress of Americanists, 1915,* 119–124.
1919 Archaeological Investigations at Paragonah, Utah. *Smithsonian Miscellaneous Collections* No. **70**(3).
Kehoe, T. F.
1966 The Small Side-Notched Point System in the Northern Plains. *American Antiquity* **31**(6):872–841.
Krieger, A. D.
1960 Archaeological Typology in Theory and Practice. In *Men and Cultures,* edited by A. F. C. Wallace. Selected Papers of the 5th International Congress of Anthropological and Ethnological Sciences. Philadelphia: Univ. of Pennsylvania Press. Pp. 141–151.
Kroeber, A. L.
1939 Cultural and Natural Areas of Native North America. *University of California Publications in American Archaeology and Ethnology* No. **38.**
Kuhn, T. S.
1970 *The Structure of Scientific Revolutions.* 2nd ed. Chicago: University of Chicago Press.
Lanning, E. P.
1963 Archaeology of the Rose Spring Site INY-372. *University of California Publications in American Archaeology and Ethnology* **49**(3):237–336.
Layton, T. N.
1970 High Rock Archaeology: An Interpretation of the Prehistory of the Northwestern Great Basin. Unpublished Ph.D. dissertation, Harvard University, Cambridge.
Libby, W. F.
1955 *Radiocarbon Dating.* Chicago: University of Chicago Press.
Loud, L. L., and M. R. Harrington
1929 Lovelock Cave. *University of California Publications in American Archaeology and Ethnology* No. **25**(1).
Madsen, D. B.
1971 O'Malley Shelter. Unpublished M.A. thesis, University of Utah, Salt Lake City.
1975 Dating Paiute-Shoshoni Expansion in the Great Basin. *American Antiquity* **40**(1):82–85.
Madsen, D. B., and M. S. Berry
1975 A Reassessment of Northeastern Great Basin Prehistory. *American Antiquity* **40**(4):391–405.
Marwitt, J. P., G. F. Fry, and J. M. Adovasio
1971 Sandwich Shelter. In Great Basin Anthropological Conference 1970, Selected Papers, edited by C. M. Aikens. *University of Oregon Anthropological Papers* **1:**27–36.
Meighan, C. W.
1959 Varieties of Prehistoric Cultures in the Great Basin Region. *Masterkey* **33:**46–58.
Merriam, C. H.
1923 The Route of Jedediah S. Smith in 1826: Earliest Crossing of the Deserts of Utah and Nevada to Southern California. *California Historical Society Quarterly* **2**(3):228–236.
Mitchell, J. L., P. Rosa, S. Castagnetto, and T. R. Hester
1977 A Preliminary Statistical Analysis of Chipped Crescents from the Great Basin. *University of California Archaeological Research Facility Contributions* **35:**23–47.
Morss, N.
1931 The Ancient Culture of Fremont River in Utah. *Papers of the Peabody Museum of American Archaeology and Ethnology* **12**(3).
Napton, L. K.
1969 The Lacustrine Subsistence Pattern in the Desert West. *Kroeber Anthropological Society Papers, Special Publication* **2:**28–67.

O'Connell, J. F.
1967 Elko-Eared/Elko Corner-Notched Projectile Points as Time Markers in the Great Basin. *University of California Archaeological Survey Reports* **70:**129–140.
1971 The Archaeology and Cultural Ecology of Surprise Valley, Northeast California. Unpublished Ph.D. dissertation, University of California, Berkeley.
O'Connell, J. F., and R. D. Ambro
1968 A Preliminary Report on the Archaeology of the Rodriguez Site (CA-LAS-194), Lassen County, California. *University of California Archaeological Survey Reports* **73:**95–192.
O'Connell, J. F., and J. Ericson
n.d. Earth Lodges of Altithermal Age in the Northern Great Basin. Manuscript to appear in Nevada Archaeological Survey Research Series.
Riddell, F. A.
1960 The Archaeology of the Karlo Site (1as-7) California. *University of California Archaeological Survey Reports* No. **53.**
Riddell, H. S., Jr.
1951 The Archaeology of a Paiute Village Site in Owens Valley. *University of California Archaeological Survey Reports* **12:**14–28.
Rogers, M. J.
1939 Early Lithic Industries of the Lower Basin of the Colorado River and Adjacent Desert Areas. *San Diego Museum Papers* No. **3.**
Roust, N. L., and C. W. Clewlow, Jr.
1968 Projectile Points from Hidden Cave (NV-Ch-16), Churchill County, Nevada. *The University of California Archaeological Survey Reports* **71:**103–115.
Roust, N. L., and G. L. Grosscup
1957 Archaeology of Hidden Cave (NV-Ch-16), Nevada. Manuscript **171,** Archaeological Research Facility, Berkeley.
Rozaire, C. E.
1963 Lake-Side Cultural Specializations in the Great Basin. 1962 Great Basin Anthropological Conference. *Nevada State Museum Anthropological Papers* **9:**72–77.
1969 The Chronology of the Woven Materials from the Caves at Falcon Hill, Nevada. *Nevada State Museum Anthropological Papers* **14:**180–186.
Sadek-Kooros, H.
1972 The Sediments and Fauna of Jaguar Cave. I. The Sediments. *Tebiwa* **15**(1):1–20.
Shutler, D., Jr., M. E. Shutler, and J. S. Griffith
1960 Stuart Rockshelter, a Stratified Site in Southern Nevada. *Nevada State Museum Anthropological Papers* No. **3.**
Shutler, M. E., and D. Shutler, Jr.
1959 Clovis-Like Points from Nevada. *Masterkey* **33:**30–32.
Shutler, M. E., and R. Shutler, Jr.
1963 Deer Creek Cave, Elko County, Nevada. *Nevada State Museum Anthropological Papers* No. **11.**
Shutler, R., Jr.
1961a Lost City, Pueblo Grande de Nevada. *Nevada State Museum Anthropological Papers* No. **5.**
1961b Correlation of Beach Terraces with Climatic Cycles of Pluvial Lake Lahontan. *Annals of the New York Academy of Sciences* **95:**513–520.
1968 The Great Basin Archaic. *Eastern New Mexico University Contributions in Anthropology* **1**(3):24–26.
Steward, J. H.
1940 Native Cultures of the Intermontane (Great Basin) Area. In Essays in Historical Anthropology of North America. *Smithsonia Miscellaneous Collections* **100:**445–502.

1954 Types of Types. *American Anthropologist* **56**(1):54–57.

Swanson, E. H., Jr.

1966 The Geographic Foundations of Desert Culture. In Current Status of Anthropological Research in the Great Basin 1964. *Desert Research Institute Technical Report* Series S-H: 137–146.

Tadlock, W. L.

1966 Certain Crescentic Stone Objects as a Time Marker in the Western United States. *American Antiquity* **31**(5):662–675.

Thomas, D. H.

1969 Great Basin Hunting Patterns: A Quantitative Method for Treating Faunal Remains. *American Antiquity* **34**(4):392–401.

1970 Archaeology's Operational Imperative: Great Basin Projectile Points as a Test Case. *University of California, Los Angeles, Archaeological Survey Annual Report* **12**:29–60.

1971a Prehistoric Subsistence-Settlement Patterns of the Reese River Valley, Central Nevada. Unpublished Ph.D. dissertation, University of California, Davis.

1971b Artiodactyls and Man in the Prehistoric Great Basin. *University of California, Davis, Archaeological Research Center Publication* **2**:201–281.

Tuohy, D. R.

1968 Some Early Lithic Sites in Western Nevada. In Early Man in Western North America, edited by C. Irwin-Williams. *Eastern New Mexico University Contributions in Anthropology* **1**(4):27–38.

1969 Breakage, Burin Facets, and the Probable Linkage Among Lake Mohave, Silver Lake, and Other Varieties of Paleo-Indian Projectile Points in the Desert West. *Nevada State Museum Anthropological Papers* **14**:132–152.

Tuohy, D. R., and M. C. Stein

1969 A Late Lovelock Shaman and His Grave Goods. *Nevada State Museum Anthropological Papers* **14**:96–130.

Warren, C. N.

1967 The San Dieguito Complex: A Review and Hypothesis. *American Antiquity* **32**(2):168–185.

Warren, C. N., and A. J. Ranere

1968 Outside Danger Cave: A View of Early Man in the Great Basin. In Early Man in Western North America, edited by C. Irwin-Williams. *Eastern New Mexico University Contributions in Anthropology* **1**(4):6–18.

Warren, C. N., and J. DeCosta

1964 Dating Lake Mohave Artifacts and Beaches. *American Antiquity* **30**(2):206–208.

Weide, M. L.

1968 Cultural Ecology of Lakeside Adaptation in the Western Great Basin. Unpublished Ph.D. dissertation, University of California, Los Angeles.

von Werlhof, J. C.

1965 Rock Art of Owens Valley, California. *University of California Archaeological Survey Reports* No. **65.**

Wheeler, R. P.

1952 A Note on the McKean Lanceolate Point. *Plains Archaeological Conference Newsletter* **4**(4):45–50.

Willey, G. R.

1966 *An Introduction to American Archaeology*. Vol. 1. *North and Middle America*. Englewood Cliffs, New Jersey: Prentice-Hall.

Williams, P. A., and R. I. Orlins

1963 The Corn Creek Dunes Site, a Dated Surface Site in Southern Nevada. *Nevada State Museum Anthropological Papers* No. **10.**

Wormington, H. M.
1957 Ancient Man in North America. *Denver Museum of Natural History Popular Series* No. **4.**

Zingg, R. W.
1939 A Reconstruction of Uto-Aztekan History. *Contributions to Ethnography: II, University of Denver.*

American Southwest

ARTHUR H. ROHN

I. INTRODUCTION

Historically, the American Southwest has been considered everything from an independent culture area to a mere marginal extension of Mesoamerican culture. Its combination of spectacular land forms, pleasing climate, and blatantly obvious archaeological remains have long attracted attention from both dilettantes and serious scholars. As a result, an extensive and complex body of published and unpublished "literature" has accumulated that threatens the patience of any prospective beginning student.

To its occupants and closest students, the Southwest presents a very diversified environment: from hot barren deserts to cool coniferous forests; from entrenched river valleys to a saltwater shoreline. Yet surprisingly, this very diversity produces a striking ecological homogeneity, especially when contrasted with other areas of North America. Most of the quite varied resources are accessible within short distances from any single point. Climatic features, vegetation zones, and faunal communities tend to be distributed according to elevation in this area of marked local relief. Thus one who lives there can usually pass through several distinct environments within a day's easy walk from home. Even varied mineralogical resources can be obtained from the extensive erosional exposures and widely scattered volcanic features.

The patterns of European exploration in the New World found the Southwest within Spain's sphere of influence. Explorers, missionaries, and colonists came from Mexico and contributed to a distinctively Southwestern blend of Native American, Spanish, Mexican, and ultimately Anglo-European culture. With the United States' acquisition of the Gadsden Purchase from Mexico in 1856, the Southwest was formally divided into two parts by an international boundary.

Active archaeological work in the Southwest began less than a century ago as the new Anglo-American explorers described in their journals, sketched, and photographed the still standing walls of long abandoned settlements, and recovered specimens of clothing, foodstuffs, and other normally perishable goods from dry caves. Museums and universities along the Atlantic seaboard and in Europe quickly recognized the informative potential of such remarkable preservation and instituted the equivalent of an extensive survey of the more spectacular archaeological remains.

The history of archaeological studies in the Southwest can perhaps be arranged in four broad stages (Rohn 1973). Early exploration began during the 1870s and lasted some 30 years. While some unabashed museum stocking occurred, most of these early studies preserved data that might easily have been totally lost. The first three decades of the twentieth century saw intensive data collecting in which agencies of the United States government played a significant role. The National Park Service and Smithsonian Institution's Bureau of American Ethnology both sent their own professional researchers and helped develop federal policy for nongovernment institutions to work on federally held lands.

While intensive data gathering and U.S. government involvement continue today, several sigificant developments began around 1930. Studies of early man in the New World received strong impetus from finds of man-made tools associated with the remains of extinct Pleistocene animals and from the welding of geologic–climatic studies to archaeology. Serious paleoecological investigations attempted to assess the environmental adaptations of various Prehistoric societies. The rapidly accumulating mass of data required the development of systems for organizing, comparing, and describing all these data.

All three of these courses contributed heavily to the development of chronological methods and culture historical sequences in the Southwest, both of which are the focus of this paper. Since World War II, comprehensive programs have been pursued in the Southwest to train students, to provide accessible exhibits-in-place, to salvage endangered resources, and to answer questions concerning population shifts, external relationships, resource management, and social history.

The international border formed an effective southern boundary to this evolution of Southwestern archaeological studies. Mexican archaeologists and foreigners who took the trouble to seek permission to work in Mexico concentrated their efforts on the high culture areas of central Mexico and Yucatan. Only a few southwesternists, such as J. C. Kelley (e.g., 1953), W. W. Taylor (1956), and C. C. DiPeso (1966, 1974), have pursued intensive studies in that part of the Southwest now under Mexican governance.

II. DEVELOPMENT OF CHRONOLOGICAL METHODS

Southwestern archaeology has benefited immeasurably from the applicability of many distinct chronological approaches to its historical problems. Although most of these approaches originated elsewhere, their application in the Southwest often led to useful refinements and offshoots.

A. Ethnohistory

Two fortunate circumstances have aided ethnohistory's application as a chronological tool in the Southwest. The Spanish missionaries and officials produced many documents describing their activities to bring about change among the aboriginal inhabitants. Virtually all culture–historical events following Coronado's expedition in 1540–1542 can be dated through ethnohistorical studies.

In addition, Southwestern native cultures—especially Pueblo—are perhaps the best preserved of any in North America. Their oral traditions contain considerable chronological information. Unfortunately, none of these peoples paid close attention to precise time measurement and accurate details, so only limited value has so far been realized from these sources.

The most effective use of ethnohistoric studies preceded the development of other chronological techniques. Adolf Bandelier synthesized documentary histories for the Zuñi and other Southwest Indian tribes prior to 1900 (Bandelier 1890a, 1892), and employed Rio Grande Pueblo legends to recreate the life and events just preceding the Spanish arrival (Bandelier 1890b). J. W. Fewkes attempted to write Hopi history from their oral traditions, but with very little success. However, several major excavation projects have employed ethnohistoric data as a primary dating tool: Kidder at Pecos 1915–1929 (Kidder 1924, 1958), Hodge at Hawikuh 1917–1923 (Smith *et al.* 1966), and Brew at Awatovi 1935–1939 (Montgomery *et al.* 1949). Recent land claims cases have revived interest in archival documents and oral literature alike, yet neither resource has been fully tapped even now.

B. Stratigraphy

The superposition of one set of archaeological materials upon another had long been recognized in Europe and the Near East as an indicator of relative antiquity even though exact dates were unobtainable. Richard Wetherill recognized this principle in the American Southwest perhaps before anyone else. In his 1893 expedition to Grand Gulch, Utah, he recorded burials with different physical characteristics and without pottery beneath the houses and graves of the pottery-making Cliff Dwellers (McNitt 1957:64–72). Wetherill lacked formal education beyond his boyhood schooling in Fort Leavenworth, Kansas, but he had read widely and benefited immensely from the prolonged visit of the young Swede Gustav Nordenskiold to the Wetherill Ranch in Mancos, Colorado, in 1891.

Three years following the pioneering work of Manuel Gamio in Mexico (Adams 1960), Nels C. Nelson introduced controlled stratigraphic excavating techniques in his 1914 work at the San Cristobal Site in the Galisteo Basin of New Mexico (Nelson 1916). Although inspired by the excavations of naturally stratified deposits in European caves and California shellmounds, he applied the principle of superposition to apparently homogeneous rubbish deposits by establishing uniform arbitrary stratigraphic levels. Like Gamio, Nelson excavated San Cristobal's refuse mound in standard levels and tabulated the changing proportions of ceramic styles from one level to the next (Woodbury 1960a,b).

In 1915, A. V. Kidder adopted Nelson's techniques at Pecos Pueblo. In the ruined buildings, Kidder traced the natural layers formed by construction, collapse, and intentional filling. At the same time he dissected some 26 feet of rubbish in standard arbitrary levels, producing a detailed seriation of ceramics cross-referenced into the successive occupations of the Pecos buildings (Kidder and Amsden 1931; Kidder and Shepard 1936). Over a span of some 10 fieldwork seasons at Pecos through 1929, Kidder shared his knowledge and methods with students and workers, who later employed them throughout the New World.

Stratigraphic excavation has become the standard *modus operandi* in Southwestern archaeology since Nelson's and Kidder's work (e.g., Beals *et al.* 1945). Unfortunately, however, some potentially important sites—notably caves (e.g., Martin *et al.* 1952)—have been excavated solely in arbitrary standard-thickness levels even though natural layers were discernible in at least a part of the deposits. In deep homogeneous refuse, though, Nelson's technique remains unsurpassed.

C. Geologic–Climatic Dating

Like stratigraphy, the dating of Prehistoric human events by association with geologic evidence for past climatic episodes had been practiced on Old World Paleolithic remains long before its entry into New World archaeology. Two Pleistocene geologists pioneered this technique in the Southwest, coming from two different directions.

As a geomorphologist, Kirk Bryan began analyzing recent channel erosion and sedimentation in the semiarid lands of Arizona and New Mexico during the early 1920s. He quickly recognized the relationships between these processes and archaeological data. Consequently, when man-made projectile points were found with extinct forms of bison at Folsom, New Mexico, in 1926, he launched geological studies to provide specific paleoclimatic contexts for the occupations at several Paleo-Indian sites. Among these were the Folsom Site (Bryan 1937), Sandia Cave (Bryan 1941), Ventana Cave (Haury *et al.* 1950), and Cerro Pedernal (Bryan 1939), although perhaps his most thorough study concerned the Lindenmeier Site (Bryan and Ray 1940).

Bryan also examined the geologic–climatic associations of much more recent Southwesterners. His study of Chaco Canyon, New Mexico, showed how a rapidly increasing Pueblo population probably accelerated erosional processes, thereby lowering levels of groundwater and perhaps leading to the canyon's eventual abandonment during the thirteenth century A.D. (Bryan 1954).

Ernst Antevs came from Sweden in 1921 as a student of the climatic events involved in the sporadic retreat of the last major Pleistocene glaciation (Wisconsin) in North America. He counted varves throughout New England and Canada and attempted "telecorrelations" with similar records in Scandinavia. Within a few years he was postulating correlations between the New England sequence and the record of "pluvial" activity in the Great Basin.

By the 1930s, Antevs too had begun to concentrate on the geological contexts for various Early Man sites. For a time, he and Bryan were consulted for their sometimes divergent interpretations concerning all major Southwestern sites of potentially great antiquity. Both men engaged directly in Early Man research—Bryan at the San José sites in New Mexico (Bryan and Toulouse 1943) and Antevs on the Cochise Culture of southeastern Arizona (Sayles and Antevs 1941). If anything, their differences inspired archaeologists toward more thorough collection of paleoclimatic evidence.

Besides his many collaborative accounts dealing with specific sites, Antevs formally outlined the procedures of geologic–climatic dating for archaeologists (Antevs 1955). He also divided post-Pleistocene climatic history in the Southwest into three major episodes based on relative temperature gradient (Antevs 1953). The Anathermal saw rising temperatures following the last minor glacial advance (Cochrane) to roughly 5500 B.C. The Altithermal was a time of warmer and drier conditions than present, marked by active water and wind erosion. From approximately 2500 B.C. until the present, the Medithermal involved gradually decreasing temperatures with more moisture.

Aside from the purely chronological value of this method, geological studies have become important standard increments to the archaeologist's reconstruction of past human environments. John T. Hack's study on "The Changing Physical Environment of the Hopi Indians of Arizona" (Hack 1942) during the late 1930s essentially set the standards to which others have generally aspired. Salvage archaeological projects in Glen Canyon and the Navajo Reservoir considered such studies a necessary part of the information to be recovered (Cooley 1958, 1959a,b; Schoenwetter and Eddy 1964). In recent years, C. Vance Haynes of the University of Arizona has assumed the role of successor to both Bryan and Antevs in Early Man studies.

D. Dendrochronology

The lone chronological technique developed exclusively in the Southwest is the analysis of annual growth rings in certain trees. Andrew Ellicott Douglass sought in tree-rings longer climatic records than those available at established weather stations. Astronomer Douglass sought possible correlations between sunspot activities and climatic episodes on Earth.The tree-rings could provide lengthy sequences of yearly precipitation, which could be analyzed for cyclical patterns matching the calculated cycles of sunspot activity.

In his search for older and older wood specimens, Douglass examined first historic Pueblo Indian buildings, then prehistoric ruins. He also perfected the process of cross-dating between separate specimens. Here were all the requirements for successfully dating the prehistoric sites in which suitable wood or charcoal specimens could be found.

Douglass began his tree-ring studies while at the Lowell Observatory in Flagstaff, Arizona. In 1906, he moved to the University of Arizona in Tucson (Anonymous 1962). His voracious collecting of wood samples produced two lengthy chronologies—one tied to the present with precise year dates for each ring, and one floating chronology for which only relative dates could be given. A dramatic moment occurred in 1929 when a beam unearthed at an archaeological site near Winslow, Arizona, bridged the gap between the two sequences and created a 1500-year continuous tree-ring calendar (Douglass 1929; Haury 1962).

The Laboratory of Tree-Ring Research was founded at the University of Arizona in 1938. It has continually provided tree-ring dates for archaeologists while supporting basic research in hydrology (e.g., Schulman 1956) and in tree growth and physiology (Fritts 1966). The tree-ring calendar now covers more than 2000 years for the northern Southwest, and dendrochronological studies have been initiated in Alaska, the Plains, and the Near East.

E. Geochronology

A direct outgrowth of geologic–climatic studies is the field of geochronology. In the Southwest, the University of Arizona became a confluence for several separate channels of chronological development. The interests of archaeologists E. W. Haury and E. B. Sayles sought collaboration with geologist Antevs, dendrochronologist Douglass, and paleontologist Lance, and encouraged the establishment of laboratories for palynology and radiocarbon dating.

A formal program was drawn together in 1957 with the establishment of the Geochronology Laboratory by Terah L. Smiley (1955, 1958). He has particularly encouraged the growth of palynology, paleoclimatic studies, and radiocarbon determinations, but the laboratory has especially helped to remove traditional disciplinary barriers to the application of chronological techniques to studies of both human prehistory and recent geological events.

Pollen studies have ranged over Late Pleistocene and post-Pleistocene times, adding useful paleoclimatic knowledge to Paleo-Indian and Cochise investigations. From this base, palynologist Paul S. Martin advanced his hypothesis that Paleo-Indian big-game hunters played a major role in exterminating North America's Late Pleistocene megafauna (Martin 1963, 1973).

Because of the efficacy of dendrochronology, radiocarbon dating has never become as important in the Southwest as in other areas. It has been employed in some regions where tree-ring records have been unavailable—such as the Southern Arizona Desert—and for ages beyond the range of dendrochronology—more than 2000 years old.

The first radiocarbon dates for the Southwest dealt with the Cochise sites Bat Cave, Tularosa Cave, Wet Leggett, and others (Libby 1952). Of greatest interest was the surprising early date of 3500 B.C. for domesticated maize in the Chiricahua Stage at Bat Cave (Dick 1965). Since then, radiocarbon determinations have been made for Early Man sites and for early stages of the Hohokam and Mogollon cultural traditions.

In recent years, archaeomagnetism has shown promise of becoming a significant dating tool for the Southwest. It has been largely refined by physicist Robert DuBois at the University of Oklahoma. Using baked earth samples from archaeological sites accurately dated by dendrochronology, DuBois has calculated the migration route of the north magnetic pole through most of the last 2000 years. Thus he has begun to produce some dates, especially in southern Arizona and the Colorado Plateau.

F. Typology

With the documentation of ceramic stylistic changes in stratified deposits in the Galisteo Basin and at Pecos, it was but one more step to arrange unrelated pottery collections in a stylistic order. Two ethnographers were the first to take this additional step. In 1915, A. L. Kroeber arranged surface collections from 15 sites at Zuñi, New Mexico, into a hypothetical sequence using three or four color and texture attributes (Kroeber 1916). The following year, Leslie Spier, working with Nels C. Nelson, combined shallow stratigraphic excavations with collections of sherds from the surfaces of trash mounds to construct a seriation of sites in the Zuñi region (Spier 1917).

As Spier described his method, he performed essentially a quantitative seriation. Both this technique and the stylistic approach of Kidder have continued in use up to the present time, but primarily in conjunction with other chronological methods. Thus they have rarely been separately presented as seriations. Amsden's design analysis of Hohokam pottery may be the most outstanding exception (Amsden 1936).

For example, both kinds of seriation have played significant roles in the growth of type classification so prominent in Southwestern archaeology. In fact, both Kidder and Spier describe and use pottery types. Other workers have described additional types for each region investigated (Hawley 1936). As the numbers of named types proliferated, Lyndon L. Hargrave and Harold S. Colton at the Museum of Northern Arizona in Flagstaff assumed the leadership for systematizing the process. In their "Handbook of Northern Arizona Pottery Wares" (Colton and Hargrave 1937), they included suggested standards for the naming, description, and use of pottery types. One major use was as time indicators in the same manner as index fossils. Colton, especially, continually refined the dated spans of pottery types through their association with tree-ring dated ruins. His systematic influence has helped make pottery styles perhaps the most widely used chronological tool in the Southwest.

Before retiring, Colton initiated the *Ceramic Series* (Colton 1955), a loose-leaf manual of pottery type descriptions designed for periodic revision as new knowledge accrues. In a sort of culmination of Colton's goals, David Breternitz further refined the chronological value of pottery styles from northern Arizona by reexamining all tree-ring dates associated with them (Breternitz 1966).

The major chronologies of the Southwest have been developed through a blend of type classification and seriation. From Neil Judd's lengthy excavations in Pueblo Bonito during the 1920s (Judd 1954, 1964), Frank H. H. Roberts, Jr. described a seriation of ceramic styles for the Chaco Canyon of New Mexico. Unfortunately, this study has never been published. Shortly afterward, however, Florence Hawley combined pottery type descriptions with newly devised tree-ring dates from the Chaco ruin of Chetro Ketl into a basic chronology (Hawley 1934).

In the Mimbres Valley of southwestern New Mexico, Wesley Bradfield's excavations at Cameron Creek Village produced the nucleus of a Mimbres ceramic and cultural chronology (Bradfield 1929) later refined by Haury (1936). Elsewhere in New Mexico, Harry P. Mera codified ceramics in the Rio Grande Valley (Mera 1935).

Certainly the most controversial chronology in the Southwest grew out of Gila Pueblo's lengthy excavation at Snaketown in southern Arizona. Emil W. Haury seriated the ceramics according to design, shape, and technological attributes. He then segmented the two continua of painted and plain pottery into types defined from attribute clusters. The correct order for both continua was determined from stratigraphic relationships, but the complete sequence of seven phases depended on the seriation (Haury, in Gladwin *et al.* 1937). No one disputed Haury's seriation, but several scholars have questioned the estimated absolute dates he assigned to the beginning of this Hohokam chronology (e.g., Bullard 1962).

Typological principles have been applied also to artifacts other than ceramics, although without extensive consequences. Both artifact types and attributes form a part of all Southwestern cultural classifications, whether they emphasize stages or phases. The stages of Cochise culture depend on recognized categories and proportions of grinding stones and projectile points. Major indicators of stage within the Pecos Classification include site arrangement and architectural style. Separate stylistic seriations have been described for grinding tools (Bartlett 1933), projectile points (Rohn 1977), sandals, clay figurines (Morss 1954), stone palettes, shell working, and basketry (Morris and Burgh 1941).

Archaeological typology in the Southwest has benefited greatly from the opportunities to associate absolute dates with artifact and cultural styles. Despite such opportunities, we are still unable to present a historical picture free from controversy over chronological interpretations.

III. DEVELOPMENT OF CHRONOLOGICAL UNIT LABELS

Cultural classifications developed along with the categorization of artifacts into type classifications and seriations. These were designed to encapsulate the rapidly growing body of descriptive and chronological data into usable historical outlines. Essentially, two kinds of chronological units have been recognized—stages and cultural phases.

Both unit concepts have continued in remarkably consistent use into the present; yet both have been modified. Each possesses a somewhat different utility. Concepts of "period," "industry," and "idealized marker trait" have seen little or no use. In recent years, the concept of "tradition" has helped translate the chronological outlines of stages or phases into narrative histories.

A. Stage Classifications

A "stage" describes any given set of economic, architectural, or technological practices in relation to other sets. Thus, Richard Wetherill's first separation of Basket Makers without houses from pottery-making Cliff Dwellers marked a crude observation of stages. Subsequently, A. V. Kidder and S. J. Guernsey tabulated the various cultural differences between the two from their explorations in Marsh Pass and Tsegi Canyon of northeastern Arizona (Kidder and Guernsey 1919). Their work of several seasons (see also Guernsey and Kidder 1921; Guernsey 1931) also recognized a "slab-house culture" and a "post basket-maker culture" as intermediates. Quickly the fieldwork of Earl Morris (1919, 1939), Frank Roberts (1929, 1930, 1931, 1932), Jesse Fewkes (1909, 1911), and Neil Judd (1930) around the Four Corners furnished so much new information that Kidder convened the first conference of Southwestern archaeologists at Pecos in the summer of 1927.

That first Pecos Conference initiated a series of informal annual gatherings at different locations each summer. It also produced a consensus on terminology and on a stage sequence for describing Puebloan culture history. The Pecos Classification (Kidder 1927) outlined eight numbered stages of culture change—Basket Maker I through III, followed by Pueblo I through V. Although descriptive refinements and absolute dates have been added, this system is still in use as an integrative framework for outlining some 2000 years of Pueblo Indian history (see chronology chart—Figure 7.1—and outline—Section IV).

There was a brief tendency to use the Pecos classificatory units as pure time periods once tree-ring dates could be associated with them. However, these same dates showed the stages did not exist everywhere on the Colorado Plateau at precisely the same time. Consequently, as a sequence of developmental stages for which reasonably accurate dates can be provided in different regions, the Pecos Classification has become a useful tool for analyzing diffusion patterns throughout the geographic area occupied by the Pueblos.

In an effort to avoid numbered units, Frank Roberts proposed a series of named stages (Roberts 1935). His terms relate to the Pecos Classification as follows:

Pecos	*Roberts*
Pueblo V	Historic Pueblo
Pueblo IV	Regressive Pueblo
Pueblo III	Classic Pueblo
Pueblo II }	Developmental Pueblo
Pueblo I }	
Basket Maker III	Modified Basket Maker
Basket Maker II	Basket Maker
Basket Maker I (hypothetical)	———

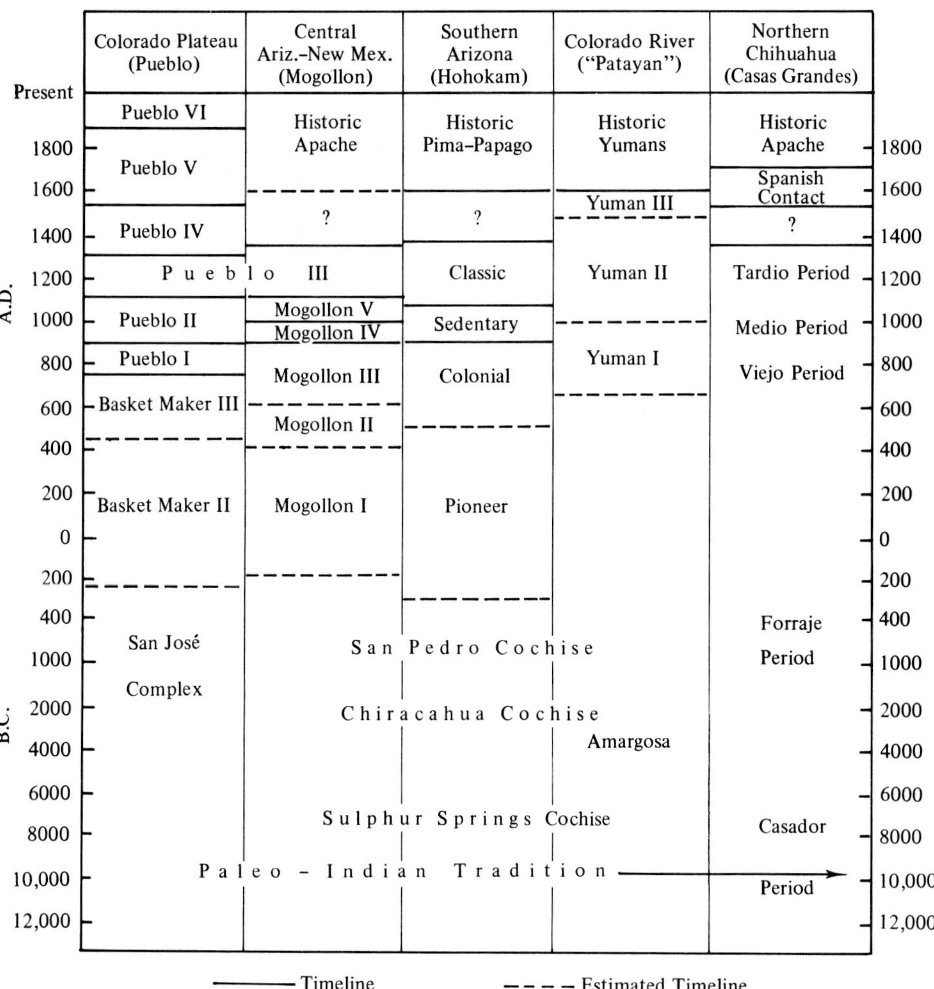

Figure 7.1. American Southwest: an outline of chronological units.

Robert's terminology is used by the National Park Service in exhibits and brochures in the National Parks and Monuments of the Southwest and by Wormington (1947) in her summary of Southwestern prehistory.

At first, the Pecos Classification was applied to the entire Southwest. But Harold S. Gladwin's systematic researches in southern Arizona led him not only to devise a different set of classificatory units—including the phase—but also to put forth a separate stage classification for the Hohokam cultural tradition. While he described detailed regional sequences—labeled *branches* in his "phase" classificatory scheme—as series of phases, he used the stage chronology as an integrative concept.

Gladwin published the Hohokam Chronology in the report of investigations at Snaketown (Gladwin *et al.* 1937), as four named stages—Pioneer, Colonial, Sedentary, and Classic. The names and basic descriptions remain intact, although E. W. Haury, Gladwin's protégé and successor, has provided additional insight from his reinvestigations at Snaketown.

Research at Mogollon sites in the mountains of New Mexico and Arizona resulted in numerous separate phase descriptions initially from every project. Consequently, in 1955, Joe Ben Wheat proposed a sequence of four numbered Mogollon stages broadly similar to parts of the Pecos Classification, but with finer divisions (Wheat 1955).

Elsewhere in the Southwest, distinct stage chronologies are lacking, although many regional phase sequences have been described. Charles DiPeso has presented a sequence of seven "periods" for the Casas Grandes Valley of Chihuahua that more closely resembles a nascent series of stages (DiPeso 1966). He further subdivides some periods into phases and links the periods together into four broader "horizons." Malcolm Rogers has proposed a similar skeletal outline for lower Colorado River prehistory (Rogers 1939, 1945).

One attempt has been made to synthesize all Southwestern prehistory in a series of 12 periods. In his book *Southwestern Archaeology,* John McGregor established a set of temporal units that cross cut the geography and cultures of the entire Southwest (McGregor 1941, 1965). These units are shown in Table 7.1. Unfortunately, McGregor's periods fail to account for differing cultural developments in different regions. He uses stagelike names, but adheres rather closely to temporal distribution when assigning cultural manifestations to the periods. Readers may compare this scheme with the chart presented in Figure 7.1, to test its utility. To my knowledge, no other Southwesternists have adopted McGregor's periods.

Table 7.1

McGregor's Classification of Southwestern Prehistory

Time	Period
	Modern
1900	
	Historic
1600	
	Culminant
1300	
	Classic
1100	
	Dissemination
900	
	Adjustment
700	
	Settlement
500	
	Founder
B.C./A.D.	
	Exploitation
200	
	Collector
5000	
	Hunter
10,000	
	Ancient

B. Phase Classification

While stages are useful integrative units, they do not facilitate detailed comparative analyses through both space and time. Harold Gladwin drew a model from the Biological world to propose several levels of cultural classificatory units (Gladwin and Gladwin 1934). Like assemblages from two or more nearby sites of the same age constituted a *phase*. Two or more sequential phases in the same geographic region represented a *branch*. Two or more branches combined into a *stem,* which emanated from a common *root* with one or more stems.

The Gladwins included both geographical and temporal criteria in their phase descriptions. At first, they placed greatest emphasis on architecture and ceramics in describing the formal content of phases. Later they added other cultural items, such as burial practices, stone artifacts, and the like. But Harold Colton (1939) formally proposed several modifications to Gladwin's system to make it more effective.

Colton adopted several concepts from the Midwestern Taxonomic System: *component* representing one occupation at a single site, and *focus* in place of Gladwin's phase. He also included as full descriptions of the cultural inventory as possible.

When Gordon Willey and Philip Phillips presented their codification of all New World prehistory (1958), they essentially followed Colton's usage for *component* and *phase* (preferring Gladwin's term over "focus"). Most active Southwestern archaeologists tend to follow this usage today; some also follow Willey and Phillips organization of geographic space—site, locality, region, area—whereas others continue to use Gladwin's term *branch* as a primarily geographic unit. The concepts of horizon, horizon style, tradition, and cotradition (Wheat 1954) have all been tried at one time or another. In general, these usages follow those suggested by Willey and Phillips and by the Society for American Archaeology Seminars in Archaeology (Wauchope 1956).

IV. PRESENT CHRONOLOGICAL UNITS

In this section, the preceding history is capped by an outline of our present knowledge of Southwestern culture history. I have made no attempt to present any new schema or to show alternative interpretations. Instead, I have chosen to reproduce the major stage sequences as a broad overview, avoiding the detail of local and regional phase sequences. More recent refinements and modifications of the originally defined stages are incorporated. A brief capsule description for each named or numbered unit follows, for the benefit of readers unfamiliar with Southwesten literature. (The outline is presented as a chronology chart in Figure 7.1.)

EARLY MAN AND ARCHAIC

Paleo-Indian Tradition (approx. 11,000–8000 B.C.): Primarily dependent on hunting large Pleistocene animals such as mammoth and bison. Represented by the Llano Complex (marked by Clovis and Sandia points) and the Lindenmeier Complex (marked by Folsom points). Many sites are kill and butchering locations; some appear to be revisited campsites.

Casador Period (approx. 11,000–8000 B.C.): The equivalent of a Paleo-Indian Tradition in northern Chihuahua, although positive remains are still scarce.

Amargosa (approx. 6000–400 B.C.): A hunting and gathering culture adapted to desert life, marked by distinctive atlatl dart points and a crude stone industry of choppers, scrapers, planes, and knives. Stone mortars and pestles are uncommon. Malcolm J. Rogers (in Haury *et al.* 1950) has postulated several subdivisions based on stylistic changes in the stone artifact classes.

Sulphur Springs Cochise (approx. 8000–4000 B.C.): The earliest stage of an economic pattern relying heavily on the gathering of wild plant products. Stone grinding tools predominate over projectile points in an otherwise nondescript artifact inventory. Open temporary campsites predominate.

Chiricahua Cochise (approx. 4000–1000 B.C.): A continuation of plant-gathering economy, although primitive pod corn appears about 3500 B.C. Stone grinding tools still predominate over projectile points of Pinto and Chiricahua styles. Some perishable materials have been found in numerous rock shelter sites.

San Pedro Cochise (1000–1 B.C.): The final stage of the Cochise plant-gathering tradition, perhaps ancestral to both the Hohokam and Mogollon cultural traditions. Purposefully shaped stone grinding tools outnumber San Pedro points. Natural rock shelters continued in use, although one open campsite contained simple house floors.

Forraje Period (approx. 8000 B.C.–?): Very poorly known hunting and gathering pattern, perhaps related to the Cochise.

San José Complex (approx. 4000–250 B.C.): A generalized hunting and gathering culture utilizing a simple stone technology and occupying temporary campsites. Several small point styles occur consistently in larger proportions than grinding stones. The terms *Basket Maker I* and *Archaic* have both been used at various times to describe this material and the closely related Concho and LaSal complexes.

COLORADO PLATEAU (PUEBLO)

Basket Maker II (est. 250 B.C.–A.D. 450): A mixed horticultural and hunting–gathering economy with positive evidence of maize and squash. Some built roughly circular houses in small clusters; others occupied natural rock shelters. In the absence of pottery, food products were stored in several styles of pits and carried in baskets. Dry conditions have preserved a sophisticated basketry and cord-weaving industry producing sandals, sashes, aprons, rabbit-fur robes, nets, tumpbands, bags, in addition to many forms of baskets. Wooden items include atlatls and darts, flexible cradles, throwing sticks, and clubs. Stone and bone technology produced dart points, atlatl weights, grinding tools, awls, scrapers, and jewelry. The dead were often buried, tightly flexed, in abandoned storage cists.

Basket Maker III (A.D. 450–750): Greater reliance on horticulture leading to sedentary villages of semisubterranean earth lodges and the first appearance of hard gray pottery. Additional new characteristics included beans, domestication of turkeys (for feathers, not meat), the bow and arrow, clay figurines, and turkey feather robes. The textile industry improved slightly. Stone tool styles changed, pottery appeared as funeral offerings with flexed inhumations. Stockaded villages and larger structures possibly designed for ceremonial use have been reported.

Pueblo I (A.D. 750–900): A stable economy, resulting in marked increases in population and technological changes. Former storage buildings and ramadas are enlarged into jacal- or adobe-walled living rooms arranged in contiguous groups; pithouses become wholly subterranean; ceramic vessels acquire new shapes and designs painted in black on a white slip or a distinctive banding around the neck; stone and bone tool styles change; cotton textiles appear, but basketry loses importance; stone axes become common; hard wooden cradles deform the crania of infants. Some large settlements house more than one hundred people and support sizable specialized ceremonial structures, or great kivas.

Pueblo II (A.D. 900–1100): Clusters of small, contiguous-room pueblos, built of stone masonry or jacal, each usually associated with one or more small circular underground kivas. Reservoirs, ditches, and check-dam systems are employed to conserve water and tillable soil. Distinctive corrugated cooking pottery appears as styles change in most aspects of material culture.

Pueblo III (A.D. 1100–1300): Settlements of large, multiroom, multistory stone masonry pueblos with many kivas, built in open valleys, at canyon heads, or in natural rock shelters. The largest settlements probably held 2000–2500 people and focused on a great kiva or a triwall structure. Water management systems diverted, transported, and stored water for domestic and irrigation uses. Domesticated turkeys appear in the diet and their bones in the tool kit. Most other aspects of material culture undergo further style changes. At the end of this stage, most of the San Juan drainage has been abandoned by Pueblo peoples.

Pueblo IV (A.D. 1300–1540): Relocation of Pueblo populations from the San Juan among their relatives in the northern Rio Grande Valley, around Zuñi, and along the south edge of Black Mesa. They continued to build large pueblos of stone and adobe brick, but with fewer small kivas, and usually arranged around a central plaza. Elaborate murals were painted on many kiva walls. In ceramics, coal was used to fire hard yellow and polychrome vessels on Black Mesa, glaze painting developed near Zuñi and spread to the Rio Grande, and corrugated vessels began to diminish. Other features of the culture changed in style only.

Pueblo V (A.D. 1540–1850): Contact and subjugation by Spanish expeditions from Mexico beginning in 1540. With the Spanish came new political domination; missionaries; many new agricultural products and animals; metal tools, weapons, and ornaments; majolica pottery; and many Mexican Indians with cultural ideas.

Pueblo VI (A.D. 1850–Present): The introduction of Anglo-American influences, wage work, and, finally, modern technology following acquisition of what is now Arizona and New Mexico by the United States in the mid-nineteenth century. Despite 400 years of enforced acculturation, the Pueblo Indians still retain much of their cultural heritage.

CENTRAL ARIZONA–NEW MEXICO (MOGOLLON)

Mogollon I (est. 200 B.C.–A.D. 400): Sedentary villages of simple wood-and-earth houses in pits, associated with a large ceremonial structure, storage pits, outside hearths, and flexed inhumations. Subsistence depended on cultivating maize, beans, and squash, in addition to hunting and gathering. Plain brown ware and red slipped pottery vessels were constructed by the paddle-and-anvil technique. An extensive industry in stone and bone included grinding stones, knives, scrapers, awls, jewelry, and tubular pipes. Sandals, baskets, matting, and fur robes were also made.

Mogollon II (est. A.D. 400–600): A continuation of the same cultural pattern, with minor changes in architectural styles and the appearance of broad red line decoration on pottery bowls. Smudging the interiors of some vessels black became common.

Mogollon III (est. A.D. 600–900): Further architectural style changes; narrow red line decoration on pottery vessels.

Mogollon IV (A.D. 900–1000): Larger villages of substantial pithouses. Red changing to black decoration is painted over a white slip on brown ceramic. Some culinary pottery shows banding or corrugation on the necks of vessels.

Mogollon V (A.D. 1000–1100): Small stone masonry pueblos, replacing pithouse villages, and brown corrugated utility pottery. These mark an intrusion of Pueblo characteristics into the

Mogollon Tradition. Subsequent developments parallel the Pueblo Tradition until abandonment of most of the Mogollon area by around 1350.

Historic Apache: The historic occupants of the former Mogollon territory since at least 1580, although they were not mentioned by Coronado in 1540. Apache culture of nomadic foraging is almost certainly not descended from sedentary horticultural Mogollon culture, but represents an intrusion.

SOUTHERN ARIZONA (HOHOKAM)

Pioneer Hohokam (est. 300 B.C.–A.D. 500): Earliest known agricultural economy in the Southern Arizona Desert. Apparently, sedentary villagers lived in wood and earth (jacal) houses set in shallow pits; cultivated maize, beans, and squash with the aid of irrigation ditches; manufactured brown and red pottery, some decorated with red designs and/or sets of exterior grooves; and practiced cremation of their dead. Stone and bone technology remained relatively simple. The first ball courts appear at the end of this stage.

Colonial Hohokam (est. A.D. 500–900): An intensification of Pioneer economic practices with a marked increase in population. The basic living pattern remains the same, although house styles and ceramics change. A buff slip forms the background for red painted vessels, many in effigy form. Stone technology produces elaborately carved vessels and palettes, jewelry, figures, ground axes, and delicate arrow points. Shell imported from the Gulf of California is carved into bracelets, pendants, and beads. Ball courts are a regular part of many villages where rubbish is collected in large heaps.

Sedentary Hohokam (A.D. 900–1100): A further elaboration of the Hohokam Tradition with easily identifiable style changes in most aspects of technology. Acid etching of shell and low platform substructure mounds appear; the presence of copper bells indicates a widening of already extensive trade networks.

Classic Hohokam (A.D. 1100–1350): Irrigation agriculture and population at their peak in this stage. New practices include construction of coursed adobe contiguous room houses—some multistory—within compounds, inhumation, black-on-white-on-red polychrome pottery, and the manufacture of shell mosaic pendants. Earlier Hohokam features, such as jacal houses in shallow pits, cremation, and red-on-buff pottery, continue.

Historic Pima–Papago (A.D. 1600–Present): Pima and Papago present in the same habitat, although a time gap intervenes. This suggests that they represent the ethnohistoric descendants of the Prehistoric Hohokam, even though many standard Hohokam practices are missing.

COLORADO RIVER ("PATAYAN")

Yuman I (est. A.D. 650–1000): Simple maize horticulture, jacal houses, trough metates, and paddle-and-anvil-made brown pottery in the first stage of a distinctive tradition extending into Historic times. Some of these characteristics appear to have existed earlier, but the evidence is incomplete.

Yuman II (est. A.D. 1000–1500): A continuation of the Yuman I pattern with changes in pottery vessel shapes, the addition of red-on-buff painted ceramics, and some style changes in stone artifacts and shell jewelry. Positive evidence for cremation occurs, although it may have been practiced much earlier.

Yuman III (est. A.D. 1500–1600): Population expansion to the Pacific Coast, resulting in exploitation of marine shellfish, in addition to horticulture and plentiful plant products. Leads directly into Historic Yuman-language tribes.

Historic Yumans (A.D. 1600–Present): The numerous tribes of the Lower Colorado River and southern California, speaking languages of the Yuman family. They are clearly the descendants of the Yuman Tradition.

NORTHERN CHIHUAHUA (CASAS GRANDES)

Viejo Period (?–est. A.D. 900): Small villages of shallow pithouses around a larger ceremonial structure. Some rock shelters were also used. Semiflexed inhumations, red-brown pottery decorated with red paint, and a presumed mixed subsistence of horticulture with hunting and gathering.

Medio Period (est. A.D. 900–1050): Single-story, contiguous-room pueblos with coursed adobe footings and walls, built around plazas with great kivas. An agricultural economy relied partly on a complex water system of irrigation ditches, besides domestic water ditches and subterranean drains. Polychrome ceramics make their appearance.

Tardio Period (est. A.D. 1050–1350): Large, multistory, coursed adobe house blocks arranged around plazas. Pyramidal platform mounds, ball courts, and market places in the larger settlements suggest a partly urban society with extensive trade. The largest city, Casas Grandes, may have held 5000 persons, some belonging to special artisan groups. Human sacrifice and the placing of secondary burials in large jars seem to have become new religious practices. Technology included fine polychrome ceramics and shell work. With the destruction of Casas Grandes about 1340, there is a gap in knowledge for this region.

Spanish Contact Period (A.D. 1540–1850): Initial contacts by the Spanish leading to colonization in the 1620s until Apache bands took control after 1684.

V. SUMMARY

The Southwest has benefited from the development of chronological techniques perhaps more than any other part of the world. Accurate absolute dating from dendrochronology has permitted precise cross-dating through typology. Radiocarbon and geologic–climatic dating not only provide dates for the earlier occupations but also help link culture history to past environmental change.

In spite of these favored developments and the great amount of work expended here, the Southwest is far from the proverbial "squeezed lemon." Many chronological and historical–genetic relationships are still unclear. Divergent interpretations are common. Some regions remain largely unknown. Now that sufficient precise descriptive data, accurately dated, have been assembled, we can realistically pose the broader and more significant questions regarding culture history: demographic changes, ecological responses, resource management, origins and dispersals, culture contact, and the like. A century of chronological studies has turned the American Southwest into one of the most promising laboratories for the study of cultural processes and change.

BIBLIOGRAPHY

Adams, R.E.
1960 Manuel Gamio and Stratigraphic Excavation. *American Antiquity* **26**(1):99.

Amsden, C.A.
1936 An Analysis of Hohokam Pottery Design. *Medallion Papers* No. **23.**

Anonymous
1962 Andrew Ellicott Douglass, 1867–1962. *Tree-Ring Bulletin* **24**(3–4):3–10.
Antevs, E.
1953 Geochronology of the Deglacial and Neothermal Ages. *Journal of Geology* **61**(3): 195–230.
1955 Geologic-Climatic Dating in the West. *American Antiquity* **20**(4):317–335.
Bandelier, A.F.
1890a Contributions to the History of the Southwestern Portion of the United States. *Papers of the Archaeological Institute of America, American Series* **V,** Peabody Museum of American Archaeology and Ethnology, Harvard University.
1890b *The Delight Makers*. New York: Dodd, Mead.
1892 An Outline of the Documentary History of the Zuñi Tribe. *A Journal of American Ethnology and Archaeology* **3:**1–115.
Bartlett, K.
1933 Pueblo Milling Stones of the Flagstaff Region and Their Relation to Others in the Southwest. *Museum of Northern Arizona Bulletin* No. **3.**
Beals, R.L., G.W. Brainerd, and W. Smith
1945 Archaeological Studies in Northeast Arizona. *University of California Publications in American Archaeology and Ethnology* **44**(1):1–236.
Bradfield, W.
1929 Cameron Creek Village. *School of American Research Monographs* No. **1.**
Breternitz, D.A.
1966 An Appraisal of Tree-Ring Dated Pottery in the Southwest. *Anthropological Papers of the University of Arizona* No. **10.**
Bryan, K.
1937 Geology of the Folsom Deposits in New Mexico and Colorado. In *Early Man, A Symposium,* edited by G.G. MacCurdy. Philadelphia: Lippincott. Pp. 139–152.
1939 Stone Cultures near Cerro Pedernal and Their Geological Antiquity. *Bulletin of the Texas Archaeology and Paleontology Society* **2:**9–43.
1941 Correlation of the Deposits of Sandia Cave, New Mexico, with the Glacial Chronology. Appendix to Evidences of Early Occupation in Sandia Cave, New Mexico, and Other Sites in the Sandia-Manzano Region, by Frank C. Hibben. *Smithsonian Miscellaneous Collections* **99**(23):45–64.
1954 The Geology of Chaco Canyon, New Mexico, in Relation to the Life and Remains of the Prehistoric Peoples of Pueblo Bonito. *Smithsonian Miscellaneous Collections* **122**(7).
Bryan, K., and L.L. Ray
1940 Geologic Antiquity of the Lindenmeier Site in Colorado. *Smithsonian Miscellaneous Collections* **99**(2).
Bryan, K., and J.H. Toulouse, Jr.
1943 The San José Non-Ceramic Culture and Its Relation to Puebloan Culture In New Mexico. *American Antiquity* **8**(3):269–280.
Bullard, W.R.
1962 The Cerro Colorado Site and Pithouse Architecture in the Southwestern United States Prior to A.D. 900. *Papers of the Peabody Museum of American Archaeology and Ethnology* No. **44**(2).
Colton, H.S.
1939 Prehistoric Culture Units and Their Relationships in Northern Arizona. *Museum of Northern Arizona Bulletin* No. **17.**
1955 Check List of Southwestern Pottery Types. *Museum of Northern Arizona Ceramic Series* No. **2.**
Colton, H.S., and L.L. Hargrave
1937 Handbook of Northern Arizona Pottery Wares. *Museum of Northern Arizona Bulletin* No. **11.**

Cooley, M.E.
1958 Physiography of the Glen–San Juan Canyon Area, part I. *Plateau* **31**(2):21–33.
1959a Physiography of the Glen–San Juan Canyon Area, part II. *Plateau* **31**(3):49–56.
1959b Physiography of the Glen–San Juan Canyon Area, part III: Physiography of Glen and Cataract Canyons. *Plateau* **31**(4):73–79.

Dick, H.W.
1965 Bat Cave. *School of American Research Monograph* No. **27.**

DiPeso, C.C.
1966 Archaeology and Ethnohistory of the Northern Sierra. In *Handbook of Middle American Indians,* edited by G.F. Ekholm and G.R. Willey. Vol. 4. Austin: University of Texas Press. Pp. 3–25.
1974 Casas Grandes: A Fallen Trading Center of the Gran Chichimeca. *Amerind Foundation Inc.,* Series No. **9.**

Douglass, A.E.
1929 The Secret of the Southwest Solved by Talkative Tree Rings. *National Geographic Magazine* **56**(6):736–770.

Fewkes, J.W.
1909 Antiquities of the Mesa Verde National Park: Spruce Tree House. *Bureau of American Ethnology Bulletin* No. **41.**
1911 Antiquities of the Mesa Verde National Park: Cliff Palace. *Bureau of American Ethnology Bulletin* No. **51.**

Fritts, H.C.
1966 Growth-Rings of Trees: Their Correlation with Climate. *Science* **154**(3752):973–979.

Gladwin, W., and H.S. Gladwin
1934 A Method for the Designation of Cultures and Their Variations. *Medallion Papers* No. **15.**

Gladwin, H.S., E.W. Haury, E.B. Sayles, and N. Gladwin
1937 Excavations at Snaketown, Material Culture. *Medallion Papers* No. **25.**

Guernsey, S.J.
1931 Explorations in Northeastern Arizona. Report on the Archaeological Fieldwork of 1920–1923. *Papers of the Peabody Museum of American Archaeology and Ethnology* No. **12**(1).

Guernsey, S.J., and A.V. Kidder
1921 Basket-Maker Caves of Northeastern Arizona. *Papers of the Peabody Museum of American Archaeology and Ethnology* No. **8**(2).

Hack, J.T.
1942 The Changing Physical Environment of the Hopi Indians of Arizona. *Papers of the Peabody Museum of American Archaeology and Ethnology* No. **35**(1).

Haury, E.W.
1936 The Mogollon Culture of Southwestern New Mexico. *Medallion Papers* No. **20.**
1962 HH-29: Recollections of a Dramatic Moment in Southwestern Archaeology. *Tree-Ring Bulletin* **24**(3–4):11–14.

Haury, E. W., K. Bryan, E.H. Colbert, N.E. Gabel, C.L. Tanner, and T.E. Buehver.
1950 *The Stratigraphy and Archaeology of Ventana Cave, Arizona.* Albuquerque: University of New Mexico Press.

Hawley, F.M.
1934 The Significance of the Dated Prehistory of Chetro Ketl, Chaco Canyon, New Mexico. *University of New Mexico Bulletin, Monograph Series* No. **1**(1).
1936 Field Manual of Prehistoric Southwestern Pottery Types. *University of New Mexico Bulletin* No. **291.**

Judd, N.M.
1930 The Excavation and Repair of Betatakin. *Smithsonian Institution Publication* No. **2828.**

1954 The Material Culture of Pueblo Bonito. *Smithsonian Miscellaneous Collections* No. **124.**

1964 The Architecture of Pueblo Bonito. *Smithsonian Miscellaneous Collections* No. **147.**

Kelley, J.C.

1953 Reconnaissance and Excavation in Durango and Southern Chihuahua, Mexico. *American Philosophical Society Yearbook:* 172–176.

Kidder, A.V.

1924 An Introduction to the Study of Southwestern Archaeology. Dept. of Archaeology, Phillips Academy, *Papers of the Southwestern Expedition* No. **1.**

1927 Southwestern Archaeological Conference. *El Palacio* **23**(22):554–561.

1958 Pecos, New Mexico: Archaeological Notes. *Papers of the Robert S. Peabody Foundation for Archaeology* No. **5.**

Kidder, A.V., and C.A. Amsden

1931 The Pottery of Pecos, I. Dept. of Archaeology, Phillips Academy, *Papers of the Southwestern Expedition* No. **5.**

Kidder, A.V., and S.J. Guernsey

1919 Archeological Explorations in Northeastern Arizona. *Bureau of American Ethnology Bulletin* No. **65.**

Kidder, A.V., and A.O. Shepard

1936 The Pottery of Pecos, II. Dept. of Archaeology, Phillips Academy *Papers of the Southwestern Expedition* No. **7.**

Kroeber, A.L.

1916 Zuñi Potsherds. *Anthropological Papers of the American Museum of Natural History* **18**(1).

Libby, W.F.

1952 *Radiocarbon Dating.* Chicago: University of Chicago Press.

Martin, P.S.

1963 *The Last 10,000 Years: A Fossil Pollen Record of the American Southwest,* Tucson: University of Arizona Press.

1973 The Discovery of America. *Science* **179**(4077):969–974.

Martin, P.S., J.B. Rinaldo, E. Bluhn, H.C. Cutler, and R. Grange, Jr.

1952 Mogollon Cultural Continuity and Change, the Stratigraphic Analysis of Tularosa and Cordova Caves. *Fieldiana: Anthropology* No. **40.**

McGregor, J.C.

1941 *Southwestern Archaeology.* New York: Wiley.

1965 *Southwestern Archaeology.* 2nd ed. Urbana: University of Illinois Press.

McNitt, F.

1957 *Richard Wetherill: Anasazi.* Albuquerque: University of New Mexico Press.

Mera, H.P.

1935 Ceramic Clues to the Prehistory of North Central New Mexico. *Laboratory of Anthropology Technical Series Bulletin* No. **8.**

Montgomery, R.G., W. Smith, and J.O. Brew

1949 Franciscan Awatovi. *Papers of the Peabody Museum of American Archaeology and Ethnology* No. **36.**

Morris, E.H.

1919 The Aztec Ruin. *American Museum of Natural History Anthropological Papers* **26**(I):1–108.

1939 Archaeological Studies in the La Plata District, Southwestern Colorado and Northwestern New Mexico—with an Appendix, "Technology of La Plata Pottery," by A.O. Shepard. *Carnegie Institution of Washington Publication* No. **519.**

Morris, E.H., and R.F. Burgh

1941 Anasazi Basketry, Basket Maker II through Pueblo III. A Study Based on Specimens from the San Juan River Country. *Carnegie Institution of Washington Publication* **533.**

Morss, N.

1954 Clay Figurines of the American Southwest. *Papers of the Peabody Museum of American Archaeology and Ethnology* No. **49**(1).

Nelson, N.C.

1916 Chronology of the Tano Ruins, New Mexico. *American Anthropologist* **18**(2):159–180.

Roberts, F.H.H., Jr.

1929 Shabik'eschee Village, a Late Basket Maker Site in the Chaco Canyon, New Mexico. *Bureau of American Ethnology Bulletin* No. **92.**

1930 Early Pueblo Ruins in the Piedra District, Southwestern Colorado. *Bureau of American Ethnology Bulletin* No. **96.**

1931 The Ruins at Kiatuthlanna, Eastern Arizona. *Bureau of American Ethnology Bulletin* No. **100.**

1932 The Village of the Great Kivas on the Zuñi Reservation, New Mexico. *Bureau of American Ethnology Bulletin* No. **111.**

1935 A Survey of Southwestern Archeology. *American Anthropologist* **37**(1):1–35.

Rogers, M.J.

1939 Early Lithic Industries of the Lower Basin of the Colorado River and Adjacent Desert Areas. *San Diego Museum Papers* No. **3.**

1945 An Outline of Yuman Prehistory. *Southwestern Journal of Anthropology* **1**(1):167–198.

Rohn, A.H.

1973 The Southwest and Intermontane West. In *The Development of North American Archaeology,* edited by J.E. Fitting. New York: Anchor Press and Doubleday.

1977 *Cultural Change and Continuity on Chapin Mesa.* Lawrence: The Regents Press of Kansas.

Sayles, E.B., and E. Antevs

1941 The Cochise Culture. *Medallion Papers* No. **29.**

Schoenwetter, J., and F.W. Eddy

1964 Alluvial and Palynological Reconstruction of Environments, Navajo Reservoir District. *Museum of New Mexico, Papers in Anthropology* No. 13.

Schulman, E.

1956 *Dendroclimatic Changes in Semiarid America.* Tucson: University of Arizona Press.

Smiley, T.L. (Editor)

1955 Geochronology. *University of Arizona Physical Science Bulletin* No. **2.**

1958 *Climate and Man in the Southwest.* Tucson: University of Arizona Press.

Smith, W., R.B. Woodbury, and N.F.S. Woodbury

1966 *The Excavation of Hawikuh by Frederick Webb Hodge,* New York: Museum of the American Indian Heye Foundation.

Spier, L.

1917 An Outline for a Chronology of Zuñi Ruins. *Anthropological Papers of the American Museum of Natural History* No. **18**(3).

Taylor, W.W.

1956 Some Implications of the Carbon-14 Dates from a Cave in Coahuilla, Mexico. *Bulletin of the Texas Archaeological Society* **27:**215–234.

Wauchope, R. (Editor)

1956 Seminars in Archaeology: 1955. *Society for American Archaeology Memoirs* No. **11.**

Wheat, J.B.

1954 Southwestern Cultural Relationships and the Question of Area Co-Tradition. *Ameri-*

can Anthropologist No. **56**(4).
1955 Mogollon Culture Prior to A.D. 1000. *Society for American Archaeology Memoirs* No. **10.**

Willey, G.R., and P. Phillips
1958 *Method and Theory in American Archaeology*. Chicago: University of Chicago Press.

Woodbury, R.B.
1960a Nels C. Nelson and Chronological Archaeology. *American Antiquity* **25**(3):400–401.
1960b Nelson's Stratigraphy. *American Antiquity* **26**(1):98–99.

Wormington, H.M.
1947 *Prehistoric Indians of the Southwest*. Denver: Denver Museum of Natural History.

California

CLEMENT W. MEIGHAN

I. INTRODUCTION

The boundaries of modern political units seldom coincide well with significant groupings of people in the past. In setting up California as a separate region of study, however, there is a geographic unit that may justifiably be treated as a distinct entity with a somewhat distinct archaeological history.

California is basically that region bounded by the Pacific Ocean on the west and the Sierra Nevada on the east. When first entered by aboriginal man an unknown number of millennia ago, the earliest humans moved into a geographically diversified region, blocked off by major geographic barriers from significant contact with other peoples. The Californians were thus left to pursue their history in relative isolation and detachment from the many changes taking place elsewhere in North America. The result was a gradual adaptation to ecological niches by a multiplicity of small tribes, none of which ever had agriculture (except for minor use on the Colorado River). The first significant contact with alien peoples for most indigenous Californians came not with more complex tribes of Indians but with sixteenth-century Europeans. In Northern California, for example, the first real outsider in the cultural sense was none other than Sir Francis Drake in 1579. His arrival was an experience for the Indians that was clearly the kind of shock we would have on observing the landing of men from Mars.

Because of isolation and generally simple technology, California developed a great diversity of small, local, individualistic groups, all hunters and gatherers but by no means all alike. At historic contact, there were some 120 languages spoken, several physical subraces, and major differences in the details of the lifeway. These distinct groups are what are generally called "tribes," but in an early report Kroeber referred to the aboriginal Californians as "little nations"—a more meaningful term. A tribe is a group of people, but a little nation is more; it is a territorial unit with its own language, culture, traditions, history, and mores.

If then, we think of Indian California as a land of 120 little nations, largely isolated from one another by cultural factors and almost completely isolated from everyone else in the world by geographic barriers, it makes sense to look at this region as an entity worth separate study. Chronologically, we have the problem of projecting back into time, for a minimum of 10,000 years and perhaps much more, our dozens of little nations, with their many changes through time: divisions, combinations, adaptations, and specializations. This is a very complex undertaking and one which is hardly begun.

II. HISTORY OF CHRONOLOGICAL THINKING

Quite distinct kinds of curiosity motivate man to study the past. Archaeology is not done because of a general and formless urge to study what went before, but because of more specific interests. Some of the strong motivations for the study of prehistory in other regions are not applicable to California (for example, interest in one's direct ancestry or interest in visible monuments and ruins). There seem to be two kinds of curiosity that began California archaeology, and these two are still dominant.

The first is an interest, perhaps a common awe, at recognizing ancient man, of finding the beginnings of human life, of seeing the first people to enter a region. California archaeology first came to attention because of this interest when the miners of the gold rush days came upon artifacts and human bones in a series of discoveries in the caves, stream banks, and auriferous gravels of the Sierra Nevada gold-mining districts. Calaveras Man is the most famous of these early discoveries. It can be said that California archaeology began with what we would now call "Early Man" archaeology, and this kind of curiosity still has strong devotees in California, sometimes to the exclusion of any other kind of interest in the past.

Another kind of curiosity starts with a quite different intellectual perspective at the late end of the time scale—an interest that begins with the contemporary Indians and seeks to develop their history and origins. Such curiosity was exceedingly rare among the early settlers of California, who saw little of interest or romance in the Indian population around them. Although a few writers, even back to the days of the Spanish missions, commented on Indian historical traditions, there was no development of what would now be called culture–historical archaeology, probably because the native populations were generally considered to have no culture worthy of note. The culture–historical kind of curiosity about archaeological remains can be said to begin with the development of anthropology in the state, and, like so many other significant developments, the beginnings of this approach should probably be attributed to A. L. Kroeber and his colleagues and students, beginning about 1900. Most of the early archaeologists in California were also ethnographers who were keenly sensitive to archaeology as a means of extending their ethnographic knowledge into the past. Of this early California group, some of the scholars who wrote both ethnographic and archaeological monographs (not necessarily on the same regions) included S. A. Barrett, E. W. Gifford, Julian Steward, Ralph Beals, and of course Kroeber himself.

These two lines of interest, "early man" and "culture history" correlate with two kinds of early efforts at chronology for aboriginal California. The first was the observation of human remains apparently associated with fossil animals or geological strata (Warren 1973:213–217, provides a good brief summary of this kind of find). The other was the effort to see time depth in the distribution of languages and cultural elements, survivals of primitive technology, and comparative ethnography. Purely archaeological dating methods, such as cultural stratigraphy, were weakly developed in California until the 1930s, and real chronology in absolute time was not really present until the advent of radiocarbon dating, although some of the earlier "guess dates" developed by reasoning out the chronology from a variety of evidences proved to be fairly close to the mark.

As a historical note, the first California archaeologist who seems to have attempted chronology on the basis of stratigraphy was Max Uhle, who excavated the Emeryville Shellmound in 1902. Published a few years later (Uhle 1907), this effort was a preliminary attempt of limited scope, but it anticipated later results with relative chronology. At that time, there were only the vaguest notions of what the absolute chronology of aboriginal California might be.

In addition to the pioneer efforts by Uhle, several workers made some tentative chronological efforts in the period 1900–1929, mostly based on typological comparison and with very limited application of stratigraphic studies. The decade 1929–1939 provided the first real chronological framework for California, in the form of several regional chronologies developed independently and with no coordination or correlation into a comprehensive chronology for the state as a whole. Starting in 1939, increasing efforts have been expended on recognition of broad horizons and relationships from one area to another.

The pioneer chronologies included two for the southern part of the state and one in the north. M. J. Rogers (1929), working in the San Diego and desert areas, devised a sequence of three cultures based on a technological sequence of artifact types and a seriation of sites. He dealt, perforce, largely with surface collections, particularly in the deserts, and his chronology has been extensively modified by later workers having excavation data (as well as radiocarbon dates) to depend upon.

In the Santa Barbara Channel area, another tripartite sequence was proposed, by D. B. Rogers, also in 1929. The sequence (Oak Grove, Hunting, and Canaliño, in that order) was based on stratigraphic excavation of many coastal sites, and his basic sequence is still valid although much expanded and refined by later workers.

For Northern California, Schenck and Dawson (1929) worked out the beginnings of a chronological scheme for some Central California sites, based in part on excavation data but relying primarily on seriation of artifact forms and their relationship to known historic sites. This work can be considered a forerunner of the much more extensive and important chronological studies published by Lillard *et al.* 10 years later (1939). The latter work deserves special mention, since it described, tabulated, and compared a whole series of site assemblages, to develop a chronological framework based on the stratigraphic excavation and comparative typology of cemetery collections.

The sequence developed for Central California included a number of named assemblages and local variants, grouped into a broad three-period division of horizons designated, somewhat unfortunately as it later appeared, as Early, Middle, and Late Central California. Although this scheme was carefully defined to apply primarily to the delta of the Sacramento River, and a separate chronology was developed for areas as close by as San Francisco Bay (Beardsley 1954), there is still a tendency to generalize this chronological framework to much wider areas of California. Since the Early Horizon, as defined, is only 4000–5000 years old, it is confusing in comparisons with much older sites elsewhere in California, some of them not too distant from the delta region originally studied. For this reason, contemporary archaeologists do not generally use an "Early–Middle–Late" terminology but refer to specific named complexes in their chronological schemes.

Since the 1950s, chronological summaries of California have become complex because there is a wide diversity of artifact assemblages, at least 140 of which are named in the literature. No single named assemblage has a statewide distribution, and many are so far known only from limited areas (or even single sites). The chronological complexity results in part from the absence of the conventional landmark changes, of which the most prominent are the inception of agriculture and the introduction of such diagnostic technological features as pottery, metallurgy, and architecture. Since California remained almost entirely on a hunter–gatherer level, the archaeological chronology is a succession of variations in the hunter–gatherer lifeway—a kind of chronology less well defined and less well understood than the shift from preagriculture to agriculture. The variant archaeological assemblages in California are most often not related to development through time, but rather to ecological adaptation to California's widely varying environmental regions. Some of the assemblages defined as individual archaeological cultures will be shown to be the products of the same group of people, differentiated solely by such differences as can result from a seasonal round of utilizing different ecological zones at different times of the year.

Several scholars have reviewed the chronology of all or part of California, among them Fredrickson (1973), Heizer (1964), and Wallace (1955, 1963). Specific discussions of Early Man chronology include Berger *et al.* (1971), Carter (1957), Davis *et al.* (1969), Glennan (1972), Heizer (1952), Johnson and Miller (1958), Krieger (1964), and Orr (1968). In my own previous attempts to summarize California chronology, I prepared a general chronological chart (Meighan 1959) and a specialized discussion of Early Man material (Meighan 1965). My 1959 chronological chart is now outdated and has some chronological placements that have been shown to be incorrect, in some cases by thousands of years. In general, the sequence of regional cultures as previously presented is valid, but the placement in time has been changed for some of the individual archaeological assemblages, as better dating evidence has accumulated.

III. NEW CHRONOLOGICAL DEVELOPMENTS

California Prehistoric studies have benefited especially from two recent advances in dating methodologies. The first is the development of radiocarbon dating on bone collagen, making it possible to determine ages directly on skeletal remains. This has been most valuable for Early Man skeletons, many of which have no cultural materials associated (Berger *et al.* 1971). Application of obsidian dating has also provided California archaeologists with valuable dating evidence, sometimes as a supplement to radiocarbon dates, but most importantly with remains for which radiocarbon dating is not available or may not be possible (Clark 1965).

In spite of the new methods and the great increase in dating evidence in recent years, there still remain a number of important sites, particularly claimed Early Man locations, that cannot be dated directly by either radiocarbon or obsidian dating. Dating by artifact time markers or geological estimates is therefore still relied upon in some individual cases. For example, there is no direct date for the important Lake Mohave Site, which is dated by association with ancient beach lines.

A. Radiocarbon Data

Application of radiocarbon dating to the bone collagen of ancient skeletons has provided important dating evidence for several finds, some of which have been controversial for years. Unfortunately, the majority of these finds are isolated skeletons, so the ages, even if valid, cannot be applied to any known cultural remains. Acceptance of the collagen dates therefore tells us when man was present but does not tell us anything about the tools he used nor his way of life.

A brief summary of important early collagen ^{14}C dates is given in Table 8.1. Of this group of dates, only one (Tranquility) was associated with an assemblage of artifacts. These were classified as in the Middle Central California Tradition, and this is correct according to the age of the skeletons, which are fairly recent. Pleistocene animal bones associated are not of the same age as the human bones.

The other dates in Table 8.1 are much older and include the oldest date on human skeletal remains in the New World. In the case of Los Angeles Man, we have a gap of at least 10,000 years between the apparent age of the skeleton and any accepted stone tool tradition known in California. This is possible but raises an interesting question, since it has always been easier for archaeologists to find the stone tools than the remains of the ancient men who made them, and, in both Old World and New, there are tremendous assemblages of artifacts known and described before skeletal remains were recovered. In some cases, there are still large tool collections without any

TABLE 8.1

Some ^{14}C Collagen Dates from California

Find	UCLA sample number	Age (years ago)
Santa Rosa Island (mammoth)	705	8,000 ± 250
Laguna Beach (skeleton)	Skull: 1233 A	17,150 ± 1,470
	Longbone: 1233 B	More than 14,800
Los Angeles Man (skull)	1430	More than 23,600
La Brea Tar Pits (human bones)	1292 B	9,000 ± 80
Tranquility (human bones)	1623	2,550 ± 60

skeletons associated—Clovis and Folsom remains are a case in point. Acceptance of the date for Los Angeles Man therefore means either that archaeologists have failed to find assemblages covering at least 10,000 years of California history or that some of the existing collections in museums include tools far older than we have been willing to accept.

It must be noted that all of the old collagen dates have problems of archaeological context and possible contamination. All the dated bones were recovered years ago and have an uncertain history. The Laguna Beach skeleton, for example, is remembered to have come from between levels that yielded radiocarbon dates of 8300 (UCLA 1364) and 8950 years ago (UCLA 1349). Use of the collagen date therefore requires explanation of how a 17,000-year-old skeleton got inserted between two soil levels less than 9000 years old.

It is not surprising to find older and older remains as archaeological work progresses, and I consider all of the collagen dates to be possible for California. On the other hand, because of uncertainties like those mentioned above, I think it is premature to rewrite New World prehistory on the basis of these early dates on bone collagen.

An additional series of ancient dates for burial remains has resulted from the work of Bada, based on amino acid racemization. The old dates are considered impossible by some archaeologists, and data are not yet available to allow for detailed evaluation of this dating method and its results.

The number of radiocarbon dates for California has almost doubled since 1965, from 164 to 292 published dates (Ericson and Hagan 1972). A number of unpublished determinations have also been used in preparing this article.

While many individual sites are as yet undated, a radiocarbon sample of 300 dates allows some preliminary general statements. First, there is a great increase in the number of dates as one approaches the recent end of the time scale. For ^{14}C determinations done so far, 38% are less than 2000 years old, 62% are less than 4000 years old, and 87% are less than 8000 years old (Table 8.2). If the purely geological and questionable dates are eliminated from the very old determinations, the percentage of dates less than 8000 years old goes to over 95%.

Even allowing for the many difficulties in finding and dating early sites, the extensive archaeology done in California suggests that 90% of all the aboriginal inhabitants lived in the state in the last 8000 years, and more than half of them lived in the state during the past 4000 years. There was clearly a tremendous population growth over the past few thousand years. Elsewhere, a population increase of this magnitude would be most likely explained by the introduction of agriculture, but in California it took place solely on increased hunter–gatherer efficiency.

The geographical distribution of radiocarbon dates in California is also worth comment. All of the old dates are in the southern third of the state, and with three exceptions all are from south of the Tehachapi Mountains (the

TABLE 8.2

Summary of Published Radiocarbon Dates from California

	Number of dates	
	As of 1965[a]	As of 1972[b]
Less than 4,000 years ago	122	181
4,000–7,500 years ago	30	65
7,500–9,500 years ago	0	15
9,500–12,500 years ago	5	5
More than 12,500 years ago	7	26
Total	164	292

[a] From Meighan (1965:709).
[b] From Ericson and Hagan (1972).

exceptions are three dates between 7600 and 8200 years ago for the Buena Vista Lake area, just north of the Tehachapis). For Northern California, the oldest published radiocarbon date is associated with the milling stone component of the Borax Lake culture, about 5000–6000 years ago (Fredrickson 1973:156). Because of this absence of early radiocarbon dates from Northern California, I suggested (Meighan 1965:713) that Southern California was settled earlier than the northern part of the state, by a flow of migrants traveling around the southern end of the Sierra Nevada from the inland deserts. We have abundant evidence that Southern California was rather thickly inhabited along the coast from San Diego to Santa Barbara by 7500 years ago, millennia before the earliest radiocarbon-dated site in the northern part of the state.

However, while my general conclusion may be valid, the radiocarbon evidence does not tell the whole story. Many fewer ^{14}C dates are available for Northern California, the search for early sites has been much more intensive in the arid south, and other kinds of dating evidence (in particular obsidian dating) suggests greater ages for some northern sites than is documented by the present list of radiocarbon dates. Since this was written, a ^{14}C collagen date in excess of 10,000 years has been reported for the Mosden site in Lake Co, confirming the suggestion just made.

B. Obsidian Hydration Data

Although by no means on as firm a basis as radiocarbon dating, there has been extensive and increasing use of obsidian dating in California. The original work by Clark (1965), plus the dates done at the UCLA hydration laboratory, total about 1200 obsidian hydration determinations. Some obsidian dating has been done on 73 California sites, but many of these have only a few determinations. About half of the total California readings are on a single site in Mono County (Michels 1964) and only about 15 sites have sufficient hydration data to be very useful for chronological problems.

California has excellent potential for obsidian dating, since obsidian is found in sites throughout the state. However, there is very little obsidian in Southern California sites and many important collections have no obsidian artifacts. In addition, there is a marked increase in use of obsidian in the later periods, so only a few of the older sites have sufficient obsidian to permit use of obsidian dating. The important San Dieguito site, for example, which is shown to be over 9000 years old, has no obsidian at all, and obsidian is generally absent or extremely rare in Southern California sites older than about 7000 years.

The central problem of obsidian dating is determination of the rate at which the hydration surface forms on a freshly chipped fragment. Measuring the thickness of the hydration layer is easy, but translating this thickness into "years ago" is difficult and subject to large errors. The rate of hydration has been shown to be affected by temperature and by the chemical composition of the obsidian. Since California has fairly wide temperature variations and numerous obsidian flows of somewhat differing chemical composition, it is impossible to determine a single hydration rate and apply it mechanically to all California obsidian. An original hydration rate determined by Donovan Clark (1965) for Central California obsidian is pretty close to the truth and has been confirmed by repeated associations of obsidian with radiocarbon-dated levels. This rate will be refined but will not have any major correction made.

Work elsewhere in California shows that there are at least two hydration rates for the state (one southern rate and one northern rate), and there may well be three or four rates for the state as a whole. However, fortunately, the rates do seem applicable to extensive areas, so a small number of hydration rates will allow obsidian dating to be used throughout the state.

Despite the uncertainties in obsidian dating, use of the method in California has had extensive effects on our understanding of California's archaeological chronology. A brief list of some of the principal effects includes:

1. Michels' (1964) pioneer study of the obsidian from a single site in Mono County showed the value of obsidian dating for sequencing artifact types. This use of obsidian dating is extremely valuable in dealing with surface collections, collections from shallow sites, and collections from badly disturbed sites, for all of which stratigraphic information may not be sufficient to arrange artifact types in time. Michels' work is of general application to other sites and areas, but it has so far not been extensively duplicated.

2. In the northern part of California, obsidian dates have been used to

supplement, and in some cases to question, radiocarbon results. In the San Francisco Bay area, Gerow and Force (1968) used obsidian dates to draw conclusions about the age of their site relative to other sites. In the North Coast Ranges, Fredrickson (1973) used obsidian dating extensively to extend his chronological findings and expand on the few radiocarbon dates available to him. A study of the controversial Borax Lake Site was done to attempt clarification of that site's chronology (Meighan and Haynes 1970). Obsidian dating was used both to estimate the absolute age of the site and to sequence the artifact types from a badly mixed collection. In this case, obsidian dating was critical, since there are no radiocarbon dates for the site.

C. Early Man

The Early Man picture has been changed in the past few years by the following findings:

1. Some previously undatable skeletons have been dated by radiocarbon dating on bone collagen, as previously discussed. These dates have eliminated some controversial finds from Early Man status (cf. Tranquility) and confirmed some other finds as older than 9000 years. Amino acid dating, while still exploratory, may well be a key tool for skeletal dating.
2. Obsidian dating has suggested the Borax Lake Site (Northern California) to include some artifacts as old as Clovis finds elsewhere in the West, possibly to as much as 12,000 years ago (Meighan and Haynes 1970).
3. The radiocarbon evidence in 1965 showed no dates in the time period 7500–9500 years ago (Table 8.2). I speculated about this apparent chronological gap (Meighan 1965:711), but it has proven a nonexistent problem, since no less than 15 radiocarbon dates have appeared in this time period during the last few years.

The number of ancient radiocarbon determinations, defined here as older than 12,500 years ago, has risen sharply, from 7 such dates in 1965 to 26 at present. However, nearly all of these dates apply to geological features, and most are not even claimed to apply directly to archaeological remains. Two of the dates in this group are collagen dates previously discussed, and a couple more apply to charcoal believed by the discoverers to be associated with human activity. The rest are geological dates. More than half (14) are dates on fauna of the La Brea Tar Pits and do not apply to man. Although a fair amount of evidence of humans has come from the tar pits excavations, all of it that has so far been dated directly is much later than 12,500 years ago. Dated human materials include the human bones (Table 8.1) and some wooden spear fragments (4400 years ago). It is still not demonstrated that any human remains belong with the levels more than 12,500 years old, although the site is among the best possibilities for human remains of this antiquity. Indeed, if truly early human remains are not found in the extensive La Brea excavations, it will be most significant for Early Man claims in California. If Early Man was in the state more than 12,000 years ago, he should have left some evidences among the massive faunal assemblage at La Brea, representing as it does most of the larger game animals trapped at water holes by underlying tar layers.

The most extravagant claims for human antiquity in California are those of Carter (1957) for San Diego County, and of the investigators for the excavation still under way at Calico in the Southern California Desert. Carter's work has been partially published, and his conclusions are disputed (Johnson and Miller 1958), although he has recently made new excavations at the Texas Street Site and is still concerned about the site's validity. Only a preliminary statement about Calico has been published by the excavators (Leakey *et al.* 1968; see also other references and evaluation in Glennan 1972; Haynes 1975; Schuiling 1972). The site cannot be fairly discussed until the evidence is forthcoming, so judgment should be withheld until the full results are available. If valid, the sites of Carter (such as Texas Street) and the Calico Site are older by at least 30,000 years than any other known sites in the New World.

IV. CULTURAL STAGES

To attempt an overview of present thinking about the chronology of California, the dozens of assemblages are not here treated individually but are combined into some suggested cultural stages of wide areal extent. Such broad cultural stages are outlined below and in Figure 8.1.

A. Pre–Projectile Point Stage

Over the years, a large number of finds have been put forward as representing a cultural stage prior to the development of projectile points (of stone, at least). Such a level would represent the basement cultures of California archaeology. All this material has recently been reviewed by Glennan (1972) from first-hand examination of the sites and assemblages. He concludes that a pre–Projectile Point stage in California is not yet demonstrated or validated, and that it remains a hypothetical level of development in this area. This is not to say that one or more of the claimed pre–Projectile Point Sites may not prove to be ancient. It is unfortunate that for all of these sites the claims of great age have been published without waiting for adequate fieldwork or for the presentation of the data required by basic descriptive scholarship.

Despite this, a couple of the claims look to me as if they are worth careful

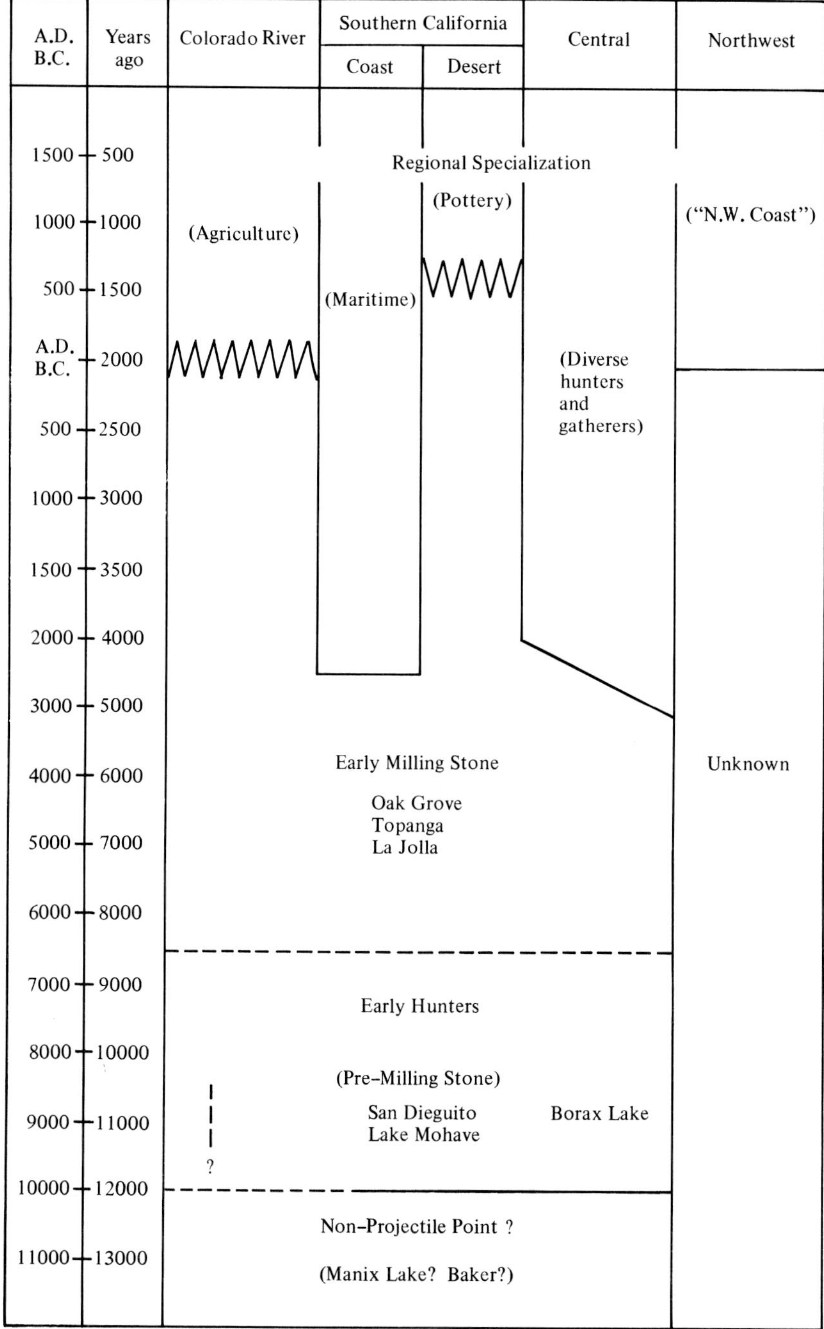

Figure 8.1. California cultural stages.

additional study, which may yet validate the non–Projectile Point stage at some future time. Among these are the Manix Lake Lithic Industry (Simpson 1964), which is believed by many to represent quarry activity but could be of great age. Also a possibility is the Baker Site (Glennan 1972), which has similar stone bifaces and appears on logical grounds to be a site that is very old and lacks projectile points. Since neither of these examples has been dated, however, a pre–Projectile Point stage remains a possible, theoretical, but undemonstrated archaeological level in California. If such a stage exists, it would appear to have an age prior to 12,000 years ago and to be distributed entirely in Southern California. The artifacts seem to comprise only bifaces and an assortment of scrapers. Some of the bifacial tools are quite small, but most are over 10 cm in length. Both the origins and evidence for characteristic subsistence behavior are obscure. The only claimed culture of this type in Northern California is the Farmington assemblage, which appears dubious for several reasons (Meighan 1965:175).

B. Early Hunting Stage

The Early Hunting Stage, dating from ca. 12,000 years ago to ca. 8500 years B.P., would be represented in Southern California by sites of the San Dieguito and Lake Mohave types (Warren 1966; Warren and True 1961; Campbell *et al.* 1937) and in Northern California, from the San Joaquin Valley, north, by fluted-point sites like Borax Lake (Fredrickson 1973; Meighan and Haynes 1970). From limited evidence, this stage probably existed over the whole state, being derived from the Interior Great Basin area. The artifact assemblages are dominated by fluted points, crescents, and abundant core tools, scrapers, and choppers, in addition to assemblages with leaf-shaped points but no fluted points; crescents are associated with both. All sites in this group lack mortars, metates, and other plant-preparation tools. The absence of such tools (with the exception of scraper planes perhaps used in the preparation of *Agave* stalks) suggests an orientation toward hunting, rather than the harvesting of wild plants. These sites are also of an antiquity that would make possible the hunting of large animals, including ground sloth and mammoth. However, there are no faunal remains from any of the sites mentioned.

C. Early Milling Stone Stage

The name Early Milling Stone Stage is taken from the original definition by Wallace (1955). This stage was at first based on several assemblages in Southern California; it is much like the "Desert Culture" as defined for the Great Basin. It is likely that this stage existed at one time over the whole state of California except for the heavily forested northwestern area. However, it disappeared from Northern California by about 5000 years ago, persisting to protohistoric times in parts of the Southern California Desert and Baja California. Milling Stone assemblages are known in the Sierras and in Northern California from sites like Borax Lake. Most sites for this stage are in Southern California and generally dated in that area at 8500–3500 years B.P. In the great Central Valley, Early Milling Stone sites would be buried in the alluvium. A couple of sites (for example, Diablo Canyon) have basal radiocarbon dates of about 9000 years, but it is not clear whether this age can be assigned to the Milling Stone cultural assemblages. Sites in Southern California assigned to this stage include a series of localities from San Luis Obispo County down into Baja California, with a number of cultural assemblages including Oak Grove, La Jolla, Topanga, and Zuma Beach. Artifact materials associated include manos and metates in great abundance, along with crude percussion-flaked stone tools, with a predominance of choppers and scraper planes. Ornaments and possible ritual objects are few, but crudely engraved pebbles occur as well as occasional shell beads and cog-stones or discoidals. Projectile points are very rare and in the earlier sites are no more frequent than one point to every 400 stone artifacts of other types. The heavy predominance of seed-grinding implements indicates a plantfood gathering, "flour mush cookery" subsistence of Desert Culture type. Even on the coast, the sites show limited adaptation to ocean resources and contain few fish and relatively little shellfish (and those of the varieties most easily gathered by hand on the beach). There was some sea mammal hunting along the coasts, but again probably on the beach only. The artifact inventory and cultural activities argue strongly that this stage began in the desert inland and spread toward the Pacific Coast, reaching it about 8500 years ago in Southern California. There is no evidence to show whether the Milling Stone Stage involved a movement of people or a conquest of earlier residents; perhaps the early hunters simply adopted this way of life as game animals became more scarce. Whatever the inception, there appears to have been a marked population increase with the adoption of the Milling Stone way of life.

D. Regional Specialization Stage

From about 5000 years ago, Californians began an in-place adaptation to various ecological niches, resulting in a wide variety of local specializations distributed over the whole state.

The southern desert peoples received influences from the Colorado River and the Southwest, and, while they never became farmers, they adopted such elements as pottery and cremation. In the protohistoric period along the southern border, such distinctive Hohokam features as reburied cremations in pottery vessels are found, although again without agriculture or many of the most characteristic elements of the Hohokam.

On the Colorado River itself, the only agriculture in California was practiced. The origin is clearly the Hohokam area, but the dates are uncertain. The region remained one of mixed agriculture, with significant use of wild plant harvesting, to the Historic period.

Along the Southern California coasts, specialization moved in the direction of maritime adaptation to an ocean-fishing economy that was elaborate and well developed by the time of Spanish missionization. Plank canoes were used, along with several kinds of fishing devices including circular shell fishhooks, and not only the subsistence but all aspects of life including religion came to reflect adaptation to the sea. These assemblages include an abundance of diversified and elaborate ornamental items, including much shell inlay work, steatite bowls and carvings, and in general the richest material culture found in aboriginal California.

Central California remained basically land-oriented hunters and gatherers, but with regional specializations toward riverine economy in some places. There was extensive use of plant resources as well as hunting of deer, elk, and other game. The artifacts include a great deal of work in shell and bone, and common ritual objects include plummets or charmstones. Shellmounds occur throughout the coastal zones, but without the ocean fishing economy found in the south.

In Northwestern California, the distinctive river fishing, centering on salmon as a principal subsistence element, developed. The origins of this adaptation are unknown since the archaeology in this region does not go back beyond about 2000 years ago.

The above summary of specializations includes only the most distinctive groups; many subtypes and specialized minor groups also existed. In general, the greatest complexity and diversity of native cultures existed at the time of Historic contact.

V. CONCLUSIONS

A detailed chronology for California prehistory is not solely a pedantic concern. Chronology here, as elsewhere, is a central issue because of its relevance to the major issues of contemporary archaeology. Among these issues is the criticism of much previous work as being descriptive rather than interpretative. Through time, archaeologists have described what conditions were like at the beginning of a period and what they were like at the end, without explaining (or often even describing) the cultural processes that led from the beginning to the end. Such procedures fall short of archaeological objectives, but they result in large part from the archaeologist's inability, particularly in hunter–gatherer areas, to place archaeological finds in time and, most especially, to measure fine time divisions in the archaeology of a region with no inscriptions or even ceramic styles and similar sharp time markers. If the smallest time division one can recognize is a millennium, it is not possible to say much about the processes of change within that thousand years. It is important to note that prior to radiocarbon dating, California archaeologists could not even sort out the millennia reliably, and until the 1930s some writers were still saying that there was no culture change in aboriginal California.

Since the development of the radiocarbon method, we have got the millennia sorted out pretty well. However, to make other than very gross interpretations of culture change, we need still finer chronologies than are available for all but a very few locations—preferably chronologies that can discriminate centuries rather than millennia. As an example of the difference this makes, on one site I recorded from midden analysis that the inhabitants exploited a favored kind of shellfish so intensively that they reduced its relative abundance by some 80%. Unfortunately, chronological information is so imprecise that it is impossible to say whether this depletion is an example of overexploitation by a couple of generations or whether it represents a gradual change over many centuries. Further, we have only fuzzy notions of what other sites are exactly contemporaneous to this observed event. Therefore we can make a significant observation but cannot offer other than speculative explanations until we know not only the general time but also the duration of the observed change.

Future efforts in California chronology will be devoted in part to improving the accuracy and sensitivity of obsidian dating methods. Once the hydration rates are more clearly understood, the combination of radiocarbon and obsidian dating will allow time placement of the great majority of California sites to within a century or two. It should be possible to develop an archaeological chronology for California that is as accurate and precise as the ceramic chronology used in the Southwest, for example. Not until this kind of chronology is available will California archaeology be able to contribute other than very general statements about culture process.

The imperfect chronological data now available in California suggest a number of important conclusions, however, none of which were clearly apparent even 10 years ago:

1. California was inhabited at least 10,000 years ago and possibly more. This is no news to the Early Man enthusiasts, but in my 1965 summary I felt that a continuum of occupation could not be firmly demonstrated for more than 8000 years in the state. New data have pushed that figure back in time by 25% in the past few years. Nobody believes that the oldest site in California has been found yet.

2. On present evidence, it still appears that man entered California at the south end rather than coming down the coast from the north.

3. The history of California cultures is one of fragmentation rather than consolidation. Even allowing for fragmentary data, the earlier cultures appear much more uniform over much larger areas than the later cultures,

which were much more diversified. Because of increasingly specialized adaptation to small environmental areas, this is probably a normal trend for hunters and gatherers, but it contrasts sharply with the centralizing and unifying effects visible in the history of agricultural societies.

BIBLIOGRAPHY

Beardsley, R.K.
1954 Temporal and Areal Relationships in Central California Archaeology, parts I, II. *University of California Archaeological Survey Reports* No. **24, 25.**

Berger, R., R. Protsch, R. Reynolds, C. Rozaire, and J. Sackett
1971 New Radiocarbon Dates Based on Bone Collagen of California Paleoindians. *University of California Archaeological Research Facility Contributions* No. **12**:43–49.

Campbell, E.W., W.H. Campbell, E. Antevs, C. Amsden, J. Barbieri, F. Bock
1937 The Archaeology of Pleistocene Lake Mohave. *Southwest Museum Papers* No. **11.**

Carter, G.F.
1957 *Pleistocene Man at San Diego*. Baltimore: Johns Hopkins University Press.

Clark, C.L.
1965 Archaeological Chronology in California and the Obsidian Hydration Method. *University of California Archaeological Survey, Annual Report 1963–64,* 139–228.

Davis, E.L., C.W. Brott, and D.L. Weide
1969 The Western Lithic Cotradition. *San Diego Museum of Man Papers* No. **6.**

Ericson, J.E., and T.A. Hagan
1972 The Establishment of an Archaeological Data Bank for California Manuscript, Archaeological Survey, UCLA.

Frederickson, D.A.
1973 Early Cultures of the North Coast Ranges, California. Unpublished manuscript, Dept. of Anthropology, University of California, Davis.

Gerow, B.A., and R.W. Force
1968 *An Analysis of the University Village Complex*. Stanford, California: Stanford University Press.

Glennan, W.S.
1972 The Hypothesis of an Ancient, Pre-Projectile Point Stage in American Prehistory: Its Application and Validity in Southern California. Unpublished Ph.D. dissertation, University of California, Los Angeles.

Haynes, Vance
1973 The Calico Site: Artifacts or Geofacts? *Science* **181**:305–310.

Heizer, R.F.
1952 Observations on Early Man in California. *University of California Archaeological Survey Reports* **7**:5–9.
1964 The Western Coast of North America. In *Prehistoric Man in the New World,* edited by J.D. Jennings and E. Norbeck. Chicago: University of Chicago Press. Pp. 117–148.

Johnson, F., and J.P. Miller
1958 Review of Pleistocene Man at San Diego. *American Antiquity* **24**(2):206–210.

Krieger, A.D.
1964 Early Man in the New World. In *Prehistoric Man in the New World,* edited by J.D. Jennings and E. Norbeck. Chicago: University of Chicago Press. Pp. 23–81.

Leakey, L.S.B., R.D. Simpson, and T. Clements

1968 Archaeological Excavations in the Calico Mountains. California: Preliminary Report. *Science* **160:**1022–1023.

Lillard, J.B., R.F. Heizer, and F. Fenenga
1939 An Introduction to the Archaeology of Central California. *Sacramento Junior College, Dept. of Anthropology Bulletin* No. **2.**

Meighan, C.W.
1959 California Cultures and the Concept of an Archaic Stage. *American Antiquity* **24**(3): 289–305.
1965 Pacific Coast Archaeology. In *The Quaternary of the United States,* edited by H.E. Wright and D. Frey. Princeton, New Jersey: Princeton University Press. Pp. 709–720.

Meighan, C.W., and C.V. Haynes
1970 The Borax Lake Site Revisited. *Science* **167:**1213–1221.

Michels, J.W.
1964 Lithic Serial Chronology Through Obsidian Hydration Dating. Unpublished Ph.D. dissertation, University of California, Los Angeles.

Orr, P.C.
1968 *Prehistory of Santa Rosa Island.* Santa Barbara: Santa Barbara Museum of Natural History.

Rogers, D.B.
1929 *Prehistoric Man of the Santa Barbara Coast.* Santa Barbara: Santa Barbara Museum of Natural History.

Rogers, M.J.
1929 Stone Art of the San Dieguito Plateau. *American Anthropologist* **31:**454–467.

Schenck, W.E., and E.J. Dawson
1929 Archaeology of the Northern San Joaquin Valley. *University of California Publications in American Archaeology and Ethnology* **25**(4):289–413.

Schuiling, W.C. (Editor)
1972 *Pleistocene Man at Calico.* San Bernardino: San Bernardino County Museum Assoc.

Simpson, R.D.
1964 The Archaeological Survey of Pleistocene Manix Lake (an Early Lithic Horizon). *Proceedings of the 35th International Congress of Americanists* **1:**5–9.

Uhle, M.
1907 The Emeryville Shellmound. *University of California Publications in American Archaeology and Ethnology* **7**(1).

Wallace, W.J.
1955 A Suggested Chronology for Southern California Coastal Archaeology. *Southwestern Journal of Anthropology* **11:**214–230.
1963 Prehistoric Cultural Development in the Southern California Deserts. *American Antiquity* **28**(2):172–180.

Warren, C.N.
1966 The San Dieguito Type Site: M.J. Rogers 1938 Excavation on the San Dieguito River. *San Diego Museum Papers* No. **5.**
1973 California. In *The Development of North American Archaeology,* edited by J.E. Fitting. Garden City, New York: Anchor Books. Pp. 212–249.

Warren, C.N., and D.L. True
1961 The San Dieguito Complex and Its Place in California Prehistory. *University of California Archaeological Survey, Annual Report 1960–61,* 264–338.

Western Mesoamerica before A.D. 900

PAUL TOLSTOY

I. INTRODUCTION

The difficulty of reviewing the evidence for three dozen or more regional sequences in a concise yet useful manner has led me to the following solution: to discuss only one of these sequences, that of the Basin of Mexico, in any detail. This choice is influenced by the present need for a recent picture of this very important chronology, and also by my greater familiarity with the Central Highlands than with other regions. More important, it reflects a conviction that the Central Highlands, and the Basin of Mexico in particular, are more suited than any other region to provide a "master sequence'' (Rowe 1962) for the remainder of the area west of the Isthmus, at least after 3000 B.C. For the period prior to 3000 B.C., however, the absence of suitably firm and complete data from any one region precludes the use of that device (Tehuacán comes to mind, but is not helpful beyond the seventh millennium B.C.). In consequence, I have used Willey's ''major American periods'' I through V as reference terms in discussion. The master sequence (described in Section 3 below) follows these and falls entirely into Willey's Period VI, at least if we grant that the 2000 B.C. threshold for that period is a ''round figure'' that can be moved back a few centuries (cf. Willey 1966:93).

By ''master sequence,'' I mean a time scale firm enough and fine enough to make it convenient to ask questions of the form with which part of the master sequence is a given phase, X, elsewhere contemporaneous? Naturally, this is not meant to bear in any way on the use of independent, local evidence (cultural or extracultural) in the construction of other regional time scales, nor is it an invitation to a procrustean fitting of regional phases elsewhere into a sequence imposed from the outside. On the contrary, local evidence must be the basis of local phasing and of local dating and, in the present attempt at least, invariably has been weighed before and over outside evidence. The purpose of instituting a master sequence, however, is to ensure that, ultimately, both the questions and the answers that concern dating are always phrased in comparable terms. Thus, we can aim to say, for example, that the Early Morett Phase of the Colima Coast is probably First Intermediate 6 (FI-6) to First Intermediate 9 (FI-9) in date, and then, as needed, we may turn to the Basin of Mexico for a definition of these intervals. The emphasis here is not so much on the correctness or accuracy of the above placement of Early Morett, as on the definiteness of its meaning. If it is, in fact, incorrect, we have, in the Basin of Mexico, a potential measure of its error and a set of terms with which to rectify it by using units that have a definite and uniform meaning for Western Mesoamerica as a whole. In dwelling on the Basin of Mexico sequence, I am urging, therefore, a more formal use of it as a standard, or yardstick, in discussions of chronology west of the Isthmus. In effect, it has filled this role fitfully and informally over the last 50 years, and my procedure is not novel. I am assuming, however, that the distinctness of temporal correlation from stylistic phasing, stage assignment and other kinds of classification is now more generally understood than it used to be (for a fuller discussion, see Rowe 1962), and that the reluctance of Mesoamericanists in making it operational is becoming increasingly inconvenient and difficult to defend.

In dealing with other regions, the burden of my conclusions is inevitably relegated to the accompanying charts (Figures 9.1–9.5). In filling them, I have been selective, and have stopped far short of placing all phases, let alone all isolated finds reported in the literature. Admittedly, the choice of material included at times verges on the arbitrary, though I have attempted in general to balance the quality of the available evidence, which is often poor, with the intrinsic or potential importance of some assemblages in filling gaps in time and space. Generally, discussion of phasing and dating outside the Central Highlands is brief and confined to the citation of principal sources, a mention of the more important evidence for absolute dating or synchronism with other sequences, a statement of some crucial problems and uncertainties, and a general rating of the reliability and precision of the sequence or group of sequences in question. Where the evidence was available, I have tried a fresh approach to the problem of correlation and dating, and to review the data rather than accept the opinions or syntheses of others. Such a procedure, despite its obvious dangers, has at least the advantage of suggesting the degree to which the conclusions of others can be independently replicated. By and large, discrepancies between temporal placements made herein and those previously published are not great, and are predictably greater for regions where the least data has been collected or reported.

Radiocarbon assays have been mostly accepted within some portion of their 1-sigma ranges wherever they were internally compatible with one another within the sequences to which they pertain. This proved to be possible for well over two-thirds of available dates, as might reasonably be expected in the light of the theoretical meaning of such dates and that of their 1-sigma ranges. Whenever dates to either side of a cultural boundary suggested a placement of the latter somewhat before or after a correlative boundary in a neighboring and related sequence, such a placement was allowed to stand, unless it conflicted strongly with the cultural evidence. This applies particularly to the matching of the Basin of Mexico, Tehuacán, and Valley of Oaxaca columns. Despite its tendency to suggest a degree of precision that other data often cannot presently confirm, this procedure was deemed more productive, potentially, than the prevailing and somewhat circular practice of matching correlative phases in a one-to-one fashion. In some cases, for example, in displacing upward in time the boundaries of the San José and Guadalupe phases of Oaxaca from published estimates, this proved enlightening in accounting for some of the cultural evidence. In other cases, cultural correlations were found to be neutral to the issue, and radiocarbon-set boundaries were adopted simply as best current estimates whose implications may or may not become apparent in the light of further work. Finally, I have made consistent use of the curve published by Suess (1970) in converting radiocarbon time to sidereal time (these are abbreviated from here on as RT and ST, respectively), though in the absence of published tabular values, my reading of the Suess curve may differ somewhat from that of others. Unlike Johnson and Willis (1970), I have been particularly concerned with fluctuations of atmospheric radiocarbon over time

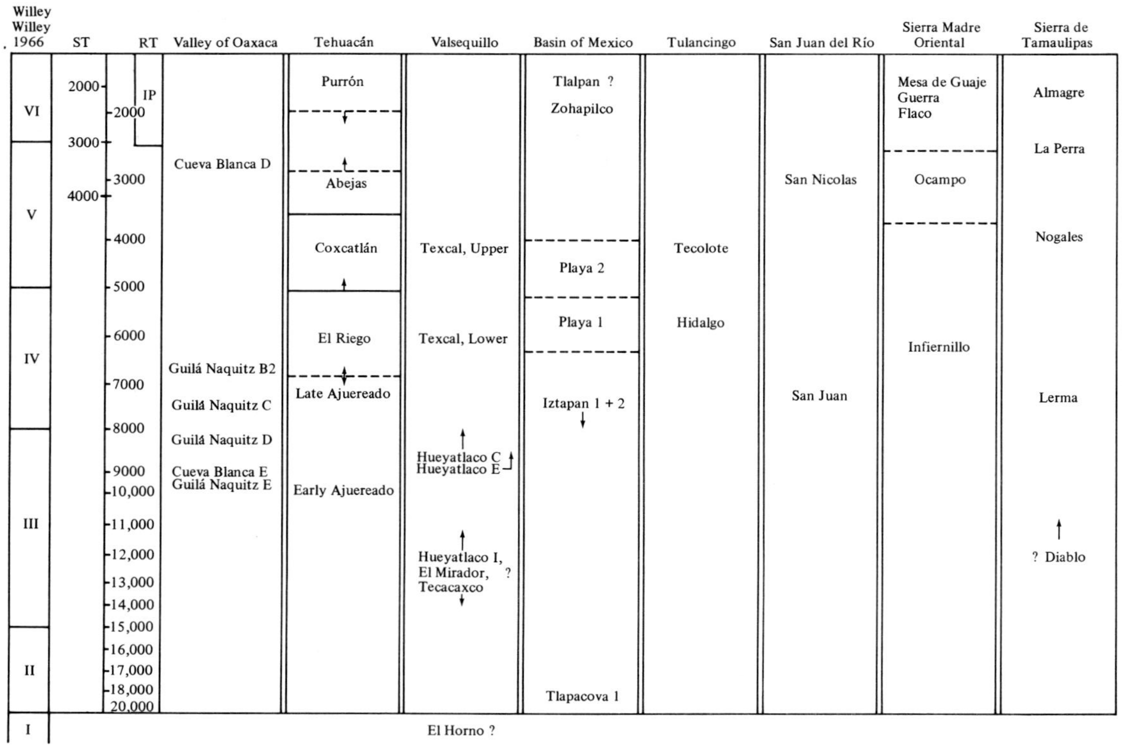

Willey Willey 1966	ST	RT	Valley of Oaxaca	Tehuacán	Valsequillo	Basin of Mexico	Tulancingo	San Juan del Río	Sierra Madre Oriental	Sierra de Tamaulipas
VI	2000	IP 2000		Purrón		Tlalpan ? Zohapilco			Mesa de Guaje Guerra Flaco	Almagre
	3000									La Perra
V	4000	3000	Cueva Blanca D	Abejas				San Nicolas	Ocampo	
		4000		Coxcatlán	Texcal, Upper	Playa 2	Tecolote			Nogales
		5000								
IV		6000		El Riego	Texcal, Lower	Playa 1	Hidalgo		Infiernillo	
		7000	Guilá Naquitz B2	Late Ajuereado		Iztapan 1 + 2		San Juan		Lerma
		8000	Guilá Naquitz C Guilá Naquitz D							
III		9000 10,000	Cueva Blanca E Guilá Naquitz E	Early Ajuereado	Hueyatlaco C Hueyatlaco E					
		11,000 12,000 13,000			Hueyatlaco I, El Mirador, ? Tecacaxco					? Diablo
II		14,000 15,000 16,000 17,000 18,000 20,000				Tlapacova 1				
I					El Horno ?					

Figure 9.1. Western Mesoamerica before 3000 B.C. ST.

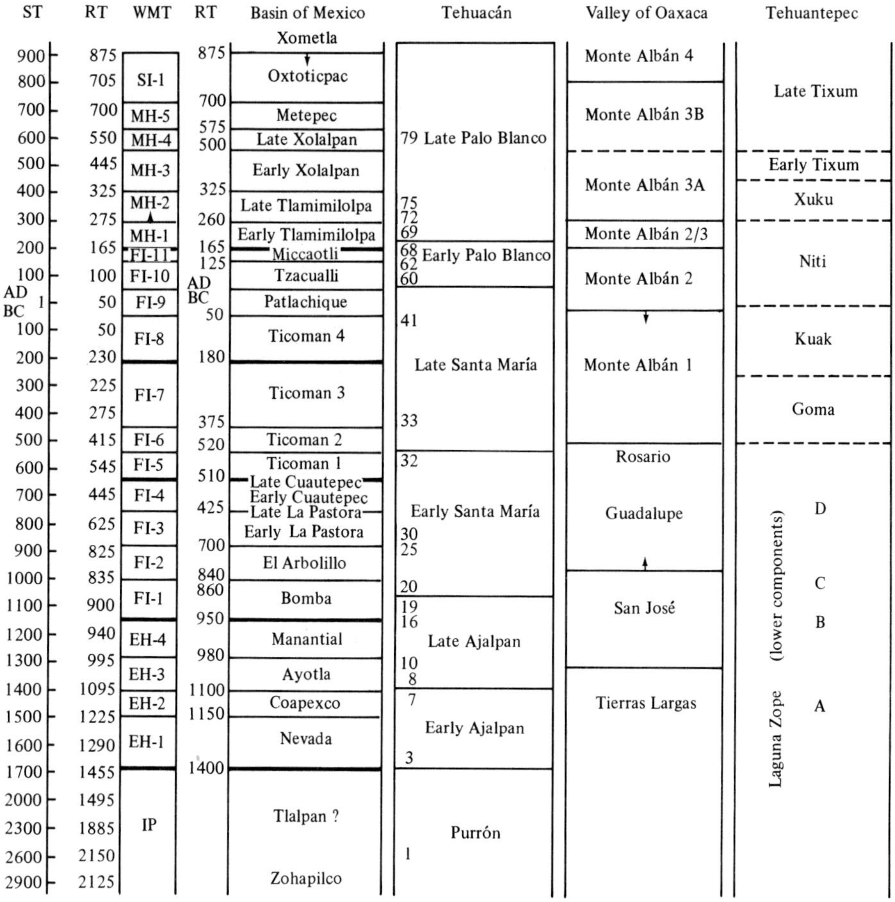

ST	RT	WMT	RT	Basin of Mexico	Tehuacán	Valley of Oaxaca	Tehuantepec
900	875		875	Xometla		Monte Albán 4	
800	705	SI-1		Oxtoticpac			Late Tixum
700	700	MH-5	700	Metepec		Monte Albán 3B	
600	550	MH-4	575 500	Late Xolalpan	79 Late Palo Blanco		
500	445	MH-3		Early Xolalpan			Early Tixum
400	325		325			Monte Albán 3A	
300	275	MH-2	260	Late Tlamimilolpa	75 72		Xuku
		MH-1		Early Tlamimilolpa	69	Monte Albán 2/3	
200	165	FI-11	165 125	Miccaotli	68 62 Early Palo Blanco		Niti
100	100	FI-10		Tzacualli	60	Monte Albán 2	
AD BC 1	50	FI-9	AD BC 50	Patlachique			
100	50	FI-8		Ticoman 4	41		Kuak
200	230		180		Late Santa María	Monte Albán 1	
300	225	FI-7		Ticoman 3			
400	275		375		33		Goma
500	415	FI-6	520	Ticoman 2			
600	545	FI-5	510	Ticoman 1 / Late Cuautepec	32	Rosario	Laguna Zope (lower components)
700	445	FI-4	425	Early Cuautepec / Late La Pastora			
800	625	FI-3		Early La Pastora	Early Santa María	Guadalupe	D
900	825	FI-2	700		30 25		
1000	835		840	El Arbolillo			
1100	900	FI-1	860 950	Bomba	20 19 16	San José	C
1200	940	EH-4		Manantial	Late Ajalpan		B
1300	995	EH-3	980		10 8		
1400	1095		1100	Ayotla			
1500	1225	EH-2	1150	Coapexco	7	Tierras Largas	A
1600	1290	EH-1		Nevada	Early Ajalpan		
1700	1455		1400		3		
2000	1495						
2300	1885	IP		Tlalpan ?	Purrón		
2600	2150				1		
2900	2125			Zohapilco			

Figure 9.2. Central and Southern Highlands, 3000 B.C.–A.D. 900.

wherever these make possible a choice between several central values on the ST scale, a choice between differing durations of a given time segment, or the reconciliation of seemingly reversed estimates for sequent phases (as in the case of what would have been called formerly the Late Middle Preclassic and the early Late Preclassic). In those portions of the sequence under discussion, in which the Suess curve leads one to expect radiocarbon ages inversely related to age in ST, RT values are cited in order of ST age, from older to younger (e.g., 925 to 960 B.C. RT).

The choice of period designations has been a difficult one. Initially, I had considered a nomenclature in which the Preclassic was divided into Initial,

Date	Phase	San Lorenzo	Tres Zapotes	Cerro de Las Mesas	El Trapiche	Lower Tecolutla	Huasteca		
900									
800	SI-1					La Isla A	Zaquil	La Salta	
700	MH-5		Tres Zapotes 4	Nopiloa					Palmillas
600	MH-4								
500	MH-3				El Trapiche 4 (Trapiche B, 1–9)	Cacahuatal	Pithaya	Eslabones	
400			Tres Zapotes 3	C de Las M 3 (Late Lower 2)					
300	MH-2								
200	MH-1, FI-11					Tecolutla			
100	FI-10							Laguna	La Florida
AD/BC	FI-9						El Prisco		
100	FI-8				El Trapiche 3 (Trapiche B, 10-13 Trapiche A, 1–4)				
200		Remplás	Tres Zapotes 2	C de Las M 2 (Early Lower 2)		Arroyo Grande			
300	FI-7								
400									
500	FI-6								
600	FI-5					Esteros B	Chila		
700	FI-4	Palangana	Tres Zapotes 1	C de Las M 1 (Lower 1)	El Trapiche 2 (Chalahuite, upper, Trapiche, middle)				
800	FI-3								
900	FI-2	Nacaste				Esteros A	Aguilar		
1000									
1100	FI-1				El Trapiche 1 (Trapiche A, 12–15 Chalahuite A, 22–44 Chalahuite B, 14–15)		Ponce		
1200	EH-4	San Lorenzo A				Ojite			
1300	EH-3	San Lorenzo							
1400	EH-2	San Lorenzo B					Pavón		
1500		Chicharras							
1600	EH-1	Bajío							
1700		Ojochi							↑ Mesa de Guaje
2000									
2300	IP							Almagre	Guerra Flaco
2600									
2900									

Figure 9.3. The Mesoamerican Gulf regions west of the Isthmus, 3000 B.C.–A.D. 900.

Date	Phase	Chalchihuites: Suchil Valley	Chalchihuites: Colorado Valley	Durango	Sinaloa–Nayarit Coast: Chametla	Sinaloa–Nayarit Coast: Peñitas	Sinaloa–Nayarit Coast: Amapa	South Nayarit & Western Highlands: Ixtlán	South Nayarit & Western Highlands: Etzatlán	South Nayarit & Western Highlands: Chapala–W. Michoacan	South GTO	Armería–Tuxpan Basin: Autlán	Armería–Tuxpan Basin: Tuxcacuexco	Armería–Tuxpan Basin: Armería	Jalisco–Colima Coast: B. de Navidad	Jalisco–Colima Coast: Morett
900																
800	SI-1			Las Joyas	Lolandis		Tuxpan	Middle Ixtlán, Los Cocos		Chapala				Armería		Late Morett
700	MH-5	Vesuvio	Retoño													
600	MH-4		Calichal	Ayala	Baluarte		Amapa					Cofradía	Coralillo	Colima	Barra (Early and Middle)	
500	MH-3															
400			Alta Vista		Tierra del Padre	Chala	Gavilán ↓		El Arenal	El Otero?						
300	MH-2							Early Ixtlán								
200	MH-1					Tamarindo			Ameca							
200	FI-11	Canutillo												Chanchopa		
100	FI-10												Tuxcacuexco	Ortices		
1	FI-9															
100	FI-8								San Sabastian							
200											Chupicuaro Black Poly					
300	FI-7										Brown Poly					Early Morett
400																
500	FI-6															
600	FI-5															
700	FI-4							San Blas								↓
800	FI-3									El Opeño Tomb 3, II						
900	FI-2															
1000																
1100	FI-1															
1200	EH-4															
1300	EH-3									El Opeño Tomb 3, I?						
1400	EH-2															
1500										↑						
1600	EH-1													Capacha		
1700																
2000	II-															
2300																
2600																
2900																

Figure 9.4. The North Central Frontier of Mesoamerica and West Mexico, 3000 B.C.–A.D. 900.

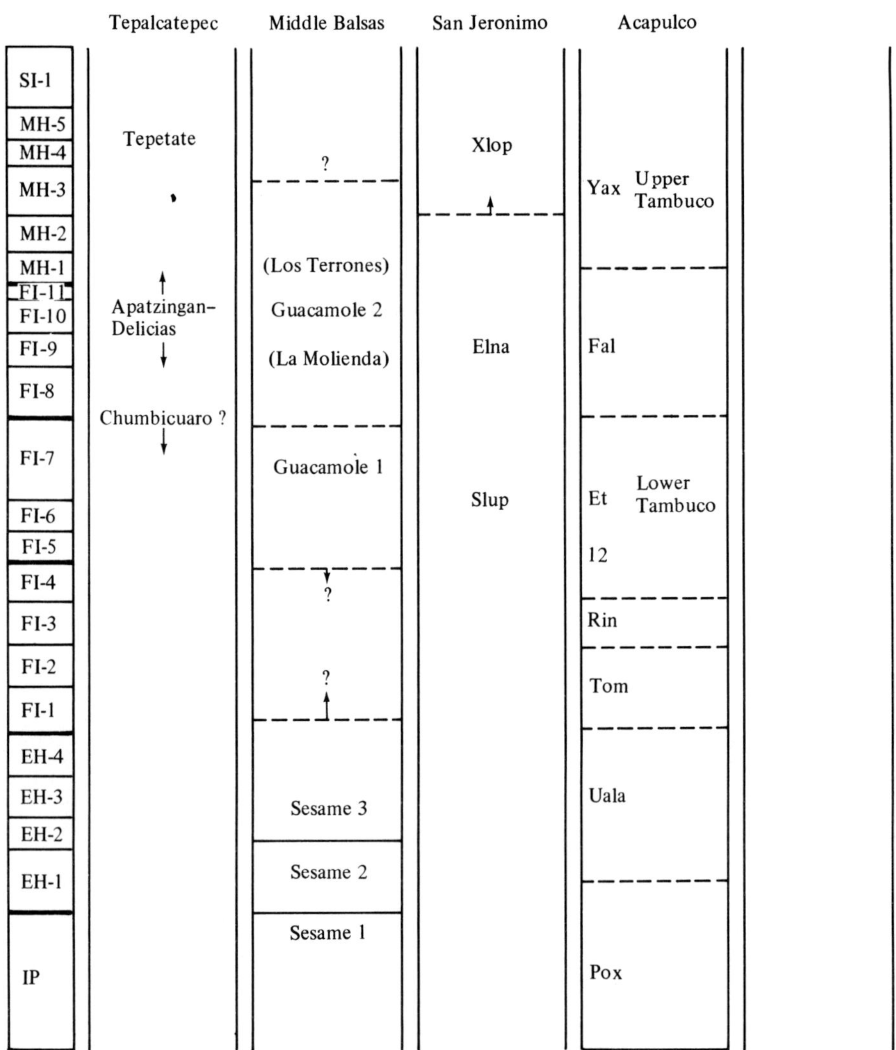

Figure 9.5. Guerrero and the Balsas–Tapalcatepec Depression, 3000 B.C.–A.D. 900.

Early, Middle, Late, and Terminal, and these periods were, in turn, subdivided numerically. Similarly, the Classic was segmented into a twofold Early and a threefold Late. Like its many predecessors over the last decade, this scheme perpetuated for chronological usage a set of terms heavily invested with evolutionary meaning (e.g., Willey and Phillips 1958). I then learned that, quite independently of my own efforts, a study group meeting in June of 1972, in Santa Fe, to discuss cultural developments in the Basin of Mexico, had not only agreed to adapt Rowe's "master sequence" concept to

Mesoamerican chronology but also to implement it with a set of period names closely modeled after the designations used by Rowe and his students in Peru (Price 1976). The desirability of a "neutral" terminology has, in fact, been argued by Millon since 1959 (cf. Willey *et al.* 1964:477–478). I have therefore adopted the scheme and it is used throughout the text that follows and in Figures 9.2–9.5. It has the effect of freeing such terms as "Classic" to designate developmental stages, a function they often already perform on occasions that need to be recognized from the context (e.g., as in Willey and Phillips 1958).

II. EARLY PERIODS

Paleoenvironmental sequences for the Pleistocene in Mesoamerica are still scarce, but recent work by J. L. Lorenzo and his students at Tlapacoya in the Basin of Mexico is now beginning to provide Basin-floor equivalents for glacial events outlined by White (1962) for the slopes of Ixtaccíhuatl. It appears increasingly that the intra- or postglacial climatic optima of North America may have been times of increased moisture in the tropical highlands of Mexico, whereas, conversely, the colder events were dry (Lorenzo 1961). Post-Pleistocene fluctuations of lake level, climate, and vegetation currently emerging at Tlapacoya (Gonzales n.d.; Goodliffe and Goodliffe 1966; Haynes 1967; Mirambell 1967; Niederberger 1969) can be related to several cultural assemblages at the same locality. These include a hearth, atypical andesite implements, and a chalcedony scraper at Tlapacoya I. The overlapping ranges of three dates (A-790A, A-793 and A-794B) would place these remains at ca. 19,000 B.C. RT, that is, in Willey's Period II, shortly after a high stand of Lake Chalco (ca. 2242 m). There are also three later occupations (Playa 1, ca. 5100 B.C.; Playa 2, ca. 4250 B.C.; and Zohapilco, ca. 2300 B.C.) at Tlapacoya IV (Niederberger 1976), which provide an assortment of chipped and ground stone, along with evidence of teosinte (Playa 1) and cultivated corn (Zohapilco). A high stand of the lake and then a dry interval intervene between Playa 2 and Zohapilco. Playa 1 and Playa 2 fall into Willey's Periods IV and V, respectively. Zohapilco is taken here to fit into the Initial Period (see Section 111.A). Two radiocarbon dates (L-161, M-776; see Johnson and MacNeish 1972:33) suggest that the mammoth kills of the Basin of Mexico (Ixtapan 1 and 2, San Bartolo Atepehuacan) date from the eighth millennium B.C., that is, from early Recent times, early in Willey's Period IV, before Playa 1 but well after Tlapacoya I. The associated projectile point forms, bipointed ones in particular, recall those of Late Ajuereado Phase of Tehuacán (MacNeish *et al.* 1967:56–57), Hueyatlaco near Puebla, Unit E (Irwin-Williams 1967), the San Juan Phase of a cave in Querétaro (MacNeish *et al.* 1967:238–239) and the Lerma Phase levels of caves in the Sierra de Tamaulipas (MacNeish 1958), the latter dated at ca.

7300 B.C. (M-499). Thus, the bipoint may well be a good eighth-millenium marker for the Mexican Highlands, though its initial appearance in Puebla could go back earlier.

Edge-retouched flake and crude blade tools underlie bifacial projectile points at Hueyatlaco (Unit I), and similar remains occur at El Mirador, Tecacaxco, Caulapan, and El Horno, in association with the rich Pleistocene fauna of the Valsequillo Gravel Formation. A date of 19,900 B.C. on shell from Caulapan (W-1896) does not contradict estimates that the Valsequillo gravels began to be deposited some 30,000 years ago. The El Horno materials may even go back close to that time, that is, to Period I in Willey's scheme.

The Tehuacán sequence prior to the Purrón Phase is exceptionally well described (MacNeish *et al.* 1967). Unfortunately, acceptable ^{14}C determinations are lacking for Early Ajuereado, an assemblage of a very few stone artifacts that do not include any projectile points and are associated with fauna suggestive of a colder and perhaps drier climate (Byers 1967:65; Flannery 1967:144). Evidence from Cueva Blanca, near Mitla, in the Valley of Oaxaca, may mean that 9000 B.C. marks approximately the onset of modern conditions in the highlands of southern Mexico (Flannery *et al.* n.d.). After that boundary, both Cueva Blanca (Zone E) and neighboring Guilá Naquitz (Zones E, D, C, and B-2) indicate occupations that radiocarbon dates put between 9000 and 6700 B.C. RT (Periods III and IV). Unlike the Late Ajuereado sites of Tehuacán, which must be contemporary, these Oaxacan cave levels yield *Cucurbita pepo* and stemmed projectile points. The latter, as well as the presence of manos by 8000 B.C., brings to mind comparably early occurrences both of stemmed points and of manos in caves of western North America (e.g., Fort Rock and other sites for the former; Danger Cave 1 for the latter). Also in the Mitla area, Geo Shih and Zone C of the Martínez Rockshelter may correlate with the El Riego Phase of the Coxcatlán Phase of Tehuacán, or both, whereas Zone D at Cueva Blanca (also Zone B of Martínez?) is somewhat later. Evidence of moist conditions at that time (Lindsay 1968) again hints at a recent climatic history different from that of more northern latitudes.

On the northeastern fringe of our area, two sequences were constructed by MacNeish (1958, 1971) between 1940 and 1955. There, the relatively moist conditions attendant on the Lerma Phase are thought to have been followed by a dry interval, contemporary with Nogales remains, and then by a return to a damper regime ca. 2500 B.C. (La Perra Phase). This is suggestive of the climatic sequence for western Texas (e.g., at the Clovis Site, Haynes and Agogino 1966) and western North America in general, rather than of the trends now emerging for the Mesoamerican Highlands. The Diablo assemblage at the base of the Sierra de Tamaulipas column evidently dates from a humid interval earlier than 7300 B.C. RT and is associated with horse. Like Early Ajuereado, it is known from a small collection in which bifacial projectile points are absent. It probably belongs in Period III. Outside of the highlands, early sites have been reported only in the sketchiest manner. The Palo Hueco Phase of the lower Tecolutla region of North-Central Veracruz (Wilkerson 1973) and the Ostiones Phase at the base of C. Brush's Puerto Marquez sequence near Acapulco (Guerrero; Brush n.d.) evidently represent shellfish collectors early in the third millennium B.C., as suggested by one date for the first (N-913) and two for the second (HO-1263, HO-1264). Other assemblages, such as those of Ford's Palma Sola Site in Central Veracruz (referred to but not named in MacNeish *et al.* 1967:244), Cerro de las Conchas in Southern Veracruz (Lorenzo 1961:16) and Mountjoy's Matanchén near San Blas on the coast of Nayarit (Porter Weaver 1972:78) may represent approximately the same period and the same way of life, but little has been reported about them in print.

III. THE CENTRAL HIGHLANDS TO A.D. 900

At the core of the Central Highlands, in the Basin of Mexico, stratigraphic work got an early start through the activities of the International School headed by Boas and Gamio (Boas 1913; Gamio 1913) at the beginning of the century. It received a second major impulse in the late 1920s and 1930s from the work of George C. Vaillant, which has been published only in part (Vaillant 1930, 1931, 1935a,b, 1944). Over the last three decades, refinements and correlations of the pre-A.D. 900 portions of the Vaillant sequence have come out of the work of Armillas at Teotihuacán (1950), Piña Chán at Tlatilco (1958), Tolstoy in the north of the Basin (1958), the University of California group at Cuicuilco (Heizer and Bennyhoff 1958), Instituto Nacional (INAH) and the University of Rochester teams at Teotihuacán (Bennyhoff 1966; Millon 1966; Muller 1966), and, more recently, Tolstoy (Tolstoy and Guénette 1965; Tolstoy and Paradis 1970; Tolstoy 1975; Tolstoy *et al.* 1977) and Niederberger (1976) at several Preclassic sites. The result is now a sequence for the Basin of Mexico, which, though still imperfect in many parts and incompletely published, consists of units sometimes a century or less in length.

Work in adjacent subregions of the Central Highlands is less advanced. Some data are available for Hidalgo to the north (Acosta 1940, 1944; García Cook 1967; Muller 1960) and the Toluca Valley to the west (García Payón 1941). Recent research has improved substantially the picture for Puebla–Tlaxcala (Aufdermauer 1970; Dumond and Muller 1972; Fowler 1969; García Cook 1976; Snow 1969; Spranz 1968; Walter 1970) to the east, while progress in Morelos to the south (Grove 1974a,b, n.d.; Grove *et al.* 1976) has been marked for Early Horizon and the beginning of First Intermediate.

The Initial Period (IP) of the Central Highlands master sequence is defined here conventionally as beginning ca. 2400 B.C. RT (ca. 3000 B.C. ST), at the somewhat hypothetical moment when fired pottery first appears. It is followed by the Early Horizon (EH) and First Intermediate (FI) periods, the latter, like the Preclassic of earlier nomenclatures, extending to the end of the Miccaotli (Teotihuacán 2) Phase at Teotihuacán (ca. A.D. 200 ST). The Middle Horizon (MH) is taken to span the remainder of the effective occupation of Teotihuacán. Beyond it, Division 1 of the Second Intermediate (SI) is assumed to last until ca. A.D. 900 ST, that is, at least to the appearance of San Juan Plumbate and to the end of the Oxtoticpac Phase (Dumond and Muller's "Transition").

A. Initial Period (3000–1700 B.C. ST; 2400–1400 B.C. RT)

At present, there is only one significant body of material from the Central Highlands that can be assigned securely to the first thousand years or so of the master sequence, the Zohapilco assemblage from Tlapacoya, which is essentially aceramic though including a single figurine (illustrated in Neiderberger 1969, 1976). The site of Las Bocas (Caballo Pintado) tested by Piña Chán (Paddock 1968) near Izúcar de Matamoros, near the Morelos boundary in southern Puebla, has yielded coarse-tempered pottery not unlike that of the Purrón and Early Ajalpan phases of the Tehuacán Valley (see p. 265). In the Tehuacán Valley, such pottery predominates from at least 1950 B.C. (2460 ST; MacNeish estimates 2300 B.C., i.e., 3000 B.C. ST) to ca. 1300 B.C. or 1600 B.C. ST or even later. A different kind of ware, found at the site of Cuicuilco in the Basin of Mexico, is postulated by Bennyhoff (Fergusson and Libby 1963, 1964; Heizer and Bennyhoff 1972) to present a phase that he names Tlalpan. This pottery is well made, relatively thin, burnished, with a sandy paste and interior scored surfaces not unlike the bulk of Ixtapaluca Phase undecorated monochrome from Tlapacoya. The complex as a whole, however, is much more limited in its range of variation than that of Tlapacoya.[1] Though this could be due to sampling, it must also be acknowledged that it exhibits some distinctive attributes of surface finish (a bright orange-red burnish), shape (a tall flare-sided, flat-bottomed flower-pot form, a deep hemispherical bowl), and decoration (vague red designs). It also offers a few, somewhat imprecise, parallels to the Tierras Largas pottery of Oaxaca (simple red-on-buff decoration, the bowl shape mentioned earlier, gently rounded olla necks, and figurines with "Valdivia-like" hair). The uncertainties connected with Tlalpan pottery are many:

1. Its integrity as an assemblage is questionable, since most of it has been segregated on typological grounds out of mixed construction fill.

[1] I am grateful to Dr. James Bennyhoff who showed me samples of this material in storage in the Lowie Museum at Berkeley.

2. In particular, the association between the pottery and the figurines (Vaillant's Types O, M, and J) is, for the same reason, uncertain.
3. The relationship of this material to six very early ^{14}C dates from Cuicuilco is tenuous: five of the dates are on charcoal unassociated directly with Tlalpan material, only one (1870 B.C. ± 100) applies to a deposit containing Tlalpan sherds. None of the deposits are primary.

Despite these flaws, there is a seductive case to be made for a Tlalpan Phase distinct from, and earlier than, other early pottery presently known from the Basin. Whatever its radiocarbon age or figurine associations (the Tlapacoya figurine from the Zohapilco Level resembles somewhat the Type O specimens from Cuicuilco), Tlalpan pottery fits well the requirements of a simple predecessor of the Ixtapaluca Complex, from which it differs mainly in lacking the elaborations characteristic of that phase.

B. Early Horizon (1700–1150 B.C. ST; 1400–950 B.C. RT)

Recent excavations (Niederberger 1976; Tolstoy and Paradis 1970) have led to the recognition, in the Basin of Mexico, of pottery that predates the initial occupation of El Arbolillo and of similar sites that Vaillant, 40 years ago, had placed at the bottom of his ceramic chronology. At Tlapacoya, on the northern shore of Lake Chalco, these remains are bracketed between 1360 and 950 B.C. RT, with most of the materials from the site probably dating to the second half of that span (i.e., from 1400 to 1150 B.C. ST or 1100 to 950 B.C. RT; I-4406; Y-2354; Y-2353; I-2524) and assigned to the Ixtapaluca Phase. The inventory is notable for the following: the flat-based dish, which is the prevailing form, and tends to be dark in color, well-burnished, and, when decorated, to bear incised, excised, rocker-stamped and/or zoned motifs; elaborate red-on-buff painted decoration, sometimes combined with resist painting; white ware with elaborate exterior incision, often of "Olmec" style, sometimes also combined with resist painting; differentially fired ware; figurines of the plow-eyed (Niederberger's Pilli and related forms), "baby-face," D and K varieties; and small pointed-stem projectile points (Niederberger 1976; Tolstoy and Paradis 1970). Changes through time occur in this inventory, an Ayotla Subphase being marked by a tendency toward darker backgrounds in red-on-buff ware, a lower proportion of D-1 and D-2 figurines than in later levels, and a kind of very fine incision on the inside of the base of some dishes, seemingly absent in the following subphase. In Niederberger's 1969 trench at Tlapacoya IV (adjacent to the locality tested by Tolstoy and Paradis in 1967), Ayotla materials are overlain by those of a phase termed Manantial, similar in some respects to, but more clearly defined than the subphase earlier named Justo (Tolstoy and Paradis 1970). Some distinctive characteristics of Manantial include the abundance of flat-based white ware with interior basal incision and the double line break motif on the lip or rim, "imitation" differentially fired ware with painted white rim bands, an increased use of gadrooning and other phytomorphic effects, masks, and the relative abundance of red ware compared to its rarity later on. Unlike the Bomba Subphase that follows, Manatial is characterized not by C-2 figurines but, instead, by figurines in the earlier D tradition. I am taking Manantial to mark the end of the Early Horizon (see Section C).

The excavations at Tlapacoya aid (without resolving definitively) the placement in time of the Tlatilco graves, a long-debated problem (Piña Chán 1958; cf. Porter 1953; Tolstoy 1971a; Tolstoy and Guénette 1965; Tolstoy and Paradis 1970). It is clear now that the graves of Tlatilco contain materials quite similar to the refuse at Tlapacoya and that they must be placed, therefore, in a broad Ixtapaluca phase, designed to accommodate Olmec-related materials in our region. Three ^{14}C dates (M-661, Y-2380, Y-2381) are consistent with this assignment. A recent attempt to seriate the Tlatilco graves (Tolstoy 1971a, n.d.) suggests four sequential groups. Group 4, the latest, is notable for a set of features (which belong to what Grove has called the Tlatilco or Rio Cuautla style) such as carinated tubular-neck bottles, stirrup spouts, masks, and certain effigies. Some of these are unknown at Tlapacoya, and most of them are scarce at that site, perhaps in view of their funerary function. Their occurrence, however, when determinable, clusters in Niederberger's Manantial Phase at that site. Group 4 graves at Tlatilco probably date from ca. 975 B.C. RT and from the decades that follow, though some of the features noted in them may be older in West Mexico (Grove 1974a; Tolstoy 1971a) and, perhaps, even in Morelos (Grennes 1974). By contrast, Group 1, the earliest in the seriation, is short on "Rio Cuautla" elements (two kinds of bottle and D figurines are among the very few) but is dominated by features known from the southern Gulf Coast in the San Lorenzo Phase of the Early Preclassic (flat-based dishes, spouted trays, certain "Olmec" design motifs, thin-walled tecomates). Groups 2 and 3 are intermediate in content and perhaps in age. Along with a few elements confined to them (oval bowls, tripod ollas), these graves contain both "Olmecoid" and "Rio Cuautla" materials, and also show the largest number of cross ties with Ayotla refuse. This may mean that Group 1 graves are somewhat earlier than our and Niederberger's earliest Ayotla refuse.[2] Niederberger's earliest fully ceramic level at Tlapacoya (her Nevada Phase) may, moreover, be earlier still: This is suggested by the ^{14}C date of 1360 (± 110) B.C. (I-4406) from her trench and hinted also by certain attributes of the

[2]Since this was written (1973), fieldwork by the author and Suzanne K. Fish on the site of Coapexco, near Amecameca (Basin of Mexico) has revealed a settlement that probably also dates from that interval, i.e., from EH-2 times. We are using it to define a Coapexco Subphase within the Ixtapaluca Phase (cf. Tolstoy *et al.* 1977).

pottery itself (Niederberger 1976 and personal communication). We are suggesting, therefore, four presently recognizable segments, or periods, within the Early Horizon of the Basin of Mexico.

Evidence from outside the Basin in the Central Highlands reveals general parallels and specific differences with the sequence just outlined. The lower levels of Pit G at the site of Moyotzingo (near Texmelucan in Puebla) gave a date of 1330 (± 85) B.C. The material has a generalized Early Horizon appearance, with a streaky "pebble-polished" surface rather frequent (Aufdermauer 1970:16–17). It may be significant that a streaky finish (reported as "stick-polishing") also prevails in a phase from Morelos labeled La Juana by Grove (1974a) and is important in the Early and Late Ajalpan phases of the Tehuacán sequence. As redefined recently from refuse in Levels 10 to 8 of an excavation at the Nexpa Site on the Cuautla River, La Juana (Early Nexpa) in turn shares the bolstered-rim dish form with Groups 1 and 2 of the Tlatilco graves. It underlies the San Pablo A Phase (Middle Nexpa), marked by attributes found both in the Ixtapaluca pottery of Tlapacoya and in graves of Groups 2 and 3 at Tlatilco (oval bowls, tall tripod supports, rocker-stamping). Four stratigraphically consistent ^{14}C dates place San Pablo A between 1150 and 980 B.C. RT at Nexpa (N-942, N-941, N-946, N-945), that is, between 1490 and 1290 B.C. ST. Ixtapaluca-like materials, though not directly dated, also occur in Pits 2A, F, and H at Moyotzingo in Puebla. In Morelos, refuse of the San Pablo B Phase (Late Nexpa), presumably contemporaneous with the later Ixtapaluca materials at Tlapacoya, shows some "Olmecoid" features, at least at Nexpa (cylindrical forms, "carved" ware), whereas five graves (Graves 1, 6, 7, 8, and 9) from Nexpa fit perfectly within Tlatilco Group 4. Two other graves (5, NC-3-L) can be placed comfortably in Group 2 and thus probably correspond in time to late La Juana or early San Pablo A refuse. The importance of these Morelos materials lies, particularly, in confirming consistent differences between refuse and grave goods in the Early Horizon of the Central Highlands, above all ca. 1000 B.C. (^{14}C time), as already suggested by the comparison of Tlatilco graves with Tlapacoya refuse. For the Toluca Valley, west of the Basin (García Payón 1941) and the Tulancingo Valley to the North (Muller 1960), there are reports of Ixtapaluca-like materials: K, D-2, and 0 figurines, and incised white cylinders at Calixtlahuaca and Metepec; and similar figurines and rocker-stamped and excised pottery in test pits at Huapalcalco (particularly Test Pit 23).

C. First Intermediate 1–4 (1150–640 B.C. ST; 950–500 B.C. RT)

Unlike the preceding interval, known from a very few sites, the earlier part of the First Intermediate (formerly, the Middle Preclassic) is represented at over 60 known locations in the Basin of Mexico alone (Blanton 1972; Parsons, 1971, n.d.; Sanders 1965)—among them Zacatenco and El

Arbolillo, dug by Vaillant (1930, 1935a) and others—some of them investigated over half a century ago by Boas (1913), Gamio (1913), and Kroeber (1925). Tests at Tlatilco (Piña Chán 1958; Tolstoy and Guénette 1965), El Arbolillo, and Tlapacoya (Tolstoy and Paradis 1970) have clarified the dating of these remains and the changes within the time span they represent.

Conventionally, the First Intermediate can be said to begin as "Olmecoid" features fade from the refuse sequence, probably ca. 1200 B.C. ST (940 RT), and are eclipsed by a roster of attributes that include white-slipped vessels decorated with the "double-line-break" and "sunburst" motifs and pointed-face figurines of Vaillant's C-2 and C-1 types. Overall characteristics of Periods 1–4 of the First Intermediate (FI 1–4) in the Basin (not necessarily present from the start) include a prevalence of round-based, tall-rise, composite-silhouette ("carinated") bowls in burnished monochrome ware that is, on the average, somewhat lighter in color than in earlier times; a relative rarity of decoration, including incision in several sequential styles as well as painting in red-white, white-red, and red-buff; a notable crudity of figurine styles; and stemless projectile points of "teardrop" outline (Tolstoy 1971b: Fig. 2 e, f). Taken together, these traits define a broad phase, which has been called Zacatenco. Four successive periods can be recognized within the span of Zacatenco in the Basin, although their Basinwide value needs confirmation:

1 and 2: Coincident with the Bomba and El Arbolillo subphases. The date earlier published for Bomba (Y-2352; 1030 ± 100 B.C.), like Niederberger's date of 1040 ± 100 B.C. (I-5242), may well apply to Manantial rather than to the appearance of C-2 figurines at Tlapacoya. In view of Y-2353, a date of 940 (±80) B.C. on "Justo" material, with three possible ST readings (ca. 1200 B.C., 1160 B.C. and 1120 B.C.), both Manantial dates are acceptable only in the upper part of their 1-sigma ranges, that is, they should be interpreted to fall after 1320 B.C. ST and, most likely, after 1200 B.C. ST (925 to 960 B.C. RT). The Bomba Subphase is now relatively well known from the contents of several storage pits at the site of Santa Catarina, east of Tlaltenco, excavated in 1971 and 1972. It is characterized by many of the features found in the El Arbolillo Subphase but differs in the continuing importance of flat bases in white ware, the absence of the true Stiff Geometric style, and several other characteristics, most of them quantitative in nature and involving elements found in El Arbolillo as well. El Arbolillo Subphase materials occur in the lower two meters of our eastern test at the El Arbolillo Site, in which the Stiff Geometric style of incision prevails, accompanied by relatively large amounts of round-bottomed, often brown-paste, white vessels with parallel lines incised on the upper rim or lip (the "double-line-break" motif and its variants), the "sunburst" motif, or panel designs cut into the interior, such as occur in Bomba as well. Whereas, in Bomba, the most common interior-base design in white ware is the star or "sunburst," panels (consisting of opposed sets of parallel lines meeting at right angles) are more frequent in El Arbolillo. C-1 and C-2 figurines predominate. Tests at Tlatilco reveal an equivalent occupation in the form of a rather inadequately represented Iglesia Subphase (Piña Chán 1958; Tolstoy and Guénette 1965). A date of 810 B.C. RT (ca. 900 B.C. ST) from Tlatilco (Y-1629), three dates from Santa Catarina (N-1808, N-1809, N-1987) and two dates from El Arbolillo (N-1811, N-1991) suggest the combined duration of 250 or more years for Periods 1 and 2 of the First Intermediate.

3: Occupied by the Early La Pastora Subphase, known from the upper three meters of the eastern test at El Arbolillo, and marked by the relative importance of white-red decoration, the predominance of broad-line incision over other styles, and the presence of the crude C-3 and C-5 figurine types defined by Vaillant. The Totolica Subphase is its equivalent at Tlatilco where, like the preceding subphase, it appears to be represented by domestic refuse but so far not by graves.

4: Containing the Late La Pastora and Cuautepec subphases. The Late La Pastora subphase is one represented in Vaillant's Levels 6, 5, and 4 of Trench D at Zacatenco, as well as in MacBride's (n.d.) Test 2 at Atlamica, Levels 8–10. The earlier part of the Cuautepec Subphase is abundantly found in our western test at El Arbolillo and, in a variant form, at Atoto, a part of the Tlatilco Site. It is also found in Levels 3–7 of Test 2 in MacBride's Atlamica material. It is defined by a high representation of the cursive style of incision, the presence of the distinctive "yellow-white" ware, and the occurrence of figurine styles B and F. It is the equivalent of Vaillant's "El Arbolillo II" and seems well represented in fill at the site of Cuicuilco (Heizer and Bennyhoff 1972). In our test at Tlapacoya, First Intermediate Periods 3 and 4 were not represented. In Niederberger's trench, they may be compressed into one depositional unit with remains of Period 2. A later portion of the Cuautepec Subphase appears in MacBride's Test 3 at Atlamica (Levels 6–10) and is marked by the decline of "yellow-white" and the dominance of figurine style A. Related materials occur at the site of Copilco, on the southern edge of modern Mexico City.

The Early La Pastora–Totolica interval is directly dated by seven samples. The seeming lateness of one of these (Y-1628: 480 ± 60 B.C.) appears to leave little room for Period 4 of the First Intermediate and the intervals that follow. It is important to note, therefore, that the bristlecone pine scale (Suess 1970) shows ^{14}C dates in this range to deviate markedly from sidereal time and to cut in half the apparent duration of the interval 800 to 400 B.C. ST. As a result, the beginning of Period 4 can be estimated at ca. 750 B.C. ST on the bristlecone pine scale, thus leaving at least some five centuries of calendar time for Periods 4 through 7.

Before leaving this time interval in the Basin, note should be taken of the researches of the Berkeley team in 1957 at Cuicuilco. Both at the main pyramid at that site (Cuicuilco A-1) and at Mound 1 of the former Peña Pobre Quarry (Cuicuilco B-1), these revealed a series of construction stages, respectively four and six in number, apparently preceding the threshold of Ticomán (FI 5–7). Three dates (UCLA-594, UCLA-595, UCLA-596) on fill containing both Period 4 and earlier First Intermediate sherds are compatible with the notion that these stages do indeed reach back prior to Ticomán times. The importance of this possibility should not be overlooked. It may make of the inhabitants of many of the Middle Preclassic sites a peasantry subservient to a major ceremonial center, rather than self-sufficient villagers, which they are commonly assumed to be.

Elsewhere in the Central Highlands, materials related to the ones described have been found in Morelos and Puebla, and in the valleys of Toluca and Tulancingo. To the south, in Morelos, pottery not unlike that of the Zacatenco periods of the Basin has come from Chalcatzingo, where it occurs above Early Horizon remains (Grove 1974b) in deposits that have produced a ladder of dates compatible with those of the Basin of Mexico. The FI 1–4 are also represented by Occupation I at the Cerro Chacaltepec Site, near Tlaltizapan (Grove n.d.). In Puebla, to the east, some of the feature pits (Pits K and G, upper levels) at Moyotzingo, and refuse at that site in and around adobe structures, also recall the Bomba and El Arbolillo subphases, both by their figurines and by their pottery (Aufdermauer 1970). ^{14}C dates of 740 (± 80) and 600 (± 90) B.C. (Hv-2513, Hv-2515) are broadly consistent with these parallels, though it would seem that (as in Morelos) precise parallels to La Pastora and Cuautepec are lacking in Early First Intermediate pottery, which tends to be conservative in appearance. In the Toluca Valley to the west, at Calixtlahuaca and Metepec, García Payón (1941:216) reports examples of most of the main figurine types that span the early FI in the Basin, and illustrates a white vessel with interior and double-line-break incision. To the north, in the Tulancingo Valley, Muller (1960:604) reports white-on-red, fugitive white, and impressed pottery—all of them suggestive of La Pastora—from her "Zupitlan Intermediate" levels (17 though 28) in Mound 6 at Huapalcalco. Outside of Morelos and Puebla, these First Intermediate assemblages have not been dated directly, and time gradients across the Central Highlands can be suspected for some of their features.

D. First Intermediate 5–7 (640–225 B.C. ST; 500–150 B.C. RT)

For the interval between the end of FI 4—Vaillant's (1944) "Lower Middle Period"—and the beginning of Teotihuacán, the basis of phasing was laid in the Ticomán report (Vaillant 1931), where an Early, a Middle, and a Late Ticomán are described. These are now more commonly referred to as Ticomán 1, 2, and 3, and are used here to define three consecutive time intervals within the middle part of the First Intermediate. To these, Bennyhoff at Cuicuilco and Sanders and his group in the Teotihuacán Valley (see West 1965) have added later units, which Bennyhoff (1966:22) considers Terminal Preclassic (FI 8–11; Section F).

Taken as a whole, Ticomán pottery tends to be relatively light in color and includes a higher proportion of red ware than Zacatenco Phase ceramics. Shapes are, on the whole, different, though many are variants of earlier forms, such as the round-bottomed carinated bowl which now exists in several new variants, generally with thicker walls and rims than those of earlier times. Among them there is a high-rise form with an attenuated shoulder angle; a shorter-rise variety with a pronounced "Z-angle," or camber; and a restricted-bowl variant with a short, sharply incurving upper rim. Ollas, unlike most of those of the Zacatenco Phase, tend increasingly to have straight, outslanting rims, which join the shoulder at a sharp angle. Tripod supports, for the first time, are fairly abundant and include conical, ball-shaped, and fanciful forms. Red-on-buff is the basic color scheme in painted decoration. It is applied in a distinctive angular style, often in combination with incision and bands of white paint (in the latter case, it is referred to as polychrome). Projectile points are small, and have bulbous or expanding stems or corner notches (Tolstoy 1971b).

Within Ticomán, Phase 1 is distinguished by the abundance of red-on-buff relative to polychrome, the relative scarcity of vessel supports in the early part (Bennyhoff has proposed a Ticomán 1A on this basis), and, on ollas, the importance of reinforced lips and the persistence of significant amounts of Zacatenco-like outcurving rims. The predominant figurine types are E-1 and E-2, with I figurines perhaps also characteristic. Phase 2 is marked by the peak of polychrome, of vessel supports, and of G-1, G-2, and L figurines. Phase 3 sees the decline or disappearance of white ware (moderately represented in 1 and 2) and of red-on-buff, the overwhelming predominance of straight olla necks with simple lip shapes, and the distinctive presence of H-1, H-2 and H-3 figurines.[3]

Radiocarbon dates for the middle of the First Intermediate are few and unsatisfactory. Aside from two Chicago solid-carbon measurements, there is a date for Ticomán 1 from Mound 4 at Cuicuilco B (UCLA 207: 650 ± 70 B.C.), which appears unacceptable within its 1-sigma range. Also for Cuicuilco, two dates, each run twice, apply to Ticomán 3 fill in Mound 2: UCLA 209–603: average 310 (± 50 B.C.); UCLA 208–602: average 190 (± 30 B.C.).They are in correct stratigraphic sequence between superimposed floors. They correspond to sidereal dates of ca. 400 and 200 B.C., respectively, though at the lower end of its 1-sigma range, the second of these dates can even be brought back to ca. 300 B.C. Outside of the Basin, probable equivalents to Ticomán 1–3 occur in Morelos, in Puebla, and in the valley of Tulancingo. In Morelos, closely related pottery was found at the site of Gualupita near Cuernavaca by the Vaillants (Vaillant and Vaillant 1943) and is noted by Grove at Pantitlán, further south. Other reported Morelos assemblages seem specifically less similar, for example, the upper occupations at the site of Chacaltepec (Chacaltepec II: Grove n.d.a), and at the sites of Chimalactlán and Tepoztlán. It is difficult with existing information to know whether this is a cultural or a temporal difference. General trends at Cerro Chacaltepec are consistent, however, with a broad Ticomán equivalence of Occupation II: the diminution of white ware, the increase of red, and the occurrence of several other attributes of form. In Puebla, Totimehuacán (Spranz 1968), Amalucan (Fowler 1969), and Acatepec (Walter 1970), all of them in the Puebla–Cholula region, yield ceramic figurines among which Vaillant's E type and variants thereof strongly predominate. Both the radiocarbon dates and the pottery—the latter briefly described and illustrated for Acatepec—suggest a dating mainly in the late range for Ticomán (perhaps 400–100 B.C. ST) and imply, therefore, a persistence, aside from an

[3]This description draws on a sequencing of the Ticomán lots given in Tolstoy (1958), though it does not differ greatly from the one provided by Vaillant (1931).

elaboration, of the E figurine style beyond its presently posited time range in the Basin. However, regional phasing remains to be worked out, and both the integrity of those assemblages and their precise relation to published ^{14}C assays are unclear. A late Ticomán date for Muller's "Zupitlán Superior B" (Levels 17–6 of her test in Mound 6, Huapalcalco) is similarly suggested both by ceramic evidence (e.g., support forms) and a ^{14}C date of A.D. 1 (± 200), which should probably be accepted only at the lower end of its 1-sigma range. Both the Acatepec and the Huapalcalco pottery exhibit characteristics that are scarce or absent in Ticomán 1–3, for example, flat-bottom bowls and, at Huapalcalco, comales. Both of these forms are considered "Terminal Preclassic" (FI 8–12) in the Basin.

E. End of First Intermediate and Beginning of Teotihuacán (225 B.C.–A.D. 200 ST)

Four sequential divisions have been recognized after Ticomán 3 and prior to the "inception of . . . the fully formed Teotihuacán tradition [Bennyhoff 1966:25]." They represent the decline of the Ticomán complex, as originally described by Vaillant, and the gradual appearance of the inventory of Classic Teotihuacán. The earliest one of these divisions is represented by manifestations that have been variously labeled Cuicuilco 4, Early Chimalhuacán, Tezoyuca, and Ticomán 4. The taxonomic status and interrelationships of these assemblages remain imprecise. Ticomán 4, in particular, remains a conjectural entity, inferred at the type site by Bennyhoff from Vaillant's illustrations but stratigraphically unidentified. A unifying feature of the group as a whole appears to be the H-4 figurine style which, in its filleted eyes and eyebrows, is generally acknowledged to be related to the Chupícuaro "slant-eyed" type, of which several actual examples have been found at Cuautitlán in the Basin of Mexico (McBride 1969). Other characteristic items include the cup on a tall pedestal base with cut-outs (seemingly absent from the Basin since the time of the Group 2 graves of Tlatilco), increasingly common flat-based dishes (anticipating Teotihuacán), resist ware, and, in a burial complex at Tlapacoya, black ware with elaborate and unusual forms, such as large mammiform supports, the "teapot" with unsupported spout and the tall jar with tripod or annular supports. Also typical is a "blobby" style of white-on-red painting, reported to be very common at Tezoyuca and related sites in the Teotihuacán Valley (West 1965:196).

The next time interval is that occupied by the Patlachique Phase of the Teotihuacán sequence and by closely similar occupations at Cuicuilco (Cuicuilco 5), Temesco (Dixon 1969), Chimalhuacán (Noguera 1943; West 1965), and Teotihuacán (Blucher n.d.). It retains such Ticomán-like characteristics as the presence of short-rise composite-silhouette bowls and the abundance of brownish utility vessels (San Martin Coarse Brown; West

1965), which now often have expanded lips and wedge-shaped rims. H-4 figurines have disappeared, both nubbin supports and flat-based dishes occur, and white-on-red decoration is rare or absent.

Tzacualli or Teotihuacán I occupies the next period recognizable in Basin chronology, which is centered, from now on, at the site of Teotihuacán and derived from the work there of the University of Rochester and Instituto Nacional teams. Tzacualli has a repertory of simple shapes in which the flat-based dish predominates. Dark colors prevail in burnished ware and continue to do so in the following Miccaotli Phase. Early Tzacualli is distinguished by the occurrence of resist painting and the presence of several three-color painted types. Late Tzacualli (Bennyhoff 1966:25; Muller 1966:33–34) sees the introduction of the cylindrical jar ("vaso"), of the florero (a tall bottle-like jar with flaring mouth), and possibly of Thin Orange, a widely traded ware made in the Nuiñe or Mixteca Baja region on the western slopes of the Southern Highlands (Cook de Leonard 1953; Paddock 1966:176–178). However, the definition of Late Tzacualli has undergone substantial revision through recent work, and other attributes published for that subphase are evidently invalid (Millon, personal communication).

Miccaotli (Teotihuacán II) is marked by the appearance of dishes with nubbin supports inset from the edge of the flat base (in monochrome burnished ware) and of the typical Teotihuacán vase with tall tripod supports. Monochrome burnished ware remains predominantly dark in color and often has a stick-burnished finish. Red-on-buff is still rare.

Radiocarbon dates for the late portion of the First Intermediate are few and difficult to interpret. A date of 430 (± 140) B.C. from the basal level of a test at Chimalhuacán, even at the upper end of its 1-sigma range and converted to sidereal time, is definitely too early and is barely suitable for Ticomán 3. Difficulties in phase identification may be involved here. A date from the uppermost floor of Mound 2 at Cuicuilco B may apply to the Patlachique Phase (UCLA-206: A.D. 1 ± 80), as do, presumably, at least two of eleven dates obtained by Dixon at Temesco (GaK-1805, GaK-1519), though their value is negligible in view of the broad range of other dates from fill of uncertain cultural context at that site (Dixon 1969). Patlachique presumably ends at or just after A.D. 50 ST (ca. A.D. 1 on the ^{14}C scale), though it may last longer at Cuicuilco (Cuicuilco 5-B) and even at Temesco, in view of the latest fill dates from these sites (UCLA-205: A.D. 160 ± 75; GaK-1804: A.D. 230 ± 80). At Cuicuilco, Tzacualli trade sherds are associated with the latest construction stage of Mound 2, Cuicuilco B. Three radiocarbon dates from Teotihuacán apply specifically to Tzacualli: Y-644: A.D. 20 (± 80); M-1118: A.D. 145 (± 120); and M-1283: A.D. 80 (± 75), the first two from structures at Ostoyohualco, a section of Teotihuacán with Phase I occupation, the third from the fill of the Pyramid of the Sun, also predominantly of that phase. M-1118 seems a bit late, and perhaps only the lower part of its

1-sigma range should be accepted. There are no direct dates on Miccaotli, except for the one Chicago solid-carbon date of A.D. 72 (± 200), which is acceptable in the upper part of its 1-sigma range. The end of Miccaotli can be suggested to fall between A.D. 200 and 250 in sidereal time, the earlier figure making it somewhat easier to accept available assays (St-162, Y-264, Y-265) for the phases that follow. Depending on where this upper boundary is drawn, a group of seven dates (UCLA 609–612, UCLA-615, UCLA-616, UCLA-618) on structural wood from buildings on the Street of the Dead clusters at the end of this phase or in the early part of the next. They probably apply to the early stages of growth of several large trees from which beams were later cut and, in some cases, used twice.

F. Middle Horizon (A.D. 200–700 ST)

The Early Tlamimilolpa Phase, once thought to follow Xolalpan in time (Armillas 1950), sees the fading away of remaining elements of the Ticomán tradition (e.g., white-on-red ware, which disappears after Early Tlamimilolpa) and the rounding out of the "typical" Teotihuacán inventory with such elements as dishes with nubbin supports flush with the basal angle, and biconical censers. One-hole candeleros and three-pronged cooking stoves appear at the end of the phase. (Millon personal communication; Muller 1966:35).

Late Tlamimilolpa differs in such ceramic features as champlevé (plano-relief), stucco decoration, and the cylindrical vase with elaborate supports and conical lid. Candeleros with two holes now occur, as do pottery spindle whorls (Millon, personal communication). The phase is also marked by a considerable expansion of symbolic and ritual motifs in pottery decoration and the occurrence of decoration in Gulf Coast (Tajín) scroll style. The beginning of the phase, according to Millon (personal communication) is represented by the contents of Linne's Tomb 1 at Tlamimilolpa, which has yielded a ^{14}C date of A.D. 230 (± 65) or ca. A.D. 250 ST (ST 162). A rough cross-check on this assay is afforded by the presence, from Early Tlamimilolpa onward, of Oaxacan settlers at Teotihuacán (Millon 1967). Their earliest refuse at Teotihuacán is probably best phased to the Monte Albán 2/3A transition, which available ^{14}C dates both from Oaxaca (M-2107, M-2106) and, indirectly, from Tehuacán (I-656, I-671, I-657, I-663) would bracket in the A.D. 170–370 range ST. It is in view of ST 162 that I favor a beginning of Early Tlamimilolpa ca. A.D. 200 ST. The span attributed to Late Tlamimilolpa depends, in turn, on the placement of the threshold of Early Xolalpan, which follows it.

The Xolalpan phases, Early and Late, constitute most of Teotihuacán's "great" period, the one during which Teotihuacán appears to have had its major impact on the rest of Mesoamerica. There is firm evidence of Early Xolalpan cross-ties with Tikal in the A.D. 400 to 500 ST range (Coe 1972), and a strong suggestion from Zaculeu that these may hold as late as the Tzakol-Tepeu boundary A.D. 550?; Woodbury and Trik 1953:192–193). An Early Xolalpan grave at Teotihuacán has produced a ^{14}C date (Y-1264) whose central value can be interpreted as ca A.D. 400 ST. Early Xolalpan attributes appear to predominate in the other components in Mesoamerica in which the Teotihuacán presence is felt. Many, however, yield radiocarbon dates that go back earlier than the range just suggested. This is true not only of the Maya highlands (Esperanza), Oaxaca (Monte Albán 3A), and the Tehuacán valley (beginning of Late Palo Blanco), but also of ceramic contexts in the Maya lowlands (Middle Tzakol equivalents) at Tikal (T. Patrick Culbert, p.c.) and elsewhere, that can be dated to the fourth century A.D. ST. Many of the Teotihuacán attributes present occur also in Late Tlamimilolpa and a number last into Late Xolalpan. Until their definition and the contexts of their occurrence both at Teotihuacán and elsewhere are better documented than they are presently, they cannot be used to set very accurately the lower boundary of Early Xolalpan, which appears to lie somewhere between A.D. 300 and 400 ST. The central value of Y-1265 (ca. A.D. 310 ST) for Burial 24 of the Zacuala Patios hints that the later of the two figures is closer to the truth, if that burial is Late Tlamimilolpa in date (Millon, p.c.).

Ceramically, Xolalpan is characterized by most of the features earlier noted for Late Tlamimilolpa and several new ones, including elaborations of the cylindrical vase, a red-on-white ware, and proliferation of motifs and scenes of religious and symbolic nature executed in a variety of incised and painted techniques. This repertory is expanded further in Late Xolalpan, at which time square vessels, molded adornos on cooking stoves, Thin Orange miniatures, and stamped decoration are stated to appear. Since cross ties at Early Classic Maya sites seem to be mainly with the preceding phase, Millon concludes that Late Xolalpan overlaps with the Maya Late Classic. Current dates for the latter have it begin ca. A.D. 550 ST (T. Patrick Culbert, personal communication).

Metepec is the last phase during which the great city of Teotihuacán was a going concern, and, in the opinion of some, may postdate the burning of its central portion at the end of Xolalpan times (Dumond and Muller 1972). It falls entirely within the Late Classic as defined in Maya lowland chronology. The ceramic inventory retains many earlier traits. New traits include annular-based bowls imitating a major Thin Orange form, pottery stamps, and, possibly, floreros with annular bases. These last three are significant as forerunners of Early Postclassic pottery in the Basin and at Tula. Stamped decoration, dentate stamping on candeleros, and spindle whorls become particularly characteristic.

A date from Yayahuala (M-1484), run twice, suggests that the Metepec phase lasted at least until ca. A.D. 700 ST. This date should be close to that of the "effective abandonment" of the city. Late Classic Maya trade sherds have been found in association with Metepec debris at Teotihuacán and include a problematical variety of Fine Orange (René Millon, personal communication). This material, however, mostly does not appear to have originated in the Petén and so far has eluded precise phasing within the Classic of the Maya regions.

G. Beginning of Second Intermediate (A.D. 700–900 ST)

A ceramic phase termed Oxtoticpac has been shown to postdate the abandonment of the city and probably represents the refuse of a small group of settlers in the already deserted and ruined metropolis. It is marked by certain unique vessel forms, primarily tripods of several kinds, and other attributes that carry through into later times: ladles, censers, and red–buff decoration in the so-called Coyotlatelco style. This pottery has been found also at Cerro Portezuelo in the Texcoco region and on the western side of the Basin (Hicks and Nicholson 1964) and near Tenayuca (Rattray 1972). It fits within the interval that Dumond and Muller (1972) have named the Transition. The main clue to its age, though hardly a solid one, is the seeming absence of San Juan Plumbate, a trade ware present in early levels at Tula and in the Xometla Phase of the Teotihuacán sequence. The Tehuacán chronology and the Chiapas–Guatemalan highland sequences suggest that its spread *need be* no earlier than A.D. 800 ST and that it could have taken place a century or so later. It is therefore uncertain how much of the Xometla Phase itself falls before A.D. 900. We are provisionally placing it above that date.

Outside of the Basin of Mexico but within the Central Highlands, material falling in the A.D. 1–900 interval is known from Cholula, where the sequence would seem to parallel closely that of Teotihuacán (Dumond and Muller 1972; Muller 1970). The Tulancingo sequence to the north also offers close parallels, from Zupitlán A (a Tzacualli equivalent) through the "Huapalcalco Horizon" (Muller 1956–1957). The Tlaxcala ceramic chronology, at least for the upper Zahuapan drainage, though interpreted to be rather different (Snow 1969), shows evident cross-ties with the Basin. In Morelos, to the south, at Chimalacatlán and Xochicalco, cross-ties go back to Miccaotli (Saenz 1964: P1. 11) and are particularly clear for Transition (SI-1) times, though the sequence, here again, is regionally distinct. Metepec and Oxtoticpac parallels (Saenz 1964: Pl. 14, 16) and ties with Veracruz (Chadwick 1971a:246), Oaxaca, and the Maya lowlands indicate an MH-4 to SI date for the bulk of the pottery from the ceremonial center itself (Saenz 1964:14, 19). To the west, in the Toluca Valley, the coexistence of Teotihuacán pottery with local wares, including local resist-decorated tripods, is asserted by Payón (1941). The chronology of these finds, however, remains unclear. If local Middle Horizon pottery is indeed as described, then the Toluca Valley in this period should be excluded from the Central Highlands region and grouped with Michoacán, Guanajuato, and Querétaro (cf. Porter Weaver 1969:13).

IV. TEHUACÁN VALLEY[4]

The Valley of Tehuacán, at present, offers the most completely dated, best published full-length sequence of western Mesoamerica (Johnson and MacNeish 1972; MacNeish *et al.* 1970). Its main weakness, for comparative purposes, is the limited power of resolution it offers for close dating, and the pattern of its cross-ties, which tend to be with neighboring Oaxaca, or else to the "softer" sequences of the Gulf Coast. It helps anchor the latter in time but can draw from them relatively little support in return. In what follows, I single out those outside parallels, of the many discussed by MacNeish, that seem to be the most specific and temporally meaningful.

There seems, at present, no compelling reason to have the Purrón Phase (Lots 1 and 2) begin before 2500 B.C. ST, the earliest of four ST positions for an RT date of ca. 1900 B.C. (I-757). This leaves an intriguing gap of about 1000 years between the latest Abejas and earliest Purrón materials. 1400 B.C. RT seems a better guess date than 1500 B.C. for the beginning of Early Ajalpan (Lots 3–7), in view of assays I-570 and I-929 for Lots 2 and 3, respectively. Vessel shape similarities with Tierras Largas (Oaxaca) and Ojochi and Bajío (southern Gulf) are consistent with a span 1400 to 1100 B.C. RT indicated or implied by I-929, I-565, I-934 and I-935—the last a date of 1030 (± 130) B.C. for Lot 8, the first of the Late Ajalpan series. Coatepec Red–Buff, first present in Lot 8, bears designs also found in Tierras Largas (Valley of Oaxaca), suggesting that the latter may last beyond 1100 B.C., as confirmed also by the Oaxacan ^{14}C dates (see Section V). Clouded white bottle and bowl fragments, rocker-stamped sherds, and other intrusive "Olmecoid" items seem late in Tehuacán by the Basin of Mexico scale, but could emanate from regions where they probably last longer, for example, the southern Gulf Coast or the Valley of Oaxaca. In Tehuacán, their range is roughly from Lot 14 (late Late Ajalpan) through 24 (early Early Santa María). The peak of white with double-line-break incision follows in Lots 25–29 (Canoas White) and seems to fall ca. 875–850 B.C. ST (750–625 B.C. RT), a century ST or so later than in the Basin of Mexico. This is plausible if we consider the figurines (which include D-like and baby-faced varieties) and such ceramic attributes as flat bottoms and differential firing. These clearly lag even more, by Central Highland standards, lasting to the end of Early Santa María. In the case of many of these, there is independent evidence for

[4]In the discussion that follows, I have numbered the lots of the MacNeish sequence from 1 through 79 consecutively, in the order in which they appear in Table 1 of MacNeish *et al.* 1970:8.

their survival into FI-4 and even FI 8–9 times outside the Central Highlands, for example, in the Gulf and Isthmian regions (for figurines, see Drucker 1943a,b; Lee 1969:7–23).

The beginning of Late Santa María (Lot 33) is cross-dated to the Tzec Phase of the Tikal sequence (ca. 450 B.C. RT) by the appearance of Mars Orange. Its end (Lot 43) and the beginning of Early Palo Blanco (Lot 60) is cross-tied to Ticomán 4 and Chiapa 7 (FI 8–10) by the occurrence of "slot-featured" type figurines, and to Ticomán 4 and Chiapa 6 (FI 8–9) by the appearance of mammiform supports (Lot 58). Radiocarbon suggests (I-918, I-921) an upper boundary for Late Santa María between A.D. 5 and 55 RT (ca. A.D. 50 ST). The general FI 6–9 range of Late Santa María is confirmed by a number of generalized resemblances to contemporary Ticomán figurine types and the abundance of Quachilco Grey, closely allied to types of the Monte Albán 1 and 2 phases.

Early Palo Blanco (Lots 60–68) must be brief, with an upper boundary between A.D. 180 RT (I-656) for Lot 68 and A.D. 200 RT (the upper 1-sigma limit of I-673) for Lot 72. The presence of Thin Orange from Lot 62 onward cross-ties the latter with Late Tzacualli (FI-10). In Late Palo Blanco, Lot 71 contains stucco polychrome, suggestive of Late Tlamimilolpa or Early Xolalpan ties. Thin Orange peaks early in the phase, whereas Lots 76–79 contain San Martin Stamped sherds. The occurrence of the latter suggests contemporaneity with the Late Xolalpan and Metepec phases of Teotihuacán. It is uncertain whether Lot 80, the first of the succeeding Early Venta Salada Phase, falls before A.D. 900 ST (A.D. 875 RT).

Generally, the Tehuacán sequence of the Preclassic and Classic offers a picture that is consistent both internally and in the ties it shows with other sequences. Some doubt lingers as to absolute dating in the range from Lot 14 to Lot 29, in which elements found in EH-3 to FI-2 in the Basin of Mexico appear in their expected order but with a lag of some 100 to 150 years. Since independent evidence, both internal and external, reveals other similar lags in the sequence at that time, the late dating proposed by MacNeish and adopted here with some modification may be correct. The lateness of some traits to appear and to fade would then reflect the rural, conservative stance of the Tehuacán region through time.

V. VALLEY OF OAXACA

As presently known, the Oaxaca chronology is the product of two major efforts: an earlier one by Caso, Acosta, and Bernal (the results are summarized in Bernal 1965; Bernal and Caso 1965), which gave us the succession Monte Albán 1–5; and a later one, by Flannery and his group (Flannery 1968; Flannery *et al.* n.d.), which defined the pre–Monte Albán phases.

While less segmented than that of the Basin of Mexico, and less securely tied to radiocarbon than that of Tehuacán, this is nevertheless one of the more reliable sequences of our area. Some of its strength derives from cross-ties with Middle and Late FI phases at Chiapa de Corzo, in Eastern Mesoamerica.

Radiocarbon indicates that Tierras Largas may go back to ca. 1330 B.C. (M-2330), though one of its specific outside links (the designs of Coatepec Red–Buff) is with Late, rather than Early Ajalpan. An overlap with Late Ajalpan is, in any case, indicated by three out of five assays published for the phase (M-2353, M-2352, M-2351) and by the eight acceptable dates (out of 10 determined) for San José, the phase that follows. San José appears to begin ca. 1050 B.C. RT, or even a decade or two later. It shares with other Early Horizon phases in Mesoamerica an abundant repertory of "Olmec" features (Flannery 1968:79–118), yet it dates (GX-0875, M-2354, SI-463, M-2355) range into FI-1 and FI-2. Some of its figurines share attributes with the C-1 and C-2 types of the Basin of Mexico, while other forms resemble the D-related "helmeted" and "bunned-helmet" varieties of Early Santa María. These observations favor an end date for San José in FI-2 or even in FI-3 times. This still leaves room for the prevalence of white ware with double-line-break incision in the following Guadalupe Phase, contemporaneously with the peak of Canoas White in Tehuacán. In line with this dating, Guadalupe figurines share attributes with types C-3, C-5, and A of FI-3 and FI-4 of the Basin of Mexico. As in Early Santa María after Lot 25, grey pottery gradually replaces white (Flannery 1968:94), eventually to dominate in Monte Albán 1.

The latest date for Guadalupe (GX-1312) and the earliest acceptable date for Monte Albán 1 (M-2109) are almost precisely contemporaneous, and suggest a boundary between the two phases a decade or two before 500 B.C. ST, that is, in FI-6.[5] Possible Mamom trade sherds in early Monte Albán 1 would confirm a pre-400 B.C. RT beginning date (Flannery *et al.* n.d.:98). Wide-everted lips, bridged spouts, stucco decoration, flanges, and mammiform supports in late Monte Albán 1 suggest Chiapa 4, 5, and even 6 parallels. Other parallels with Chiapa 6 (cylinders, tetrapods) occur in Monte Albán 2, consistent with a Monte Albán 1–2 boundary near the beginning of our era, as also suggested by the overlap in ranges of GX-1310 (A.D. 65 ± 105) for Monte Albán 1 and HO-1300 (240 ± 150 B.C.) for Monte Albán 2. If HO-1210 (390 ± 275 B.C.) applies to Monte Albán 2 (Bernal 1971:47) rather than late Monte Albán 1 (Paddock 1966:120), then the boundary between the two should perhaps be dropped about one century. However, as Paddock

[5]Since this was written, workers in the Valley of Oaxaca have reinstated the Rosarío phase, as the final distinguishable entity there prior to Monte Albán 1. GX-1312 therefore dates the end of Rosario (see Drennan 1976).

points out (1966:112), the two phases may overlap, with Monte Albán 2 a primarily "aristocratic and ceremonial" manifestation, possibly late or absent at such rural sites as Huitzo, which provided GX-1310.

The Monte Albán 2–3 transition anticipates the stronger Teotihuacán connections evident in Monte Albán 3A. Suggestive Monte Albán 2–3 forms include the florero, dishes with tripod supports, the Tlaloc olla, and vases. These features recall Early Tlamimilolpa and, less strongly, Miccaotli. At Teotihuacán itself, a group of Oaxacan immigrants, using Monte Albán 2–3 pottery, has left refuse in conditions implying their arrival there at least by Early Tlamimilolpa (MH-1) times (Millon 1967:42, 44). In Oaxaca, ^{14}C dates bracket the 2–3 transition between A.D. 170 ST (M-2107, which applies to Monte Albán 2) and A.D. 370 ST (the earliest of three ST central values for M-2106 on Monte Albán 3A material). A date of about A.D. 275 ST for the beginning of Late Tlamimilolpa at Teotihuacán (St-162) would mean that the 2–3A transition at Monte Albán had begun shortly before that time, in MH-1 or FI-11.

On the basis of abundant ceramic parallels, Monte Albán 3A equates with Teotihuacán's "great" period, that is, MH-2 to MH-3, as M-2106 confirms (see earlier). Its duration, however, has not been directly measured. A point in time perhaps equivalent to its end in the Mixteca Alta is dated by a log from a tomb at Yucuñudahui, whose solid heart provided a date of A.D. 320 (± 100) RT (I-3259; Paddock 1970), while the outer, worm-eaten layer was dated to A.D. 540 (± 100) RT (I-2680; Spores 1972:172). Pending more reliable indications, it is perhaps best to draw the 3A–3B division arbitrarily at ca. A.D. 550 ST, at the end of MH-3, with the understanding that it may be as much as 150 years too late, though perhaps no more than 60 years too early. Monte Albán 3B is, by definition, that part of the Middle Horizon in Oaxaca when Teotihuacán contacts are no longer apparent in the pottery. Maya jades in 3B deposits, if contemporaneous, would mean an early seventh-century date in the Goodman-Martinez-Thompson (GMT) correlation (Caso 1965, p. 906). The end of Monte Albán 3B and the beginning of Monte Albán 4 is now bracketed by seven dates (M-2096, I-3258, I-2679, I-3257, SI-514, M-1151, and M-2105) and by the occurrence of Balancán Fine Orange in Monte Albán 4 contexts at Lambityeco (Paddock 1970:8) and Miahuatlán (Scott 1969:514). Radiocarbon gives a margin of A.D. 740–840 ST, for the beginning of Monte Albán 4, while the presence of Balancán Fine Orange, a Tepeu 3 marker of the Maya lowlands, may further narrow this range to A.D. 790–830 ST (Culbert, personal communication). It follows from these estimates that the beginning of Monte Albán 4 falls into SI-1.

Before leaving the Oaxacan area, mention should be made of two other sequences which relate, in some degree, to that of the Valley of Oaxaca. The first of these is that outlined by Spores (1972) for the Nochixtlán Valley of the Mixteca Alta. In the range that concerns us here, it contains three exceedingly broad divisions: Cruz, correlative of the EH and FI 1–8 phases of the Valley of Oaxaca, from Tierras Largas through Monte Albán 1; Ramos, broadly equivalent to Monte Albán 2 and 2/3 transition; and Las Flores, which ties into Monte Albán 3A, 3B, and 4. This sequence is still in need of refinement, and some of the radiocarbon measurements pertaining to it seem out of line with both Tehuacán and Valley of Oaxaca evidence. The other sequence is that of the Tehuantepec region, originally constructed by Wallrath (1967) at Tehuantepec and Salina Cruz, and recently extended downward by Robert Zeitlin (personal communication) at the site of Laguna Zope, near Juchitán. Wallrath's phases, from Goma through Tixum, are shown in Figure 2, where they are placed primarily in consequence of ties with Chiapa de Corzo for the FI 6–9, and of Monte Albán parallels for the later phases. For Laguna Zope, Zeitlin (personal communication) reports a long occupation with ceramics that parallel those of the Pacific Coast of Chiapas and Guatemala, ranging from an Ocós-equivalent complex (shown provisionally as "A" in Figure 2) through correlatives of Cuadros, Jocotal, and Conchas. Zeitlin's analysis is expected eventually to substitute phase names for the letter designations provisionally given to these units in the chart.

VI. GULF COAST

The Gulf Coast sequences rate among the more imperfect ones of Western Mesoamerica. They are generally deficient in radiocarbon support, the EH portion of Coe's San Lorenzo sequence being an exception. Most are not full-length, and their divisions are gross. Wilkerson's (1973) recently established Lower Tecolutla chronology, with eight radiocarbon dates (as of 1973), and the Pavón time scale of the Huasteca originally built by Ekholm (1944) and extended downward by MacNeish (1958), with no radiocarbon dates, are important exceptions. For correlation purposes, the Gulf sequences cluster in three groups: the San Lorenzo, Tres Zapotes, and Cerro de las Mesas group of southern Veracruz, the latter two closely tied to each other (Coe 1965, 1970; Drucker 1943a,b); the sequence of El Trapiche, in Central Veracruz, with some links to the first three (García Payón 1966, 1971); and the northern group, with few outward ties but convincing links to one another through the Pavón column of the Huasteca. The first two groups show significant links with Tehuacán; Tres Zapotes and Cerro de las Mesas connect with Chiapa de Corzo; and San Lorenzo can be related to the Chiapas–Guatemala Pacific Coast sequence of Eastern Mesoamerica. A few Central Highland parallels can be recognized in the northern sequences, among which I am including MacNeish's Sierra de Tamaulipas and Sierra

Madre columns (MacNeish 1958, 1971), inasmuch as they are obviously connected to the Huasteca and provide a few radiocarbon dates that bear on it.

For the earlier phases, parallels are few and scattered. In several ways, Ojochi resembles Ocós, which it helps date, as well as Moyotzingo and Early Nexpa, in its predilection for stick-burnishing. Bajío gadrooned bottles bring to mind the somewhat later Tlatilco graves of Group 1 (EH-2). Pavón's angle-neck ollas are compared by MacNeish to those of Early Ajalpan (MacNeish, Petersen, and Flannery 1970:39). Almagre, Flaco, and Guerra are nonceramic, Flaco being perhaps somewhat younger than its Chicago solid-carbon date indicates (MacNeish 1971:579). Mesa de Guaje pottery is simple, but its date of ca. 1500 B.C. may also be too early if it resembles that of the Ponce Phase of Pánuco (MacNeish 1971:580).

The twelve dates for the San Lorenzo Phase and the single dates for Chicharras and Bajío are particularly important for Mesoamerica as a whole, in that they apply to the widely distributed Olmec style of figurine and pottery making. They seem to show quite clearly that some 150 years, at least, separate its beginnings at San Lorenzo from its first appearance in the valleys of Tehuacán and Oaxaca and on the Pacific Coast of the Isthmus. These events would appear to have taken place during the San Lorenzo B Subphase in EH-3 and EH-4 times, when trade contacts, as shown by obsidian imports, suddenly become more numerous and more extended (Cobean *et al.* 1971). Interestingly, the Tlatilco Group 1 graves and some recently dated Guerrero finds (see Section VII) do not conform to this pattern and seem to date from EH-1 and EH-2. As in Peru, we may be reaching the point when "the precision of our chronology [has] increased beyond the point where the appearance of 'horizon styles' could be taken as a sufficient indication of contemporaneity [Rowe 1962:48]."

Unfortunately, such precision is far from attained for other parts of the Gulf Coast sequences. Not only are absolute dates few, but San Lorenzo Phase parallels are relatively scarce and sometimes demonstrably long-lived, as in Southern Veracruz itself, where baby-faced and cut-featured figurines last into Tres Zapotes (Drucker 1943a) and Cerro de las Mesas (Drucker 1943b), and in Central Veracruz, where they abound in El Trapiche 2 (as defined in Figure 3; García Payón 1966). The basis for placing Trapiche 1 in EH-4 and FI-1, aside from some correspondence with San Lorenzo, is the prevalence of dentate rocker-stamping, which it shares with Lots 14 to 21 in Tehuacán. Parallels with Tehuacán continue in Trapiche 2, which has an abundance of white ware with double-line-break incision, and an assortment of figurines similar to that of Early Santa María, including punched-eye forms in a tradition that begins with Nacaste and Chiapa 2 and continues into the early portions of Chiapa 4, Tres Zapotes, and Cerro de las Mesas 1. I agree with Coe's phasing of the latter two sites (1965:686 ff.) and will note here only that their beginnings (bottoms of Trench 42 at Cerro de las Mesas and Trench 26 at Tres Zapotes) must follow closely on the peaks of white ware noted in FI-2 and FI-3 in so much of Mesoamerica. The general range of Phases 1 and 2 at both sites[6] is defined by that of a distinctive dark incised pottery (in "simple," "cursive" and "complex" styles), shared with El Trapiche 2 and 3 (García Payón 1966); its long span evidently parallels that of Quachilco Grey in Tehuacán. Cerro de las Mesas 2 (particularly the deeper levels in Trench 13) cross-ties specifically with Chiapa 4 through 6 or 7 on the basis of its I-C figurines (compare Drucker 1943b: Pl. 27, m-s; and Lee 1969: Fig. 6, a-n). These figurines relate to the Incised-Eye type of Lower Remojadas 1 (McBride 1971:24). Cerro de las Mesas Trench 13 also helps define the range of another type of figure (Drucker's Type IV) which has been called the Triangular-Face type of Upper Remojadas 1 (McBride 1971: 25): it is found in the upper levels of Phase 2 (48–96 inches) and continues into Phase 3. A peak of red-on-brown in Phase 2 appears to match one in El Trapiche 3. Finally, Tres Zapotes 3–4, Cerro de las Mesas 3, and Trapiche 4 share several quantitative trends as well as Teotihuacán traits that match the Late Tlamimilolpa and Early Xolalpan phases. The Long Count dates of Stelae 6 and 8 (A.D. 468 and 533, respectively) would fit Phase 3, as does a radiocarbon date (I-5791: A.D. 350 ± 95) recently obtained by Barbara Stark (1977) on Teotihuacán-related remains from her Camaron 2 Phase from the site of Patarata near Alvarado. The stratigraphic definition of the Late Classic occupation at Tres Zapotes (Coe's TZ 4) is more than ordinarily poor, while the presence of a similar component at Cerro de las Mesas cannot be altogether excluded. In South-Central Veracruz, this interval is generally thought to contain the "smiling figure" style of the Nopiloa tradition.

Wilkerson's (1973) recently described sequence at Santa Luísa in the Lower Tecolutla drainage is important in at least two ways: It links the Huasteca to the remainder of Veracruz, providing it with badly needed absolute time estimates; and it brings El Tajín into the fabric of current Mesoamerican chronology. At the early end, attribute overlaps between Trapiche 1, Ojite, and Ponce suggest rough contemporaneity, with Ponce also sharing figurine types with Trapiche 2 (e.g., the puffed-cheek and bulging-eye kinds). Aguilar is more like Early FI phases elsewhere, in its vessel forms (carinated bowls, expanded lips) and in its punched-eye figurines. It shared with Esteros A the highly specific triangular-loop sup-

[6]I am taking the following levels of Drucker's cuts at these sites as illustrative of the phases described by Coe:

TZ 1: All of Trench 26; Trenches 1 and 19 below 60 inches; Trench 13 below 30 inches.
TZ 2: Trench 1: 42–60 inches; Trench 19: 48–60 inches; Trench 13: 12–30 inches.
TZ 3 and 4: Trenches 1, 19, 13—upper levels.
CM 1: Trench 42 below 132 inches.
CM 2: Trench 42: 96–132 inches; Trench 13: 84–132 inches.
CM 3: Trench 42: 48–96 inches; Trench 13: 0–84 inches.

port. Esteros B resembles Chila in possessing the type Chila White. Like contemporary Central Highland phases, it sees the decline of double-line-break decoration. Chila shares vessel forms with Ticomán. El Prisco links with Ticomán 4, and other late FI phases include short-rise carinated bowls, fresco decoration, horizontal ribbing, spouts, and a decline of supports. Arroyo Grande, like El Prisco, is marked by the first appearance of ladles and of Pánuco figurines, and is dominated by black ware. At Santa Luísa, the ceramic complex associated with the site of El Tajín then emerges in the Tecolutla Phase, and goes through two Middle Horizon phases, with the first of these, Cacahuatal, showing figurine parallels both with Teotihuacán and Pánuco. Cacahuatal and the two Isla phases represent the major occupation of the site of El Tajín, with Isla B falling after A.D. 900. In the Pánuco region, Pithaya is tied to Teotihuacán by the occurrence of a slab support in Level 11 of the Pavón Site (Ekholm 1944: Fig. 7w). On the northern periphery of the Huasteca, the Laguna and Eslabones phases are characterized by trade items and attributes of the Pithaya and Zaquil phases, which indicate overlap in time. Eslabones (Laguna de Moctezuma site) has yielded dates of A.D. 1 ± 110 (HO-1055) and A.D. 600 ± 105 (HO-1054). Palmillas, a correlative of Eslabones and of La Salta, which follows it, is dated A.D. 236 ± 200 (M-506). These three dates thus help anchor the latter part of the Pánuco sequence in absolute time.

In general, the Gulf sequences may be characterized as "soft." With the exception of the San Lorenzo phase and, to some degree, the phases of the Lower Tecolutla drainage, they are dated in a very rough manner, and their boundaries and content alike are imprecise. The units recognized at Tres Zapotes, Cerro de las Mesas, and El Trapiche, in particular, are almost certain to compress in misleading fashion elements which, on closer study, would be found to be noncontemporaneous.

VII. NORTH-CENTRAL FRONTIER AND WESTERN MEXICO

Sequences in this immense area have in common our poor control of them, their erratic coverage both in time and in space, and the suspicion that most of them, west of the Balsas River, at least, lie outside of Mesoamerica proper, particularly before A.D. 900. For correlation purposes, primary divisions trending northwest to southeast may be seen between (*a*) the North-Central Frontier, a strip of highland that follows the eastern edge of the Sierra Madre Occidental and reaches south to include the region known as the Bajío, and, more generally, the upper Lerma basin; (*b*) West Mexico, that is, the West Coast from Sinaloa to the border of Michoacán, as well as most of the Lower Santiago Basin, and the adjacent Western Highlands; and (*c*) the Balsas–Tepalcatepec depression and coast of Guerrero, south of the Central Highlands. The first two show some cross-correlations, the third remains a virtually unknown entity, with interesting but chronologically not always helpful ties to the Central Highlands and even to the Gulf Coast.

Southern Guanajuato was the locus of the Chupícuaro mortuary complex, with links on the one hand northward in the Bajío, that is, in Central and Northern Guanajuato, and beyond it to the Canutillo Phase of the Chalchihuites sequence; and, on the other hand, westward among shaft-tomb and related assemblages of West Mexico, for example, to Jalisco and Nayarit. Two groups of graves have been distinguished (Porter 1956): the "black polychrome" group, represented at Ticomán 4 sites of the Basin of Mexico by trade items and shared elements such as the H-4 figurine style, and the "brown polychrome" group, now thought to precede it (Bennyhoff 1966:24; Porter Weaver 1969:9) in view of its figurines, which resemble the E-2 and H-2 types of earlier Ticomán phases. Chupícuaro sites are known to exist eastward as close to the Basin of Mexico as Tepejí (Cook de Leonard 1956–1957) and westward in Michoacán (Chadwick 1971b:668). In Central Guanajuato, a closely related phase, Morales (Braniff 1972:278–280), bridges the geographic gap between Chupícuaro and the Chalchihuites sequence. Further to the northwest, still in Guanajuato, the lower occupation at the site of El Cóporo is dated by Morales trade sherds, while the middle level above it contains Thin Orange. Middle Cóporo also contains "Valle de San Luis" pottery which, in turn, occurs in neighboring San Luis Potosí with Zaquil Black, a type characteristic of the Zaquil Phase of the Pánuco sequence (see Section 4).

By far the most thoroughly reported and best-dated chronological column of the North-Central Frontier is the threefold one provided by J. Charles Kelley for the Chalchihuites remains of Zacatecas and Durango (Kelley 1971). Like the ceramics of the less-studied sequences of the Bolaños and Juchipila drainages, those of Chalchihuites appear ultimately related to those of Chupícuaro. Radiocarbon dates bearing on the development of the Chalchihuites tradition provide not only anchor points for the coastal sequence of Sinaloa and Nayarit (Kelley and Winters 1960), but also a number of links with the North American Southwest.

A badly needed summary of West Mexican sites and phases has been provided by Bell (1971). Radiocarbon dates for the region are discussed by Taylor *et al.* (1969). Trade items serve to equate the Alta Vista and Ayala phases of MH-2 and MH-3 times to Tierra del Padre and Baluarte of the coast. This dating can be extended to the correlative Gavilán and Amapa phases of the Amapa sequence and to the Chala Phase of Peñitas. A check on the age of the latter is provided by a date (UCLA-973) on the Tamarindo Complex, which precedes it. Gavilán Phase material includes figurines in "Chinesca" style, one of several commonly represented in the shaft tombs of the region to the south and east. The placement in the Middle Horizon of at least some shaft tombs of highland Nayarit, Jalisco, and Colima is confirmed by similarities between Tierra del Padre and Early Ixtlán and by several radiocarbon dates (Meighan and Nicholson 1970) for example those thought to apply to "El Arenal Brown" figures in a tomb near Etzatlán, Jalisco (UCLA-966, UCLA-593-C), and to Ortices pottery in a Colima tomb (M-2341-a).

A somewhat larger body of dates, however, shows that many shaft tombs and phases with similar material go back earlier, well into the First Intermediate. This seems to be the case not only of Tamarindo, mentioned earlier, but also of the Tequilita tomb in Nayarit (UCLA-1012), of the "San Sebastian Red" component at Etzatlán (UCLA-593-A, 593-B), of "horned" figures and other burial goods from a grave near Teocaltiche in the Los Altos region of Northeastern Jalisco (UCLA-1647; Bell 1972) and of Tuxcacuexco, Ortices, Chanchopa, and related materials from tombs and habitation sites in Jalisco and Colima. The Tequilita date implies that the Chinesca style, and probably the Early Ixtlán and Gavilán phases as well, had begun by this time. Many of these assemblages have features reminiscent of Chupícuaro. The tomb at Chanchopa evidently contained a Thin Orange vessel and, roughly in keeping with this, provided a date in the first century A.D. (UCLA-1066). Chanchopa-like materials from the Coahuayana Valley on the Colima–Michoacán border have been dated at A.D. 140 ± 140 RT (M-2340). Ortices-related material from the same area appears to be some three centuries older (M-2396). The Early Phase at the Morett Site, with nine dates, may be older still and go back to FI-4 times or even beyond. By implication, Mountjoy's briefly reported San Blas complex of the Nayarit south coast (Scott 1969:353), which underlies Early Ixtlán and is said to resemble Early Morett, may be comparably old.

No continuous sequence in West Mexico can be shown at present to extend earlier than FI-4. Two remarkably early dates, however, apply to some highly interesting materials: those associated with the initial occupation of a twice-used tomb at El Opeño (UCLA-1659; Arturo Oliveras, personal communication), and those of the Capacha Phase of the Armería Basin in Colima (GX-1784; Kelly 1970). The El Opeño materials are highly similar to those of some Tlatilco graves, particularly those of Group 4. The corrected UCLA date of 1270 (± 80) B.C. ST would make the two precisely contemporary. The Capacha date of 1450 B.C. RT would appear to be considerably earlier and applies to ceramics that resemble both El Opeño and Tlatilco. The possible implications of this are discussed elsewhere (Kelly 1970; Tolstoy 1971a).

On a later time level, the Las Joyas Phase of the Durango column can be cross-tied to the Lolandis and Acaponeta phases of Southern Sinaloa. The uncertainty as to how late Las Joyas extends beyond ca. A.D. 800 ST is thereby transferred to the Sinaloa sequence. In view of the lateness of Guasave (UCLA-964), a correlative of the post–Acaponeta La Divisa Phase of Sinaloa, I have assumed that, of the two phases, only Lolandis is pre-A.D. 900. The placement of other West Mexican phases on the post-Baluarte level is further made difficult by the inapplicability of markers used to recognize the Second Intermediate in the Basin of Mexico. It would appear that many of these, for example, "shadow-striped" pottery (cf. Tula Watercolored, Tolstoy 1958), red-on-buff bowls, molcajetes, spindle whorls and conceivably even metal, are earlier in West Mexico and in the Bajío than they are further east. At this point, a reasonable decision is to place prior to A.D. 900 those phases in which the "Aztatlán Complex" features of Guasave are relatively undeveloped. A number of such phases seemingly constitute a local horizon, dominated by red-on-buff pottery not unlike that of the Oxtoticpac, Xometla, and Mazapan phases of the Basin of Mexico. Direct dates on Armería (M-2339: A.D. 690 ± 130 RT), Late Morett, and Playa del Tesoro (which probably overlaps with Middle and Late Morett, cf. Bell 1971:745) are in keeping with this estimate, particularly for the closely related Cofradía, Coralillo, and Colima phases.

Descending into the Balsas–Tepalcatepec trough, we find that we do not have here a culturally valid region. There is, in fact, a strong possibility that the boundary of Mesoamerica itself (at least before the Second Intermediate) separated Kelly's Apatzingán sequence from contemporary developments along, and south of, the Balsas. The Apatzingán sequence thus fits better with West Mexico, and within it the Tepetate Phase appears related to the set of MH-4 to SI-1 phases just enumerated for Jalisco and Colima (Kelly 1947:187). There are also general grounds for grouping the Delicias Phase with Tuxcacuexco and other late FI cultures of western Mexico. The date of Chumbícuaro is conjectural.

In the Middle Balsas and on the Guerrero Coast, known materials, though regionally quite distinctive, have links to the Central Highlands of a kind that are conspicuously absent in West Mexico. The only full-length sequence for Guerrero region is that of Charles Brush (n.d.), which applies to the coast, near Acapulco. A short sequence exists also for San Jerónimo. The Acapulco sequence, based principally on a deep shaft at Puerto Marquez, begins with the Pox Phase, dated to ca. 2300 B.C. RT by the overlap of a direct date (HO-1248) with one on the underlying preceramic occupation (HO-1264). The Uala Phase, which follows, contains bowls with graterlike scoring on the interior base and an assortment of simple forms that include cylindrical-neck ollas and restricted bowls with short inslanting upper sections. Figurine fragments suggest the baby-face type, definitely present in the following Tom and Rin phases. Recent dates from Amuco on the Middle Balsas (1530 ± 230 and 1220 ± 110 B.C. RT) would confirm a very early date for such figurines in Guerrero, inasmuch as they refer to an occupation at that site (the Sesame 2 Subphase) above one that yielded a ceramic mask in Olmec style (Sesame 1 Subphase; Louise Paradis, personal communication).

In Tom, ledge rims, incised double lines, interior basal incision and the importance of white ware combine to suggest the earlier Zacatenco phases of the Central Highlands. Burnished ware is frequent, as it is in the later Rin and Et. Level 12, an Et level at Puerto Marquez, is directly dated (HO-1262: 540 ± 115 B.C. RT). The carinated bowl appears in Et and therefore would seem to be late here, as in Oaxaca. Resist painting and earspools recall

Ticomán. Incised guilloche motifs are shared with Ekholm's Early Tambuco (1948: Fig. 2 k), the Slup levels at San Jerónimo, and some of the Middle Balsas pottery from La Molienda and other sites recently investigated by Paradis. Mammiform supports and ring bases become characteristic in Fal, partly correlative with Elna at San Jerónimo. Elna and Xlop at that site (the latter with a direct date of A.D. 590 (± 75) RT: M-1166) contain unmistakable Teotihuacán features, for example, two-hole condeleros, flat-based tripods, and figurine types. Comparable attributes occur in pottery of the Late Tambuco–Yax portion of the Acapulco sequence. Thin Orange has been found at the site of Los Terrones in the Middle Balsas region (Paradis, personal communication). These and other finds indicate that Guerrero in general, unlike much of Western Mexico, had links to the Central Highlands in Middle Horizon times. Like the earlier Olmec presence, these ties are only now beginning to be seen in the perspective of extended regional sequences.

VIII. CONCLUSION

Western Mesoamerica's most solid chronological supports, at present, occur in the highlands. They consist of the Basin of Mexico and Tehuacán columns. The first is chosen here as the master sequence for the area, in view of its length, refined phasing, strategically distributed outside ties, and good radiocarbon support, further improved by cross-ties with the Maya lowlands in Middle Horizon times. In tightness, Tehuacán runs a close second and has very solid radiocarbon support. It suffers from grosser phase definition and somewhat more localized cross-ties. These, however, are helpful in dating events in Oaxaca and on the Gulf Coast. The Valley of Oaxaca provides yet another first-rate sequence which, like those of the Basin of Mexico and of Tehuacán, is long and relatively well anchored in absolute time. The three sequences just mentioned are, at the moment, by far the most reliable of those constructed west of the Isthmus, and others are, to a considerable degree, dependent on one or two of them.

The remaining sequences of western Mesoamerica suffer from one or more of the following weaknesses: deficient radiocarbon support, incompleteness, or vague phase definition. These flaws affect, for example, the Mixteca Alta and Tehuantepec chronologies of Oaxaca, the latter profiting from cross-ties east of the Isthmus. On the Gulf, San Lorenzo is firm for EH times, when, moreover, it ties in with much of the rest of Mesoamerica. It becomes weaker for later periods when, like Tres Zapotes and Cerro de las Mesas, it acquires some support from east of the Isthmus, on the one hand, and Tehuacán, on the other. The vaguely phased El Trapiche sequence similarly depends on Tehuacán, though it is also supported to some degree by the Santa Luísa chronology of the lower Tecolutla region. The latter combines length, satisfactory phasing and moderate radiocarbon support more than any other lowland sequence so far established. Jointly with that of the Basin of Mexico and that of the Sierras to the north, it helps date the Pánuco column, which is long but lacks direct chronometric support.

To the north and west, coverage is spotty. The most solid sequence is that of Chalchihuites, on the North-Central Frontier, which, however, begins no earlier than FI-10. Much of West Mexican chronology, which also tends to cover only late FI and later periods, is based on correlations with the North-Central Frontier, extended southward, and aided by a scattering of radiocarbon dates and scarce links to the Basin of Mexico. West Mexican phases tend to be vaguely defined and irregularly distributed in both space and time. Finally, the Balsas drainage and coastal Guerrero seem, at present, the least adequately covered and the least firmly tied to the remainder of our area, despite one long unpublished sequence from the coast near Acapulco, intriguing early radiocarbon dates recently obtained at Middle Balsas sites, and a number of promising links to the Central Highlands. Guerrero and coastal Oaxaca to the east and south thus seem, at present, to be the regions where further chronological work is most urgently needed.

AUTHOR'S NOTE

This chapter was completed essentially in its present form in June of 1973. In the 4 years that have followed, significant contributions have been made to the chronology of parts of Western Mesoamerica, both through fieldwork and by the publication of data previously less completely or less easily accessible. It has not been possible to rewrite the present chapter to give this new information the place it would deserve in a truly contemporary review. It is hoped that future editions of this volume can be more satisfactory in this respect. Here, only a few of the more important titles to appear since 1973 have been added to the bibliography, and a small number of very essential changes have been made in the text, mainly to incorporate recent improvements in the chronology of the EH and early FI periods of the Basin of Mexico.

BIBLIOGRAPHY

Acosta, J. R.

1940 Exploraciones en Tula, Hidalgo. *Revista Mexicana de Estudios Antropológicos* **4:**172–194.

1944 La Cuarta y Quinta Temporadas de Exploraciones Arqueológicas en Tula, Hidalgo. *Revista Mexicana de Estudios Antropológicos* **7:**1–13.

Armillas, P.

1950 Teotihuacán, Tula y los Toltecas. *Runa* **3:**37–70.

Aufdermauer, J.

1970 Excavaciones en Dos Sitios Preclásicos de Moyotzingo, Puebla. *Communicaciones I, proyecto Puebla-Tlaxcala. Fundación Alemana para la investigacion científica* 9–24.

Bell, B.

1971 Archaeology of Nayarit, Jalisco and Colima. In *Handbook of Middle American Indians*, Vol. 2, edited by R. Wauchope, G. F. Ekholm and I. Bernal. Austin: University of Texas Press. Pp. 694–735.

1972 Archaeological Excavations in Jalisco, Mexico. *Science* **175:**1238–1239.

Bernal, I.

1965 Archaeological Synthesis of Oaxaca. In *Handbook of Middle American Indians,* Vol.

3, edited by R. Wauchope, G. F. Ekholm and I. Bernal. Austin: University of Texas Press. Pp. 788–813.

1971 The Olmec Region—Oaxaca. *University of California Archaeological Research Facility Contributions* No. **11**:29–50.

Bernal, I., and A. Caso

1965 Ceramics of Oaxaca. In *Handbook of Middle American Indians,* Vol. 3, edited by R. Wauchope. G. F. Ekholm and I. Bernal. Austin: University of Texas Press. Pp. 871–895.

Bennyhoff, J. A.

1966 Chronology and Periodization: Continuity and Change in the Teotihuacán Ceramic Tradition. In *Teotihuacán-XI Mesa Redonda.* Vol. 1. Pp. 19–30 Mexico:Sociedad Mexicana de Antropología.

Blanton, R. E.

1972 Prehispanic Adaptation in the Ixtapalapa Region, Mexico. *Science* **175**:1317–1326.

Blucher, D.

n.d. Late Pre-Classic Cultures in the Valley of Mexico: Preurban Teotihuacán. Unpublished Ph.D. dissertation. Brandeis University, Waltham, Massachusetts.

Boas, F.

1913 Archaeological Investigations in the Valley of Mexico by the International School, 1911–1912. *Proceedings of the 18th International Congress of Americanists,* 176–179.

Braniff, B.

1972 Secuencias Arqueológicas en Guanajuato y la Cuenca de México: Intento de Correlacíon. In *Teotihuacán-XI Mesa Redonda*. Vol. 2. Pp. 273–324. Mexico:Sociedad Mexicana de Antropología.

Brush, C. F.

n.d. A Contribution to the Archaeology of Coastal Guerrero, Mexico. Unpublished Ph.D. dissertation, Columbia University, New York.

Byers, D. S.

1967 Climate and Hydrology. In *The Prehistory of the Tehuacán Valley.* Vol. 1. Pp. 48–65. Austin: University of Texas Press.

Caso, A.

1965 Lapidary Work, Gold Work and Copper Work from Oaxaca. In *Handbook of Middle American Indians,* Vol. 3, edited by R. Wauchope, F. G. Ekholm, and I. Bernal. Austin: University of Texas Press. Pp. 896–930.

Chadwick, R.

1971a Postclassic Pottery of the Central Valleys. In *Handbook of Middle American Indians,* Vol. 10, edited by R. Wauchope, G. F. Ekholm, and I. Bernal. Austin: University of Texas Press. Pp. 228–257.

1971b Archaeological Synthesis of Michoacán and Adjacent Regions. In *Handbook of Middle American Indians,* Vol. 11, edited by R. Wauchope, G. F. Ekholm, and I. Bernal. Austin: University of Texas Press. Pp. 657–693.

Cobean, R. M., M. D. Coe, E. A. Perry, Jr., K. K. Turekian, and D. P. Kharkar

1971 Obsidian Trade at San Lorenzo Tenochtitlán, Mexico. *Science* **174**:666–671.

Coe, M. D.

1965 Archaeological Synthesis of Southern Veracruz and Tabasco. In *Handbook of Middle American Indians,* Vol. 3, edited by R. Wauchope, G. F. Ekholm, and I. Bernal. Austin: University of Texas Press. Pp. 679–715.

1970 The Archaeological Sequence at San Lorenzo Tenochtitlán, Veracruz, Mexico. *University of California Archaeological Research Facility Contributions* **8**:21–34.

Coe, W. R.

1972 Cultural Contact between the Lowland Maya and Teotihuacán as Seen from Tikal, Petén, Guatemala. In *Teotihuacán-XI Mesa Redonda,* Vol. 2. Pp. 257–272. Mexico: Sociedad Mexicana de Antropologia

Cook de Leonard, C.
1953 Los Popolocas de Puebla: Ensayo de Una Identificación Etnodemográfica e Histórico-Arqueológica. In *Huastecos, Totonacas y sus vecinos,* edited by I. Bernal and E. Davalos. *Revista Mexicana de Estudios Antropológicos* **13** (2–3).
1956–57 Algunos Antecedentes de la Cerámica Tolteca. *Revista Mexicana de Estudios Antropológicos* **14:**37–43.

Dixon, K. A.
1969 A Comparison of Radiocarbon and Obsidian Hydration Dating as Applied to Ceremonial Architecture at Temesco, Valley of Mexico. *Proceedings of the 8th International Congress of Anthropological and Ethnological Sciences, 1968,* pp. 187–189.

Drennan, R. D.
1976 Fábrica San José and Middle Formative Society in the Valley of Oaxaca. *Memoirs of the Museum of Anthropology, University of Michigan* **8.**

Drucker, P.
1943a Ceramic Sequences at Tres Zapotes, Veracruz, Mexico. *Bulletin of American Ethnology* **140.**
1943b Ceramic Stratigraphy at Cerro de las Mesas, Veracruz, *Bulletin of American Ethnology* **141.**

Dumond, D., and F. Muller
1972 Classic to Postclassic in Highland Central Mexico. *Science* **175:**1208–1215.

Ekholm, G. F.
1944 Excavations at Tampico and Pánuco in the Huasteca, Mexico. *American Museum of Natural History Anthropological Papers* No. **35**(5).
1948 Ceramic Stratigraphy at Acapulco, Guerrero. In *El Occidente de México: Cuarta Reunión de Mesa Redonda sobre problemas Antropológicos de México y Centro América.* Mexico: Sociedad Mexicana de Antropologia. Pp. 95–104.

Fergusson, G. J., and W. F. Libby
1963 UCLA Radiocarbon Dates II. *Radiocarbon* **5:**1–22.
1964 UCLA Radiocarbon Dates III. *Radiocarbon* **6:**318–339.

Flannery, K. V.
1967 The Vertebrate Fauna and Hunting Patterns. In *The Prehistory of the Tehuacán Valley,* Vol. 1. Austin: University of Texas Press. Pp. 137–177.
1968 The Olmec and the Valley of Oaxaca: A Model for Inter-Regional Interaction in Formative Times. In *Dumbarton Oaks Conference on the Olmec,* edited by E. P. Benson. Washington: Dumbarton Oaks Research Library and Collection. Pp. 79–118.

Flannery, K. V. (Ed.)
n.d. Preliminary Archaeological Investigations in the Valley of Oaxaca, Mexico, 1966–1969. Report submitted to *Instituto Nacional de Antropológia e Historia.*

Fowler, M. R.
1969 A Preclassic Water Distribution System in Amalucan, Mexico. *Archaeology* **22**(3):208–215.

Gamio, M.
1913 Arqueología de Atzcapotzalco, D.F., Mexico. *Proceedings of the 18th International Congress of Americanists,* pp. 180–193.
1920 Las Excavaciones del Pedregal de San Angel y la Cultura Arcaica del Valle de México. *American Anthropologist* **22**(2):127–143.

García Cook, A.
1967 Análisis Tipológico de Artefactos. *Instituto Nacional de Antropología e Historia Investigaciones* **12.**
1976 El Desarrollo Cultural en el Norte del Valle Poblano: Inferencias. *Serie Arqueología, Publicaciones del Departamento de Monumentos Prehispánicos* **1.**

García Payón, J.
1941 La Cerámica del Valle de Toluca. *Revista Mexicana de Estudios Antropológicos* **5**(2–3):209–238.

1966 Prehistoria de Mesoamérica. Excavaciones en Trapiche y Chalahuite, Veracruz, Mexico. *Cuadernos de la Facultad de Filosofía, Letras y Ciencias,* **31,** Jalapa.

1971 Archaeology of Central Veracruz, In *Handbook of Middle American Indians*, Vol. 11, edited by R. Wauchope, G. F. Ekholm and I. Bernal. Austin: University of Texas Press. Pp. 505–542.

Gonzalez, L.

n.d. Paleobotánica. Paper read at a special session—Excavationes en Tlapacoya, Estado de México, at the 25th Annual Meeting of the Society for American Archaeology (1970).

Goodliffe, E., and M. Goodliffe

1966 Un sitio Pleistocénico en Tlapacoya, Estado de México, *Instituto Nacional de Antropología e Historia Boletín* **23:**30–32.

Grennes, R. A.

1974 Dating the Olmec Presence at Iglesia Vieja, Morelos. In *Mesoamerican Archaeology. New Approaches*, edited by N. Hammond. Austin: University of Texas Press. Pp. 99–108.

Grove, D.

n.d. The Morelos Preclassic and the Highland Olmec Problem. An Archaeological Study. Unpublished Ph.D. dissertation, University of California, Los Angeles.

1974a San Pablo Nexpa and the Early Formative Archaeology of Morelos, Mexico. *Vanderbilt University Publications in Anthropology* **12.**

1974b The Highland Olmec Manifestation: A Consideration of What It Is and Isn't. In *Mesoamerican Archaeology. New Approaches,* edited by N. Hammond. Pp. 109–128. Austin: University of Texas Press.

Grove, D. C., K. G. Hirth, D. E. Bugé, and A. M. Cyphers

1976 Settlement and Cultural Development at Chalcatzingo. *Science* **192:**1203–1210.

Haynes, C. V.

1967 Muestras de C-14 de Tlapacoya, Estado de México. *Instituto Nacional de Antropología e Historia Boletín* **29:**49–52.

Haynes, C. V. and G. Agogino

1966 Prehistoric Springs and Geochronology of the Clovis Site, New Mexico. *American Antiquity* **31** (6):812–821.

Heizer, R. F., and J. Bennyhoff

1958 Archaeological Investigation of Cuicuilco, Valley of Mexico, 1957. *Science* **127:**232–233.

1972 Archaeological Investigations at Cuicuilco, Mexico, 1957. *National Geographic Society Research Reports, 1955–1960 Projects,* 93–104.

Hicks, F., and H. B. Nicholson

1964 The Transition from Classic to Postclassic at Cerro Portezuelo, Valley of Mexico. *35th Congreso Internacional de Americanists, México, 1962, Actas y Memorias* **1:**493–506.

Irwin-Williams, C.

1967 Associations of Early Man with Horse, Camel and Mastodon at Hueyatlaco, Valsequillo (Puebla, Mexico). In *Pleistocene extinctions: The search for a cause,* edited by P. S. Martin and H. E. Wright, Jr. New Haven: Yale University Press.

Johnson, F., and R. S. MacNeish

1972 Chronometric Dating. In *The Prehistory of the Tehuacán Valley,* Vol. 4. edited by R. S. MacNeish. Pp. 3–55. Austin: University of Texas Press.

Johnson, F., and E. H. Willis

1970 Reconciliation of Radiocarbon and Sidereal Years in Mesoamerican Chronology. *Nobel Symposium* **12:**93–104.

Kelley, J. C.

1971 Archaeology of the Northern Frontier: Zacatecas and Durango. In *Handbook of Middle American Indians,* Vol. 11, Austin: University of Texas Press. Pp. 768–801.

Kelley, J. C., and H. D. Winters
1960 A Revision of the Archaeological Sequence in Sinaloa, Mexico. *American Antiquity* **25**(4):547–561.
Kelly, I. T.
1947 Excavations at Apatzingán, Michoacán. *Viking Fund Publications in Anthropology* No. **7.**
1970 Vasijas de Colima con Boca de Estribo. *Instituto Nacional de Antropología e Historia Boletín,* **42:**26–31.
Kroeber, A. L.
1925 Archaic Culture Horizons in the Valley of Mexico. *University of California Papers in American Archaeology and Ethnology* **17:**374–408.
Lee, R. A. Jr.
1969 The Artifacts of Chiapa de Corzo, Chiapas, Mexico. *Papers of the New World Archaeological Foundation* No. **26.**
Lindsay, A. J.
1968 Current Research: Western Mesoamerica. *American Antiquity* **33**(3):418.
Lorenzo, J. L.
1961 La Revolución Neolítica en Mesoamerica. *Dirección de Prehistoria, Instituto Nacional de Antropología e Historia Publicación* **6.**
MacNeish, R. S.
1958 Preliminary Archaeological Investigations in the Sierra de Tamaulipas, Mexico. *American Philosophical Society Transactions* No. **48**(6).
1971 Archaeological Synthesis of the Sierra. In *Handbook of Middle American Indians,* Vol. 11, edited by R. Wauchope, G. S. Ekholm, and I. Bernal. University of Texas Press. Pp. 573–581.
MacNeish, R. S., A. Nelken-Terner, and I. Weitlaner de Johnson
1967 The Non-Ceramic Artifacts. In *The Prehistory of the Tehuacán Valley,* Vol. 2. Austin: University of Texas Press.
MacNeish, R. S., F. Peterson, and K. V. Flannery
1970 Ceramics. In *The Prehistory of the Tehuacán Valley*, Vol. 3. Austin: University of Texas Press.
McBride, H. W.
1969 The Extent of the Chupícuaro Tradition. In *The Natalie Wood Collection of Pre-Columbian Ceramics from Chupícuaro, Guanajuato, México*, edited by J. D. Frierman. Pp. 31–49. Los Angeles: Occasional Papers of the Museum and Laboratories of Ethnic Arts and Technology, 1.
1971 Figurine Types of Central and Southern Veracruz. In *Ancient Art of Veracruz.* Los Angeles: Ethnic Arts Council.
1974 Formative Ceramics and Prehistoric Settlement Patterns in the Cuauhtitlán Region, Mexico. Unpublished Ph.D. dissertation, University of California, Los Angeles.
Meighan, C. W., and H. B. Nicholson
1970 The Ceramic Mortuary Offerings of Prehistoric West Mexico: An Archaeological Perspective. In *Sculpture of Ancient West Mexico, Nayarit, Jalisco, Colima.* Los Angeles: Los Angeles County Museum of Art. Pp. 17–32.
Millon, R.
1966 Cronología y Periodificación: Datos Estratigráficos Sobre Períodos Cerámicos y Sus Relaciones con la Pintura Mural. In *Teotihuacán XI Mesa Redonda*, Vol. 1. Pp. 1–18. Mexico: Sociedad Mexicana de Antropologia.
1967 Una urna de Monte Albán IIIA encontrada en Teotihuacán. *Instituto Nacional de Antropología e Historia Boletín* **29:**42–44.
Mirambell, L.
1967 Excavaciones en un Sitio Pleistocénico de Tlapacoya, México. *Instituto Nacional de Antropología e Historia Boletín* **29:**37–41.

Muller, F.
1956–57 El Valle de Tulancingo. *Revista Mexicana de Estudios Antropológicos* **14:**129–138.
1960 The Preclassic Ceramic Sequence of Huapalcalco, Tulancingo, Hidalgo. In *Selected Papers of the 5th International Congress of Anthropological and Ethnological Sciences, 1956*, edited by A. T. C. Wallace. Philadelphia: University of Pennsylvania Press. Pp. 601–611.
1966 Secuencia cerámica de Teotihuacán. In *Teotihuacán XI Mesa Redonda*, Vol. 1N. Pp. 31–44. Mexico: Sociedad Mexicana de Antropología.
1970 La cerámica de Cholula. In *Proyecto Cholula*, edited by J. Marquina. *Instituto Nacional de Antropología e Historia Investigaciones* **19:**129–142.

Niederberger, C. B.
1969 Paleocología Humana y Playas Lacustres Post-Pleistocénicas en Tlapacoya. *Instituto Nacional de Antropología e Historia Boletín* **37:**19–24.
1976 Zohapilco. Cinco Milenios de Ocupación Humana en un Sitio Lacustre de la Cuenca de México. Instituto Nacional de Antropología e Historia. *Colección Científica. Arqueología, Departamento de Prehistoria* **30.**

Noguera, E.
1943 Excavaciones en El Tepalcate, Chimalhuacán, México. *American Antiquity* **9**(1):29–32.

Paddock, J.
1966 *Oaxaca in Ancient Mesoamerica.* Stanford: Stanford University Press
1968 Current Research: Western Mesoamerica. *American Antiquity* **33**(1):122–128.
1970 A Beginning in the Ñuiñe. Salvage Excavations at Ñuyoo, Huajuapan. *Boletín de Estudios Oaxaqueños* **26.**

Parsons, J. R.
1971 Prehistoric Settlement Patterns in the Texcoco Region, Mexico. *University of Michigan Memoirs of the Museum of Anthropology* No. **3.**
n.d. Prehispanic Settlement Patterns in the Chalco Region, Mexico, 1969 Season. Report submitted to Departamento de Monumentos Prehispánicos, Instituto Nacional de Antropología e Historia, México, D. F., 1971.

Piña Chán, R.
1958 Tlatilco, L. *Instituto Nacional de Antropología e Historia Investigaciones* **1.**

Porter, M. N.
1953 Tlatilco and the Pre-Classic Cultures of the New World. *Viking Fund Publications in Anthropology* No. **19.**
1956 Excavations at Chupícuaro, Guanajuato, Mexico. *American Philosophical Society Transactions* **46**(1).

Porter Weaver, M.
1969 A Reappraisal of Chupícuaro. In *The Natalie Wood Collection of Pre-Columbian Ceramics from Chupícuaro, Guanajuato, México*, edited by J. P. Frierman Occasional Papers of the Museum and Laboratories of Ethnic Arts and Technology, 1, Los Angeles. Pp. 3–15.
1972 *The Aztecs, Maya and Their Predecessors*. New York: Seminar Press.

Price, B. J.
1976 A Chronological Framework for Cultural Development in Mesoamerica. In *The Valley of Mexico: Studies in Pre-hispanic Ecology and Society,* edited by E. R. Wolf. Pp. 13–22. Albuquerque: University of New Mexico Press.

Rattray, E. C.
1972 El Complejo Cultural Coyotlatelco. In *Teotihuacán-XI Mesa Redonda,* Vol. 2. Pp. 201–210.

Rowe, J. H.
1962 Stages and Periods in Archaeological Interpretation. *Southwestern Journal of Anthropology* **18**(18):40–54.

Saenz, C. A.
1964 Ultimos Descubrimientos en Xochicalco. Departamento de Monumentos Prehispánicos. *Instituto Nacional de Antropología e Historia Informes* **12.**
Sanders, W. T.
1965 *Cultural Ecology of the Teotihuacán Valley*. Pennsylvania State University, Department of Sociology and Anthropology.
Scott, S. D.
1969 Current Research: Western Mesoamerica. *American Antiquity* **34**(3):351–353.
Snow, D. R.
1969 Ceramic Sequence and Settlement Location in Pre-Hispanic Tlaxcala. *American Antiquity* **34**(2):131–145.
Spores, R.
1972 An Archaeological Settlement Survey of the Nochixtlán Valley, Oaxaca. *Vanderbilt University Publications in Anthropology* No. **1.**
Spranz, B.
1968 Präklassische Figuren aus Totimehuacan. Puebla/Mexico. *Zeitschrift für Ethnologie* **93**(1–2):107–118.
Stark, B. L.
1977 Prehistoric Ecology at Patarata 52, Veracruz, Mexico: Adaptation to the Mangrove Swamp. *Vanderbilt University Publications in Anthropology* **18.**
Suess, H. E.
1970 Bristlecone-Pine Calibration of the Radiocarbon Time-Scale 5200 B.C. to the Present. *Nobel Symposium* **12:**303–311.
Taylor, R. E., R. Berger, C. W. Meighan, and H. B. Nicholson
1969 West Mexican Radiocarbon Dates of Archaeologic Significance. In *The Natalie Wood Collection of Pre-Columbian Ceramics from Chupícuaro, Guanajuato, Mexico,* edited by J. P. Frierman. Los Angeles: Occasional Papers of the Museum and Laboratories of Ethnic Arts and Technology, 1. Pp. 17–30.
Tolstoy, P.
1958 Surface Survey of the Northern Valley of Mexico: The Classic and Post-Classic Periods. *American Philosophical Society Transactions* **48**(5).
1971a Recent Research into the Early Preclassic of the Central Highlands. *University of California Archaeological Research Facility Contributions* No. **11:**25–28.
1971b Utilitarian Artifacts of Central Mexico. In *Handbook of Middle American Indians,* Vol. 10, edited by R. Wauchope, G. F. Ekholm, and I. Bernal. Austin: University of Texas Press. Pp. 270–296.
1975 Settlement and Population Trends in the Basin of Mexico (Ixtapaluca and Zacatenco Phases). *Journal of Field Archaeology* **2:**331–340.
n.d. A New Look at the Tlatilco Graves. Paper read at the 12th Meeting of the University Seminar on Primitive and Pre-Columbian Art, Columbia University, New York, 1972.
Tolstoy, P., and A. Guénette
1965 Le Placement de Tlatilco dans le Cadre du Pré-Classique du Bassin de Mexico. *Journal de la Société des Americanistes* **54**(1):47–91.
Tolstoy, P., and L. Paradis
1970 Early and Middle Preclassic Culture in the Basin of Mexico. *Science* **167:**344–351.
Tolstoy, P., S. K. Fish, M. W. Boksenbaum, K. B. Vaughn, and C. E. Smith
1977 Early Sedentary Communities of the Basin of Mexico. *Journal of Field Archaeology* **4:**1.
Vaillant, G. C.
1930 Excavations at Zacatenco. *American Museum of Natural History Anthropological Papers* No. **32**(1).
1931 Excavations at Ticoman. *American Museum of Natural History Anthropological Papers* No. **32**(2).

1935a Excavations at El Arbolillo. *American Museum of Natural History Anthropological Papers* No. **35**(2).
1935b Early Cultures of the Valley of Mexico: Results of the Stratigraphical Project of the American Museum of Natural History in the Valley of Mexico, 1928–1933. *American Museum of Natural History Anthropological Papers* No. **35**(3).
1944 *Aztecs of Mexico*. New York: Doubleday Doran.

Vaillant, S. B., and G. C. Vaillant
1934 Excavations at Gualupita. *American Museum of Natural History Anthropological Papers* No. **35**(1).

Wallrath, M.
1967 Excavations in the Tehuantepec Region, Mexico. *American Philosophical Society Transactions* **57**(2).

Walter, H.
1970 Informe Preliminar Sobre una Excavación Realizada en el Sitio Preclásico de San Francisco Acatepec, Puebla, México. *Proyecto Puebla-Tlaxcala, Fundación Alemana para la Investigación Científica. Communicaciones* **1**:25–36.

West, M.
1965 Transition from Preclassic to Classic at Teotihuacán. *American Antiquity* **31**(2):193–303.

White, S. E.
1962 El Iztaccíhuatl. *Instituto Nacional de Antropología e Historia Investigaciones* **6**.

Wilkerson, S. J. K.
1973 An Archaeological Sequence from Santa Luísa, Veracruz, Mexico. *University of California Archaeological Research Facility Contributions* No. **18**:37–50.

Willey, G. R.
1966 *An Introduction to American Archaeology*. Vol. 1. *North and Middle America*. Englewood Cliffs, New Jersey: Prentice Hall.

Willey, G. R., G. F. Ekholm, and R. Millon
1964 The Patterns of Farming Life and Civilization. In *Handbook of Middle American Indians*, Vol. 1, edited by R. Wauchope, G. F. Ekholm, and I. Bernal. Austin: University of Texas Press. Pp. 44–498.

Willey, G. R., and P. Phillips
1958 *Method and Theory in American Archaeology*. Chicago: University of Chicago Press.

Woodbury, R. B., and A. S. Trik
1953 *The Ruins of Zaculeu, Guatemala*. Richmond: United Fruit Company.

Western Mesoamerica: A.D. 900–1520

H. B. NICHOLSON

I. INTRODUCTION

The previous chapter is a very useful summary of the pre–A.D. 900 archaeological chronology of Western Mesoamerica. Between 900 and the Conquest extends a period of over six centuries, the Postclassic. A treatment similar to that of Tolstoy for this epoch, applying his proposed new sequential scheme, would have been worthwhile. However, this paper takes quite a different tack. It focuses on one key problem of Postclassic Western Mesoamerican culture history: the contribution the dated native historical traditions possibly can make to the attainment of greater chronologic precision. The reason for this choice of emphasis is that an entirely new dimension is added to Postclassic culture history by the availability of a sizable corpus of dated native histories.[1] Although some ostensibly extend back well before 900, the period for which most might be able to supply relatively accurate dates falls subsequent to that date. It is only the archaeologist working with Postclassic materials, therefore, who can effectively add to his arsenal of chronometric techniques the relevant data contained in these indigenous histories. (The "ethnohistorical periods" are charted in Figure 10.1). They add a potentially valuable new string to his bow, but they also present difficult challenges and possible pitfalls. It will be the principal purpose of this chapter to survey concisely the major Western Mesoamerican dated native histories—with particular attention to Central Mexico—and to discuss some of the methodological problems encountered by the archaeologist–ethnohistorian interested in utilizing them for chronological purposes.

The Mesoamerican "chronicle consciousness" and the historiographical techniques employed in Central Mexico to record past events have been previously discussed by the writer (Nicholson 1955, 1959, 1971a). Briefly, a strong interest in history, which was closely correlated with the political interests of the powerful ruling dynasties, was a major diagnostic of the Mesoamerican Area Co-Tradition. By Late Postclassic times, and probably much earlier, each major sociopolitical entity appears to have maintained an "official" history, which provided a kind of charter, saturated with religious ideological concepts, sanctioning its political legitimacy and status. Historical events in both the oral and the pictorial chronicles were frequently dated in the native calendric system. The years were designated by one of the 52 days in the 260-day divinatory cycle, *tonalpohualli,* which, for structural reasons, either ended (360th day) or began the 365-day year composed of 18 periods of 20 days (*veintenas*), plus 5 supernumerary days. In Contact Central Mexico these were Calli, Tochtli, Acatl, and Tecpatl, with their "numerical coefficients" 1–13, in the order 1. Tochtli, 2. Acatl, 3. Tecpatl, 4. Calli, 5. Tochtli, and so on, creating the 52-year permutating round ending with 13. Calli, the next cycle commencing again with 1. Tochtli. Most events were dated only by years, but occasionally the day was specified and/or its position within the *veintena*.

The dated histories can be divided into two major categories: (*a*) those that provide some dates but not in a continuous sequence; (*b*) those that date their events in terms of an unbroken sequence of years (the surviving examples, however, sometimes contain gaps). In the case of the former, one is immediately confronted with the problem of the repeating 52-year cycles.

[1]The most comprehensive listings of Mesoamerican native tradition sources are Gibson and Glass (prose) (1975) and Glass and Robertson (pictorial) (1975). To avoid tedious overcitation, the numbers of the items in these two censuses, which provide full bibliographic coverage, will be utilized abbreviating the compilers' names as GG and GR, respectively.

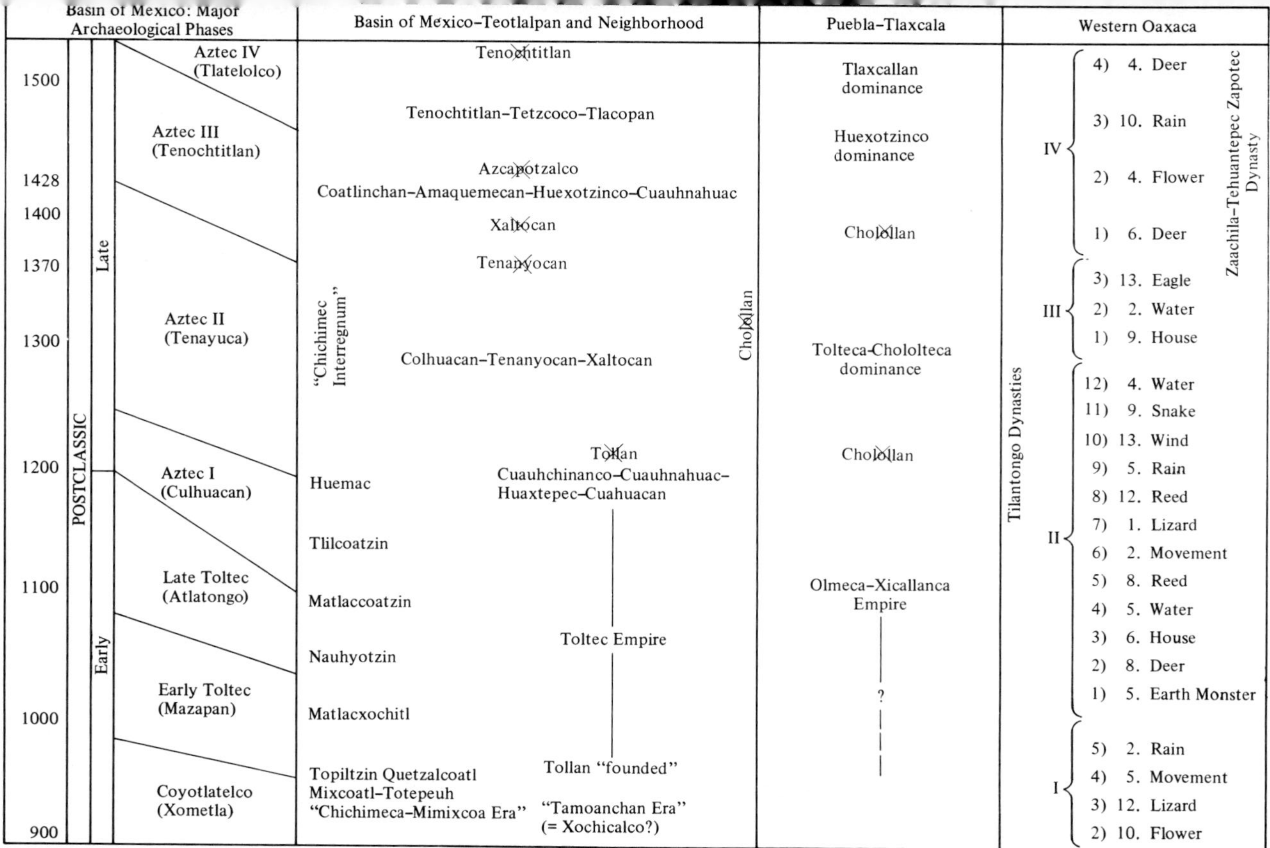

Figure 10.1. Major "ethnohistorical periods" of Postclassic Western Mesoamerica. (Note: The highly selective data and very tentative temporal assignments (particularly pre-1370) of this preliminary chart must be emphasized. It is intended to provide only a hypothetical braod overview to complement the text discussion. A cross superimposed on a community name signifies conquest or drastic loss of political power. The Western Oaxaca column follows the Caso chronology, with the caveat noted in the text.

In the case of the latter, if no significant gaps occur, this problem is ostensibly eliminated, by definition ("ostensibly" is used advisedly, since, as will be seen, there are still serious difficulties in ascertaining the correct Christian equivalents in some of these sources). Because of their particular value, therefore, the most important extant members of the second group are listed, with their most probable Christian year chronological spans indicated, in Table 10.1.

The archaeologist faces various problems when he attempts to utilize those dated native histories. The greatest, perhaps, is simply the difficulty of successfully synchronizing "the deeds of mighty kings and slow shifts in pottery and other artifact styles." Or, to put it another way, "the would-be correlator faces the problem of a genuine 'gap' between the emphasis in the native traditions on political and dynastic history and the sequent modifications in artifact form which are the chief concern of the excavator (Nicholson 1955: 596–597)." I have discussed this problem in two previous articles (Nicholson 1955, 1959; cf. 1972); subsequently, I have become, if anything, more than less convinced of the inherent difficulties that confront the archaeologist interested in these correlations. I would, however, still strongly urge that these correlative hypotheses, no matter how tentative, be advanced. "Dirt" archaeology and ethnohistory should, in my view, always be integrated as closely as possible.

Assuming that at least some general correlations are possible between excavationally derived cultural sequences and the dated native historical traditions, the basic question must again be posed: to what extent can the latter really contribute to achieving greater chronologic precision for the Postclassic? On the face of it, those events that are dated in terms of specific years would apear to offer very promising data permitting a high degree of chronologic accuracy. However, numerous complications frequently intrude. One is the simple fact that the fundamental mechanisms and structures of the late pre-Hispanic Western Mesoamerican calendric systems are still the subject of considerable controversy (Caso 1967, 1971; Nicholson 1960). Even the exact correlation of the Christian and Central Mexican native system(s) is still not universally agreed upon, although the Caso (1967: 41–90) correlation (August 13, 1521 = 1. Coatl 2 Hueymiccailhuitl–Xocotlhuetzi) has received the most acceptance. And the problem of the repeating 52-year cycles, particularly in the sporadically dated annals, is omnipresent.

However, an even more formidable problem has recently been recognized. Earlier students generally assumed that the system current in Central Mexico at Contact (1. Acatl = 1519) was universal throughout the area and had prevailed there for many centuries. At the end of the 1930s, however, there emerged a strong awareness of the possibility of differing year counts, used simultaneously by different groups, in Western Mesoamerica. The first to be convincingly demonstrated was that of the Mixtec and Popoloca-speaking area of Western Oaxaca–Southern Puebla (1519 = 13. Acatl;

TABLE 10.1

Some Significant Western Mesoamerican Continuous Year-Count Annals[a]

A. PICTORIAL

I. *Basin of Mexico and Neighborhood*

1. *Codex Boturini* (GR 34) (probably 1116–1303 [1168–1355?]; unfinished) (Tenochtitlan?)
2. *Codex Aubin* (GR 13) (probably 1116 [1168?]–1608; one 52-year cycle possibly omitted in middle of sequence) (Tenochtitlan)
3. *Códice Azcatitlan* (GR 20) (ostensibly 1168–1382, possibly 1116–1330; 2nd part [Tenochca rulers and conquests] undated) (Tenochtitlan?)
4. *Codex Mexicanus* (GR 207) (1168–1590) (Tenochtitlan)
5. *Codices Telleriano-Remensis/Vaticanus A* (GR 308 and 270) (1195–1562) (?; possibly Tenochtitlan?)
6. *Histoire Mexicaine depuis 1221 jusqu'en 1594* (Aubin-Goupil #40) (GR 201) (probably 1116–1259 [1168–1311?]; 1364–1559; 1565–1573) (Tenochtitlan?)
7. *Tira (Mapa) de Tepechpan* (GR 317) (1298–1596) (Tepechpan)
8. *Codex Mendoza* (GR 196) (1324–1521) (Tenochtitlan)
9. *Códice en Cruz* (GR 84) (1402–1559) (Chiauhtla?)
10. *Fragment de l'Histoire des Anciens Mexicains* (Aubin-Goupil #85) (GR 202) (1196–1405) (Tenochtitlan?)
11. *Codex Saville* (GR 282) (1407–1535) (Tenochtitlan or neighborhood?)

II. *Morelos*

12. *Códices de Tlaquiltenango* (GR 343) (?–?) (Tlaquiltenanco)

III. *Teotlalpan and neighborhood*

13. *Anales de Tula* (GR 369) (1361–1521) (Tollan?)
14. *Códice de Huichapan* (GR 142) (1403–1528, with gaps) (Hueychiappan)

IV. *Puebla*

15. *Historia Tolteca–Chichimeca* (GR 359) (1116–1544) (Cuauhtinchan)

V. *Guerrero*

16. *Códices de Azoyu:*
    - #1 (GR 21) (1300–1565?) (Tlappan–Azoyoc area)
    - #2 Obverse (GR 22) (1429–1564)? (Azoyoc area)
    - #3 Reverse-*Humboldt Fragment 1* (GR 147) (1487–1498; 1504–1522?)

B. TEXTUAL (Native Calendric System)

I. *Basin of Mexico and Neighborhood*

1. *Anales de Cuauhtitlan* (GG 1033) (635–1519; probably spurious time depth) (Cuauhtitlan and various other Central Mexican communities)
2. Chimalpahin:
   a. *Relaciones* (GG 1027):
      #2 (*Memorial Breve acerca de la Fundación de la Ciudad de Culhuacan* (670–1299; probably spurious time depth) (Chalco province *cabeceras,* Tenochtitlan, and various other Central Mexican communities)
      #3 (1063–1519)
      #4 (1064–1241)
      #5 (1269–1334)
      #6 (1258–1612)
      #7 (1272–1591)
      } (Chalco province *cabeceras,* Tenochtitlan, and various other central Mexican communities)
   b. *Diario* (GG 1115 and 1026) (1426–1615) (Tenochtitlan, Chalco communities, etc.)

TABLE 10.1 ***(Continued)***

3. *Anales de Tlatelolco-5* (GG 1073) (1155–1522; truly continuous, 1367–1522) (Tlatelolco)
4. *Anales Mexicanos, 1398–1596* (GG 1058) (1398–1596) (Tenochtitlan)

II. *Puebla-Tlaxcala*

5. *Anales de Tecamachalco* (GG 1112) (1398–1590) (Tecamachalco)
6. *Historia Cronología de la N. C. de Tlaxcala* (Juan Bentura Zapata y Mendoza and Manuel de los Santos y Salazar) (GG 1139) (1163?–1527; 1310–1692; truly continuous, 1477–1692) (Tlaxcallan)
7. *Anales de Tlaxcala #1* (GG 1124) (1453–1603) (Tlaxcallan)

C. TEXTUAL (Other Systems: Reign Lengths, etc.)

8. *Juan Cano Relaciones:*
   a. *Origen de los Mexicanos* (GG 1061) (749 [778?]–1532) (Tenochtitlan–Colhuacan)
   b. *Relación de la Genealogía . . .* (GG 1038) (767 [772?]–1532)
9. *Historia de los Mexicanos por Sus Pinturas* (GG 1060) (986–1532) (Tenochtitlan)

[a] All temporal spans are given in Christian Era years based on the equation: 1. Acatl (1. Malinalli, *Códices de Azoyu* system) = 1519, although this may not actually hold for some of the earlier dates (see discussion in text). The pictorials frequently contain textual glosses (Spanish, Nahuatl, Otomi), while the textual items occasionally contain minor pictographic elements. Full bibliographic data for each source listed are provided in Glass and Robertson (1975) (GR) and Gibson and Glass (1975) (GG). A brief resumé of this list was published in Nicholson (1971a:45–49).

Jiménez Moreno 1940). Accepting Caso's hypothesis that the eponymous day fell at the end of the last *veintena,* it was suggested that the reason for its different "numerical coefficient" was that the Mixtec–Popoloca year must have commenced with Atemoztli (instead of Izcalli, as in the Caso system). The hypothesis of another late pre-Hispanic year count was advanced soon after by Caso (1967:226–240) in his reconstruction of the Matlatzinca system (1519 = 2. In Thihui [Acatl]), the year beginning with In Thacani (= Hueytozoztli). During the next few years, a series of articles appeared, authored by the two leading students of pre-Hispanic Central Mexican ethnohistory, Jiménez Moreno (1953, 1956, 1961, 1966a, n.d.) and Kirchhoff (1949, 1950, 1955a,b, 1956a, 1964), wherein many differing Central Mexican year counts were hypothesized, the latter even eventually suggesting the simultaneous use of many different *tonalpohualli* counts. More recently, Davies (1973: Apéndice), in his study of early Mexica history, also hypothesized various distinct Central Mexican year counts. In contrast to his three principal predecessors, who stressed that the main reason for these differing year counts were certain structural features of the native calendric systems (the years commencing with different *veintenas* or [Kirchhoff] distinct *tonalpohualli* counts as well), Davies bases his reconstructed counts mostly on "empirical" grounds, making extensive use of comparative tables and "fechas claves."

Jiménez Moreno, Kirchhoff, and Davies sometimes agree concerning their reconstructed counts, sometimes not. A basic assumption they share is that the native annalists themselves were often unaware they were employing different year counts—which can be discerned only by the modern analyst. Their calendric hypotheses deserve a thorough critique and appraisal. Unfortunately, this is made difficult by the fact that only Davies has presented the detailed evidence for his schemes (see also Jiménez Moreno 1961 and Kirchhoff 1955a, 1956a, for partial presentation of evidence favoring some of their counts). Space limitations preclude detailed comment, but, in general, it can be said that Kirchhoff's views, particularly, often appear somewhat radical, such as when he suggests (1956a) different *tonalpohualli* counts in communities so close in ethnic background and unified politically (post-1473) as Tenochtitlan and Tlatelolco (cf. Caso 1967:48), or (1955b:192) differing year counts in the hypothesized four sectors of the territory dominated by the same community (Colhuacan). Also, statements (1950:129) such as "No longer do we have to select from several dates one as 'the most acceptable.' Every one of them turns out to be correct, though only within a given year count used by a particular people or in a particular city" do not appear to be altogether defensible. Other reasons for these differences must also be recognized, especially the well-known penchant of the native annalists to rearrange their community's past events to conform to various political advocatory positions and religious preconceptions (and Kirchhoff himself often clearly recognized this tendency). However, the greatest difficulty in accepting Kirchhoff's hypotheses is that nowhere did he publish in full the evidence that must be marshaled in their support—and the same goes, although to a somewhat lesser degree, for Jiménez Moreno's generally more cautious reconstructions. Davies has presented his arguments for each of his systems. Although they often appear reasonable, in my view none of them should be considered as convincingly demonstrated beyond question. They, and those of his predecessors, should rather be regarded as stimulating working hypotheses that require further analysis and testing against all available data. These few general remarks must suffice pending an exhaustive examination of the whole question, which has become an obvious desideratum in Mesoamerican studies.

Clearly, from this brief resumé of outstanding problems, face value acceptance of the dates in these native histories is a highly questionable procedure. Because of the considerable amount of confusion and contradiction with regard to calendrics they frequently display, each chronological problem must be thoroughly analyzed in context—particularly by the field archaeologist who attempts to integrate his excavated data with those of the dated native histories. Even after careful critiques, it is difficult enough to synchronize their calendric information with the archaeological record; without them, scant success in this area must be expected.

II. REGIONAL SURVEY OF HISTORICAL SOURCES

We now turn to a rapid survey of those dated native historical traditions that appear to provide the most promise of contributing significantly to greater chronological precision for the Postclassic. Each principal region will be considered in turn.

A. West Mexico

The extensive western subdivision of Mesoamerica can be conveniently divided (e.g., Taylor *et al.* 1969) into two major zones, Tarascan Michoacan and Trans-Tarascan Michoacan West Mexico. It seem doubtful that *dated* historical records were ever compiled in either, although a version of the typical Mesoamerican calendar appears to have been in use at least in late pre-Hispanic Michoacan (Caso 1967:241–252; Kirchhoff 1956b:XXI). For the former region, only two traditions seem to display any significant temporal depth, the "*Francisco Pantecatl Relación*" (GG 1006) of central Nayarit and the "Otomi" Amula (Jalisco) dynastic history, both recorded in the 1653 chronicle of Fray Antonio Tello (1891:202–203). The value and authenticity of the Pantecatl account is controversial. Brand (1971:651–653) has dismissed it as virtually a falsification. Jiménez Moreno (1970 , 1973), on the other hand, clearly regards it more sympathetically. The Amula account, although its source is unknown, appears generally acceptable (cf. Kelly 1949:29–30). Neither contains any precise dates. The Amula dynastic list includes 13 sequent names of rulers; if all of these represent different generations, which is perhaps doubtful, then a fairly respectable time depth of about 150 to 200 years might be possible.

For Michoacan—aside from some minor, temporally rather shallow historical notices in various scattered sources—there is available an unusually rich, detailed chronicle of the Tarascan dynasty which ultimately ruled in Tzintzuntzan at Contact, the *Relación de Michoacan* (GR 213), probably compiled by Fray Jerónimo de Alcalá in 1539–1541. The dynastic history appears to cover about 11 generations, thus, again, possibly around 150 to 200 years (commencing ca. 1350?)—but none of the events are dated in any native calendric system. An interesting sixteenth-century pictorial item, the *Lienzo de Jucutacato* (GR 177), apparently narrates the migration from the Gulf Coast of a Nahua-speaking group, of "Nonoalca" affiliation (cf. Carrasco 1969), to western Michoacan, and their subsequent search for mines. If this movement was connected with other Nonoalca wanderings (see Jiménez Moreno 1942:136–137; 1948) to the east, a fairly respectable period of time might be involved, but, since—as usual in these Western sources—the *lienzo* contains no dates, the temporal coverage is quite uncertain. Pre-Hispanic West Mexico, therefore, has so far not yielded the kind of dated chronicle that constitutes the subject of this paper, and we can pass on to an area from which stem by far the greatest number of these records, Central Mexico.

This large region can be conveniently divided into various subzones: West (Toluca Basin); North (Teotlalpan [Cook 1949] and neighborhood); Central (Basin of Mexico and neighborhood); Northeast (Sierra de Puebla and neighborhood); and Southeast (Puebla–Tlaxcala). Each will be concisely discussed in turn.

B. Central Mexico West: Toluca Basin

This area, the rugged western edge of which constituted a buffer zone between the Tarascan and Triple Alliance (Tenochtitlan–Tetzcoco–Tlacopan) empires at Contact, was a thriving, well-populated region dominated by Otomian-speakers (Matlatzinca, Mazahua, Otomi, Ocuilteca, etc.). The archaeology indicates that this prosperity had considerable time depth. No significant local dated history, however, appears to be extant—although the area is frequently referred to in the annals of the adjacent Central region, particularly during the time (post–1470s) it was incorporated into the Triple Alliance empire (Hernández Rodríguez 1952).

C. Central Mexico North: Teotlalpan and Neighborhood

The arid, rolling steppe region north of the Basin of Mexico was, like the Toluca Basin with which it had close linguistic–cultural ties, a prosperous zone at Contact, with a number of important Otomi (the predominant element)–Nahua *cabeceras,* most of which had probably belonged to the sequent Toltec, Xaltocan, Tepanoc, and Triple Alliance empires. Two continuous year annals stem from this region, *Códice de Huichapan* and *Anales de Tula,* but the time depth of both is, unfortunately, relatively shallow (see Table 10.1). For the earlier period of Tollan's preeminence, various dated histories are available. In every case, however, they appear to constitute the earlier portions of histories of communities located in the Central area, to the south. For this reason, they will be discussed with that region, consideration of which follows. This nuclear region of Western Mesoamerica, however, is so rich in dated histories that it is convenient to divide it into further subzones: North, Northwest, West, South, Southeast, and East.

D. Central Area: Basin of Mexico and Neighborhood

1. Basin of Mexico: North

Only one significant local history has been preserved (although the area is often referred to in annals from adjacent areas), from Xaltocan, the predominantly Otomi-speaking capital of a fairly extensive domain stretching some distance to the north and west during the fourteenth century and probably earlier (Carrasco 1950:255–268; Jiménez Moreno 1950). A 1566 source, Latin letter to Philip II from the Xaltocan cacique, Pablo Nazareo (GG 1075; Zimmermann 1970:23–31, Tafel 19–29), contains, in addition to a valuable listing of the communities that constituted the Xaltocan empire and some important pan-Basin genealogical data, a few significant historical notes on Xaltocan, including an eight-member dynastic list. If the genealogical information can be taken literally, it indicates that Huemac, the last Toltec ruler, was the great-great-great-great-grandfather of Motecuhzoma Ilhuicamina, fifth ruler of Tenochtitlan (1440–1469), a fact of some relevance to the problem of the date of the crack-up of the Toltec Empire. The most interesting historical information is a listing of sequent peoples (''Chichimecorum, Vixtocanorum, Nonovalcanorum, Texcalpanoroum'') who ruled the area in pre-Toltec times, extending over a period, as the writer put it, ''millia millium annorum.'' This source is one of the few from Central Mexico that extends this far back in time, almost certainly well into the Classic (or even Preclassic?). Unfortunately, none of this historical material is dated in terms of either the native or European calendars.

2. Basin of Mexico: Northwest

At Contact this was an important Nahua–Otomi province dominated by Cuauhtitlan, which, in turn, was controlled by the Triple Alliance. It had earlier been part of the Xaltocan, then Tepanec domains. For Cuauhtitlan we possess, in a substantial portion of the *Anales de Cuauhtitlan* (GG 1033), one of the most detailed, precisely dated histories of any Mesoamerican community, ostensibly covering the period 635–1570,[2] including a dynastic chronicle with no less than 24 *tlatoani* listed in order. The original Cuauhtitlancalque are described as typical roving, hunting Chichimeca from Chicomoztoc, who settled in the Cuauhtitlan region about 700. They maintained this same basic culture throughout the Toltec and ''Chichimec Interregnum'' periods until, in 1347, Colhuaque, fleeing the internal disorders that resulted in the downfall of that important center, settled in the region and, in effect, ''civilized'' them. Forty years later, in 1395, Cuauhtitlan claims to have conquered Xaltocan after a long struggle, only to succumb, in 1408, to the Tepanec—whom they later help to overthrow during the 1427–1431 Tepanec War, subsequently becoming a major tributary province of the Triple Alliance empire.

If the year count of the *Anales de Cuauhtitlan* is accepted at face value, for Cuauhtitlan we possess the longest continuous exactly dated history of any Mesoamerican community. On the other hand, we may be dealing here with the well-recognized penchant of the native chroniclers to exaggerate the

[2]From this point on, all native–Christian year correlations are those of the source (explicit or calculated), unless otherwise specified.

time depth of their histories for political reasons. If the usual view is accepted, that the flow of barbarous Chichimeca into the Basin of Mexico did not occur until after the fall of Tollan, then the dating of the earlier portion of this history must necessarily be rejected. However, the possibility cannot be entirely discounted that some "Chichimeca" settled in and around the Basin of Mexico before or during the period of the Toltec imperium and managed to maintain their way of life until post-Toltec times (cf. Barlow 1947:520; Carrasco 1950:242–243). Even at Contact, with imperial Tenochtitlan and Tetzcoco only miles away, some groups pursuing an essentially Chichimec life style and still speaking their original language are reported in parts of the Northeast Basin and territory to the north (Carrasco 1950:265). Perhaps the archaic Nahua-speaking, Itzpapalotl-worshipping "Chichimeca" of Pochutla and neighboring communities on the Oaxaca Coast (C 45)[3] can possibly be associated with an early series of interconnected migratory movements that might have included the Cuauhtitlancalque. It may also be significant that the "Chichimeca–Mimixcoa Era" (prominently involving Mixcoatl and Itzpapalotl, major Cuauhtitlan deities) in Central Mexican history is usually assigned to the immediate pre-Toltec Period (Nicholson 1957; 1971b:402–403). However, the principal alternative hypothesis, that the Cuauhtitlan Chichimeca migration to their historic habitat actually occurred in the wake of Tollan's collapse, with the necessary corollary that the chronology of their history in the *Anales de Cuauhtitlan* has been enormously and artificially lengthened, must also be seriously considered. And this reconstruction would probably better fit the most likely dating of other post-Toltec Chichimeca movements, to be discussed later. Unfortunately, what little is known of the Classic–Postclassic archaeology of the Northwest Basin (e.g., McBride 1974) cannot be sufficiently tied in with the *Anales de Cuauhtitlan* history of the community from which it takes its name to clarify the problem.

3. Basin of Mexico: West

This zone was the political power heart of all Western Mesoamerica for at least a century and a half before the Conquest and, not surprisingly, provides a particularly large number of dated native histories. Already an important area during the Preclassic and Classic periods (as is known from archaeological evidence), during the Postclassic this zone steadily forged ahead politically, particularly at the expense of Xaltocan in the north and Colhuacan in the south, ultimately to dominate much of Western Mesoamerica. There are many indications that the Sierra de Guadalupe region was a veritable hive of "Chichimec" political activity not too long after the collapse of Tollan (or

[3]For convenience, all *relaciones geográficas* of the 1579–1585 series are cited by the numbers utilized in Cline's comprehensive census (1972), abbreviating the compiler's name as C.

even before?), with Tenanyocan, Cuitlachtepec, Zahuatlan, Tecpayocan, etc., standing out as early power centers, particularly the first named. Gradually, however, this region declined in political strength, particularly vis-à-vis the Azcapotzalco–Tlacopan–Coyoacan zone just to the south, culminating in the definitive conquest of Tenanyocan in 1470–1471—followed by a considerable emigration of diehard groups, who moved to two main locations, Metztitlan and Tlaxcallan. Perhaps because of this, no significant local histories of this area are extant.

Our knowledge of the history of Azcapotzalco, ultimate capital of the Tepanec empire, is somewhat better, but, for the same reason, that its political power had been destroyed long before Cortés, only a rather sketchy record of the Tepanec dynasty is available. The most reliable dynastic listing is probably that contained in the *Anales de Tlatelolco-3, 4, 5* (GG 1073), compiled shortly after the Conquest in Tlatelolco, whose own dynasty was derived from that of Azcapotzalco. The only other significant versions are those of Torquemada (GG 1130)—and the cognate *"Anónimo Mexicano"* (GG 1013)—and the *Códice Xolotl* (GR 412). These accounts only partially agree; the problem may be compounded by Azcapotzalco's dual *tlatoani* pattern (Tepanecapan versus Mexicapan; Barlow 1952). The *Anales de Tlatelolco-5* dates the commencement of the Tepanec dynasty, for which it provides six names, through Maxtla, at ca. 1150 (cf. Barlow 1948: Chart). Chimalpahin (GG 1027; *Relación 2*), on the other hand, assigns the founding of Azcapotzalco Tepanecapan to 995, while the *Códice Xolotl* initiates the dynasty (for which it names only three members) apparently in 1168. Of particular interest is Torquemada's (Book III, Chapter 6) statement that Azcapotzalco was founded as early as ca. 50—which might indicate that an authentic tradition was still extant recalling its importance as a major center during the Classic. A key question is the date of the accession of Tozozomoc, the chief forger of the Tepanec empire, which ranges in the annals from 1331 to 1372. Jiménez Moreno (1966a:108) prefers 1363, Davies (1973:202), 1371; until recently, the generally accepted date was 1343 (putatively supported by the *Anales de Tlatelolco-5* and the *Códice Xolotl*). It is highly unfortunate that the dynastic history of Azcapotzalco is so sketchy and chronologically unsatisfactory, since this imperial center must have maintained quite detailed records, most of which appear to have been superseded or lost after its defeat in 1428.

The political power of Azcapotzalco was inherited by its former subject, out in the lake to the southeast, Mexico Tenochtitlan (with Tlatelolco always playing a significant role, even after its conquest by the former in 1473). As Table 10.1 indicates, there are many more continuous year histories for Tenochtitlan than for any other Western Mesoamerican community. The one that ostensibly extends furthest back in time is the prototype for the *Cano Relaciones* (GG 1038, 1061), compiled by anonymous Franciscans as early as 1532. The focus of this key source is the tracing of the royal ancestry of Doña Isabel (wife of the Spaniard Juan Cano), most prominent of Motechuzoma II's daughters. No years are given in the native calendar, the chronology being presented rather in reign lengths. Unfortunately, the good fathers' arithmetic seems to have been rather slipshod, nor do the two extant versions always agree. According to the *Relación de la Genealogía's* own calculation, human history in Central Mexico began in 767 (= 772?), while the *Origen de los Mexicanos* places its start in 749 (= 778?).

The account commences with a migration from Central Mexico (where man was created) to the distant northwest, where a community, Teocolhuacan, was founded, its first ruler, Totepeuh, acceding 28 years later (ca. 800). He was assassinated by his brothers, and his son, Topiltzin Quetzalcoatl, avenged the murder but then abandoned Teocolhuacan, leading a migration to the southwest and founding Tollan about 885. Topiltzin Quetzalcoatl was forced to abandon his capital after a 10-year reign; no ruler acceded for the next 97 years. The final ruler, Huemac, acceded in ca. 995, ruling 62 years until the collapse of Tollan (ca. 1055). Huemac fled to Chapoltepec with some followers, where he hung himself in desperation in a cave. Back in Tollan, a new ruler, Nauhyotl, persisted for another 16 years, then led the remaining Tolteca south into the Eastern Basin of Mexico, dying, after a 60-year reign, "on the road." His son, Cuauhtexpetlatl, in the sixth year of his reign, founded, ca. 1125, the second, Basin of Mexico Colhuacan; the leaderless Chapoltepec group soon thereafter joined the new settlement. Colhuacan maintained its status as a major political–cultural center for about 215 years (ca. 1125–1340), during which time it exerted a positive civilizing force on various "Chichimec" centers (Azcapotzalco, Tenanyocan, Xaltocan, Coatlinchan, etc.) and with whose rulers it entered into dynastic marital alliances. Finally, after 16 rulers, a royal assassination and ensuing internal disorders broke the power of Colhuacan, and most of the Colhuaque dispersed to other Basin communities. Its dynastic tradition, however, was carried on by the nine successive rulers of Mexico Tenochtitlan, who claimed direct descent from Acamapichtli I, the next-to-last Colhuacan *tlatoani*. Motecuhzoma II, for example, was apparently considered to have been the twenty-seventh member of this putatively unbroken Tollan–Colhuacan–Tenochtitlan dynasty.

Only three other histories from the Western Basin compare, in the temporal scope of their coverage, with the *Cano Relaciones:* the equally early *Historia de los Mexicanos por Sus Pinturas* (GG 1060), the *Leyenda de los Soles* (1558; GG 1111), and one portion of the *Anales de Cuauhtitlan*. The first is an exceptionally valuable source for the Mexica conception of their history, but, precisely because it focuses so strongly on the Mexica at the expense of other groups, it is much less satisfactory for the earlier Toltec and Colhuaque periods. The chronology is again expressd in reign lengths and other durations, rather than the native year count. Although one serious gap apparently occurs, the total sequence appears to be reconstructable; the historical era begins with the creation of the present earth in 1. Tochtli, 986. A "Chichimeca–Mimixcoa Era" (1012–1051?) ends with an account somewhat similar to that of the *Cano Relaciones*. Tollan is apparently founded in 1. Tecpatl, 1064, by Topiltzin Quetzalcoatl (here called "Ce Acatl"—born to Mixcoatl–Camaxtli in 1. Acatl, 1051), who becomes its first ruler. After Topiltzin Quetzalcoatl's flight from Tollan, in 1091, however, other than stating that Tollan was abandoned and without a ruler for nine years, no account is given of later Toltec history or its downfall during the reign of Huemac; nor is the Basin of Mexico Colhuacan mentioned until the time of its military expedition against the Mexica at Chapoltepec (1299). The remainder of the account is almost exclusively concerned with the Mexica (Tenochca): their long migration to Chapoltepec from Aztlan (commencing in 1116); their defeat there and subsequent "Babylonian captivity" in the Colhuacan area; the founding of Mexico Tenochtitlan (1324); their domination by Azcapotzalco through their first three rulers, beginning with Acamapichtli who accedes in 1376; and their subsequent rise to paramount political power in Western Mesoamerica during the reigns of their final six rulers, 1428–1519.

The *Leyenda de los Soles,* like the major portion of the source just discussed, is an explanation of a lost pictorial Mexica "world history," unfortunately—though it has the advantage of being in Nahuatl—much sketchier than the *Historia*. After a similar cosmogonical beginning, events of the Chichimeca–Mimixcoa Era, initiated in 1. Tecpatl (1116?), are narrated in some detail, concluding with the birth, apparently in 1. Acatl (1155?), of Mixcoatl–Camaxtli's son, Topiltzin Quetzalcoatl, who, after avenging his father's murder, becomes ruler of Tollan (its founding, however, is not explicitly mentioned). Fifty-two years later, in another 1. Acatl (1207?), Topiltzin Quetzalcoatl abandons Tollan, traveling to Tlapallan, where, four years later, in 4. Tochtli (1210?), he dies and is cremated. Huemac (with three corulers?) appears to succeed shortly after Topiltzin Quetzalcoatl's departure. In 1. Tecpatl (1220?) Tollan is abandoned, and the remainder of the narrative is devoted to Mexica history, presented in essentially standard fashion. The equations with the Christian years are quite tentative; if they are correct, they are notably later than in most other sources.

The early portion of the *Anales de Cuauhtitlan,* in addition to the Cuauhtitlan chronicle, is devoted to cosmogonical beginnings, followed by an account of Toltec and Colhuaque, then Mexica history. The Chichimeca–Mimixcoa Era is, in effect, omitted. The present earth is created and the Toltec year count is stated to have commenced in 1. Tochtli, 726. In 1. Tecpatl, 752, one year after the creation of the Fifth sun (13. Acatl), Mixcoamazatzin acceded to power and initiated the Toltecayotl. Nothing is recounted of Toltec origins or Teocolhuacan, although an entry for 9. Calli, 721, states that the "Colhuaque Chichimeca" established their community, which, as Kirchhoff (1955b:178–179; cf. 1964:81–82) has suggested, could relate to Teocolhuacan. Mixcoamazatzin died in 817 and was succeeded by Huetzin. Then, without further mention of Huetzin or of his demise, it is stated that in 834 Totepeuh, identified specifically as the father of Topiltzin Quetzalcoatl, died and was succeeded as Tollan ruler by Ihuitimal. He was succeeded in 873 by Topiltzin Quetzalcoatl, after various earlier adventures. In 895 he was driven from Tollan by the machinations of Tezcatlipoca and other "demons" and was succeeded by Matlacxochitl (895–930), Nauhyotzin (930–945), Matlaccoatzin (945–973), Tlilcoatzin (973–994), and, finally, Huemac, during whose reign Tollan, wracked by disasters and malevolent supernatural persecutions, was abandoned in 1. Tecpatl, 1064; Huemac fled and hanged himself six years later, 1070, in a Chapoltepec cave.

In 1064 the Colhuaque, under Nauhyotzin, emigrated from Tollan. As in the *Cano Relaciones,* he died en route, in 1072, and was succeeded by his son Cuauhtexpetlatzin, who, with his followers, founded the Basin of Mexico Colhuacan in 1127. Following his death in 1129, the same 14 successors are listed in the same order but occasionally with somewhat different reign lengths until the death of the last, the usurper Achitometl II, in 1347, the year of the Colhuaque crack-up and dispersion. The Mexica migration from Aztlan to Chapoltepec, 1. Tochtli, 1090–1. Tochtli, 1193, is traced in detail, as well as the Chapoltepec defeat in 1240, followed by the period of Colhuacan servitude, with the founding of Tenochtitlan very cursorily mentioned *twice,* once in 2. Calli, 1273 (Tlacocomolco), and again in 8. Tochtli, 1318. The Tenochca dynasty begins with the accession in 1350 of Acamapichtli, whose origin in Coatlinchan is mentioned but whose genealogical connection with the Colhuacan dynasty is not.

The principal other accounts of the history of Tenochtitlan form a distinct group. They do not commence with cosmogonical eras and proceed through the Chichimeca–Mimixcoa, Toltec, and Colhuaque epochs; instead, they begin only with the departure from Aztlan–Colhuacan–Chicomoztoc (usually dated at 1116, or one cycle later, 1168). They then narrate the migration to Chapoltepec, following which nearly all agree in main outline concerning subsequent leading events: Chapoltepec defeat (majority: 1. Tochtli, 1298), Colhuaque servitude, founding of Tenochtitlan (majority: 1. Tecpatl, 1324, or 2. Calli, 1325), and Tepanec servitude during the reigns of the first three "official" *tlatoani,* Acamapichtli, Huitzilihuitl, and Chimalpopoca, whose most common regnal dates are, respectively, 1376–1396, 1396–1417, and 1417–1427. A significant exception within this group is the *Codex Mendoza* (GR 196), which commences with the founding of Tenochtitlan (1324–1325). In addition to the Mexica continuous year count histories included in Table 10.1, the "*Crónica X* group" (Durán [GR 114], Alvarado Tezozomoc [GG 1012], Tovar [GR 365]), *Mapa Sigüenza* (GR 290; migration period only), and Torquemada stand out as important sources for Mexica history; they rarely, however, provide very precise dates. Although most of the principal accounts of Azteca–Mexica (Mexitin)–Tenochca history agree concerning major events, their dates often differ considerably—although, expectably, these discrepancies steadily lessen during the last few decades before the Conquest.

The history of Tenochtitlan's sister city, Tlatelolco, receives a fair amount of attention in the Tenochca annals, but, in addition, one important early Nahuatl account (actually a five-piece collection) is extant which focuses primarily on Tlatelolco, the *Anales de Tlatelolco*. As with so many Tenochca histories, this source omits any consideration of pre-Toltec and Toltec history, beginning instead with various "Chichimec" foundations in the Basin of Mexico. As mentioned earlier, because of dynastic ties, it provides the seemingly most reliable version of the Azcapotzalco dynasty. Its account of the Mexica migration (commencing with an unusual year, 1. Acatl, 1155) and post-Chapoltepec defeat history closely parallels the Tenochca accounts.

A particularly interesting historical tradition, in Nahuatl, was collected by Sahagún probably in Tlatelolco between 1561 and 1565 (*Manuscrito de Tlatelolco* [GG 1099; *Códice Matritense de la Real Academia de la Historia*]: fols. 172r–199v; *Florentine Codex* version of *Historia General de las Cosas de Nueva España* [GG 1104]: Book X, Chapter 29). While it contains no dates (on the contrary, it includes various disclaimers of precise chronological knowledge, emphasizing the great antiquity of the earliest events), it appears to extend back in time substantially further than the other Mexica "world histories" discussed above. Unlike those, it contains no cosmogonical preamble but commences with the landing, from boats, of the first inhabitants of Central Mexico at Panuco, followed by a migration, via Cuauhtemallan, to Tamoanchan (apparently a kind of "terrestrial paradise," associated at Contact with the ruins of Xochicalco, Morelos). They were led by *tlamatinime*, "wise men," known as *amoxhuaque*, "book possessors," most of whom migrated to the East, followed, after an interval, by the Olmeca Huixtotin and the Cuexteca (Huaxtecs), the latter returning to Panuco. Those who remained, after inventing *octli* (pulque), eventually established their kingdom in Xomiltepec (Morelos), then Teotihuacan, where, with the help of some of the surviving Giants (Quinametin), they constructed the Pyramids of the Sun and the Moon and the other great edifices and where they buried their (apotheosized) lords. Advised by their gods, they migrated north to Chicomoztoc, from whence various groups prominent in late pre-Hispanic times—Tolteca, Teochichimeca, Michhuaque (Tarascans), Tepaneca, Acolhuaque, Chalca, Huexotzinca, Tlaxcalteca, Tlalhuica, Cohuixca, and, finally, Mexica (from Colhuacan in the far West)—returned and reestablished themselves in Central Mexico. Much has been made of this tradition, and an ambitious attempt has been made to correlate it with the archaeological record (Piña Chan 1972; cf. Jiménez

Moreno 1942:129–131); but it is obviously not of much aid on the strictly chronological side. Its most significant aspect, perhaps, is the tantalizing glimpse it provides of a "Tamoanchan Era" (connected with the floruit of Xochicalco?) and, much more hazily, of a "Teotihuacan Era"—although interestingly, this follows the former in time. Noteworthy, however, is the essentially mythological and legendary cast of the events narrated as having transpired in both centers. For this reason, the attempts, such as those of Jiménez Moreno and Piña Chan and others, to correlate them with the archaeology must be treated with some reserve.

4. Basin of Mexico: South

The great *cabecera* here, of course, was Colhuacan. Earlier, its most important immediate satellites were Huitzilopochco, Mexicatzinco, and Itztapallapan; at Contact, together they were known as the Nauhtecuhtli, the "Four Lords." As we have seen, since the Tenochtitlan dynasty was derived from that of this center, much attention was devoted to its dynastic history in the Tenochca annals. No local history of consequence certainly compiled in Colhuacan itself is known, but apparently some were available to the compilers of the *Cano Relaciones* (and the *Anales de Cuauhtitlan?*). The early seventeenth-century Indian chronicler, Chimalpahin, however, in his "*Memorial Breve acerca de la Fundación de la Ciudad de Culhuacan*," part of his *Segunda Relación* (GG 1027), might have had access to a local history, although it is perhaps just as likely derived from Mexica sources. It is the only portion of Chimalpahin's extensive corpus devoted to the Toltec period. His account is quite aberrant and has generated sharp differences of opinion concerning its reliability and value.

It begins as early as 10. Tochtli, 670, with the foundation of what is putatively the Basin of Mexico Colhuacan. In 717 the Colhuaque dynasty is initiated with Nauhyotzin (717–767), followed by Nonochualcatl (767–845) and Yohuallatonac (845–904). In his twelfth year, 857, a political "triple alliance" was organized, Colhuacan–Tollan–Otompan. The Colhuaque dynasty continued with Quetzalacxoyatzin (904–953), Chalchiuhtlatonac (953–985), and Totepeuh (985–1026), who, in 993, installed his son, Hueymac, in Tollan as ruler. During Hueymac's reign "Topiltzin Acxitl Quetzalcoatl" was born in 1002 in Tollan (or perhaps came to Tollan from elsewhere). In one account, Hueymac died in 1029, and Topiltzin Quetzalcoatl succeeded. In 1. Tecpatl, 1040, Tollan broke up and the Tolteca dispersed to distant regions, including Cholollan, while Topiltzin Quetzalcoatl departed in 1. Acatl, 1051, journeying to the eastern coast, to "Poctlan Tlapallan." At this point it is stated that 342 years had elapsed since Tollan's foundation (= 10. Calli, 709). An alternative account is narrated that a still living Hueymac also abandoned Tollan in 1051 in pursuit of his enemy, Topiltzin Quetzalcoatl; failing to overtake him, he entered "Cincalco Chapultepec" (this version implies that the pair were involved in some kind of joint rulership in Tollan). In 1047, Otompan having also been overthrown, a new triple alliance was organized, Coatlinchan substituting for Tollan, Azcapotzalco replacing Otompan, with Colhuacan continuing to play the dominant role. The narrative then shifts abruptly to the Mexica migration from Aztlan–Chicomoztoc, in 1. Tecpatl, 1064, but continues throughout the remainder of the *Segunda Relación* to provide the chronology of the successive Colhuaque rulers, whose names, but not dates, agree almost exactly with the regnal lists in the *Cano Relaciones* and the *Anales de Cuauhtitlan*.

Chimalpahin's account is apparently the principal basis for Jiménez Moreno's well-known view (e.g., 1966c:192) that the Basin of Mexico Colhuacan was founded *before* Tollan and that from there Topiltzin Quetzalcoatl, probably under pressure from the "historical Olmecs," with their capital at Cholollan, moved the capital north, first to Tollantzinco, then to Tollan. Kirchhoff (1964) and I (Nicholson 1957:195–198, 349) have dissented from this view, arguing that Chimalpahin's version appears to be the result of misunderstanding and chronological juggling.

Colhuacan obviously occupies a crucial place in any consideration of pre-Hispanic Central Mexican chronology, as the apparent key link between the Toltec imperium and those lesser domains that succeeded it, eventuating in the Tepanec empire of Azcapotzalco. Unfortunately, there are strong indications that the different versions of the Colhuaque dynasty, in spite of the basic agreement in names, cannot be taken entirely at face value. Various accounts of the interaction between the Colhuaque and the Mexica following the Chapoltepec defeat of the latter, for example, indicate that there were four contemporaneous *tlatoani* ruling in the Colhuaque domain. When these are named together, they are often the same as the rulers who are listed in sequence in the dynastic lists. Kirchhoff (1955b:190–193; cf. Davies 1973:57–58), therefore, has suggested that the Colhuaque dynasty has been artificially elongated by putting, in effect, end-to-end the reigns of rulers some of whom were actually contemporaries (he also connects this with differing year counts, but this is not really crucial to the hypothesis). As was earlier suggested as a possibility in the case of the Cuauhtitlan dynasty, the wish to provide an exaggeratedly ancient dynastic pedigree might well have been operative here. Another complication is that there appear to have been unusually close ties between the Coatlinchan and Colhuacan dynasties. There are similarities in names and perhaps actual overlap in rulerships; the question, however, is quite embroiled (cf. Davies 1973:55–56). Another difficult question (see p. 229) connected with Colhuacan history is that of the precise date of the "fall" of this center (largely, it would seem, the result of internal dissension) and the consequent Colhuaque dispersion, which had such transcendent cultural repercussions in the Basin of Mexico. It seems clear, therefore, that, although we appear to have available accounts of the Colhuacan dynasty which were accepted as authentic by the Contact period Colhuaque and their epigones, the Mexica, themselves, they must be approached by modern students with considerable caution, particularly their chronological aspects.

Closely linked ethnically and culturally to the realm of the "Four Lords" were other major *cabeceras* in the freshwater *chinampaneca* region, above all, Xochimilco, Cuitlahuac, and Mizquic. The first named, before its Tepanec and later Triple Alliance conquest, had clearly controlled a fairly wide domain in the extreme Southern Basin of Mexico, extending down into eastern Morelos and adjoining Puebla as far east as Tochimilco–Ocopetlacayocan (e.g., Durán 1967, Vol. 2:22). Regrettably, no primary local history seems to have survived for this important center, although it is often referred to in the chronicles of neighboring groups and a few of its later rulers, in its *tri-tlatoani* (Olac, Tepetenchi, Tecpan) governmental system, are mentioned. Alva Ixtlilxochitl (GG 1043–1044), however, in his *Relación Sucinta,* presents, from an unknown source, a brief sketch of Xochimilca history that contains no dates but includes a 20-name ruler list, with the reign length of each (the total, after the first legendary reign [600+ years], is 250 years). The three distinct *cabeceras* are not mentioned. Whether this dynastic listing was considered to belong to only one of them or includes the names of rulers of one or both of the others is uncertain, nor is it clear whether all these reigns were sequent, rather than overlapping. A 180-year migration is described, from "Aquilazco" to Tollan, which they reach during the reign of Tlotzin (1263–1298?), the supposed Chichimec "emperor," who granted them the right to settle in Xochimilco. This relatively late arrival contrasts strikingly with Durán's (1967, Vol. 2:22) account of the peopling of the Basin of Mexico and adjoining territory, wherein the Xochimilca are the first to arrive (before the Chalca, Topaneca, Acolhuaque, Tlalhuica, Tlaxcalteca, and Mexica), ca. 902; and the *Anales de Cuauhtitlan* describes Xochimilca–Colhuaque struggles as early as years equated with 1130–1142. There are even some data in the *Historia Tolteca–Chichimeca* (GR 359) and Chimalpahin (see Jiménez Moreno 1942:125–126) that appear to extend the history of the Xochimilca back to pre-Toltec, Olmec times.

For the *cabecera* immediately to the east, Cuitlahuac, we possess, in a portion of the *Anales de Cuauhtitlan,* a fairly detailed history, focusing particularly on one of its four *tlatoani* dynasties, that of the subdivision of Tizic, although the other three (Teopancalecan, Tecpan, Atenchicalcan) are not entirely neglected. This dynasty apparently stemmed from Xicco, an island in Lake Chalco to the east, which was the source also of some of the Chalco province dynasties. It commenced in 1222 and was reinforced in 1233 by further migration from this island, whose political power appears to have essentially ended at this time. Fourteen rulers are named, with reign lengths, in côntinuous sequence, from 1230 to 1545. In addition, the history of a special dynasty is presented, that of the Tzompantecuhtin, or Nahualtecuhtin, "sorcerer lords," distributed through the four divisions—a particularly interesting lineage since they claimed direct descent from (Iztac) Mixcoatl himself; unfortunately, exact dates for the earlier members of this dynasty are not given.

Mizquic, although the least powerful of the three, was nevertheless a *cabecera* of considerable significance, whose rulers claimed Toltec descent (Durán 1967, Vol. 2:88–89); the Mizquica are listed in some accounts as one of the original migrating groups from Aztlan–Chicomoztoc. No local history is extant, although Mizquic is occasionally referred to in the histories of neighboring communities; but these scattered references are not sufficient to reconstruct a complete dynastic list, much less a satisfactory chronology.

5. Basin of Mexico: Southeast

This area constituted the superprovince of Chalco. At one time it appears to have possessed no less than 25 distinct *tlatoani* lineages, although at Contact these had apparently been reduced to 9 (cf. Gibson 1964:42–44), when four *cabeceras* dominated: Tlalmanalco (including Chalco Atenco), Amaquemecan, Chimalhuacan Chalco, and Tenanco. For this complex province, we have particularly detailed dynastic histories compiled by Chimalpahin, an Indian ecclesiastic descended from one of the royal lineages of Amaquemecan—which were based on earlier pictorial native histories and oral traditions (Zimmermann 1960; Rendón 1965: Introducción). According to Chimalpahin, Chalco was settled in Postclassic times by many distinct groups arriving at different times. He provides detailed dynastic chronicles for most of them. The earliest begins, in his system, in 1160, with the emigration of the Tecchichimeca Totollinpaneca Itztlacozauhque, the later Amaquemeque Chalca (Chimalpahin's own ancestral group), from Aztlan–Chicomoztoc–Teocolhuacan, finally settling in the Amaquemecan area in 1259. Chimalpahin's chronological orderings need much more analysis than they have yet received. A special "Chalca" year count (Kirchhoff: Mexica 1. Acatl = Chalca 5. Tochtli; Jiménez Moreno, 11. Acatl) has been claimed (Kirchhoff 1949; Jiménez Moreno 1961), but the full evidence has never been presented. Chimalpahin also provides some information on a more ancient, indigenous element in the Amaquemecan area when the Chichimeca Totollinpaneca arrived, the Olmeca Xicallanca Xochteca Quiyauhuizteca Cocola, but he does not narrate any genuine history for them. As Jiménez Moreno (1942:125–126) has suggested, they may have been connected with the "historical Olmecs," the Olmeca Xicallanca of Cholollan (see later). Chimalpahin's complete oeuvre, now finally almost completely published, deserves much more comparative analysis, both chronological and otherwise, a task that Zimmermann, regrettably, did not live to complete. Jacqueline de Durand-Forest is presently working toward this end and has already published (1973) a very useful preliminary analysis, hopefully the first of many.

The *Anales de Cuauhtitlan* also includes at least one Chalco province history, apparently one of the Tlalmanalco–Chalco Atenco dynasties. It begins in Xicco, in 1. Acatl, equated with 1051, when a group, identified simply as "Chalca," emigrates from this island. An 11-ruler dynasty is chronicled, ending in 1465 with the Triple Alliance conquest. Other Chalcan groups are identified as arriving later, at different times: Chalca Tenanca in 1132; Chalca Mihuaque, Huitznahuaca Chichimeca in 1135; Chalca Tlahuacan in 1138; and Chalca Tlacochcalca (apparently Chimalpahin's Nonohualca Teotlixca Tlacochcalca) in 1168.

6. Basin of Mexico: East

This area constituted the province of Acolhuacan, second only to Tenochtitlan in political power in the late pre-Hispanic period, and a number of valuable native histories are extant. Unfortunately, they tend to be relatively weak on the chronological side. As Table 10.1 indicates, only two continuous year annals stem from this region. However, in compensation, the geographically most comprehensive and genealogically most detailed Central Mexican pictorial history hails from Acolhuacan, the *Códice Xolotl.* The *Mapas Quinatzin* (GR 263–264) and *Tlotzin* (GR 356) also provide important historical–genealogical data—but almost no dates. In addition, six of the *relaciones geográficas* of the 1579–1585 series (C 19, 22, 29, 111, 116, 123) cover 18 significant Acolhuacan communities, including Tetzcoco, and some of them supply valuable historical information, including a few dates. As is well known, the greatest amount of Acolhuacan history is contained in the seventeenth-century *Relaciones* and *Historia Chichimeca* of the mestizo chronicler, Alva Ixtlilxochitl, a descendant of the royal dynasty of Tetzcoco. However, it is precisely Alva Ixtlilxochitl's highly confused and artificial chronology that causes the greatest problems in the utilization of his historical data. Torquemada also devotes considerable attention to the history of Acolhuacan, derived either from Alva Ixtlilxochitl's writings or from sources available to both. Finally, the *Relaciones* of Chimalpahin provide a few data on Acolhuaque dynastic history, much of it seemingly based on Alva Ixtlilxochitl and/or Torquemada (Chimalpahin's dates, however, often are quite discrepant) or on sources utilized by them.

As indicated, preeminent among Acolhuaque histories is the remarkable *Códice Xolotl,* seemingly a colonial copy of a lost pre-Hispanic original(s) and probably compiled in either Coatlinchan or Tetzcoco (Nicholson 1972:163–164). Most of its sheets (1–7 [including 1–2bis] and 9–10) depict historical events and genealogical connections superimposed on schematic maps of the Basin of Mexico and adjoining territory. Only a handful of dates are sprinkled throughout these pages. Their correlation with the Christian calendar has given rise to many differences of opinion, and the problem has been compounded by Jiménez Moreno's (1961) hypothesis that they are in at least three different year counts, the most important being his "Tetzcocan" system (Mexica 1. Acatl = Tetzcocan 8. Acatl). I have previously suggested (Nicholson 1972:193–194) that the total time span covered is from 1. Tecpatl,

1116, to 13. Acatl, 1427, a period of 312 years (which generally agrees with the old Veytia reconstruction, accepted by Orozco y Berra and Chavero). Dibble (1951:122), who has made the most thorough study of this source, prefers a 1220 beginning, while Jiménez Moreno (1966a:104) has implicitly opted for 1240, considering it to be in his Tetzcocan system. In any case, the earliest dates in the *Códice Xolotl*—some of which necessitate obviously impossible reign lengths—appear to be quite stylized and probably should not be taken too seriously.

The *Códice Xolotl* clearly presents a rather distorted account of post-Toltec Central Mexican history, particularly in the greatly exaggerated political role ascribed to "Xolotl," founder of a putative widespread "Chichimec empire," a figure virtually ignored (and, if mentioned at all, apparently under different names) in most other primary native histories. When the detailed genealogies the *Códice Xolotl* provides for the ruling dynasties of many leading Central Mexican communities can be checked against relevant local sources for these same dynasties, many glaring discrepancies become evident. Nevertheless, the plethora of historical–genealogical information pictorialized in this extraordinary history must always be taken seriously into account; unfortunately, its chronological aspect appears to be its weakest element.

As is known from archaeological evidence, the eastern Basin of Mexico was occupied in certain areas by agricultural groups from a very early period. However, at some point—either in the immediate wake of Tollan's fall or perhaps earlier—a great flow of barbarous Chichimeca groups must have settled in the area. The dating of these movements (which may have been very complex) is quite difficult. As is all too typical, the basic sources are in great disagreement. The *Anales de Cuauhtitlan,* for example, gives a date as early as 13. Tochtli, equated with 686, for the start of the year count of the "Tetzcoco in Chichimeca." Sahagún's Tepepolco informants (*Primeros Memoriales* [GR 271]: Chapter 3, Par. 1B, C) provided him with the royal dynastic lists of Tetzcoco and Huexotla. The start of the former, which begins with (Quinatzin) Tlaltecatzin (*Códice Xolotl:* great-grandson of Xolotl), can be calculated, from the reign lengths, at about 1255. However, complications arise—caused by what appears to be confusion, in the case of the earlier rulers, between life and reign lengths—which unduly elongates the chronology. Elsewhere (*Florentine Codex* [GR 274]: Book VIII, Chapter 5) Sahagún states that the Chichimeca established themselves in Tetzcoco 22 years after the fall of Tollan (see p. 322) and their first ruler (unnamed) acceded in 1246 (cf. Pomar [C 123], who describes the Tetzcoco dynasty as lasting "casi de mil años").

The ruler list from neighboring Huexotla is much longer, beginning with the Acolhuaque founder, Mazatzinteuctli, who, from the reign lengths, can be calculated to have acceded in 1000 (1070?). Again, however, there appears to have been confusion between life and reign lengths, and the order of names in the final portion of the list disagrees with other primary sources. Mazatzin (Mazatl) is also named as the Acolhuaque "founding father" in the *Anales de Tlatelolco-5,* but the *Códice Xolotl* specifies the second name on the Sahaguntine list, Tochintecuhtli, as the initiator of the Huexotla dynasty. His accession is given as 13. Acatl, possibly intended to be equatable with 1219 (1271?). Chimalpahin (*Relacíon 2*), on the other hand, apparently has Tochintecuhtli leaving Chicomoztoc in 1116, arriving at Azcapotzalco with his wife, Miahuatotocihuatzin, in 1148, and subsequently establishing themselves at Huexotla in 1. Acatl, 1155. Actually, considerable confusion reigns in the sources concerning the origin of Tochintecuhtli, but discussion of this problem must be reserved for another occasion.

Even more important than Huexotla, however, in Acolhuaque beginnings was Coatlinchan, which by the fifteenth century had clearly become one of the great Central Mexican powers. Whether the *Códice Xolotl* derives from here or not, the history of the Coatlinchan zone is covered in this source with particular fullness. I have summarized (Nicholson 1972) the earliest history of this area as chronicled by the *Códice Xolotl* and a few other sources. Nopaltzin, son of Xolotl, encountered at Tlatzallan (possibly identifiable with the Corro Portezuelo–San Antonio archaeological site) Toltec survivors, who moved to Colhuacan and initiated the new dynasty there. Tlatzallan was subsequently occupied by Tlotzin Pochotl, Nopaltzin's son, and abandoned in 1. Tochtli (1298?; 1350?) due to military pressure from nearby Coatepec. The Coatlinchan area was settled by Acolhuaque under Tzontecomatl, who, with two related rulers, Acolhua (established in Azcapotzalco), and Chiconcuauh (established in Xaltocan), supposedly migrated from the West in 1. Tecpatl (1168?). Acatonal, a chieftain who accompanied Xolotl, founded the Coatepec dynasty at about the same time. The *Anales de Tlatelolco-3, 4* also name those two Acolhuaque founders, but provide no dates. The *relaciones geográficas* of Chicoloapan and Coatepec (C 29) state that Acolhuaque Chichimeca from Chicomoztoc settled the area in the mid-twelfth century. They were later "civilized" and Nahuatized by the Colhuaque in the early fifteenth century. This Colhuaque movement to this area and north to the Tetzcoco zone is also depicted in the *Códice Xolotl* (4. Calli, 1405) and the *Mapa Quinatzin,* during the reign of Techotlalatzin. The Coatepec *relación geográfica* includes a detailed dynastic listing, dated in terms of reign lengths, which only agrees in part with that of the *Códice Xolotl.* A similar dynastic history is provided in the *relación geográfica* of neighboring Chimalhuacan (C 29), but this regime was apparently established about a century later, from Colhuacan.

Northern Acolhuacan was also politically important, especially between the decline of Xaltocan and the rise of Tetzcoco. Its principal center was Acolman, which became a bastion of Tepanec control (ruled by a son of Tezozomoc) after the conquest of Tetzcoco in 1416–1418. According to the *Códice Xolotl,* this area was settled by various Chichimec chieftains connected with Xolotl. It was the major theater of the two "Chichimec Wars" (1. Tecpatl, 1220; and 1. Tecpatl, 1324, or 1. Tochtli, 1350?), led by Yacanex (Yacatzotzoloc) of Tepetlaoztoc, when these northerners apparently attempted to maintain their more barbarous life style in the face of increasing acculturative pressure from the south. The *relaciónes geográficas* for Tecciztlan, Tepechpan (C 116), Tepepolco (C 111), Cempoallan, and Epazoyocan (C 19) provide other names of Chichimeca founders in this region (which do not agree with those of the *Códice Xolotl*). Only the Tepepolco *relación* provides any dates, 1146 (sic) for the supposed unsuccessful attempt of Tezozomoc of Azcapotzalco to conquer this community. In the *Tira de Tepechpan* (GR 317) a Colhuaque–Chichimeca lord, Icxicuauhtli (Acxocuauhtzin in the Tepechpan *relación geográfica*), initiates the dynasty as late as 11. Tochtli, 1334. The *Codex Kingsborough* (GR 181), from Tepetlaoztoc, depicts its Chichimeca founders, which it is stated settled the region early in the twelfth century, then lists its complete dynasty into the colonial period (interestingly, Yacanex is missing, but a Contact period *principal* bears that name).

As mentioned, fundamental for Acolhuaque history are the writings of Alva Ixtlilxochitl and the somewhat briefer cognate version in Torquemada's *Monarquía Indiana* (Books I–II, passim). Their accounts of the "Chichimec period" were obviously derived from the *Códice Xolotl* or a very similar source. Of special interest is their account of Toltec history. It is usually considered to be an Acolhuaque version, and Torquemada does specifically cite "Historias Aculhuas" in connection with it. It is strongly at variance with those other accounts previously discussed, mostly from the Mexica orbit. It goes into much more chronological and geographical detail than any other version concerning the Toltec migration, from Huehuetlapallan (Hueyxalac), which Alva Ixtlilxochitl locates in the northwest. From the itinerary presented, however, a southeastern location appears more likely—and this is supported by other data on Tlapallan (Lehmann 1920–21, Vol. II:1019, 1922:290; Melgarejo Vivanco 1950:47). Accepting this notion, Jiménez Moreno (1966b:63–80) has developed a bold hypothesis that Alva Ixtlilxochitl's Huehuetlapallan Tolteca were really the Nonoalca, connected with the Nahuat-speaking Pipil (themselves ultimately of Teotihuacan affiliation), one group of which, after an early (ca. 650) migration to the eastern Gulf Coast area and ultimately down the Pacific Coast at least as far as Panama (Ecuador–North Peru?), returned to Central Mexico to participate in the Toltec florescence (ca. 900).

Torquemada's (Book I, Chapter 14) account (the first portion of which virtually duplicates Alva Ixtlilxochitl's *Relación Sucinta*) contains no dates, but Alva Ixtlilxochitl's *Sumaria Relación . . . de los Tultecas* provides a detailed chronology. The emigration from Huehuetlapallan commences in 1. Tecpatl, 440, the founding of Tollan occurs in 1. Calli, 557. The ensuing nine-ruler dynasty, beginning with Chalchiuhtlanetzin and ending with

Meconetzin Topiltzin, covers a period of 449 years (7. Acatl, 563, to 1. Tecpatl, 1012). Only two of the names, Huetzin and Totepeuh, the third and fourth rulers, correspond with names in the more familiar lists. The whole flavor of Alva Ixtlilxochitl's account of Toltec history is markedly more European than these previously discussed, and it contains elements (such as a 52-year limitation on reign lengths) that are obviously absurd. Although putatively based on native pictorial sources, nothing resembling them are extant. It was earlier quite influential, especially in the nineteenth century syntheses of Brasseur de Bourbourg, Bancroft, Orozco y Berra, and Chavero, but it has never been thoroughly analyzed from a modern ethnohistorical viewpoint (see Nicholson 1957:164–188 for a preliminary analysis of the material relating to Topiltzin Quetzalcoatl). Its chronological aspect, especially, appears very suspect, but it cannot be altogether ignored in any discussion of the temporal problems of Postclassic Central Mexico.

E. Central Mexico Northeast: Sierra de Puebla and Neighborhood

The western portion of this zone might be termed "far northern Acolhuacan," since it was largely controlled politically from that province in late pre-Hispanic times and closely tied to it ethnically and culturally. At Contact it was quadrilingual: Nahua, Otomi, Totonac, and Tepehua. The overall area provides a fair-sized corpus of local historical materials, including a few pictorial items (listed, with other major Pueblan pictorials, in Nicholson 1968). The most important is a local history of Zacatlan–Tenamitec (Atenamitic)–Mizquihuacan, in the Totonac–Nahua mountain zone, collected in 1600 by Torquemada (Book III, Chapter 18) and certain *relaciónes geográficas* of the 1579–1585 series from various Totonac–Nahua communities in the eastern Sierra de Puebla and extending down into the coastal plain.

The Torquemada account provides a sketchy but circumstantial narrative of a nine-generation Totonac dynasty at "Mizquihuacan" (= modern San Francisco–Izquihuacan?; Kelly and Palerm 1952:18; cf. García Payón 1963, who attempts, very speculatively, to identify it with the archaeological site of Tajín, Veracruz). Its purported total duration was 800 years (each ruler's reign was set at exactly 80 years!). These Totonac had supposedly migrated from Chicomoztoc, and, en route, had constructed the Pyramids of the Sun and Moon at Teotihuacan, subsequently moving east, populating the Sierra de Puebla and extending down into the littoral as far as Cempoallan, the great lowland Totonac metropolis at Contact. Most of the rulers' names appear to be Nahua (three are calendric). During the reign of the second, Xatontan, the "Chichimeca," coming from the west, settled at "Nepoalco," six leagues distant. Hundreds of years later, after civil strife between two coruling brothers (the ninth generation) had destroyed the power of the

Totonac regime, these Chichimeca assumed political control of the area under their ruler Xihuitlpopoca. After his disappearance, two more Chichimec rulers followed in succession, during the reign of the last of which the Mexica incorporated the area into their empire.

Most scholars (e.g., Krickeberg 1933:63, 133; Kelley 1953:306) have rejected, for obvious reasons, the purported chronology of this tradition. Krickeberg and Melgarejo Vivanco (1943:88–89; 1950:29–30) have even suggested that some kind of formalized calendric computation is involved—but this is very dubious (see Caso 1953:338–339). The Zacatlan-Tenamitic area also receives some limited attention in the *Códice Xolotl*. On Sheet 2, two sons of Xolotl's son, Nopaltzin (1232–1263?), Toxtequihuatzin and Atocatzin, establish themselves at those two places. On Sheet 5, during the reign of Techotlalatzin of Tetzcoco (1357–1409?), the Zacatlan ruler is indeed shown as Xihuitlpopoca, while a Cuauhquetzale rules at Tenamitec—after which this area receives no further depiction. Zacatlan also figures as one of the stations on Alva Ixtlilxochitl's Toltec migration itinerary from Huehuetlapallan to Tollan, which, as mentioned earlier, Jíménez Moreno has hypothesized only pertains to one Toltec subgroup, the Nonoalca, a Tajínized Nahua–Pipil group originating in Teotihuacan who migrated via the Gulf Coast to Central America and eventually backtracked to Tollan. Zacatlan additionally plays a prominent role as one of the principal communities to which the refugee Olmeca Xicallanca fled after being driven from Tlaxcallan by the Teochichimeca (see p. 313).

The only other local dynastic history of consequence from this region is that of Tollantzinco, a major Nahua–Otomi *cabecera* politically subject to Tetzcoco in the late pre-Hispanic period. A document published by Carrasco (1963) provides a six-generation dynasty for its southern (Nahua) division, Tlatocan, which is temporally rather shallow (initiated by Hueymihuatzin, "el primer cazique chichimeco poblador," ca. 1350–1400?). As is known from archaeological data, however, the community itself was established long before this, and it is mentioned in various accounts as a Toltec center founded before Tollan; it also figures as a stopping place in Alva Ixtlilxochitl's migration account (as noted earlier). Two pictorials from the northern Sierra de Puebla region, the *Lienzo de Metlaltoyuca* (GR 199) and the *"Papers of Itzcuintepec"* (GR 161), provide considerable genealogical information concerning what must have been ruling dynasties of this area (the latter includes a number of dates), but they have not yet been adequately studied.

Some significant information concerning the original Totonac settlement of various communities in Southern Totonacapan and the subsequent "Chichimec" and final Mexica conquest is contained in certain *relaciones geográficas* (C 67, 118, 118bis, 141) of the 1579–1585 series from various Nahua and Nahua-Totonac towns in northern Puebla and central Veracruz: Xonotlan, Totzamapan, Ayotochco, Ehecatlan, Tetellan, Tzanacuauhtlan

(Teocuauhtenco), Calpolalpan, Tzotzonpan, Tototlan, Xalapan, Tlacuilolan, Mazatlan (Misantla), etc. Tzanacuauhtlan and Tototlan were supposedly founded originally by Totonaca from the east in 818. Tlacuilolan was also founded by Totonaca (from the sea); their regime endured for 400 years before the Chichimec conquest, which was followed 109 years later by the Mexica domination. All of these communities were eventually conquered by Chichimeca, who in some cases are specified as having come from Colhuacan, over 300 leagues distant, in a range of years falling between 1100 and 1280, the majority clustering around 1200. Most of these specifications of years are so precise that it seems likely they were derived from authentic local dated histories. The "Chichimeca" who overran much of Totonacapan appear to have been closely connected with those who similarly moved into the Basins of Mexico and Puebla no later than wake of Tollan's fall.

F. Central Mexico Southeast: Puebla–Tlaxcala

This region was one of the climax zones of Mesoamerican civilization and at Contact was a particularly thriving, well-populated zone, one sector of which (Tlaxcallan–Huexotzinco) still possessed enough military muscle to maintain its political autonomy in the face of the sustained, enveloping power of the Triple Alliance. A well-developed local historical tradition, therefore, characterized the area. However, many fewer dated chronicles are available than for the Basin of Mexico. The most important centers at Contact appear to have been Tlaxcallan, Huexotzinco, Chalollan, Tochimilco (Ocopetlayocan), Cuauhquechollan, Totomihuacan, Cuauhtinchan, Tecamachalco–Quecholac, Tepeyacac, Itzyocan, Teohuacan, Cozcatlan, Teotitlan, and Tepexi—excluding those communities in the far south that belong to the Mixteca Baja. Some local historical information is available for nearly all of these (and for various lesser centers as well), but only Cuauhtinchan provides a continuous year chronicle with much time depth (*Historia Tolteca–Chichimeca;* GR 359). Its coverage includes many neighboring communities, although in a rather sporadic fashion.

The *Historia Tolteca–Chichimeca* presents a continuous chronology ostensibly from 1. Tecpatl, 1116, to 13. Tecpatl, 1544. It describes the movement to Tollan from Colhuatepec–Chicomoztoc of two groups, the Tolteca Chichimeca and Nonoalca Chichimeca; their brief coexistence and internecine struggles in Tollan; the movement of the latter to southeastern Puebla; the subsequent migration of the former to Chalollan; their initial servitude under and later overthrow of the Olmeca Xicallanca (then ruling most of Central Puebla); their ensuing harassment by various allies of the latter; their recruitment of seven Chichimeca groups (Cuauhtinchantlaca, Totomihuaque, Texcalteca [Tlaxcalteca], [Chi]malpaneca, Acolchichimeca [Acolhuaque], Tzauhteca, and Zacateca) at Chicomoztoc–Colhuacatepec to aid them in their final takeover of the area; the consequent settlement in the region of their Chichimec allies; and the later history of these groups, with particular emphasis on the Cuauhtinchantlaca and the neighboring Totomihuaque. It is one of the most detailed, authentically native Mesoamerican histories that has survived. Unfortunately, its chronology, particularly in its earlier portions, cannot be taken at face value, nor can the earlier events chronicled, which are obviously quite stylized. The basic sequence of major events, many of which are corroborated in other sources (particularly, for the earlier migratory portion, the *Mapa de Cuauhtinchan 2* [GR 95], which frequently agrees even in specific dates [Bittmann Simons 1968]), probably can be accepted. It is precisely the dating of these events that poses the greatest problem.

In the 1. Acatl = 1519 equation, the following chronology would emerge: arrival at Tollan of the Tolteca Chichimeca and the Nonoalca Chichimeca, 1116; collapse of Tollan, 1117–30; Tolteca Chichimeca arrival at Chalollan, 1168; final defeat of the Olmeca Xicallanca and their allies, and the Chichimeca settlement of the area, 1174–1175. Earlier students (Preuss and Mengin, Kirchhoff, Berlin, *et al.*) of this source tended to accept this chronology, but Jiménez Moreno (1953, 1961), in probably his most comprehensive chronological reappraisal of any major Mesoamerican native history, has hypothesized three distinct year counts (Mixtec–Popoloca, Tetzcocan, and Mexica), plus 52-year backshifts in the earlier portions. In his reconstruction, the Tolteca Chichimeca arrival at Chalollan is dated 1292 (1168 + 52 + 52 + 20) and, on the same basis, the final defeat of the Olmeca Xicallanca allies, 1298–1299. Subsequent events up to the late fourteenth century are adjusted similarly, adding 104 years plus 20 (Tetzcocan) or 40 (Mixtec–Popoloca). Beginning with 1386 (his adjusted chronology), only one 52-year cycle is added, plus, where indicated, the same additional shifts. A number of the later events in the *Historia Tolteca–Chichimeca* are also included, with the same dates and Christian calendar equations, in the *Anales de Cuauhtitlan*, and Jiménez Moreno would, of course, make the same shifts for them.

The sixteenth-century Tlaxcalteca mestizo, Muñoz Camargo (GG 1072), provides the fullest history of Tlaxcallan, undoubtedly derived from both pictorial and oral local annals. Only the earlier portion, up to the establishment of the ancestors of the Tlaxcalteca at Texcaltepec–Tepeticpac, is dated (but not continuously) in terms of the native system. The beginning of Muñoz Camargo's chronicle is lost. However, Torquemada (Book III, Chapters 7–17), whose account of Tlaxcalteca history was almost literally copied from that of Muñoz Camargo, probably substantially preserves it. It consists of a particular version of the Topiltzin Quetzalcoatl of Tollan tale (summarized and discussed in Nicholson 1957:157–164). After an ethnographic digression the history is resumed with an account of the migration of the Olmeca Xicallanca through the Basin of Mexico and on to (a previously unpopulated) Tlaxcallan. No dates are provided, but, in describing their

Xochitecatl fortress, Muñoz Camargo states that it was abandoned 360 years before, that is, ca. 1230. Although mentioned rather casually and confusedly, the settlement of ChololIan is placed in a year 1. Acatl, by "otras cuadrillas de Chichimecas" (= Tolteca Chichimeca).

The migration of the ancestors of the Tlaxcalteca and related Teochichimeca groups is recounted in some detail. After departing from "aquel pasaje del agua y rio e estrecho de mar," they arrived at the "siete cuevas" in a year 5. Tochtli, moving down to and occupying the Cuauhtitlan area for some time, following which (2. Tecpatl) they settled in the plains of Poyauhtlan near the southeastern margin of Lake Tetzcoco. In 1. Tochtli or 1. Tecpatl (both versions are given), after a bloody battle with their neighbors, they resumed their wandering, moved south through Amaquemecan (2. Calli) and east into the Huexotzinco area (3. Tochtli), and finally settled, in 5. Tecpatl, at Texcaltepec–Tepeticpac after conquering and expelling the indigenous inhabitants, the Olmeca Xicallanca, who fled north to the Zacatlan area. In 9. Tecpatl, they consolidated their position at Tepeticpac by decisively defeating an enemy coalition led by Huexotzinco. A rather sketchy, undated history of Tlaxcallan follows, concentrating on the formation of the four traditional *cabeceras* (Tepeticpac, Ocotelolco, Tizatlan, Quiahuiztlan) and the ruler sequence in each—plus fifteenth and early sixteenth century struggles with the Triple Alliance powers and neighboring Huexotzinco.

Muñoz Camargo himself makes no equations between his native system and European dates. In one place he speaks of the Tlaxcalteca migration as having occurred about 300 years before (= ca, 1290); in another, of a 300-year period of "Chichimec" colonization of much of New Spain following the founding of Tlaxcallan (= ca. 1220). Most earlier students (e.g., Orozco y Berra 1960, Vol. 3:110) equated 9. Tecpatl, year of the Battle of Tepeticpac, with 1384. Accepting this equation, if the years are in continuous sequence with no 52-year gaps, the earliest, 5. Tochtli (arrival at Chicomoztoc), would correspond to 1302. Subtracting one cycle would take it back to 1250, in better conformity with Muñoz Camargo's round figure—and this is apparently favored by Jiménez Moreno (1966a:103, n.d.), who equates 5. Tecpatl, the date of the arrival at Tepeticpac, with 1348 (1328 + 20); and, consequently, the 9. Tecpatl year of the Battle of Tepeticpac, with 1352. This latter date is also given in the *Historia Tolteca–Chichimeca* and the *Anales de Cuauhtitlan* for what appears to be the same event, but equated with 1228. As Gibson has pointed out, however, Muñoz Camargo's dynastic histories of the four Tlaxcalteca *cabeceras* cover spans of at most seven average reigns, "or, as most reigns are commonly computed, somewhat less than 200 years [1952:5]," which would support the later dating. The *Anales de Tlatelolco-5* describes a series of Chichimeca emigrations from the Sierra de Guadalupe region (one eminence of which was apparently called Tlaxcaltecatepetl) connected with the Tepanec–Mexica conquest of Tenanyocan in

1370–1371, including one to Tliliuhquitepec, a major (Otomi) ally of Tlaxcallan at Contact. These movements, however, were probably subsequent to the major migration via the Cuauhtitlan and Poyauhtlan zones described by Muñoz Camargo.

A late seventeenth-century chronicle, in Nahuatl, still unpublished, that of Zapata y Mendoza and Santos y Salazar (GG 1139), also rather sketchily outlines major events of Tlaxcalteca history, beginning with the departure in 1. Tecpatl from Chicomoztoc (no Christian year equation). In the second part, the arrival to Tlaxcallan is dated at 9. Tecpatl, equated with 1332. No further specific Tlaxcalteca historical events are chronicled until 13. Calli, 1453, when Chalca migrated to Tlaxcallan (the year count is continuous, 1477–1692). Tlaxcallan is also peripherally covered in the *Códice Xolotl.* On Sheet 3, its place sign first appears, associated with the date 1. Tecpatl (1220?; 1272?), with three rulers (who apparently arrived from Huexotzinco)— Xiuhquetzaltzin, son of Tlotzin, and Cuauhtlachtli and Memexoltzin, sons of Huetzin (third ruler of Coatlinchan). Alva Ixtlilxochitl in his *Historia Chichimeca,* probably influenced by Torquemada's account (derived, in turn, from Muñoz Camargo), connects the Tlaxcalteca emigration from Poyauhtlan with the "Second Yacanex War" (1. Tecpatl, 1324?; 1. Tochtli, 1350?), when the northern (Tepetlaoztoc area) barbarians were finally defeated by an Acolhuaque coalition—but this is not authorized by the depictions on *Códice Xolotl* Sheet 4. On Sheet 5, devoted to the reign of Techotlalatzin (1357–1409?), a Mitl rules Tlaxcallan, while on Sheets 7 and 9, concerned with the Tepaneca–Acolhuaque war (1414–1428), he is replaced by a Cuauhatlapal. None of these rulers, known by these names, are included in the Muñoz Camargo dynastic lists.

No local chronicle for Huexotzinco, Tlaxcallan's chief ally, seems to be extant, but many brief references to its history are contained in the *Historia Tolteca–Chichimeca* and other annals, including the *Códice Xolotl.* On Sheet 3, three of its four founders are members of the Basin of Mexico Acolhuaque dynasty (son of Tlotzin and two sons of Huetzin), apparently in the same 1. Tecpatl year as the founding of Tlaxcallan. The *Anales de Cuauhtitlan* gives the same year but equates it with 804, also naming three, but distinct, founders. Muñoz Camargo specifies 3. Tochtli (1326?) as the foundation year, and mentions the names of six Chichimeca chiefs as founders of six major divisions of the province, none of which appear in other sources. The *Historia Tolteca–Chichimeca* gives short shrift to Huexotzinco in its earlier portion, ostensibly not even including it in the seven Chichimeca groups, but the Huexotzinca probably were included in the "Acolchichimeca." In its later portion, on the other hand, Huexotzinco figures frequently in major events—most of which, as indicated, also appear in the *Anales de Cuauhtitlan.* The later great Huexotzinca lords (Miccacalcatl, Xayacamachan, Tenocelotzin, Toltecatzin, Tecayehuatzin, *et al.*) are frequently mentioned in both Basin of Mexico and Pueblan annals.

Cholollan, the third member of the Pueblan "Triple Alliance" also has yielded no significant local chronicle, which is particularly unfortunate because of the well-known antiquity of this leading mercantile and religious center. The early portion of the *Historia Tolteca–Chichimeca,* however, is much concerned with Cholollan, and other Central Mexican histories often refer to it. The *Historia Tolteca–Chichimeca* only goes back to the final days of the Olmeca Xicallanca rule in Cholollan. Jiménez Moreno (1966a:62–63), further developing the well-known "Olmeken–Tyrannei" hypothesis of Lehmann (1920–1921, Vol. 2:792, 1004–1006, 1088–1090; 1922:289–291), has suggested that a triethnic (Mixtec–Popoloca–Nahua) Olmeca Xicallanca regime dominated Cholollan between ca. 800 and 1292. The relevant passages in Torquemada (Book I, Chapter 14; Book III, Chapter 40), on which both rely, however, do not explicitly refer to Cholollan, and this reconstruction must be regarded as quite speculative. Alva Ixtlilxochitl assigns the Olmeca Xicallanca occupation of Cholollan to his third cosmogonical era, the "Wind Sun," Ehecatonatiuh, to which, in his *Sumaria Relación . . . de los Tultecas,* he gave a duration of 1715 years. These Olmeca Xicallanca were the second occupiers of the Pueblan area, seizing it from the "Giants," the Quinametin, whom they exterminated after entertaining them at a banquet (cf. similar tale in Durán). Clearly, no real history of the Olmeca Xicallanca before the period of the Tolteca Chichimeca invasion is extant, nor is the record of Toltec Cholollan much better preserved. Even the date of the latter's "founding" varies: Muñoz Camargo, 1. Acatl (no Christian equivalent); *Historia Tolteca–Chichimeca* and *Anales de Cuauhtitlan,* 1. Tecpatl, 1168. The last two sources describe a Chololteca defeat by Huexotzinco in 3. Acatl, 1235, after which Cholollan does not appear to have played a very significant military–political role; Huexotzinco dominated until at least the late fifteenth century, Tlaxcallan after that.

Cholollan was ruled from Olmec times on by two co-high priests, the Aquiach and the Tlalchiach (a four-ruler and six-ruler system is also described; see Carrasco 1971), but no satisfactory dynastic list has been preserved. In the *Códice Xolotl* some coverage is devoted to Chololteca dynastic history. Unfortunately, neither Alva Ixtlilxochitl nor Torquemada provide much interpretation of the relevant scenes, which in two cases (Sheets 1, 3) feature numerical year tallies whose interpretation is somewhat uncertain. Only one specific year is pictured (Sheet 2), 1. Tochtli (1194?), for the accession of Iztaccuuhtli and a co-ruler, apparently grandsons of Texpolcatl, one of the two co–founding high priests. The last ruler shown (Sheets 5, 6, 9), Chichimecatlacpayantzin, was contemporaneous with the Tepanec War (1427–1431).

Considerable historical data are available for other important Pueblan centers, above all, Tochimilco, Cuauhquechollan, Totomihuacan, Tepeyacac, Tecamachalco–Quechollac, and Cozcatlan, but the time depth is generally rather shallow. The *Historia Tolteca–Chichimeca* refers to some degree to most of these centers during the post-Chichimec settlement period, particularly Totomihuacan and Tecamachalco–Quechollac. An especially prominent Chocho–Popoloca/Nahua dynasty (seemingly ultimately derived from Coaixtlahuacan, Oaxaca) ruled the latter province, beginning toward the close of the fourteenth century, whose history can be sketchily reconstructed from various primary sources, particularly the *Anales de Tecamachalco* (GG 1112), which provides a continuous year count from 1398 (Nicholson n.d.). An extensive, but insufficiently studied, pictorial genealogy stems from Cuauhquechollan (GR 91), but more time depth is probably provided for this important center in the *Códice Xolotl,* where its dynasty is founded by a pair of sons of a Toltec couple resident at Tlatzallan (Nicholson 1972:165) at the time of Xolotl's arrival—and at least three successive rulers are pictured to the time of the Tepanec War. The accession of Matlacxochitl, who succeeded the two co-founders, is specified (Sheet 2) as 1. Tochtli (1194?). Cuauhquechollan suffered some major military defeats, which were finally so serious that the community had to be shifted some miles south down the Atlixco Valley and its ancestral lands ceded to Huexotzinco and Calpan (seemingly pictorialized in *Códice Xolotl,* Sheet 6). The *Historia Tolteca–Chichimeca* and the *Anales de Cuauhtitlan* date these defeats in 1. Acatl, 1259, and 2. Acatl, 1299, but Motolinia, in his *Memoriales* (GG 1071; Part I, Chapter 64), describes them as occurring in the early fifteenth century—with which the Jiménez Moreno (1961) chronology (1383 and 1403) and that of the *Códice Xolotl* would essentially agree.

For nearby Tochimilco (Ocopetlayocan) we have, in the final section of the *Historia de los Mexicanos por Sus Pinturas,* a brief dynastic listing, unfortunately undated, which is significant because it covers only six generations from the apparent crack-up of Tollan (the founder emigrated from there) to the time of the Conquest (cf. Nazareo Xaltocan genealogy, cited earlier, which covers eleven generations from Huemac to Motecuhzoma II). According to Motolinia's *Memoriales* (Part I, Chapter 64), Tochimilco–Ocopetlayocan was "la cosa más antigua de todo este valle" (Atlixco), from which both Huexotzinco and Calpan were colonized.

An incomplete dynastic history can also be reconstructed for Tepeyacac, a leading Nahua-speaking *cabecera* of central Puebla. According to the *Anales de Cuauhtitlan,* it was founded in the same year as Toltec Cholollan, 1. Tecpatl, 1168. Its 1580 *relación geográfica* (C 110), however, specifies the same year but correlates it with 1267–1270 (= 1272). It was settled by Chichimeca from Chicomoztoc, led by Cuauhtliztac, who, as Kirchhoff (1947:lxi) suggested, might be identifiable with a Tolteca Chichimeca of that name mentioned in the *Historia Tolteca–Chichimeca.* Some later rulers, to the trio in power at Contact, are also named, including Chichtli, pictured on Sheet 5 of the *Códice Xolotl* (reign of Techotlalatzin). This source (Sheet 2) depicts a different founder, Iztacmitl, a Chichimec chieftain who accompanied Xolotl. Muñoz Camargo describes a Chichimeca conquest of the

Tepeyacac–Tecalpan (Tecali) area in 5. Tecpatl (1224?) and a settlement there by a lord called Cuauhtzintecuhtli (= Cuauhtliztac?). The later history of Tepeyacac, particularly its long, ultimately successful struggle for supremacy with Cuauhtinchan and its conquest, in turn, in 1466 by the Triple Alliance, is sketchily chronicled in the *Historia Tolteca–Chichimeca.*

The Nahua-speaking southeastern Pueblan centers (Teohuacan, Cozcatlan, Teotitlan, Tzonquiliuhcan, etc.) were, according to the *Historia Tolteca–Chichimeca,* settled shortly after the collapse of Tollan by the Nonoalca Chichimeca, led by Xelhuan and other leaders, and this is generally confirmed by the 1580 *relación geográfica* of Cozcatlan (C 42–43) and Motolinia (Epístola Proemial). Except for some genealogical data in the *Historia Tolteca–Chichimeca,* however, the subsequent history of this region, until its conquest in the middle years of the fifteenth century by the Triple Alliance, is not well covered in the extant sources. One of the "Coixtlahuaca Group" of genealogical *lienzos* (Smith 1973:182–184), the *Lienzo de Ihuitlan* (Caso 1951), from Santiago Ihuitlan, Oaxaca, includes some limited, very late (undated) pre-Hispanic dynastic information for Teohuacan and Cozcatlan.

As indicated, the Pueblan sources do not appear to provide any validly dated historical information much prior to the Toltec–Chichimec movement to, and political takeover of, Olmec Cholollan and neighboring territory. However, a cosmogonical tradition possibly collected in Puebla by Motolinia (see Nicholson 1956:115) and preserved (truncated?) in his *Memoriales* (Part II, Chapter 28) and, more sketchily, in López de Gómara (1943, Vol 2:211–212) ostensibly carries a continuous dated historical record back to 1. Tochtli, 726, the commencement of the fifth and present era. Unfortunately, Motolinia provides no historical information of significance derived from these supposed long-range annals.

G. Other Central Mexican Regions

Some limited historical data, including a few dated events, but usually with rather shallow temporal coverage, can be gleaned from various indigenous records from other areas in or adjacent to Central Mexico, particularly Morelos, Guerrero, and the Gulf Coast. Space limitations prevent consideration of these zones. It is worth noting, however, that from the south coastal region of one of them, Guerrero, hail some significant continuous year pictorial annals, the *Códices de Azoyu* (see Table 10.1), although the time depth is not very great.

H. Central Mexican "Alliance Sequence"

Before leaving this region, a brief summary should be made of the various systems of political alliances at different periods, a sequence that has considerable relevance to chronological problems. The ostensibly earliest of these would be Chimalpahin's Tollan–Colhuacan–Otompan triple alliance supposedly set up in 1. Tecpatl, 856, and subsequently, in 10. Acatl, 1047, reorganized, with Azcapotzalco replacing Tollan and Coatlinchan, Otompan. Our skepticism concerning the validity of this account has been expressed earlier. Probably much more reliable is the quintuple alliance described in the *Anales de Cuauhtitlan* for the (late?) Toltec Period: Tollan–Cuauhchinanco–Cuauhnahuac–Huaxtepec–Cuahuacan. Probably functioning not too long after Tollan's collapse was the triple alliance mentioned in the *Codex Vaticanus A:* Colhuacan–Tenanyocan–Xaltocan. The next stage would be represented by the triple alliance described in the *Anales de Cuauhtitlan* and by Sahagún (Book X, Chapter 29): Azcapotzalco–Colhuacan–Coatlinchan, which reflects the power shift represented by the rise of the Tepaneca and the Acolhuaque. The succeeding political order, recorded in the *Codex Vaticanus A* and the 1580 *relación geográfica* of Acolman (C 116B), must have flourished following the crack-up of Colhuacan: Azcapotzalco–Coatlinchan–Acolman. Apparently the final Tepanec imperial system devised by Tezozomoc would be represented by the quintuple alliance referred to in the *Cano Relaciones:* Azcapotzalco–Coatlinchan–Huexotzinco–Amaquemecan–Cuauhnahuac. The last, of course, was *the* Triple Alliance, Tenochtitlan–Tetzcoco–Tlacopan, which, from ca. 1434 to the Conquest played the dominant political role in Western Mesoamerica. Similar alliances were seemingly also characteristic of the Pueblan (and Toluca?) area, but these are not nearly as well documented—although a kind of Tlaxcallan–Huexotzinco–Chalollan triple alliance appears to have functioned vis-à-vis its Basin of Mexico counterpart during the last few pre-Hispanic decades.

I. Oaxaca

Western Oaxaca, the Mixteca, yields the ostensibly most extensive temporal coverage in terms of precisely dated historical events of any Western Mesoamerican region, in the five screenfold "meander histories" (*Bodley, Selden, Vindobonensis, Zouche–Nuttall, Colombino–Becker I*). Caso (1951) has correlated the historically relevant dates in these sources with those in the Christian calendar, working out a continuous sequence extending back to 692. His data and arguments need hardly be repeated here. His reconstruction has been almost mechanically accepted by most other Mesoamericanists; but, as I have pointed out elsewhere (Nicholson 1967), there were some very challenging problems facing Caso when he attempted to establish his synchronizations, and they should be regarded only as stimulating working hypotheses subject to further refinement and modification. The early portion of Caso's widely accepted Mixteca chronology has recently (Rabin 1974) been seriously challenged on some very cogent grounds, wherein it is proposed that its beginning (692) be shifted forward no less than three 52-year cycles (156 years). Perhaps the greatest current need is the fuller integration of these extensive Mixteca dynastic histories with the Western Oaxacan archaeological record.

The predominantly Zapotec-speaking area of Eastern Oaxaca has not yielded dated historical chronicles even approaching in richness of content those from Western Oaxaca. Burgoa (1934a,b) and some of the 1579–1585 *relaciones geográficas* provide a few data, with rather shallow time depth. The pictorial corpus (see Cline 1966; Glass and Robertson 1975) is disappointing in this regard, although the colonial *Lienzo de Guevea* (GR 130), from a community near Tehuantepec, provides a brief listing of the Zaachila (Teozapotlan)–Tehuantepec Zapotec dynasty—possibly covering five generations—with numerical tallies (which, however, appear to be much too long for reign lengths). Although the most "historical" of all the Zapotec pictorials, no specific year dates, unfortunately, are included.

III. CONCLUSION

From this concise review of major Western Mesoamerican dated native histories, a few observations can be drawn. The most obvious is that a tremendous amount of confusion and contradiction prevails in this scattered and disparate corpus, which poses a formidable challenge to those attempting to utilize these records to improve the precision of Postclassic chronology. No simple keys to unlock their complexities apppear to be available. The hypothesis of many different, simultaneous functioning year counts, for example, hailed as a major breakthrough, has not, in my opinion, clarified chronological problems nearly to the extent expected—and, to some degree, has actually compounded them. In the absence of any shortcuts, the ordinary methodological canons of critical historical scholarship must be rigorously applied to all relevant data provided by these highly uneven sources.

I have dealt briefly with the question of the reliability and value of the pre-Hispanic Central Mexican histories elsewhere (Nicholson 1971a). To that discussion I would like to add a few more observations of particular relevance to chronological aspects. Expectably, the nearer the event to the time of the Conquest, the greater the probability of basic chronological accuracy. Particularly for the final pre-Hispanic century, the temporal precision of the best accounts often appears to be quite impressive. However, after the first two or three decades of the fifteenth century, chronological reliability seems to fall off almost at an exponential rate, particularly for events earlier than about 1350. One obvious reason is simply the "fade-out factor," that is, the more remote in time any record is from the event, the more chance that recollection of its details will gradually fuzz and eventually disappear altogether. The tendency to merge and telescope chronologically separated events is also well known. Even when records are kept in a fully developed phonetic writing system, this fade-out factor can be significantly operative. In pre-Hispanic Western Mesoamerica, where most historical information could only be conveyed orally or by somewhat limited picto–ideographic (with some limited phoneticism in place and name signs) techniques, it must have been operative to an even greater degree. This problem seems to have been recognized by the native annalists themselves, for the compilers of the *Cano Relaciones* reported the uncertainty of their informants concerning the relationship of Huetzin, the third Colhuaque ruler, to his predecessor, "por ser tan de lejos no lo saben todos que parentesco se habían estos señores."

Another factor causing major problems was simple politics. Each politically significant community clearly sought to portray its past in the most favorable possible light—and "rewriting" directed to this end must have been virtually continuous. This could seriously affect chronological aspects, for dynastic primacy was often a major consideration in certain political–military conflict situations. For quite recent events it would obviously be difficult to tamper successfully with chronological notations (reign lengths, town foundation dates, conquests, etc.); more remote events, on the other hand, could be manipulated with much greater facility. The essentially political and dynastic purposes of these histories must be constantly kept in mind. If it is objected that the frequent recording of the exact dates of some "natural" (versus "human") events, such as eclipses, earthquakes, droughts, etc., would not have been influenced by political considerations, it should be emphasized that most of these are recorded only for the final pre-Conquest century, when all chronological problems are much less acute. For earlier centuries, the great bulk of the historical data are political, dynastic, and military, precisely the type of event whose dating would be most likely to be modified if an obvious political advantage was apparent.

Another significant factor contributing to chronological unreliability was the disruptive effects of major conquests, dispersions, abandonments, and migrations, which caused serious breaks in historical record-keeping continuities. Deliberate destruction of records certainly frequently accompanied pre-Hispanic as well as post-Conquest military take-overs. As always, one of the principal prizes of military victory was the past (cf. Orwell's "Who control the past controls the future; who controls the present controls the past"), and conscious alteration of existing records for political advantage in the wake of conquests and related upheavals must have been common—and creates problems in long-range chronological interpretation. Even if the famous Itzcoatl case reported by Sahagún has probably been exaggerated and possibly misunderstood, there can be no doubt that politically motivated modification of historical records must have been common. If the multiplicity of calendars hypothesized by Jiménez Moreno, Kirchhoff, Davies, and others has validity, this too can be related to political factors, for each system was probably largely sustained by conditions of political autonomy.

Examination of Old World calendric systems and their acceptance and propagation reveals that calendric standardization is normally connected with the establishment of particular political and religious systems. Conversely, in an atmosphere of political–religious fragmentation, a multiplicity of calendric systems appears to have been common. Acceptance of a single, unified system was usually associated with political and/or religious unification, and similar cultural processes were probably operative in Mesoamerica. More adequate understanding of the calendric systems of this area co-tradition might emerge from more careful analyses of their religio–political correlates.

Also, there must always be clear recognition of the pervasive influence on all Mesoamerican historiography of various religious ideological conceptions: ceremonial numbers (Kirchhoff 1947: xxxiv–xxxviii), sacred directional associations, deified ancestral leaders and patron god "covenants" (Nicholson 1971b:409–410), calendric divinatory connotations (e.g., "proper" years for migratory departures and community foundations: 1. Tecpatl, 1. Acatl, etc.), and many others. These ideological preconceptions particularly pervaded accounts of the historical beginnings of ethnic entities. The line here between cosmogony and history is often very difficult to draw. Certainly, the complex welter of acutual past events was often restructured and altered to conform to fundamental cosmological–cosmognical notions, resulting in a kind of "pattern history" for the earlier portions of the more authentically native tradition annals. Another complicating factor is the obvious rapidity of the formation of colorful narratives, saturated with folkloristic and mythological motifs, around such major political events as conquests and political collapses (e.g., fall of Tollan, Spanish conquest of Tenochtitlan–Tlatelolco, etc.).

Much more discussion could profitably be devoted to those problems, but it is time now to conclude with a few final remarks concerning the fundamental question that motivated this chapter: to what extent can events of the Postclassic be accurately dated by the surviving native histories? Although it appears that the Indians themselves believed at Contact that quite a few centuries of accurately dated history were available to them (cf. Torquemada, Book X, Chapter 36: "se podía tener noticia de sus cosas, y referir con puntualidad lo sucedido de mil Años atrás"), critical examination of the extant corpus reveals that only the broadest overall chronological outline can be reconstructed before the mid-fourteenth century. Western Oaxaca may be the exception that Caso's sequence back to 692 ostensibly indicates, but more analysis of his influential reconstruction is in order before it can be unequivocally accepted. I tend to agree with Jiménez Moreno (1972:197, n.d.) that a major political–chronological watershed was the conquest of Tenanyocan, 1370–1371, which decisively established Azcapotzalco's supremacy in the Western Basin of Mexico and cleared the way for the explosive expansion of the Tepanec Empire. Whether a basic calendric unification resulted, as Jiménez Moreno holds, or whether the consequent unfolding of Tepanec power merely created the basis for fuller and more accurate record keeping, from this time forward most principal Central Mexican events—with some notable exceptions—seem to be datable within a year or so of their occurrence. Before 1370 this is generally not the case, in spite of the plethora of specific dates provided by the sources, putatively stretching back for centuries. Some, but by no means all, of these pre-1370 chronological problems may be the result of the simultaneous use of different year counts. More probably stem from the disruptive political conditions that prevailed between the break-up of the Toltec Empire and the rise of Azcapotzalco. The chronological confusion of this "Chichimec Interregnum" probably directly reflects the prevailing political confusion. Even key events, therefore, can usually be dated only approximately, with all dating becoming steadily more approximate the further back in time the events are removed from 1370.

Significant examples of pre-1370 events whose dating has created serious problems are the accession of Tezozomoc (see p. 296), the "fall" of Colhuacan, and the "founding" of Tenochtitlan–Tlatelolco. One problem is that perhaps only the first was really an abrupt event. Davies (1973:96–100) may be correct in suggesting that the second may have been a more gradual affair than is usually recognized, probably beginning about 1345. Although nearly all the Mexica histories provide a specific "official" year for the founding of the future metropolis, historically it may also have been—like the "founding" of Rome—a gradual process of settlement and colonization. This could be one factor partly accounting for the considerable divergencies in the sources concerning this date, which have led, in turn, to similar differences of opinion among modern students (cf., apart from the majority who still probably favor the "traditional" date of 1324–1325, Kirchhoff [1950]: 1369–1370; Jiménez Moreno [e.g., 1966a: 112] and Davies [1973:198–199]: 1345). The chronology of many other important events of the Chichimec Interregnum deserve discussion, but we must pass on to some consideration of perhaps the single most significant question of Postclassic chronology, the date of the collapse of Tollan, whose political and cultural repercussions constituted such a fundamental watershed in Mesoamerican history.

The majority of students of the perennial "Toltec problem," above all Jiménez Moreno (e.g., 1966c:191–192—1156) and Kirchhoff (1961:264—1200), still appear to favor a middle or late twelfth-century date. As we have seen, however, some data appear to support an early thirteenth-century Toltec collapse. In any case, ca. 1250 would probably represent a *terminus ante quem*. A *terminus post quem* might be ca. 1050. Aside from the difficult problem of the date of the destruction of the Toltec Empire, the question can be legitimately raised as to whether any kind of reliably dated history can be compiled for the period of Tollan's floruit. Without falling into the trap of Brintonian hyperskepticism, an objective appraisal of the available information relevant to this period requires the conclusion that only the most generalized outline can be legitimately blocked out—and even here widely divergent interpretations (e.g., Kirchhoff 1955b versus Jiménez Moreno 1966a:95–102; 1966c:191–193) are possible. As has been noted, the leading sources differ greatly concerning the names, proper sequence, and dates of the Toltec dynasts. And, if establishing an accurate date for the finale of Tollan is difficult enough, attempting to ascertain the complementary date of the founding—or at least rise to power—of this imperial center is much more difficult.

One method of approaching this question might be to try to establish a reliable total duration for the period of Tollan's supremacy. Again, however, the disagreements among the prime accounts are tremendous, ranging from Sahagún's millennium (on his confused and highly aberrant Toltec chronology, see Nicholson 1957:341) to the *Historia de los Mexicanos por Sus Pinturas'* possible 52 years (104?; cf. *Leyenda de los Soles*). The *Cano Relaciones* ca. 190 and the *Anales de Cuauhtitlan's* 260 might be considered to be the most "reasonable" (cf. Jiménez Moreno 1941), particularly the latter if its dynastic list (differing, however, from any other source) can be accepted. Chimalpahin's 342 years is perhaps as suspect as his anomalous dynastic history; and Alva Ixtlilxochitl's figure of 455 can be considered only within the context of his even more aberrant dynastic history. If a figure of 150–250 might be favored, then a Toltec "founding," working back from 1050–1250 for the collapse, would fall somewhere between 800 and 1000. The currently most favored date (e.g., Jiménez Moreno 1966c:192) of ca. 900 splits this period rather neatly—and also corresponds fairly well with archaeological estimates. Certainly, any Toltec duration over 300 years would appear to face serious difficulties; even a period about half that length might be supported with various cogent arguments.

Finally, we arrive at a question of considerable interest: Do the dated native historical traditions of Western Mesoamerica—aside from the possible special case of the Mixteca meander histories—really penetrate with any degree of reliability into the Epiclassic and Classic periods? In my view, the possibility of reconstructing any kind of more or less accurate chronology on the basis of the scant allusions to these periods in the native histories is very slight. A quite hazy, immediately pre-Toltec "Tamoanchan Era" (Jiménez Moreno 1966b:59–60; Nicholson 1971b:403), based largely on the Sahaguntine tradition summarized earlier and probably connected with Xochicalco, can perhaps be dimly discerned, but no specific dates in the native calendar appear to be available. How this would relate to another immediately pre-Toltec epoch, the somewhat hypothetical "Chichimeca–Mimixcoa Era," is unclear. Perhaps a more northerly locus for the latter might be involved. As we have seen, a few dates are cited in accounts of this era, but they seem to be highly stylized and to express concepts more cosmogonical than historical. One more step back, and we are squarely in the epoch of the "Giants,"

Quinametin (which Jiménez Moreno [1945:11–12; 1966b:50] has identified with the Teotihuacanos), and the great cosmogonical eras, or "suns." At this point, any question of reliable historical specifics becomes virtually meaningless. The great Epiclassic and Classic centers (Xochicalco, Tajín, Teotihuacan, Cholula, Monte Albán, etc.) may well have compiled dated historical annals, perhaps covering considerable temporal spans, but, if so, only their most ghostly echoes appear to have been audible at the time of the Conquest.

These rather critical observations concerning the value and reliability of pre-1370 dated events in the native histories should not be interpreted to mean that I am suggesting that the archaeologists should, in effect, ignore them in their chronological analyses. On the contrary, I would urge the constant advancement of fresh working hypotheses, even for earlier centuries, particularly of the type so stimulatingly advanced for so many years by Jiménez Moreno. But all of these pre-1370 schemes must be clearly recognized as *hypotheses,* to be modified or discarded when fresh evidence or more penetrating analyses become available. I am convinced that students have been frequently misled by the "seductive specificity" of the sophisticated Western Mesoamerican calendric system. They have also tended to underestimate, I feel, the adverse effect on the maintenance of long-term, chronologically accurate histories by the frequent political–military upheavals that were typical of the area—not to speak of the effects of local propagandistic bias and other distorting influences discussed above. Stable, temporally extensive history is a normal concomitant of political stability, apparently a rather rare condition in pre-Hispanic times. The dated native histories of Western Mesoamerica can certainly contribute significantly to the attainment of greater chronological precision for the last few centuries before the Conquest, but only if they are utilized critically and perceptively—a task in which close collaboration is necessary between the field archaeologist and the ethnohistorian.

BIBLIOGRAPHY

Barlow, R.H.

1947 Review of P.F. Velázquez Edition of the *Anales de Cuauhtitlan* and the *Leyenda de los Soles* (Mexico, 1945). *Hispanic American Historical Review* **27**(3):520–526.

1948 Resumen Analítico de "Unos Anales Históricos de la Nación Mexicana." In *Anales de Tlatelolco. Unos Anales Históricos de la Nación Mexicana y Códice de Tlatelolco.* Fuentes para la historia de México 2, edited by H. Berlin. Robredo, Mexico. Pp. ix-xiii.

1952 Los Tecpaneca Después de la Caída de Azcapotzalco. *Tlalocan* **3**(3):285–287.

Bittmann Simons, B.

1968 Los Mapas de Cuauhtinchan y la Historia Tolteca-Chichimeca. *Instituto Nacional de Antropología e Historia, México, Serie Investigaciones* **15.**

Brand, D.

1971 Ethnohistoric Synthesis of Western Mexico. In *Handbook of Middle American Indians,* Vol. 11, edited by R. Wauchope, G.F. Ekholm, and I. Bernal. Austin: University of Texas Press. Pp. 632–635.

Burgoa, Fray F. de

1934a Geográfica Descripción de la Parte Septentrional, del Polo Ártico de la América, y Nueve Iglesia de las Indias Occidentales, y Sitio Astronómico de Esta Provincia de Predicadores de Antequera Valle de Oaxaca. 2 vols. *Archivo General de la Nación, México, Publicaciones* **25–26.**

1934b Palestra Historial de Virtudes, y Exemplares Apostólicos. Fundada del Zelo de Insignes Héroes de la Sagrada Orden de Predicadores en Este Neuvo Mundo de América en las Indias Occidentales. *Archivo General de la Nación, México, Publicaciones* **24.**

Carrasco, P.

1950 Los Otomíes; Cultura e Historia de los Pueblos Mesoamericanos de Habla Otomiana. *Universidad Nacional Autónoma de México, Instituto de Historia, Publicaciones, Primera Serie* **15.**

1963 Los Caciques Chichimecas de Tulancingo. *Estudios de Cultura Náhuatl* **4:**85–91.

1969 Nuevos Datos Sobre los Nonoalca de Habla Mexican en el Reino Tarasco. *Estudios de Cultura Náhuatl* **8:**215–221.

1971 Los Barrios Antiguos de Cholula. *Instituto Poblano de Antropología e Historia, Estudios y Documentos de la Región de Puebla-Tlaxcala* **3.**

Caso, A.

1951 Base Para la Sincronología Mixteca y Cristiana. *Memoria de El Colegio Nacional* **6**(6):49–66.

1953 Calendarios de los Totonacos y Huastecos. *Revista Mexicana de Estudios Antropológicos* **13**(2–3):337–350.

1967 Los Calendarios Prehispánicos. *Universidad Nacional Autónoma de México, Instituto de Investigaciones Históricas, Serie de Cultura Náhuatl, Monografías* **6.**

1971 Calendrical Systems of Central Mexico. In *Handbook of Middle American Indians,* Vol. 10, edited by R. Wauchope, G. F. Ekholm, and I. Bernal. Austin: University of Texas Press. Pp. 333–348.

Cline, H. F.

1966 Native Pictorial Documents of Eastern Oaxaca, Mexico. In *Summa Anthropologica en Homenaje a Roberto J. Weitlaner,* edited by A. Pompa y Pompa. Mexico: Instituto Nacional de Antropología e Historia. Pp. 101–130.

1972 A Census of the Relaciones Geográficas of New Spain, 1579–1612. In *Handbook of Middle American Indians,* Vol. 12, edited by R. Wauchope and H. F. Cline. Austin: University of Texas Press. Pp. 324–369.

Cook, S. F.

1949 The Historical Demography and Ecology of the Teotlalpan. *Ibero-Americana* **33.**

Davies, C. N.

1973 Los Mexicas: Primeros Pasos Hacia el Imperio. *Universidad Nacional Autónoma de México, Instituto de Investigaciones Históricas, Serie de Cultura Náhuatl, Monografías* **14.**

Dibble, C. E.

1951 Códice Xolotl. *Universidad Nacional Autónoma de México, Instituto de Historia, Publicaciones, Primera Serie* **22.**

Durán, Fray D.

1967 *Historia de las Indias de Nueva España e Islas de la Tierra Firme,* 2 vols., edited by A. M. Garibay K. Mexico: Porrúa.

Durand-Forest, J. de
1973 Chimalpahin et l'Histoire de la Vallée de Mexico. *Atti del XL Congresso Internazionale degli Americanisti* **1**:379–387.

García Payón, J.
1963 Quienes Contruyeron El Tajín y Resultados de las Ultimas Exploraciones de la Temporada 1961–1962. *La Palabra y el Hombre* **7**:243–252.

Glass, J., and D. Robertson
1975 A Census of Native Middle American Pictorial Manuscripts. In *Handbook of Middle American Indians,* Vol. 14, edited by R. Wauchope, H. F. Cline, C. Gibson, and H. B. Nicholson. Austin: University of Texas Press. Pp. 81–252.

Gibson, C.
1952 *Tlaxcala in the Sixteenth Century.* New Haven, Connecticut: Yale University Press.
1964 *The Aztecs under Spanish Rule: A History of the Indians of the Valley of Mexico, 1519–1810.* Stanford: Stanford University Press.

Gibson, C., and J. Glass
1975 A Census of Middle American Prose Manuscripts in the Native Historical Tradition. In *Handbook of Middle American Indians,* Vol. 15, edited by R. Wauchope, H. F. Cline, C. Gibson, and H. B. Nicholson. Austin: University of Texas Press. Pp. 322–400.

Hernández Rodríguez, R.
1952 El Valle de Toluca; su Historia: Época Prehispánica y Siglo XVI. *Boletín de la Sociedad Mexicana de Geografía y Estadística* **74**:(1–3):9–124.

Jiménez Moreno, W.
1940 Signos Cronográficos del Códice y Calendario Mixteco. In *Códice de Yanhuitlan; Edición en Facsimile y con un Estudio Preliminar por Wigberto Jiménez Moreno y Salvador Mateos Higuera.* Mexico: Secretariá de Educación Pública, Instituto Nacional de Antropología, Museo Nacional. Pp. 69–76.
1941 Tula y los Toltecas según las Fuentes Históricas. *Revista Mexicana de Estudios Antropológicos* **5**(2–3):79–83.
1942 El Enigma de los Olmecas. *Cuadernos Americanos* **1**(5):113–145.
1945 Introducción. In *Guía Arqueológica de Tula,* by A. R. Lhuillier. Mexico: Ateneo Nacional de Ciencias y Artes de México. Pp. 7–18.
1948 Historia Antigua de la Zona Tarasca. In *El Occidente de México; Cuarta Reunión de Mesa Redonda Sobre Problemas Antropológicos de México y Centro América.* Mexico: Sociedad Mexicana de Antropología. Pp. 146–157.
1950 The Importance of Xaltocan in the Ancient History of Mexico. *Mesoamerican Notes* **2**:133–138.
1953 Cronología de la Historia de Veracruz. In *Huastecos, Totonacos y sus Vecinos,* edited by I. Bernal and E. Dávalos Hurtado. *Revista Mexicana de Estudios Antropológicos* **13**(2–3):311–313.
1956 Síntesis de la Historia Precolonial del Valle de México. *Revista Mexicana de Estudios Antropológicos* **14**(1):219–236.
1961 Diferente Principio del Año Entre Diversos Pueblos y Sus Consecuencias Para la Cronología Prehispánica. *El México Antiguo* **9**:137–152.
1966a *Compendio de Historia de México* (with J. Miranda and M. T. Fernández). Editorial E.C.L.A.L.S.A., Mexico.
1966b Mesoamerica before the Toltecs. In *Ancient Oaxaca; Discoveries in Mexican Archaeology and History,* edited by J. Paddock. Stanford: Stanford University Press. Pp. 3–82.
1966c Los Imperios Prehispánicos de Mesoamérica. *Revista Mexicana de Estudios Antropológicos* **20**:179–195.

1970 Nayarit: Etnohistoria y Arqueologia. In *Historia y Sociedad en el Mundo de Habla Española: Homenaje a José Miranda,* edited by B. García Martínez, V. Lerner, A. Lira, G. Palacios, and I. Vásquex Mexico: El Colegio de México. Pp. 17–25.

1972 Historiografía Prehispánica y Colonial de México. *Enciclopedia de México* **6:**537–555.

1973 La Migración Mexica. *Atti del XL Congresso Internazionale degli Americanisti* **1:**166–172.

n.d. Historia Antigua de México. (Transcription of class notes, corrected by WJM, duplicated).

Kelley, D.

1953 Historia Prehispánica del Totonacapan. In *Huastecos, Totonacos y Sus Vecinos,* edited by I. Bernal and E. Dávalos Hurtado. *Revista Mexicana de Estudios Antropológicos* **13**(2–3):303–313.

Kelly, I.

1949 The Archaeology of the Autlán-Tuxcacuesco Area of Jalisco; II: The Tuxcacuesco-Zapotitlán Zone. *Ibero-Americana* **27.**

Kelly, I., and A. Palerm

1952 The Tajín Totonac; Part 1. History, Subsistence, Shelter and Technology. *Smithsonian Institution, Institute of Social Anthropology Publication* **13.**

Kirchhoff, P.

1947 La Historia Tolteca-Chichimeca: Un Estudio Histórico-Sociológico. In *Historia Tolteca—Chichimeca; Anales de Cuauhtinchan.* Fuentes Para la Historia de Mexico 1, edited by H. Berlin and S. Rendón. Mexico: Robredo. Pp. xix–lxiv.

1949 A New Analysis of Native Mexican Chronologies. Paper presented at the 24th International Congress of Americanists, New York.

1950 The Mexican Calendar and the Founding of Tenochtitlan-Tlatelolco. *Transactions of the New York Academy of Sciences, Series II,* **12**(4):126–132.

1955a Las Fechas Indigenas Mencionadas Para Ciertos Acontecimientos en las Fuentes, y su Importancia como Índice de Varios Calendarios. Paper presented at the Sociedad Mexicana de Antropologia Mesa Redonda on Calendric Problems of Pre-Hispanic Mesoamerica, Castillo de Chapultepec.

1955b Quetzalcoatl, Huemac y el Fin de Tula. *Cuadernos Americanos* **14**(6):163–196.

1956a Calendarios Tenochca, Tlatelolca y Otros. *Revista Mexicana de Estudios Antropológicos* **14**(1):257–267.

1956b La "Relación de Michoacán" como Fuente para la Historia de la Sociedad y Cultura Tarascas. In *Relación de las ceremonias y ritos y población y gobierno de los indios de la provincia de Michoacán (1541); reproducción facsimil del Ms. c. IV. 5 de El Escorial,* edited by J. Tudela. Madrid: Aguilar. Pp. xix–xxxiii.

1961 Das Toltekenreich und sein Untergang. *Saeculum* **12**(3):248–265.

1964 La Aportación de Chimalpahin a la Historia Tolteca. *Anales de Antropologia* **4:**77–90.

Krickeberg, W.

1933 *Los Totonaca; Contribución a la Etnografía Histórica de la América Central.* Mexico: Secretariá de Educación Pública, Talleres Gráficos del Museo Nacional de Arqueología, Historia y Etnografía.

Lehmann, W.

1920–21 *Zentral-Amerika. I. Teil, Die Sprachen Zentralamerikas,* 2 vols. Berlin: Reimer.

1922 Ein Tolteken-Klagegesang. In *Festschrift Eduard Seler; dargebracht zum 70. Geburststag von Freunden, Schulern und Verehrern,* edited by W. Lehmann. Pp. 281–319. Spanish trans. by P. R. Hendrichs, with introduction and annotations by W. Jiménez Moreno: Una elegía Tolteca. Mexico: Publicaciones de la Sociedad "México-Alemana Alejandro de Humboldt," Folleto No. 2, 1941.

López de Gómara, F.
1943 *Historia de la Conquista de México. Con una Introducción y Notas por D. Joaquín Ramírez Cabañas,* 2 vols. Mexico: Robredo.
McBride, H.
1974 Formative Ceramics and Prehistoric Settlement Patterns in the Cuauhtitlan Region, Mexico. Unpublished Ph.D. dissertation. University of California, Los Angeles.
Melgarejo Vivanco, J. L.
1943 *Totonacapan.* Xalapa, Veracruz: Talleras Gráficos del Gobierno del Estado.
1950 *Historia de Veracruz (Época Prehispánica).* Jalapa-Enriquez, Veracruz: Talleres Gráficos del Gobierno de Veracruz.
Nicholson, H. B.
1955 Native Historical Traditions of Nuclear America and the Problem of Their Archeological Correlation. *American Anthropologist* **57**(3):594–613.
1956 The Temalacatl of Tehuacan. *El México Antiguo* **8**:95–134.
1957 Topiltzin Quetzalcoatl of Tollan: A Problem in Mesoamerican Ethnohistory. Unpublished Ph.D. dissertation, Harvard University.
1959 The Synchronization of Culture Historical Sequences Derived from Archaeological Excavation with Native Meso-American Historical Traditions. Paper presented at the 58th annual meeting of the American Anthropological Association, Mexico City.
1960 Native Mesoamerican Calendric Systems: A Summary of Recent Research. Paper resented at the 34th International Congress of Americanists, Vienna.
1967 Review of Alfonso Caso, "Interpretación del Códice Selden 3135 (A 2)." *American Antiquity* **32**(2):257–258.
1968 Native Tradition Pictorials from the State of Puebla, Mexico: A Preliminary Classification and Analysis. Paper read at the 38th International Congress of Americanists, Stuttgart.
1971a Pre-Hispanic Central Mexican Historiography. In *Investigaciones Contemporáneas sobre Historia de México. Memorias de la Tercera Reunión de Historiadores Mexicanos y Nortamericanos, Oaxtepec, Morelos, 4–7 de Noviembre de 1969.* Mexico: Universidad Nacional Autónoma de México, El Colegio de México, the University of Texas at Austin. Pp. 38–81.
1971b Religion in Pre-Hispanic Central Mexico. In *Handbook of Middle American Indians,* Vol. 10, edited by R. Wauchope, G. F. Ekholm, and I. Bernal. Austin: University of Texas Press. Pp. 395–446.
1972 The Problem of the Historical Identification of the Cerro Portezuelo/San Antonio Archaeological Site: An Hypothesis. In *Teotihuacán: XI Mesa Redonda.* Mexico: Sociedad Mexicana de Antropología. Pp. 157–200.
n.d. The Late Pre-Hispanic Ruling Dynasty of Tecamachalco-Quechollac, Puebla, and Its Antecedents: A Tentative Reconstruction. Unpublished manuscript.
Orozco y Berra, M.
1960 *Historia Antigua y de la Conquista de México* (republication of original edition of 1880, with added materials by A. M. Garibay K. and M. León-Portilla), 4 vols. Mexico: Porrúa (Biblioteca Porrúa **17–20**).
Piña Chan, R.
1972 Historia Arqueología y Arte Prehispánico. Mexico: Fondo de Cultura Económica.
Rabin, E.
1974 Some Problems of Chronology in the Mixteca Historical Manuscripts. Paper presented at the 41st International Congress of Americanists, Mexico City.
Rendón, S. (Editor, translator)
1965 *Relaciones Originales de Chalco Amaquemecan Escritas por Don Francisco de San Antón Muñón Chimalpahin Cuauhtlehuanitzin.* Mexico-Buenos Aires: Fondo de Cultura Económica.

Smith, M. E.
1973 *Picture Writing from Ancient Southern Mexico; Mixtec Place Signs and Maps.* Norman: University of Oklahoma Press.

Taylor, R. E., R. Berger, C. W. Meighan, and H. B. Nicholson
1969 West Mexican Radiocarbon Dates of Archaeologic Significance. In *The Natalie Wood Collection of Pre-Columbian Ceramics from Chupícuaro, Guanajuato, México, at UCLA,* edited by J. D. Frierman. *Occasional Papers of the Museum and Laboratories of Ethnic Arts and Technology, University of California, Los Angeles* **1**:17–30.

Tello, Fray A.
1891 *Libro Segundo de la Crónica Miscelanea en Que se Trata de la Conquista Espiritual y Temporal de la Santa Provincia de Xalisco en lel Nuevo Reino de la Galicia y Nueva Vizcaya y Descubrimiento del Nuevo México.* Guadalajara: Imprenta de "La República Literaria."

Zimmerman, G.
1960 Das Geschichtswerk des Domingo de Muñon Chimalpahin Quauhtlehuanitzin (Quellenkritsche Studien zur frühindianischen Geschichte Mexikos). *Beiträge zur mittelamerikanischen Völkerkunde Herausgegeben vom Hamburgischen Museum für Völkerkunde und Vorgeschichte* **5.**
1970 Briefe der indianischen nobilität aus Neuspanien an Karl V und Philipp II um die Mitte des 16. Jahrhunderts. *Beiträge zur mittelamerikanischen Völkerkunde Herausgegeben vom Hamburgischen Museum für Völkerkunde und Vorgeschichte* **10.**

Eastern Mesoamerica

GARETH W. LOWE

With an Endnote by E. WYLLYS ANDREWS V

I. PROBLEMS IN MAYA CHRONOLOGY

A. Introduction

Eastern Mesoamerica extends from the southeastern borders of Oaxaca and Veracruz at the Isthmus of Tehuantepec in the northwest to central Honduras in the south (Figure 11.1). This is the greater Maya area, both lowland and highland; Willey (1971, Fig. 1) terms it "the Maya territory."

The relative ethnic and linguistic uniformity of the Maya territory is culturally deceptive. The physiographically diverse area has many ecological regions and subregions, most of which have distinctive culture histories. It is the task of the chronologist to determine which particular local traits or trait complexes within these many and varied regions are in fact contemporaneous. Only with the establishment of reasonably accurate cross-dating

Figure 11.1. Map of Eastern Mesoamerica showing modern political divisions and the location of archaeological sites included in Figures 11.2–11.5.

between many regions will it become possible to compare rates of cultural development and divergence across this area of unusually high civilization or to postulate the events involved or the processes at work. Fortunately, there are several chronometric aids available to the Mayanist, the most outstanding of which has been the Maya calendar system.

Eastern Mesoamerica is unique among the cultural divisions of the New World for having within it regions in which cyclical calendrical dates were inscribed on numerous stone monuments during a period of over 600 years, from before A.D. 300 to about 900. A few other inscriptions extend the dated period both back to the century before our era and forward into the present millennium. The deciphering of the core-area lowland Maya dates, and the determination of their relative alignment with the Christian calendar, has permitted archaeologists to date associated architectural and artifactual contexts in these regions with exactness during what has come to be called the Classic Period. Stylistic cross-dating with these aspects of the southern Classic Maya Lowlands civilization and with its pottery types in particular has been a principal chronological guide throughout Mesoamerica during much of the present century.

In spite of the calendrical inscriptions of the Classic period in the central Maya regions, an adequate chronological understanding for the whole breadth and depth of the greater Maya territory has come about very slowly, and, in fact, still eludes us. Confident remarks about chronological control are occasionally offered us by investigators with Maya area experience (Longyear 1951; Michels 1972: 124; Woodbury 1972), but such control may be considered adequate for very few and very restricted zones in Eastern Mesoamerica. Within this diverse area, the earliest human occupations and the first sophisticated societies have been the slowest to be recognized. The relatively late full Maya civilization that developed in the central and northeastern extremities of our area, on the other hand, had left standing ruins and carved stone monuments that very early attracted wide attention, wonder, and speculation about possible dating. Nevertheless, serious chronological investigation even in these Maya ruins did not begin until the present century, and then only as a secondary consequence of the search for additional carved inscriptions.

The Spanish colonizers and missionaries viewed the few Maya cities and ruins that came to their attention in Yucatan and Guatemala with understandable awe and puzzlement as to their beginnings and antiquity but were able to learn little from the local populace. Though some native legendary or historical accounts ascribed origins to migrations from the west or east, for instance, it was useless to conjecture when these took place. Even such scant information as was recorded by the early chroniclers lay buried in Spanish or New World archives and was subject to little or no subsequent study or use for centuries. When these documents began to come to light again in the nineteenth century, they proved of "little service in writing Classic-stage history" (Morley and Brainerd 1956:78). Only with the painstaking analysis of hieroglyphic documents rediscovered in the mid-nineteenth century and of the carved stone monuments discovered and recorded in increasing numbers by the beginning of the present century did an adequate understanding of the Maya calendar itself and of the Classic Maya centers begin to unfold.

Very little archaeological excavation was done in the central Maya area until the 1920s, when the original preoccupation with epigraphical problems began to give way to a wider concern with the Maya society and its environment, past and present (see Tozzer in foreword to Merwin and Vaillant 1932). Summaries of early epigraphical research and of the belated archaeological beginnings in the Maya area are found in many sources

(Thompson 1950:28–34; 1966:32–41; M. D. Coe 1966:28–30), with more specific discussions offered by, for instance, Merwin and Vaillant (1932:1–4), Pollock (1940), Thompson (1940), Kidder (1958), Lothrop (1961), and Zimmerman (1971). Unequaled episodical accounts of the early explorers and their initial excavations in the Maya area forests have been assembled by Wauchope (1965); these are both thrilling and required background reading for any Mayanist, explaining the real difficulties in the way of early investigations.

As field research increased, albeit slowly, during the 1930s and 1940s to widely separated zones across much of the Maya area, it was joined by the technological triumph of radiocarbon dating at mid-century. Calendrical dates, ceramic style horizons and trade pieces, and radiocarbon dates have thus become a reliable threesome aiding the chronological placement of cultural phases at site after site today. Of the thousands of ruin sites in the Maya territory, perhaps a hundred have had their occupation histories determined by serious excavations. Unfortunately, the details have been published for only a handful of these announced but often incomplete site sequences.

B. Ceramic Complexes, Phasing, and Cross-Dating

A half century of gradually accelerating field archaeology, building upon the epigraphical base, is bringing into increasingly sharpened chronological focus long developmental sequences at various points in the greater Maya territory. Radiocarbon dating has made invaluable contributions toward the Preclassic horizons in several regions. A few additional discovered inscriptions have enlarged slightly the calendrical written basis of Maya area chronology (Prem 1971; M. D. Coe 1976; Marcus 1976). Inasmuch, however, as most archaeological regions within Eastern Mesoamerica have produced neither dated stone monuments nor adequate radiocarbon dates, the archaeological occupations of such regions continue to be dated by external comparisons. Locally recoverable materials or features are cross-dated with other stylistically similar materials and features having parallel stratigraphy or known relationships with dated monuments or ^{14}C-dated series where these do occur. Pottery is the only class of material object consistently found over the Maya territory that is sufficiently sensitive to change through time to be useful for refined cross-dating. Ceramic complexes, accordingly, will receive major emphasis in the remainder of this article.

The determination of what constitutes a given "ceramic complex," and subsequently the composition of a chronologically delimited archaeological phase when the ceramics are combined with presumably contemporaneous architectural and other classes of material culture, has been a subjective process in the Maya area, as it has elsewhere. The correct assessment of what we may call a true chronological phase of ancient human occupation—let us say of a given century or two of unrecorded history—is dependent upon several variable factors. First, the original degree of preservation of cultural elements in the ground is subject to a combination of the archaeologist's luck and perspicacity in recovering both a representative sample of the surviving material and evidence of its inter-relationships. Then, the analytical skill or "feel" of the investigator is challenged in putting related elements of this past "culture" together realistically in the laboratory. Finally, the information must be communicated understandably in a published or readily available field report. The subjective element is intensified when traits are arbitrarily selected for comparison by archaeologists lacking first-hand acquaintance with the nonlocal materials being compared or their relevant find circumstances.

The contingencies of archaeological phasing have been well summarized by Michels (1972), who expresses a hope for more precise "attribute-system analysis, artifact typology, archaeological-component discrimination, and archaeological-unit classification" but is forced to conclude that "traditional techniques of archaeological-unit classification, with their reliance upon monothetic groupings, and intuitively derived artifact typologies still prevail and will continue to prevail within the near future [p. 114]."

The modern human element needs particular consideration in Maya area archaeology. Many regional cultures varied markedly, and to still unknown degrees, during both the Formative and Classic eras. Strong horizon markers or trade goods are often lacking or scarce in recoverable samples of many short occupations. Ancient settlement histories usually were noncontinuous in nonpredictable patterns even within single site localities (see Lowe, in Green and Lowe 1967:75, 76). Occupation disruptions are often difficult or impossible to discern from limited investigations, particularly in the forested tropical climes of Eastern Mesoamerica. Extensive field research together with open-minded and open-ended first-hand comparative studies will tend to reduce human error. Science, withal, is still a long way from an ideal understanding of Maya area culture history in any of its regions; all culture-historical reconstructions in this area are tentative and subject to change.

Distinctive Classic Maya pottery groupings from burial offerings in stratigraphic architectural superimposition were identified at Holmul, Guatemala, as early as 1914 (Merwin and Vaillant 1932). The first comprehensive sequence of "phases" relating broad ceramic complexes to dated monuments and architectural stages beginning in Preclassic times, however, was determined at Uaxactun, Guatemala (Figure 11.2), in the late 1920s and early 1930s (Ricketson 1928; Ricketson and Ricketson 1937; Smith 1936a, b; 1955). The pioneer Uaxactun phases have found parallels of varying degrees of similarity in additional site sequences across the Maya territory, growing from 8 reported in 1940 (Hay and others 1940; Table X) to over 90 at the

Chronological Periods	Dates B.P. AD/BC	Yucatan: DZIBIL-CHALTUN (a)	Yucatan: CHICHEN MAYAPAN (b)	Quintana Roo: COZUMEL (c) TANCAH (d)	Belize: SAN JOSE (e) BARTON RAMIE (f)	Campeche: CAMPECHE COAST (g) JAINA (h)	Campeche: AGUACATAL (i) DZIBILNOCAC (j)	Campeche: BECAN (k)	Maya Calendar Dates (11.16.0.0.0 or GMT Correlation)
Colonial	1550		Chauaca	Aguada Grande					11.16.10.0.0
Protohistoric	1450		Chikinchel				Late Plantacion		11.11.10.0.0
Postclassic: Late Postclassic	1300	Chechem	Tases	Tulum Group B		IV	Early Plantacion	Lobo	
	1200		Hocaba						10.19.0.0
Postclassic: Early Postclassic	1 1100	Zipche	Sotuta	Vista Alegre	New Town	II-b	Mangle		
	1000								10.8.10.0.0
Classic: Terminal Classic	900	Copo 2	Cehpech	Group A San Miguel	V Spanish IV Lookout	III II-a	Conchada 2	Xcocom	
	800							Chintok	9.18.10.0.0
Classic: Late Classic	650	Copo 1	Motul	Transition	III Tiger Run		Dz-IV Conchada 1	Behuco	9.11.0.0.0
Classic: Middle Classic	450	Piim		Late Tancah		II I		Sabucan	9.1.0.0.0
Classic: Early Classic	250	?	Cochuah	Early Tancah	II Hermitage		Peninsula III	Chacsik	8.10.0.0.0
Protoclassic	100	Xculul 2	Chakan		Floral Park	I	Tarpon	Pakluum 2	8.5.0.0.0
Formative: Late Preclassic II	2 AD 0 BC 100	Xculul 1			Mount Hope		Pinzon 2		8.0.0.0.0 7.15.0.0.0 7.10.0.0.0
Late Preclassic I	200 300 400	Komchen	Tihosuo		I Barton Creek	I	II Pinzon 1	Pakluum 1	
Formative: Middle Preclassic III	500	Nabanche 2	Culpul		2	Tixchel			
Middle Preclassic II	600 700 800	Nabanche 1			Jenney Creek 1	?	I	Acachen ?	
Middle Preclassic I	3 900 1000	?			Lopez (l)				
Early Preclassic III	1100 1200							?	
Early Preclassic II	1300 1400 1500 1600		Mani Formative (m) ?						
Early Preclassic I	4 1700 1800 1900 2000				Swasey (l)				First Mesoamerican pottery ?
? Preformative	2500								
	5 3000								
Late Archaic (Hunters Gatherers, Incipient Agriculturists)	3500								
	6 4000								
Early Archaic (Hunters Gatherers, Incipient Agriculturists)	4500								
	7 5000								
	5500								
	8 6000								
	9 7000								
	10 8000								

Figure 11.2 Principal chronological sequences of the Peninsula of Yucatan. (a) Joesink-Mandeville 1973; Ball 1977a, Table 1; (b) R. E. Smith 1971, Chart 1; (c) Sanders 1960:223–224, Chart 3; Sabloff and Rathje 1972:2; (d) Sanders 1960; (e) Thompson 1939, Fig. 93, Table 17; (f) Willey *et al.* 1965; Gifford 1976: Fig. 8; (g) Ruz 1969:239, Table 11; (h) Piña Chan 1968:62–63; Ruz 1969:239–240; (i) Matheny 1970: Chart 1; (j) Nelson 1973; (k) Ball 1977a; (l) Cuello site: Pring 1976b; Hammond et al. 1976; n.d.; Hammond 1977a; (m) Brainerd 1958:24; Hammond 1977a:130.

Era	Chronological Periods	Dates B.P. AD/BC	Tabasco: LA VENTA (a) CHONTALPA (b)	Tabasco: TRINIDAD (c)	Chiapas: CHIAPA DE CORZO (d) MIRADOR (e) STA' MARTA (f)	Chiapas: SANTA CRUZ (g) SANTA ROSA (h)	Chiapas: HIGHLANDS (i) PALENQUE (j)	Chiapas: SAN ISIDRO-MAL PASO (k)	Chiapas: IZAPA (l) ALTAMIRA (m)	Maya Calendar Dates (11.16.0.0.0 or GMT Correlation)
Postclassic	Colonial	1550				Santa Rosa 7		Santiago		11.16.10.0.0
Postclassic	Protohistoric	1450	?		Urbina	Chiapanec				11.11.10.0.0
Postclassic	Late Postclassic	1300 / 1200	Cintla		Tuxtla		Lum	Quejpomo		10.19.0.0
Postclassic	Early Postclassic	1100 / 1000	?	Chacbolay	Ruiz		Yash	Pecha	Remanso	10.8.10.0.0
Classic	Terminal Classic	900 / 800	Comalcalco	Naab	Paredon	6	Isah Balunte 2	Mechung	Peistal	9.18.10.0.0
Classic	Late Classic	650		Taxinchan	Maravillas	Late Santa Cruz	1 Murcielagos Otolum		Metapa Loros Kato	9.11.0.0.0
Classic	Middle Classic	450			Laguna		Motiepa	Kundapi		9.1.0.0.0.0
Classic	Early Classic	250	Palmas (?)	Kaxabyuc	Jiquipilas	5 Early Santa Cruz	Picota	Juspano	Jaritos	8.10.0.0.0
Classic	Protoclassic	100			Istmo	4		Ipsan	Izapa	8.5.0.0.0
Formative	Late Preclassic II, I	0, 100, 200, 300, 400	Castañeda	Chacibcan	Horcones, Guanacaste, Late Francesa	Late Chiapilla 3	Sak	Guanamo	Hato, Crucero, Guillen	8.0.0.0.0, 7.15.0.0.0, 7.10.0.0.0
Formative	Middle Preclassic III, II, I	500, 600, 700, 800, 900, 1000	IV Franco, III, II Puente, I Palacios	Xot, Chiuaan	Early Francesa, Escalera, Quequepac, Dili	Early Chiapilla 2, Late Burrero 1	Pre-Picota ?	Felisa, Equipac, Dombe	Frontera, Escalon, Duende	
Formative	Early Preclassic III, II, I	1100, 1200, 1300, 1400, 1500, 1600, 1700, 1800, 1900, 2000	Pre-Comp A, Molina, Pellicer	Pre-Chiuaan ?	Pac, Cotorra, Cotorra (SM)	Early Burrero, Santa Rosa Ocos		Cacahuano, Bombana	Jocotal, Cuadros, Ocos, Barra	First Mesoamerican pottery ?
?	Preformative	2500 / 3000							Chantuto (n)	
Hunters-Gatherers, Incipient Agriculturists	Late Archaic	3500 / 4000								
Hunters-Gatherers, Incipient Agriculturists	Early Archaic	4500 / 5000								
		5500 / 6000			Santa Marta 5359±300					
		7000			Santa Marta 6769±400					
		8000					Teopisca "Arqueolitica" (o)			

Figure 11.3 Principal chronological sequences of Tabasco and Chiapas. (a) Drucker, Heizer, and Squier 1959:264–267; Berger, Graham, and Heizer 1967; (b) Sisson 1970; (c) Rands 1969; (d) Navarrete 1960, 1966; Lowe and Mason 1965, Fig. 3; Lee 1969, Table 1; (e) Peterson 1963; Agrinier 1970; 1975b; Wainer 1970; (f) MacNeish and Peterson 1962; (g) Sanders 1961:50–521; (h) Delgado 1965:79–81; Brockington 1967:4. (i) Culbert 1965:4; (j) Willey, Culbert, and Adams 1967:292; Rands 1974; (k) Lee 1974; (l) Ekholm 1969:19; Lee 1973; Lowe, Lee, and Martínez 1976; (m) Green and Lowe 1967:52; Lowe 1975; (n) Lorenzo 1955; Voorhies 1976; (o) Mirambell 1974:62–63.

present time. The most complete of these phase sequences are listed in Figures 11.2–11.5 according to geographical provenience.

Dating of the ceramic phases in the sequences devised up to 1950 was based upon the relative positions of internal stratigraphy before, during, and after the "Initial Series" or Classic Maya period. Alignments usually were made by cross-dating with traits known in the key Uaxactun sequence because of its priority of discovery and relative completeness. Some use was made of local historical traditions for the Postclassic Period. The favored Christian calendar correlation for the Initial Series dates was that of 11.16.0.0.0, or Goodman–Thompson–Martínez, confining the Early and Late Classic developments to within approximately A.D. 300 to 900 (Thompson 1935; Kidder and Thompson 1938; Andrews IV 1940: 161); this situation continues to prevail.

Following 1950, radiocarbon dating began to influence Maya area chronology. Some unexpectedly early age determinations pushing back the Preclassic and Archaic horizons in Mesoamerica were usually accepted warmly by Mayanists. An early series of dates from Classic Maya samples tending to favor the older 12.9.0.0.0 correlation, however, was less warmly, even antagonistically received by most investigators. Some resultant confusion was subsequently dispelled through improved radiocarbon techniques and reruns of questionable samples (Satterthwaite and Coe 1968). Only a slight and noncritical difference in data and interpretative possibilities persists today between the central lowlands and Northern Yucatan (see Andrews V, endnote to this chapter). The charts in Figures 11.2–11.5 follow the 11.16.0.0.0 correlation; adoption of the 12.9.0.0.0 correlation would move the Initial Series dates (for the Maya Classic in its homelands and all cross-dated Classic period cultures) back in time approximately 260 years, with some necessary adjustment of the periods before and after (see Willey, Culbert, and Adams 1967: Fig. 10; Andrews V, endnote to this chapter).

Other correlations of the Maya and Christian calendar have been suggested and continue to be suggested sporadically but receive little support today (see Satterthwaite and Coe 1968:3). Some further commentary on phase dating problems is included in the periodization discussion in Section D.

In addition to the improved quantity and quality of radiocarbon dates becoming available, many improvements to chronological understanding in the 1960s and 1970s have come from the sheer volume of new data made available from a few intensive investigations scattered over the greater Maya area. Also important have been the intensive and extensive stratigraphic studies in regions to the west of the Maya area, particularly at San Lorenzo, Veracruz, Tehuacan, Puebla, and the Valley of Oaxaca, where radiocarbon-dated complexes permit some improved cross-dating for the early ceramic complexes found in the marginal Maya areas (Coe, Diehl, and Stuiver 1967; M. D. Coe 1970; MacNeish 1962; MacNeish and others 1970;

	Chronological Periods	Dates B.P. AD/BC	Peten: UAXACTUN (a), TIKAL (b)	Peten: ALTER DE SACRIFICIOS (c), SEIBAL (d)	Western Highlands: ZACULEU (e), ZACUALPA (f)	Northern Highlands: COTZAL (g), VERAPAZ (h)	Central Highlands: KAMINALJUYU (i)	Pacific Coast: EL BAUL (j), BILBAO (k)	Pacific Coast: LA VICTORIA (l), SALINASILA BLANCA (m)	Maya Calendar Dates (11.16.0.0.0 or GMT Correlation)
	Colonial	1550								11.16.10.0.0
	Protohistoric	1450			Yaqui; Xinabahul	Chajul				11.11.10.0.0
Postclassic	Late Postclassic	1300; 1200				Chipal 3	Chinautla	Peor-es-nada		10.19.0.0
	Early Postclassic	1 1100; 1000	Caban		Tohil; Quankyak	Chipal 1b, 2; Chama 5; Late Cotzal	Ayumpac	Tohil		10.8.10.0.0
Classic	Terminal Classic	900; 800	Tepeu 3; Eznab	Bayal; Jimba; Boca	Pokom; Chinaq	Chipal 1a	Pamplona	San Juan Plumbate; Santa Lucia	Marcos	9.18.10.0.0
	Late Classic	650	Tepeu 2; Imix	Tepejilote; Pasion		Early Cotzal; Chama 3,-4	Amatle	San Juan		9.11.0.0.0
	Middle Classic	450	Tepeu 1; Ik; Tzakol 3	Chixoy; Veremos; Late Ayn	Atzan; Late Balam	Late Tuban; Chama 2	Esperanza	Laguneta; San Francisco		9.1.0.0.0
	Early Classic	250	Late Manik; Tzakol 1,2; Early Manik	Junco; Early Ayn		Early Tuban	Aurora	Mejor-es-Algo	Tiestal	8.10.0.0.0
	Protoclassic	100	Matzanel; Cimi	Salinas; Late Cantutse	Early Balam	Chama 1	Santa Clara			8.5.0.0.0
Formative	Late Preclassic II	2 AD BC 0	Cauac	Late Plancha		Porton	Arenal			8.0.0.0.0
	Late Preclassic	100; 200; 300	Chicanel; Chuen	Early Cantutse; Early Plancha		Sakajut	Miraflores	Ilusiones	Crucero	7.15.0.0.0; 7.10.0.0.0
	Late Preclassic I	400	Tzec	Late San Felix			Providencia	Algo-es-Algo	Conchas 2	
	Middle Preclassic III	500	Mamom	Escoba; Early San Felix		Tol Sakajut	Las Charcas		?	
	Middle Preclassic II	600; 700; 800	Eb							
	Middle Preclassic I	3 900; 1000		Xe; Real		Max	Arevalo		Conchas 1; Jocotal	
	Early Preclassic III	1100; 1200				Sakajut			Cuadros	
	Early Preclassic II	1300; 1400; 1500; 1600				Xox				
	Early Preclassic I	4 1700; 1800; 1900; 2000							Ocos	First Mesoamerican pottery
?	Preformative	2500; 5 3000		Maize pollen (d')						
	Late Archaic	3500; 6 4000					?????; El Chayal (n)			
Early Archaic; Hunters-Gatherers, Incipient Agriculturists		4500; 7 5000					?????			
		5500; 8 6000								
		9 7000								
		10 8000			Los Tapiales, Totonicapan (o)					

Figure 11.4 Principal chronological sequences of Guatemala. (a) Smith 1936, 1955; (b) W. R. Coe 1965, 1967; Willey, Culbert, and Adams 1967; Culbert 1977; (c) Adams 1971; (d) Willey 1970:319; Sabloff 1975; (d') Rice 1976:424; (e) Woodbury and Trik 1953; (f) Wauchope 1948; see also Lothrop 1936; (g) Becquelin 1969;112–122; Adams 1972:14; (h) Butler 1940; Sedat 1971 (Porton); Sedat and Sharer 1972; 1973 (Sakajut and Salama); (i) Shook 1951, 1957; Shook and Kidder 1952; Borhegyi 1965; (j) Thompson 1948; (k) Parsons 1967; (l) M. D. Coe 1961; (m) Coe and Flannery 1967:66–70; (n) M. D. Coe 1966:39–40; (o) Bryan 1971; Gruhn and Bryan 1976; n.d.

	Chronological Periods	Dates B.P.	AD/BC	El Salvador: CHALCHUAPA (a)	El Salvador: QUELEPA (b)	Honduras: COMAYAGUA (c)	Honduras: CHOLUTECA (d)	Honduras: ULUA-YOJOA (e)	Honduras: LOS NARANJOS (f)	Honduras: COPAN (g)	Maya Calendar Dates (11.16.0.0.0 or GMT Correlation)
	Colonial		1550								11.16.10.0.0
	Protohistoric		1450					Naco			11.11.10.0.0
Postclassic	Late Postclassic		1300 1200	Ahal			Malalaca				10.19.0.0
Postclassic	Early Postclassic	1	1100 1000	Matzin		Las Vegas	Amapala		Rio Blanco	Post Classic	10.8.10.0.0
Classic	Terminal Classic		900 800	Payu	Lepa	Yarumela 4	Fonseca	Ulua Polych.			9.18.10.0.0
Classic	Late Classic		650			Lo de Vaca 3	San Lorenzo		Yojoa	Full Classic	9.11.0.0.0
Classic	Middle Classic		450	Xocco	Shila 2					Early Classic 2	9.1.0.0.0
Classic	Early Classic		250	Vec	Shila 1		Chismuyo		Eden 2	Early Classic 1	8.10.0.0.0
Classic	Protoclassic		100	Late Caynac		Yarumela 3				Archaic	8.5.0.0.0
Formative	Late Preclassic II	2	AD 0 BC 100	Early Caynac	Uapala	Lo deVaca 2		Ulua Bichrome	Eden 1		8.0.0.0.0 7.15.0.0.0 7.10.0.0.0
Formative	Late Preclassic I		200 300 400	Chul		Yarumela 2					
Formative	Middle Preclassic III		500	Kal	Early Uapala?	Lo de Vaca 1		Playa de los Muertos			
Formative	Middle Preclassic II		600 700 800	Colos		?		Yojoa Monochrome	Jaral	?	
Formative	Middle Preclassic I	3	900 1000			Yarumela 1				?	
Formative	Early Preclassic III		1100 1200	Tok		?		?	?	Copan Caves? ?	
Formative	Early Preclassic II		1300 1400 1500 1600								
Formative	Early Preclassic I	4	1700 1800 1900 2000								First Mesoamerican pottery ?
?	Preformative	5	2500 3000							Preceramic ????	
Incipient Agriculturists	Late Archaic	6	3500 4000								
Hunters-Gatherers, Incipient Agriculturists	Early Archaic	7	4500 5000								
Hunters-Gatherers	Early Archaic	8	5500 6000								
Hunters-Gatherers	Early Archaic	9	7000								
Hunters-Gatherers	Early Archaic	10	8000			La Esperanza (h) Intibuca					

Figure 11.5 Principal chronological sequences of El Salvador and Honduras. (a) Sharer and Gifford 1970:444–446; Sharer 1969, 1972, 1974; (b) Andrews V 1976:42–45; (c) Canby 1951 (Yarumela); Baudez 1966:334–338; (d) Baudez 1966; (e) Strong, Kidder, and Paul 1938:119, Table I; Baudez 1966; (f) Baudez and Becquelin 1973, Table 16; (g) Gordon 1898; Longyear 1952; Graham and Berger 1972; (h) Bullen and Plowden 1963.

Johnson and MacNeish 1972; Flannery 1968; Marcus 1976). Within the central Maya lowlands, and increasingly for much of the remainder of Eastern Mesoamerica, radiocarbon dating with its usual 150- to 200-year 1-sigma margin of error is at the present time less precise than ceramic cross-dating; where there arises a controversy between local radiocarbon dates and ceramic cross-dating, the Maya archaeologist will almost inevitably rely upon the latter.

Laboratory refinements may eventually reduce the range of error in radiocarbon analyses, but it appears more reasonable to expect that regional ceramic histories can be more assuredly refined once sufficient material is produced and correctly charted (Rowe 1959). A present chronological challenge for the Mayanist is the perfection and ample publication of broad-based regional ceramic sequences, so that new site complexes may be cross-dated promptly, leaving the investigator more free to pursue weightier cultural-behavioral problems (Michels 1972:124). We are yet a long way from this ideal, in spite of a long history of wishful thinking to the contrary, as noted earlier. This situation is the result of too few intensive excavations of undisturbed primary deposits and of a failure adequately to publish existing material with good associations clearly demonstrated. These are remediable failings, but the perfecting process is still a long and hard one. Many regions of the Maya area remain poorly known ceramically and a few are unknown altogether.

C. Cultural Regions and Subareas

The difficulties in the way of deriving satisfactory regional ceramic chronologies for the numerous ancient Maya peoples become obvious when we realize that they need to "deal comprehensively with the immense variety of what must be one of the world's most complex and diverse ceramic areas [Willey, Culbert, and Adams 1967:289]."

In the accompanying charts local chronological phase sequences are charted by modern political–geographic divisions (states in Mexico, countries and physiographic regions in northern Central America). These are valid subareas, culturally, but too gross for good science (see, for instance, Palerm and Wolf 1957; Sanders and Price 1968:101–105; Lowe 1971). Inasmuch as this paper is concerned with time rather than with space, however, little further attention is given here to regional definitions. The regionally as well as chronologically useful concepts of ceramic complex, phase, horizon, and sphere, and their known Lowland Maya components, were clarified in an important conference held in Guatemala City in 1965; the coordinative results of this conference are necessary reading for all Maya area investigators (Willey, Culbert, and Adams 1967; see Ball in Gifford 1976 for some updating). Future conferences may be expected to define similar problems in the other regions of Eastern Mesoamerica.

D. Chronological Periods: Old and New

The refinement of regional time divisions continues to be a prime goal in the Maya area. Good local and regional time control is paramount to the construction of lasting developmental hypotheses. Most of the concern of midcentury archaeological theory, on the other hand, was with the design of broader taxonomic systems applicable to wide areas of pre-Hispanic America. The latter included functional developmental theories (Armillas 1948; Steward 1948); culture-historical integration schemes (Willey and Phillips 1955, 1958); socioeconomic terminology (Wauchope 1950); and a period–number age system for the Preclassic (Sorenson 1955). While all of these theoretical considerations were and continue to be useful, none of them were widely adopted. Snowballing data overwhelmed most developmental schemes for organizing chronology faster than such schemes were invented (Wauchope 1964:335). Writing in 1960, Lothrop wryly observed:

> The current flood of theoretical discussions and taxonomic schemes undoubtedly is a sign of healthy progress in New World archaeology. I foresee far greater concurrence of thought and definition, however, perhaps not so much the result of discussions and conferences as by the stagnation and elimination of theories and concepts which do not stand the test of time [1961:14].

More specifically, this was preceded by the observation that

> There are signs of active revolt in recent literature against the present expanding complexity. Rowe (1959:318) writes "one of the objects of typological classification is to reduce the number of units of study to a more manageable size." Thus Ledyard Smith (1955), in discussing highland Maya architecture, has junked 28 more or less unintelligible terms in favor of a self-explanatory Preclassic, Early and Late Classic, Postclassic and Protohistoric. George Brainerd (1958) has classified the pottery of the Yucatan Maya in four stages—Formative, Regional, Florescent and Mexican [Lothrop 1961:13].

The "self-explanatory" units favored by Smith in 1955 (and by Willey and Phillips also in 1955), slightly modified, were pretty well set in concrete by Willey and Phillips in 1958 as part of a revised series of "stages" for the New World (Lithic, Archaic, Formative, Classic, and Postclassic), except that today these are conceived of as Middle American periods of time only, rather than as stages of development. The terms *Preclassic* and *Formative* continue to be interchanged at will, and concepts regarding the preceramic eras have been modified. Major Classic and Postclassic divisions seem here to stay, having been adopted in recent years by everyone in the Maya area except Andrews IV, who, as did Brainerd earlier, favored a locally distinguishing periodization for Northern Yucatan.

In an important text written in 1966, the culture history of Mesoamerica was divided into the five chronological periods of Paleo-Indian, Food-collecting and Incipient Cultivation, Preclassic, Classic, and Postclassic (Willey 1966, Fig. 3.9); the standardized Early, Middle, and Late subdivisions are shown for the Preclassic, as are Early and Late subdivisions for the Classic and Postclassic. The periods are conceived of as "strictly horizontal time divisions, adhering to absolute dating insofar as this is possible. They are not stages [Willey 1966:89]." The periods and their subdivisions embrace all of Mesoamerica indifferently. The basic format of the above periodization is changed only little in a later chart by Sanders and Price, which is cross-cut by stepped organizational or evolutionary stage concepts (1968, Fig. 2); there are some minor changes in terminology, substituting *Early Hunters–Gatherers* for Paleo-Indian, and *Archaic* for the subsequent period of Food Collecting and Incipient Cultivation, and using the term *Formative* in place of Preclassic. Sanders and Price also include a fourth or uppermost subdivision of the Formative Period labeled "Terminal Formative or Protoclassic," expressing favor for the latter designation (1968:29). Here again, the periods extend indiscriminately across Mesoamerica.

During the past decade, the basic Preclassic, Classic, and Postclassic temporal divisions have been followed everywhere in Eastern Mesoamerica except for Northern Yucatan, where Brainerd's culture-historical scheme (1958, Chart 22) was replaced by Andrews IV in 1960, Fig. 1 (see also Andrews IV 1965a:289, Fig. 1, 1965b, Table 4) with a revised "cultural evolution" terminology formulated for the Tulane Project at Dzibilchaltun; each of these period schemes was designed to set Yucatan apart from the better-known (and dated) Peten area to the south. More recently, Dzibilchaltun phase names have been published (see Figure 11.2, this chapter), but the Northern Maya area period names continue in use (see Andrews V in endnote to this chapter).

Terminology for the Tulane Project ceramic sequence at Becan in the Rio Bec-Xpuhil region of Southern Campeche has reverted to the basic Middle and Late Preclassic, Protoclassic, Early and Late Classic, Terminal Classic, and Early and Late Postclassic period frame of reference for its local phase names (see Figure 11.2 this chapter; Ball 1977, Table 1).

The current tendency is to accept fixed date approximations for the Maya area periods and subperiods (Willey, Culbert, and Adams 1967: Fig. 10), though some differences of opinion remain. In particular, there survives some lack of agreement about the relative dating and separation of divisions in the long Formative Era (see later in this chapter; also discussions in Sanders and Price 1968:25–26, and by Lowe in Green and Lowe 1967:54–55); but in general the standardized before-, during-, and after-Classic (Initial Series) periods and their subdivisions are serving as firm, uniform, steps on a recognized ladder of Maya area chronology.

The near-standard period designations are used in Figures 11.2–11.5, rather than any adaptation of "culture-historical horizon" terms (Lowe 1971) or stage concepts (Sanders and Price 1968; see also Willey 1960:303, Figs. 11.1 to 11.3). Our concern is first of all chronological. The periods and subperiods are blocks of time, literally sections or divisions of the Christian calendar that will aid the temporal alignment of local phases across Eastern Mesoamerica. Insofar as possible, nevertheless, the periods are designed to represent major cultural horizon lifetimes (see Section III-A). Changes in style noted in site phase complexes may have extralocal, extraregional, or even extra-areal historical explanations, as is known to be true for certain times in the Classic and Postclassic eras. On the Preclassic time levels, the precise period limits and their neatly divided subperiods crossing Figures 11.2–11.5 are more obviously artificial. These subdivisions are of suspected historical significance, of course, and some may in fact represent approximate turning points in prehistory, even though these are not yet proven theses. Lifetimes of particular local ceramic complexes may as likely fall abreast of present area period and subperiod dividing lines as between them, except when the placements have been determined by especially strong event-impelled horizon styles that moved rapidly across Eastern Mesoamerica.

The problem of cultural lag is a difficult one, inasmuch as some conservative societies apparently failed to adopt popular style changes altogether or adopted them only slowly and incompletely. By and large, however, culture change was pervasive in Eastern Mesoamerica, a relatively small area (only a few weeks' walk from one end to the other!). Despite pockets of resistance, horizon markers make their impact everywhere, sometimes in modified form. Only more intensive investigation of cultural centers and of intervening regions alike will resolve questions of cultural lag, for which socioethnic causes must be as responsible as is the matter of distance. At the present time, withal, horizon markers are superior to isolated radiocarbon dates for the chronological placement of "marginal" complexes. The real need, of course, is for lengthy radiocarbon date series to accompany more adequate field exploration programs everywhere; lacking these, there is little justification for calling upon cultural lag, marginality, or "diffusion slope" to explain problematic radiocarbon dates.

Because of their importance and because they are less well understood, some of the critical temporal markers, ceramic distribution patterns, and other dating problems for the earlier Preclassic periods in the greater Maya territory are discussed in some detail later in the next section.

The accompanying charts (Figures 11.2–11.5) include data from those sites in Eastern Mesoamerica that have produced the most critical or lengthy phase sequences. Radiocarbon dates with some bristlecone pine allowances (MASCA correction factors in Ralph 1971, Table 1.5) have been used to locate approximately the Preclassic phases, with the result that some placements have slightly earlier positions than originally published. Full use of the Suess (1970) and other correction schemes would permit other, often earlier, dating possibilities (see discussion of the Middle Preclassic II Subperiod later in this chapter; and R. E. Taylor, Chapter 1, this volume).

II. ARCHAIC AND FORMATIVE ERAS

A. Archaic and Preformative

Being primarily a humid tropical area, Eastern Mesoamerica has well hidden most of the evidence of its preceramic occupations. There is little local basis for dividing these long eras of human habitations in this area other than some very simple cross-dating of a few artifact types and a handful of radiocarbon dates. The only well-described and dated complex for the Archaic periods in the greater Maya area continues to be that of the Santa Marta Cave in West-Central Chiapas, where radiocarbon dates of 6780 (± 400) B.C. and 5370 (± 300) B.C. (non-MASCA) are said to relate a lithic assemblage of scrapers, mullers, choppers, and points to the Desert Culture of Mexico and the American Southwest (MacNeish and Peterson 1962; Johnson and MacNeish 1972:40). No further Desert Culture occupations have been positively identified, despite a report by J. L. Lorenzo of preceramic lithics in highland Chiapas caves at Teopisca near Comitan (Mirambell 1974; see also MacNeish and Peterson 1962:15).

Activities even older than the Santa Marta small-game hunting and seed gathering are suggested by a Clovis-like obsidian point found near San Raphael west of Guatemala City (M. D. Coe 1960b; 1966:36, Pl.5). This slight evidence for positing an Early Hunting Era during the Ice Age is supported by the presence of fossilized glyptodon, elephas, and mastodon bones in various departments of Guatemala (Shook 1951:93–96). A possibly related, fine-grained, andesite flake complex from Los Tapiales, Totonicapan, Guatemala, has a combined charcoal sample radiocarbon date of 7550 (± 150) B.C. (Gak-2769) reported by Bryan (1971) and Gruhn and Bryan (n. d.). Three additional uncorrected radiocarbon dates for the nearby "Paleo-Indian" basalt flake-industry site of La Piedra del Coyote are 8700, 8070, and 7480 B.C. (Tx 1632, 1634, and 1635), according to Gruhn and Bryan (1976:86). Numerous other preceramic sites have been reported in the La Esperanza Intibuca region of Honduras at 5000 to 6500 feet above sea level, but these are undated (Bullen and Plowden 1963).

Distinctive obsidian tools scattered widely at the famed central Guatemalan El Chayal obsidian source may more likely represent later Archaic hunting groups (M.D. Coe 1963:28–31; 1966:36–41, Fig. 4). Eventual careful research of favored habitats in the Maya highlands and elsewhere may be expected to fill in our charts for the Archaic Era during which Mesoamerica presumably was experiencing a warmer and drier climate. Evidences of incipient agriculture should appear also, as this is a characteristic of the era in other areas.

Several early brief explorations in the shell middens among the mangrove-lined estuaries on the Pacific Coast of Chiapas failed to produce evidence for their dating or of any transition from a gathering to a farming way of life (Drucker 1948:165–166); Lorenzo 1955; Navarrete in preparation). Despite a tendency to place this apparently preceramic Chantuto culture very early on chronological charts (Johnson and MacNeish 1972: Fig. 4) we have had no correct idea of its age until recently. Several pits dug to 6- and 11-meter depths in three large middens near Las Palmas, east of Chantuto, cut through highly bedded aceramic shell deposits beneath a distinctive surface layer with late pottery; the aceramic bulk produced a few stone artifacts, some animal bone, and abundant charcoal for which radiocarbon dates now provide an age of c.a. 3000 to 2000 B.C. for the bulk of the preceramic component (Voorhies 1975:7; 1976). The available evidence continues to indicate that there were periods of midden disuse both preceding and following deposition of the first ceramic-bearing refuse atop the tremendous aceramic accumulations of small clam shells; there are a few Barra sherds in this material (Voorhies 1976) but none of the Ocos Early Preclassic ceramics that are more widely found across the Soconuscan Pacific Coast (most of the Chantuto ceramic deposit is of the Protoclassic and Early Classic periods).

Some river-mouth sites and several small islands within the Chiapas estuaries do have heavy deposits of Ocos tecomate (neckless olla) sherds, little other pottery, and comparatively few shells (Ceja 1974; Navarrete in preparation; see Lowe 1966:454). It appears, then, that the Chantuto and Ocos estuarine sites represent distinct eras and separate ways of life, with the Ocos society certainly codependent upon inland villages and cultivated crops as well as upon some fishing, shrimping, and shell gathering (Ceja 1974). The Chantuto culture may also have been no more than a seasonal facet of an inland preceramic population, but the large dimensions of some of their middens suggest either a very intensive occupation or, if casual, an accumulation running over a very long period.

The early placement of a preceramic occupation at Copan (Figure 11.5) is hypothetical. What appear to be lithic artifacts were reported by Longyear (1952) to have come from a buried stratum separated by sterile layers from overlying Formative deposits. No further information has been obtained to either date the complex or to substantiate its archaic characteristics.

The Preformative Era, placed in Figures 11.2–11.5 at the close of the Archaic, is an unwitting resurrection of a concept discarded by Willey and Phillips (1958:73–74 and 145); it is presented here as a supposed period of transition for growing populations living in farming or fishing but prepottery villages. At this writing, the Preformative is purely a conjecture, in that sense, for Mesoamerica, though it may be substantiated by the recent dating of Chantuto to the third millennium B.C. The Chantuto shellmound dwellers may have had some rudimentary village life despite the present failure of limited investigations to identify more than stratified living floors or to find other, onshore, contemporaneous habitation areas.

The earliest known Formative Era village cultures in Eastern Mesoamerica appear to have had a developed agriculture and certainly did have excellent pottery (ceramics being a criterion for Preclassic or Formative status in this chapter).

B. Early Preclassic I Subperiod

The Early Formative, or Early Preclassic, Period in Eastern Mesoamerica encompasses two distinct and regionally consistent, very lengthy, cultural traditions which appear to have intermingled very little until after 1000 B.C. These geographically separate divisions represent an extensive but as yet little-known pre-Maya (or earliest Maya?) society in the Yucatan Peninsula (Hammond 1977) and what appears to be a widespread distribution of the Mixe-Zoque peoples with pre-Olmec and Early Olmec cultures (Lowe 1977) astride the Isthmus of Tehuantepec and the Cordilleran mainland to the southeast. These will be discussed separately for this beginning Early Preclassic subperiod, but treated jointly thereafter.

1. The Peninsula of Yucatan

A striking cultural distinction between the postulated early Mixe-Zoque and Lowland Maya territories is most obvious during the beginning Early Preclassic period of initial pottery usage in both areas (between ca. 2000 and 1500 B.C.); the quite completely opposed ceramic traditions (compare Figures 11.6 and 11.7) indicate societies that must be very nearly mutually exclusive at this critical period. The explanation for this situation may lie in outright ethnic differences of a very ancient character or it may more simply be the result of the local reception or adaptation of dissimilar ceramic techniques and styles (and functional associations) arriving from two disparate diffusion sources into a basically similar preceramic society (with or without significant immigration). The very distinctive nature of these two early area traditions, even on the domestic level, is best dramatized by the peculiar early distribution pattern of necked ollas and olla handles and spouts across the Yucatan Peninsula and their general absence during contemporaneous horizons in the greater isthmian region.

Necked ollas are completely absent in most Barra and Ocos ceramic complexes of Chiapas and Pacific Coast Guatemala, and they are nearly absent on the Gulf Coast at this time, as has been commented upon at some length elsewhere (Green and Lowe 1967:62–72; Lowe 1971, 1977:241–242). Necked ollas are now known to be dominant not only in the earliest central Mexican cultures but in all of the first Maya-area ceramic complexes also, with the neckless olla or tecomate relatively rare in either area tradition (cf. Willey 1966: Fig. 3.12, a-c; Flannery et al. 1969:97, Figure for Tierras Largas Phase; Pring 1976a: Figs. 10–11, 20–22, 29; 1976b: Fig. 15).

The recent dating of the beginning of the newly discovered but highly sophisticated pre-Mamom Swasey ceramic complex at the Cuello site in northern Belize (Figure 11.6) to between 2500 and 2000 B.C. (Hammond

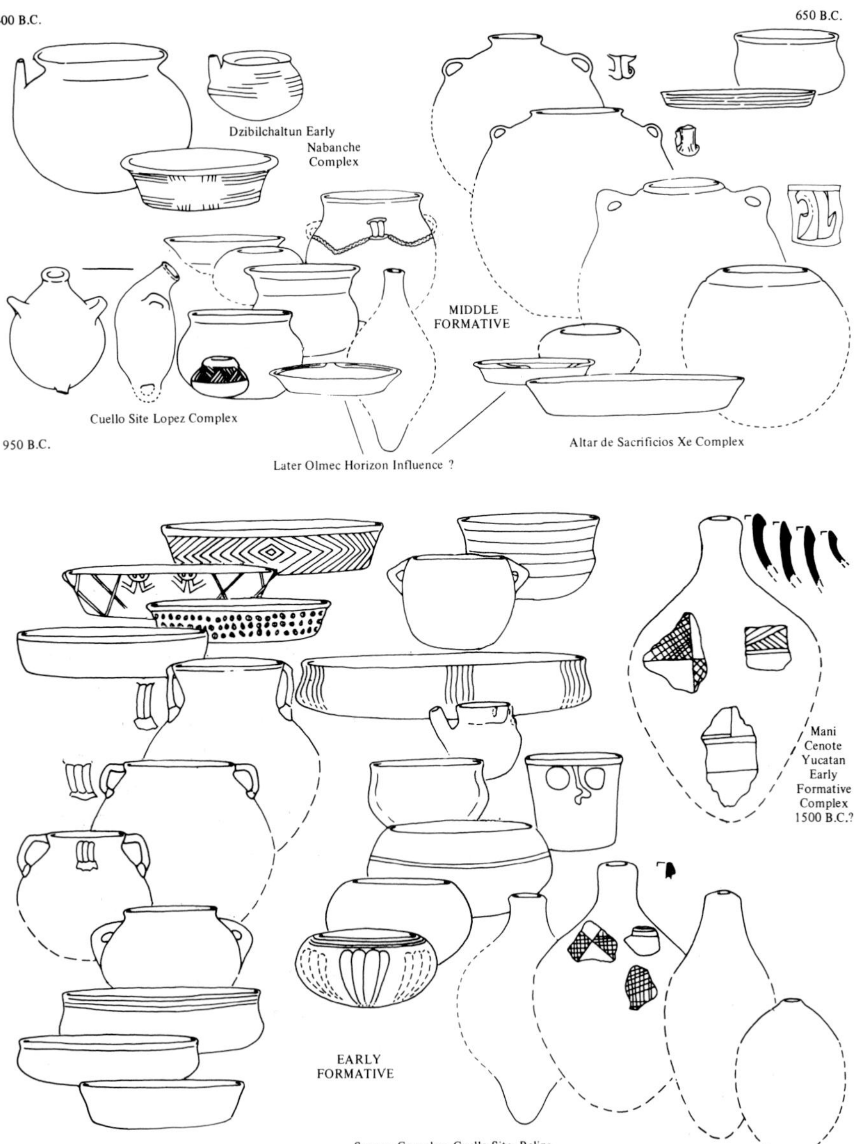

Figure 11.6. The earliest ceramic form traditions of the Yucatan Peninsula and Río Pasión zone (Swasey and Lopez forms redrawn from Pring 1976a, 1976b; Mani Cenote from Brainerd 1958, Fig. 30e; Xe from Adams 1971; Nabanche from Andrews IV 1968:40).

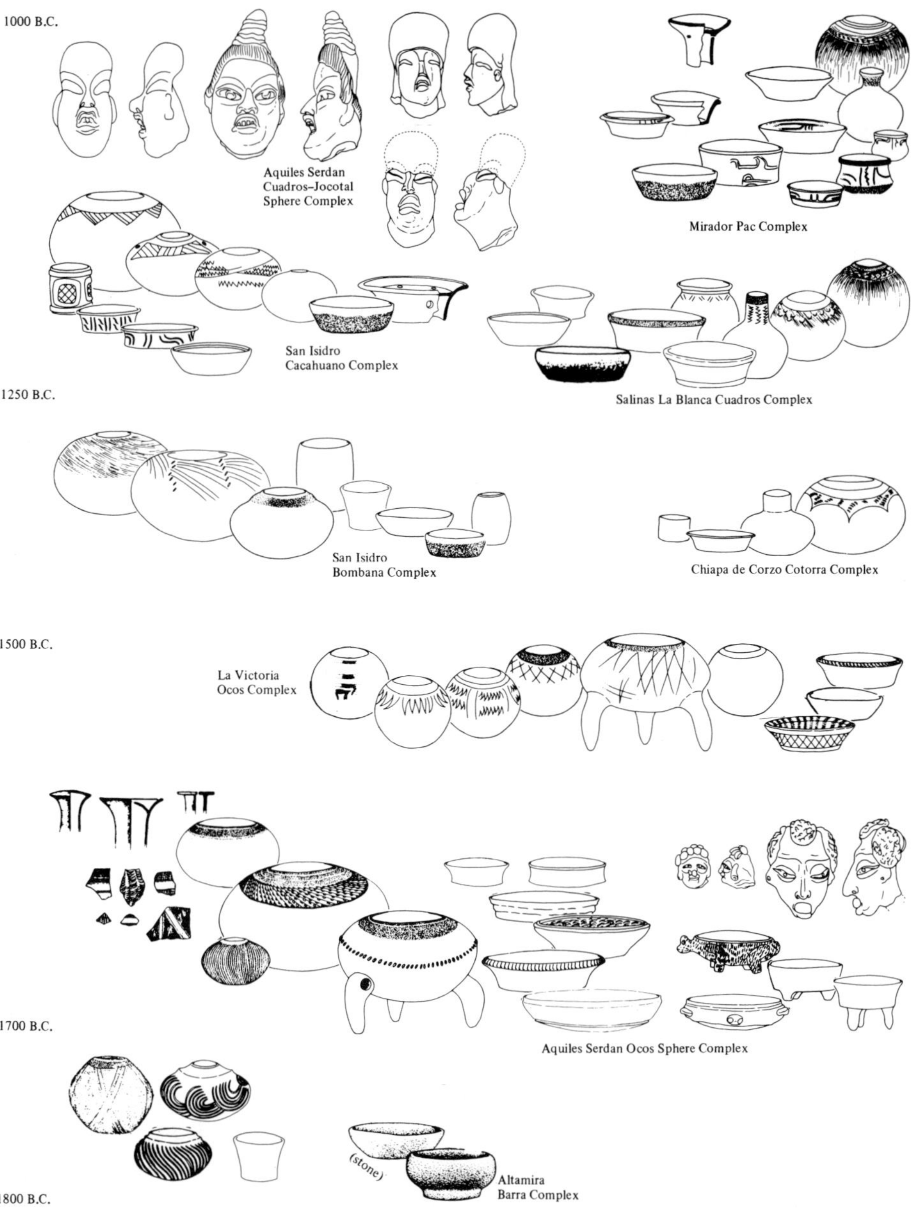

Figure 11.7. The Early Preclassic ceramic form tradition in the Western and Southern regions of Eastern Mesoamerica (La Victoria and Salinas La Blanca forms adapted from M.D. Coe 1961, and Coe and Flannery 1967, Fig. 11; remainder from New World Archaeological Foundation).

et al. 1976; Hammond 1977a) now suggests that the true hearth of bottles, spouts, and handled necked ollas in Mesoamerica will all be in that region. It is significant too that such form modes appear very early within Swasey, together with fragments of "Early Formative" pattern-burnished water bottles (Pring 1976a, Fig. 11; Hammond 1977a:130); the latter were reported originally by Brainerd (1951; 1958) from a deep cenote cave deposit at Mani in Yucatan. The descriptions of the Cuello Swasey Phase with their confirmation of Brainerd's "Yucatan Early Formative" horizon (Pring 1976b:14; Hammond 1977a:130) now appear to firmly establish the existence of a widespread, early, sedentary, Lowland Maya-area society in the Yucatan Peninsula contemporaneous with the pre-Olmec and Olmec stylistic developments in the Isthmian and Cordilleran mainland regions that we are attributing to the early Mixe-Zoque. The ultimate origins of neither of these high culture traditions are apparent at this time in spite of supposedly very ancient shared linguistic precedents.

It is noteworthy that "narrow-necked bottles" do occur in the San Lorenzo, Veracruz, Ojochi Phase complex of the Ocos horizon, the earliest pottery so far reported in the Gulf Coast "Olmec heartland." Even more interestingly, in the following, and still pre-Olmec, Bajio Phase are "large numbers of bottles which appear . . . with bodies which are either fluted or deeply gadrooned to resemble gourds or squashes; necks are straight or slightly restricted towards the mouth (M. D. Coe 1970:24)." Similar bottles are common in the Tabascan Chontalpa Molina Phase (Sisson 1970:44). Certainly this situation does suggest a meeting in the Gulf Coast of the Early Formative water bottles of Yucatan and Belize with the grooved gourd-like tecomates so common to the Barra and Ocos phases on the Pacific Coast of Chiapas, but Sisson (personal communication) postulates a stronger Central Mexican connection.

The distribution pattern of Preclassic modelled anthropomorphic figurines is another excellent evidence of early differentiation: geographically and chronologically limited interaction between the distinctive Mixe-Zoque and Maya culture areas. It is significant that: (*1*) figurines are absent in the Maya Early Preclassic and their interchange is mainly confined to the later Middle Preclassic; (*2*) that such Preclassic figurines appear almost always to have been much more abundant in the regions of known or supposed closer Mixe-Zoque affiliation; (*3*) that they are almost never found in the Yucatan Peninsula proper (Yucatan, Quintana Roo, Campeche, Belize), the area with which the Early Preclassic Maya pottery has been identified; and (*4*) that the few described Middle Preclassic Maya figurines (mainly from the Peten and Río Pasión) show a logical evolution from Middle Preclassic late Olmec antecedents generally limited in abundant distribution to the greater isthmus and southern Pacific Coast regions. More unique figurine traditions appear in the Southeastern Highlands in late Middle and Late Preclassic times.

Detailed publication of the abundant human figurines from several Preclassic sites in El Salvador, Guatemala, and Chiapas, all in preparation, will make possible more meaningful evaluation of the interareal relationships which seem now to indicate that the Mixe-Zoque area contributed the early figurine tradition to the central Maya lowlands, whereas the Yucatan Peninsula proper, farther removed from the source of diffusion, rejected its adoption. This trend is also reflected in the regionally distinct nature of most early Yucatan Formative pottery.

The Cuello, Belize archaeological sequence is now one of the best dated Preclassic developments in Mesoamerica, with 18 radiocarbon dates providing an "internally consistent radiocarbon chronology" (Hammond, et al. n.d.); twelve of these dates, from the Swasey Phase, lead these authors to propose that the Maya "Early Formative would span the period 2500–1300 B.C., coinciding with the limits proposed for the Initial Ceramic period of Mesoamerica in the Valley of Mexico," suggesting further that "The Middle Formative would then occupy the period 1300–450 B.C." This very early dating proposal has not yet been widely accepted by Mayanists.

2. The Isthmian-Cordilleran Mainland

Judging from advanced and massive sculptural and architectural terrace developments, the Olmec area cultural tradition appears to have climaxed well before 1000 B.C. (M. D. Coe 1968a; 1968b). Following the introduction of one or more ceramic (and other?) technologies, five or six centuries of Early Preclassic occupation on the western and southern margins of the Maya territory culminated in several remarkable Early Olmec centers and multitudinous small hinterland sites by about 1200 B.C. The Ocos ceramic system was certainly a principal contributing ancestor of this Olmec development; as now known from Veracruz and the interior and Pacific coast regions of Chiapas, Ocos pottery has an even more remarkable sophistication and distribution pattern than that first published for it from Guatemala by M. D. Coe in 1961. The antecedent but little known Barra ceramic complex restricted to the Pacific Coast was equally well made and more "formative" than Ocos only with regard to its more limited known shape inventory and spatial distribution.

Some typical Barra Complex and Ocos sphere pottery forms are shown in Figure 11.7. These phases have produced little architectural evidence, but low mounds and a type of village plaza arrangement are found at Paso de la Amada near Altamira (Ceja 1974). Both phases do include an obsidian chip complex thought to be related to manioc grating. Obsidian chips are also common in some of the Central Chiapas Grijalva River Ocos Horizon occupations but were not noted with the Pacific Coast estuary island Ocos deposits presumably left purely by fishermen.

Most typical of the Barra ceramic complex are rather small red tecomates or squashlike vessels with thin walls, distinguishable from similar Ocos forms by their diagonal or curvilinear grooving. Larger unpolished Barra Phase tecomates have unique crossed, multiple-diagonal incisions. Red, slipped, flat-bottom, straight-wall bowls or jars are frequent, and a zoned punctate, black-brown ware in apparently restricted orifice forms is rare (Green and Lowe 1967:97–104; Lowe 1975).

The original Ocos pottery complex identified at La Victoria, Guatemala, also has tecomates and flat-bottom bowls as the predominant shapes, with a "surprising sophistication"; "most smoothed zones contrast with zones roughened by rocker stamping, shell back stamping or fine cord-wrapped paddle impressions (M. D. Coe 1966:43–45, Fig. 5)." Red and buff bowls received a variety of surface incision and highly polished rim grooving (M. D. Coe 1961: Figs. 19, 21; see also, for Izapa, Ekholm 1969: Figs. 18, 25). Faint iridescent paint striping like that found at comparable levels in Ecuador and Peru was common on both bowl and tecomate forms at La Victoria (M. D. Coe 1960a) but has been little noted elsewhere in Mesoamerica. Another surprising mode in this ceramic complex are tall tripod supports for some tecomates (M. D. Coe 1961: Fig. 14; 1966: Fig. 5). This trait has been found subsequently with Ocos Horizon complexes in Chiapas (see Fig. 11.7) at Aquiles Serdan (Navarrete in preparation) and Paso de la Amada (Ceja 1974) on the Pacific Coast and at El Carmen, an Upper Grijalva River Angostura Basin site (I.N.A.H. Dept. of Arch. Salvage).

Other Ocos ceramic modes common at Aquiles Serdan and Paso de la Amada include numerous flat-bottom bowls with either poorly formed solid-slab tripod feet (also found at Izapa—Ekholm 1969: Fig. 44) or a variety of hollow rounded feet. Many shell-back-stamped animal effigies and finely modeled, human female figurines are also found at Aquiles Serdan (see Figure 11.7); these heads resemble those of La Victoria (M. D. Coe 1966: Fig. 5), but their bodies are armless or nearly so, with strongly exaggerated breasts and thighs.

Neither Ocos nor Barra have been very adequately dated. Two radiocarbon dates (I-8162, I-8161) corrected to 1649 (± 160) and 1710 (± 225) B.C. (Lowe 1975:29) are available for the Barra phase; these are from a fully developed, functioning complex. Ocos Horizon dating is more problematical, but its components are found stratigraphically beneath the Early Olmec-related Cuadros complexes at various sites on the Pacific Coast of Chiapas and Guatemala and are well below the San Lorenzo Phase Early Olmec levels at San Lorenzo, Veracruz. The Ocos Horizon Complex (Ojochi Phase) at San Lorenzo is separated from the San Lorenzo Phase by two apparently transitional phases, Bajio and Chicharras (M. D. Coe 1970). The Bajio Phase with the MASCA dendrochronological adjustment of radiocarbon dates begins at approximately 1500 B.C. A Bajio parallel has not been identified on the Pacific Coast, but some such transitional complex may exist there, for there is an apparent stylistic and technological gap between the hard-fired, rather thin, well-polished and often highly embellished Ocos ceramics and the overlying poorly fired, heavier Cuadros sphere pottery. There is then a general agreement that Ojochi and Ocos were fully developed well before 1500 B.C., but the lifespan is conjectural. Conservatively allowing Ocos 200 years (rather than 400 or 500 as is often done), it appears safe to conclude that Barra beginnings must antedate 1800 B.C., as the existing radiocarbon dates require. A ca. 1700 beginning date for Ocos appears to align well with the Chorrera Phase in Ecuador, with which M. D. Coe saw direct design parallels in 1960 (see also Evans and Meggers 1966:247–253, Figs. 2, 3).

As noted above, it is supposed that the Ocos Complex was a principal forerunner of the Olmec society, but the full evolutionary process is unknown. The sophistication of the Ocos Ceramic Complex does not indicate its mere development out of Barra as we presently know that complex, suggesting that diffusion was a continuing process. This supposition is particularly sustained by the La Victoria Ocos and Conchas Phase stylistic relationships to northern South America noted by M. D. Coe (1960a).

Additional or continuing diffusion from unknown centers, together with undiscovered local developmental site complexes, very probably does explain both the Ocos situation and the formation of the following Olmec civilization (Lowe 1971:222–225). A major unknown is the role possibly played by local preceramic or nonceramic cultures that must have interacted with any immigrant groups responsible for the massive introduction of sophisticated ceramic systems. It may even be argued that such ceramic systems were simply adopted, if not invented, by a local preceramic and gourd-using populace; but there is no evidence to support this argument, and it appears to be an unlikely explanation of the known facts. Careful dating of a larger series of aceramic Chantuto-type middens and of more Barra and Ocos sites is a first requirement of further investigation.

C. Early Preclassic II Subperiod

As indicated, in Eastern Mesoamerica there are few identified cultural components comparable to the intermediate Bajio Phase at San Lorenzo, Veracruz. Bajio ceramics are described by M. D. Coe (1970:24) as including flat-bottom pots with restricted necks and greatly outflaring rims, as well as large numbers of "bottles" with fluted gourd- or squashlike bodies. Both of these forms are very rare in Eastern Mesoamerica, which suggests either an unusual independent development or that exotic influences helped form this early pre-Olmec phase at San Lorenzo. Other Bajio ceramic traits, more familiar to the Early Preclassic of our area, include modified Ocos attributes, differentially fired black-and-white ware, and hollow human figurines. On the other hand, there is now a complete absence everywhere of several Ocos traits such as vessel supports, and effigy forms and stamping are rare in Chiapas during this and following subperiods.

Only in the Chontalpa region of the Tabasco floodplain is good Bajio-like complex reported within Eastern Mesoamerica; it is significant that this region of occupied river levees is adjacent to the La Venta zone and was no doubt subsidiary to that great Olmec center (Sisson 1970). The Molina Phase of the Chontalpa is "characterized by brushed tecomates, a black-and-white ware, effigy vessels, plain and dentate rocker stamping, plain and 'gourd-shaped' bottles, stone vessels, and amorphous obsidian flakes [with] closest similarities with that of the Bajio and Chicarras phases [Sisson 1970:44]." All of the eight identified sites of the Molina Phase were said to be small; they were "covered by from one to three meters of overburden and were exposed in the sides of drainage ditches [Sisson 1970:45]."

Eastward from the Chontalpa, in Tabasco, at the Usumacinta River site of San Jose del Rio, Ferree reports very scarce sherds of "fabric-impressed tecomates and rocker-stamped vessels [1971:3]," which suggests an occupation of Early Preclassic I or II date for that region.

South from the Chontalpa, in Western Chiapas, a Bajio- or Chicharras-like pottery complex named Bombana was found in the deepest levels under Mound 20 at San Isidro in the now flooded Mal Paso Dam Basin of the Middle Grijalva River (Lowe 1969). Curious two-legged metates occur both at San Isidro and at San Lorenzo in the Chicharras contexts; legged metates are otherwise absent from the Mesoamerican Formative, but an identical two-legged example was recovered from an "Early Classic" mound at Tiquisate on the Pacific coast of Guatemala (Shook 1965: Fig. 2, *O*). The Santa Marta Cotorra and Chiapa de Corzo Cotorra complexes, as noted following, may correspond with at least part of the Chicharras Phase of San Lorenzo, and thus may be largely pre-Olmec in Chiapas. Santa Marta Cotorra, in addition, has some characteristics that appear to be even earlier (Johnson and MacNeish 1972:34) and better aligned with the Bajio Phase.

A radiocarbon date for the Santa Marta Cave Cotorra Phase of 1330 (± 200) B.C. (non-MASCA) falls within the Early Preclassic II Subperiod, a further indication that it may align with Chicharras at San Lorenzo. However, a date for the typologically later Pac Phase (a San Lorenzo and Cuadros Phase equivalent) at nearby Mirador of 1290 (± 90) B.C. (non-MASCA) is almost identical to that from Santa Marta, and older than most of the few San Lorenzo, Veracruz, dates available for this phase. Inasmuch as the Santa Marta and Mirador dates are single examples, it is possible that they will be modified by additional analyses; Figures 11.3 and 11.7 follow dating for the Early Preclassic Period based on the fuller San Lorenzo indications (Coe *et al.* 1967; M. D. Coe 1970).

Some shapes and decorative modes in Western Honduras, such as zoned rocker stamping and long-necked bottles with lobed bodies (Gordon 1898) suggest the presence of an intermediate Early Preclassic occupation in various parts of that country. Both the Honduras and the Tabasco situations suggest some interaction with the Belizian Swasey Complex or Central Mexico by mid-Early Preclassic times.

D. Early Preclassic III Subperiod

As presently understood, the final two or three centuries of the second millennium B.C. saw the climax of the Early Preclassic Period, with the rise and demise of the remarkable Early Olmec society in the Isthmian region. The best-known Early Olmec ceremonial center is San Lorenzo, Veracruz, which has given its name to this horizon. The San Lorenzo Phase is typified both at San Lorenzo and elsewhere by the erection of great terrace platforms and the skilled carving of massive Olmec stone altars, colossal human heads, and smaller sculpture in the round (Stirling 1955; M. D. Coe 1968a; 1968b:73–89; 1970). This activity at the Gulf Coast heartland sites was accompanied by the development and wide diffusion of the carved black excised-incised Olmec pottery style, and evolution of the continuing controlled smudging tradition (M. D. Coe 1970; Green and Lowe 1967:67, 108, Fig. 80). Other typical modes of this subperiod include the smudged white-rimmed black bowls, several red and white wares, heavy tecomate types, large coarse ware pedestal-base incensarios, and a variety of distinctive clay figurines, all of which are common at many sites in the interior and on the Pacific coast of Chiapas and Guatemala during the Cuadros Phase (see Figure 11.7, upper groups), as well as farther south. Considering this normal ceramic evolution from preceding phases and the violent ending of the Early Olmec Horizon described elsewhere (see following subperiod), it makes better sense to think of the Early Olmec Horizon as climaxing the Early Preclassic Period rather than as beginning the Middle Preclassic Period (a decision ending doubts raised in Green and Lowe 1967:55).

The San Lorenzo Phase cultural horizon and its violent close are both well represented at La Venta, Tabasco, by huge stone monuments subsequently defiled and moved to secondary positions and by numerous smaller battered and discarded sculptures, as well as by carved stone drain-line segments found well buried beneath the later "Sterling Acropolis" platform (Heizer, Graham, and Napton 1968). A ceramic complex similar to that of the San Lorenzo Phase was also identified in various zones at La Venta (Hallinan, Ambro, and O'Connell 1968:155, 161–165). Other ceramic materials related to both early and late subphases of the Early Preclassic Period were reported by R. J. Squier to be "very abundant" in deeply buried levels of two test pits dug in 1964 at La Venta (see *Comments* in Berger and Libby 1966: 474–475). Unfortunately, these materials have not been described.

Much of the development of the Early Olmec society and its culture appears to have taken place in the regions around the general Los Tuxtlas zone of Southern Veracruz (M. D. Coe 1968a: 63–64). Further work in the

Veracruz sector will make it easier properly to define recognized Olmec relationships to the south and east. We do know now that within Eastern Mesoamerica the distribution of the Early Preclassic III or "Early Olmec" ceramic system followed rather closely the pattern of the Ocos Horizon sites, with some expansion into additional river basins and estuary zones. The distribution pattern across the Greater Isthmus area has been discussed by Lowe (1971: 222–224; 1977: 212–218, Fig. 9.2; and in Green and Lowe 1967: 65–68).

Ample Pac Phase trash deposits recently excavated at Mirador and Plumajillo (Miramar), Chiapas, show strong ceramic parallels with the San Lorenzo and Cuadros complexes (see Figure 11.7, upper right); such stylistic faithfulness (Wainer 1970: 44–50, Fig. 12; Agrinier 1975a: Figs. 3–18) may be explained only by very close contact with the Southern Veracruz or Western Tabasco Early Olmec centers. The closely related Cacahuano sherd complex at San Isidro, Chiapas (Lowe 1969), indicates that part of this early intercommunication was via the Middle Grijalva River and its western, or Rio La Venta, tributary, which passes between Mirador and Plumajillo as the Rio Flores. Quite probably these were workshop and way stations between the Gulf Coast and Pacific Coast Soconuscan sites at this early time (Agrinier 1975a: 24–25).

The Chiapa de Corzo Cotorra ceramic complex (Dixon 1959: Figs. 2–20; Lowe and Mason 1965: Fig. 6) is so conservative alongside the Mirador Pac Phase Complex that we must suppose it to be a puzzling regional variant or else in fact older, as postulated earlier, and thus at least partly in line with the Chicharras Phase (the position taken in Figures 11.3 and 11.7). Particularly notable is the absence of white-rimmed black ware and excised decoration in the Cotorra Complex. The Cotorra component at Padre Piedra (Navarrete 1960: 10–12, Figs. 22–24), also in Southern Chiapas, is a closer parallel to the Pac Complex and does include white-rimmed black sherds (Green and Lowe 1967: 43–45, Figs. 53, 57).

Some Pacific Coast site components of what we may term the Cuadros ceramic sphere at Salinas La Blanca, Guatemala, and Izapa, Altamira, and Aquiles Serdan, Chiapas, have been fully described (Coe and Flannery 1967; Ekholm 1969; Green and Lowe 1967; Navarrete in preparation). Three radiocarbon dates (non-MASCA) based on charcoal from Cuadros Phase hearths are 978, 765, and 928 (±105) B.C. (Coe and Flannery 1967: 68). These dates run a century or two later than a set of five dates secured for the San Lorenzo Phase at that Veracruz site (Coe, Diehl, and Stuiver 1967), so that our claims for the fully contemporaneous status of Cuadros and San Lorenzo are based on the remarkable similarity of their ceramic complexes (Coe 1970).

Full characterization of the Early Preclassic III Subperiod awaits publication of the Isthmian San Lorenzo ceramic typology (M. D. Coe in preparation) with its definition of San Lorenzo A and B subphases. The latter is characterized by the addition of new traits (M. D. Coe 1970: 27) not so far distinguished in the greater Maya territory except, apparently, for the Palacios Phase of the Chontalpa in Western Tabasco (Sisson 1970: 45). A better-known transitional phase is that of Jocotal (described in E. following), which develops out of Cuadros everywhere on the Pacific Coast. Jocotal in most respects appears to be a reaffirmation of the Olmec Tradition and a heralding of the La Venta–Olmec Period of Middle Preclassic domination (Green and Lowe 1967: 118–120, Figs. 90–91; Coe and Flannery 1967: 44–46, Figs. 22–24).

The farthest-south extension of the Early Preclassic III San Lorenzo–Olmec-related ceramic style horizon so far reliably reported is the initial Tok Phase ceramic complex at Chalchuapa, El Salvador (Sharer 1969: 64–68; Sharer and Gifford 1970: 445). Some representative vessel forms are shown in Figure 11.9, lower right. A radiocarbon date from a stratified Tok context with MASCA correction is 998 (± 55) B.C. (P-1551, R. J. Sharer, personal communication). Some other late Early Preclassic pottery identified in the collections from Monte Alto on the central Pacific Coast of Guatemala suggests that this southward Early Olmec-related occupation was constant (E. M. Shook, personal communication). The Honduras late Early Preclassic is still problematical (see Section E. following and Fig. 11.5).

Recent explorations and excavations in two neighboring regions (Sakajut, Alta Verapaz, and El Porton, Baja Verapaz) by Sedat and Sharer (1972: 25–28; 1973) have confirmed an Early and Middle Preclassic occupation for the northern highlands of Guatemala. Preliminary descriptions of sherds from both surface sites and a submound humic layer at Sakajut leave no doubt of their early date (Sedat and Sharer 1972: 27); closest affiliations appear to be with the Cuadros sphere complexes of the Pacific Coast and that of Mirador (Pac Phase) in West-Central Chiapas. The Verapaz discoveries open a welcome new door on the problem of Lowland Maya Río Pasión zone ceramic origins during the early Middle Preclassic Period (Willey 1973: 25–26). The northern Guatemalan highlands and their northern drainage appear to represent expectable zones of transition between the Mixe-Zoque and Maya area traditions.

As described above in Section II-B1 and in Figure 11.6, recent evidence indicates that much of the Yucatan Peninsula and some Maya Lowlands regions were already being occupied during or soon after Early Preclassic times, but by peoples with a ceramic complex quite different from that of the Isthmian and Cordilleran mainland Olmec-related societies. This early Peninsular culture was the direct and principal forerunner of the Middle Preclassic Maya Pre-Mamom and Mamom horizons (Pring 1976), but apparently an infusion of Mixe-Zoque Isthmian-Cordilleran traits, perhaps from both the west and south, helped to bring about those stylistic transformations. Some of the earliest Olmec figurines and sherds moving eastward have been noted at Tierra Blanca and Trinidad, Tabasco (Rands 1977: 168, Fig. 7.1).

E. Middle Preclassic I Subperiod

The human occupation of Eastern Mesoamerica during the first two centuries of the Middle Preclassic Period is still somewhat better known in the western and southern regions, of presumed Mixe-Zoque affiliation (Lowe 1977: 218–222. Fig. 9.3). The 1000 B.C. beginning date obviously is simply a convenient round figure, but an actual period of marked cultural change does seem to take form at most studied sites at about this time. The changed pattern is seen in disrupted site occupations, more and more-extended settlements, new artifact types, and varied ceramic styles (see Figure 11.6, upper, and Figure 11.8).

As noted previously, the end of the San Lorenzo Phase occupation at San Lorenzo was preceded by a thorough destruction (M. D. Coe 1968b:89), which had apparent repercussions over a wide area (M. D. Coe 1968a:63) including Tabasco and Chiapas (Lowe 1971: Fig. 1). These developments are most ostentatiously seen at La Venta during its Complex A heyday, but artifact and ceramic complexes are better known elsewhere. The post–San Lorenzo Phase La Venta Complex A architectural sequence, with its extraordinary buried offering ceremonialism (Drucker, Heizer, and Squier 1959), accompanied an apparently gradual renovation of pottery norms having much in common with both Tres Zapotes, Veracruz, and much of the Maya territory. This evolution, however poorly understood it may be at the La Venta Site, is rather well known in several other regions; it makes a logical development throughout Eastern Mesoamerica within the Middle Preclassic Period, and it is described here as a separate tradition for the Tabasco and Chiapas regions (see Figure 11.8).

Phases I and II of Complex A at La Venta may be transitional from Early to Middle Preclassic status. Unfortunately, published knowledge of the ceramics from these phases at La Venta is almost limited to the four vessels shown at bottom right in Figure 11.8. These few bowls do indicate an almost certain alignment with the Middle Preclassic I style horizon, in approximate conformity with recent reconsideration of the radiocarbon dates for Phases I and II (ca. 1000 to 600 B.C.; Berger, Graham, and Heizer 1967:5), but they give no clue to full complex content and its wider external relationships.

It is apparent that Complex A at La Venta was begun after or at the close of the San Lorenzo Phase component at that site; it is probable also that the Colossal Heads (Monuments 2, 3, 4) were already defiled and placed in secondary positions north of Complex A prior to beginning the construction of Complex A and the Stirling Acropolis platform (see preceding discussion of Early Preclassic III). In this context, La Venta clearly begins the Middle

Figure 11.8. The Middle Preclassic ceramic form traditions in the Western and Southern regions of Eastern Mesoamerica (La Victoria forms redrawn from Coe and Flannery 1967, Fig. 11; La Venta from Drucker 1952, and Drucker, Heizer, and Squier 1959; remainder from New World Archaeological Foundation).

Preclassic Period in at least one or two new settings; or, stated better, the changes in architectural settings at La Venta with the start of the Complex A construction marked the beginning of the new historical era that is being called here the Middle Preclassic Period.

The small Phases I and II pottery sample does indicate that the earliest La Venta Complex A offering vessels, at any rate, were in the expected style norm of the terminal Early Preclassic or transitional Jocotal ceramics as known on the Pacific Coast and the related earliest Middle Preclassic complexes such as Dili at Chiapa de Corzo (see Figure 11.8). More problematical is the nature of the ceramic evolution following at La Venta, for there is a marked shift in style noted in the offerings from Phases III and IV in Complex A. An actual hiatus at about this time is postulated for San Lorenzo because of a similar disjunction in style traditions related to modified structural practices, but it seems probable that this abandonment must largely coincide with La Venta Complex A Phases I and II and the Dili Phase development in Chiapas, from whence much of the subsequent ceramic complex of the Nacaste Phase reoccupation of San Lorenzo may have been derived (M. D. Coe 1970:29). The ubiquitous Dili ceramic sphere is further discussed later in this section.

The Middle Preclassic is almost everywhere recognized at its beginning by the remarkably increased presence (frequently predominant) of a whitish or "white-to-buff" ceramic ware in which a flat-bottom, flaring-wall bowl is the most common form. These bowls typically, though not always, have one or more lines incised around the interior lip; when double, the upper will usually break and the ends turn upward, in a characteristic trait conveniently labeled the "double-line break" by M. D. Coe (1961:61). Various types of upright vessels as well as rather plain tecomates and deeply punched-eye human figurines accompany this complex (see Figure 11.8, lower left). A wide distribution of the white ware incised-rim bowl mode throughout Middle Preclassic occupations in Oaxaca and Central Mexico is noteworthy; it is the hallmark of the Guadalupe Phase in the Valley of Oaxaca (Flannery 1968: 90), common in Tehuacan (MacNeish, Peterson, and Flannery 1970:59–64), and sufficiently abundant even in the Valley of Mexico to merit comment (Tolstoy and Paradis 1971:10, 16–17).

Good deposits of Middle Preclassic I pottery, including enormous quantities of the white-to-buff, double-line-break bowl sherds, are most abundantly known at numerous sites in Central and Southern Chiapas, belonging to what we have referred to as the Dili ceramic sphere. Components have been described for the Upper Grijalva River (Lowe 1959: Figs. 3, 35, 51b); Chiapa de Corzo (Dixon 1959:19–36); the Frailesca or Villaflores region (Navarrete 1960: Figs. 25, 26); Santa Rosa (Brockington 1967:37–43, Figs. 29, 32, E–L, 46); and Padre Piedra (Green and Lowe 1967: Figs. 55–62). A pure Dili sphere component has been located as a heavy refuse zone at Miramar (Agrinier 1975a). A closely related complex has been tested at Vistahermosa near Cintalapa, on the southwestern edge of the Central Depression of Chiapas, which includes a small contingent of a red-and-white trait (Treat 1969) carried over into the succeeding Quequepac Phase at Mirador, as shown in Figure 11.8, upper center (Wainer 1970).

Recent explorations in the initial occupation levels of Tzutzuculi at Tonala on the Pacific Coast of Chiapas (Navarrete 1959:6) have produced a refuse deposit closely approximating both the inland Dili complexes and the coastal Jocotal complexes of the Soconusco (McDonald 1971). A single radiocarbon date from this deposit gives a date (I-5995) of 800 (±125) B.C. (non-MASCA).

The Chiapa de Corzo Dili Complex, in particular, displays many Olmec ceramic design traits (Lowe and Mason 1965:210, Figs. 7, 9) and may be considered to be a late development out of the Early Olmec San Lorenzo Phase influence in Central Chiapas (as best known for the Pac Phase of Mirador), and thus apparently is pre-Nacaste in San Lorenzo terms (M. D. Coe 1970). Dili must be approximately coeval with the transitional Complex A Phases I and II at La Venta, and at least partly in line with the late Jocotal Phase at Altamira (Green and Lowe 1967:112–120), Salinas la Blanca (Coe and Flannery 1967:69), and Izapa (Ekholm 1969).

The Jocotal Phase on the Pacific coast of Chiapas and Guatemala was terminal at Aquiles Serdan, Altamira, and Salinas la Blanca (though Aquiles Serdan experienced rather little of the Jocotal evolution). This circumstance leads to the placement of Jocotal in the Early Preclassic Period in Chiapas (see Figure 11.3, far right column). There is also a probable disruption in the occupation pattern at Izapa following Jocotal (Ekholm 1969:97, Fig. 1 chart). The belated recognition of a "thin layer of Jocotal material" beneath Conchas 1 at La Victoria (Coe and Flannery 1967:67), however, seems to justify consideration of Jocotal as an at least partially transitional phase (Coe and Flannery 1967:23), and it is so indicated for the Salinas la Blanca–La Victoria region (see Figure 11.4, far right).

From another point of view, there exists a possibility that the well-developed Conchas 1 Complex of Southwestern Guatemala includes more direct survivals of the old Ocos ceramic and cultural tradition (Lowe in Green and Lowe 1967:68). Certainly Conchas 1 does manifest a developmental history that is different from its Mexican neighbors of the period; S. M. Ekholm has observed that "Conchas phase at resettled La Victoria developed somewhat distinctively, perhaps as a result of seemingly stronger contacts with the Huasteca and coastal Ecuador than has been noted elsewhere at this time on the Pacific coast [1967:96]."

The maintenance of relationships with South America during Conchas 1 times (M. D. Coe 1960a:366, 369–371, Figs. 4–7; Evans and Meggers 1966:248–250, Figs. 4–10) is in keeping with the precedent set during the Ocos Phase at La Victoria, but it is not noted for the presumably intervening Cuadros and Jocotal phases identified at other sites. Similarly, the tripod grater bowls and the evidences for interaction with South America suggest some socioeconomic independence from Olmec traditions for the Conchas society. Additional field research and improved chronological controls are needed to enlighten this puzzling regional situation.

A technological continuity from Ocos times is suggested by the hard-fired nature of Conchas 1 pottery, which distinguishes it from known Jocotal or Cuadros complex ceramics. The "hard, white, monochrome pottery of the Conchas White-to-buff type" along with unburnished red tecomate sherds have been reported from a dozen sites in the Ocos area, where Conchas is the "most widespread and important of the Formative phases" (Coe and Flannery 1967:87, 89, Fig. 46). A number of additional Conchas sites, some of them very large and with once-important mounds, have been called to my attention by E. M. Shook, who was similarly impressed by the "Ocos-like" technical superiority of the Conchas sherds in this region (personal communication, 1973, regarding the superabundance of excellent pottery and figurines in what appear to be Conchas 1 ceramic types found in the scattered debris left from numerous mound sites recently razed by road building operations of North American contractors along the west bank of the Rio Naranjo upstream from Ocos and La Victoria, Guatemala). A single radiocarbon date is available for the Conchas 1 Phase (Y-1167) of 790 (±60) B.C. (non-MASCA), obtained from an exposed river-cut mound face at a site on the east side of the Rio Naranjo, upstream from the Salinas la Blanca Site (Coe and Flannery 1967:68, 89).

Other beginning Middle Preclassic ceramic developments in upper Central America are less well understood. On the southeastern periphery, pottery with some good Early Olmec characteristics in the Jaral Phase at Los Naranjos, Honduras, appears to be an outrider of the Early Preclassic III horizon, but it is thought by its excavators to be a more delayed, Middle Preclassic horizon, arrival (Baudez and Becquelin 1973), and it is so placed in Figure 11.5. The Yojoa Monochrome complex (Strong, Kidder, and Paul 1938) is apparently identical to Jaral, as both seem to have sampled the same buried stratum. Yarumela I, from the Comayagua Valley in Southcentral Honduras, remains undated, but its stratigraphic position and peculiar character with many flattish comale- or griddle-like plates (Canby 1951), suggest a very early date and differing, perhaps lower Central American, relationships. The Colos Complex of Chalchuapa, in Western El Salvador (Sharer and Gifford 1970:445), includes new pottery types and forms (mainly spouted and handled jars), similar to those which figured in the first settlements in both Belize and the Petén-Pasión regions of Guatemala (compare Figures 11.6, 11.9, 11.10, lower left in all). The earlier occurrence of these forms in Northern Belize suggests that diffusion was from that direction.

There are few proved ceramic occupations within the central Maya Lowlands at the beginning of the Middle Preclassic Period, but surely the push in that direction was well under way, from both the east and the west. The Chiuaan Phase at Trinidad and Tierra Blanca, Tabasco, includes the farthest northeastward ceramic complex emphasizing tecomates and flat-based flaring-wall bowls so far confidently reported (Rands 1969:6, Fig. 3; 1974; 1977:168). The cream or white paste ware in this Eastern Tabasco regional early Middle Preclassic tradition may be related to the early white-to-buff sherds of the Isthmian-Cordilleran Mixe-Zoque regions as well as to the initial Xe pottery of the Rio Pasion zone (Rands 1977:170–171). This eastward push (or pull) appears to have carried the Mixe-Zoquean tradition as

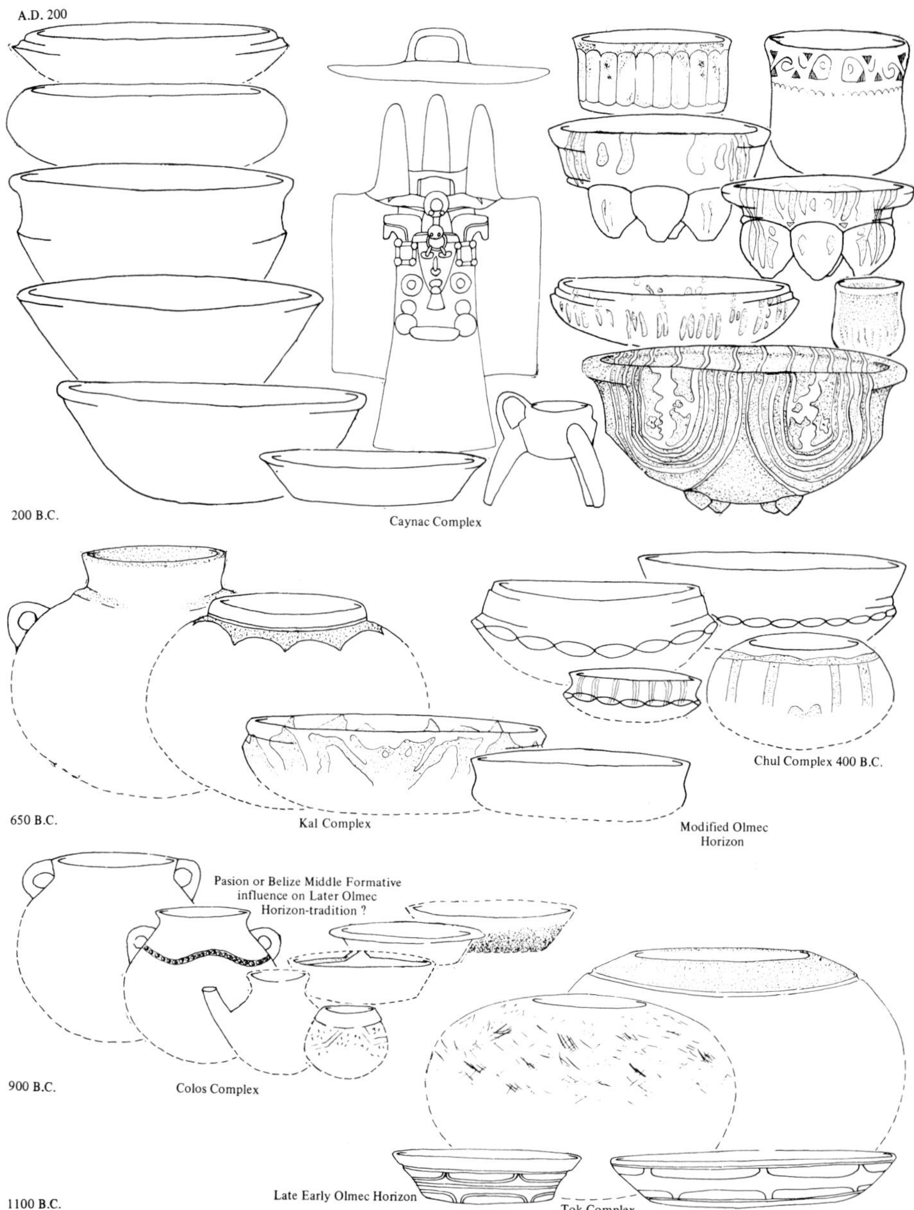

Figure 11.9 Sequence of ceramic form traditions in the Southern Highlands at Chalchuapa, El Salvador (redrawn from Sharer 1972 except Colos forms, which are reconstructed from Sharer and Gifford 1970, Figs. 5, 6, 9, and Sharer 1974 descriptions).

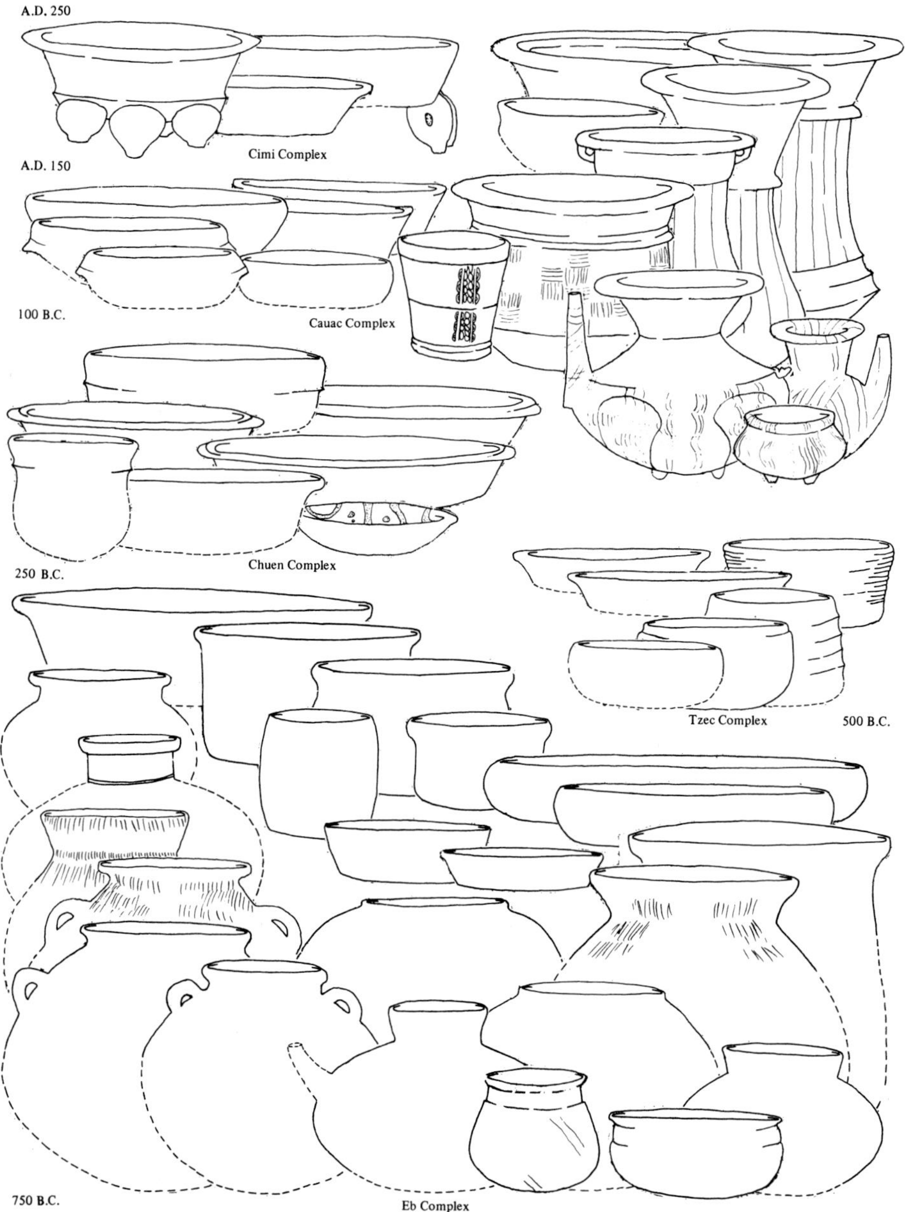

Figure 11.10 The Middle to Late Preclassic ceramic form sequence in the Central Peten at Tikal, Guatemala (after Culbert n.d., and W. R. Coe 1965).

far as the Carribean, if we are correct in attributing to it a role in the process leading to the development of the Lopez Complex (Figure 11.6, upper left) which marks the Middle Preclassic Period's appearance in Northern Belize at about 1000 B.C. (Pring 1976b). Other, probably related, people also influenced by both the eastern and western ceramic traditions then appear to have established the pioneering Xe ceramic sphere at least along the lower Pasion River before 800 B.C. (Willey 1977a:135). Inasmuch as the Xe phases are thought to have continued up to 700 or 600 B.C., they will be discussed with the following subperiod.

F. Middle Preclassic II Subperiod

The two centuries from 800 to 600 B.C., from present evidence, witnessed for the first time a strong ceramic occupation of all extremes of the Yucatan Peninsula, including the Southern Peten region, where the earliest ceramic complexes show some close resemblances to evolving traditions on both the west (or south?) and northeast. It is difficult, nevertheless, to generalize about this subperiod during which ceramic forms and finishes became greatly varied and increasingly regionalized throughout Eastern Mesoamerica.

Even within the Isthmus region, pottery traditions were now markedly modified, with the emphasis on round-side and composite-silhouette bowls, effigy and punctate-wall vessels, simplified tecomates, and the application of highly polished colored slips to both composite and flat-bottom outcurving-wall bowls (see Figure 11.8). The polished slips are frequently eroded to the point of nonexistence at La Venta (thus leading to much confused typology), but they are well preserved at many sites in Veracruz and Chiapas (for examples of the latter, see Lowe and Mason 1965, Fig. 11).

The vessel profiles from Drucker's poorly stratified 1952 La Venta pottery study, shown at the extreme right in Figure 11.8, are ranked by their resemblances to both the offering pottery from La Venta Complex A Phases III and IV and to ceramics from Chiapa de Corzo, San Isidro, and Mirador in Chiapas (with consideration also for observations made at San Lorenzo, Veracruz, during the Nacaste and Palangana phases by M. D. Coe 1970:28–30). Perhaps reflecting another influence arriving from sites in Central or Western Mexico, La Venta shows more annular bases on bowl forms than do most other sites in Eastern Mesoamerica at this time; there is also at least one example of a fine-paste black-ware hollow stirrup spout in the La Venta collections made by the Instituto Nacional de Antropologia e Historia (Ceramoteca, Museo Nacional de Antropologia, Mexico City).

An Escalera Phase double-chamber whistling vessel with loop handle and unsupported spout, found at Chiapa de Corzo, is another example of presumably Central Mexican (and ultimately South American?) influence in Eastern Mesoamerica during the Middle Preclassic (Lowe 1962: Fig. 28, Pl.

25; Lowe and Mason 1965: Figs. 10, 11). This object is of a whitish to gray-black smudged paste with a black-to-white incised surface that is typical of a group of white, gray, and smothered black-and-white wares being widely traded at this time (Warren 1959:101–103; Ekholm 1969:87–90; Agrinier 1975: Figs. 32–33). These wares are thought to have their origin in Southern Veracruz, particularly at Tres Zapotes, where the squat, wide "cuspidor" or composite-silhouette bowl predominates (Ortíz-Ceballos 1975:111–112). This class of pottery has not been identified in the Maya Lowlands or Highlands, and thus seems restricted to the more conservative Mixe-Zoque regions.

Varieties of early red-to-orange "waxy" wares, often having lighter-color blotches and occasional patterns, may have been widely exchanged before 600 B.C., eventually occurring almost everywhere between Tres Zapotes in Southern Veracruz and Western El Salvador; this "cloudy resist" ware is the type fossil for the Escalera Phase sphere in Central Chiapas. It or a modified red-on-buff resist ware appears in the Maya Lowlands during the following subperiod (Willey, Culbert, and Adams 1967:294–295), and its distribution and significance will be discussed there (Section G, following).

Single unbridged spout jars appear to tie together the earliest Yucatan, Peten, Belize, and El Salvador Middle Preclassic components (see Figures 11.6, 11.9, and 11.10). It is also noteworthy that the Structure 605 Burial 8 vessels from the earliest complex at Dzibilchaltun, Yucatan (Figure 11.6, upper left), suggest at once some descent from the flat-based bowl incised-ware tradition in the Greater Isthmus area and the early spouted jar forms of the southern regions. Other resemblances between the Yucatan Middle Preclassic Nebanche Complex and La Venta Complex A Phases III and IV have been cited by Joesink-Mandeville and Meluzin (1976).

A separate Middle Preclassic cultural tradition in the Yucatan Peninsula is indicated by the perseverance pattern of Mani- (or Swasey-) style water "bottles" or jars (Brainerd 1958:170) at numerous sites. Narrow-based "unipod" or "monopod" jars with narrow necks and bolster-rim mouths have been found at Xcalumkin (Holactun) in Northwestern Campeche, at the base of a dry cenote cave deposit (Matheny and Berge 1971:4), and in a cave at Sacalum, Yucatan (Folan 1970), all without line burnishing. According to Ball (1977b:105), this mode "appears restricted to a zone extending from the Mani-Chacchob-Sacalum district [of Yucatan] southward to the Becan-Xpuhil locality" of Southern Campeche (see also Ball 1977a, passim). To this distribution should of course be added the Cuello Site Lopez Complex occurrence (Figure 11.6, upper left), a Middle Preclassic Period continuity of the form (Pring 1976a) which was first known in the Early Preclassic Swasey Complex at that and several neighboring sites in Northern Belize (Pring 1976b); the narrow-mouth water jar thus has its source in this region, with little doubt, and seems never to have spread southward.

The monopod jar did reappear, or continue, in much heavier ceramics during what are presumed to be Late Preclassic times at various Quintana Roo sites (Sanders 1960: Fig. 10d). Apparently identical jars have been found *in situ* in some numbers by J. Eaton along the Rio Lagartos estuary at the northeastern tip of Yucatan (personal communication, and Andrews IV 1971:92).

In the Guatemalan Highlands, the beginning of the Las Charcas ceramic tradition (Shook 1951) is generally assigned to the Middle Preclassic II time period. Despite certain minor trait correspondences noted with complexes to the north and south (M. D. Coe 1961:128; Rands and Gifford 1965:123–125), nevertheless, Las Charcas has relatively little in common with Middle Preclassic complexes elsewhere except reportedly in El Salvador during the Colos and Kal phases at Chalchuapa (Sharer and Gifford 1970:445). The Kal Complex at Chalchuapa witnessed a consolidation of northern and western influences and it shared in the beginning formation of the long Usulutan resist-multiple-striping tradition (see close of Section G following) which was soon to dominate the Southeastern Highlands for the remainder of the Preclassic (Figure 11.9), becoming an all-important cultural export from that region throughout Eastern Mesoamerica.

The relatively numerous strap and loop handles on water or storage jars in the Lopez, Jenney Creek, Xe, Real, Eb, Las Charcas, and Colos-Kal complexes is particularly striking (Figures 11.6, 11.9, 11.10) and is complementary to the similar distribution of jar spouts mentioned earlier (see also Sharer and Gifford 1970: Figs. 5, 6, 9). This eastern abundance of early strap handles contrasts with an almost complete absence of the trait west of Guatemala, where handled water jars almost never appear until the Postclassic Period. The Quequepac example at Mirador (see Figure 11.8) is so unusual, in fact, that this daub-painted Chiapas instance appears to be derived from the southern highlands. A few strap handles and a buff ware unbridged jar spout also appear in the early Middle Preclassic II Duende Phase at Izapa (Ekholm 1969:70, 74, 78, 80). This phase is further discussed later in this section.

Other Xe Phase pottery at Altar de Sacrificios (see Figure 11.6, upper right), in addition to the unslipped low-neck water jars with strap handles high on the shoulders, emphasize thin-wall tecomates and a variety of monochrome, and rarely bichrome, flat-bottom dish and bowl forms having occasional wall grooving and lip incision (Adams 1971, Figs. 1–7). The Real Phase at Seibal adds to this typical Xe inventory a thick white slipping as well as both bowls and large tecomates with bolstered lips; the latter traits seem to indicate somewhat earlier dating for the Real Complex (Willey, Culbert, and Adams 1967:293). Jenney Creek I Subphase may align with Real and Xe (Sharer and Gifford 1967:452).

Precise dating of the Middle Preclassic II Subperiod in the Maya area is made difficult by the particularly unreliable nature of radiocarbon dates at this time: Suess (1970) indicates a bristlecone-pine year range of 775–525

B.C. for a radiocarbon date of 450 B.C., a bristlecone-pine year range of 775–550 B.C. for a radiocarbon date of 550 B.C., and a bristlecone-pine year range of 850–775 B.C. for a radiocarbon date of 650 B.C. (see Chapter 1, this volume). These differences have been leveled out in the MASCA correction factors for this period by the simple addition of 50 years to the radiocarbon age (Ralph 1971: Table 1.5), but this may not completely dispose of the unreliability of particular dates. In addition to these changes, apparently due to fluctuations of magnetic intensity or climate, many other unknowns afflict the few dates available for the Middle Preclassic Maya area.

We have two dates for the initial phase of occupation at Dzibilchaltun, Yucatan, which are in nonagreement: LJ-505, 975 (± 340) B.C. and LJ-508, 180 (± 200) B.C. Inasmuch as both of these ages are said to date approximately the same artifactual complex (Hubbs, Bien, and Suess 1963:263; Andrews IV 1965b:61), the frequent citation of the first date and rejection of the second is an arbitrary judgment. Probably neither of these dates is reliable, as their wide latitudes indicate, though they possibly do represent, at their latest and earliest ranges respectively, the approximate early and late margins of the Nabanche Phase, that is, ca. 635 to 380 B.C.; the MASCA factor would push this range back 50 years. This interpretation fits with the opinion of contemporary workers on the peninsula who see a general Nabanche–Mamom correspondence (Ball 1977a, 1977b:104–106; see also Joesink-Mandeville 1973), but these particular radiocarbon dates have become secondary to typological arguments.

Available radiocarbon dates assignable to the Xe Phase at Altar de Sacrificios are somewhat equivocal but permit Adams (1971:146) to argue for a beginning date between 900 and 750 B.C. At Seibal, Willey places the Real Xe Phase between 800 and 600 B.C. (1970:318, Fig. 2), and he would include Xe at Altar in this same time span (1973:18; 1977a:135). A Real Xe cache at Seibal has an unpublished radiocarbon date (UCLA-1437) of 660 (± 75) B.C. "which calibrates to around 900 B.C." according to Hammond (1977b:51); a group of six jade celts with this cache (Willey, 1970:321) indicates some affinities of Xe with the cultural practices common in La Venta Phases III–IV and the early Equipac Phase at San Isidro, Chiapas (Lowe 1969). The initial Eb complex at Tikal (Figure 11.10) is dated to between 750 and 500 B.C. and shows an unusual independence of style (Culbert 1977:35–36); see following Section G.

A series of seven unpublished radiocarbon dates from reliable circumstances within the Quequepac Phase at Mirador, Chiapas, provides the best available dating of the Middle Preclassic II Subperiod. These dates are from refuse associated with the floors and walls of clay-surfaced platform structures in Mounds 12 and 27 (Agrinier in preparation). The Quequepac Phase has an early aspect that lacks the cloudy resist polished orange ware. A single date (I-6222) from the early aspect in Mound 27 is 720 (±95) B.C. (or 820 [± 95] B.C. with MASCA correction). The six dates (all non-MASCA) from the last aspect in Mounds 12 and 27 are as follows: I-6470, 435 (± 90) B.C.; I-6221, 450 (± 90) B.C.; I-1658, 510 (± 120) B.C.; I-6220, 535 (± 90) B.C.; I-1657, 560 (± 140) B.C. and I-6469, 590 (± 120) B.C. With the addition of 50 years for the MASCA factor, these dates give an average of 563 (± 108) B.C.

The rather peculiar Duende ceramic complex within Mound 30a at Izapa, which is post-Conchas 1 and pre-cloudy resist polished orange as well as "pre-Mamom" in general character, has three radiocarbon dates from associated charcoal that average 628 ± 177 B.C. (MASCA) if one inconsistently late date is eliminated (Ekholm 1969:21, Fig. 10). Either way, the 10-m high Duende structure at Izapa remains the earliest dated pyramid in Eastern Mesoamerica.

A number of the Middle Preclassic II ceremonial centers on the Upper Grijalva River (San Mateo, Vergel, and Finca Acapulco) were abandoned at the close of the Escalera Phase; these terminal occupations included ball courts, pyramids, and huge platform structures (Gussinyer 1972). The ancient abandonment of these three unusual early intact centers (Lowe 1977:224–227, Fig. 9.4) does suggest historical factors at work leading to the close of the Middle Preclassic II Subperiod; we tend to relate these factors to events responsible for the demise of the La Venta Olmec center in Complex A at that site. A slightly later but less permanent lapse in construction after the late Middle Preclassic of all or a principal part of the great San Isidro ceremonial center in the Middle Grijalva basin following the Felisa Phase has been postulated by Lowe (in preparation; see also Lee 1974), and this hiatus in activity may coincide better with the end of La Venta as an important center, falling after the next subperiod.

G. Middle Preclassic III and Beginning of Late Preclassic

The establishment of the Mamom horizon occupation throughout the Maya Lowlands by about 600 B.C. resulted from population expansion and a general move toward ceramic uniformity across much of the central zone of Eastern Mesoamerica. By about 400 B.C. this relative crystallization of culture had produced the full Mamom ceramic sphere in regions of the Pasión, Petén, and Western Belize (Willey 1977b:387–388; Willey, Culbert, and Adams 1967:308, Figs. 1, 4). The full Middle Preclassic-to-Late Preclassic transition can be adequately understood only by including sites remote from the Guatemalan Peten, however, as a comparison of even the incomplete illustrations of pottery form evolution shown in Figures 11.6, and 11.8–11.10 will demonstrate. An interplay of traditions, of exceptional culture-historical portent (see close of section), can be seen (Figure 11.9) in the Southeastern Highlands (Sharer and Gifford 1970:452–454; Sharer 1974). Yucatan and Campeche provide other developmental histories recently discussed by Ball (1977a; 1977b) and Joesink-Mandeville (1973; see also Nelson 1973). Despite such diversity, some ceramic cross-ties can, nevertheless, be seen to relate all of the varied Mixe-Zoque and Maya-area regions at this time.

An early facet of the Mamom Phase suggested originally by R. E. Smith (1955:13–14, Fig. 77, a) on the basis of excavations made prior to 1936, but only recently confirmed and adopted in the literature (Willey, Culbert, and Adams 1967:295), now is seen as related to early Eb Phase (Culbert 1977:30). This early pottery was poorly defined at Uaxactun (refuse in a single deep trench), but is more amply represented in the Eb Complex at nearby Tikal (W. R. Coe 1965). The Eb ceramics (see Figure 11.10) emphasize low-neck water jars—with and without striations and handles and some simple spouts, as well as vertical-wall bowls and thin-wall tecomates each with bolstered lips, and flat-bottom dishes with both flaring and rounded walls (Culbert 1963). The succeeding Tzec Complex, dating to 500–250 B.C. and described by Culbert (1977:29) as being transitional between the Mamom and Chicanel horizons, seems to represent a simplified gamut of styles and forms, in keeping with "a discernible overall trend from ceramic heterogeneity to homogeneity in the three to four hundred years of the Mamom horizon (Willey 1977b:387)." Both Eb and Tzec are common in the Lake Yaxha area, according to a series of test pits and a survey reported by Rice (1976).

Thin-wall tecomates, handled jars, flaring-side plates, resist-painted red-on-buff ware, some surviving Xe types, and the absence of the fine paste Mars Orange ware are said to distinguish the early facet of the San Felix ceramic complex at Altar de Sacrificios (Willey, Culbert, and Adams 1967:294–295; Adams 1971:84–85). A somewhat different list of traits is rather generally shared by the Felisa Phase at San Isidro, Chiapas (see Figure 11.8, upper left), and Complex A Phase IV at La Venta (Figure 11.8, upper right). The Early Francesa Phase at Chiapa de Corzo differs little from the Felisa and La Venta Phase IV complexes except for a lack of known pedestal bases (see Lowe and Mason 1965: Fig. 12, lower two rows except for left center jar and far right chalice).

La Venta itself seems to become an unimportant center after the Middle Preclassic Period, its functions passing to other sites as populations expanded across the breadth of Eastern Mesoamerica. It seems probable, nevertheless, that some of the major Olmec stone monuments, particularly the great relief carvings (the Tres Zapotes Monument C carved stone box and La Venta Stelae 2 and 3) were actually carved and erected, along with much of the huge Complex C pyramid, during some part of the Middle Preclassic III Subperiod (see M. D. Coe 1968b, discussion at end of article). If this is so, then La Venta presents another example of a ceremonial center collapsing at its zenith.

The abandonment of La Venta Complex A (and Complex C also) provides a major historical event related to the conceptual shift from Middle to Late Preclassic positioning in our chronological scheme. Stated in overly simple terms, this shift marks the decline of certain Olmec heartland centers as peripheral communities took on increased ceremonial significance. Until perhaps 200 B.C. or even later, however, some older Olmec centers, notably Tres Zapotes in Veracruz, continued to be as important, to all appearances, as any known Preclassic Maya site in the Lowlands; other centers in Chiapas, Guatemala, and El Salvador, such as Chiapa de Corzo, Izapa, Kaminaljuyu, and Chalchuapa, also continued on their own already well-advanced if abortive trajectories toward Preclassic civilization (Lowe in Green and Lowe 1967:73–74; Lowe 1977:228–240; a brief description of the Izapan civilization and the highland Kaminaljuyu Formative Period is provided by M. D. Coe 1966:60–69; and Chalchuapa's brilliant but equally truncated career is described succinctly by Sharer 1969, 1974).

A late or "Modified Olmec" horizon within the Mixe-Zoque area (Lowe 1977:222–228, Fig. 93) is definable due to dramatic internal cultural changes briefly portrayed for us at La Venta by the offerings in Complex A Phases III and IV and more fully, before its end, by the bulk of the ceramics described for that site by Drucker (1952: Figs. 25–27, 28d-g, 29, 31-32, 34, 36, 38e-j, 41d, 42, Pls. 18, 19a-b, f, 20). By far the majority of the famed La Venta jade celt and figurine offerings, the several equally famed Olmec low-relief stelae and monuments, the basalt column enclosures, sandstone cist tomb, and probably most of the great pyramid are also attributable to this horizon before its close at ca. 400 B.C. (Drucker, Heizer, and Squier 1959:133–189, Appendix 1; Heizer 1971:51–52; Clewlow 1974:180, Table 20).

As might be expected, this late modification of heartland Olmec society, or civilization, involved some continuity of earlier structural features, but in the peripheral southern regions many remarkable new cultural components appeared with revolutionary suddenness at the beginning of the horizon, shortly before or soon after 600 B.C. These innovations included numerous formal architectural platform-plaza complexes established widely across southern Chiapas for the first time (Lowe 1977: Fig. 9.4); the plazas centered around a long mound and facing pyramid, forming a solstice observatory (McDonald n.d.). Accompanying this appearance of formal platform architecture through central Chiapas was a new ceramic technology substituting a highly polished reddish-orange slip for the previous dull finishes so characteristic of the earlier Olmec horizons; many portions of the rather waxy surface include "cloudy," "accidental," or definite geometric resist-painted designs, as discussed briefly in F above and more fully in Lowe 1977 (pp. 223–224).

Though believed to be most abundant across Southern Chiapas (Lowe and Mason 1965: 212, Fig. 11, left center and lower right two vessels; Ekholm 1969: 18, 20; Agrinier 1975c: Figs. 32, 36), cloudy resist ware is spread during the late Middle Preclassic from El Salvador on the southeast to Southern Veracruz on the northwest. At Tres Zapotes in the latter region the type is common in deeper sub-ash levels; it has been labeled there as

Naranja Pulido, and it has a *Nebulosa* or Cloudy variety (Ortíz Ceballos 1975:35–36, 107–10, Figs. 38–48; collections in the Museum of Anthropology, Jalapa, Veracruz). Very similar vessels were common at La Venta, Tabasco (personal observation), where, having lost their slip, they presumably were subsumed under other categories in the analysis by Drucker (1952) of the very poorly preserved La Venta ceramics. At Laguna Zope near Juchitan on the Pacific side of the Isthmus of Tehuantepec, Zeitlin (1976: 20) has reported also the "Usulutan clouding on gloss-orange pottery" as being typical of the Middle Preclassic Goma phase.

Within the Lowland Maya area, a few examples of orange-resist pottery have been reported from Uaxactun (Ricketson and Ricketson 1937: 236; Smith 1955: 60, Fig. 14a, *17*) and Altar de Sacrificios (Adams 1971: 85, Fig. 11) in the Middle Preclassic Mamom sphere of the Peten. Only at Seibal is it common, however, occurring in "refuse . . . in all parts of the site" (Sabloff 1975: 71–74, 76, Figs. 109–118); Sabloff gives by far the best description and illustration of this class of ceramic in print, as the Tierra Mojada Resist and Timax Incised types, in Flores Waxy ware.

With less than 200 of some 2,100 Escoba Mamom Complex sherds, we may presume the Tierra Mojada group at Seibal to be a relatively minor and quite possibly an introduced component or technique. This supposition is strengthened by the minute numbers reported from sites farther into the Peten and by its greater frequency to the south and west. For instance, identical cloudy resist orange pottery found in abundance at Río Blanco on the headwaters of the Río Negro, not far east of Huehuetenango in western highland Guatemala (E. M. Shook collections, Antigua), has been compared by M. D. Coe (1961:79) to Río Blanco Orange, a very minor type with a "milky lustrous sheen" of the Conchas 2 phase at La Victoria on the Pacific coast. For the interior regions, a movement eastward from the uppermost Grijalva Valley in southern Chiapas (where the ware is especially abundant and widespread) through the adjacent interior valleys of western highland Guatemala and then northward may be proposed as a most probable diffusion route, although water transport may also have favored diffusion up the Usumacinta from the Gulf Coast.

Within the southeastern highlands, the Middle Preclassic III Subperiod is best represented by the Kal Phase at Chalchuapa, El Salvador (Sharer and Gifford 1970:445), which is now believed to align with late Las Charcas and the Providencia Phases of Kaminaljuyu dating from about 650 to 400 B.C. (Sharer 1974). The Kal ceramic complex includes examples of the resist-decorated ware just described and a type of true Usulutan and Mars Orange ware as well as large, handled, red-on-buff painted water jars (Figure 11.9, left center). Horizon markers for the Chul and Providencia Phases, transitional to the Late Preclassic Period, include the faceted-shoulder bowl and the common occurrence of true Usulutan resist pottery (Figure 11.9, right center). These two traits appear at Izapa as trade ware during the Frontera

Phase (Lowe, Lee, and Martinez 1976). Labial flanges and nubbin feet accompany these vessels, emphasizing the exotic nature of the southern highlands tradition.

Within the Peninsula of Yucatan, the recently published Dzibilnocac I ceramic complex appears typologically comfortable in the Middle Preclassic III subperiod (Nelson 1973: Figs. 57–62). This placement is sustained by a radiocarbon date (I-4641) of 480 (± 80) B.C. (non-MASCA) that was obtained from charcoal on a deeply buried earthen floor associated with Dzibilnocac I sherds (Nelson 1973:29, 43, 81, 127). This complex lacks handled or striated ollas, which are reported as present in the contemporaneous but regionally distinct Acachen Complex of Becan in Southern Campeche (Ball 1977b:103).

There are few other reliable radiocarbon dates for the Middle Preclassic III Subperiod in the Maya Lowlands, although several rather controversial dates can be accommodated to the 600- to 400-B.C. interval suggested here (see discussions by Adams 1971:146; and Willey 1973:18). A Tikal date for the earlier Eb Phase (P-750) is 683 (± 53) B.C. (MASCA), and another for the contemporaneous Tzec Phase (P-759) is 506 (± 47) B.C. (MASCA); both samples dated were scattered midden charcoal (Stuckenrath, Coe, and Ralph 1966:374–376). Away from the Lowlands, two late Felisa Phase floor-dates from the San Isidro, Chiapas, zone average about 400 (±80) B.C. with the MASCA correction (Lee 1974:5–6). Two other pertinent dates are available for charcoal recovered from the fill immediately behind a stairway flanked by late Olmec relief carvings of a were-jaguar face and stylized serpent head (Navarrete 1977, Lam.2,a) at the base of a pyramidal structure at Tzutzuculi, Tonala, Chiapas (McDonald 1971). These dates (I-5996, 2290 (±95) years; I-5997, 2490 (±90) years) give a MASCA average of 490 (±90) B.C.; associated ceramics indicate a Tzutzuculi II or Escalera-Early Francesa Phase upper limit for the architectural and sculptural complex.

More abundant radiocarbon dates from the Late Preclassic Period of the Maya area often are cited to place the upper limit of the Middle Preclassic Period, with 400 to 300 B.C. being the preferred century for this (Adams 1977, Fig. 1.3). An "intermediate period of transition" would appear to be a more realistic concept for this time, when separate regions made their own peculiar intensifications of widely shared horizon traditions. The Tzec-Chuen ceramic complexes at Tikal (Figure 11.10, center) and the Chul complex at Chalchuapa (Figure 11.9 center) are representative of this transition in the Maya Lowlands and Southeastern Highlands, respectively. In the latter region, a new ceramic style soon became dominant, utilizing the Usulutan technique of decoration (Figure 11.9, upper right). A pottery type or types with multiple-stripe resist lines formed a "major part" of the Chul Complex, and "predominated" the Caynac Complex, at Chalchuapa (Sharer 1972:31), and it comprised 60% of the Uapala Complex and 47% of the Chila Complex at Quelepa (Andrews V 1976:190). At Copan in far western Honduras, Usulutan made up 70% of the Archaic, 55% of the Early Classic, and 20% of the Middle Classic complexes, whereas it comprised only 7.2% of the Eden 1 and 8 to 14% of the Eden 2 complexes at Los Naranjos in Northcentral Honduras (Baudez and Becquelin 1973:183). In Southcentral Honduras the Usulutan pottery composed 24% of the Yarumela 3 Complex and was lacking in the preceding phase (Canby 1951:81). To the west in the Central Guatemala Highlands at Kaminaljuyu, Usulutan pottery constituted only 4% of the Middle Formative Las Charcas Complex and 5% of the Late Formative Providencia Complex, but 15% of the Terminal Formative Miraflores-Arenal complexes (Wetherington 1974).

The above-cited distribution pattern for Usulutan indicates both a center of popularity and probably an origin for the technique in El Salvador or Western Honduras (Baudez and Becquelin 1973:409), but the transitional or developmental stages for this sphere of strong stylistic affiliations are not yet well known in spite of the important beginning work done at Chalchuapa and Quelepa in El Salvador. The technique may owe some inspiration to sites and societies in Southcentral Honduras, where the pre-Usulutan and apparently transitional Middle-to-Late Preclassic Yarumela II Complex of the Comayagua Valley, underlying one of the principal centers in Preclassic Central America, included an unusual or unique emphasis upon pattern-burnished vertical striping on jar necks and bowl walls (Canby 1951:81). This trait of multiple-line burnishing may logically have been joined with the resist-painting techniques of the apparently southward-moving, late Middle Preclassic ceramic tradition of the Isthmus to contribute toward the perfection of the formal, Usulutan multiple-brush striping style in resist paint or slip. Withal, only pending and future research results will clarify the chronologically significant evolution of regional and horizonal styles within the almost 1000-year-long Usulutan tradition (see especially Sharer in press).

Farther west in the greater Isthmus region, Usulutan pottery appears only as trade ware, with occasional offering vessels and rare sherds being recovered from Francesa to Istmo-Phase deposits at Chiapa de Corzo, for instance. At this site, the ceramic transition from Middle to Late Preclassic may best be seen in the burial offerings of the Francesa and Guanacaste Phases (Agrinier 1964:10–37); these regional complexes are thought to represent a local Mixe-Zoque pottery distinct from ceramics of the Maya Lowlands Chicanel sphere which occur in elite domestic and burial situations only (cf. Lowe and Agrinier 1960, Figs. 18–28). The Northern Yucatan Komchen Complex and the Northern Belize Cocos Complex also demonstrate regional variations of the Chicanel Horizon ceramic styles (Ball 1977b:114–116; Pring 1976b:32–33). Belize in slightly later times would again draw strong trait diffusion, and perhaps immigrants, from the south (Floral Park Complex at Barton Ramie—Sharer and Gifford 1970:454–461; see also Pring 1976b:35, 39–40 and Ball in Gifford 1976:326–327), and even during the Late Preclassic Mount Hope phase, Central Belize was remarkably isolated culturally from the remainder of the Maya Lowlands, according to Ball (in Gifford 1976:326).

By the second or first century B.C., large architectural complexes had been constructed in most regions of Eastern Mesoamerica, during a period of intense competition with restricted interaction. Within the first century A.D., regional cultural frontiers and communications lines seem to have been well established, however, and most-favored regions passed the threshhold of the brief Protoclassic Period rise toward Maya civilization.

III. LATER MAYA CHRONOLOGY

As reasonable a consensus as can be ascertained of the Protoclassic, Classic, and Postclassic sequences in the Maya Territory is reflected in Figures 11.2–11.5, and the reader is referred to authors cited therein for details. An earlier and revised article by Gordon Willey (1971), "An Archaeological Frame of Reference for Maya Cultural History," should also be consulted. Up-to-date discussions of the relationships between Middle and Late Preclassic, Protoclassic, and Early Classic Period Maya site components for most regions are to be found in the recent book "Origins of Maya Civilization" (Adams 1977), with a concise and insightful Summary View provided by Willey (1977b). The Classic and Postclassic Periods of the Maya civilization are carefully reviewed in the earlier companion volume "The Maya Collapse" (Culbert 1973). The closing Endnote (B) to this chapter offers recent thinking regarding the Maya calendar correlation problem. One other aspect of the Chronological Tables, Figures 11.2–11.5, does remain to be explained here, and that is the addition of two Period divisions to the Classic Era that have not been customary, namely the Middle Classic and the Terminal Classic.

A. Classic Era Period Divisions

The increasingly acute dating of certain stylistic horizon markers—ceramic, iconographic, and socioeconomic—has resulted in the recent addition of new periods to the Eastern Mesoamerica chronology. The two most generally accepted of these new time horizons are the Middle Classic and Terminal Classic period subdivisions of the Classic Era.

The Middle Classic Period adopted in Figures 11.2–11.5 conforms to part of the greater Middle Classic Horizon proposed by Parsons (1969:157–184). Corresponding only to, and combining, the last 100 years of Parsons' Teotihuacan Horizon and the first 100 years of his Teotihuacanoid Horizon (1969: Fig. 16), the period is indicated here in round numbers as enduring from A.D. 450 to 650. Some future adjustment of these dates may result from further research and consensus.

A middle subdivision of the Classic Era appears to be a logical and useful temporal unit; it is a time of peculiar historical significance in much of our area. Many of the major sites in Western Chiapas, for instance, were abandoned during or at the close of this period (Lowe and Mason 1965:226; Agrinier 1970:81–82). A similar apparent abandonment has been noted at Seibal on the Río Pasión, Guatemala, from about A.D. 500 to 700 or 750 (A. L. Smith and Willey 1968:151; Willey 1970:320; Sabloff 1975:15, 233–234). Contemporaneously, nearby Altar de Sacrificios was experiencing first a maximum decline and then a cultural peak (the Veremos and Chixoy phases—Adams 1971:5; cf. chart in Willey 1970:319, Fig. 1). In the Guatemalan central highlands, the Middle Classic Period corresponds fully with the Esperanza Phase, which saw an intrusive Teotihuacan ceremonial and trade center established at Kaminaljuyu (Kidder, Jennings, and Shook 1946; Borhegyi 1965:23–30; Sanders and Michels 1969). The Teotihuacan style is clearly dominant also at Izapa at this time (Lee 1973), as well as at Mirador in Central Chiapas before that site was abandoned as a ceremonial center (Peterson 1963:73–75, 124, Figs. 10, h–j, 13, 109; Agrinier 1975b, n.d.).

Apparently reflecting strong civic–religious pressures of the Teotihuacan period of influence (or of its withdrawal), the Middle Classic Period includes an inscriptional hiatus in the Maya lowlands (Willey 1974). Almost no dated monuments were erected between A.D. 535 and 600, and none were erected at Tikal between A.D. 550 and 700 (Parsons 1969:159). The Middle Classic Period almost everywhere reflects the turmoil and political or economic realignments associated with the final rise and fall of Classic Period Teotihuacan and its apparently far-flung territorial involvements. The Middle Classic Period in much of Eastern Mesoamerica is thus a time of established (not necessarily original) contact with Central Mexico, followed by times of often violent reactions and reorientations. Even at sites where there was not the decline or outright discontinuity of occupation noted at Mirador, Chiapa de Corzo, and Seibal, a Middle Classic Period ties together the Early Classic and Late Classic configurations, as in reality they should be; many authors comment upon the continuity evident (Willey, Culbert, and Adams 1967:300–301):

Tikal: Transitional complexes show up at Tikal with an Ik–Imix transition detectable in burial pottery and a Manik–Ik transition also possible. There is a coexistence of Early Classic and Late Classic monochrome types during the latter transition.

Altar de Sacrificios: As at Tikal, there is a strong continuity between Tzakol 3-like material and Tepeu 1 (Veremos and Chixoy locally).

Piedras Negras: The Balche Complex corresponds to the early part of Tepeu 1 in content but shows a continuation of the Tzakol Horizon Aguila Orange type.

Yucatan: At Dzibilchaltun, the Copo Complex, which had started toward the end of the Tzakol Horizon, continues through both the Tepeu 1-2 and the Tepeu 3 horizons.

The recognition of a Middle Classic Period, which to all appearances reflects true historical factors, makes for a less arbitrary and less artificial chronology (for a full discussion of the upsetting "Mexican influences" in the Maya area, see W. R. Coe 1965:34–41; Parsons 1969:157–169). The hiatus in Maya sculpture from about A.D. 524 and the succeeding slightly changed sculptural style characterizing the period from A.D. 593 to 692 (unfortunately labeled the "Late Classic Formative Phase") is discussed at length by Proskouriakoff (1950:111–124).

Figures 11.2–11.5 also include a Terminal Classic Period. This chronological division was first defined by Sabloff as follows:

> The designation "Terminal Late Classic" refers here to the century dating from 10.0.0.0.0 to 10.5.0.0.0, in the Mayan calendar, or from about A.D. 830 to 930 (11.16.0.0.0 Correlation). This is the period which corresponds, approximately, to the Tepeu 3 phase at Uaxactun. By some authorities, it is considered incipient Postclassic. From a strictly chronological viewpoint, the whole question depends on the date one chooses on the time scale at which to draw a Classic–Postclassic dividing line. Leaving aside, for now, the developmental or cultural configurational implications of this dividing line, we are inclined to consider the A.D. 830 to 930 time span as the final century of the Lowland Maya Classic period—hence the name, "Terminal Late Classic" [1970:360 n.2].

More recently, Sabloff and others (1974) and Ball(1977a)have widened this period to the 200 years from A.D. 800 to 1000, and labeled it Transition and Terminal Classic, respectively. The latter practice is followed in Figures 11.2–11.5. The Terminal Classic thus encompasses the pre-Florescent Transition of Andrews IV (1965b: Table 4) and includes most of the Puuc architectural style (see the 9.18.0.0.0 to 10.8.0.0.0 or A.D. 790 to 987 duration suggested by Andrews V in the endnote to this chapter).

B. Endnote: The Northern Maya Lowlands Sequence

E. Wyllys Andrews V

E. Wyllys Andrews IV, of the Middle American Research Institute at Tulane University, began excavations at the site of Dzibilchaltun, in Northwestern Yucatan, in 1956. At that time a correlation of the Maya and Christian calendars at about 11.16.0.0.0 was widely accepted. Indeed, Andrews was one of the strongest proponents of this correlation—his 1940 paper on astronomy and the Maya calendar in *The Maya and Their Neighbors* provided well-received evidence that an earlier 12.9.0.0.0 was unacceptable as an exact solution and that astronomical evidence could well support a later correlation at 11.16.0.0.0.

At Dzibilchaltun, however, Andrews' excavations indicated a long, and partially unexpected, sequence following the Classic Period in the southern lowlands. From 1957 until 1971 he believed that an 11.16.0.0.0 solution left insufficient time for the complex sequence of cultural developments in Yucatan after the Classic Period, and he suggested in many papers that Maya archaeologists consider a correlation that would allow a greater span for the development of Maya culture. Most radiocarbon determinations from the northern Maya area have seemed to support him in this opinion. Andrews' arguments for an earlier correlation have rested on two major judgments of the archaeological record in Northern Yucatan:

1. A period of 150 years must be allowed for a transition period between the Modified Florescent and the Decadent periods. At Dzibilchaltun this intermediate period saw the dominance of black-on-cream pottery, which had previously been encountered superficially at Chichen Itza and in early levels at Mayapan.
2. At Dzibilchaltun the Pure Florescent, characterized by the Puuc architectural style, followed the end of Tepeu 2 and was in fact separated from the Early Period (Classic) architecture by a long transition period. In one of his last papers Andrews assigned the beginning of the Pure Florescent to a position at 10.6.0.0.0 in the Maya long count (1968:39). A subsequent development of 200 years for the Puuc sites could only with difficulty be accommodated in an 11.16.0.0.0 correlation.

The final reports on the archaeology of Dzibilchaltun are now in preparation, and my present comments on the above questions must be considered interim statements. In all cases these remarks represent the thinking of the present author and should not be regarded as reflecting opinions of E. Wyllys Andrews IV.

Black-on-cream pottery at Chichen Itza derived primarily from above-floor refuse in limited areas, although several small building additions contained sherds of this ware. At Mayapan, Black-on-cream appeared near the center of the site in early levels, and here it is always associated with Mayapan Red Ware. At Dzibilchaltun, where Chichen Slate is relatively rare, Black-on-cream is a major ware found in poststructural refuse from buildings used into the Decadent Period and also found in stratigraphic samples from a small vaulted building near the center of the site (Structure 39). Ceramic lots from this structure indicate that Black-on-cream was a major ware considerably before the arrival of Mayapan Red Ware and Mayapan modeled censers at Dzibilchaltun. The presence of Black-on-cream in sealed lots antedating Mayapan Red Ware led Andrews to suggest a transition period of 150 years following the disappearance of Chichen Slate and preceding the appearance of Mayapan Red Ware.

Michael P. Simmons, who is preparing the final report on the post-Formative ceramics from Dzibilchaltun, believes that Black-on-cream cannot be limited to the period following the Modified Florescent ("Toltec") Period. Whereas others have thought that Puuc Slate was replaced by Chichen Slate, which was in turn replaced by Black-on-cream, he views Chichen Slate as a ceramic unit geographically centered around Chichen Itza itself. Its presence at other sites in Northern Yucatan may well be the result of trade. At Dzibilchaltun, Simmons sees an indigenous sequence from Puuc

Slate to Xlacah Slate (a coarse slateware) to Black-on-cream, with considerable overlap between adjacent members of the sequence, and he believes that Black-on-cream pottery made its appearance near the middle of the Modified Florescent.

The stratigraphy at Structure 39 bears out Simmons' new interpretation of Yucatan ceramic history. Chichen Slate appeared in most ceramic units of the Structure 39 complex, and in every unit it was associated with larger quantities of Xlacah Slate and Black-on-cream. Chichen Slate was very likely always a minor type at Dzibilchaltun, and its appearance may not have long preceded Black-on-cream; in fact, Structure 39-sub, which contains a large amount of Xlacah Slate and Black-on-cream in its fill, included only traces of Chichen Slate. This reinterpretation of the position of Black-on-cream avoids the necessity of a 150-year "Black-on-cream Transition" between the Modified Florescent and Decadent periods.

Early Period II architecture at Dzibilchaltun has been securely cross-dated by trade polychromes to Tepeu 1-2. The immediately subsequent "Transitional" architecture (e.g., Structure 57, the "Standing Temple") is equally surely cross-dated to the last half of Tepeu 2 (ca. 9.16.0.0.0–9.19.0.0.0), and buildings utilizing true Puuc veneer masonry at Dzibilchaltun unquestionably follow 9.19.0.0.0, the end of Tepeu 2. Andrews allowed 140 years (9.19.0.0.0–10.6.0.0.0) between Structure 57 and the beginning of Puuc architecture. This gap is probably excessive.

Structure A-3 at Seibal, Guatemala, utilizes true Puuc veneer masonry in walls and vaults. Five Initial Series dates on stelae associated with the building read 10.1.0.0.0, and a Calendar Round date in stucco, probably from the upper facade, reads 10.0.0.0.0. The stucco date may have been altered by now missing elements to correspond to the dates on the stelae. This type of masonry originated hundreds of miles to the north, and we must allow several katuns for the previous evolution of Puuc architecture in its homeland.

At Oxkintok, Yucatan, a period of Puuc architecture postdates buildings characterized by cruder wall stones and cantilevered slab vaults. The masonry of these earlier buildings is identical to that of Andrews' Early Period "Transition" at Dzibilchaltun and other northern sites and should therefore date to late Tepeu 2. Oxkintok, far from exhibiting a large gap between the two masonry types, indicates that the two overlap. Structure 2-B-8, a portal vault, has a true Puuc wall and vault, but the north room adjacent to the vault, built at the same time, is of "Transitional"masonry. The walls below the spring include carefully cut Puuc facing stones, used with considerable spalling, which contrast dramatically with other rough wall stones and with the slab vault. The inescapable conclusion is that on the northern fringes of the Puuc hills the two masonry styles coincide in time.

The acropolis at Edzna, Campeche, near the southwestern corner of the Puuc area, shows a mixture of Puuc and earlier architectural styles. The rooms of the main pyramid and temple are of both Puuc boot-shaped stones and slabs, although the two types never appear in the same room. The combination of veneer walls and slab vaults is a transitional feature.

The main temple atop the pyramid, representing one construction period, contains five rooms. Four have corbeled slab vaults, but the vault of the east room is a true Puuc veneer. On the second level, Room 15 has a corbeled vault above a true veneer wall; directly behind it the earlier Room 17 has a beautifully finished, slightly convex vault of Puuc boot-shaped stone.

The simple two-member medial and superior moldings, and the absence of Puuc mosaic compositions on the upper facades, of the main pyramid at Edzna suggest a date early in the Pure Florescent for the latest construction. Here, as at Oxkintok, early Puuc architecture and slab vault construction seem to overlap in time.

Andrews visited Yaxcopoil, a large site about 30 km south of Merida, in 1942. He described in detail a series of adjoining vaulted rooms (the Aka'na) which span a transition from Early Period II (Tepeu 1-2) into the Pure Florescent (1965a:313, Fig. 18). Of Andrews' three superimposed construction periods the third, of late Puuc veneer masonry and sculpture showing non-Classic Maya influence, has today fallen, but the first two remain.

The interior and exterior walls of the first set of rooms are faced by a veneer of variable quality. Although the vaults are of rough slabs, the end walls have false springs with fine veneer stones for several courses above them. This advanced feature suggests a construction time shortly following Structure 57 at Dzibilchaltun (about the end of Tepeu 2). The four later rooms composing the east side of the Aka'na have an interior wall facing identical to that of the earlier building (the outer facade has peeled off since 1942), but the latter's vault stones are carefully beveled and tapered. They do not, however, have the fine, boot-shaped tenons of true Puuc vault stones, so that the second phase of construction probably dates to the very beginning of the Pure Florescent or a time immediately preceding it.

A long interval could not have separated the two building phases. Exterior walls of the earlier rooms were covered by only one coat of stucco, to judge from protected sections of the upper facade. When the east range of rooms was added, this finely modeled and painted stucco was still in excellent condition, indicating that at Yaxcopoil crude slab vaults preceded vaults of beveled and tapered veneer stones by very few years.

These observations, in conjunction with other evidence from the northern lowlands, lead me to suggest a beginning of Puuc veneer masonry late in the ninth cycle, possibly around 9.17.0.0.0 or 9.18.0.0.0. Present evidence substantiates a beginning neither as early as the start of Tepeu 2 nor as late as 10.6.0.0.0. If the Pure Florescent (the Puuc architectural style) begins about 9.17.0.0.0, 220 years are allowed for its growth, and we do not need the expanded chronological scale of a 12.9.0.0.0 correlation. Andrews' Transition, between Early Period II and Pure Florescent, falls in the last katuns of the ninth cycle and probably continues into the first few decades of the tenth at some sites.

Clearly, the vast bulk of Puuc architecture in Yucatan and Campeche postdates the end of the Tepeu 2 ceramic subphase in the Peten. Late Puuc architecture, represented, for example, by the latest constructions at Uxmal, is replete with Central Mexican stylistic motifs, as is much of the excavated Pure Florescent architecture at Dzibilchaltun. This late stylistic horizon probably follows 10.3.0.0.0 and is possibly much later.

Twenty-two radiocarbon dates from the northern and central lowlands (not including sample reruns, which have invariably supported the previous determinations) bear on the correlation problem.[1] Of five dates from Chichen Itza, four support a 12.9.0.0.0 and one supports either correlation. Two dates from Uxmal indicate a 12.9.0.0.0, and one suggests an 11.16.0.0.0. The single date from Sayil suggests a 12.9.0.0.0. Of the two dates from Dzibilchaltun that bear on the problem, one supports an 11.16.0.0.0, and the other supports either. Two important dates from Balancanche Cave, near Chichen Itza, have been rerun, providing almost identical dates on the second counting, and these probably indicate a correlation at 12.9.0.0.0.

In the central lowlands, nine recent dates from the Rio Bec sites of Becan and Chicanna provide some slight additional data on the problem. Five dates support an 11.16.0.0.0 correlation, one date supports a 12.9.0.0.0, and three dates may indicate either solution. These depend for their interpretation on Joseph W. Ball's (1977a:186–187) analysis of the Becan and Chicanna pottery.

If all 22 dates are used, we are faced with 7 favoring a correlation at 11.16.0.0.0 and 10 favoring the earlier 12.9.0.0.0 correlation; 5 additional dates are equivocal. From Yucatan, only 2 dates support the later correlation, 9 the earlier, and 2 either. It appears that, given the Peten dates favoring an 11.16.0.0.0 solution, radiocarbon determinations from the Maya area will not solve the correlation problem for us.

I believe the archaeological data from the northern and central Maya lowlands can be accommodated to either an 11.16.0.0.0 or a 12.9.0.0.0 correlation. They do not appear to force an earlier correlation at 12.9.0.0.0. Nevertheless, because radiocarbon dates are presently contradictory, a 12.9.0.0.0 correlation should not be discarded out of hand.

BIBLIOGRAPHY

Adams, R.E.W.

1971 The ceramics of Altar de Sacrificos. *Papers of the Peabody Museum of Archaeology and Ethnology 63* (1).

[1]Most of these dates are published in Andrews IV (1965b:63, Table 5).

1972 Maya highland prehistory; new data and implications. *In* Studies in the archaeology of Mexico and Guatemala, edited by J.A. Graham, pp. 1–21. *Contributions of the University of California Archaeological Research Facility* No. 16.

Adams, R. E. W. (Ed.)

1977 *The origins of Maya civilization.* Albuquerque, New Mexico: University of New Mexico Press.

Agrinier, P.

1964 The archaeological burials at Chiapa de Corzo and their furniture. *Papers of the New World Archaeological Foundation* No. *16.*

1969a Dos tumbas tardias y otros descubrimientos en Chinkultic. *Boletin Instituto Nacional de Antropología e Historia 36*:21–28.

1969b Excavations at San Antonio, Chiapas, Mexico. *Papers of the New World Archaeological Foundation* No. *24.*

1970 Mound 20, Mirador, Chiapas, Mexico. *Papers of the New World Archaeological Foundation No. 28.*

1975a Un Complejo Ceramico, Tipo Olmeca, del Preclasico Temprano en El Mirador, Chiapas. *XIII Mesa Redonda, Sociedad Mexicana de Antropologia,* Vol. II.

1975b Mounds 9 and 10 at Mirador, Chiapas, Mexico. *Papers of the New World Archaeological Foundation* No. 39.

1975c Mound 1A, Chiapa de Corzo, Chiapas, Mexico. *Papers of the New World Archaeological Foundation* No. 37.

n.d. Classic Period Occupation in the Zoque Area of Chiapas and the Teotihuacan Style. *In* Cultural ecology and human geography in Southern Chiapas: A Symposium. *Papers of the New World Archaeological Foundation No. 42.* (in press)

Andrews, E. W., IV

1940 Chronology and astronomy in the Maya area. In *The Maya and their neighbors,* edited by C. Hay, *et al.* Pp. 150–161. New York: Appleton-Century-Crofts.

1960 Excavation at Dzibilchaltun, northwestern Yucatan, Mexico. *Proceedings of the American Philosophical Society 104:*254–265.

1965a Archaeology and prehistory in the northern Maya lowlands. In *Handbook of Middle American Indians,* edited by R. Wauchope, Volume 2. Austin: University of Texas Press.

1965b Progress report on the 1960–1964 field seasons, National Geographic Society—Tulane University Dzibilchaltun program. *Middle American Research Institute Publication 31:*23–67.

1968 Dzibilchaltun: A northern Maya metropolis. *Archaeology 21*(1):36–47.

1971 The emergence of civilization in the Maya lowlands. *University of California Archaeological Research Facility, Contribution* No. 11:85–96.

Andrews, E. Wyllys, V

1976 The Archaeology of Quelepa, El Salvador. *Middle American Research Institute Publication* 42.

Armillas, P.

1948 A sequence of cultural development in Mesoamerica. *In* A reappraisal of Peruvian archeology, edited by W. C. Bennett. *Memoirs of the Society for American Archaeology* No. *4.*

Ball, J. W.

1977a The Archaeological ceramics of Becan, Campeche, Mexico. *Middle American Research Institute Publication* 43.

1977b The rise of the Northern Maya chiefdoms: A socioprocessual analysis. In *The origins of Maya civilization*, edited by R. E. W. Adams. Albuquerque, New Mexico: University of New Mexico Press. Pp. 101–132.

Baudez, C. F.
1966 Nieveaux ceramiques au Honduras: Une reconsideration de l'evolution culturelle. *Journal de la Société des Americanistes 55*(2):299–342.

Baudez, C. F., and P. Becquelin
1973 *Archéologie de los Naranjos, Honduras*. Mexico City, Mexico: Mission Archéologique Francaise au Mexique.

Becquelin, P.
1969 Archeologie de la region de Nebaj (Guatemala). *Memoires de l'institut d'Ethnologie 12*.

Berger, R., J. A. Graham, and R. F. Heizer
1967 A reconsideration of the age of the La Venta site. *In* Studies in Olmec archaeology. *Contributions of the University of California Archaeological Research Facility* No. *3*:1–24.

Berger, R., and W. F. Libby
1966 UCLA radiocarbon dates V. *Radiocarbon 8*:467–497.

Borhegyi, S. F. de
1965a Archeological synthesis of the Guatemala highlands. In *Handbook of Middle American Indians,* edited by R. Wauchope, Volume 2. Austin: University of Texas Press.

Brainerd, G. W.
1951 Early ceramic horizons in Yucatan. In *The civilizations of ancient America*, edited by S. Tax. New York: Cooper Square. Pp. 72–78.
1958 The archaeological ceramics of Yucatan. *University of California Anthropological Records 19*.

Brockington, D. L.
1967 The ceramic history of Santa Rosa, Chiapas, Mexico. *Papers of the New World Archeological Foundation* No. *23*.

Bryan, A.
1971 Current Research: Mesoamerica. *American Antiquity 36*(2):236.

Bullen, R. P., and W. W. Plowden, Jr.
1963 Preceramic archaic sites in the highlands of Honduras. *American Antiquity 28*(3):382–385.

Butler, M.
1940 A pottery sequence from the Alta Verapaz, Guatemala. In *The Maya and their neighbors,* edited by C. L. Hay, *et al*. New York: Appleton-Century-Crofts. Pp. 250–267.

Canby, J. S.
1951 Possible chronological implications of the long ceramic sequence recovered at Yarumela, Spanish Honduras. In *The civilizations of ancient America,* edited by S. Tax. New York: Cooper Square. Pp. 79–85.

Ceja, J. F.
1974 Coatan, una provincia preclásica temprana en el Soconusco de Chiapas. Paper presented at the 41st International Congress of Americanists, Mexico City. (*Papers of the New World Archaeological Foundation,* No. *42,* in press).

Clewlow, C. W., Jr.
1974 A stylistic and chronological study of Olmec monumental sculpture. *Contributions of the University of California Archaeological Research Facility* No. *19*.

Coe, M. D.
1960a Archaeological linkages with North and South America at La Victoria, Guatemala. *American Anthropologist 62*:363–393.
1960b A fluted point from highland Guatemala. *American Antiquity 25*:412–413.

1961 La Victoria: An early site of the Pacific coast of Guatemala. *Papers of the Peabody Museum of Archaeology and Ethnology 53.*
1963 Cultural development in southeastern Mesoamerica. *In* Aboriginal cultural development in Latin America: An interpretative review, edited by B. J. Meggers and C. Evans. *Smithsonian Miscellaneous Collections 146*(1):27–44.
1966 *The Maya. Ancient peoples and places.* Mexico, D. F.: Lara.
1968a San Lorenzo and the Olmec civilization. In *Dumbarton Oaks conference on the Olmec,* edited by E. Benson. Washington, D.C.: Dumbarton Oaks. Pp. 41–78.
1968b *America's first civilization.* Washington: Smithsonian Institution of Washington Press.
1970 The archaeological sequence at San Lorenzo Tenochtitlan, Veracruz, Mexico. *Contributions of the University of California Archaeological Research Facility* No. 8:21–40.
1976 Early Steps in the Evolution of Maya Writing. In *Origins of religious art and iconography in Preclassic Mesoamerica,* edited by H. B. Nicholson. Los Angeles: UCLA Latin America Publications. Pp. 107–122.

Coe, M. D., and K. V. Flannery
1967 Early cultures and human ecology in south coastal Guatemala. *Smithsonian Contributions to Anthropology 3.*

Coe, M. D., R. A. Diehl and M. Stuiver
1967 Olmec civilization, Veracruz, Mexico: Dating of the San Lorenzo phase. *Science 155*(3768):1399–1401.

Coe, W. R.
1965 Tikal: Ten years of study of a Maya ruin in the lowlands of Guatemala. *Expedition 8* (1).
1967 *Tikal, a handbook of the ancient Maya ruins.* Philadelphia: Univ. of Pennsylvania.

Culbert, T. P.
1963 Ceramic research at Tikal, Guatemala. *Ceramica de Cultura Maya 1* (2–3): 34–42.
1965 Ceramic history of the central highlands of Chiapas, Mexico. *Papers of the New World Archaeological Foundation* No. *19.*
1973 *The Classic Maya Collapse* (edited by T. Patrick Culbert). University of New Mexico Press, Albuquerque.
1977 Early Maya Development at Tikal, Guatemala. In *The origins of Maya Civilization,* edited by R. E. W. Adams. Albuquerque: University of New Mexico Press. Pp. 27–43.
n. d. Tikal Ceramic Sequence; preliminary work sheets (mimeograph).

Delgado, A.
1965 Excavations at Santa Rosa, Chiapas, Mexico. *Papers of the New World Archaeological Foundation* No. *17.*

Dixon, K. A.
1959 Ceramics from two Preclassic periods at Chiapa de Corzo, Chiapas, Mexico. *Papers of the New World Archaeological Foundation* No. *5.*

Drucker, P.
1948 Preliminary notes on an archaeological survey of the Chiapas coast. *Middle American Research Records 1* (2).
1952 La Venta, Tabasco; a study of Olmec ceramics and art. *Bureau of American Ethnology Bulletin 153.*

Drucker, P., R. F. Heizer, and R. J. Squier
1959 Excavations at La Venta, Tabasco, 1955. *Bureau of American Ethnology Bulletin 170.*

Ekholm, S. M
1969 Mound 30a and the early preclassic ceramic sequence at Izapa, Chiapas, Mexico. *Papers of the New World Archaeological Foundation* No. *25.*

Evans, C., and B. J. Meggers
1966 Mesoamerica and Ecuador. In *Handbook of Middle American Indians,* edited by R. Wauchope, Volume 4. Austin: Univ. of Texas Press. Pp. 243–264.
Ferree, L.
1971 Excavations at San Jose de Rio, Tabasco, Mexico. Mimeograph of article published in *American Philosophical Society Yearbook 1971.* Pp. 578–580.
Flannery, K. V.
1968 The Olmec and the Valley of Oaxaca: A model for interregional interaction in formative times. In *Dumbarton Oaks conference on the Olmec,* edited by E. Benson. Washington: Dumbarton Oaks. Pp. 79–118.
Folan, W. J.
1960 Un botellon monopodio del centro de Yucatan, Mexico. *Estudios de Cultura Maya 8:*67–77.
Gifford, J. C.
1976 Prehistoric pottery analysis and the ceramics of Barton Ramie in the Belize Valley. *Peabody Museum Memoirs 18.* Cambridge: Harvard University.
Gordon, G. B.
1898 Caverns of Copan. *Memoirs of the Peabody Museum 1*(5).
Graham, J. A., and R. Berger
1972 Radiocarbon dates from Copan, Honduras. *In* Studies in the archaeology of Mexico and Guatemala, edited by J. A. Graham. *Contributions of the University of California Archaeological Research Facility* No. *16.* Pp. 37–40.
Green, D. F., and G. W. Lowe
1967 Altamira and Padre Piedra, early preclassic sites in Chiapas, Mexico. *Papers of the New World Archaeological Foundation* No. *20.*
Gruhn, R. and A. L. Bryan
1967 An archaeological survey of the Chichicastenango area of Highland Guatemala. *Ceramica de Cultura Maya et al.* No. 9:75–119.
n.d. Los Tapiales: A Paleo-Indian campsite in the Guatemalan Highlands. Proceedings of the American Philosophical Society. Philadelphia. In press.
Gussinyer, J.
1972 Primera temporada de salvamento arquelogico en la presa de la Angostura. *ICACH,* Tuxtla Gutierrez, Chiapas.
Hallinan, P. S., R. D. Ambro, and J. F. O'Connell
1968 La Venta ceramics, 1968. Appendix I of the 1968 investigations at La Venta by R. F. Heizer, J. A. Graham and L. K. Napton. *Contributions of the University of California Archaeological Research Facility 5:*155–170.
Hammond, N.
1977a The earliest Maya. *Scientific American 236*(3):116–133.
1977b Ex Oriente Lux: A view from Belize. In *The origins of Maya civilization,* edited by R. E. W. Adams. Albuquerque: University of New Mexico Press. Pp. 45–76.
Hammond, N., D. Pring, R. Berger, V. R. Switsur, and A. P. Ward
1976 Radiocarbon chronology for early Maya occupation at Cuello, Belize. *Nature 260*(5552):579–581.
n.d. Maya Formative radiocarbon chronology: New dates from Belize. Manuscript prepared for publication in *Science,* 1977.
Heizer, R. F.
1971 Commentary on the Olmec Region and Oaxaca. *Contributions of the University of California Archaeological Facility* No. *11*:55–69.
Heizer, R. F., J. A. Graham and L. K. Napton
1968 The 1968 investigations at La Venta. *Contributions of the University of California Archaeological Research Facility* No. *5*:127–154.

Hubbs, C. L., G. S. Bien and H. E. Suess
1963 The La Jolla natural radiocarbon measurements III. *Radiocarbon 5*:254–272.
Joesink-Mandeville, L. R. V.
1973 Yucatan and the Chenes during the Formative: A comparative synthesis. *Katunab 8*(2):1–38.
Joesink-Mandeville, L. R. V. and S. Meluzin
1976 Olmec-Maya Relationships: Olmec Influence in Yucatan. In *Origins of religious art and iconography in Preclassic Mesoamerica,* edited by H. B. Nicholson. Los Angeles: U.C.L.A. Latin American Center Publication. Pp. 87–105.
Johnson, F., and R. S. MacNeish
1972 Chronometric dating. In *The prehistory of the Tehuacan Valley.* Edited by F. Johnson. Volume 4, Austin: Univ. of Texas Press. Pp. 3–55.
Kidder, A. V.
1958 Middle American archaeology since 1906. *In* Middle American anthropology (special symposium of the American Anthropological Association). *Social Science Monographs 5*:1–10.
Kidder, A. V., and J. E.
1938 The correlation of Maya and Christian chronologies. *In* Cooperation in research. *Carnegie Institution of Washington Publication 501.*
Kidder, A. V., J. D. Jennings, and E. M. Shook
1946 Excavations at Kaminaljuyu, Guatemala. *Carnegie Institution of Washington Publication 561.*
Lee, T. A., Jr.
1969 The artifacts of Chiapa de Corzo, Chiapas, Mexico. *Papers of the New World Archaeological Foundation* No. *26.*
1973 The post-formative phase sequence at Izapa, Chiapas, Mexico. *Estudios de Cultura Maya 9*:75–84.
1974 Mound 4, San Isidro, Chiapas, Mexico. *Papers of the New World Archaeological Foundation* No. *34.*
Longyear, J. M.
1951 An historical interpretation of Copan archaeology. In *The civilizations of ancient America,* edited by S. Tax, New York: 29th Congress of Americanists. Pp. 86–92.
1952 Copan ceramics: A study of southeastern Maya pottery. *Carnegie Institution of Washington Publication 597.*
Lorenzo, J. L.
1955 Los concheros de la costa de Chiapas. *Anales del Instituto Nacional de Antropologia e Historia 7*:41–50.
Lothrop, S. K.
1936 Zacualpa, a study of ancient Quiche artifacts. *Carnegie Institution of Washington Publication 472.*
1961 Archaeology, then and now. In *Essays in Pre-Columbian art and archaeology,* by S. K. Lothrop *et al.* Cambridge: Harvard University.
Lowe, G. W.
1959 Archaeological exploration of the Upper Grijalva River; Chiapas, Mexico. *Papers of the New World Archaeological Foundation* No. *2.*
1962 Mound 5 and minor excavations, Chiapa de Corzo, Chiapas, Mexico. *Papers of the New World Archaeological Foundation* No. *12.*
1966 Current research: Southeastern Mesoamerica. *American Antiquity 31*(3):453–463.
1969 The Olmec horizon occupations of Mound 20 at San Isidro in the middle Grijalva region of Chiapas. Unpublished manuscript thesis, University of the Americas, Mexico.
1971 The civilizational consequences of varying degrees of agriculture and ceramic depen-

dency within the basic ecosystems of Mesoamerica. *In* Observations on the emergence of civilization in Mesoamerica, edited by R. F. Heizer, J. A. Graham, and C. W. Clewlow, Jr. *Contributions of the University of California Archaeological Research Facility* No. *11*:212–249.

1975 The Early Preclassic Barra Phase of Altamira, Chiapas; A review with new data. *Papers of the New World Archaeological Foundation,* No. *38*.

1977 The Mixe-Zoque as Competing Neighbors of the Early Lowland Maya. In *The origins of Maya Civilization,* edited by R. E. W. Adams. Albuquerque: University of New Mexico Press. Pp. 197–248.

Lowe, G. W., and P. Agrinier

1960 Mound 1, Chiapa de Corzo, Chiapas, Mexico. *Papers of the New World Archaeological Foundation* No. *8*.

Lowe, G. W., and J. A. Mason

1965 Archaeological survey of the Chiapas coast, highlands, and upper Grijalva Basin. In *Handbook of Middle American Indians,* edited by R. Wauchope, Volume 2. Austin: Univ. of Texas Press. Pp. 195–236.

Lowe, G. W., T. A. Lee, Jr., and E. Martínez

1976 Izapa: An introduction to the ruins and monuments. *Papers of the New World Archaeological Foundation* No. *31*.

MacNeish, R. S.

1962 *Second annual report of the Tehuacan archaeological-botanical project.* Andover: Robert S. Peabody Foundation for Archaeology.

MacNeish, R. S., and F. A. Peterson

1962 The Santa Marta rock shelter, Ocozocoautla, Chiapas, Mexico. *Papers of the New World Archaeological Foundation* No. *14*.

MacNeish, R. S., F. A. Peterson and K. V. Flannery

1970 Ceramics. In *The prehistory of the Tehuacan Valley,* edited by F. Johnson, Volume 3. Austin: Univ. of Texas Press.

Marcus, J.

1976 The Origins of Mesoamerican Writing. *Annual Review of Anthropology 5*:35–67. Palo Alto: Annual Reviews Inc.

Matheny, R. T.

1970 The ceramics of Aguacatal, Campeche, Mexico. *Papers of the New World Archaeological Foundation* No. *27*.

Matheny, R. T., and D. L. Berge

1971 Investigations in Campeche, Mexico. *Ceramica de Cultura Maya et al. 7*:1–15.

McDonald, A. J.

1971 Tzutzuculi, a preclassic site of coastal Chiapas. Unpublished M.A. thesis, University of the Americas, Cholula.

n. d. Middle Preclassic Ceremonial Centers in Southern Chiapas. *Papers of the New World Archaeological Foundation,* No. *42* (in press).

Merwin, R. E., and G. C. Vaillant

1932 The ruins of Holmul, Guatemala. *Memoirs of the Peabody Museum of Archaeology and Ethnology 3*(2).

Michels, J. W.

1972 Dating methods. In *Annual review of Anthropology,* edited by B. J. Siegel, A. R. Beals and S. A. Tyler, Volume 1. Palo Alto: Annual Reviews Inc. Pp. 113–126.

Miles, S. W.

1965 Sculpture of the Guatemala-Chiapas highlands and Pacific slopes and associated hieroglyphs. In *Handbook of Middle American Indians,* edited by R. Wauchope. Volume 2. Austin: Univ. of Texas Press. Pp. 237–275.

Mirambell, L.
1974 La etapa litica. *Historia de Mexico,* Vol. 1, pp. 55–76. Salvat Editores de Mexico. S. A.

Morley, S. G., and G. W. Brainerd
1956 *The ancient Maya.* Stanford: Stanford University Press.

Navarrete, C.
1959 A brief reconnaissance of the Tonala region, Chiapas, Mexico. *Papers of the New World Archaeological Foundation* No. *4.*
1960 Archaeological exploration of the Frailesca, Chiapas, Mexico. *Papers of the New World Archaeological Foundation* No. *7.*
1977 Aportaciones a la iconografía Post-Olmeca del Altiplano Central de Guatemala. *Anales de Anthropología 14*:91–108.

Nelson, F. W., Jr.
1973 Archaeological investigations at Dzibilnocac, Campeche, Mexico. *Papers of the New World Archaeological Foundation* No. *33.*

Ortiz Ceballos, P.
1975 La Cerámica de los Tuxtlas. Tesis de Maestria en Ciencias Antropológicas, Universidad Veracruzana, Jalapa.

Palerm, A., and E. R. Wolf
1957 Ecological potential and cultural development in Mesoamerica. *Pan American Union Social Science Monograph.* No. *3.*

Parsons, L. A.
1967 *Bilbao, Guatemala, an archaeological study of the Pacific coast Cotzumalhuapa region,* Volume 1. Milwaukee: Milwaukee Public Museum Publications in Anthropology 11.
1969 *Bilbao, Guatemala, an archaeological study of the Pacific coast Cotzumalhuapa region,* Volume 2. Milwaukee: Milwaukee Public Museum Publications in Anthropology 12.

Pendergast, D. M.
1971 Evidence of early Teotihuacan-lowland Maya contact at Altun Ha. *American Antiquity 36*(4):455–460.

Peterson, F. A.
1963 Some ceramics from Mirador, Chiapas, Mexico. *Papers of the New World Archaeological Foundation* No. *15.*

Piña Chan, R.
1968 *Jaina, la casa en el Agua.* Mexico, D.F.: Instituto Nacional de Antropologia e Historia.

Pollock, H. E. D.
1940 Sources and methods in the study of Maya architecture. In *The Maya and their neighbors,* edited by C. L. Hay *et al.* New York: Appleton-Century-Crofts. Pp. 179–201.

Porter, M. N.
1953 Tlatilco and the pre-classic cultures of the New World. *Viking Fund Publications Anthropology* No. *19.*

Prem, H. J.
1971 Calendrics and writing. *In* Observations on the emergence of civilization in Mesoamerica, edited by R. F. Heizer, J. A. Graham and C. W. Clewlow, Jr. *Contributions of the University of California Archaeological Research Facility* No. *11*:112–132.

Pring, Duncan
1976a Illustration for Preclassic Ceramic Complexes in Northern Belize. Cambridge, England: Center of Latin American Studies, Cambridge University.
1976b Outline of the Northern Belize Ceramic Sequence. *Ceramica de Cultura Maya et al.* No. *9*:11–51.

Proskouriakoff, T.
1950 A study of classic Maya sculpture. *Carnegie Institution of Washington Publication 593.*

Puleston, D. E., and O. S. Puleston
1971 An ecological approach to the origins of Maya civilization. *Archaeology 24*(4):330–337.

Ralph, E. K.
1971 Carbon-14 dating. In *Dating techniques for the archaeologist,* edited by H. N. Michael and E. K. Ralph. Cambridge: MIT Press. Pp. 1–48.

Rands, R. L.
1969 Mayan ecology and trade: 1967–1968. *Research Records of the University Museum, Mesoamerican Studies Series* '69 M, 2 A. Southern Illinois Univ.
1974 The ceramic sequence at Palenque, Chiapas. In *Mesoamerican Archaeology: New Approaches,* edited by Norman Hammond. Austin: University of Texas Press. Pp. 51–75.
1977 The Rise of Classic Maya Civilization in the Northwestern Zone: Isolation and Integration. In *The Origins of Maya Civilization,* edited by R. E. W. Adams. Albuquerque: University of New Mexico Press. Pp. 159–180.

Rice, D. S.
1976 Middle Preclassic Maya Settlement in the Central Maya Lowlands. *Journal of Field Archaeology 3*(4):425–445.

Ricketson, O. G., Jr.
1928 A stratification of remains at an early Maya site. *Proceedings of the National Academy of Sciences 14*(7):505–508.
1929 Excavations at Baking Pot, British Honduras. *Carnegie Institution of Washington Publication 403.*

Ricketson, O. G., and E. B. Ricketson
1937 Uaxactun, Guatemala: Group E—1926–1931. *Carnegie Institution of Washington Publication 477.*

Rowe, J. H.
1959 Archaeological dating and cultural process. *Southwestern Journal of Anthropology 15*(4).

Ruz Lhuillier, A.
1969 La costa de Campeche en los tiempos prehispanicos. *Instituto Nacional de Antropologia e Historia, Serie Investigaciones* No. *18.*

Sabloff, J. A.
1970 Type descriptions of the fine paste ceramics of the Bayal Boca complex, Seibal, Peten, Guatemala. *Papers of the Peabody Museum of Archaeology and Ethnology 61:*359–419.
1975 Excavations at Seibal, Department of the Peten, Guatemala: The Ceramics. *Memoirs of the Peabody Museum of Archaeology and Ethnology, 13,* No. *2.*

Sabloff, J. A., W. L. Rathje, D. A. Freidel, J. G. Connor, and P. L. W. Sabloff
1974 Trade and power in Postclassic Yucatan; initial observations. In *Mesoamerican archaeology: New approaches,* edited by Norman Hammond. University of Texas Press, Austin. Pp. 397–416.

Sanders, W. T.
1960 Prehistoric ceramics and settlement patterns in Quintana Roo, Mexico. *Carnegie Institution of Washington Publication 606:*155–264.
1961 Ceramic stratigraphy at Santa Cruz, Chiapas, Mexico. *Papers of the New World Archaeological Foundation* No. *13.*

Sanders, W. T., and J. W. Michels
1969 The Pennsylvania State University Kaminaljuyu Project—1968 season; part 1, the excavations. *Pennsylvania State University Occasional Papers in Anthropology* No. *2.*

Sanders, W. T., and B. Price
1968 *Mesoamerica, the evolution of a civilization.* New York: Random House.

Satterthwaite, L., and E. K. Ralph
1960 New radiocarbon dates and the Maya correlation problem. *American Antiquity 26*(2).

Sedat, D. W.
1971 The preclassic lowland Maya and their northern highland neighbors. Mimeographed paper read at 37th Annual Meeting of the Society for American Archaeology, Claremont, California.

Sedat, D. W. and R. J. Sharer
1972 Archaeological investigations in the northern Maya highlands: New data on the Maya preclassic. *Contributions University of California Archaeological Research Facility* No. *16:*23–36.
1973 Preclassic populations and writing systems in the Salama Valley, Guatemala. Mimeographed paper read at 72nd Annual Meeting, American Anthropological Association, New Orleans.

Sharer, R. J.
1969 Chalchuapa: Investigations at a highland Maya ceremonial center. *Expedition 11*(2):36–38.
1972 Investigaciones preclasicas en Chalchuapa, El Salvador. *Anales Museo Nacional "David J. Guzman." xi* (37–41):27–34.
1974 The Prehistory of the Southeastern Maya Periphery. *Current Anthropology 15*(2):165–187.
n.d. The Pottery of Chalchuapa, El Salvador. In *The prehistory of Chalchuapa, El Salvador*, edited by Robert J. Sharer. Volume 3, Number 1. Philadelphia: University of Pennsylvania. (in press)

Sharer, R. J., and J. C. Gifford
1970 Preclassic ceramics from Chalchuapa, El Salvador and their relationships with the Maya lowlands. *American Antiquity 35:*441–462.

Shook, E. M.
1951 The present status of research on the pre-classic horizons in Guatemala. In *The civilizations of ancient America,* edited by Sol Tax. New York: Cooper Square. Pp. 93–100.
1957 Lugares arqueologicos del altiplano meridional central de Guatemala. In *Arqueologia Guatemalteca*. Guatemala. Pp. 65–128. Also published in *Antropologia e historia de Guatemala, IDAEH* 1952, *4*(2):3–40.

Shook, E. M., and A. V. Kidder
1952 Mound E-III-3, Kaminaljuyu, Guatemala. *Carnegie Institution of Washington Publication 596.*

Sisson, E. B.
1970 Settlement patterns and land use in the northwestern Chontalpa, Tabasco, Mexico: A progress report. *Ceramica de Cultura Maya et al.* No. *6.*

Smith, A. L.
1955 Archaeological reconnaissance in central Guatemala. *Carnegie Institution of Washington Publication 608.*

Smith, A. L., and G. R. Willey
1969 Seibal, Guatemala, in 1968: A brief summary of archaeological results. *38th International Congress of Americanists 1:*151–157.

Smith, R. E.
1936a Preliminary shape analysis of the Uaxactun pottery. Carnegie Institution of Washington. Mimeographed.
1936b Ceramics of Uaxactun: A preliminary analysis of decorative technics and design. Carnegie Institute of Washington. Mimeographed.

1955 Ceramic sequence at Uaxactun, Guatemala. *Middle American Research Institute Publication 20.*

1971 The pottery of Mayapan (2 volumes). *Papers of the Peabody Museum of Archaeology and Ethnology 65.*

Smith, R. E., and J. C. Gifford

1965 Pottery of the Maya lowlands. In *Handbook of Middle American Indians,* edited by R. Wauchope. Volume 2. Austin: Univ. of Texas Press. Pp. 498–534.

Sorenson, J. L.

1955 A chronological ordering of the Mesoamerican pre-classic. In *Middle American Research Records 2:*43–68.

Steward, J. H.

1948 A functional-development classification of American high cultures. *In* A reappraisal of Peruvian archaeology, edited by W. C. Bennett. *Memoirs of the Society for American Archaeology* No. *4.*

Stirling, M. W.

1955 Stone Monuments of the Rio Chiquito, Veracruz, Mexico. *Bureau of American Ethnology Bulletin 157.*

Strong, W. D., A. Kidder, II, and A. J. D. Paul, Jr.

1938 Preliminary report on the Smithsonian Institution–Harvard University archaeological expedition to northwestern Honduras. *Smithsonian Miscellaneous Collections 97*(1).

Stuckenrath, R., W. R. Coe, and E. K. Ralph

1966 University of Pennsylvania radiocarbon dates IX. *Radiocarbon 8.*

Suess, H. E.

1970 Bristlecone-pine calibration of the radiocarbon timescale 5200 B.C. to the present. In *Radiocarbon variations and absolute chronology, Twelfth Nobel Symposium,* edited by I. U. Olson. New York: Wiley.

Thompson, J. E. S.

1935 Maya chronology: The correlation question. *Carnegie Institution of Washington Publication 456.*

1939 Excavations at San Jose, British Honduras. *Carnegie Institution of Washington Publication 506.*

1940 Archaeological problems of the lowland Maya. In *The Maya and their neighbors,* edited by C. L. Hay et al. New York: Appleton-Century-Crofts. Pp. 126–138. (Reprinted 1962 by the Univ. of Utah Press, Salt Lake City).

1948 An archaeological reconnaissance in the Cotzumalhuapa region, Escuintla, Guatemala. *Carnegie Institution of Washington Publication 574.*

1950 Maya hieroglyphic writing. *Carnegie Institution of Washington Publication 589* (Reprinted 1960 by the Univ. of Oklahoma Press, Norman).

Tolstoy, P., and L. I. Paradis

1971 Early and middle preclassic culture in the Basin of Mexico. *In* Observations on the emergence of civilization in Mesoamerica, edited by R. F. Heizer, J. A. Graham and C. W. Clewlow, Jr. *Contributions of the University of California Archaeological Research Facility* No. *11*:7–29.

Treat, R. C.

1969 Excavations at Vistahermosa, Chiapas, Mexico. Unpublished M.A. thesis, Department of Anthropology, University of the Americas, Mexico.

Voorhies, B.

1975 Los Conchales de la Zona de Chantuto, Chiapas, Mexico. XIII Mesa Redonda, Sociedad Mexicana de Antropologia, Vol. II. Mexico. D.F.

1976 The Chantuto People: An Archaic Society of the Chiapas Littoral, Mexico. *Papers of the New World Archaeological Foundation,* No. *41.* Provo.

Wainer, J. C.
1970 A redefinition of the ceramic sequence at Mirador, Chiapas. Unpublished manuscript. New World Archaeological Foundation, Chiapas, Mexico.
Warren, B. W.
1959 New discoveries in Chiapas, southern Mexico. *Archaeology 12*:98–105.
1961 The archaeological sequence at Chiapa de Corzo. In *VIII Mesa Redonda de la Sociedad Mexicana de Antropologia, Los Maya del sur y sus relaciones con los Nahuas meridionales*. Pp. 75–83.
Wauchope, R.
1948 Excavations at Zacualpa, Guatemala. *Middle American Research Institute Publication* No. *14*.
1950 A tentative sequence of preclassic ceramics in Middle America. *Middle American Research Records 1*(14).
1964 Southern Mesoamerica. In *Prehistoric man in the New World,* edited by J. D. Jennings and E. Norbeck. Chicago: Univ. of Chicago Press. Pp. 331–386.
1965 *They found the buried cities: Exploration and excavation in the American tropics.* Chicago: Univ. of Chicago Press.
Willey, G. R.
1956 New World prehistory. *Science 131*:73–86.
1966 *An introduction to American archaeology.* Volume I, *North and Middle America.* Englewood Cliffs, New Jersey: Prentice-Hall.
1970 Type description of the ceramics of the Real Xe Complex, Seibal, Peten, Guatemala. *In* Monographs and papers in Maya archaeology, edited by W. R. Bullard, Jr. *Papers of the Peabody Museum of Archaeology and Ethnology 61*:313–355.
1971 An archaeological frame of reference for Maya cultural history. In *Desarrollo cultural de los Mayas* (augmented 1964 edition), edited by E. Z. Vogt and A. Ruz. L. Mexico, D.F.: Universidad Nacional Autonoma de Mexico.
1973 The Altar de Sacrificios excavations; general summary and conclusions. *Papers of the Peabody Museum of Archaeology and Ethnology 64*(3).
1974 The Classic Maya hiatus: A rehearsal for the collapse? *Mesoamerican Archaeology: New Approaches,* edited by Norman Hammond. Austin: University of Texas Press. Pp. 417–430.
1977a The rise of Maya civilization: A summary view. In *The origins of Maya Civiliza-Maya civilization,* edited by R. E. W. Adams. Albuquerque: University of New Mexico Press. Pp. 133–157.
1977b The rise of Maya civilization: A summary view. In *The origins of Maya Civilization,* edited by R. E. W. Adams. Albuquerque: University of New Mexico Press. Pp. 383–423.
Willey, G. R., and P. Phillips
1955 Method and theory in American archaeology II: Historical-developmental interpretation. *American Anthropologist 57*:723–819.
1958 *Method and theory in American archaeology.* Chicago: Univ. of Chicago Press.
Willey, G. R., W. R. Bullard, J. B. Glass, and J. C. Gifford
1965 Prehistoric Maya settlements in the Belize Valley. *Papers of the Peabody Museum of Archaeology and Ethnology 54.*
Willey, G. R., T. P. Culbert, and R. E. W. Adams (editors)
1967 Maya lowland ceramics: A report from the 1965 Guatemala City conference. *American Antiquity 32*(3):289–315.
Woodbury, R. B.
1972 Archaeology in Anthropology. *American Antiquity 37*(3):337–338.

Woodbury, R. B., and A. S. Trik
1953 *The ruins of Zaculeu, Guatemala*. New York: United Fruit Co.
Zeitlin, Robert N.
1976 Long-distance exchange and the growth of a regional center on the southern isthmus of Tehuantepec, Mexico. Mimeographed. Paper presented at the 41st Annual Meeting of the Society for American Archaeology, St. Louis.
Zimmerman, G.
1971 La escritura jeroglifica y el calendario como indicadores de tendencias en la historia cultural de los Mayas. In *Desarrollo cultural de los Mayas,* edited by E. Z. Vogt and A. Ruz L. Mexico, D.F.: Universidad Nacional Autonoma de Mexico. Pp. 242–256.

Lower Central America

WOLFGANG HABERLAND

I. HISTORY OF LOWER CENTRAL AMERICAN ARCHAEOLOGY

A. Nineteenth Century

The first archaeological descriptions of this region—apart from ethnohistorical information dating from the time of Conquest—were provided by travelers from about the middle of the nineteenth century. As far as can be ascertained, the first object to be mentioned was a stone statue of the Chontales type from the Sierra de Amerisque (Nicaragua), described in 1841 by Emanuel von Friedrichsthal. This Austrian explorer even brought back one of these monuments, now in the Museum für Völkerkunde, Vienna (Nowotny 1956, 1961). The stone statues of Nicaragua, especially those from the Lake region, aroused the curiosity of many travelers during the third quarter of the last century. Squier, who investigated—and removed—these statues in 1849, was the first to publish them intensively (Squier 1852). A special publication, dedicated exclusively to the Zapartera statues, was written by Bovallius in 1886. After this publication, however, interest in the Nicaraguan stone statues declined, and only during the last few years have photographs of some of them been published (Baudez 1970: Figs. 78–89; Willey 1971: Figs. 5-113, 5-114; Thieck 1971; Haberland 1969: Figs. 124; etc.). Only preliminary attempts have been made to classify these monuments (Haberland 1973).

Whereas stone statues were the main point of interest in the Lake region of Nicaragua, gold was the stimulating factor for the birth of Chiriquian archaeology in Western Panama. While sporadic finds had been made for some centuries, the great find of 1858–1859 at Bugavita, yielding more than 150 lbs of this precious metal (Bollaert 1963; Holmes 1887; Lüders 1888) caused a rush of excavations and the rise of full-time *huaqueros* in this part of Central America. As shown for example by the minutes of the American Ethnological Society for 1860 (*Historical Magazine,* Vol. IV, pp. 144, 176–177, 240–241, 274) pottery and stone objects from these graves were also collected and sent abroad. They formed the early "Chiriquian Collections" present in every major museum and the basis of studies by Holmes (1888) and MacCurdy (1911) that were outstanding for their time. Because of these publications, Chiriquian pottery during the early twentieth century was one of the best-known ceramics from all of Latin America. However, as with the stone statues, interest declined subsequently, and no further investigations were conducted until 1955 (Haberland 1961a).

A third subject of early archaeological discovery and interest were the footprints of El Sauce and Acahualinca (Nicaragua), first mentioned by Earl Flint in 1884. He claimed that these were "pre-Adamite" (1886); others attacked him vehemently, challenging the age of the footprints (e.g., Peet 1889) and their nature (McA 1885). In 1891, the heated discussion suddenly died down and for half a century no new investigations of this interesting phenomenon took place (Williams 1952).

Not all investigations of the last century were the result of fortuitous encounters, sensations, and pot- or gold-hunting. At least some of the early travelers and excavators made intelligent reports about their finds: Bovallius (1886) regarding the stone statues of Zapatera Island and Brandford (1881) on his excavations at Ometepe Island. Among early excavators, Carl Hartman, a Swedish archaeologist, was outstanding. He introduced scientific excavation methods of high standard to Central America at a very early date (Rowe 1959). His reports on excavations in Highland Costa Rica and at the "Linea Vieja" (1901) as well as on Nicoya Peninsula (1907a) are still models for this type of publication and have rarely been surpassed in Lower Central America. Thus, on the eve of World War I, knowledge about the archaeology of Lower Central America was concentrated in a few spots. Pre-Columbian remains were known from Chiriquí, Highland Costa Rica, the Linea Vieja, Nicoya Peninsula, the vicinity of Managua (footprints), the Lake region, and Chontales. None of these remains, nor the many isolated objects already in collections, showed any temporal depth, and all were unrelated to one another. The travels of Walter Lehmann in Central America

(1907–1909) provided a rare opportunity to advance the archaeology of these regions, but Lehmann never published his archaeological results except for brief preliminary reports (1908, 1910).

B. Early Twentieth Century

During the 1920s, several developments took place, still more or less on an individual basis—a trend that continues to the present. While there were no important excavations in Nicaragua or Costa Rica, the publication of Lothrop's book (1926) on the pottery of these two republics marked a further advance because, for the first time, most of the known ceramics from these regions were illustrated—some of them even in color—and given a certain order. From today's vantage point, the book is badly lacking in some respects, for example, in actual fieldwork, time depth, grave associations, identification of the source of objects already published, and so on. But, for that time, it was a step forward. Unfortunately, it did not induce other individuals—with the exception of *huaqueros,* dealers, and collectors—to engage in the archaeology of these countries.

Important fieldwork occurred in Panama, where A. Hyatt Verrill excavated in the province of Coclé, hitherto untouched. He followed some leads provided by Karl Curtis, a famous resident of the Canal Zone since 1915. In 1925–1926, Verrill excavated a large stone enclosure (the so-called "Verrill Site") near Penonomé with a large number of stone statues, most of which are now in the Museum of the American Indian and the American Museum of Natural History, both in New York. Unfortunately, apart from a plan and some photographs, only very flimsy descriptions have been published by him (1927, n.d.). Of more scientific value was the Swedish expedition to Panama in 1927 under the direction of Erland Nordenskiöld, with Sigvald Linné in charge of the archaeological investigations. Their excavations, on the Pearl Islands and on the Pacific coast of Darién, are still our only source for those regions, archaeologically speaking. Even today the report (Linné 1929) is still usable by modern standards. Panama continued to play a leading role in the archaeology of Lower Central America between the two world wars—and it is still the best-known. It gained further fame through the 1930–1933 excavations by the Peabody Museum expedition at Sitio Conte and other sites in Coclé—first under the direction of H. H. Roberts and later under S. K. Lothrop. In this investigation an attempt was made, for the first time in Panama archaeology, to interpret the evidence and assess the stratigraphic situation among the graves in chronological terms (Lothrop 1937–1942).

Progress in the archaeology of Lower Central America in the interwar years was minimal, with the exception perhaps of Panama, where two new regions, Coclé and Darién, had been added to the roster of provinces from which pre-Columbian remains were somewhat better known. In the other, already known regions, scarcely any advance was made, and sometimes knowledge that had been gained was actually lost. Therefore, by 1940, good stratigraphic series in many areas were still missing; something that in 1910 had been usual for all parts of Latin America was now an exception, especially in Nuclear America. Only in the description of a few graveyards had a chronological ordering been attempted (by Hartman and Lothrop). Furthermore, none of the regions known archaeologically up to that date could be linked either among themselves or with cultures or phases outside Lower Central America. While the creation of Mesoamerica as a cultural entity by Kirchhoff (1943) did touch upon Lower Central America because some parts of it were included, this did not have any positive influence on the development of archaeological investigations in the region.

C. Post–World War II Developments

Since World War II, especially during the 1950s and 1960s, considerable progress has occurred. It can only be summarized here because a detailed history of archaeological developments over the last 25 years would take up too much space. The work done during that time in Lower Central America has been more or less basic. Its most important problem was, and still is, the establishing of stratigraphic sequences of sufficient depth, of chronologies and links between the regions, and so on. Because this has not yet been accomplished in many areas, no further "problem-oriented" research has been done, except in connection with the questions already mentioned. Even today a single excavation often characterizes a whole region.

One of the first—and still the best—defined areas was Greater Nicoya. Here stratigraphic excavations by Michael D. Coe in the Tamarindo Zone of Nicoya Peninsula and Santa Elena Peninsula (Baudez and Coe 1962; Coe 1962; Coe and Baudez 1961), by Claude F. Baudez in the Tempisque Valley (1962, 1967), by Frederick W. Lange in the Sapoa Valley (1971), by Albert H. Norweb on the Isthmus of Rivas (1964), and by Wolfgang Haberland on Ometepe Island (1964, 1966) provided a number of chronological sequences, which are basically similar and can be synchronized. Another sequence, further south, was established by William J. Kennedy in the Reventazon Valley (personal communication; Haberland 1969b:358). It should link the regions of Highland Costa Rica and "Linea Vieja," for which, however, stratigraphic sequences are still missing in spite of the investigations by Doris Stone (1958, 1961, etc.; Stone and Balser 1957, 1965), Carlos Balser (1959, 1961, 1967, 1969), Matthew W. Stirling, and others. Another chronological sequence was found by the investigations of Olga Linares on the Pacific coast of Chiriquí (1968). Others, like Matthew W. Stirling (1949, 1950), Stirling and Stirling (1964b), Samuel K. Lothrop (1963), Doris Stone (1943, 1963), S. Henry Wassén (1949), L. L. and L. Minelli (1966), and Wolfgang Haberland (1955, 1959, 1960, 1961a, 1961b, 1962), either excavated single-component sites or were unable to establish good sequences. During the 1960s, many new sites and grave associations were reported by Roberto de la Guardia and his associates in their Boletín del Museo Chiricano, adding valuable details to our knowledge.

The first chronological sequence established for Lower Central America was in the Parita region of Central Panama, at the base of the Azuero Peninsula. Here, in 1948 and 1952, Matthew W. Stirling and Gordon R. Willey together with various assistants excavated a number of sites, which yielded the necessary information (Willey and Stoddard 1954; Willey and McGimsey 1954). The already long sequence was further lengthened by the discovery of the Cerro Mangote Complex in the same region (McGimsey 1956, 1958). Later, John Ladd refined and revised the stratigraphy of the Sitio Conte Sequence (1957) and that of the Polychrome time of the Parita Sequence (1964). Since then, a sequence on the Azuero Peninsula has been established by Alain Ichon (personal communication; Linares 1971; Ichon 1970); this is in the Tonosí district, where Mitchell and Heidenreich (1965) made the first discoveries and reported some stratigraphic evidence. Further explorations on the Azuero Peninsula were conducted independently by Thelma Bull and myself in the Guararé region (personal communication) as well as by various members of the now defunct Archaeological Society of Panama (see the *Panama Archaeologist,* Vols. 1–6, 1958–1965). Excavations to be mentioned in Coclé Province are those by Neville A. Harte on Cerro Guacamayo (1966; E. M. Harte 1958) and by Matthew W. and M. Stirling at El Limón (1964a). The latter also excavated on the islands of Taboga, Urabá, and Taboguilla (1964c). None of these excavations resulted in any stratigraphic evidence or series.

Such a sequence is also missing in the region around the Panama Canal. Neither the excavations at Panama Viejo (Biese 1964) nor those in the famous Venado Beach cemetery, of which only preliminary reports exist (Bull 1958, 1961; Lothrop 1954, 1960; Sander *et al.* 1958), allow a chronological ordering. More recent investigations by Donald L. Crusoe (1970); Crusoe and Felton (1971) give a certain sequence, especially for Preceramic and Formative times. The data are in some instances controversial and lacking a factual basis, because the stratigraphy of some key regions like Madden Lake is virtually nonexistent. Important results were also obtained through paleobotanical "palynological" (pollen-analytical) investigations of muck cores from the Gatun Lake, yielding early maize pollen (Stewart 1968).

To complete this enumeration of achievements during the last 25 years, many small investigations ought to be mentioned. They do not appear here either because they have not been reported on as yet or because they are still so isolated spatially and/or temporally that they do not have major consequences for this chapter. They include Bull's excavations at Chamé (1959), Meggers and Evans' investigations on the Atlantic coast of Nicaragua near Bluefields (Haag 1970), and Lothrop's report on the Veraguas graves (1950).

While the array of excavations and stratigraphies for Lower Central America is quite impressive, it has to be borne in mind that many of them have not yet been published in final form. This may be a reason for the rarity of comparative studies and general accounts. In the first category there is only Peter J. Schmidt's investigations on burial customs (1968) and, on a smaller scale, one that I have done on stone statues (Haberland 1973). The first general accounts were written by Lothrop (1959b, 1966), while a modern summary was included by Willey in a larger study (1971:254–359). The only book exclusively dedicated to the archaeology of Central America is by Baudez (1970). Ford, in his basic study of the Formative cultures (1969), has not a single sequence for Lower Central America.

II. PRESENT STATUS OF ARCHAEOLOGICAL KNOWLEDGE

A. Delineation of Archaeological Areas

Lower Central America is by no means a uniform archaeological province in the sense of an area co-tradition. On the contrary, it comprises a number of important cultural frontiers and independent archaeological areas, with affiliations to the north and the south at various times. The cultural history of these areas is widely different and, therefore, often difficult to correlate. Due to the uneven distribution of excavations, the absence of final reports on many of the most important of them, and the lack of comparative studies, only two of these areas are to a certain degree understood.

One of the better-known areas—and the best understood—is Greater Nicoya, a term first used by Norweb (1961) and today generally accepted. The core of it is the base of Nicoya Peninsula, that is, the northern part of Guanacaste Province in Costa Rica, and the Isthmus of Rivas in Nicaragua. Other parts, such as Ometepe Island, the vicinity of Nindirí (Nicaragua), Zapatera Island, and so on, were only sometimes integrated ino this cultural entity. Despite the fact that this is the best investigated area of all of Lower Central America, its real extensions during various time periods are still uncertain. The other better-known area is Greater Chiriquí, which, at least during the last 400 years before Conquest, includes western Chiriquí Province in Panama, Burica and Osa peninsulas, and the valleys of the Diquis, Rio Grande del General, and Rio Brus with their tributaries (all in Costa Rica). Whether Bocas de Toro (Panama) belonged to this area is still an open question. Excavations by the Stirlings (1964b) and by Linares (Linares and Ranere 1971) indicate many differences—enough to exclude this region from Greater Chiriquí for most time periods.

A third area is probably the Coclé–Azuero region. Here, the extent of the region is still more unknown than that of the previous two. A name has not even been coined, since, to date, each sequence of this area has been treated as a separate and unconnected entity. There is, however, enough uniformity—at least during certain periods—to warrant grouping the sequences together to form a cultural area. At the moment the term "Gulf of Panama area" might be appropriate enough, because most of the sites or sequences cluster around this body of water. Among the criteria for suggesting this area are the El Hatillo, Parita, and Macaracas Polychrome types (Ladd 1964). They are encountered in the following sites, regions, or sequences, which are all included in this area: Parita, Coclé, Guararé, Tonosí, Islas de Perlas, Venado Beach, Taboga, Taboguilla, Urabá, and perhaps Chamé. In addition, there are numerous other sites, mostly unreported and uninvestigated scientifically, in the provinces of Los Santos, Herrera, Coclé, and Panama. Sites in the scantily reported but not unknown province of Veraguas might also be included here. Perhaps the Mariato Site, excavated by J. A. Schultz but not yet published despite some ^{14}C dates (Crane and Griffin 1965:143–144), also belongs to the area; others, like the Rio de Jesus cemetery (personal information), certainly do.

A fourth area, distinguishable from the three already mentioned, is here called Central Costa Rica. It comprises what is otherwise known as Highland Costa Rica (or Meseta Central), the Linea Vieja, and the Reventazon Valley (see also Stone 1958). All other regions of Lower Central America are so unknown archaeologically that they can neither be designated as cultural zones nor incorporated into one of the four entities here delineated.

The basis for the chronological ordering of all the phases named or known to date are stratigraphic sequences. Their absolute age determination depends upon the ^{14}C dates available. Unfortunately, there are at this moment (1972) only 56 dates run for the whole of Lower Central America. Furthermore, their distribution among and in the areas is very uneven and a number of them are still unrelated to any phase, that is, it is not yet known exactly what material is dated by them (e.g., B1, B2, B4, B5, B10, B13, D5, D7, D10, D11, D16). Despite these handicaps, I will try in the following sections to correlate the different sequences in each of the areas outlined and connect them with the corrected ^{14}C dates. After establishing a "generalized sequence" for each of the four areas, these will be correlated with one another—as far as possible—to give a more or less coherent, if tentative, picture of the cultural development of Lower Central America.

B. Greater Nicoya

Beginning in the north, Greater Nicoya is the first of the areas to be discussed. Here, no less than six regional sequences have been established, three of which—those of the Tempisque Valley (Baudez 1962, 1967), the Tamarindo Zone of Nicoya Peninsula (Coe 1962), and the Santa Elena Peninsula—have given birth to a seventh more generalized one with a period system (see Figure 12.1). Their correlated form was first mentioned by

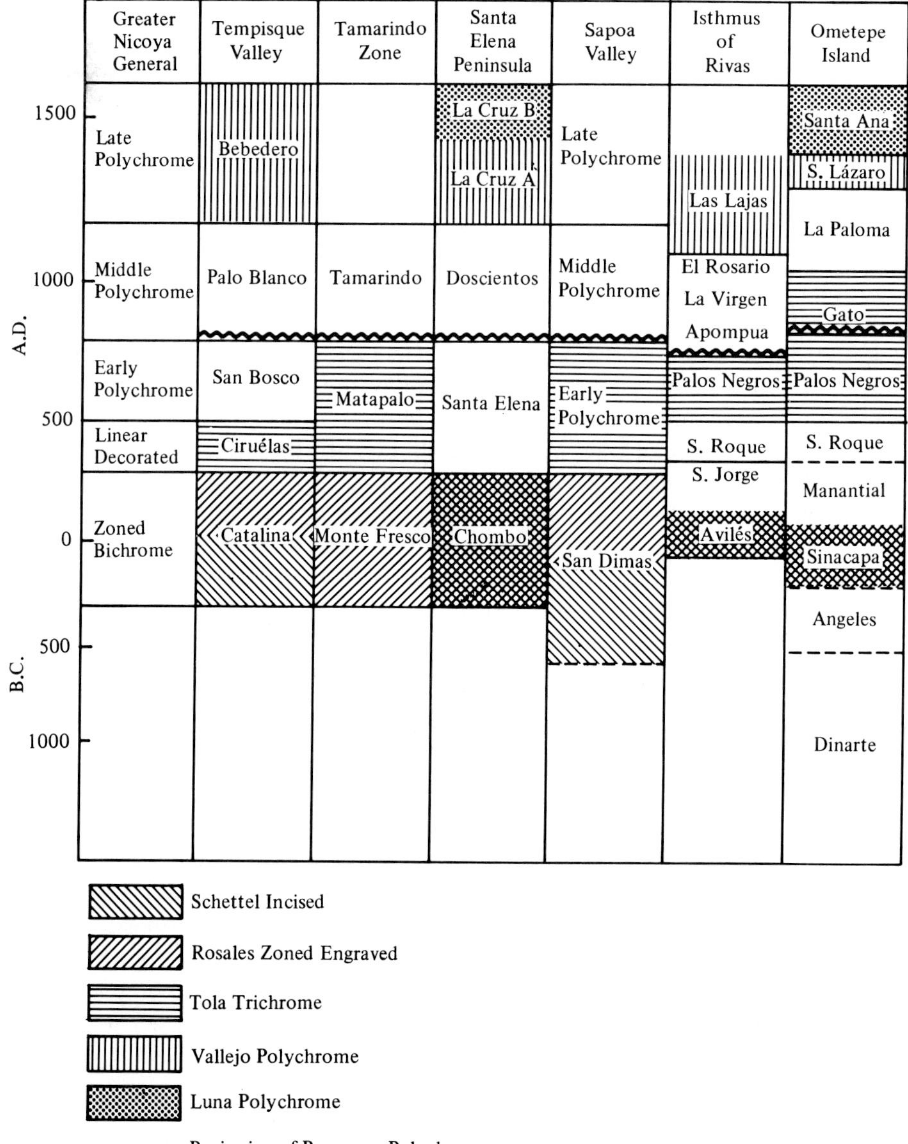

Figure 12.1 Greater Nicoya sequences as given by excavators.

Baudez and Coe (1962; see also Coe and Baudez 1961). Later sequences are those of the Sapoa Valley (Lange 1971; Lange and Scheidenhelm 1972), the Isthmus of Rivas (Norweb 1961, 1964), and Ometepe Island (Haberland 1963, 1964, 1966). One has to bear in mind, however, that only the Tempisque sequence has been published in extenso (Baudez 1967); for all others there are only preliminary reports or generalized accounts. The authors of the later sequences, especially those of the northern part of Greater Nicoya, tried to fit them and their phases into the system devised by Baudez and Coe, but they encountered great difficulty—as can be deduced from Figure 12.1. One of the reasons for these discrepancies may be the basic assumption of Coe and Baudez that many of the cultural impulses came from the north, that is, from Mesoamerica, and that all advancements had their origin in migrations of northern tribes into Lower Central America. For example, they correlated the Early Polychrome Period (at that time still called Early Polychrome B) with the Tepeu Phase of Classic Maya Lowland culture and with the Uloa Valley (Baudez and Coe 1962:369–370); Papagayo Polychrome, the leading pottery type of the Middle Polychrome Period, with X Fine Orange (Baudez and Coe 1962:370); and Vallejo Polychrome, of the first part of the Late Polychrome Period, with Mexican sources (Baudez and Coe:370). These ideas also contributed to the dating of the generalized periods, especially if there were no ^{14}C dates. The dating itself was only slightly changed later by Baudez (1967). The different sequences of Greater Nicoya as given by the various authors are shown in Figure 12.1.

A correlation of the phases in Greater Nicoya is very much facilitated through the distribution of some distinctive pottery types, which act as horizon markers. The earliest of these is Schettel Incised (Norweb 1964:559; Lange 1971: Fig. 35 a–b). This type obviously characterizes an early part of the Zoned Bichrome Period (Lange 1971:131–148). It is present in the early part of the Catalina Phase (Tempisque Valley), in the Avilés Phase of Rivas, in the Sinacapa Phase of Ometepe, in the Chombo Phase of Santa Elena Peninsula, and in the San Dimas Phase of the Sapoa Valley. Here, Schettel Incised was found stratigraphically beneath Rosales Zoned Engraved (Lange 1971:131–148). The same temporal difference may be true for the Tempisque sequence, where Rosales Zoned Engraved (Baudez 1967:68–71) is typical for the second half of the still undivided Catalina Phase. However, in the Avilés and Sinacapa phases, Schettel Incised and Rosales Zoned Engraved always appear together (Norweb 1964:554). Since this fact has been checked on Ometepe Island at a number of sites, it is scarcely possible that this connection is due to a mixing of different cultural layers (see also Haberland 1969a).

The next clue for the alignment of phases is Tola Trichrome. It is present in what has been called the Linear Decorated Period by Baudez (1967:194, 207–208) and the Early Polychrome Period by others (e.g., Norweb, 1964:554). In the Ciruelas Phase of the Tempisque Valley and the Matapalo

Phase of the Tamarindo Zone, Tola Trichrome is called Lopez Polychrome (Haberland 1969a:232–233). It was also found in the Early Polychrome of the Sapoa Valley, the Palos Negros phases of Rivas and Ometepe, and the Gato phase of Ometepe. The first appearance of true Polychrome is at the beginning of the San Bosco Phase (Tempisque Valley), the Matapalo Phase (Tamarindo Zone), the Santa Elena Phase (Santa Elena Peninsula), the Middle Polychrome of the Sapoa Valley, the Apompua Phase (Rivas), and the Gato Phase (Ometepe). Probably of more value is the distribution of the Papagayo Polychromes, a horizon marker for the Middle Polychrome Period. They are present during the following phases: Palo Blanco (Tempisque), Tamarindo (Tamarindo), Doscientos (Santa Elena), Middle Polychrome of the Sapoa Valley, Apompua (Rivas), La Virgen (Rivas), El Rosario (Rivas), La Paloma (Ometepe), and the second part of Gato (Ometepe). Vallejo Polychrome is the significant pottery type of the first half of the Late Polychrome Period. It links Bebedero (Tempisque) together with La Cruz A (Santa Elena), Las Lajas (Rivas), and San Lázaro (Ometepe). It is also probably present in the Late Polychrome of the Sapoa Valley. The final horizon marker is Luna Polychrome, found in the Santa Ana Phase of Ometepe. Coe reports it for his La Cruz B Phase (Coe 1962:362). In the absence of illustrations it is not certain whether "Luna Polychrome" represents the true type or only one of the so-called Lunoid ceramics, which might or might not be contemporaneous.

This enumeration shows that many links exist between the different sequences of Greater Nicoya and their phases. The signs for the different horizon markers in Figure 12.1 make it clear, however, that at least some sequences have to be corrected. This is especially true when the revised ^{14}C dates are linked with these horizon markers. There are, at the moment, 20 ^{14}C dates for Greater Nicoya, marked in the first column of Table 12.1 with the letter A. Of these, 4 are not accepted, leaving 16 samples for the dating of the sequences. Of these, 4 belong to the Zoned Bichrome Period, 5 to the Early Polychrome Period, 4 to the Middle Polychrome Period, and 3 to the Late Polychrome Period.

The Zoned Bichrome dates (A1–A4) have a corrected range from 512 B.C. to A.D. 850, that is, more than 1350 years, which may be too long for this period. Especially A4 (Y-809), dating the Monte Fresco Phase (Tamarindo Zone), has a very large 1-sigma range of 560 years, which, with correction, is even more extended. Eliminating this date, which in its earlier part is overlapped by A3 (Y-850) and A2 (Y-810), would compress the time range to about 450 years (to A.D. 390). Baudez, using the same dates but uncorrected, thought that the Zoned Bichrome Period lasted from 300 B.C. to A.D. 300 (Baudez 1967:205–207). He accepted these dates because he also saw connections between Rosales Zoned Engraved and the Late Formative "Utatlán Ware" of Guatemala and between certain bichromes painted with a multiple brush (Charco Black-on-red, Zelaya Bichrome, etc.) and the

TABLE 12.1

Annotated List of ^{14}C Dates

Number	Institution number	Provenience	B.P. date	Old sigma range	Range with Suess effect	Phase/Period	Remarks
A1	GsY-100	Ortega 3/L6	2195 ± 130	375–115 B.C.	512–450—125–115 B.C.	Catalina	Date composed of two runs.
A2	Y-810	Matapalo, G 11/ 2J, Cut 2, 135–150 cm	1870 ± 200	120 B.C.–A.D. 280	120 B.C.–A.D. 320	Monte Fresco	
A3	Y-850	Ortega 170 cm	1700 ± 70	A.D. 180–320	A.D. 230–235 to 380–388	Catalina	
A4	Y-809	Matapalo, G 11/ 1 K, Cut 1, 150–165 cm	1530 ± 280	A.D. 140–700	A.D. 212–ca. 850	Monte Fresco	Slightly too late; Coe thinks it to be contaminated by air.
A5	Y-811	Matapalo, G 11 / 1 E, Cut 1, 60–75 cm	1395 ± 90	A.D. 465–645	A.D. 540–675	Matapalo	
A6	Y-1124	Ayala (Gr-5), Cut 2, 285 cm	1390 ± 100	A.D. 460–660	A.D. 535–665	Beginning of Early Polychrome	
A7	Y-1122	Ayala (Gr-5), Cut 2, 195 cm	1380 ± 70	A.D. 500–640	A.D. 575–670	Beginning of San Roque	
A8	M-1173	Matapalo, Cut 1, 60–75 cm	1270 ± 75	A.D. 575–725	A.D. 653 to 775–850	Matapalo	
A9	Y-1125	Cruz (Ri-7), Cut 2, 260 cm	1170 ± 120	A.D. 660–900	A.D. 685–940	End of San Roque	
A10	GsY-99	La Bocana, 1/ M3	1005 ± 90	A.D. 855–1035	A.D. 858 to 1068–1174	Zoned Bichrome	Contaminated, not used.
A11	Y-815	Huerta del Aguacate, G 2 / 2 E, Cut 2, 60–75 cm	990 ± 70	A.D. 890–1030	A.D. 920–ca.1200	Tamarindo	
A12	Hv-2688	Los Angeles, F 1	970 ± 60	A.D. 920–1040	A.D. 980–1070	Gato	
A13	M-1172	Chahuite Escondido, Cut 4, 105–90 cm	920 ± 75	A.D. 955–1105	A.D. 1025–ca. 1200	Late Chombo or Early Santa Elena	Contents mixed through intrusive graves.
A14	Y-816	Chahuite Escondido, B 1 / 1 B, Cut 1, 15–30 cm	840 ± 70	A.D. 1040–1180	A.D. 1070–1183 to 1180–1275	La Cruz	Too late. Not used for sequence.
A15	Hv-2690	La Paloma, 4-F, 100–120 cm	675 ± 50	A.D. 1225–1325	A.D. 1230–1290	La Paloma	
A16	Hv-2691	La Paloma, 4-I, 160–180 cm	660 ± 50	A.D. 1240–1340	A.D. 1240–1310	La Paloma	
A17	GsY-98	La Bocana, 1 / G 1	515 ± 150	A.D. 1285–1585	A.D. 1275 to 1467–1511	Late Polychrome	
A18	Hv-2692	San Lázaro 3-B, 20-40 cm	505 ± 30	A.D. 1415–1475	A.D. 1380–1410	End of San Lázaro	
A19	Hv-2669	Los Angeles, B-9	460 ± 75	A.D. 1415–1565	A.D. 1420–1450	Gato	Much too late; probably contaminated. Not used for sequence.
A20	Y-814	Miramar, G 10/3C, Cut 3,30–45 cm	220 ± 100	A.D. 1630–1830	A.D. 1490–1590 to 1670–1750	Colonial	Pottery used for salt production, thick-walled.

TABLE 12.1 *(Continued)*

Number	Institution number	Provenience	B.P. date	Old sigma range	Range with Suess effect	Phase/Period	Remarks
B1		Mercocha, grave	1820 ± 140	10 B.C.–A.D. 270	15 B.C.–A.D. 60 to A.D. 305–325	Unknown	Jade in grave. Only known from remark in Balser 1969.
B2		Porvenir, grave	1685 ± 120	A.D. 145–385	A.D. 196–460	Unknown	Jade in grave. Only known from remark in Balser 1969.
B3	Sh 5-5475A	El Cardel	1530 ± 210	A.D. 210–630	ca. A.D. 260–665	Middle Period A	
B4	SI-147	Marin (W-2), Grave 11	1360 ± 90	A.D. 500–680	A.D. 575 to 705–727	Unknown	
B5	SI-146	Marin (W-1), Grave 4	1330 ± 120	A.D. 500–740	A.D. 575 to 765–832	Unknown	
B6	Sh 50-5592A	Platanillo	1140 ± 220	A.D. 590–1030	A.D. 645 to 1045–1165	Middle Period A	Better for Middle Period B; disregarded in dating sequence.
B7	Sh 29-5592A	Aquiarres, Section 2-B	1030 ± 290	A.D. 630–1210	A.D. 665 to 1210–1230	Middle Period B	
B8	Sh 45- 5211A	Rosa Maria	980 ± 170	A.D. 800–1140	A.D. 937–ca.1200	Middle Period B	
B9	Sh 6-5475A	Monte Cristo	960 ± 430	A.D. 560–1420	A.D. 630–1378	Middle Period B	
B10	SI-144	Marin (W-4), Grave 7	900 ± 90	A.D. 960–1140	A.D. 1030–1042 to ca.1200	Unknown	
B11	Sh 8-5475A	Descanso	870 ± 390	A.D. 690–1470	A.D. 715–745 to 1410	Middle Period B	
B12	Sh 28-5592A	Guayabo 4	730 ± 210	A.D. 1010–1430	A.D. 1055–1130 to 1385	Middle Period B	
B13	SI-145	Marin (W-6), Grave 2	480 ± 90	A.D. 1480–1560	A.D. 1347 to 1460–1467	Unknown	
C1		Trapiche, Stratum E	5850 ± 110	.4010–3790 B.C.	4855–4600 B.C.	Phase 2	
C2		Casita de Piedra, Stratum D	4075 ± 105	2230–2020 B.C.	2945–2870 to 2493–2425 B.C.	Before beginning of Phase 3	
C3	GrN-1516	El Volcán	2290 ± 45	385–295 B.C.	547–460 to 397–391 B.C.	Scarified??	Not known for certain which material is dated.
C4	M-1470	Palenque Island, Pit 2, 90–100 cm	1190 ± 100	A.D. 660–860	A.D. 685–693 to 868	End of Burica	
C5	M-1308	El Cangrejal (SL-1), Pit 3, 60–70 cm	930 ± 100	A.D. 920–1120	A.D. 973–ca.1200	"San Lorenzo"	Now probably Chiriquí Phase, as San Lorenzo has been abandoned.
C6	GrN-1520	Pueblo Nuevo	330 ± 50	A.D. 1570–1770	A.D. 1460–1485 to 1605–1642	Unknown	May date shaft-and-chamber grave, but then much too late.
C7	M-1309	Las Secas Island (IS-11), Pit 1, 40–50 cm	115 ± 100	A.D. 1735–1935	A.D. (1900) to 1613–1644	(Chiriquí)	Much too late, cannot be accepted.

D1	FSU-300	Alvina de Parita, hearth	11399 ± 330	9649–9049 B.C.	Outside of range		Dates hearth, without any cultural material associated.
D2	Y-458-d	Cerro Mangote, Pit V, 130–145 cm	6810 ± 110	4970–4750 B.C.	Outside of range	Cerro Mangote	
D3	Y-585	Monagrillo (He-5)	4090 ± 70	2210–2070 B.C.	2940–2790 to 2585–2510 B.C.	Monagrillo	
D4	GIF-1643	La India (T1-1)	1930 ± 100	80 B.C.–A.D. 120	97–80 B.C. to A.D. 163	Búcaro	
D5	M-1474	Mariato Region, MO-1, Mound 4, 215–225 cm	1760 ± 130	A.D. 60–320	A.D. 87 to 463–470	Unknown	
D6	Y-125	Venado Beach, Area A, Trench 8, between A-7 and B-2, 29 inches	1750 ± 60	A.D. 140–260	A.D. 188 to 288–290	Early Coclé	Should be the same as D12; Lothrop thought it too early.
D7	M-1472	Mariato Region, MO-1, Mound 2, 355–370 cm	1700 ± 120	A.D. 130–370	A.D. 175–445	Unknown	
D8	GIF-1641	Tonosí	1560 ± 100	A.D. 290–490	A.D. 335–350 to 565	El Indio	Shell
D9	GIF-1642	Tonosí	1500 ± 100	A.D. 350–550	A.D. 425–625	El Indio	Shell
D10	M-1471	Mariato Region, MO-1, Mound 2, 190–205 cm	1480 ± 120	A.D. 350–590	A.D. 425–645	Unknown	
D11	M-1475	Mariato Region, MO-1, Mound 4, 130–150 cm	1400 ± 120	A.D. 430–670	A.D. 505 to 695–710	Unknown	
D12	GrN-2200	Venado Beach	1125 ± 65	A.D. 760–890	A.D. ca. 850–920	Early Coclé	Probably too late; see D6.
D13	GIF-1520	La Bernardina (T1-10)	1100 ± 95	A.D. 755–945	A.D. ca. 850–1016	Bijaguales	
D14	GX-1545	Guanaquito Abajo (T1-28)	955 ± 120	A.D. 875–1115	A.D. 894–ca. 1200	Bijaguales	
D15	M-11	Monagrillo (He-5)	800 ± 250	A.D. 900–1400	A.D. 937–1363	Unknown	Shell
D16	I-637	El Hatillo, shaft-and-chamber grave	415 ± 90	A.D. 1445–1625	A.D. 1402 to 1487–1581	Unknown	

Usulután ceramics. All these arguments are very weak and obviously of no chronological value. Lange, in discussing the Zoned Bichrome Period, argues that Schettel Incised has some similarities with certain Conchas II types of coastal Guatemala (Lange 1971:129–149; Lange and Scheidenhelm 1972:244). He therefore begins his "Schettel-dominated Zoned Bichrome"—the first part of the San Dimas Phase—at 500 B.C., which would be in accordance with the present ^{14}C dates. This extension, which would hold true for Catalina and most other Zoned Bichrome phases, makes it necessary to revise the guess dates for the Angeles and Dinarte phases of Ometepe Island. As shown elsewhere (Haberland 1966:401), the Angeles Phase clearly antedates stratigraphically the Sinacapa Phase (at that time called "Avilés-like"). Since Schettel Incised is an integral part of the Sinacapa Phase, Angeles should end—and Sinacapa begin—at about 500 B.C. The open questions are: How long was the duration of the Angeles Phase? What time was consumed by the gap between the Angeles and Dinarte phases, which is indicated by the sterile layers in Pits 1 and 2 of Los Angeles? And how long did the Dinarte Phase—the oldest phase known to date from Ometepe Island and also from Greater Nicoya (Haberland 1966)—continue? To date the Dinarte Phase, there is a certain amount of similarity between the few decorated sherds and material from the Cuadros Phase of coastal Guatemala (Coe and Flannery 1967). Since Meggers and Evans also saw certain similarities between Dinarte sherds and their Machalilla material (Haberland 1966:402) a dating of Dinarte at about 1000 B.C. might be justified. Coe and Baudez ended the Zoned Bichrome Period at A.D. 300 (1961:512–514), but an end date of about A.D. 400 is more compatible with dates A2 (Y-810) and A3 (Y-850).

The correlation of the beginning of the Middle Polychrome Period is quite easy, since it is characterized by the appearance of Papagayo Polychrome. This event is, at the same time, used by most authors and excavators as an indication of a new phase. The only exception is the Gato Phase of Ometepe Island, where Papagayo Polychrome is thought to appear at about the middle of the phase, probably as imports or the ceramics of a new immigrating population element. There are four usable ^{14}C dates for the Middle Polychrome Period: A11, A12, A15, and A16. One of them, A12 (Hv-2688), dates the Gato Phase and might, therefore, be only partly relevant for the period, but it may also date more or less the phase's beginning at about A.D. 950. Its end, as shown by A15 (Hv-2690) and A16 (Hv-2691), occurs at about A.D. 1300. This time bracket, A.D. 950–1300, is confirmed by the fact that Papagayo Polychrome is sometimes found together with Tohil Plumbate at the southern fringes of Mesoamerica (Baudez (1966:337–338; Baudez and Becquelin 1969:224). These contexts are usually assigned to the end of the Late Classic and to the Early Postclassic of Mesoamerica. This leaves about 250 years for the last period, Late Polychrome. Sometimes this period is composed of two consecutive phases, the earlier one characterized by Vallejo Polychrome, which stems from the Papagayo Tradition, the later one by the intrusive Luna Polychrome. This was already recognized by Coe, who distinguished between La Cruz A and La Cruz B. Unfortunately his ^{14}C date for this phase, A14 (Y-816), can be connected only with the La Cruz Phase and not with one of its subdivisions. Furthermore, the range of this date (A.D. 1070–1215) falls well inside the Middle Polychrome Period as defined earlier. It is, therefore, more than equivocal and will not be used for dating purposes. The Late Polychrome date of Baudez, A17 (GsY-98), relates to the Bebedero Phase. While this is a "Vallejo Phase," lacking Luna Polychrome, it is not certain whether there are any Luna Polychromes in the Tempisque Valley at all. Therefore, A17 cannot be assigned only to the "Vallejo time." Certainly dating that time is A18 (Hv-2692), which comes from a single-component site. It would indicate that the Luna phases did not begin earlier than A.D. 1400 and probably began later than that date.

This leaves only the time between the end of the Zoned Bichrome Period and the beginning of the Middle Polychrome Period unaccounted for—a time that poses the greatest difficulties. Baudez filled it with two periods, Linear Decorated and Early Polychrome. The first of them, represented by the Ciruelas Phase, includes Tola Trichrome, while true polychromes appear in the Early Polychrome Phase of San Bosco. Obviously there exists in the Tempisque Valley a clear-cut division between the two phases. In no other sequence, however, has anything comparable been found. The Matapalo Phase of the Tamarindo Zone includes Tola Trichrome as well as the early Carillo and Gallo Polychromes (Coe 1962:363). In the Santa Elena sequence, as far as can be verified through the preliminary report, Tola Trichrome is completely missing, as are all other bichromes of the same group (Chavez White-on-red, León Punctate, etc.) (Norweb 1964:559). In the Rivas and Ometepe sequences, Tola Trichrome characterizes the Palos Negros Phase, which occupies the second half of Norweb's Early Polychrome Period. It is absent from the earlier San Roque Phase, which, however, contains the closely related types of Chavez White-on-red, León Punctate and others (Norweb 1964:554). This shows a local development that, on Ometepe Island, can be traced back into the Manantial Phase of Zoned Bichrome affiliation. Since these antecedents are missing in Northern Costa Rica, it is probable that Tola Trichrome and related types have been imported into this region. On the other hand, Coe claims to have found Chavez White-on-red "in relatively high frequency" in the Santa Elena Phase (Coe 1962:362). Lange found Tola Trichrome and related types together with Carillo Polychrome in his Early Polychrome Phase (Lange 1971:150–157). The Toloid types at least did not seem to be imported. In any case, Tola Trichrome and related types should in Northern Costa Rica, that is, the southern part of Greater Nicoya, appear at about the same time or later than in Southern Nicaragua, but not earlier, as implied by the sequences (see Figure 12.1).

Another difficulty in correlating the two parts of Greater Nicoya during this time of (probably) maximum extension is the fact that in Southern Nicaragua there is no phase with "early polychromes" (Carillo and Gallo) exclusively. In the Rivas sequence, polychromes appear with the beginning of the Apompua Phase, but obviously only Papagayo and other "late polychromes" are present, and none of the early ones. These have been found sometimes in the Gato Phase of Ometepe Island but are associated with Tola Trichrome and similar types. Papagayo Polychrome, emerging about the middle of this phase, is also associated with Toloid ceramics, the hallmark of the Gato Phase.

In correlating the different sequences one has to take into account several still unproven ideas. First of all, the distinction between Linear Decorated and Early Polychrome should be dropped because in most of the sequences such a division cannot be proved. This is also advocated by Lange (1971: 148–150). Then, we have to assume either that there is a break in the Tempisque sequence, with something missing between Catalina and Ciruelas, or that Catalina lasted longer than the Zoned Bichrome phases of other regions. If one of these hypotheses is accepted, we can place Ciruelas opposite Palos Negros, as indicated by the presence of Tola Trichrome in both phases. San Bosco would in this case equal the first part of Gato, while the place of San Roque would not be occupied by any Tempisque Phase.

The five ^{14}C dates, two for the Matapalo Phase, two for Palos Negros, and one for San Roque (A5–A9) cover a corrected range of A.D. 540 to 940. A dating of the "new" Early Polychrome Period at A.D. 500 to 950 might be in accordance with the dates. The end of the Zoned Bichrome Period would, therefore, be corrected to A.D. 500 instead of A.D. 400 as proposed earlier. The beginning of the Palos Negros Phase and of the Tola Trichrome should be placed at about A.D. 600. The result of these adjustments is shown in Figure 12.2. The generalized sequence (Column 1), which will be used for comparison with other areas, reads as follows: 500 B.C.–A.D. 500, Zoned Bichrome; A.D. 500–950, Early Polychrome; A.D. 950–1300, Middle Polychrome; A.D. 1300–1600, Late Polychrome. The phases before 500 B.C.—to date known only from Ometepe Island—are included in a "Formative Period" tentatively dated 1200–500 B.C.

C. Central Costa Rica

This area has only a single dated sequence, developed by William J. Kennedy through his investigations in the Reventazon Valley. The sequence has not yet been published and is, therefore, scarcely usable for chronological comparison. Of the 13 ^{14}C dates for Central Costa Rica, 7 belong to this sequence while 6 others date graves at the Linea Vieja. Nothing is yet known, however, about these excavations by the Stirlings, except that the dates B1 and B2 (both with unknown laboratory numbers) are connected with jade objects (Balser 1969:245–246). Two of the Reventazon dates, B3

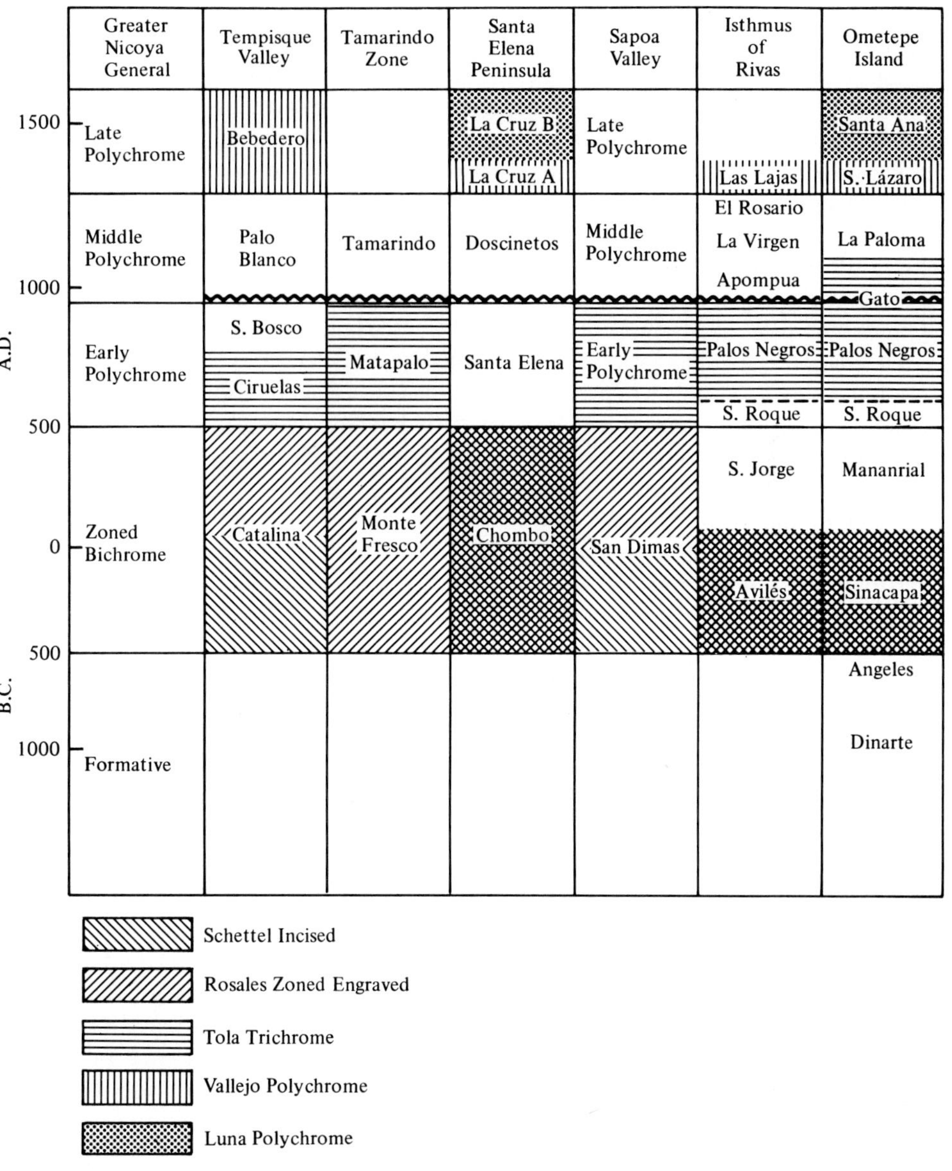

Figure 12.2 Greater Nicoya, revised sequences.

(Sh 5-5475A) and B6 (Sh 50-5592A), are connected with Middle Period A, distinguished by ceramics with appliqué and/or punctate decoration and grit temper (Kennedy, personal communication). Kennedy dated this period A.D. 400–850. The corrected range, however, is from A.D. 260 to 1165, which is very long. Since B6 more or less completely overlaps several of the Middle Period B dates—B7, B9, and B11—it might, rather, be part of that period. The lack of detailed publication prevents a checking of its possible association and it is therefore better to disregard B6 entirely for the dating. The five Middle Period B dates, B7–B9, B11–B12, are all clustered inside the same time span, in spite of the fact that some 1-sigma ranges are very long, including B9 with 860 years. A certain redating is, however, necessary because the new dates require the Middle Period A to begin at about A.D. 200 and end at A.D. 700, while Middle Period B ends, as in Kennedy's original scheme, at about A.D. 1400. This period, I might mention in passing, has line-decorated ceramics as well as a few Mora Polychrome sherds, the latter imported from Nicoya.

While the Late Period covers the remaining time until the European conquest and is, therefore, fixed in time, the Early Period was assigned by Kennedy a time from 300 B.C. to A.D. 400. The reason for this dating is unknown. However, it begins at 300 B.C., the same time as the Zoned Bichrome Period of Greater Nicoya was originally thought to begin. Since rocker stamping and red-on-buff painting are the most important ceramic decoration modes, a connection with Zoned Bichrome might be correct. A dating commencing about 300 B.C. or even slightly earlier is, therefore, justified.

Several attempts have been made during the last decades to establish a chronology in the Meseta Central of Costa Rica, especially through a reevaluation of Hartman's excavations (e.g., Baudez 1963). The most successful of them was by Rowe (1959:275–276), adapted in Figure 12.3, Column 2 and also used, for example, by Baudez (1970:225). But even this sequence remains controversial because it lacks a true stratigraphy. Only the end of the sequence can be dated, through glass beads found in some Orosí V graves. For purposes of comparison, this sequence cannot be used. As mentioned earlier, no stratigraphic sequence has been established to date for the "Linea Vieja," despite the fact that this is one of the most intensively excavated regions in all Lower Central America.

D. Greater Chiriquí

There is again only one stratigraphic column for all of Greater Chiriquí. It is based on several excavations by different archaeologists. Although stratigraphic evidence was often missing, it is generally thought to be correct and applicable in all regions. The phases are sometimes known by local names, such as Boruca Phase in the Valle del General, which has slightly

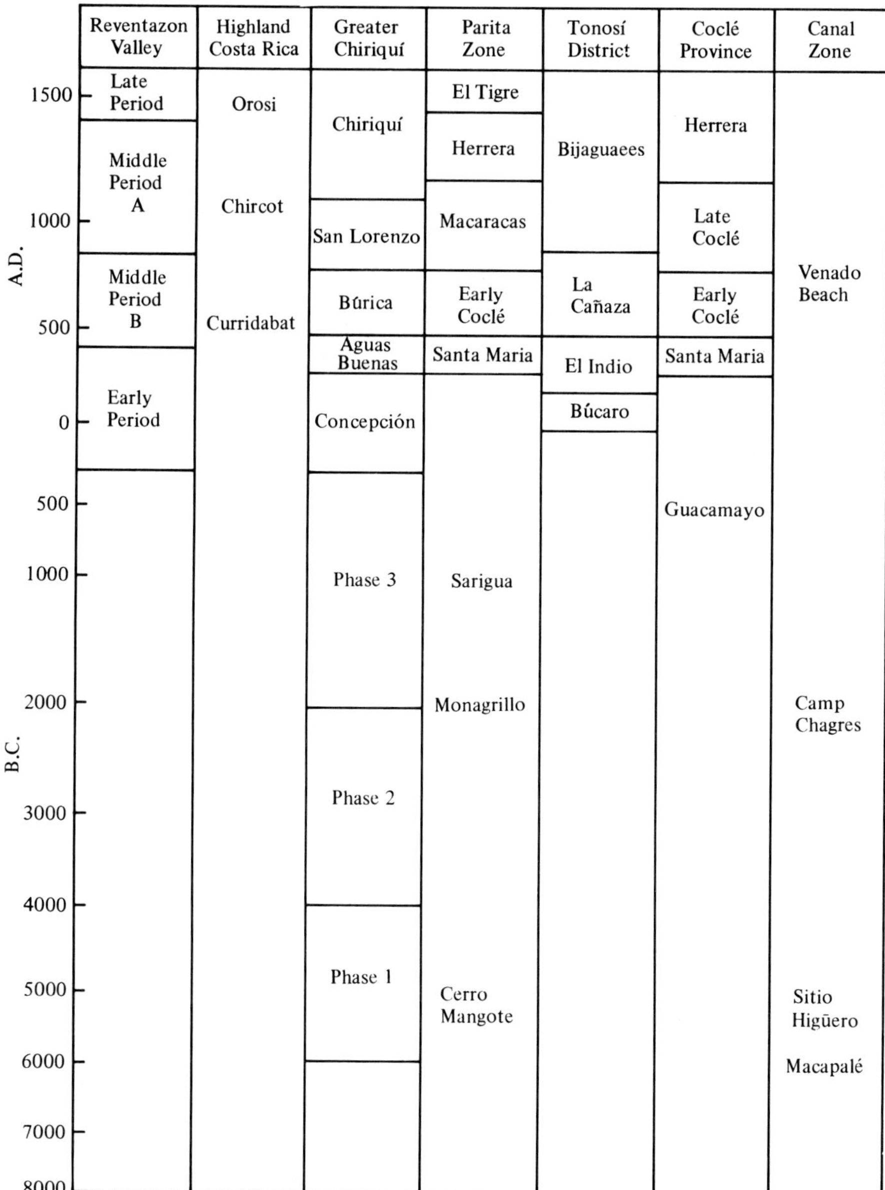

Figure 12.3. Central Costa Rica Greater Chiriquí, Gulf of Panama sequences as given by excavators.

different content but is intimately related to and contemporaneous with the Chiriquí Phase (Haberland 1959).

The first true stratigraphy was quite recently developed by Linares on the Pacific coast of Chiriquí, where three phases were found (Linares 1968). Since publishing these data, however, Linares now doubts the San Lorenzo Phase and would like to eliminate it from the sequence (personal communication). I completely agree with Linares, having found typical San Lorenzo ceramics together with Chiriquí types in the same grave (Haberland 1961a:35–36). Taking this as well as the corrected ^{14}C dates C5 (M-1308) into account, the Chiriquí Phase with its polychrome and negative painted pottery could begin about A.D. 950. For the stratigraphically earlier Burica Phase, there is only one ^{14}C date, C4 (M-1470), which, according to Linares, covers the end of this entity. The beginning of the phase was fixed by the excavator at about A.D. 300–500, as some Coclé sherds, probably of Early Coclé affiliation, have been found and because Linares thinks that Early Coclé began about A.D. 500 (Linares 1968:86).

As I have shown elsewhere (Haberland 1961a, 1962, 1969), and as corroborated by Linares (1968:85–86), the Aguas Buenas and Concepción phases are older than Burica. The stratigraphic proof of this is, however, still lacking—or at least still not satisfactory. Recent deliberations make it likely that Concepción is older than Aguas Buenas (Haberland 1969a:234–235). Their dating—Aguas Buenas from A.D. 300 to 500, Concepción from 300 B.C. to A.D. 300—is speculative, although based on diverse lines of reasoning (Haberland 1969a: especially p. 240). The ^{14}C sample C3 (GrN–1516) always used for the dating of "Scarified Ware," that is, the Concepción Phase, has to be rejected, since nothing is really known about the material with which it was associated. Certainly it has no connection with Pueblo Nuevo, as is often argued. Feriz (1959:732; 1961:266) explicitly states that the sample was collected at El Volcán. The Pueblo Nuevo excavations are dated by C6 (GrN-1520), which Feriz rejected—probably correctly—as too young (1959:732; 1961:266).

This reconstructed sequence has recently been greatly expanded through excavations in rockshelters along the Rio Chiriquí by Linares and Ranere (1971). At least three preceramic phases have been found, which were tentatively dated. Linares and Ranere think that their Phase 1 lasted from 6000 to 4000 B.C., Phase 2 from 4000 B.C. to "before 2000 B.C.," and Phase 3 from that date to about 300 B.C. (1971:348–351). Phases 2 and 3 of this sequence possess one ^{14}C date each. Correcting them gives a different picture and necessitates shifting the phases in time. While Linares and Ranere give the date C1 (unknown laboratory number) as 3900 B.C., the corrected range, including the sigma, is 4855–4600 B.C. This date shows that Phase 2 began probably no later than 5000 B.C., with Phase 1 beginning perhaps as early as 7000 or 8000 B.C. (see also later discussion). Date C2 (unknown laboratory number) is given as 2125 B.C. by the authors. It antedates the outset of Phase 3 at Casita de Piedra, as it comes from Level D. Unfortunately the report does not state whether this level was a sterile layer or not. Yet Stratum E was connected with Phase 2 and Strata C and B with Phase 3. The corrected date, ranging from 2940 to 2510 B.C., makes it possible that Phase 3 may have begun as early as 2500 B.C. Overlaying Phase 3 of the preceramic sequence are ceramic complexes that, judging from the illustration (Linares and Ranere 1971:354), look very much like Aguas Buenas.

E. Gulf of Panama

While Central Costa Rica and Greater Chiriquí had only one good sequence each, here we have a deal with four sequences (Columns 4–7, Figure 12.3). Of these, the youngest, established by Ichon in the Tonosí district of Los Santos Province (Linares 1971:238–239; Ichon, personal communication) is the most completely dated. Four phases have been set up (Figure 12.3, Column 5), with a probable fifth covering Conquest time. The oldest is Búcaro, dated through D4 (GIF-1643). Ichon thinks that this phase covers the first two centuries after Christ; but the corrected range of D4 indicates that a beginning about 100 B.C. is probably correct (see revised sequence in Figure 12.4). Two dates, D8 (GIF-1641) and D9 (GIF-1642) apply to the subsequent El Indio Phase, which Ichón thinks covers the time between A.D. 200 and 500. The corrected dates, including their sigma, make it necessary to lengthen the time in which El Indio flourished to A.D. 650. Whether it began about A.D. 200 as Ichón thinks (personal communication) or a century later cannot yet be verified, since none of the ^{14}C dates covers this time. As a compromise, a date of A.D. 250 for the ending of Búcaro and the beginning of El Indio is proposed.

The next phase, La Cañaza, has no ^{14}C dates. On account of the surrounding dates and the Early Coclé polychromes found, Ichon places it between A.D. 500 and 900 (personal communication). The beginning must, however, be postponed, since the El Indio Phase does not end before A.D. 650. The end of La Cañaza depends on two ^{14}C dates, D13 (GIF-1520) and D14 (GX-1545), connected with the following Bijaguales Phase. Their range covers the time from A.D. 850 to 1200. Therefore, a beginning around A.D. 800 seems justified, a century earlier than Ichon places it. Ichon also thinks that Bijaguales ends at about Conquest. However, there are no dates for the last four centuries, and it is possible that there might be yet another unnamed phase between A.D. 1200 and 1550, as Linares indicated (1971:239).

The sequence for Coclé was established through contributions by Lothrop (1937–1942) and Ladd (1957). Ladd also revised the late parts of the Parita sequence (1964), while the older phases were published by Willey and McGimsey (1954), Willey and Stoddard (1954), and McGimsey (1956). Unfortunately, there are no ^{14}C dates for the later parts of these intimately

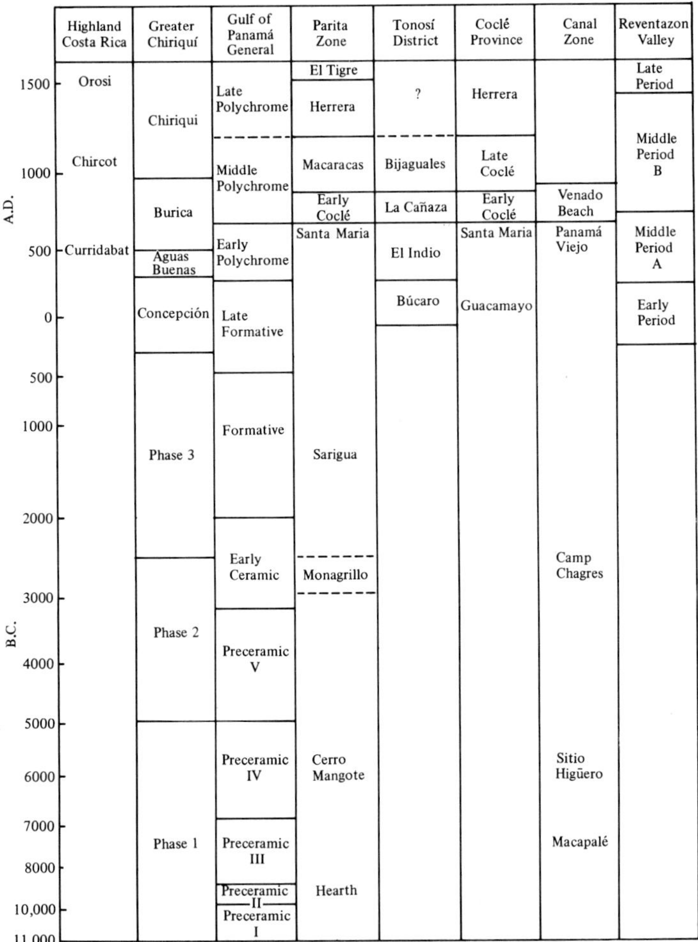

Figure 12.4. Central Costa Rica, Greater Chiriquí, Gulf of Panama, revised sequences.

related sequences. All dates by which the phases are ordered in Figure 12.3 (Columns 4 and 6) are guess dates as proposed by Ladd (1957, 1964) and discussed by Linares (1968:87–89, Fig. 47). A key phase may be "Early Coclé," which Ladd (1964:222) placed in the second half of the first millennium, while Linares dated it A.D. 500–800 (1968:88). Since much "Early Coclé" material has been found in the La Cañaza Phase (Tonosí), a dating of Early Coclé similar to that phase, that is A.D. 650–850, would seem justifiable and at least as good as the guess dates used up to now. This places the beginning of Late Coclé at A.D. 850. Its end might well be A.D. 1200, as given by Linares (1968:88), because that would conform to the known end of Bijaguales. Contemporaneity between Late Coclé, Macaracas—its Parita counterpart—and Bijaguales is demonstrated by the Macaracas Polychrome pottery found in all three phases. The dating of the Herrera Phase in Parita and Coclé by Linares (1968:89) on the basis of Ladd's investigations (especially 1964:223) from A.D. 1200 to 1500 is accepted here, as well as that of the El Tigre Phase (Parita), thought to have flourished at about Conquest and in colonial times (Willey and McGimsey 1954:134; Ladd 1964:22, 224–225). The presence of another phase after A.D. 1200 confirms the probability of one more phase after Bijaguales in the Tonosí sequence.

The Santa María Phase precedes Early Coclé in Parita and Coclé. As pointed out by Ladd (1964:221), no absolute dates can be given except that this phase is earlier than Early Coclé. Linares in her chronological chart (1968: Fig. 47) dates Santa María from A.D. 300 to 500. This may be correct, but a verification is urgently needed, especially since Santa María ceramics are often associated with Early Coclé ones (Ladd 1964:221). Santa María may, therefore, be only a local variant at certain sites and not a true phase at all. For the moment it is placed opposite El Indio in the revised chronological table (Figure 12.4, Columns 4 and 6). There is a gap in the Parita sequence prior to the Santa María Phase. Santa María is also the first more or less firmly established phase in Coclé. In this province, however, another complex has been found that is antecedent to Santa María. For this Guacamayo Phase, only graves are known as yet (N. A. Harte 1966; E. M. Harte 1958; Stirling and Stirling 1964a). Linares places Guacamayo at about 300 B.C., that is, opposite the Concepción Phase of Chiriquí, as the pottery types of both phases are decorated with groups of incisions ("scarifications"). As pointed out elsewhere (Haberland 1969a:236–239) there are a relatively large number of sites, phases, and complexes with such ceramics. One of them, found by Mitchell and Heidenreich (1965: Pl. 7-9) at Tonosí was called "Lower Level" (Haberland 1969a:236–239, Fig. 6). It is now the Búcaro Phase of Ichon. Guacamayo should, therefore, be placed opposite Búcaro. Preceding the gap mentioned earlier, are two ceramic and one preceramic phases in the Parita sequence. One of the two ceramic phases, Monagrillo, has a single ^{14}C date, D3 (Y-585). Through it, Monagrillo with its simple ceramics (Willey and McGimsey 1954) has always been placed at about 2000 B.C. (see for example Willey 1971: Fig. 2-2). The corrected date has, however, a range of from 2940 to 2510 B.C., putting this phase closer perhaps to Puerto Hormiga in Colombia (see Reichel-Dolmatoff 1971) and Valdivia in Ecuador (Meggers *et al.* 1965), with which it shares a number of ceramic modes. The subsequent Sarigua Phase has no dates at all. Willey (1971: Fig. 5-7) places it at the beginning of his "Formative Period," that is, at about 1500 B.C., a date that is as good as any and is, therefore, retained here. The preceramic Cerro Mangote Phase also has only one ^{14}C date, D2 (Y-458-d) (McGimsey 1958). With a dating of 6810 ± 100 B.P., it is outside the calculated Suess corrections and cannot at present be corrected. Its future correction will probably make it about 800 to 1000 years older. That places Cerro Mangote at about 6000 B.C and not at 5000 B.C. as in older publications.

The oldest date for the Parita region, D1 (FSU-300), was collected by Donald L. Crusoe (Crusoe and Felton 1971); it is reported to date a hearth at La Alvina de Parita—probably the same site as La Mula of Willey and McGimsey (1954:110–115) and is associated with some Sarigua sherds. The date of 9350 ± 250 B.C. is, however, impossible for this ceramic material. Crusoe now thinks (personal communication) that the sherds came accidentally into the hearth area and that the sample dates only the hearth itself—as well as probably some other hearths on the same site. All are certainly of human construction. No artifacts have so far been recovered from these hearths which, nevertheless, indicate the presence of man in this part of the New World as early as 10,000 B.C.

Crusoe and Felton also constructed a tentative early sequence for the Canal Zone—Madden Lake—Chamé region (1971), tying finds from there to known material by comparison, especially with the Parita region. The Camp Chagres Complex, especially its projectile points and choppers, is thought to be similar to Monagrillo. This idea is further strengthened by the fact that the ceramic complex is in both cases topped by Sarigua or Sarigua-like material. Crusoe and Felton also see many links between their site Sitio Higuero in the Chamé region (Crusoe 1970) and Cerro Mangote. Finally, the oldest finds—from Macapalé Island in the Madden Lake—including the fluted points (Sander 1959, 1964), are aligned with the El Inga material from Ecuador (Bell 1960, 1965). While Crusoe and Felton give this Macapalé Complex a "conservative dating" at about 6000 B.C., I would put these objects, according to the El Inga I ^{14}C dates, at about 7000 B.C. if not earlier (see also Willey 1971:45–46, Fig. 2-2).

For the later part of the Canal Zone sequence, there is only scanty evidence, in spite of the large cemetery of Venado Beach, which Lothrop intended to publish at the time of his death. It is dated by D6 (Y-125) and D12 (GrN-2200), which differ at their nearest sigma point by about 450 years. Since the urn burials from which the samples came were in Lothrop's opinion alike, he thought the Yale date (D6) was too early (Lothrop 1959a, 1960) and that a correct date should lie halfway between D6 and D12 (personal communication). Since no pottery has as yet been published, there is no possibility to compare this cemetery with other phases nor to decide whether it belongs in one or more phases. Linares thinks that its ceramics are of Early Coclé types (1968:88) and puts it opposite that phase (Fig. 47). Since there is no better argument, I have placed it at the outset of this phase, that is, between A.D. 650 and 920—the end of the D12 sigma—covering, therefore, also some parts of Late Coclé.

The situation at Panamá Viejo is also very confused. No real stratigraphy is present or presented (Biese 1964). It is possible that the relief modeled ceramics ("Votive Ware" and Incised Relief Brown Ware; Biese 1964, Pls.

3–8, 12–14, 16–18, etc.) are contemporaneous with the Santa María Phase of Parita and Coclé. The link is provided by the urn covers, which look very similar to Girón Polychrome (cf. Biese 1964: frontispiece and Fig. 1 with Ladd 1964: Fig. 60 and Pl. 13). Of the 16 ^{14}C dates for the Gulf of Panama area—lettered D—5 have not yet been mentioned. Four of them, D5, D7, D10, and D11, are from the Mariato region of Veraguas. They are said to have been collected by J. A. Schultz from shellmounds (Crane and Griffin 1965:143–144) and to be connected with polychromes (Linares 1968:87, Fig. 47), some of which might be similar to the El Indio ceramics of Tonosí (Linares 1971:239). The fifth date, D16, from El Hatillo, is also so far unconnected with pottery types.

For the Gulf of Panama area, then, the only task that remains is that of developing a general terminology acceptable and flexible enough to accommodate future additions. Willey (1971: Fig. 5-7) adopted certain terms for his ceramic chronology of the Intermediate Area that were first used by Meggers for Ecuador (1966). They might be useful; but I prefer smaller entities, to facilitate possible coordinations. As shown in Figure 12.4, Column 3, there is, in reverse order (i.e., working back from Conquest time), a Late Polychrome Period, until A.D. 1200, preceded by a Middle Polychrome Period—A.D. 650–1200—which may later be split into two parts. Whereas there is great uniformity in the area during these two periods, the Early Polychrome Period—A.D. 250–650—shows much diversification. The time from 500 B.C. to A.D. 250 will be called Late Formative. It is preceded by the Formative Period—2000–500 B.C. This and the earlier periods have been adopted from Willey's scheme.

F. Summary

Having discussed and generalized the sequences of the four areas, we might now proceed to compare them (see Figure 12.5). Normally there should be enough trade material between the areas to check the sequences against one another and to refine datings. There might even be horizon markers covering the whole of Lower Central America. However, nothing has yet been found that might serve as a horizon marker for all areas at any time. This fact shows again the diversity of the area as a whole. It rarely—perhaps never—has been an entity. Even the sharing of certain modes, especially in pottery, between two areas is rather rare. One such instance is the "scarified pottery" of Greater Chiriquí and the Gulf of Panamá. Its distribution has been discussed at length elsewhere (Haberland 1969a) and will not be reiterated here. "Scarified" ceramics are typical for the Concepción Phase of Greater Chiriquí, dated 300 B.C.–A.D. 300, and for the Late Formative of the Gulf of Panama area, 500 B.C.–A.D. 250. They are roughly contemporaneous, although Concepción has a guess date and Late Formative is based on a single ^{14}C date, D4 (GIF-1643), which covers only the

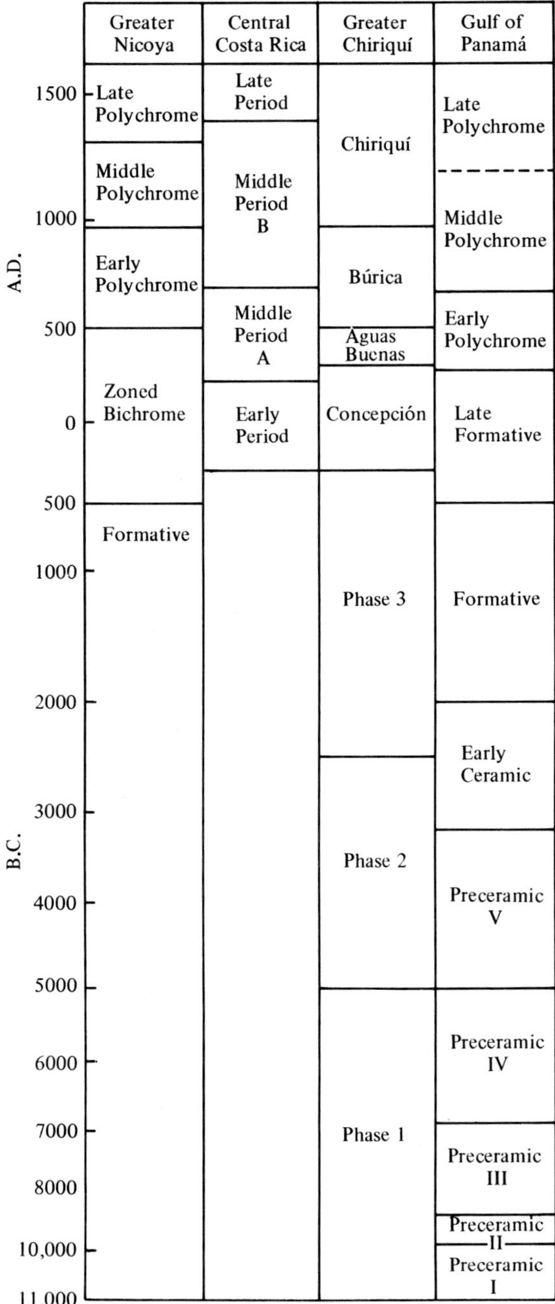

Figure 12.5. Lower Central America, general area sequences.

period 97 B.C.–A.D. 163. This contemporaneity of the two entities might indicate that their dating is basically correct.

A relationship may also exist between Middle Period B of Central Costa Rica and the Chiriquí Phase of Greater Chiriquí. In both of them, white line decoration on a reddish-brown pottery is present (Central Costa Rica: Kennedy, personal communication; Greater Chiriquí: Haberland 1959, Table VI, m–q). The possibility of imports into Chiriquí, raised by Osgood (1935:235), is present but not stringent. Since the periods overlap for a considerable time (A.D. 950–1400; see Figure 12.5, Columns 2 and 3), the connection is possible. However, it does not aid in solving the chronological problems.

A rather vague similarity exists through a ceramic form, the "double tecomate," between the Zoned Bichrome of Greater Nicoya and the Early Polychrome of the Gulf of Panama, through the El Indio Phase of Tonosí (Haberland, 1971). Whether this is a true relationship or only a coincidence cannot be decided yet. In any case the two periods are contemporaneous for 250 years; despite the large distance involved, a cultural connection is not impossible. There is also a general likeness in design, appliqué matters, and common feeling between the Curridabat ceramics (Hartman 1907a) of the Middle Period A of Central Costa Rica (Kennedy, personal communication) and the Aguas Buenas pottery of Greater Chiriquí (Haberland 1955, 1959, 1961a). Here, too, a sharing of certain ceramic traditions is possible, since the periods are contemporaneous.

These few examples exhaust the meager stock of specialized modes that might transcend their area limits. Perhaps further investigations will turn up other and better-suited modes. This is most necessary for preceramic times also. Chiriquían periods have been compared by the excavators in general terms with those of the Gulf of Panama (Linares and Ranere 1971), but the lack of adequately published material precludes detailed comparisons. They equate Phase 2 with Cerro Mangote, and Phase 3 with Monagrillo. Both comparisons are very uncertain. If they turn out to be correct, then the dating of Phase 2 and especially of Phase 1—which in the scheme (Figure 12.3) is contemporaneous with Cerro Mangote—will have to be changed. Even without this comparison, the placing of Phase 1 at from 7000 to 5000 B.C. is disappointing. The few published artifacts (Linares and Ranere 1971:349, Figs. 1a–d) are very similar to implements of those complexes that Willey has called "Flake Tradition" (Willey 1971:34–38), and Lanning and Patterson (1967), "burin industries." A comparison of the five Chiriquí instruments with those from Cerro Chivateros (Linares and Ranere 1971:349, Fig. 1c; Lanning and Patterson 1967:48, Fig. b), as well as with other lithic instruments of the same tradition illustrated by Willey, is convincing and might be enough to place Phase 1 at about 10,000 B.C. It might be of interest that a similar complex was found at Rancho Casimira in the Dominican Republic. This complex, which shares many instrument types with Phase 1, has been dated at about 5000 B.C., much too late on the light of its artifact types (Cruxent and Rouse 1969: especially pp. 50–51).

For a more general comparison, the introduction of some broad artifact categories—such as Zoned Bichrome, Polychrome, and tall tripods—might be of value. None of these, however, proved to be of any chronological aid when tested. Zoned Bichrome is known only from two areas, Greater Nicoya and Greater Chiriquí. It begins in the former about 500 B.C., in the latter about A.D. 300. This difference of 800 years, as well as the absence of this decoration in Central Costa Rica, makes unlikely its introduction from one area into the other. True Polychrome is present in all four areas. In Greater Nicoya, it appears during the Early Polychrome Period, at about A.D. 800 or 900. In Central Costa Rica, it is present during Middle Period B (A.D. 700–1400) but only in small quantities and at least partly imported from Greater Nicoya (Kennedy, personal communication). This suggests that Polychrome is not present at the outset of the period—otherwise the imported pottery would appear earlier here than in its original setting. In Greater Chiriquí, Polychrome begins in A.D. 950, while in the Gulf of Panama area it occurs as early as A.D. 250, the earliest date in Lower Central America. Perhaps later investigations will show a twofold introduction of this pottery decoration—from the north (Mesoamerica) and the south (Colombia?). Its late arrival at the innermost areas and obviously small role in Central Costa Rica (see Hartman 1901; most of his Polychrome was imported) makes this a possible explanation for the temporal differences. The third general type tested, tall tripods, is still more unsatisfactory. They too are present in only two areas—Central Costa Rica, beginning about A.D. 700, and Greater Chiriquí, from 300 B.C. on. There are a few examples in Greater Nicoya, probably only during the Zoned Bichrome Period (Baudez 1967:54, Pl. 48F), but they were never prominent and disappeared quickly. In the Gulf of Panama area they were never present as far as is known. Here, their place was occupied by tall pedestals not known further north and certainly of more southern origin (Haberland 1957).

The other possibility for correlating and checking the sequences are by trade objects. These too are rare. There was some trade in pottery from the Gulf of Panama into Greater Chiriquí, which enabled Linares to connect Late Coclé and Macaracas with her San Lorenzo Phase—a connection later abandoned—and Herrera with the later part of the Chiriquí Phase (Linares 1968:88–89). The present dating does not contradict this (Figure 12.5, Columns 3 and 4). Kennedy reports a few Mora Polychrome sherds from his Middle Period B (personal communication), which makes it contemporaneous with the Middle Polychrome of Greater Nicoya. Mora Polychrome has also been found in the Chircot cemetery in Highland Costa Rica by Hartman, together with several Birmania Polychrome vessels of the same period (Baudez 1967:199–201). There was also a single Birmania Polychrome vessel in the lower layer of Orosí V (Baudez 1967:202), while the upper layer contained Millifiori glass beads (Hartman 1901:175, Pl. 60, Fig. 1-2). These trade pieces corroborate the contemporaneity of the Middle Polychrome of Greater Nicoya and the Middle Period B of Central Costa Rica.

It might be mentioned in passing that in Nicaragua, on the Isthmus of Rivas (Norweb 1964:554), as well as on Ometepe Island, some sherds with painting in Usulután technique have been found, mostly in connection with Zoned Bichrome material. Unfortunately, this technique is of considerable time depth, and the sherds found in Nicaragua have not yet been investigated enough to assign them to one of the known Salvadorean types. Therefore, they are of no chronological value at the moment.

Of greater aid in correlating the sequences should be two materials that have been traded over large distances: gold, and jade. Unfortunately, both have only rarely been found in scientifically impeccable conditions. Gold in particular has rarely been found (with some spectacular exceptions like Sitio Conte) in controlled excavations, so that it cannot yet be dated sufficiently nor assigned with much reliability to specific regions or areas. Therefore, gold cannot yet be used here as a chronological indicator. At first glance the situation as to jade is somewhat better. It was said that the celt-shaped amulets ("ax-gods") of jadeite and similar stones were associated at Las Huacas cemetery with Early Polychrome ceramics (Baudez and Coe 1962:362; the Early Polychrome B mentioned there equates with the Early Polychrome of Baudez's scheme). However, checking the detailed list given by Baudez (1967:196–198) only one piece was found that could be assigned to this period; the majority represent ceramic types of the Catalina or Ciruelas phases, making Las Huacas either late Zoned Bichrome or early Early Polychrome. Probably this cemetery straddles the boundary of the two periods. The connection of jade with Zoned Bichrome is also demonstrated by the investigations at San Dimas (Lange and Scheidenhelm 1972). The bird-shaped "ax-god" was associated there with Zoned Bichrome ceramics, especially such early types as Schettel Incised and Rosales Zoned Engraved. This would at least date this type of jade ornament as far back as 500 B.C. A number of jade pieces with Olmec-style elements have been found in Costa Rica (Balser 1959, 1961, 1969). One of them, a stirrup-shaped object with an Olmecoid head from Nicoya Peninsula was associated with several ax-shaped pendants (Balser 1969:243–244), demonstrating the contemporaneity of these styles. The same association occurred with one of the bat-winged Olmecoid pendants from Guapiles (Linea Vieja) (Balser 1959:282). As indicated by Balser (1969), there is a possibility that the Olmecs imported at least part of their jade from Costa Rica or more likely from Greater Nicoya, where unworked "jade" pebbles have recently been found (Balser 1969:246; Weyl 1969:431–432). Balser's opinion is shared by Elizabeth Easby (1968:81–93). These connections make it probable that jade working in Costa Rica might have begun as early as 800 or 700 B.C. On the other hand, finds at La Fortuna (Costa Rica) demonstrate that ax-shaped jades were still used during the early part of the Early Polychrome Period at least (Baudez and Coe 1966; Stone and Balser 1965). But these finds and those from Guapiles (Linea Vieja) published in the same articles do not assist in establishing a useful connection of jade with the Central Costa Rica periods.

After checking all known associations—which are not numerous—one has to conclude that jade, such as the ax-shaped pendants, have been manufactured in Costa Rica for at least 1000 years. Since no detailed chronological ordering of the different types of jade carvings has been conducted to date—again due to the lack of scientific excavations in key regions—a dating of jade found outside Northern Costa Rica is more or less impossible and has no chronological value. This is true for the single jade bead found by Sander in an Aguas Buenas grave near Boquete (Haberland 1969a:240), which otherwise could well aid a better dating of the Aguas Buenas Phase. The result of these comparisons, of mode distribution as well as of trade items, is extremely meager and has been of little help in improving upon the dating of specific phases and periods. On the other hand, none of the relations established have contradicted a dating, which might indicate that the datings as given earlier are basically correct. Confirmation, however, is obviously a matter for the future.

III FUTURE RESEARCH

Generally speaking, there are no problems of any kind that do not warrant investigation in Lower Central America. Most urgent—as I hope I have demonstrated—is a coordinated effort to establish more and better sequences, complete with ^{14}C dates. These should not only be checked against existing ones but should also be distributed in such a way as to define the boundaries of the existing areas and create new ones where necessary. Cemeteries and mounds should be of only secondary interest, since they will not furnish the sequences needed.

Equally urgent is evaluation and publication of the knowledge already gathered through excavations conducted during the last 20 years. (I am myself one of the culprits who have not yet published their final results.) Other "desk work" might include a reevaluation of older excavations, such as those by Hartman or Bransford, and the stylistic comparison of such artifacts and materials as jade ax-gods or metates. These too might aid chronological ordering as well as the investigation of trade routes. As soon as a chronology of Lower Central America is on firm ground—which it is not yet—problems like the possible jade trade from Costa Rica to the La Venta region or of gold from Panama to Yucatán should be investigated. Another urgent question is that of the immigration of the historic tribes from the north (Nicarao, Chorotega, etc.) and the south (Chibcha-speaking groups) into Lower Central America, and the identification of their archaeological remains, as well as a much needed correction of the ethnohistoric records. In all, this is certainly not an ambitious or sophisticated program, but it is one that would fulfill the basic needs of the archaeology of Lower Central America. All other questions fashionable today—such as settlement patterns, sociological interpretation, ecological adaptation, and so on—will have to wait, except insofar as they can be solved in the course of fieldwork conducted for the primary purpose—chronology and distribution—very old-fashioned matters, but ones that nevertheless have not yet been settled. And these matters are urgent, since internal colonization, the spread of roads and settlements, and the rapid rise of professional *huaquerismo* is destroying the evidence at an ever-increasing pace. In such regions as Highland Costa Rica and Linea Vieja, there will soon be nothing left to excavate.

EDITORS' NOTE

Due to a field trip, the author could not receive and update his manuscript (originally submitted in 1973).

BIBLIOGRAPHY

Balser, C.
1959 Los "Baby Faces" Olmecas de Costa Rica. *33rd Congreso Internacional de Americanistas, Actas* **2**:280–285.
1961 La Influencia Olmeca en Algunos Motivos de la Arqueología de Costa Rica. *Instituto Geográfico de Costa Rica, Informe Semestral Enero a Junio* **1961**:63–78.
1967 Investigación Arqueológica en la Región de Suerre. *Associación Amigos del Museo, Boletín* **34.**
1969 A New Style of Olmec Jade with String Sawing from Costa Rica. *38th Internationaler Amerikanistenkongress, Verhandlungen* **1**:243–247.

Baudez, C. F.
1962 Rapport Préliminaire sur les Recherches Arquéologiques Entreprises dans la Vallée du Tempisque—Guanacaste—Costa Rica. *34th Internationaler Amerikanistenkongress, Akten.* 358–365.
1963 Cultural Development in Lower Central America. In Aboriginal Cultural Development in Latin America: An Interpretative Review, edited by B. J. Meggers and C. Evans. *Smithsonian Miscellaneous Collections* **146**(1):45–51.
1966 Niveaux Céramiques au Honduras: Une Reconsidération de l'Évolution Culturelle. *Journal de la Société des Américanistes* **LV**(2):299–342.
1967 Recherches Archéologiques dans la Vallée du Tempisque, Guanacaste, Costa Rica. *L'Institut des Hautes Etudes de l'Amerique Latine, Travaux et Memoires* No. **18.**
1970 *Central America; Archaeologia Mundi.* Paris: Nagel Publ.

Baudez, C. F., and P. Becquelin
1969 La Séquence de Los Anranjos, Hondures. *38th Internationaler Amerikanistenkongress, Verhandlungen,* 221–227.

Baudez, C. F., and M. D. Coe
1962 Archaeological Sequences in Northwestern Costa Rica. *36th Internationaler Amerikanistenkongress, Akten,* 366–373.
1966 Incised Slate Disks from the Atlantic Watershed of Costa Rica: A Commentary. *American Antiquity* **31**(3):441–443.

Bell, R. E.

1960 Evidence of a Fluted Point Tradition in Ecuador. *American Antiquity* **26**(1):102–106.

1965 *Archaeological Investigations at the Site of El Inga, Ecuador.* Guayaquil: Casa de la Cultura Ecuadoriana.

Biese, L. P.

1964 The Prehistory of Panama Viejo. *Bureau of American Ethnology, Anthropological Papers* No. **68** (also published as *Bulletin* **191:**1–52).

Bollaert, W.

1863 On the Ancient Indian Tombs of Chiriquí in Veragua (Southwest of Panama), on the Isthmus of Darien. *Transactions of the Ethnological Society of London* **2:**147–166.

Bovallius, C.

1886 *Nicaraguan Antiquities.* Stockholm: Swedish Society of Anthropology and Geography.

Bransford, J. F.

1881 Archaeological Researches in Nicaragua. *Smithsonian Contributions to Knowledge* **25**(2):1–96.

Bull, T. H.

1958 Excavations at Venado Beach, Canal Zone. *The Archaeological Society of Panama* **1:**6–14.

1959 Preliminary Report on an Archaeological Site in the District of Chame, Province of Panama, Republic of Panama. *Panama Archaeologist* **2:**91–137.

1961 An Urn-Burial—Venado Beach, Canal Zone. *Panama Archaeologist* **4:**42–47.

Coe, M. D.

1962 Preliminary Report on Archaeological Investigations in Coastal Guanacaste, Costa Rica. *34th Internationaler Amerikanistenkongress, Akten,* 358–365.

Coe, M. D., and C. F. Baudez

1961 The Zoned Bichrome Period in Northwestern Costa Rica. *American Antiquity* **26**(4):505–515.

Coe, M. D., and K. V. Flannery

1967 Early Cultures and Human Ecology in South Coastal Guatemala. *Smithsonian Contributions to Anthropology* No. **3.**

Crane, H. R., and J. B. Griffin

1965 University of Michigan Radiocarbon Dates X. *Radiocarbon* **7:**123–152.

Crusoe, D. L.

1970 Archaic-Formative Cultures Along the Western Coast of the Gulf of Panama. Unpublished thesis.

Crusoe, D. L., and J. H. Felton

1971 Lithic Assemblages in Panamanian Prehistory. Paper presented at the Second Symposium of Archaeology and Ethnohistory of Panama.

Cruxent, J. M., and I. Rouse

1969 Early Man in the West Indies. *Scientific American* **221**(5):42–52.

Easby, E. K.

1968 *Pre-Columbian Jade from Costa Rica.* New York: André Emmerich Inc.

Feriz, H.

1959 Zeugnisse einer unbekannten vorkolumbischen Kultur in Panama. Ausgrabungen am Rio Tabaserá (West Panama). *Die Umschau in Wissenschaft und Technik, Jahrg. 59, Heft* **23:**728–732.

1961 Bericht über Grabfunde am Isthmus von Panama in den Jahren 1956 und 1958. *Bericht über den 5th Internationalen Kongress für Vor-und Frühgeschichte*, 260–266.

Flint, E.

1884 Human Foot-Prints in Nicaragua. *American Antiquarian and Oriental Journal* **6:**112–114.

1886 Pre-Adamite Foot-Prints. *The American Antiquarian and Oriental Journal* **8:**230–233.

Ford, J. A.
1969 A Comparison of Formative Cultures in the Americas: Diffusion or the Psychic Unity of Man. *Smithsonian Contributions to Anthropology* No. **11.**
Friedrichsthal, E.
1841 Notes on the Lake of Nicaragua and the Province of Chontales in Guatemala. *Royal Geographical Journal* **11:**97–100.
Haag, W. G.
1970 Archeological Investigations in Eastern Nicaragua. Mimeographed, Louisiana State University, Baton Rouge.
Haberland, W.
1955 Preliminary Report on the Aguas Buenas Complex, Costa Rica. *Ethnos* **20**(4):224–230.
1957 Black-on-Red Painted Ware and Associated Features in Intermediate Area. *Ethnos* **22**(3–4):148–161.
1959 Archäologische Untersuchungen in Südost-Costa Rica. *Acta Humboldtiana, Series Geographica et Ethnographica* No. **1.**
1960 Cien Años de Arqueologia en Panama. *Publicaciones de la Revista "Loteria"* **12:**7–16.
1961a Archäologische Untersuchungen in der Provinz Chiriqui, Panama. *Acta Humboldtiana, Series Geographica et Ethnographica* No. **3.**
1961b Arqueología del Valle del Rio Ceiba, Buenos Aires. *Instituto Geográfico de Costa Rica, Informe Semestral, Enero a Junio 1961,* 31–62.
1962 The Scarified Ware and Early Cultures of Chiriqui (Panama). *34th Internationaler Amerikanistenkongress, Akten,* 381–389.
1963 Ometepe 1962–63. *Archaeology* **14**(4):287–289.
1964 Neue archäologische Ergebnisse in Nicaragua. *Die Umschau in Wissenschaft und Technik, Jahrg. 64. Heft* **20:**622–625.
1966 Early Phases on Ometepe Island, Nicaragua. *36th Congreso Internacional de Americanistas, Actas y Memorias* **1:**399–403.
1969a Early Phases and Their Relationship in Southern Central America. *38th Internationaler Amerikanistenkongress, Verhandlungen* **1:**229–242.
1969b Current Research: Central America. *American Antiquity* **34**(3):357–359.
1969c Die Kulturen Meso- und Zentralamerikas. In *Handbuch der Kulturgeschichte, Band: Die Kulturen Alt-Amerikas.* Frankfurt a.M.
1973 On Stone Sculpture from Southern Central America. In *The Iconography of Middle American Scripture.* Pp. 134–152.
1971 Doppel-Tecomates im südlichen Mittelameriak. *Baessler-Archiv.* **19:**311–319.
Harte, E. M.
1958 Mountain-Top Burials. *Archaeological Society of Panama* **1:**29–31.
Harte, N. A.
1966 El Sitio Guacamayo. *Boletín del Museo Chiricano* **3:**3–7.
Hartman, C. V.
1901 *Archaeological Researches in Costa Rica.* Stockholm.
1907a Archaeological Researches on the Pacific Coast of Costa Rica. *Memoirs of the Carnegie Museum* **3**(1).
1907b The Alligator as a Plastic Decorative Motive in Costa Rican Pottery. *American Anthropologist* **9**(2):307–314.
Holmes, W. H.
1887 The Use of Gold and other Metals among the Ancient Inhabitants of Chiriqui, Isthmus of Darien. *Smithsonian Institute Bulletin* **3.**
1888 Ancient Art of the Province of Chiriqui, Colombia. *Bureau of American Ethnology, Annual Report for 1884–1885,* 13–187.

Ichon, A.
1970 Vases Funéraires d'El Indio, District de Tonosi, Panama. *Objects et Mondes* **10**(1):29–36.

Kirchhoff, P.
1943 Mesoamerica. *Acta Americana* **1**:92–107.

Ladd, J.
1957 A Stratigraphic Trench at Sitio Conte, Panama. *American Antiquity* **22**(3):265–271.
1964 Archaeological Investigations in the Parita and Santa Maria Zones of Panama. *Bureau of American Ethnology Bulletin* **193.**

Lange, F. W.
1971 Culture History of the Sapoa River Valley, Costa Rica. *Logan Museum of Anthropology, Occasional Papers in Anthropology* No. **4.**

Lange, F. W., and I. K. Scheidenhelm
1972 The Salvage Archaeology of a Zoned Bichrome Cemetery, Costa Rica. *American Antiquity* **37**(3):240–245.

Lanning, E. P., and T. C. Patterson
1967 Early Man in South America. *Scientific American* **217**(5):44–50.

Lehmann, W.
1908 Reisebericht aus San José de Costa Rica. *Zeitschrift für Ethnologie* **40**:439–446.
1910 Ergebnisse einer Forschungsreise in Mittelamerika und Mexico 1907–1909. *Zeitschrift für Ethnologie* **42**:687–749.

Linares de Sapir, O.
1968 Cultural Chronology of the Gulf of Chiriqui, Panama, *Smithsonian Contributions to Anthropology* No. **8.**
1971 Current Research: Central America. *American Antiquity* **36**(2):237–239.

Linares de Sapir, O., and A. J. Ranere
1971 Human Adaption to the Tropical Forests of Western Panama. *Archaeology* **24**(4):346–355.

Linné, Sigvald
1929 Darien in the Past. The Archaeology of Eastern Panama and Northwestern Colombia. *Göteborgs Kungl. Vetenskaps och Vitterhets- Sämhalles Handlinger, Femte följden, Ser. A,* **1**(3).

Lothrop, S. K.
1926 Pottery of Costa Rica and Nicaragua. *Museum of the American Indian, Contributions* **8.**
1937–1942 Coclé. An Archaeological Study of Central Panama; Parts 1 and 2. *Memoirs of the Peabody Museum of Archaeology and Ethnology* **7–8.**
1950 Archaeology of Southern Veraguas, Panama. *Memoirs of the Peabody Museum of Archaeology and Ethnology* **9**(3).
1954 Suicide, Sacrifice, and Mutilations in Burials at Venado Beach, Panama. *American Antiquity* **19**(3):226–234.
1959a A Re-Appraisal of Isthmian Archaeology. *Mitteilungen aus dem Museum für Völkerkunde in Hamburg* **25**:87–91.
1959b The Archaeological Picture of Southern Central America. *33rd Congreso Internacional de Americanistas, Actas* **1**:165–172.
1960 ^{14}C Dates for Venado Beach, Canal Zone. *Panama Archaeologist* **3**:96.
1963 Archaeology of the Diquis Delta, Costa Rica. *Papers of the Peabody Museum of Archaeology and Ethnology* **2.**
1966 Archaeology of Lower Central America. In *Handbook of Middle American Indians,* vol. 4, edited by R. Wauchope. Austin: University of Texas Press. Pp. 180–208.

Lüders, C. W.
1888 Der grosse Goldfund in Chiriqui im Jahre 1859. *Jahrbuch der Hamburgischen Wissenschaftlichen Anstalten, VI. Jahrg. 1. Hälfte,* 19–25.

McA . . ., A.
1885 The Pre-Adamite Track. *American Antiquarian and Oriental Journal* **8**:364–367
MacCurdy, G. G.
1911 A Study of Chiriquian Antiquities. *Connecticut Academy of Arts and Sciences Memoirs* **3.**
McGimsey III, C. R.
1956 Cerro Mangote: A Precermic Site in Panama. *American Antiquity* **22**(2):151–161.
1958 Further Data and a Date from Cerro Mangote, Panama. *American Antiquity* **23**(4):434–435.
Meggers, B. J.
1966 *Ecuador; Ancient Peoples and Places.* London: Thames and Hudson.
Meggers, B. J., C. Evans, and E. Estrada
1965 The Early Formative Period in Coastal Ecuador: The Valdivia and Machalilla Phases. *Smithsonian Contributions to Anthropology* No. **1.**
Minelli, L. L. de, and L. Minelli
1966 Informe Preliminar Sobre Excavaciones Alreadedor de San Vito de Java. *36th Congreso Internacional de Americanistas, Actas y Memorias* **1:**415–427.
Mitchell, R. H., and K. F. Heidenreich
1965 New Developments on the Azueroo Peninsula, Province of Los Santos, Republic of Panama. *Panama Archaeologist* **6:**12–26.
Norweb, A. H.
1961 The Archaeology of the Greater Nicoya Subarea. Mimeographed seminar paper.
1964 Ceramic Stratigraphy in Southwestern Nicaragua. *35th Congreso Internacional de Americanistas, Actas y Memorias* **1:**551–561.
Nowotny, K. A.
1956 Ein zentralamerikanischer Monolith aus dem Besitz von Emanuel von Friedrichsthal. *Archiv für Völkerkunde* **11**:104–115.
1961 Ein zentralamerikanischer Monolith aus dem Besitz von Emanuel von Friedrichsthal, 2. *Archiv für Völkerkunde* **16:**135–139.
Osgood, C.
1935 The Archaeological Problem in Chiriqui. *American Anthropologist* **37:**234–243.
Peet, S. D.
1889 The Age of the Nicaraguan Foot-Prints. *American Antiquarian and Oriental Journal* **11:**120–121.
Reichel-Dolmatoff, G.
1971 Early Pottery from Colombia. *Archaeology* **24**(4):338–345.
Rowe, J. H.
1959 Carl Hartman and His Place in the History of Archaeology. *33rd Congreso Internacional de Americanistas, Actas* **2:**268–279.
Sander, D.
1959 Fluted Points from Madden Lake. *Panama Archaeologist* **2:**39–51.
1964 Lithic Material from Panama—Fluted Points from Madden Lake. *35th Congreso Internacional de Americanistas, Actas y Memorias* **1:**183–192.
Sander, D., R. Mitchell, and R. G. Turner
1958 Report on Venado Beach Excavations. *Archaeological Society of Panama* **1:**26–28.
Schmidt, P. J.
1968 Die Bestattungsformen der Indianer des südlichen Mittelamerika. Unpublished thesis, Hamburg.
Squier, E. G.
1852 *Nicaragua: Its People, Scenery . . . .* London.
Stewart, R. H.
1968 Geological Evidences of Ancient Man in Panama. *Boletín del Museo Chiricano* **7:**20–25.

Stirling, M. W.
1949 Exploring the Past in Panama. *National Geographic Magazine* **94**(3):373–399.
1950 Exploring Ancient Panama by Helicopter. *National Geographic Magazine* **97**(2):227–246.

Stirling, M. W., and M. Stirling
1964a El Limón, an Early Tomb Site in Coclé Province, Panama. *Bureau of American Ethnology, Anthropological Papers* No. **71** (also published as *Bulletin* **191:**247–254).
1964b Archaeological Notes on Almirante Bay, Bocas del Toro, Panama. *Bureau of American Ethnology, Anthropological Papers* No. **72** (also published as *Bulletin* **191:**255–284).
1964c The Archaeology of Taboga, Urabá, and Taboguilla Islands, Panama. *Bureau of American Ethnology, Anthropological Papers* **73** (also published as *Bulletin* **191:** 285–348).

Stone, D.
1943 A Preliminary Investigation of the Flood Plains of the Rio Grande de Terraba, Costa Rica. *American Antiquity* **9**(1):74–88.
1958 *Introducción a la Arquelogía de Costa Rica.* San José.
1961 The Stone Sculpture of Costa Rica. In *Essays in pre-Columbian art and archaeology,* edited by S. K. Lothrop, Cambridge, Massachusetts. Pp. 192–209.
1963 Cult Traits in Southeastern Costa Rica and Their Significance. *American Antiquity* **28**(3):339–359.

Stone, D., and C. Balser
1957 Grinding Stones and Mullers of Costa Rica. *Journal de la Société des Americanistes* **46:**165–179.
1965 Incised Slate Disks from the Atlantic Watershed of Costa Rica. *American Antiquity* **30**(3):310–329.

Thieck, F.
1971 *Idolos de Nicaragua,* Album no. 1. León: Universidad Nacional Autónoma de Nicaragua.

Verrill, A. H.
1927 Excavations in Coclé Province, Panama. *Indian Notes* **4**(1):47–61.
n.d. *Old Civilizations of the New World.* London: Williams and Norgate Ltd.

Wassen, S. H.
1949 Some Archaeological Observations from Boquete, Chiriqui, Panama. *Etnologiska Studier* No. **16.**

Weyl, R.
1969 Magmastische Förderphasen und Gesteinschemismus in Costa Rica. *Neues Jahrbuch für Geologie und Paläontologie, Monatshefte, Jg. 1969* **7:**423–446.

Willey, G. R.
1971 *An Introduction to American Archaeology,* Vol. *2. South America.* Englewood Cliffs, New Jersey: Prentice-Hall.

Willey, G. R., and C. R. McGimsey III
1954 The Monagrillo Culture of Panama. *Papers of the Peabody Museum of Archaeology and Ethnology* **49**(2):

Willey, G. R., and T. L. Stoddard
1954 Cultural Stratigraphy in Panama: A Preliminary Report on the Giron Site. *American Antiquity* **19**(4):332–343.

Williams, H.
1952 Geologic Observations on the Ancient Human Footprints near Managua, Nicaragua. *Contributions to American Archaeology and History* **11**(52):1–31.

Caribbean

IRVING ROUSE AND LOUIS ALLAIRE

I. INTRODUCTION

The Caribbean (as opposed to the Circum-Caribbean) area includes only the eastern half of the Caribbean Basin (see Figure 13.1). Following Willey (1971: Fig. 61), we limit it to North-Central and Northeastern Venezuela, Northern Guayana, and the West Indies. Northwestern Venezuela and the Caribbean part of Colombia are instead considered part of the Intermediate area; and Southern Venezuela and the rest of the Guianas are assigned to Amazonia.

II. HISTORY OF CHRONOLOGICAL RESEARCH

The first chronological evidence was obtained in 1869 by William M. Gabb (1872), an American geologist, who found a preceramic layer beneath a ceramic layer in a cave on the south shore of Samaná Bay in the Dominican Republic. He did not attempt to determine the nature of the cultural complex in each of these components.

The first person to note cultural variation within a single component was the Puerto Rican historian Adolfo de Hostos (1919:14). While digging the site of Ostiones on that island, he observed that the red slip and modeled-incised decoration typical of the pottery in the upper levels became rarer as he proceeded downward through the refuse, and eventually disappeared. He did not pursue the chronological implications of this observation.

It remained for a Danish anthropologist, Gudmund Hatt, to draw the first chronological conclusions. He dug a number of sites in the Virgin Islands during 1922–1923 and arranged them in the following sequence: (1) Krum Bay, which was preceramic; (2) Coral Bay–Longford, marked by white-on-red painted pottery; and (3) Magens Bay–Salt River, which had modeled-incised pottery. He put (1) first simply because it lacked pottery, and he placed (2) before (3) because "the interrelationships between the two groups is most evident in the lower and older part of the Magens Bay and Salt River deposits [Hatt 1924:33]." Comparing the pottery of (2) and (3) with that from the Lesser Antilles, to the south, and from the rest of the Greater Antilles, to the west, he came to the conclusion that (2) was the result of a "cultural movement" from the south and (3) of diffusion from the west.

Hatt's work was not followed up until 1933–1934, when Froelich G. Rainey (1940) excavated in Puerto Rico on behalf of Yale University and the University of Puerto Rico. At Canas and two other sites he encountered deposits with white-on-red pottery like that of Hatt's group (2) beneath deposits with modeled-incised pottery like that of group (3). The modeled-incised pottery also resembled the material obtained by de Hostos at Ostiones. From this stratigraphy Rainey inferred the existence of two successive cultures, which he named Crab and Shell after the food remains domi-

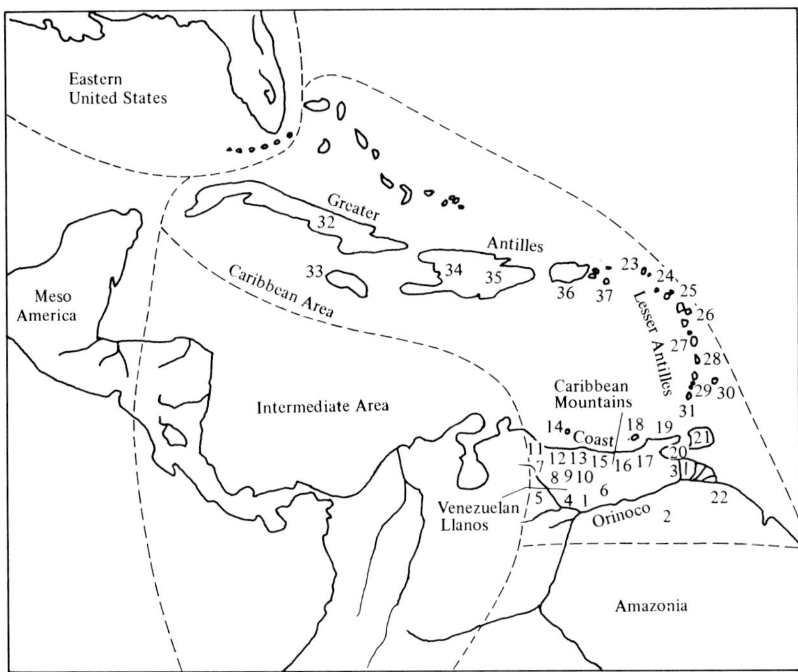

Figure 13.1. The Caribbean area, its regional divisions and subdivisions. *Orinocan subdivisions:* (1) Middle Orinoco, (2) Caroní, (3) Lower Orinoco; *Llanos subdivisions:* (4) San Fernando, (5) Barinas, (6) Valle de la Pascua; *Mountain subdivisions:* (7) San Felipe, (8) Valencia, (9) Los Teques, (10) Caracas; *Coastal subdivisions:* (11) Tucacas, (12) Puerto Cabello, (13) La Guaira, (14) Los Roques, (15) Río Chico, (16) Barcelona, (17) Cumana, (18) Margarita, (19) Carúpano, (20) Güiria, (21) Trinidad, (22) Guayana; *Lesser Antillean subdivisions:* (23) Saba-St. Eustatius, (24) St. Kitts, (25) Antigua, (26) Guadeloupe, (27) Martinique, (28) St. Lucia, (29) Grenadines, (30) Barbados, (31) Grenada; *Greater Antillean subdivisions:* (32) Cuba, (33) Jamaica, (34) Haiti, (35) Dominican Republic, (36) Puerto Rico, (37) Virgin Islands.

nant in the successive layers. Contrary to Hatt, he concluded that both cultures were the result of migrations from South America.

During 1936–1938, Irving Rouse continued Rainey's Puerto Rican research. In the pottery from Rainey's upper stratum at Canas, he observed the trend from modeled-incised pottery at the top to largely plain pottery at the bottom that de Hostos had noted at Ostiones and Hatt at Magens Bay–Salt River; and in the pottery from Rainey's lower stratum he observed a trend from white-on-red pottery at the bottom toward the same nearly plain pottery at the top. From this he inferred the existence of a continuous sequence from white-on-red through largely plain to modeled-incised pottery. He searched for the missing part of this sequence and found it in several sites (Rouse 1952). Hence, Rainey must have been wrong in postulating two successive migrations from South America.

This experience made Rouse wary of basing chronological conclusions upon theories of migration or diffusion, that is, upon horizon styles. Instead, he worked with discrete "cultures" or local styles, which he organized in terms of areas and periods (Rouse 1939:93–97, 1941). He named each culture after a typical site and numbered the periods from I to IV. The periods were assumed to be units of absolute time and hence to extend horizontally across the charts, but in the absence of radiocarbon dates they had to be defined culturally. Period I was preceramic and Periods II, III, and IV were marked respectively by the white-on-red, largely plain, and modeled-incised pottery. Rouse's first chart of the areas, periods, and cultures of the Greater Antilles (Rouse 1948: Table 1) appeared in the *Handbook of South American Indians* and has since been revised periodically as new data became available and new concepts, to be described later, were developed (Rouse 1951: Fig. 2, 1953a: Fig. 2; 1964: Figs. 4, 5,; Cruxent and Rouse 1958–1959: Vol. 2, Fig. 4).

Chronological research developed more slowly in the Lesser Antilles. In 1958–1959, Marshall McKusick (1960), a student of Rouse's, worked out a sequence of four ceramic "styles" on the island of St. Lucia, the first two of which fit into Period III and the other two into Period IV, and correlated the finds on the other islands with this sequence. Ripley P. Bullen (1964: Fig. 4) subsequently formulated a comparable sequence of six local "periods" on Grenada and used it to revise and expand Rouse's current chart. Finally, Louis Allaire (1973) produced a new version of the chart based on his excavations in Martinique during 1971–1972.

Venezuela has had a longer history of chronological research. During 1933–1934, Alfred Kidder II (1944) obtained a stratigraphic sequence of La Cabrera and Valencia "phases" at the site of La Cabrera in the north central part of the country. In 1941, George D. Howard (1943:59–60) demonstrated the existence of a comparable sequence of Early and Late Ronquin "cultures" at the site of that name on the Middle Orinoco River.

Both authors subsequently published chronological charts. Kidder (1948:432–433) compiled his for the *Handbook of South American Indians.* He limited it to Venezuela and called its constituent units "aspects" and "phases" in the terminology of the Midwestern Taxonomic System. It had only areal divisions; its vertical dimension was not marked off into periods.

Howard (1947: Tables 1–3) included charts for the Greater Antilles, Venezuela, and lowland Bolivia in his doctoral dissertation at Yale University. He based the Greater Antillean chart on Rouse's work and the lowland Bolivian chart on the findings of Wendell C. Bennett, his dissertation adviser. He divided each chart horizontally into areas and vertically into Early, Middle, and Late Ceramic periods, corresponding to Rouse's Periods II, III, and IV. (He limited himself to ceramic time.) On Bennett's advice, he applied the Peruvianist term "style" to the units in the bodies of the charts, instead of calling them cultures, aspects, phases, or periods.

In the 1950s, J. M. Cruxent and Rouse joined forces to work out a more detailed chronology of Venezuela. They distinguished five regions and drew up a chart for each region. Each chart was divided horizontally into local areas and vertically into the Period I–IV sequence Rouse had used in the Antilles, to which a Period V was added in order to take into consideration the historic remains (Cruxent and Rouse 1958–1959: Vol. 2, Figs. 9, 26, 100, 149, 170).

The units in the bodies of the charts were called "complexes" if they were preceramic and "styles" if they were ceramic. The term *complex* was adopted from Paleo-Indian archaeology and *style* from Howard's previous usage of that term in Venezuela.

The complexes and styles were originally regarded as completely discrete units, to be organized only in terms of the areas and periods. Soon, however, Cruxent and Rouse began to note strong resemblances between adjacent complexes or styles. They grouped together the units that resembled one another, called them "series" of complexes or styles, and named each series by adding the suffix "-oid" to the name of a constituent complex or style.

The Peruvianist terms *horizon* and *tradition* could not be applied to the series because most do not extend horizontally or vertically across the Venezuelan charts; they have an irregular distribution. In other words, they are relative units, occurring at different times in different places.

In a later popularization of their research, Rouse and Cruxent (1963) supplemented the periods with a parallel set of Paleo-Indian, Meso-Indian, Neo-Indian, and Indo-Hispanic "epochs." The Paleo-Indian Epoch was defined by the presence of chipped stone artifacts and big-game hunting. In the Meso-Indian Epoch, these were replaced by ground stone and shell artifacts and by an economy that emphasized gathering and fishing. The Neo-Indian Epoch was the time of appearance of pottery and agriculture; and the Indo-Hispanic Epoch, the time when European artifacts and foods began to be used.

The system of epochs was inspired by Cruxent's discovery of Paleo-Indian remains earlier than the previously known preceramic remains of Period I. In the chronological charts, therefore, the Paleo-Indian Epoch was shown earlier than Period I. The Meso-Indian Epoch was equated with Period II, the Neo-Indian Epoch with Periods II–IV, and the Indo-Hispanic Epoch with Period V (Rouse and Cruxent 1963: Fig. 3).

In the text, Rouse and Cruxent (1963:42–43; 56–59) noted that the Paleo-Indian Epoch apparently survived until the Meso-Indian Epoch in a peripheral area, and that the Meso-Indian way of life similarly survived into the Neo-Indian Epoch in several areas. They did not attempt to portray these instances of survival in their chronological charts, however.

Rouse did so in the subsequent revision of his West Indian chronologies. He had previously shown the preceramic survivals in these chronologies by drawing a heavy line across the body of each chart at the points of first appearance of pottery, higher in some areas than in others. Now he handled the epochs in the same way, delimiting them within the charts instead of putting them on the sides with the periods (Rouse 1964: Figs. 3–5). In other words, he recognized that the epochs were units of relative time and, as such, needed to be separated from the periods, which were units of absolute time.

The chronological research in Northern Guayana remains to be considered. Clifford Evans and Betty J. Meggers, of the U.S. National Museum, are responsible for our knowledge of that region. Upon excavating there in 1952–1953, they distinguished a "preceramic lithic horizon," a largely preceramic "phase," and three ceramic "phases." They placed the units in a chronological chart, but without reference to areas, periods, or other chronological devices (Evans and Meggers 1960: Fig. 126). Willey (1971: Fig. 6-2) has added these devices; as he notes, the three kinds of remains can be ascribed to the Paleo-, Meso-, and Neo-Indian epochs respectively.

The Caribbean area is well supplied with radiocarbon determinations, thanks largely to the analyses carried out by the Geochronometric Laboratory of Yale University at Rouse's instigation and by the laboratory of the Instituto Venezolano de Investigaciones Científicas on Cruxent's behalf. In 1962, Rouse and Cruxent obtained a grant from the National Science Foundation to fill the major gaps in radiocarbon coverage. They incorporated the results of this research in the latest versions of their chronologies (Rouse and Cruxent 1963; Rouse 1964). The dates published there were corrected for the recalculation of the half-life of ^{14}C current at the time. Many new corrections are now available, but since some are alternative and there is no general agreement as to their use, we have chosen to present our dates in uncorrected form.

Since the original draft of this chapter (written in 1972), an explosion of archaeological research has taken place in the Caribbean area. In particular, much new information has accumulated about the preceramic part of the chronology, prompting both Kozlowski (1974) and Plina *et al.* (1976) to revise that part. Nevertheless, we have retained our original version in modified form, because the present data are not sufficient to decide between it and the two alternatives.

The new finds have also prompted each of us to make revisions in the ceramic part of the chronology, referring to the Lesser Antilles and the Orinoco Valley respectively (Allaire 1977; Rouse n.d.). We have incorporated these revisions in the present chapter.

The 1972 version of the chapter contained tabulations of all the available radiocarbon dates. Their number has more than doubled since then, making it impracticable to include all of them. Our tables are now restricted to the dates cited in the chronological charts.

III. CARIBBEAN CHRONOLOGY AND ITS IMPLICATIONS

A. Conceptual Approach

Cruxent and Rouse's conceptual approach will be used here, but with several modifications. We now have enough radiocarbon dates to make the system of absolute periods superfluous. The periods were originally placed at the sides of the charts as substitutes for absolute dates. Now they can be replaced with the Christian calendar.

The system of relative epochs will also be abandoned. It rests on the assumption that there is a one-to-one correlation between technology and economy—for example, between chipped stonework and big-game hunting in the case of the Paleo-Indian Epoch. This assumption is no longer tenable. As we have seen, typically Paleo-Indian lithic complexes apparently survived into Period I, by which time the big game included in the definition of the Paleo-Indian Epoch had become extinct. Moreover, comparable lithic complexes have recently been found in the Greater Antilles, where there never was any big game (Cruxent and Rouse 1969). Several authors (e.g., Tabio and Guarch 1966) have similarly raised the question whether certain Meso-Indian peoples may not have acquired pottery in advance of an agricultural economy or vice versa, in which case these peoples would have been half Meso-Indian and half Neo-Indian.

Old World archaeologists have encountered the same problem in working with the corresponding system of Paleolithic, Mesolithic, and Neolithic ages. It is now clear, for example, that ground stonework and an agricultural economy, taken together, are not an adequate definition of the Neolithic Age, for stone grinding appears before an agricultural economy in some regions, such as the Middle East; at the same time in other regions, such as Western Europe; and by itself in the circumboreal zone and other places where agriculture is impossible.

To take into account variations like these, Rouse (1972:136–138) has proposed a return to the original practice of defining the ages solely in terms of technology. This will be done here. We shall abandon the system of epochs and replace it with a sequence of four "ages": Lithic, Archaic, Ceramic, and Historic. The Lithic Age is the time between the beginning of chipped stonework and the appearance of ground stone and/or shell artifacts, including those ground solely through use. The Archaic Age is the time from the first appearance of ground artifacts to the first manufacture of pottery. The Ceramic Age starts with the introduction of pottery making and ends with the appearance of European artifacts, at which time the Historic Age begins.

Finally, we believe that the time has come to drop Cruxent and Rouse's distinction between preceramic complexes and ceramic styles. Not only is this cumbersome but also it clashes with the trend among some workers to define their ceramic units in terms of pottery types rather than elements of style. In this chapter, therefore, we shall drop the term *style* and call all the local chronological units *complexes,* regardless of whether they are preceramic or ceramic. Whenever possible, the complexes will be grouped into series, as in the previous formulations.

For purposes of this paper, the Caribbean area will be divided into six regions: the Orinoco River; the Venezuelan Llanos, or lowlands west and north of the Orinoco; the Caribbean Mountains, which separate the Llanos from the coast; the Coastal region, including the islands immediately offshore; the Lesser Antilles; and the Greater Antilles (see Figure 13.1). Each region will be considered in turn.

B. Orinoco Region

This region is one of three principal routes of entry into the Caribbean area, the others being via the coast and islands to the north (see Figure 13.1). It is possible to travel without portage from the Amazon River through the Río Negro and the Casiquiare Canal into the Upper Orinoco, although rapids form a barrier some distance down the Orinoco.

Our chart (Figure 13.2 and Table 13.1) extends from the rapids at the head of navigation on the Orinoco to the Gulf of Paria and the Atlantic Ocean at the mouth of the river. The Guianan highlands of Venezuela, to the south of the Orinoco, are also included, since they are not well enough known archaeologically to be put in a separate chart (Vargas and Sanoja 1970).

Systematic research in this region has been concentrated in three widely separated parts: the great bend in the Orinoco River, just below the rapids; the drainage of the Río Caroní, a principal Guianan tributary; and the area around Barrancas and Ciudad Guayana, just above the Delta. In the chart, these local areas are termed Middle Orinoco, Caroní, and the Lower Orinoco, respectively. The sequence for the Barinas area of the Llanos and the Trinidad area of the Coastal region have been added at either end of the chart to facilitate comparison with the chronologies for those regions (Figure 13.3 and see Figure 13.5, (pp. 441, 453).

1. Lithic Age

The Caroní area has yielded the only Lithic complex yet known from the Orinocan region (see Figure 13.2). This complex, called Canaima, is assignable to the Joboid series, distinguished by Cruxent (1971:51) as the result of his research in western Venezuela. It is characterized by bifacially chipped, stemmed projectile points, resembling those at the very end of the Joboid sequence in the west. Knives, scrapers, and choppers are also present.

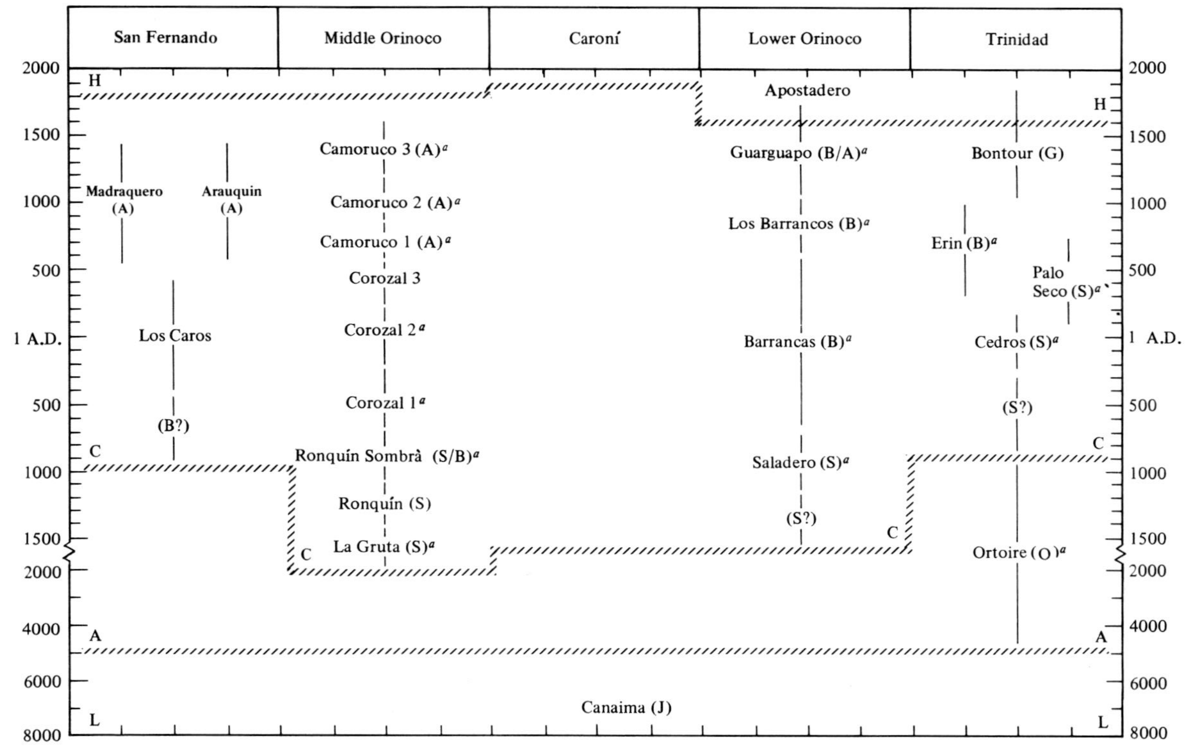

Figure 13.2. Chronology of the Orinoco region. *Ages:* L = Lithic; A = Archaic; C = Ceramic; H = Historic. [a] = Position supported by radiocarbon analyses. See Table 13.1. *Series:* (A) = Arauquinoid; (B) = Barrancoid; (G) = Guayabitoid; (J) = Joboid; (O) = Ortoiroid; (S) = Saladoid.

TABLE 13.1

Radiocarbon Dates Cited in the Orinoco Chart

Area	Age	Complex	Sample number	Site	Date B.P.	Calendric date
Middle Orinoco:	*Ceramic:*	La Gruta	I–8970	La Gruta	4090 ± 105	2140 B.C.
		La Gruta	I–8548	La Gruta	4065 ± 85	2115 B.C.
		La Gruta	I–8546	La Gruta	3710 ± 85	1760 B.C.
		La Gruta	I–9232	La Gruta	3665 ± 85	1585 B.C.
		Ronquín Sombra	I–8971	Los Merecurotes	2970 ± 85	1020 B.C.
		Corozal 1	QC–271B	Parmana	2805 ± 80	855 B.C.
		Corozal 1	QC–271A	Parmana	2650 ± 80	700 B.C.
		Corozal 2	QC–322	Corozal	1740 ± 100	A.D. 210
		Camoruco 1	QC–313A	Los Mangos	1170 ± 90	A.D. 780
		Camoruco 2	QC–326	Corozal	1200 ± 85	A.D. 750
		Camoruco 3	QC–309	Corozal	860 ± 70	A.D. 1090
		Camoruco 3	I–8543	Ronquín Sombra	750 ± 80	A.D. 1200
		Camoruco 3	I–8626	Camoruco	670 ± 80	A.D. 1280
		Camoruco 3	I–8625	Camoruco	625 ± 80	A.D. 1325
		Camoruco 3	I–8627	Tucuragua	565 ± 80	A.D. 1385
		Camoruco 3	I–8624	Camoruco	550 ± 80	A.D. 1400
		Camoruco 3	I–8623	Camoruco	470 ± 80	A.D. 1480
		Camoruco 3	I–8622	Camoruco	455 ± 85	A.D. 1495
Lower Orinoco:	*Ceramic:*	Saladero	Y–42	Saladero	2870 ± 130	920 B.C.
		Saladero	Y–43	Saladero	2700 ± 130	750 B.C.
		Saladero	Y–44	Saladero	2570 ± 130	620 B.C.
		Barrancas	Y–40	Saladero	2850 ± 120	900 B.C.
		Barrancas	Y–316	Saladero	2820 ± 80	870 B.C.
		Barrancas	Y–294	Saladero	2800 ± 150	850 B.C.
		Los Barrancos	Y–499–2	Los Barrancos	1370 ± 90	A.D. 580
	Historic	Guarguapo	Y–38–39	Saladero	300 ± 50	A.D. 1650

NOTE: A number of dates indicating a younger age for the La Gruta, Ronquín Sombra, Corozal 2, and Camoruco 1 complexes have been omitted from this table because they come from sand-dune sites. It is assumed that there has been movement of the sand since deposition of the refuse, causing intrusion of more recent charcoal from the surfaces of the sites.

2. Archaic Age

No preceramic complexes with ground stone artifacts have yet been found in the Orinoco region. They should be present, especially if Sauer (1952:46) is correct in suggesting that manioc, the staple crop of the historic Indians in the Caribbean area, was domesticated in Northern South America. Ground stone axes would have been needed to clear the forests as domestication began to take place.

3. Ceramic Age

By the time of the earliest known ceramic deposits, the process of domestication had been completed and manioc had become the staple food on the Orinoco. Clay griddles, still used today to bake the bread made from manioc flour, occur in all the ceramic complexes.

The ceramic sequence begins with a Saladoid series, which is marked by open bowls and white-on-red painted designs, like those of the first Antillean pottery discussed earlier. So far, four members of the Saladoid series have been distinguished on the Orinoco River, La Gruta, Ronquín, and Ronquín Sombra in the Middle area and Saladero in the Lower area (Figure 13.2). The three Middle Orinocan complexes are radiocarbon dated between 2100 and 800 B.C., and the Lower Orinocan complex, around 1000 B.C. (Table 13.1).

The origin of the Saladoid series is unknown. It could either have come down the Apure River from the Intermediate area or up the Casiquiare Canal from the Amazon Basin (see Figure 13.1), but no antecedents have yet been found in either region. There is, however, evidence that it moved down the Orinoco River. The Saladero Complex on the Lower Orinoco appears to be an offshoot of La Gruta on the Middle Orinoco (Rouse n.d.).

Indeed, the original La Gruta pottery contains within itself the seeds of two major ceramic developments, Barrancoid as well as Saladoid. It is decorated with complex modeled-incised as well as white-on-red painted designs. The Saladoid people who moved downstream emphasized the white-on-red painting at the expense of modeling and incision. Those who remained behind on the Middle Orinoco focused instead on modeling and incision. During the course of the development from La Gruta to Ronquín Sombra on the Middle Orinoco, the pottery became larger and bolder, flanges were added to the rims, and the flanges began to be incised and modeled with geometric designs. At the same time, vertical strap handles declined, and the lugs with which they were originally decorated became larger and began to be attached directly to the rim (Rouse n.d.).

By the end of the Ronquín Sombra Complex, as a result, the Saladoid peoples of the Middle Orinoco had become transformed into Barrancoid. They expanded northward in two directions, down the Orinoco Valley toward the east coast of Venezuela and up the Apure and Guarico rivers into central Venezuela. The Barrancoids who moved down the Orinoco appear to have pushed the Saladoid inhabitants of the Lower Valley through the Delta to the east coast and the island of Trinidad, from where they eventually expanded into the Antilles, introducing pottery and agriculture wherever they went (Rouse and Cruxent 1963:115–125). The Barrancoids who moved up into central Venezuela themselves introduced pottery and agriculture into the Valencia Basin of the Caribbean Mountains, as well as to the adjacent part of the coast (Rouse n.d.).

Following Lathrap (1970:110–112), we would correlate the Saladoid movement down the Orinoco River with the original spread of Arawakan languages from the Amazon Basin into the Orinoco Valley and then out into the Antilles. The subsequent Barrancoid development on the Middle Orinoco and the spread of that series of peoples down the Orinoco and up the Apure and Guarico rivers can similarly be correlated with the splitting off of Maipuran from the original Arawakan languages. The estimated time of divergence of the two ceramic series (Figure 13.2) corresponds quite well with that for divergence of the two linguistic groups, as calculated by the technique of glottochronology (Stark 1977).

In excavations on the Middle Orinoco during 1974–1975, Anna C. Roosevelt (personal communication) found that the Barrancoid series was followed by a sequence of three new complexes, which she provisionally terms "Corozal 1–3." These are radiocarbon dated between 800 B.C. and A.D. 500 (Figure 13.2). Stylistically, they appear to be transitional between the previous development and a new Arauquinoid series, which prevailed on the Orinoco during protohistoric time. The white-on-red painting that had been diagnostic of the Saladoid series vanished, and in its place one finds only rare examples of polychrome painting in red, brown, and black on a white background, which probably originated on the Llanos (see Section C, 3). Other Saladoid and Barrancoid traits died out more gradually; indeed, the incised flanges of the Barrancoid series survived until the end of the Corozal sequence. Sponge-spicule tempering, which is characteristic of the subsequent Arauquinoid series, began to replace the grit and fiber tempering of the previous series at the beginning of Corozal 1 time. By Corozal 3, the replacement had been completed. Other Arauquinoid diagnostics emerged during the Corozal 2 and 3 periods.

Arauquinoid pottery (Camoruco 1–3 in Figure 13.2) is characterized by a greater amount of sponge-spicule tempering than in Corozal pottery, by the absence of painted designs, and by an emphasis on appliqué-work, punctation, and rectilinear, parallel-line incision. Its origin is uncertain. It resembles the pottery on the Amazon that Lathrap (1970:164–170) calls "Fine-line Incised" and Evans and Meggers (in Pronapa, 1970:19–20), "Incised and Punctate." On the other hand, the evidences of a transition on the Middle Orinoco suggest that the new series developed in that vicinity. Within the

Orinoco region, it clearly spread downstream; the Guarguapo Complex on the Lower Orinoco is a blend of intrusive Arauquinoid and local Barrancoid traits.

4. Historic Age

Evidences of European contact are known only from the Lower Orinoco. On the basis of trade goods and a late radiocarbon date, the Guarguapo complex of that area may be said to have survived into the Historic Age. It was succeeded by a final complex, Apostadero, the affiliations of which are unknown.

C. Venezuelan Llanos

Significant research on the archaeology of the Llanos has been limited to three areas: San Fernando in the south, near the juncture of the Río Apure with the Middle Orinoco; Barinas in the west, along the Upper Apure and its tributary, the Río Portuguesa; and Valle de la Pascua in the center, extending from the Middle Orinoco to a gap in the Maritime Andes, which leads to Río Chico and Barcelona on the coast (see Figure 13.1). These three areas form the heart of our chronological chart (Figure 13.3 and Table 13.2), with the Middle Orinoco and Río Chico columns added to show the principal relationships with the neighboring regions.

1. Lithic and Archaic Ages

No preceramic sites have yet been found on the Llanos, though that area must have been well suited to hunting and gathering, as well as to incipient agriculture. This is the greatest gap in our coverage of Caribbean chronology.

2. Ceramic Age

If our migration hypotheses are correct, it should be possible to find Barrancoid pottery in the San Fernando area and along the route from there to the Valencia Basin and the central part of the Coastal area. This pottery should resemble that of Ronquín Sombra on the Middle Orinoco and should date from the beginning of the first millennium B.C., as indicated by the symbol "(B?)" in Figure 13.3.

The earliest known pottery belongs to an Osoid series, situated in the Barinas area farther west (see Figures 13.1 and 13.2). Cruxent and Rouse (1958–1959, Vol. 1:185–187) had originally attributed Osoid pottery to a single, Caño del Oso Complex. They assigned this complex to the Tierroid series of the Venezuelan Andes and concluded that it must have intruded into the Llanos from that region, that is, from the Intermediate area. However, Zucchi (1972a) has since shown that the later Caño del Oso remains

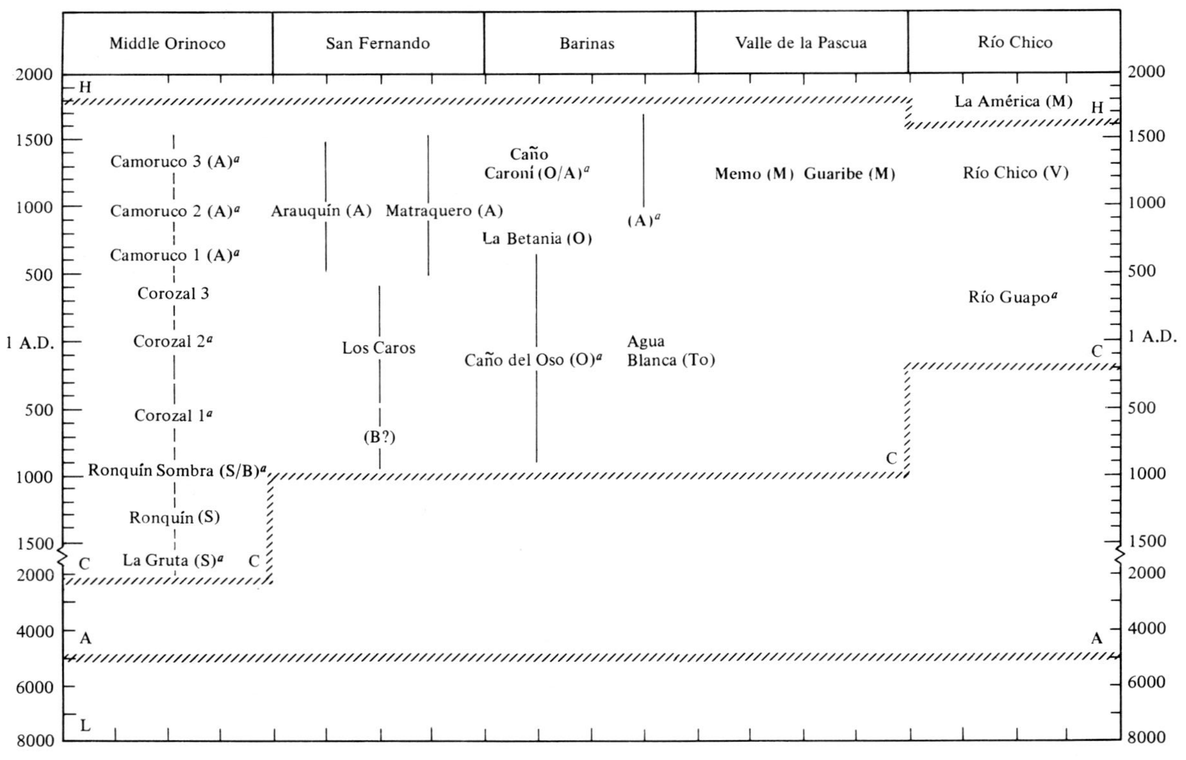

Figure 13.3. Chronology of the Venezuelan Llanos. *Ages:* L = Lithic; A = Archaic; C = Ceramic; H = Historic. [a] = Position supported by radiocarbon analyses. See Table 13.2. *Series:* (A) = Arauquinoid; (M) = Memoid; (O) = Osoid; (S) = Saladoid; (To) = Tocuyanoid; (V) = Valencioid.

must be separated off as a La Betania Complex and that Caño del Oso and La Betania together constitute a distinct series of complexes.

This series is characterized by painted pottery with polychrome designs reminiscent of those in the Intermediate area. The earlier, Caño del Oso Complex has much more elaborate shapes, however. The later, La Betania shapes are more like those in the Intermediate area. The cultivation of maize is also an Intermediate-area trait; it is indicated for Caño del Oso by the presence of corn cobs and the absence of griddles.

Zucchi has obtained 45 radiocarbon dates from the Caño del Oso components of the two sites she has dug (Table 13.2). Almost all are prior to the second millennium A.D., when the Tierroid series came into existence. Hence, the Osoid series must have been ancestral to the Tierroid series, not derived from it as Cruxent and Rouse had thought.

The dates have a surprisingly broad range, covering most of the first millennia B.C. and A.D. Zucchi (1972a) thinks this is due to the use of earlier Caño del Oso refuse by the later occupants of her two sites. About A.D. 500, the occupants began to make earthworks from the refuse, apparently in order to raise their houses and trails above the level of the water that floods the Llanos during the rainy season. Zucchi estimates that the Caño del Oso people was in existence from ca. 900 B.C. to A.D. 650 and the La Betania people, for an indefinite period after that (Figure 13.3).

These dates have aroused controversy because they are by far the earliest for polychrome pottery anywhere in the New World. They are substantiated, however, by Roosevelt's dates of 800 B.C. to A.D. 500 for polychrome pottery on the Middle Orinoco (Corozal 1–3 in Figure 13.2). Together, the two sets of dates support the hypothesis of M.D. Coe (1962:177) and Gallagher (1964:333) that polychromy originated in Venezuela and spread from there through the Intermediate area into Mesoamerica. Both Coe and Gallagher had considered Western Venezuela to be the most probable place of origin, but Zucchi's and Roosevelt's find indicate that polychromy developed further east, in the Caribbean rather than the Intermediate area.

If Zucchi is correct, polychromy spread from the Osoid series on the Western Llanos to the Tocuyanoid series of the Venezuelan Andes, in the Intermediate area. A single Tocuyanoid complex, Agua Blanca (see Figure 13.3) has been found on the Llanos, near the foothills leading into the Andes. In the absence of information about its age, we have placed it on the chart at the time of Tocuyano, a complex situated farther west in the region of the Andes which has been radiocarbon dated (Rouse and Cruxent 1963:155).

Two later series are recognized on the Llanos. One, Arauquinoid, has already been discussed in connection with the Orinoco region. According to our present evidence, this series appeared in the San Fernando area during the first millennum A.D. Lathrap (1970:164–170) has theorized that it originated in the Amazon Basin and that its peoples migrated from there into the

TABLE 13.2

Radiocarbon Dates Cited in the Llanos Chart

Area	Age	Complex	Sample number	Site	Date B.P.	Calendric date
Barinas:	*Ceramic:*	Caño del Oso	IVIC–549	La Calzada	2870 ± 150	920 B.C.
		Caño del Oso	IVIC–120	La Betania	2180 ± 110	230 B.C.
		Caño del Oso	IVIC–475	La Calzada	1990 ± 90	40 B.C.
		Caño del Oso	IVIC–45	La Betania	1820 ± 130	A.D. 130
		Caño del Oso	IVIC–583	La Calzada	1820 ± 70	A.D. 130
		Caño del Oso	IVIC–592	La Calzada	1810 ± 80	A.D. 140
		Caño del Oso	IVIC–43	La Betania	1800 ± 120	A.D. 150
		Caño del Oso	IVIC–472	La Calzada	1800 ± 100	A.D. 150
		Caño del Oso	IVIC–584	La Calzada	1800 ± 70	A.D. 150
		Caño del Oso	IVIC–436	La Calzada	1760 ± 80	A.D. 190
		Caño del Oso	IVIC–460	La Calzada	1760 ± 90	A.D. 190
		Caño del Oso	IVIC–476	La Calzada	1750 ± 70	A.D. 200
		Caño del Oso	IVIC–581	La Calzada	1740 ± 70	A.D. 210
		Caño del Oso	IVIC–590	La Calzada	1730 ± 80	A.D. 220
		Caño del Oso	IVIC–437	La Calzada	1710 ± 70	A.D. 240
		Caño del Oso	IVIC–474	La Calzada	1700 ± 100	A.D. 250
		Caño del Oso	IVIC–580	La Calzada	1690 ± 90	A.D. 260
		Caño del Oso	IVIC–452	La Calzada	1670 ± 100	A.D. 280
		Caño del Oso	IVIC–457	La Calzada	1640 ± 90	A.D. 310
		Caño del Oso	IVIC–591	La Calzada	1640 ± 80	A.D. 310
		Caño del Oso	IVIC–44	La Betania	1630 ± 130	A.D. 320
		Caño del Oso	IVIC–71	La Betania	1610 ± 115	A.D. 340
		Caño del Oso	IVIC–587	La Calzada	1570 ± 70	A.D. 380
		Caño del Oso	IVIC–459	La Calzada	1560 ± 70	A.D. 390
		Caño del Oso	IVIC–551	La Calzada	1530 ± 80	A.D. 420
		Caño del Oso	IVIC–471	La Calzada	1510 ± 70	A.D. 440
		Caño del Oso	IVIC–586	La Calzada	1510 ± 80	A.D. 440

Caño del Oso	IVIC–550	La Calzada	1490 ± 80	A.D. 460
Caño del Oso	IVIC–588	La Calzada	1480 ± 70	A.D. 470
Caño del Oso	IVIC–114	La Calzada	1460 ± 130	A.D. 490
Caño del Oso	IVIC–454	La Calzada	1410 ± 70	A.D. 540
Caño del Oso	IVIC–582	La Calzada	1400 ± 60	A.D. 550
Caño del Oso	IVIC–112	La Betania	1365 ± 95	A.D. 585
Caño del Oso	IVIC–593	La Calzada	1350 ± 70	A.D. 600
Caño del Oso	IVIC–74	La Betania	1340 ± 95	A.D. 610
(Arauquinoid)	WIS–706	Punta Fijo	1095 ± 55	A.D. 855
(Arauquinoid)	WIS–764	Punta Fijo	1065 ± 55	A.D. 885
(Arauquinoid)	WIS–602	Caño Caroní	745 ± 50	A.D. 1205
(Arauquinoid)	WIS–620	Caño Caroní	695 ± 50	A.D. 1255
(Arauquinoid)	WIS–619	Caño Caroní	610 ± 50	A.D. 1340
(Arauquinoid)	WIS–617	Caño Caroní	535 ± 55	A.D. 1415

NOTE: A number of dates indicating a younger age for the Caño del Oso complex have been omitted from this table because they are believed to have resulted from the use of that complex's refuse in mound-building by the people of the La Betania complex. It is assumed that more recent charcoal became incorporated in the refuse during the course of this process.

Middle Orinocan and San Fernando areas, bringing with them the Cariban family of languages. His theory is contradicted by the evidences of a gradual Barrancoid-Arauquinoid transition on the Middle Orinoco, as already noted. Roosevelt (personal communication) and Rouse (n.d.) are inclined to think that the Arauquinoid series originated in the San Fernando area.

Whatever the case, it is clear that that series radiated out from the Middle Orinocan and San Fernando areas between A.D. 500 and 1500 (Zucchi 1972b:Figure 8). The already mentioned diffusion of Arauquinoid traits down the Orinoco River is but one example. Zucchi (1975a) has located sites on the Llanos of Barinas belonging to still undefined Arauquinoid complexes, which she believes to be the result of migration up the Apure River and its tributaries. One of these sites, at Caño Caroní, has both Osoid and Arauquinoid characteristics, a fact which suggests that the Osoid and Arauquinoid peoples were living side by side in the Barinas area during the second millennum A.D. (Zucchi 1975b).

The second of the later series, Memoid, seems to have been a local development in the Valle de la Pascua area (see Figure 13.3). It is marked by simple shapes and by crude, largely impressed and punctated decoration.

3. Historic Age

Complexes dating from this age have yet to be discovered on the Llanos. However, it must be assumed that the Memoid series survived until historic time, for an historically dated member of the series is known from the Río Chico area on the coast (see Figure 13.5).

D. Caribbean Mountains

Since the present-day population of Venezuela is largely concentrated in the mountains and on the coast, one might expect to find a more thorough coverage of the archaeology of those parts of the country. The Caribbean Mountains are relatively poorly known, however. We are only able to distinguish four local areas, most of the remains from these areas are late, and the list of radiocarbon dates is the smallest for all of Venezuela (see Figure 13.4 and Table 13.3).

Our chronological chart (Figure 13.4) begins in the west with the San Felipe area, a low valley connecting the Llanos with the coast (see Figure 13.1). Then comes the intermontane basin draining into Lake Valencia, followed by the mountain valleys of Los Teques and Caracas. Columns for Barinas in the Llanos and La Guaira on the coast have been added on either side of the chart to illustrate the interrelationships with those regions.

1. Lithic Age

A stray projectile point of Lithic type has been found in this region (Dupouy 1945), but no sites have yet been located.

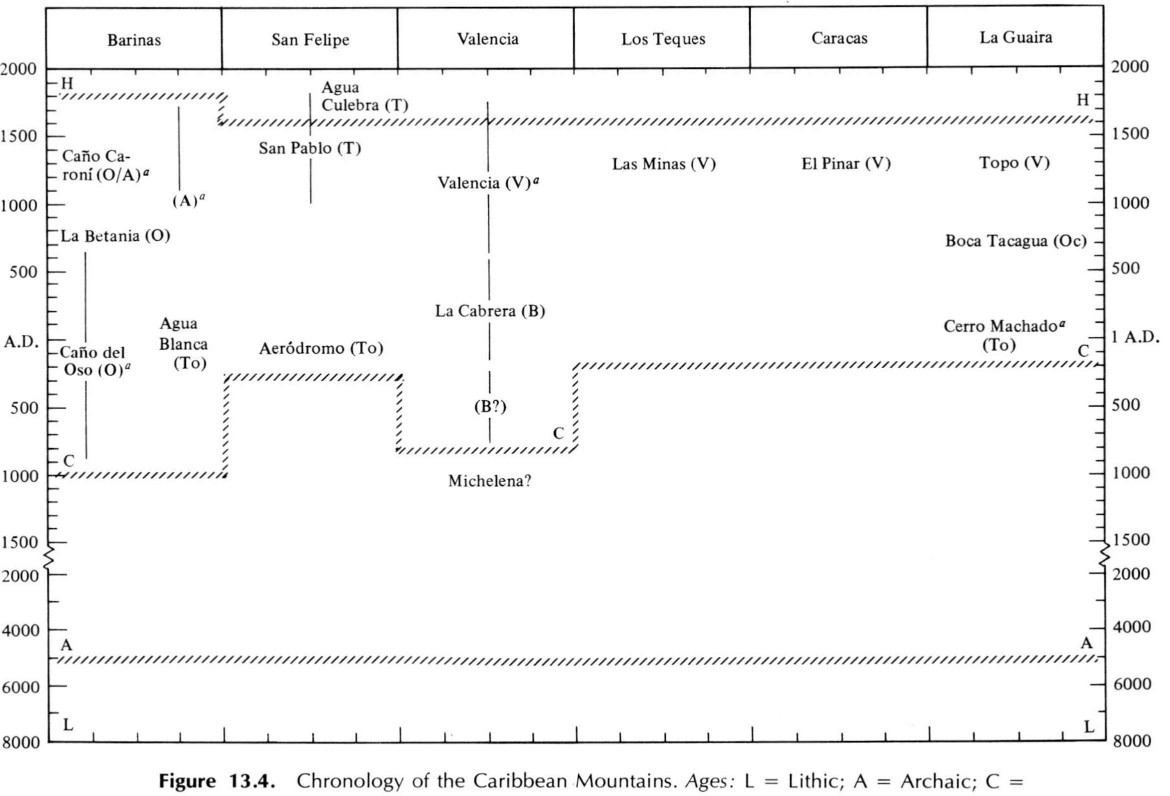

Figure 13.4. Chronology of the Caribbean Mountains. *Ages:* L = Lithic; A = Archaic; C = Ceramic; H = Historic. [a] = Position supported by radiocarbon analyses. See Table 13.3. *Series:* (A) = Arauquinoid; (B) = Barrancoid; (O) = Osoid; (Oc) = Ocumaroid; (T) = Tierroid; (To) = Tocuyanoid; (V) = Valencioid.

TABLE 13.3

Radiocarbon Dates Cited in the Mountain Chart

Area	Age	Complex	Sample number	Site	Date B.P.	Calendric date
Valencia:	*Ceramic:*	Valencia	Y–630	La Mata	1000 ± 70	A.D. 950
		Valencia	Y–632	La Mata	1000 ± 100	A.D. 950
		Valencia	Y–631	La Mata	980 ± 110	A.D. 970

2. Archaic Age

There is a single Archaic assemblage—consisting of a milling stone, pestles, grooved stone axes, and a hammerstone—which comes from the site of Michelena near the city of Valencia. Its age and affiliations are unknown.

3. Ceramic Age

While no early Barrancoid remains have yet been found in the Caribbean Mountains, they must be postulated to provide a connecting link between the Barrancoid complexes on the Middle Orinoco and those on the Caribbean coast (cf. Figures 13.2, 13.4, 13.5). If our hypothesis of Barrancoid migration is correct (Section B, 3), pottery resembling that of Ronquín Sombra on the Middle Orinoco should eventually be found in the Valencia area and should date from the first millennium B.C.

The earliest ceramic complex presently known is Aeródromo of the San Felipe area (see Figure 13.4). Like Agua Blanca on the Llanos, this is presumed to be the result of expansion from the Tocuyanoid center in Western Venezuela around the time of Christ.

It is probable that the Barrancoid series continued in the Valencia area while the Tocuyanoid series was intruding farther west. It culminated in the La Cabrera complex, which shows signs of a transition into the subsequent Valencioid series.

The west–east dichotomy continued into the second millennium A.D. At that time, the Caribbean Mountains were occupied by two different series of peoples, Tierroid in the westernmost, San Pablo area and Valencioid in the rest of the region. The Tierroid complexes seem to have intruded from a center in Western Venezuela, paralleling the earlier spread of the Tocuyanoid series from that center. Their legged vessels and polychrome decoration are typical of the Intermediate area, and as in that area, they lack griddles for cooking bread made from manioc flour.

The Valencioid complexes, on the other hand, are typically Caribbean and appear to be the result of a local development from the Barrancoid series, centering in the Valencia Basin. Their vessel shapes are relatively simple, they lack painted designs, and manioc griddles abound. The pots are typically decorated with zoomorphic figures done in appliqué work, and there are also rectilinear incised designs reminiscent of those in the Arauquinoid series along the Orinoco and on the Llanos. The construction of artificial mounds may likewise have diffused from the Llanos, and clay figurines may have spread from the Intermediate area. Effigy pipes continued from Barrancoid time (Cruxent and Rouse 1958–1959: Vol. 1;174–179).

4. Historic Age

Both the Tierroid pottery and Valencioid series survived the coming of the Spaniards. Tierroid pottery has been recovered from mission sites and

Valencioid pottery, from Nueva Cadiz, the first Spanish town (Rouse and Cruxent 1963:73, 97).

E. Coastal Region

The coast and adjacent islands are better known archaeologically than the rest of the Caribbean mainland, partly because they are more readily accessible by modern means of transportation and partly because the presence of shell refuse makes it easier to find sites there. Eleven local-area sequences have been worked out. These are shown from west to east on two chronological charts (Figures 13.5 and 13.6 and Table 13.4). The San Felipe column has been added from the chart for the Caribbean Mountains, and the Lower Orinoco column from the chart for the Orinoco region, in order to illustrate the major relationships with other parts of the mainland.

1. Lithic Age

No kill sites, where Lithic-Age peoples hunted the now-extinct Pleistocene mammals, have yet been encountered in the Coastal region. They should be there, since Cruxent (1970) has encountered them farther west along the Venezuelan Coast, in the Intermediate area. A likely place to seek them is on the Island of Trinidad, which was attached to the mainland at the time and has yielded the remains of big game (Wing 1962).

It is entirely possible that the Lithic technology survived the extinction of the Pleistocene mammals and the beginning of shell-fish collection. If so, we should eventually find shell middens laid down by peoples who lacked the grinding of stone and shell as well as ceramics.

2. Archaic Age

Shell middens without grinding and pottery-making are already known, but we cannot be sure that their lack of grinding is not due to the smallness of our artifact samples. Until the samples are increased by further excavation, it seems more prudent to assign all such sites to the Archaic Age.

Ten possibly Archaic complexes are represented on the coast and adjacent islands (see Figures 13.5 and 13.6). Cruxent (1971:39) has concluded that four of these, which share an emphasis on small stone chunks and/or flakes, constitute a single series. It will be called Ortoiroid, after a complex on the Island of Trinidad (Rouse 1953b:94–96).

The chips and flakes of the Ortoiroid complexes are highly irregular in shape. They are not worked on their side faces, like the Lithic artifacts, nor do their edges show appreciable evidences of intentional trimming. Cruxent (1971:39–40) theorizes that they were used mainly in order to produce basketry and wooden artifacts, including wood-tipped projectiles to take the place of the stone-tipped projectiles prevalent during the Lithic Age. The Ortoire Complex itself has projectile points of bone. Grinding stones and pestles are likewise characteristic, and a grooved stone ax is known.

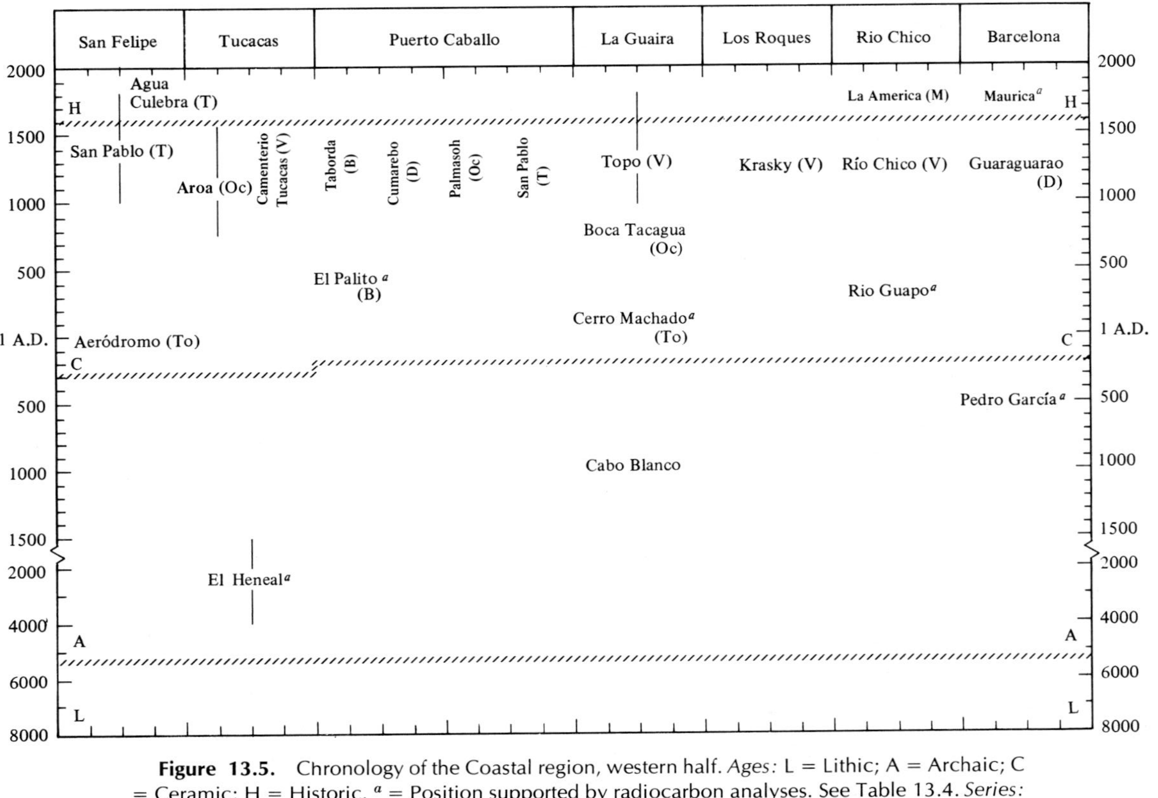

Figure 13.5. Chronology of the Coastal region, western half. *Ages:* L = Lithic; A = Archaic; C = Ceramic; H = Historic. [a] = Position supported by radiocarbon analyses. See Table 13.4. *Series:* (B) = Barrancoid; (D) = Dabajuroid; (M) = Memoid; (Oc) = Ocumaroid; (T) = Tierroid; (To) = Tocuyanoid; (V) = Valencioid.

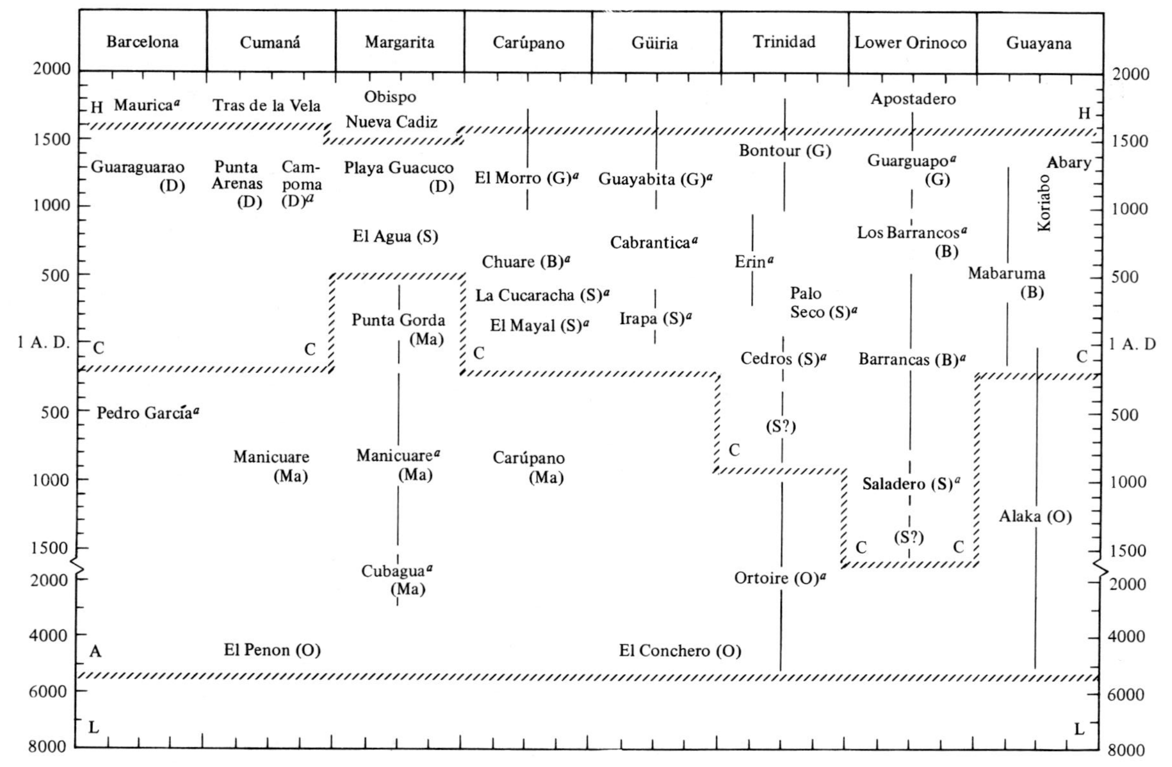

Figure 13.6. Chronology of the Coastal region, eastern half. *Ages:* L = Lithic; A = Archaic; C = Ceramic; H = Historic. [a] = Position supported by radiocarbon analyses. See Table 13.4. *Series:* (B) = Barrancoid; (D) = Dabajuroid; (G) = Guayabitoid; (Ma) = Manicuaroid; (O) = Ortoiroid; (S) = Saladoid.

The Ortoiroid series is distributed throughout the eastern part of the Coastal region (see Figure 13.6). Cruxent (1971:39) reports finding similar remains on the coast of Western Venezuela, within the Intermediate area, and notes a relationship with the San Nicolás Complex of coastal Colombia (Reichel-Dolmatoff 1965:48–50). Radiocarbon dates are available only for the Ortoire Complex of Trinidad. They range from 5250 to 800 B.C. (Table 13.4).

On present evidence, a second series developed in the east central part of the Coastal region during the third millennium B.C. It is characterized by ground shellwork and by bi-pointed, ground stone artifacts, possibly used as sling stones. There is a steady development in the shellwork from hammers and cups in the Cubagua Complex through gouges, beads, and pendants in the Manicuare Complex to celts and projectile points in the Punta Gorda Complex. The shell projectile points appear to be copies of bone points, which the Manicuaroid peoples shared with the Ortoiroid peoples (Rouse and Cruxent 1963:44–46).

The Manicuaroid complexes have a limited distribution. They have only been found in the three contiguous areas of Cumaná, Margarita, and Carúpano (see Figure 13.6). The radiocarbon dates range from 2200 to 1100 B.C. (Table 13.4), but apply only to the earlier complexes in the series. The final Punta Gorda Complex is associated with Saladoid trade sherds, which indicate that the series survived offshore in the Margarita area until after the appearance of pottery on the mainland.

In the Orinoco delta, the Archaic Age apparently survived alongside the Ceramic Age until the Historic Age, for the Warrau Indians of the delta were still without pottery when the Europeans arrived (Wilbert 1972:65–115). This survival is not shown in our chronological charts, because it has not yet been documented archaeologically.

3. Ceramic Age

Pottery did not reach the mainland part of the Coastal region until shortly before the time of Christ. It came from two sources, the Tocuyanoid series in the west (see Figure 13.5) and the Saladoid series in the east (see Figure 13.6).

The Tocuyanoid peoples apparently expanded from the Intermediate area along a route marked by the Aeródromo Complex in the San Felipe area and the Cerro Machado Complex in the La Guaira area (see Figure 13.1). Cerro Machado has a radiocarbon date of 20 A.D. (see Table 13.4).

As we have seen, Saladoid peoples apparently moved from the lower Orinoco through the delta of that river to the island of Trinidad, whence they proceeded westward into the Güiria, Carúpano, and Margarita areas (Figure 13.1). The earliest radiocarbon dates in these areas are 190 B.C. for the Cedros Complex on Trinidad and A.D. 155 for the El Mayal Complex in Carúpano (see Table 13.4).

TABLE 13.4

Radiocarbon Dates Cited in the Coastal Charts

Area	Age	Complex	Sample number	Site	Date B.P.	Calendric date
Tucacas:	*Archaic:*	El Heneal	Y–854	Cerro Iguanas	5580 ± 160	3630 B.C.
		El Heneal	Y–852	Cerro Iguanas	5550 ± 100	3600 B.C.
		El Heneal	Y–1247	Cerro Iguanas	5540 ± 250	3590 B.C.
		El Heneal	Y–853	Cerro Iguanas	5190 ± 120	3240 B.C.
		El Heneal	Y–455	El Heneal	3400 ± 120	1450 B.C.
Puerto Cabello:	*Ceramic:*	El Palito	Y–580	Aserradero	1615 ± 120	A.D. 335
		El Palito	Y–579	Aserradero	1640 ± 120	A.D. 310
La Guaira:	*Ceramic:*	Cerro Machado	Y–457	Cerro Machado	1930 ± 70	A.D. 20
Río Chico:	*Ceramic:*	Río Guapo	Y–1231	Río Guapo	1630 ± 100	A.D. 320
Barcelona:	*Archaic:*	Pedro García	Y–456	Pedro García	2450 ± 90	500 B.C.
	Historic:	Maurica	IVIC–288	Maurica	550 ± 70	A.D. 1400
		Maurica	IVIC–289	Maurica	530 ± 60	A.D. 1420
		Maurica	IVIC–285	Maurica	490 ± 50	A.D. 1460
Cumaná:	*Ceramic:*	Campoma	Tx-1435	Campoma	750 ± 50	A.D. 1200
		Campoma	Tx-1434	Campoma	720 ± 40	A.D. 1230
		Campoma	Tx-1433	Campoma	700 ± 40	A.D. 1250
Margarita:	*Archaic:*	Cubagua	Y–497	Punta Gorda	4150 ± 80	2200 B.C.
		Manicuare	Y–295	La Aduana 1	3570 ± 130	1620 B.C.
		Manicuare	Y–296g	La Aduana 1	3050 ± 80	1100 B.C.

Carúpano:	*Ceramic:*	El Mayal	Y–297	El Mayal 2	1795 ± 80	A.D. 155
		La Cucaracha	IVIC–777	El Cuartel	1660 ± 70	A.D. 290
		La Cucaracha	Y–1230	La Cucaracha	1600 ± 100	A.D. 350
		Chuare	Y–300	El Mayal 1	1355 ± 80	A.D. 595
		El Morro	Y–298	El Morro	715 ± 70	A.D. 1235
		El Morro	Y–299	Calle de la Marina	290 ± 70	A.D. 1660
Güiria:	*Ceramic:*	Irapa	Y–1113	Punta de Piedras	1680 ± 85	A.D. 270
		Irapa	Y–290	Irapa	1580 ± 40	A.D. 370
		Cabrantica	Y–1112	Cabrantica	1320 ± 95	A.D. 630
		Guayabita	Y–1111	Amacuro	690 ± 70	A.D. 1260
Trinidad:	*Archaic:*	Ortoire	IVIC–888	Banwari Trace	7180 ± 80	5250 B.C.
		Ortoire	IVIC–889	Banwari Trace	6780 ± 70	4830 B.C.
		Ortoire	IVIC–891	Banwari Trace	6190 ± 100	4240 B.C.
		Ortoire	IVIC–887	Banwari Trace	6170 ± 90	4220 B.C.
		Ortoire	IVIC–890	Banwari Trace	6100 ± 90	4150 B.C.
		Ortoire	IVIC–783	Banwari Trace	5650 ± 100	3700 B.C.
		Ortoire	IVIC–784	Banwari Trace	2550 ± 100	600 B.C.
		Ortoire	Y–260–2	Ortoire	2760 ± 130	810 B.C.
		Ortoire	Y–260–1	Ortoire	2750 ± 130	800 B.C.
	Ceramic:	Cedros	IVIC–642	Cedros	2140 ± 70	190 B.C.
		Cedros	IVIC–643	Cedros	1850 ± 80	A.D. 100
		Palo Seco	IVIC–638	Palo Seco	2130 ± 80	180 B.C.
		Palo Seco	IVIC–641	Palo Seco	2060 ± 80	110 B.C.
		Palo Seco	IVIC–640	Palo Seco	1990 ± 70	49 B.C.
		Palo Seco	IVIC–639	Palo Seco	1480 ± 70	A.D. 470
		Erin	IVIC–786	Guayaguayare	1720 ± 90	A.D. 230
		Erin	IVIC–785	Guayaguayare	1260 ± 100	A.D. 690

Further west, the Río Guapo Complex of the Río Chico region may be said to have developed out of the Saladoid series by loss of the latter's diagnostic white-on-red painting. Río Guapo has a radiocarbon date of A.D. 320.

According to our present evidence, the Barrancoid peoples were the next to arrive on the coast. If the conclusions we have drawn from the Orinoco chronology are correct (see Section B, 3), they migrated there via two routes, one across the central Llanos and through the Valencia area of the mountains into the Puerto Cabello area on the central coast, and the other down the Orinoco River and through its delta onto the eastern coast.

The first of these migrations resulted in two successive complexes, El Palito and Taborda (see Figure 13.5). El Palito has radiocarbon dates of ca. A.D. 300 (Table 13.4), which are confirmed by the presence of Saladoid trade sherds, presumably from El Mayal or another complex farther east along the coast (Figure 13.6).

The second migration took place about the same time. The Orinocan Barrancoids expanded into the northwestern part of Guayana and intermingled with the Saladoids of Trinidad and the east coast of Venezuela. They also exerted strong influence on the Saladoids in the southern half of the Lesser Antilles (see Section F, 3).

The Orinocan Barrancoids possessed an outstanding ceramic style at this time. Its modeled-incised decoration rivals that of Mexico and Peru (e.g., Chavín) in its complexity and artistic quality, and yet it appears to have developed in isolation in northeastern South America. Unfortunately, we know very little about the rest of Barrancoid culture.

During the latter part of the first millennium A.D., there was a break in the coastal chronology. In the west, the Tocuyanoid and Barrancoid series gave way to a new, Ocumaroid series, which appears to have been a local development. It combined the Tocuyanoid tradition of legged vessels and polychrome decoration with modeling and incision from the Barrancoid series and appliqué work and corrugation from Dabajuroid, a Western Venezuelan series that was spreading eastward along the coast of Venezuela at the time (Wagner 1972).

In the east, the Saladoid and Barrancoid complexes were succeeded by another local series, Guayabitoid, which is stylistically much inferior to its predecessors. Its decoration consists solely of tabular lugs and simple geometric motifs crudely executed in appliqué work and rectilinear incision. We know from the ethnohistorical accounts that this degeneration in ceramics was not accompanied by a decline in the rest of the culture (Kirchhoff 1948).

4. Historic Age

Research in Historic archaeology has been centered on the island of Cubagua in the Margarita area, where the Spaniards founded Nueva Cadiz, their first settlement in South America, in order to exploit the local pearl fisheries. Indian pottery from various parts of Venezuela has been recovered from the remains of Nueva Cadiz (Rouse and Cruxent 1963:137–138). New Indian complexes subsequently developed in Margarita and the neighboring areas (see Figure 13.6). These continued the process of decline in ceramics that had begun with the Guayabitoid series.

F. Lesser Antilles

The Lesser Antilles form an arch of small islands between the continent and the Greater Antilles (see Figure 13.1). Volcanic in origin, they are geologically distinct from Trinidad in the south and the Virgin Islands in the north. Each visible from the next, the Lesser Antilles have been compared to a bridge of stepping stones. They constitute by their situation the most likely route of migration and diffusion between the cultural centers of the mainland and the Greater Antilles.

The chart (Figure 13.7) gives the chronology of the best-known islands, each island being considered a separate local area. Trinidad and the Virgin Islands are added to show the relationships with the neighboring regions. The archaeology of the Lesser Antilles has been worked by different peoples in very different contexts and some of the classification is still tentative.

1. Lithic Age

One of the most significant developments of the last 5 years has been the discovery of preceramic sites in the Lesser Antilles (Olsen 1971). Since the original find on Long Island off Antigua lacks ground stonework as well as pottery, and offers similarities with the Lithic part of the Casimiroid series in Hispaniola (to be discussed later), this find may date from the Lithic Age. Alternatively, it may represent a workshop used by the Archaic or Ceramic occupants of Antigua.

2. Archaic Age

Davis (1974) has been able to isolate a Jolly Beach complex on Antigua, which is typically Archaic. It includes flint blades and flakes, shell celts, and ground stonework in a context of shell middens. A similar assemblage has just been excavated by R. Christopher Goodwin (personal communication) on St. Kitts. The two finds are radiocarbon dated in the second and third millennia B.C. respectively (Table 13.5).

Both Antigua and St. Kitts are situated in the Leeward Islands at the northern end of the Lesser Antilles. No preceramic complexes are known from the Windward Islands and Barbados, farther south. Since this leaves an open gap between the Greater Antilles and the mainland, the original peopling of the islands remains a problem.

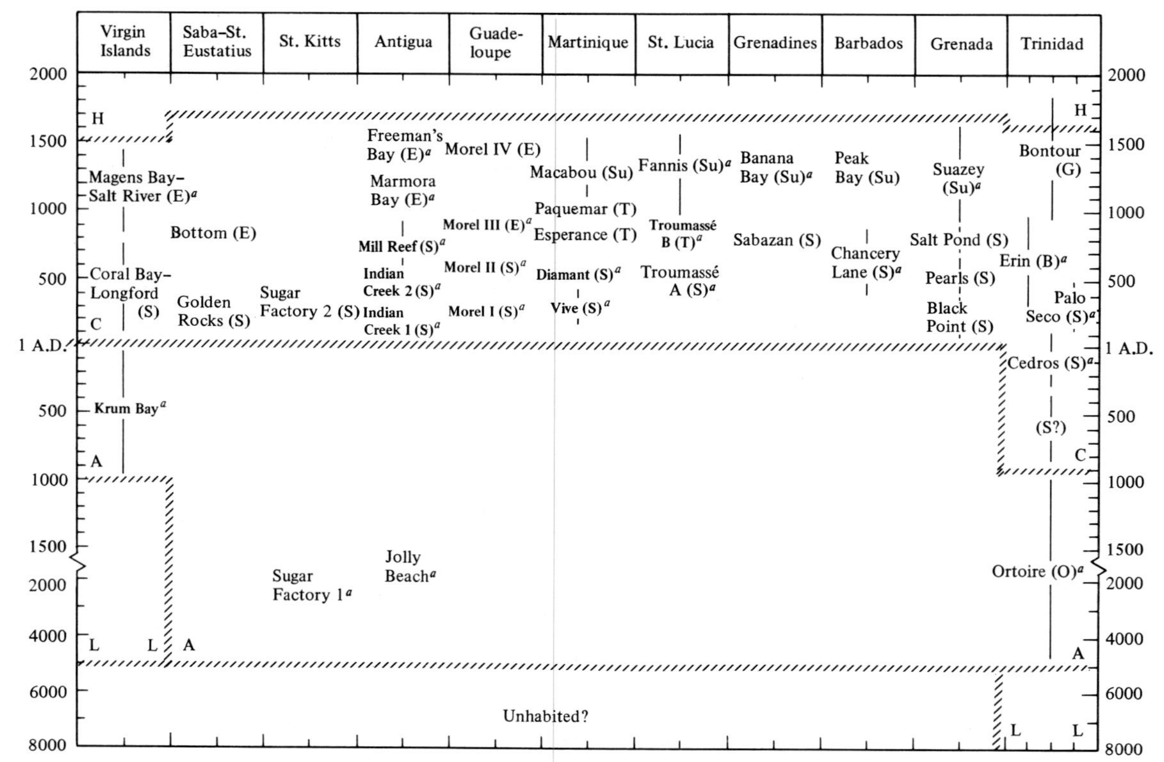

Figure 13.7. Chronology of the Lesser Antilles. *Ages:* L = Lithic; A = Archaic; C = Ceramic; H = Historic. [a] = Position supported by radiocarbon analyses. See Table 13.5. *Series:* (B) = Barrancoid; (E) = Elenoid; (G) = Guayabitoid; (O) = Ortoiroid; (S) = Saladoid; (Su) = Suazoid; (T) = Troumassoid.

3. Ceramic Age

The earliest Ceramic-Age complexes belong to the Saladoid series, discussed above in connection with the Orinoco and Coastal regions (Sections B, 3 and E, 3). These complexes certainly resulted from a migration out of eastern Venezuela and Trinidad, perhaps as early as the last centuries before the time of Christ, as evidenced by the dates for the Cedros complex of Trinidad, a possibly related component at Black Point on the southern tip of Grenada (Bullen 1964), and Indian Creek 1 on Antigua (Tables 13.4 and 13.5). The Saladoid people must have moved quite rapidly through the islands, since their earliest pottery and radiocarbon dates are relatively uniform. They introduced pottery, manioc agriculture, and possibly Arawakan languages to the Antilles (Figure 13.7). Their remains are ordinarily located on the best agricultural soils, almost exclusively close to the seashore and usually on the Atlantic coast. Although the Saladoid people may at first have moved into uninhabited islands, they replaced or mingled with the preceramic peoples of the Leeward Islands and the Greater Antilles.

The simple, well made, and delicate pottery of the first migrants to the Lesser Antilles, such as the Vivé complex on Martinique (Mattioni 1974) and the Indian Creek complex on Antigua (Rouse 1974), preserved its stylistic characteristics throughout the islands until about A.D. 350, but was enriched by the addition of polychrome painting and incense burners. Small three-pointed objects of stone, clay, or shell were present from the beginning. These are prototypes of the larger and more elaborately decorated deities or "zemis" of the later archaeology of the Greater Antilles (Olsen 1970).

A further elaboration of the existing complexes took place after A.D. 350. This development can unmistakedly be traced to the influence of the Barrancoid peoples who were then moving into Trinidad (Section E, 3). It is marked by greater emphasis on modeled-incised decoration and even by true Barrancoid imitations. The vessels become larger, more complex in shape, and more elaborately decorated, but the essential Saladoid traits are preserved. The development reaches its climax in the Diamant complex of Martinique (Pettijean-Roget 1968), but similar ceramics are found from Grenada to Guadeloupe.

The wave of Barrancoid influences seems to have peaked around A.D. 500. It may be associated with the introduction of the Maipuran branch of Arawakan languages, if Lathrap (1970) is correct in his correlation of that branch with the Barrancoid series (see Section B, 3). Island Carib, the speech of the historic Indians of the Windward Islands, is a Maipuran dialect. Consequently, the intensification of Barrancoid stylistic features in the Windward Islands may provide a date for the introduction of the historic language, although no migration can be inferred from the remains themselves.

TABLE 13.5

Radiocarbon Dates Cited in the Lesser Antillean Chart

Area	Age	Complex	Sample number	Site	Date B.P.	Calendric date
Grenada:	*Ceramic:*	Suazey	RL–76	Savanne Suazey	550 ± 110	A.D. 1400
Barbados:		Chancery Lane	I–2486	Chancery Lane	1570 ± 95	A.D. 380
Grenadines:	*Ceramic:*	Banana Bay	RL–27	Banana Bay	720 ± 100	A.D. 1230
		Banana Bay	RL–71	Banana Bay	530 ± 110	A.D. 1420
St. Lucia:	*Ceramic:*	Troumassée A	Y–1115	Grande Anse	1460 ± 80	A.D. 490
		Troumassée B	Y–650	Troumassée	1220 ± 120	A.D. 730
		Troumassée B	RL–30	Giraudy	1240 ± 100	A.D. 710
		Troumassée B	RL–31	Giraudy	1120 ± 100	A.D. 830
		Fannis	RL–26	Lavoutte	710 ± 100	A.D. 1240
Martinique:	*Ceramic:*	Vivé	Y–1116	La Salle	1770 ± 80	A.D. 130
		Vivé	RL–156	Vivé	1730 ± 110	A.D. 220
		Vivé	F–?	Vivé	1730 ± 100	A.D. 220
		Vivé	S–85	Vivé	1655 ± 150	A.D. 295
		Diamant	UGa–113	Vivé	1530 ± 75	A.D. 420
		Diamant	Y–1762	Diamant	1490 ± 60	A.D. 460
		Diamant	Y–1337	Grande Anse	1450 ± 80	A.D. 500
Guadeloupe:	*Ceramic:*	Morel I	Y–1137	Morel	1726 ± 70	A.D. 170
		Morel I	Y–1138	Morel	1705 ± 100	A.D. 190
		Morel II	Y–1245	Morel	1400 ± 80	A.D. 550
		Morel II	Y–1136	Morel	1380 ± 100	A.D. 570
		Morel III	Y–1246	Morel	1100 ± 80	A.D. 850

Antigua:	*Archaic:*	Jolly Beach	I–7687	Jolly Beach	3725 ± 90	1775 B.C.
	Ceramic:	Indian Creek 1	I–7980	Indian Creek	1915 ± 80	A.D. 35
		Indian Creek 1	I–7981	Indian Creek	1855 ± 80	A.D. 95
		Indian Creek 1	I–7979	Indian Creek	1790 ± 85	A.D. 160
		Indian Creek 2	I–7855	Indian Creek	1765 ± 80	A.D. 185
		Indian Creek 2	I–7838	Indian Creek	1750 ± 80	A.D. 200
		Indian Creek 2	I–7837	Indian Creek	1715 ± 80	A.D. 235
		Indian Creek 2	I–7854	Indian Creek	1670 ± 80	A.D. 280
		Indian Creek 2	I–7355	Indian Creek	1505 ± 85	A.D. 445
		Indian Creek 2	I–7352	Indian Creek	1440 ± 85	A.D. 510
		Mill Reef	I–7356	Indian Creek	1505 ± 85	A.D. 445
		Mill Reef	I–7834	Indian Creek	1265 ± 80	A.D. 685
		Mill Reef	I–7353	Indian Creek	1230 ± 85	A.D. 720
		Mill Reef	I–7846	Indian Creek	1140 ± 80	A.D. 810
		Mill Reef	I–7984	Indian Creek	1125 ± 80	A.D. 825
		Mill Reef	I–7983	Indian Creek	1110 ± 80	A.D. 840
		Mill Reef	I–7354	Indian Creek	1100 ± 85	A.D. 850
		Mill Reef	I–7357	Indian Creek	1080 ± 85	A.D. 870
		Mill Reef	I–7836	Indian Creek	1070 ± 80	A.D. 880
		Mill Reef	I–7982	Indian Creek	1070 ± 80	A.D. 880
		Mill Reef	I–7844	Indian Creek	1000 ± 80	A.D. 950
		Marmora Bay	I–7845	Indian Creek	1020 ± 80	A.D. 930
		Marmora Bay	I–7847	Indian Creek	900 ± 80	A.D. 1050
		Marmora Bay	I–7832	Indian Creek	855 ± 80	A.D. 1095
		Marmora Bay	I–7835	Indian Creek	845 ± 80	A.D. 1105
		Freeman's Bay	I–7839	Freeman's Bay	935 ± 80	A.D. 1015
		Freeman's Bay	I–7856	Freeman's Bay	480 ± 80	A.D. 1470
St. Kitts:	*Archaic:*	Sugar Factory 1	UCLA–?	Sugar Factory 1	4100 ± 60	2123 B.C.

The period following about A.D. 600 is characterized by local developments within the Lesser Antilles and by the introduction of new series. In the Windward Islands, the Troumassoid series (Allaire 1977; McKusick 1960) presents us with a regression in ceramic standards; it has less complex and less frequent decoration, simpler shapes, and sturdier vessels, especially in the L'Esperance and Paquemar complexes (see Figure 13.7). Saladoid hallmarks such as bell-shaped vessels and white-on-red painting decline or disappear. Plain, crude, utilitarian vessels of simple geometrical shapes become more frequent, together with incurving walled containers, known as "cazuelas." A new type of decoration consists of linear painted scrolls or spirals on a buff or red painted background, a type referred to as "Caliviny Polychrome" (Bullen 1964). It is most highly represented in St. Vincent, Grenada, and Barbados.

The contemporary developments in the Leeward Islands, including perhaps Guadeloupe, have been classified within the Elenoid series (Rouse 1976), because of closer affinities with ceramic developments in the Virgin Islands and eastern Puerto Rico. A distinctive Lesser Antillean artifact, the footed griddle, appears during this time period, but is not represented north of Antigua.

Barbados, on present evidence, appears to have been first inhabited by Saladoid peoples around A.D. 380. The subsequent ceramic developments seem peripheral, yet close, to the Troumassoid series of the Windward Islands (Bullen and Bullen 1968).

Throughout the Lesser Antilles, the transitional developments out of the Saladoid series resulted in ceramic similarities, which extend to the Ostionoid complexes of the Greater Antilles, especially in vessel shape and some appendages. The distinctions far outweigh the similarities, however, and no overall migration can be inferred to account for the changes.

Recent radiocarbon dates (Bullen and Bullen 1972; Rouse 1976) place the most striking changes in the ceramic sequence of the Lesser Antilles around A.D. 1100–1200. In the Windward Islands, but apparently not north of Martinique, the remains belong to a Suazoid series (Bullen 1964; McKusick 1960), which is characterized by some of the crudest pottery in the West Indies. Tripod vessels, scratched surfaces, and plain cooking pots are diagnostic. Decoration occurs on rare specimens; thick overall red slip, various unpatterned incisions, "Caliviny" painting, and finger-intended rims are typical. Finer vessels are occasionally encountered, but should not be mistaken for Saladoid intrusions. A greater variety of small stone, shell, and clay objects is associated with the complexes (Allaire 1977). On Antigua in the Leeward Islands, the last prehistoric period is represented by the Freeman's Bay complex, which seems to carry on Elenoid features (Rouse 1976).

No exterior origin can be established for the introduction of the Suazoid series into the Lesser Antilles, despite tenuous influences from coastal

Venezuela and the Greater Antilles. (Apparently there were none from the Guianas.) The Suazoid series seems to be entirely a local development; any evidence for a migration, as held by Bullen and Bullen (1976), is lacking and is contradicted by the pattern of distribution of the ceramics. Nowhere are Suazoid complexes more elaborate than on Barbados, and hence that island may have played a significant role in the development of the new series.

4. Historic Age

No European-contact sites have yet been identified in the Lesser Antilles. According to the documentary sources, the pottery of the historic inhabitants of the islands, the Caribs, was similar to that of the Guiana Caribs, or Galibis (Allaire 1977). This pottery is entirely different from the preceding Suazoid series. It can no longer be claimed, therefore, that Suazoid pottery marks the migration of the Island Caribs from the mainland which is narrated in their own traditions.

G. Greater Antilles

Since these islands extend westward from the Lesser Antilles to the peninsulas of Yucatán and Florida, they provide a means of passage to and from Middle and North as well as South America. However, the pair of straits separating Yucatán and Florida from the islands are broader than that between Trinidad and the Lesser Antilles, and the winds and currents are less favorable; as a result, migration and diffusion into the Greater Antilles seem to have taken place primarily from South America. The islands are so large that they offered the opportunity for the development of a cultural center, rivaling those on the South American mainland.

Our chart (Figure 13.8 and Table 13.6) extends from west to east through the islands, omitting only the Bahamas, where there is little chronological information. Each major island is treated as a single local area, except for Hispaniola, which is divided along the boundary between Haiti and the Dominican Republic.

1. Lithic Age

The major find of the past decade has been a Casimiroid series of Lithic-Age complexes on the island of Hispaniola (Cruxent and Rouse 1969). Prior to this discovery, it was assumed that man had not reached the Antilles until the Archaic Age, that is, until 2000 B.C. according to our present radiocarbon dates (see Table 13.6). Now, the estimated time of arrival has to be pushed back, possibly as far as 5000 B.C., although the earliest radiocarbon date is still only 2500 B.C.

The Casimiroid peoples were highly proficient in the working of flint, which abounds on the island of Hispaniola. In the original complex, the Casimira, they made only irregular chunks and flakes. These are comparable

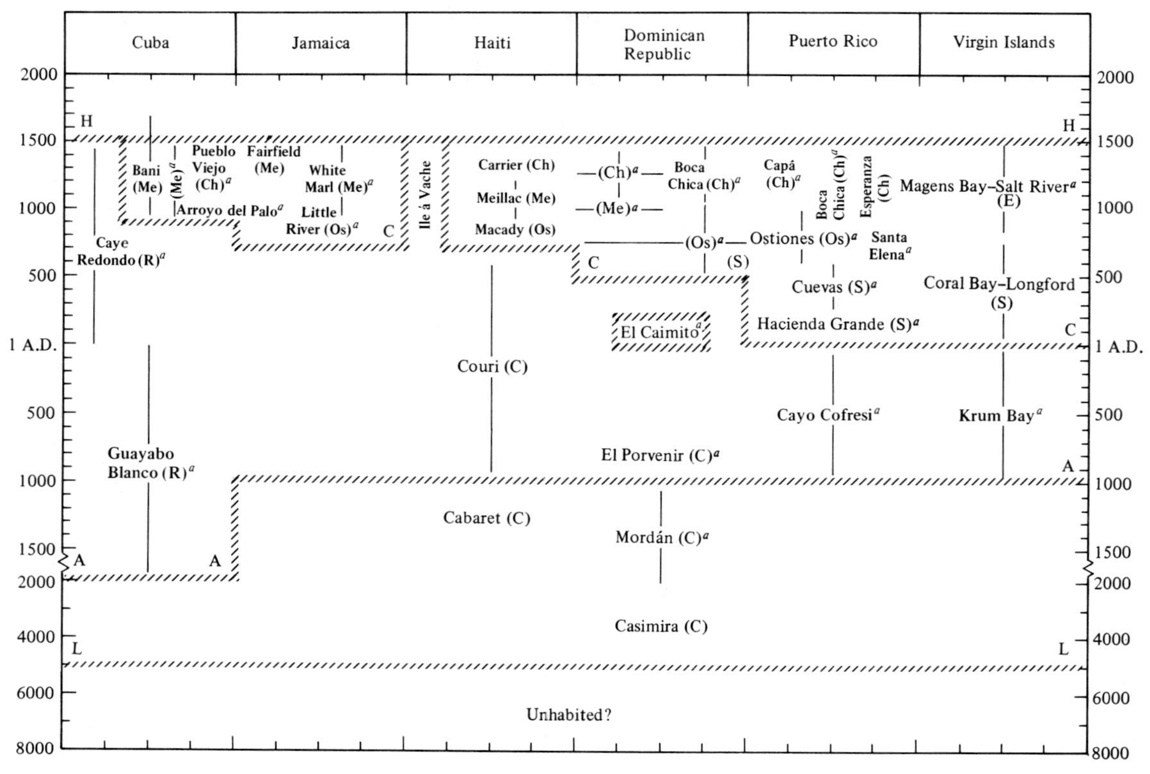

Figure 13.8. Chronology of the Greater Antilles. *Ages:* L = Lithic; A = Archaic; C = Ceramic; H = Historic. [a] = Position supported by radiocarbon analyses. See Table 13.6. *Series:* (C) = Casimiroid; (Ch) = Chicoid; (Me) = Meillacoid; (Os) = Ostionoid; (R) = Redondoid; (S) = Saladoid.

to the stone artifacts of the Ortoiroid complexes on the mainland, except for their massive size, which may be due to the high quality of the local flint (Cruxent and Rouse 1969:50–51). In the next complex, the Mordán, the flakes are even larger and tend to be lamellar in shape, prepared striking platforms are common, and trimmed edges make their appearance. Cabaret, the final complex in the Lithic part of the series, is distinguished by projectile points made from lamellar flakes by trimming one side at the base is order to produce a crude stem (Cruxent and Rouse 1969:49). Shell refuse has been found only in association with the Mordán and Cabaret complexes.

Originally, Cruxent and Rouse (1969:44–45) theorized that the Casimiroid series is likely to have come from Central America via the chain of mid-Caribbean islets and reefs that extends from Nicaragua through Jamaica to Hispaniola. They based this conclusion on the resemblances in flint working between Central America and Hispaniola, originally noted by W. R. Coe (1957), and on the absence of such artifacts along the alternative routes of migration, especially in the Lesser Antilles. However, the comparable Central American artifacts date from the Ceramic Age, and hence could just as well be due to diffusion in the opposite direction, from Hispaniola to the mainland.

Cruxent (1970:39) has since called attention to the resemblances between the earlier, Mordán complex on Hispaniola and the Ortoiroid stoneworking on the mainland of South America, and Olsen (1971) has found a possible connecting link between the two on the island of Antigua, as noted earlier (Section F, 1). It would be well, therefore, to keep open the possibility of a South rather than a Central American origin for the Casimiroid series.

2. Archaic Age

The Krum Bay complex of the Virgin Islands is unique in the presence of stone celts. Two of its middens yielded chipped and pecked celts with barely perceptible evidences of grinding, while a third contained fully ground petaloid celts, lying directly beneath the only pottery at the site (Bullen and Sleight 1963). This suggests that the practice of grinding stone celts may have developed on the island. A different complex, marked by stone pestles in addition to edge grinders, is known from Cayo Cofresí, Caño Hondo, and Cueva María la Cruz in Puerto Rico. The two complexes are radiocarbon dated between 450 B.C. and A.D. 40 (see Table 13.6).

The Casimiroid peoples had advanced from the Lithic to the Archaic Age some 500 years earlier, by the development of several new complexes in Hispaniola. In Couri, the best known of the new complexes (Figure 13.8), the Casimiroid flintwork reaches its climax in long, regularly shaped lamellar flakes, which are reminiscent of the Upper Paleolithic European flintwork, even to the presence of backed "blades" and end scrapers (Rouse 1941:Pl. 1). Again, however, they are considerably larger than their counterparts elsewhere. Projectile points continue from the previous, Cabaret Complex

TABLE 13.6

Radiocarbon Dates Cited in the Greater Antillean Chart

Area	Age	Complex	Sample number	Site	Date B. P.	Calendric date
Virgin Islands:	*Archaic:*	Krum Bay	I–8640	Krum Bay	2830 ± 85	880 B. C.
		Krum Bay	I–8693	Cancel Hill	2820 ± 85	870 B. C.
		Krum Bay	I–8642	Grambokola Hill	2785 ± 85	835 B. C.
		Krum Bay	I–8641	Krum Bay	2775 ± 85	825 B. C.
		Krum Bay	L–1380B	Aboretum	2410 ± 60	460 B.C.
		Krum Bay	I–621	Krum Bay	2400 ± 175	450 B.C.
		Krum Bay	I–620	Krum Bay	2175 ± 160	225 B.C.
		Krum Bay	L–1380A	Aboretum	1900 ± 70	A.D. 50
	Ceramic:	Magens Bay-Salt River	RL–411	Hull Bay	730 ± 110	A.D. 1220
		Magens Bay-Salt River	RL–409	Hull Bay	640 ± 110	A.D. 1310
Puerto Rico:	*Archaic:*	Cayo Cofresí	UGa–995	Caño Hondo	3010 ± 70	1060 B.C.
		Cayo Cofresí	UGa–996	Caño Hondo	2855 ± 65	905 B.C.
		Cayo Cofresí	UGa–997	Caño Hondo	2705 ± 70	755 B.C.
		Cayo Cofresí	I–7424	Cayo Cofresí	2227 ± 85	325 B.C.
		Cayo Cofresí	I–7425	Cayo Cofresí	2224 ± 85	295 B.C.
		Cayo Cofresí	Y–1234	Cueva María la Cruz	1920 ± 120	A.D. 30
		Cayo Cofresí	Y–1235	Cueva María la Cruz	1910 ± 100	A.D. 40
	Ceramic:	Hacienda Grande	Y–1233	Hacienda Grande	1830 ± 80	A. D. 120
		Hacienda Grande	Y–1232	Hacienda Grande	1580 ± 80	A. D. 370

		Cuevas	I–6595	Punta Ostiones	1545 ± 90	A.D. 405
		Cuevas	Y–1240	Monserrate	1440 ± 80	A.D. 510
		Cuevas	Y–1237	Monserrate	1360 ± 80	A.D. 590
		Ostiones	UM–398	Villa Taina	1300 ± 90	A.D. 650
		Ostiones	Y–1236	Monserrate	1240 ± 80	A.D. 710
		Ostiones	Y–1242	Punta Ostiones	1200 ± 80	A.D. 820
		Ostiones	UM–399	Villa Taina	1090 ± 100	A.D. 860
		Ostiones	UM–400	Villa Taina	1050 ± 80	A.D. 900
		Ostiones	Y–1241	Punta Ostiones	900 ± 80	A.D. 1050
		Santa Elena	Y–1239	Santa Elena	1060 ± 80	A.D. 890
		Santa Elena	Y–1238	Santa Elena	740 ± 80	A.D. 1210
		Boca Chica	Y–1243	Cayito	700 ± 80	A.D. 1250
		Capá	Y–1244	Capá	680 ± 80	A.D. 1270
Dominican Republic:	*Lithic:*	Mordán	Y–1422	Mordán	4560 ± 80	2610 B.C.
		Mordán	IVIC–5	Mordán	4400 ± 170	2450 B.C.
		Mordán	Tx–54	Mordán	4140 ± 130	2190 B.C.
	Archaic:	El Porvenir	I–6790	El Porvenir	2980 ± 95	1030 B.C.
		El Porvenir	I–6615	El Porvenir	2855 ± 90	905 B.C.
	Ceramic:	El Caimito	I–7823	El Caimito	2130 ± 85	180 B.C.
		El Caimito	I–6924	El Caimito	1965 ± 90	15 B.C.
		El Caimito	I–7822	El Caimito	1865 ± 85	A.D. 85
		El Caimito	I–7821	El Caimito	1830 ± 85	A.D. 120
		(Ostionoid)	UGa–433	San Juan de la Maguana	1255 ± 115	A.D. 695
		(Ostionoid)	I–6837	La Caleta	1220 ± 85	A.D. 730
		(Ostionoid)	CSIC–95	Juan Dolio	1130 ± 100	A.D. 820
		(Ostionoid)	I–6314	Macao	1125 ± 90	A.D. 825
		(Ostionoid)	I–?	Corrales	1090 ± 90	A.D. 860
		(Ostionoid)	I–?	Corrales	1080 ± 90	A.D. 870
		(Ostionoid)	I–6443	Macao	970 ± 90	A.D. 980
		(Ostionoid)	I–7179	La Caleta	965 ± 85	A.D. 985
		(Meillacoid)	GrN–6576	Río Verde	1145 ± 30	A.D. 805
		(Meillacoid)	GrN–6577	Río Verde	1110 ± 30	A.D. 840

(Continued)

TABLE 13.6 *(Continued)*

Area	Age	Complex	Sample number	Site	Date B.P.	Calendric date
		(Meillacoid)	CSIC–104	El Carril	1030 ± 100	A.D. 920
		(Meillacoid)	GrN–6575	Río Verde	965 ± 30	A.D. 1025
		(Meillacoid)	I–6446	López	900 ± 90	A.D. 1050
		Boca Chica	IVIC–422	La Caleta	670 ± 70	A.D. 1280
		(Chicoid)	I–6445	Macao	925 ± 110	A.D. 1025
		(Chicoid)	I–6146	Altos de Vireya	920 ± 90	A.D. 1030
		(Chicoid)	I–6147	El Pleicito	865 ± 90	A.D. 1085
		(Chicoid)	I–6313	Macao	750 ± 90	A.D. 1200
		(Chicoid)	I–6018	La Llamada	730 ± 95	A.D. 1220
		(Chicoid)	I–6592	Punta de Garza	650 ± 90	A.D. 1300
		(Chicoid)	UGa–432	Sonador	580 ± 65	A.D. 1370
		(Chicoid)	UGa–434	Sonador	480 ± 65	A.D. 1470
Jamaica:		Little River	Y–1897	Bottom Bay	1300 ± 120	A.D. 650
		White Marl	Y–1118	White Marl	1073 ± 95	A.D. 877
		White Marl	Y–1117	White Marl	1016 ± 95	A.D. 934
		White Marl	Y–1784	White Marl	820 ± 60	A.D. 1130
		White Marl	Y–1786	White Marl	780 ± 80	A.D. 1170
		White Marl	Y–1751	White Marl	760 ± 60	A.D. 1190
		White Marl	Y–1754	White Marl	720 ± 60	A.D. 1230
		White Marl	Y–1753	White Marl	650 ± 60	A.D. 1300
		White Marl	Y–1785	White Marl	650 ± 60	A.D. 1300
		White Marl	Y–1119	White Marl	617 ± 95	A.D. 1333
		White Marl	Y–1755	White Marl	600 ± 60	A.D. 1350
		White Marl	Y–1750	White Marl	460 ± 120	A.D. 1490
Cuba:	*Archaic:*	Guayabo Blanco	SI–429	Residuario Fuenche	4000 ± 150	2050 B.C.
		Guayabo Blanco	Y–1764	Damajayabo	3250 ± 100	1300 B.C.

	Guayabo Blanco	SI–428	Residuario Fuenche	3110 ± 200	1160 B.C.
	Guayabo Blanco	SI–427	Residuario Fuenche	2510 ± 200	560 B.C.
	Guayabo Blanco	SI–426	Residuario Fuenche	2070 ± 150	120 B.C.
	Cayo Redondo	SI–424	Mogote de la Cueva	1620 ± 150	A.D. 330
	Cayo Redondo	Y–465	La Vega del Palmar	960 ± 60	A.D. 990
	Cayo Redondo	SI–425	Mogote de la Cueva	650 ± 200	A.D. 1300
Ceramic:	Arroyo del Palo	SI–347	Mejías	1020 ± 100	A.D. 930
	Arroyo del Palo	Y–1556	Arroyo del Palo	970 ± 80	A.D. 980
	Arroyo del Palo	Y–1555	Arroyo del Palo	760 ± 60	A.D. 1190
	Baní	Mo–399	Aguas Gordas	1000 ± 100	A.D. 950
	Baní	SI–352	Loma de la Forestal	970 ± 100	A.D. 980
	Baní	Y–206	Potrero del Mango	810 ± 80	A.D. 1140
	Baní	SI–351	Barajagua	590 ± 100	A.D. 1360
	Baní	SI–349	Esterito	550 ± 150	A.D. 1400
	Baní	SI–350	Esterito	500 ± 100	A.D. 1450
	(Meillacoid)	Y–1994	Damajayabo	1120 ± 160	A.D. 830
	(Meillacoid)	SI–353	El Morrillo	590 ± 90	A.D. 1360
	Pueblo Viejo	SI–348	Laguna Limones	640 ± 120	A.D. 1310
	Pueblo Viejo	SI–350	Esterito	500 ± 100	A.D. 1360
	Pueblo Viejo	SI–349	Esterito	550 ± 150	A.D. 1400

and now have their stems trimmed on both sides. Double-bitted axes, bowls, beads, pendants, balls, and daggerlike ceremonial artifacts are all ground from stone, and chisels and pendants from shell. Both stone and shell artifacts are incised with rectilinear parallel-line designs. Other sites show a further elaboration of ground stonework, including eared axes and ceremonial objects.

Though Casimiroid-type flakes also occur in the Archaic sites of Cuba, they are so rare and simple, relative to the Hispaniolan finds, that they cannot be considered diagnostic. Instead, the Cuban complexes are grouped into a Redondoid series on the basis of their ground shellwork, especially the presence of gouges. The earlier, Guayabo Blanco Complex lacks ground stonework, but this becomes increasingly common and more varied in the later, Cayo Redondo Complex, apparently as the result of influence from Hispaniola.

Several authors (e.g., Alegria 1965:264) have derived the Redondoid complexes from the Manicuaroid series on the Venezuelan Coast, because both have shell gouges. However, no true gouges have been found in any of the intervening islands. Moreover, the radiocarbon dates indicate that any diffusion would have had to go in the opposite direction. The shell gouge appears before 2500 B.C. in Florida, ca. 2000 B.C. in Cuba, and not until ca. 1600 B.C. in Venezuela (cf. Guayabo Blanco in Table 6 and Manicuare in Table 4).

3. Ceramic Age

Saladoid peoples from the Lesser Antilles replaced the Lithic-Age people in the Virgin Islands and Puerto Rico during the first or second century A.D., according to our radiocarbon dates (see Table 13.6). Farther west, the Archaic Indians survived from varying lengths of time.

Before considering the Saladoid invasion, let us look at an effect it may have had on the neighboring Archaic population. Two sites, Caimito in the Dominican Republic (Ortega *et al.* 1975) and Arroyo Palo in Cuba (Tabio and Guarch 1966), have yielded pottery but not griddles indicative of agriculture. In both cases, the pottery is decorated in the style of Archaic stonework. These facts suggest that the two sites were inhabited by preceramic peoples who had learned how to make pottery as the result of stimulus diffusion from the Saladoid invaders. Alternatively, as R. C. Goodwin has pointed out to us, the stimulus may have come from the Glades potters of Florida.

In Puerto Rico, the Saladoid sequence of Hacienda Grande and Cuevas Complexes shows a decline, contrary to the contemporary development in the Lesser Antilles (see Section F, 3). Shapes become simpler, modeling and incision cease, and in the upper levels of the Cuevas deposits, the complex curvilinear designs painted in white on red give way to crude parallel lines before disappearing completely.

During late Cuevas time, ca. A.D. 500, the Saladoid peoples expanded into the Dominican Republic, taking it over from the previous Archaic population (see Figure 13.8). There and in Puerto Rico, they developed a new Ostionoid series, which is transitional from Saladoid ceramics to the later series of the Greater Antilles, as explained in Section II. In the earlier Ostionoid deposits, the bell-shaped bowls diagnostic of the Saladoid series become straight sided, but still flare outward. In the later deposits, this form gradually loses popularity in favor of closed, cazuela-type bowls that are diagnostic of all subsequent series. The earlier decoration consists only of black and/or red painting and plain, tabular lugs, but appliqué work, incision, and eventually modeled-incised lugs gradually make their appearance. Ball courts also developed at this time (Rouse, 1952).

During early Ostionoid time, ca. A.D. 700, the peoples of that series expanded into Haiti and Jamaica. There, under the influence of the previous Archaic peoples' rectilinear style of art, they developed a new Meillacoid series, which subsequently spread into Cuba and the Bahamas, bringing to an end the Ceramic-Age Indians' invasion of the Antilles ca. A.D. 1000.

By this time, the Lithic-Age Indians had entirely disappeared and the Archaic-Age Indians survived only in the most remote parts of Haiti and Cuba, where Columbus eventually encountered them. (Their historic survivors are sometimes called Ciboneys; Rouse 1948). The Meillacoid Indians of the Ceramic Age similarly persisted in Jamaica, central Cuba, and the northern Bahamas. (Their historic survivors are known in Jamaica and Cuba as Sub-Tainos and in the Bahamas as Lucayos; Rouse 1948).

Meanwhile, ca. A.D. 800 the Ostionoid people of the Dominican Republic had produced still another Ceramic-Age series, known as Chicoid (see Figure 13.8). It continued the newly developed emphasis on closed, cazuela-type vessels. These were decorated with complex incised and punctated designs and with elaborate modeled-incised lugs. The Chicoid artisans carved similar designs in stone, bone, and shell, in order to represent their *zemis* (deities).

Chicoid ceramics and the accompanying ceremonial developments spread ca. A.D. 1000 in two directions, westward into Haiti and Eastern Cuba and eastward into Puerto Rico and the Virgin Islands (see Figure 13.8). They persisted until the time of Columbus. (Their historic possessors are known as Tainos; Rouse 1948.)

The origin of the late Ostionoid and Chicoid ceramics has been the subject of much dispute. As already noted, Hatt originally concluded that they diffused from Hispaniola and Puerto Rico into the Virgin Islands, whereas Rainey considered them the result of a migration from South America. Hoffman (1972) has recently revived and extended the former theory, and Alegría (1965:248–249), the latter.

The strongest evidence in favor of a South American origin is provided by the modeled-incised lugs of late Ostionoid and Chicoid pottery, which might seem to be derived from the Barrancoid lugs on the mainland. However, it now appears that the original Saladoid peoples possessed the prototypes of these lugs and carried them into the islands. The lugs became dormant in the Greater Antilles during the early part of the Ostiones series and were subsequently revived by the late Ostionoid and Chicoid potters, possibly with the help of diffusion from the Lesser Antilles. Other traits, such as the cazuela-type bowl, seem to have diffused in the opposite direction, from the Greater to the Lesser Antilles.

This interpretation is supported by Lathrap's reconstruction of the prehistory of the Arawakan languages. If he is correct, the Saladoid peoples spoke a non-Maipuran form of Arawakan and carried it out to the Greater Antilles, where it survived until Historic time (Lathrap 1970:112), while the Barrancoid peoples subsequently transmitted a Maipuran form of Arawakan to the Saladoid peoples of the Lesser Antilles (see Sections B, 3 and F, 3), from whom it was eventually handed down to the historic Carib population. The late Ostionoid and Chicoid peoples are too recent to have introduced the second language and, moreover, it never reached the Greater Antilles, as it should have if the theory of Ostionoid or Chicoid migration from South America is correct.

The origin of the Chicoid ceremonial traits, including the ball game, is also in dispute. Some authors (e.g., Alegría 1951) have derived part or all of these traits from Mesoamerica, whereas others (e.g., Stern 1950:31) have postulated diffusion from South America. Local development must also have played a part; as we have seen, stone carving goes back to the Archaic Age in the Greater Antilles. Instead of seeking a single origin, therefore, we need to determine which traits are local and which have diffused from the South, Central, and North American mainlands, respectively.

4. Historic Age

Chicoid pottery occurs in the earliest Spanish sites on Hispaniola, but it soon died out as the local Indians became extinct. Meillacoid pottery, on the contrary, survived for an indefinite time in Central Cuba, where Spanish occupation was less intense (Rouse 1942:157–158).

H. Summary

The five regional chronologies are summarized in Figure 13.9. Only the ages and series are shown, and only they will be discussed here.

1. Lithic Age

Early Lithic remains are unknown, but it has been possible to distinguish two late series, Joboid on the mainland and Casimiroid in the Greater Antilles. The Joboid series, characterized by bifacially chipped projectile points of stone, is well documented only for the Venezuelan Guiana, which it seems to have reached from a center in Western Venezuela.

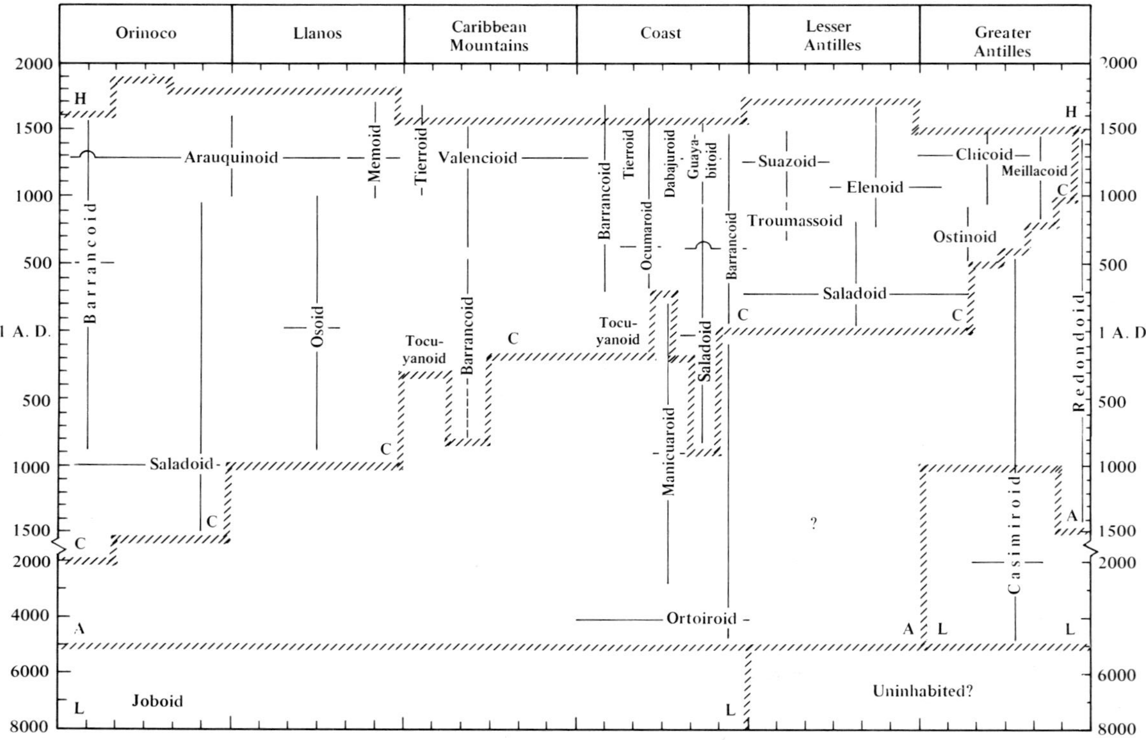

Figure 13.9. Summary of the regional chronologies. *Ages:* L = Lithic; A = Archaic; C = Ceramic; H = Historic.

The Casimiroid series has instead flakes and blades of flint, trimmed only on their edges as in the European Paleolithic. It may or may not have originated in Middle America.

2. Archaic Age

The earliest remains of the Archaic Age come from Trinidad. We have assigned them to an Ortoiroid series, which began about 5000 B.C. (see Figure 13.9). The source of its stone grinding is not known. Its chipping may be a degeneration from that of the Joboid series; it has lost almost all rechipping and, with it, any regularity of shape.

In Hispaniola, the Casimiroid peoples advanced into the Archaic Age by acquiring stone grinding, either independently or through diffusion from the Ortoiroid peoples of Trinidad. The diagnostic blades became more elaborate at this time, and a distinctive art style made its appearance.

Two more series arose in other parts of the Caribbean area, Manicuaroid on the east central coast of Venezuela and Redondoid in Cuba. We have seen that both series are characterized by shell gouges but that these appear to have had separate origins, the Manicuaroid gouges in Venezuela and the Redondoid gouges possibly in Florida. Otherwise, the two series are quite different; the Manicuaroid peoples emphasized ground shellwork and the Redondoid peoples ground stonework.

3. Ceramic Age

Pottery had reached the Caribbean area by the end of the third millennium B.C. It took the form of a Saladoid series, which was established at that time only in the Middle Orinoco area, according to our present evidence. Its origin is uncertain; it could have come down the Apure River from the Intermediate area, but we have suggested on linguistic grounds that it spread instead up the Casiquiare Canal from the Amazon Basin.

During the second millennium B.C., the Saladoid peoples expanded downstream into the Lower Orinoco area. There, as in other peripheral areas, they retained their original characteristics while the potters back in the center on the Middle Orinoco were developing a Barrancoid series. The new series moved downstream during the first millennium B.C., pushing the Saladoids of the Lower Orinoco out through the delta to the coast and adjacent islands. The Barrancoid peoples may also have spread at this time across the central Llanos to the Valencia Basin in the Caribbean Mountains, introducing both pottery and agriculture to these two places.

Farther up the Apure River, the western Llanos were occupied during the first millennium B.C. by an Osoid series, the origin of which is unknown. It is characterized by the first polychrome pottery in the New World. This appears to have diffused northwestward into the Venezuelan part of the Intermediate area, where it gave rise to a Tocuyanoid series. The latter than spread eastward, introducing pottery to the western part of our Coastal region around the time of Christ.

Meanwhile, about 800 B.C. if our radiocarbon dates are correct, the practice of polychromy spread from the Osoid series down the Apure River to the Middle Orinoco. There it combined with other, not yet completely understood, developments to cause a change from the Barrancoid series into three transitional Corozal complexes. They evolved into an Arauquinoid series about A.D. 500 (see Figure 13.9).

The remaining Barrancoid peoples were now isolated in two groups, one in the Valencia Basin of the Caribbean Mountains and the other in the Lower Orinoco area. During the first half of the first millennium A.D., these two groups expanded to the adjacent coastal areas. The Orinocan group produced the classic Barrancoid pottery that has attracted such attention because of its artistic quality.

Between A.D. 500 and 1000, the previously current ceramic series declined and gave way to a number of new series, except for a few peripheral survivors, mainly in the western part of the Coastal region. The Arauquinoid series, already mentioned, was the most prominent newcomer. It radiated out from a center in the Middle Orinoco and San Fernando areas to the rest of the Orinoco Basin and the Venezuelan Llanos, in part by diffusion and in part by migration. It also influenced the western Barrancoid people of the Valencia Basin, thereby contributing to the rise of a new Valencioid series. This series spread throughout the adjacent parts of the Caribbean Mountains and the Coastal region (see Figure 13.9).

The movement of ceramicists and agriculturalists out into the Antilles remains to be considered. This movement was a continuation of the original Saladoid invasion of the Orinoco Valley. After the Saladoid people of the Lower Orinoco had passed through the delta to the adjacent coast and islands and had become adapted to life on the seashore, they were able to proceed into the Lesser Antilles, which they occupied quickly during the first few centuries A.D. They developed to a climax there about A.D. 600, with the help of Barrancoid influences from the mainland. Thereafter they declined, giving way toward the close of the first millennium to a Troumassoid series in the Windward Islands and an Elenoid series in the Leeward Islands. The Troumassoid series was succeeded by a Suazoid series during the second millennium A.D.

The original Saladoid migrants reached the Virgin Islands and Puerto Rico during the first centuries A.D. They underwent an immediate process of decline, much sooner than in the Lesser Antilles, and about A.D. 600 gave way to an Ostionoid series, in which the decline was gradually reversed. The new series survived in western Puerto Rico and the Dominican Republic until the end of the first millennium A.D., but gave way several centuries earlier to the Elenoid series farther east and to a Meillacoid series farther west (see Figure 13.9). Meillacoid shows influences from the previous Archaic-Age complexes.

4. Historic Age

The Indians of the Greater Antilles did not long survive the discovery of America, except in Cuba. They have persisted until today in other, remote parts of the Caribbean area, but nowhere do we know enough about their ceramics to be able to establish series of complexes.

BIBLIOGRAPHY

Alegría, R. E.

1951 The Ball Game Played by the Aborigines of the Antilles. *American Antiquity* **16:**348–352.

1965 Caribbean Symposium: On Puerto Rican Archaeology. *American Antiquity* **31:**246–249.

Allaire, L.

1973 *Vers une Préhistoire des Petites Antilles.* Ste-Marie, Martinique: Centre de Recherches Caraïbes de l'Université de Montréal.

1977 *Later Prehistory in Martinique and the Island Caribs: Problems in Ethnic Identification.* Ph.D. dissertation, Yale University. Ann Arbor: University Microfilms.

Bullen, R. P.

1964 The Archaeology of Grenada, West Indies. *Contributions of the Florida State Museum, Social Sciences* No. **11.**

Bullen, R. P., and A. K. Bullen

1968 Barbados Archaeology: 1966. In *Proceedings of the Second International Congress for the Study of Pre-Columbian Cultures of the Lesser Antilles*, edited by R. P. Bullen. Gainesville: Florida State Museum. Pp. 133–144.

1972 Archaeological Investigations on St. Vincent and the Grenadines, West Indies. *The William L. Bryant Foundation, American Studies, Report* **8.**

1976 Culture Areas and Climaxes in Antillean Prehistory. In *Proceedings of the Sixth International Congress for the Study of Pre-Columbian Cultures of the Lesser Antilles,* edited by R. P. Bullen. Gainesville: Florida State Museum. Pp. 1–10.

Bullen, R. P., and F. W. Sleight

1963 The Krum Bay Site: A Preceramic Site on St. Thomas, United States Virgin Islands. *The William L. Bryant Foundation, American Studies Report* **5.**

Coe, M. D.

1962 Costa Rican Archaeology and Mesoamerica. *Southwestern Journal of Anthropology* **18:**170–183.

Coe, W. R., II

1957 A Distinctive Artifact Common to Haiti and Central America. *American Antiquity* **22:**280–282.

Cruxent, J. M.

1970 Projectile Points with Pleistocene Mammals in Venezuela. *Antiquity* **44:**223–225.

1971 Apuntes Sobre Arqueología Venezolana. In *Art Prehispánico de Venezuela*, edited by M. C. Arroy, J. M. Cruxent, and S. P. Soto de Atencio. Caracas: Foundación Eugenio Mendoza.

Cruxent, J. M., and I. Rouse

1958–

1959 An Archeological Chronology of Venezuela. 2 Vols. *Pan American Union, Social Science Monographs* No. **6.**

1969 Early Man in the West Indies. *Scientific American* **221:**42–52.

Davis, Dave D.

1974 Some Notes Concerning the Archaic Occupation of Antigua. In *Proceedings of the Fifth International Congress for the Study of Pre-Columbian Cultures of the Lesser Antilles,* edited by R. P. Bullen. Gainesville: Florida State Museum. Pp. 65–71.

Dupouy, W.

1945 Sobre un Tipo de Joya Lítica Singular en Venezuela. *Acta Venezolana* **1:**80–89.

Evans, C., and B. J. Meggers

1960 Archaeological Investigations in British Guiana. *Bureau of American Ethnology Bulletin* **177.**

Gabb, W. M.

1872 On the Topography and Geology of Santo Domingo. *Memoirs of the American Philosophical Society* **15:**146–147.

Gallagher, P. F.

1964 La Pitía: An Early Ceramic Site in Northwestern Venezuela. Ph. D. dissertation, Yale University. Ann Arbor, Michigan: University Microfilms.

Hatt, G.

1924 Archaeology of the Virgin Islands. *Proceedings of the Twenty-First International Congress of Americanists* **1:**29–42.

Hoffman, C. A., Jr.

1972 Current Research: Caribbean. *American Antiquity* **37:**272–273.

Hostos, A. de

1919 Prehistoric Puerto Rican Ceramics. *American Anthropologist* **21:**376–399.

Howard, G. D.

1943 Excavations at Ronquín, Venezuela. *Yale University Publications in Anthropology* No. **28.**

1947 Prehistoric Ceramic Styles of Lowland South America, Their Distribution and History. *Yale University Publications in Anthropology* No. **37.**

Kidder, A., II

1944 Archaeology of Northwestern Venezuela. *Papers of the Peabody Museum of American Archaeology and Ethnology* **26**(1).

1948 The Archaeology of Venezuela. In Handbook of South American Indians, Vol. 4, The Circum-Caribbean Tribes, edited by J. H. Steward. *Bureau of American Ethnology Bulletin* **143**(4):413–438.

Kirchhoff, P.

1948 The Tribes North of the Orinoco River. In Handbook of South American Indians, Vol. 4, The Circum-Caribbean Tribes, edited by J. H. Steward. *Bureau of American Ethnology Bulletin* **143**(4):481–493.

Kozlowski, J. K.

1974 Preceramic Cultures in the Caribbean. *Zeszyty Naukowe, Uniwerstytetu Jagiello* ńskiego 386, Prace Archeologiczne, Zesyt No. **20.**

Lathrap, D. W.

1970 The Upper Amazon. In *Ancient Peoples and Places*, Vol. 70. New York: Praeger.

Mattioni, M.

1974 Essai sur des Concordances Archéologiques du Venezuela à la Martinique. In *Proceedings of the Fifth International Congress for the Study of Pre-Columbian Cultures of the Lesser Antilles,* edited by R. P. Bullen. Gainesville: Florida State Museum. Pp. 21–27.

McKusick, M. B.

1960 The Distribution of Ceramic Styles in the Lesser Antilles, West Indies. Unpublished Ph.D. dissertation. Department of Anthropology, Yale University.

Olsen, F.
1970 The Arawak Religion: Cult of Yocahu. *Antigua Archaeological Society, Mill Reef Diggers' Digest,* 1–18.
1971 Did the Ciboney Precede the Arawaks in Antigua? *Antigua Archaeological Society, Mill Reef Diggers' Digest,* 1–15.

Ortega, Elpidio, Marcio Veloz Maggiolo, and Plinio Pina
1975 El Caimito: Un Antiguo Complejo Ceramista de las Antillas Mayores. In *Proceedings of the sixth International Congress for the Study of Pre-Columbian Cultures of the Lesser Antilles,* edited by R. P. Bullen. Gainesville: Florida State Museum. Pp. 276–282.

Pettijean-Roget, J.
1968 Étude d'un Horizon Arawak et Proto-Arawak à la Martinique. In *Proceedings of the Second International Congress for the Study of Pre-Columbian Cultures in the Lesser Antilles*, edited by R. P. Bullen. Gainesville: Florida State Museum. Pp. 61–68.

Plina, P., M. Veloz Maggiolo, and M. García Arévalo
1976 Esquema Para una Revisión de Nomenclaturas Arqueológicas del Poblamiento Precerámico en las Antillas. In *Actas del XLI Congreso International de Americanistas* **3:**693–697.

Pronapa
1970 Brazilian Archaeology in 1968: An Interim Report on the National Program of Archaeological Research. *American Antiquity* **35:**1–23.

Rainey, F. G.
1940 Porto Rican Archaeology. *The New York Academy of Sciences, Scientific Survey of Porto Rico and the Virgin Islands* **18**(1).

Reichel-Dolmatoff, G.
1965 Columbia. In *Ancient Peoples and Places*, vol. 44. New York: Praeger.

Rouse, I.
1939 Prehistory in Haiti, a Study in Method. *Yale University Publications in Anthropology* No. **21.**
1941 Culture of the Ft. Liberté Region, Haiti. *Yale University Publications in Anthropology* No. **24.**
1942 Archaeology of the Maniabón Hills, Cuba. *Yale University Publications in Anthropology* No. **26.**
1948 The Arawak. In *Handbook of South American Indians, vol. 4, The Circum-Caribbean Tribes*, edited by J. H. Steward. *Bureau of American Ethnology Bulletin* **143**(4):507–546.
1951 Areas and Periods of Culture in the Greater Antilles. *Southwestern Journal of Anthropology* **7:**248–265.
1952 Porto Rican Prehistory. *The New York Academy of Sciences, Scientific Survey of Porto Rico and the Virgin Islands* **18**(3–4).
1953a The Circum-Caribbean Theory, an Archaeological Test. *American Anthropologist* **55:**188–200.
1953b Indian Sites in Trinidad. In On the Excavation of a Shell Mound at Palo Seco, Trinidad, B.W.I., by J. A. Bullbrook. *Yale University Publications in Anthropology* **50:**94–111.
1961 The Bailey Collection of Stone Artifacts from Puerto Rico. In *Essays in Pre-Columbian Art and Archaeology* by S. K. Lothrop *et al.* Cambridge, Massachusetts: Harvard University Press. Pp. 340–355.
1964 Prehistory of the West Indies. *Science* **144:**499–513.
1972 *Introduction to Prehistory: A Systematic Approach.* New York: McGraw-Hill.
1974 The Indian Creek Excavations. In *Proceedings of the Fifth International Congress*

for the Study of Pre-Columbian Cultures of the Lesser Antilles, edited by R. P. Bullen. Gainesville: Florida State Museum. Pp. 166–176.

1976 The Saladoid Sequence on Antigua and Its Aftermath. In *Proceedings of the Sixth International Congress for the Study of Pre-Columbian Cultures of the Lesser Antilles*, edited by R. P. Bullen. Gainesville: Florida State Museum, Pp. 35–41.

n.d. The LaGruta Sequence and Its Implications. Paper submitted for a festschrift to J. M. Cruxent. Caracas: Instituto Venezolano de Investigaciones Científicas.

Rouse, I., and J. M. Cruxent.

1963 *Venezuelan Archaeology*. New Haven: Yale University Press (Caribbean Series 6).

Sauer, C. O.

1952 *Agricultural Origins and Dispersals*. New York: American Geographical Society.

Stark, L.

1977 Linguistic Evidence for Early Migrations in South America. Paper read at the annual meeting of the Society for American Archaeology in New Orleans, April 28–30.

Stern, T.

1950 The Rubber-Ball Game of the Americas. *Monographs of the American Ethnological Society* No. **17.**

Tabio, E., and J. M. Guarch

1966 *Excavaciones en Arroyo del Palo, Mayarí, Cuba*. La Habana: Academia de Ciencias de Cuba.

Vargas I., and M. Sanoja

1970 The Orinoco Project: Preliminary Report, 1968–69. In *Proceedings of the Third International Congress for the Study of Pre-Columbian Cultures of the Lesser Antilles,* edited by R. P. Bullen. Gainesville: Florida State Museum. Pp. 107–113.

Wagner, Erika

1972 Nueva Evidencia Arqueológica de Venezuela Oriental: el Yacimiento de Campoma. *Atti delgi XL Congresso Internazionale delgi Americanisti.* Genova: Tilgher. Pp. 239–245.

Wilbert, J.

1972 *Survivor of El Dorado: Four Indian Cultures of South America.* New York: Praeger.

Willey, G. R.

1971 *An Introduction to American Archaeology,* Vol. 2, *South America*. Englewood Cliffs, New Jersey: Prentice-Hall.

Wing, E. S.

1962 Succession of Mammalian Faunas on Trinidad, West Indies. Unpublished Ph.D. dissertation, Depart of Biology, University of Florida.

Zucchi, A.

1972a New Data on the Antiquity of Polychrome Painting from Venezuela. *American Antiquity* **37:**439–446.

1972b Tropical Forest Groups of the Venezuelan Savannas: Archaeological Evidence. In *Atti del XL Congresso Internazionale degli Americanisti*. Genova: Tilgher. Pp. 261–267.

1975a Campos Agrícolas Prehispánicos en los Llanos de Barinas, Venezuela. *Indiana: Beitrage zur Völker- und Sprachenkunde, Archäologie und Anthropologie des Indianischen Amerika* **2:**209–215.

1975b Caño Caroni: Un Grupo Prehispánico de la Selva de los Llanos de Barinas. *Universidad Central de Venezuela, Colección Anthropología* **5**.

Northern Chile

Lautaro Núñez A.

I. HISTORY OF CHRONOLOGICAL RESEARCH

Chronological studies in Chile have been based on differing ideas about the placement and arrangement of pre-Hispanic cultures in different regions and at various stages of development in a country that is strictly longitudinal (ecological difference between the Andean region and the Pacific). Efforts to establish chronology in specific subareas have not resulted from regional plans of study but rather from the particular efforts of individual investigators in the course of their independent studies.

The history of chronologies in the north of Chile begins with the works of Uhle (1919, 1922), who applied a stylistic standard to determine the first cultural sequence of the prehistoric Andean settlements of Chile. His excavations at Calama, Taltal, Pisagua, and Arica created a broad regional panorama, formulating a preceramic–ceramic sequence that remained in force for a long time.

The author thanks Prof. C. Moragas from the University of the North, for her observations and corrections to the present report.

In revising this chapter, which was originally written in 1972, I have not, in general terms, made substantial modifications. Moreover, its content shows the status of the basic chronological problems of the archaeology of northern Chile just as they were 5 years ago. The actual modifications reveal that these problems persist in one way or another. For these reasons I thought it best not to alter the original manuscript except for the addition of the footnotes which show the present day knowledge of chronological information.

Period	Culture
A.D. 1350–1450	Inca
A.D. 1100–1350	Chincha–Atacameño
A.D. 900–1100	Indigenous Atacameño
A.D. 600–900	Tiahuanaco and following epigonal
A.D. 400–600	Protonazca or contemporaries of Chavin
First centuries of the Christian Era	Aborigines of Arica
End of the pre-Christian Era	"Primordial man"

This scheme was applied by later investigators (Latcham 1938) and was generally accepted until Bird (1943) began a reevaluation of Uhle's sequence.

Uhle applied a stratigraphic criterion for the first time in Chile in a cave at Punta Pichalo, and this enabled him to determine cultural changes across different cemeteries. On the basis of his finds in preagricultural settlements, he postulated two periods; the first he called "Primordial Man," based on surface stone artifacts from the region of Arica; the second he called "Aborigines of Arica" (the Chinchorro Complex), based on extended burials showing artificial mummification. These periods can be linked to the "Paleolithic" industries of Taltal, which were appraised through Uhle's investigations at Capdeville.

For the sites with pottery and agriculture, Uhle applied an intuitive method based on the presence or absence of traits, having as chronological points of reference the penetration of the three basic Andean horizons: Chavin, Tiwanaku, and Inca. From the foundation of these three temporal levels, he succeeded in fixing in time the main prehistoric sites then known. His "Proto-Nazca" Period (Pisagua), he arranged synchronically with the Chavin culture of Peru. The "Tiahuanaco–Atacameño" stage he identified with the penetration of the Second Andean Horizon, and the "Atacameño" culture corresponded to post-Tiwanaku and immediately pre-Inca cultures. This chronological contribution is of extreme importance if we recognize that it was formulated at a very early stage of archaeological investigation.

From the beginning of this century, there was a tendency to believe that some lithic industries from the shellmounds of Taltal, because of their "Paleolithic" forms, could be linked to the first settlement of the territory. But there were no secure evidences to relate this region to the scheme of development for the earliest occupations of the New World.

Bird (1938) showed, in the extreme south of Chile, that a series of sites had occupied the area for some 5000 years. Subsequently, some local investigators began to suspect that the presence of man in the territory might go back considerably further in time. Latcham (1941) proposed a limit of 6000 years ago for the deepest deposits at Taltal. This temporal limit for the coast was more or less confirmed by Bird (1943–1946) who excavated coastal sites at Arica, Pisagua, and Taltal, providing the first program of stratigraphic evaluation in Chile. Bird developed a notable stratigraphic sequence based on a field methodology not previously used in Chile. The first of the excavated sites (at Arica) was subsequently dated by radiocarbon at 4220 B.C. (Bird 1967; Mostny 1964). The sequence formulated by Bird is as follows:

Arica	Pisagua	Taltal
	Ceramics	
Playa Miller (Arica II)		
Playa Miller (Arica I)		
	Punta Pichalo 4	
	Punta Pichalo 3	Cerro Colorado Levels A–B
	Preceramics	
Quiani	Punta Pichalo 2	
		Cerro Colorado Levels C–H
Quiani (Shell Fishhook culture)	Punta Pichalo 1	

With the exception of Taltal, Bird depended exclusively on the stratigraphy of coastal middens near river outlets, so that knowledge was limited to settlements adapted to maritime subsistence, mostly in regions with flowing rivers. Thus this sequence applies only to those sites best adapted to exploitation of the sea; it has no apparent relationship to the histories of the many inland sites found in the valleys, oases, and highlands (*altiplano*).

In 1943, Bird identified a long preceramic period with two basic divisions with shell fishhooks in the first levels and a period with pottery and agriculture also divided into two stages. At Arica were located the ceramic stages Arica I (corresponding to San Miguel) and Arica II (corresponding to Gentilar). In Pisagua the ceramic cultural change showed a division in the first brown refuse with black and red polished ceramics possibly earlier (and not yet dated). Among the black refuse were noted ceramic fragments of monochrome surface.

Dates for the beginning of the first occupation of the coast correspond to the culture Bird called Shell Fishhook, dated at 4220 to 3666 B.C., and it is probable that the first coastal sites of middle specialized type will be earlier than this date.[1] The possibility of finding post-Pleistocene evidences related

[1]The investigations performed with C. Moragas in the area of Tiliviche, a valley inward of the coast of Pisagua, show the development of a dense Archaic population with milling stone implements, shell fishhooks, and early maize. These groups occupied the coast and the inner

to sites of greater temporal depth seem very remote because the sites would by now have been eroded away by the periodic transgressions of the sea. But, in the springs level, near the pacific, there are good possibilities in study.

The end of this preceramic history is not chronologically determined, but everything suggests that about 1000 B.C. the coastal stratigraphy of Northern Chile would show the incorporation of new experimental agriculture and ceramic elements.[2]

Bird's sequence does not help to solve the preceramic chronological problems of the interior. For the agricultural stages, test excavations in the individual valleys are needed. Sectors like Punta Pichalo, the preceramic division receives an influx of ceramic and agricultural elements. The superposition shows a small change in the pattern of subsistence but does not clarify the chronological sequence of the diverse agricultural sites of the interior valleys. For example, Bird was not able to throw any light on the Tiwanaku problem, and his contribution to knowledge of pre-Tiwanaku agricultural peoples is also limited, because both populations tend to occupy valleys somewhat inland from the coast.

II. PRESENT STATE OF CHRONOLOGY

Following up on the work of Bird, the current generation of Chilean archaeologists has succeeded in contributing interesting chronological studies based on the experiences of their predecessors, and, in the subareas that make up the "Norte Grande" of the country, their advances have been stimulating.

At the present time there are various teams occupied with establishing cultural chronologies. Dauelsberg (1963, 1972a, b, c) and his collaborators have advanced knowledge of the chronology for the ceramic period in the

---

oases at 5.900 years B.C. We can point out that settlements in the coast represented the Tiliviche Culture, before the time limit given by the Quiani (coast of Arica) radiocarbon determination: 4220 B.C. This early population occupied the coastline in the Camarones River outlet, as shown in the last investigations of H. Niemeyer, V. Schiappacasse, and P. Dauelsberg.

[2]In the desert coast south of Iquique (Site Cáñamo-1), we have identified the association of ordinary brown ceramic with smooth and semipolished surfaces associated with maize, beans, and algarrobo, dated at 890 B.C. This deposit indicates an early cultural change in Late Archaic populations distant from river outlet areas and shows one of the first critical moments of an initial agrarian stability in valleys and nearby oases. C. Moragas and I are now reviewing the problem through new radiocarbon datings. Other pre-Tiwanaku settlements with ceramic and agrarian features have been localized in the area of Arica. M. Rivera and G. Focacci have dated funerary registers in Playa Miller-77 (El Laucho complex) at 530 B.C. These investigators have determined the time of burials in mounds at the area of Azapa at 490 and 410 B.C. This time period would seem to consolidate the agrarian change in the lowland valleys of Arica.

region of Arica, although until now there has been a lamentable lack of radiocarbon determinations. Rivera (personal communication) has continued the chronological studies of this area, collecting radiocarbon samples in a systematic project the results of which are in process. Schiappacasse and Niemeyer (1963) have concerned themselves with dating the Valley of Camarones, while True *et al.* (1970) have made a similar study of the valley (*quebrada*) of Tarapacá. Núñez (1971, n.d.a, n.d.c) has obtained radiocarbon determinations for Pisagua Viejo, the coast south of Iquique, the mouth of the Rio Loa and its lower drainage, and Pica. Boisset and Llagostera (n.d.) have dated the coast near Antofagasta. Le Paige (1963), Lanning and Patterson (1967), Pollard (1971), Orellana (1963), and others have made chronological determinations for the settlements of the western basin of Atacama and for the Middle and Upper Rio Loa and its tributaries.

Despite these efforts, the chronological problems continue to be fundamental, especially in relation to the first settlements of hunter–gatherers. Chronological estimates have tended toward an exaggerated age. This is because the lithic industries found especially in the highlands show artifact forms reminiscent of the types found in the Old World. Le Paige, for example, has suggested a maximum antiquity of about 40,000 years.

Without an analysis making fine discriminations between finished manufactures and cores, between camp sites and quarries, taxonomies have been applied that tend to separate lithic types on the basis of chronological criteria in sites that are not stratified. There has been a tendency to postulate a "pre–projectile point" horizon on the basis of horizontal studies, which do not provide a valid basis for such chronological propositions, and to define as preceramic artifact types lacking specific associations and therefore lacking radiocarbon dates. For these reasons, the first occupations that have been proposed for Northern Chile, on the basis of sites like Ghatchi, ought to be properly reevaluated.

Among the cases of unsubstantiated cultural inventories of supposed first settlements is the Chuqui Complex (Lanning and Patterson 1967), thought to be related to an early phase of burins, small-keeled denticulates and spokeshaves in Peru. However, it has been demonstrated that these evidences are not man-made artifacts, and their placement at about 14,000 years ago must be considered scientifically invalid. A date obtained in a nearby cave of Tulan region suggests that at 8330 B.C. Early Man was present in the region, but a specific context is not known. It is probable that between 8000 and 9000 B.C., occupations existed that used some of the industries now placed in sequence solely on typological grounds.

Dates obtained from Intihuasi (Argentina) as well as from San Pedro Viejo de Pichasca in the Norte Chico indicate the existence of projectile points at about 6000 B.C., providing some basis for the belief that still earlier evidences exist dating to between 9000 and 6000 B.C. This offers a real possibility of locating cultural remains (hunter) from the end of the Pleistocene. The finds from Tagua Tagua (in Central Chile), on a comparative basis, can be considered of Mesolithic "typology," according to the taxonomic scheme of the Atacama Desert. This warns us of the complexity of the typological problem, since the industry of Tagua Tagua is associated with an extinct fauna of mastodons and horses dating to 11,000 years ago (Montane 1972).

To complicate the chronological situation even further, a bifacial artifact with the same morphology as those found in the Salar de Talabre has been recorded in the second level of Tagua Tagua (Lanning 1967). The Salar de Talabre artifacts have been found in open quarries and are without radiocarbon dates, but they have been speculatively dated (at the Chivateros Site) at 10,000 years. Although the industry of Talabre, as part of the Andean Biface Tradition, could be early, the stratigraphic fact is that the crude bifacial artifacts found in the second level of Tagua Tagua have an antiquity of 6000 years and are associated with an assemblage of points, perforated stones, manos, and polishers (Montane 1972). A more precise temporal determination of the Biface Horizon seems the best approach to advancing the chronological studies in this region, although until now there exists no stratified deposit showing a specific chronological situation. On the other hand, the frequency of sites appears to be high.

Despite the foregoing, there is a certain emphasis on postulating a "tradition" of bifaces at the beginning of the chronological sequence as a horizon over the whole Northern Chile. However, in the same region there are bifaces that appear in such late preceramic stratified and dated sites as Conanoxa with an age of 2000 B.C. (Niemeyer and Schiappacasse 1963). On the other hand, as mentioned earlier, this "style" of bifaces has been speculatively assigned at date of 10,000 years ago at the site of Chivateros (Lanning and Patterson 1967). Subsequent studies carried out in that quarry (Fung 1972), however, seem to contradict some of Lanning and Patterson's (1967) conclusions.

Certainly sites in Peru, Bolivia, Chile, and Argentina offer a great deal of information in the form of bifaces present on the surface. But the lack of stratified finds precludes major advances in the chronology of the first Andean settlements. The presumption of Le Paige (1963b) and other investigators that a people without projectile points, such as exemplified at Ghatchi, Fundiciones, and Talabre, should exist in this region requires present-day evaluation. Separating points and bifaces (crude percussive forms) on the basis of the supposed mixture of components resulting from periodic reoccupations (Meltzer 1969) has no validity without the local control of stratigraphic columns as guidelines. In addition, some statements on favorable paleoenvironments prior to the climatic optimum (such as the "lakes" of Talabre) must be thoroughly checked in order to be correctly used as support for the early nature of the supposed first occupations. For the present, there are neither dates nor secure contexts for those sites with crude or heavy industries not associated with surface points or cores of more sophisticated forms.

Still, it must be emphasized that first occupations ought to be detectable in sites that are not quarries, for one must suppose that many lithic "types" were carried away from the site, and certainly the manufactures left behind may well be cores in different stages of workmanship, without being necessarily representative of the total assemblage of forms and functions. When we place at the beginning of the sequences the concepts of Talabre, Pampa, and Pukio Nuñez, we do not do it with a chronological criterion; we only indicate that their presence in quarries or isolated workshops is not associated with points and/or cores of finer manufacture. One could suppose a cultural stage different from the rest of the sequence (sites with a proliferation of points), but the correct chronological and even cultural position is in debate.

In the extreme south of Chile shellmounds between 8000 and 9000 years in age have been found. For the site of Marassi, Laming-Emperaire (1968) has postulated a date of 10,000 years ago. From this, it seems very probable that the first occupations in the extreme north of the country are earlier,[3] close to the terminal events of the Pleistocene, with dates intermediate between those obtained by MacNeish (1969) in the Ayacucho Complex (14,000 years ago) and those of Montané (1972) for Central Chile (11,000 years ago). Their identification is one of the most urgent problems in fitting the early chronology to the rest of the regional sequence.

In general, the chronological situation of the sites of Northern Chile can be considered satisfactory in relation to investigational advances on the national level. But, along with other regions of the Andean area, considerable effort is required to establish a better chronology supported by new radiocarbon dates and more refined excavation techniques in key sites. Until now, a combination of negative factors has made difficult the elaboration of an objective sequence:

1. The scarcity of stratigraphic studies away from the coast
2. The surplus of funerary contexts studied with methods inadequate for defining cultural and chronological changes
3. Deficiencies in the establishment of cultural traits that are diagnostic or indicative of change processes

[3]Recent radiocarbon determinations for the Tiliviche Culture suggest that the beginning of the occupations took place between 7.810 and 5.900 B.C. with a subsistence pattern that principally includes the contribution of a maritime economy, for which they controlled the littoral of Pisagua and the fertile microenvironments of the immediate inlands (watersheds). The terminal moments of this culture might be represented by groups specialized in maritime exploitation that Bird called "Fishhook Culture," with absolute determinations that fluctuate between 4.220 and 3.666 B.C., obtained in the coast of Arica (Quiani site).

4. Lack of a radiocarbon laboratory in the Andean countries
5. Emphasis on excavations without zonal, regional, or sequential planning

Despite these limitations, the present state of knowledge has been considerably advanced through the continuity established in a few selected sectors, which has permitted development of the primary sequences. These have sown the seeds of a regional chronology in a reasonably coherent manner. Nevertheless, the paucity of radiocarbon dates and of descriptions of cultural context continue to handicap further advances.

III. ANALYSIS OF THE CHRONOLOGICAL SEQUENCES

The accompanying chronological chart (Figure 14.1) provides an ordering of site types that represents stages of development across the diverse environments of the regional–ecological divisions.

1. *Preceramic Period* (8500–1000 B.C.): Corresponds to the evidences of hunter–gatherers without production of crops (preagricultural), in accordance with the more or less operational use given this term in the Andean region.

2. *Regional Formative* (800 B.C.–A.D. 500): Defined as a cultural period that includes early diversified settlements of pre-Tiwanaku chronology; in its final phase it tends to permanent communities in sectors favorable to the development of tending plants and animals. These settlements are at different stages of development related to diverse levels of the practice of hunting, gathering, horticulture, and part-time agriculture. It seems clear that they succeeded in achieving controlled animal breeding, along with metallurgy and other manufactures including pottery, which began with the establishment of fixed settlements. The term Regional Formative is used here as bordering the nuclear Andean concept, as a common denominator of the particular or regional development of early cultures marginal to the Andean centers. It constitutes the cultural matrix of the later farming society. In this sense, the formative character is given by the introduction of an irrigation agriculture with consequent village development, constituting the fundamental structure of the post-Tiwanaku social process west of the *altiplano*.

3. *Tiwanaku* (A.D. 400–1000): Tiwanaku colonizations probably were intermittent in nature and spanned a considerable time, coexisting with western Formative communities. It is generally agreed that this expansion covered all the possible ecological zones and that, in consequence, it ought to have produced a process of transculturation with respect to the local settlements. For these reasons the defined Tiwanaku, along with marking a chronological point, should show a kind of cultural change, but as yet it has not been well defined. Unfortunately the dates and phases of the *altiplano* do not have a

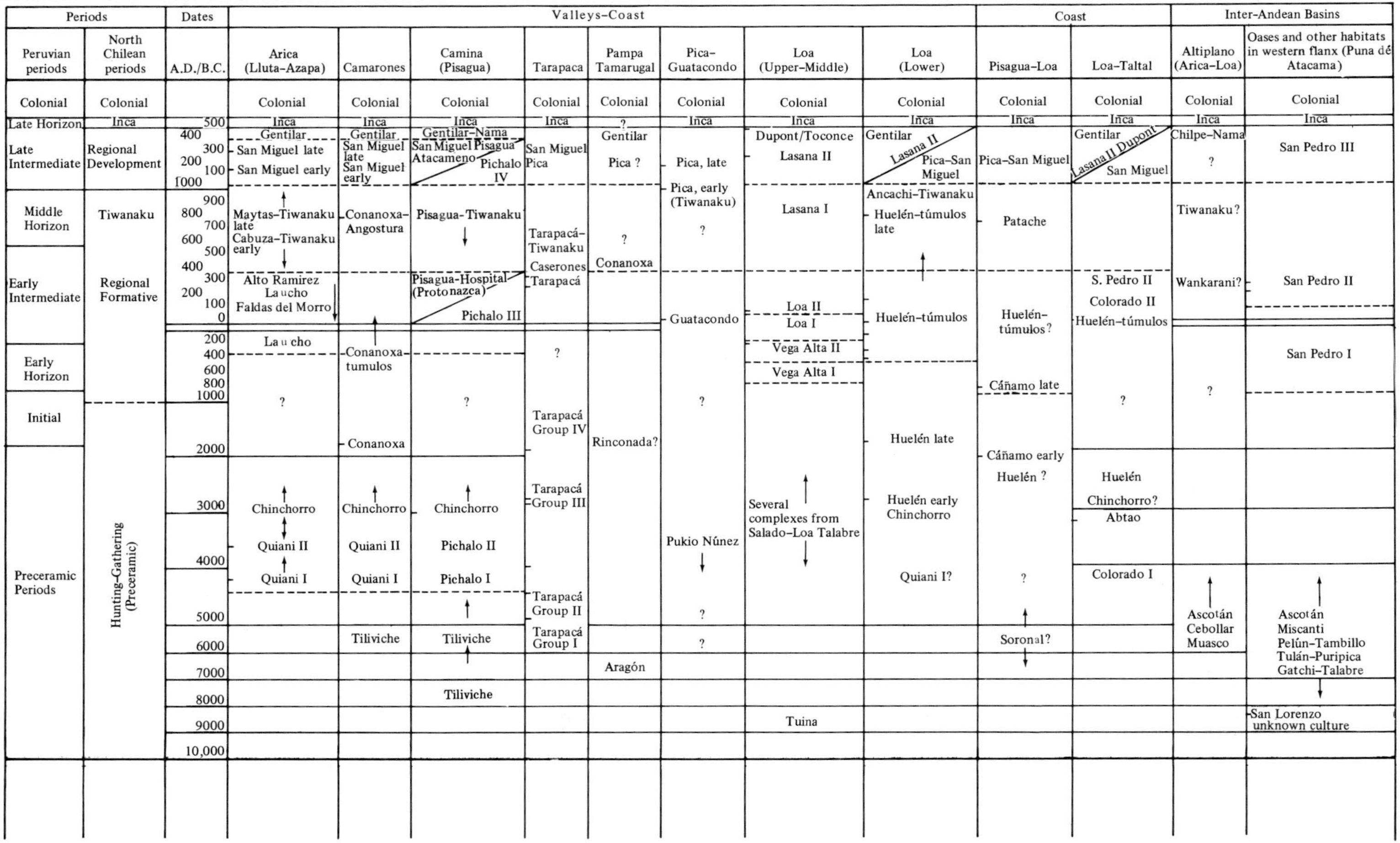

Periods		Dates	Valleys–Coast								Coast		Inter-Andean Basins	
Peruvian periods	North Chilean periods	A.D./B.C.	Arica (Lluta–Azapa)	Camarones	Camina (Pisagua)	Tarapaca	Pampa Tamarugal	Pica–Guatacondo	Loa (Upper–Middle)	Loa (Lower)	Pisagua–Loa	Loa–Taltal	Altiplano (Arica–Loa)	Oases and other habitats in western flanx (Puna dé Atacama)
Colonial	Colonial		Colonial	Colonial	Colonial	Colonial	Colonial	Colonial	Colonial	Colonial	Colonial	Colonial	Colonial	Colonial
Late Horizon	Inca	500	Inca	Inca	Inca	Inca	?	Inca	Inca	Inca	Inca	Inca	Inca	Inca
Late Intermediate	Regional Development	400 300 200 100 1000	Gentilar San Miguel late San Miguel early	Gentilar San Miguel late San Miguel early	Gentilar–Nama San Miguel Pisagua Atacameno Pichalo IV	San Miguel Pica	Gentilar Pica ?	Pica, late	Dupont/Toconce Lasana II	Gentilar Lasana II Pica–San Miguel	Pica–San Miguel	Gentilar Lasana II Dupont San Miguel	Chilpe–Nama ?	San Pedro III
Middle Horizon	Tiwanaku	900 800 700 600 500	Maytas–Tiwanaku late Cabuza–Tiwanaku early	Conanoxa–Angostura	Pisagua-Tiwanaku	Tarapacá–Tiwanaku	?	Pica, early (Tiwanaku) ?	Lasana I	Ancachi–Tiwanaku Huelén–túmulos late	Patache		Tiwanaku?	
Early Intermediate	Regional Formative	400 300 200 100 0	Alto Ramirez Laucho Faldas del Morro		Pisagua-Hospital (Protonazca) Pichalo III	Caserones Tarapacá	Conanoxa	Guatacondo	Loa II Loa I	Huelén–túmulos	Huelén–túmulos?	S. Pedro II Colorado II Huelén–túmulos	Wankarani?	San Pedro II
Early Horizon		200 400 600 800 1000	Laucho	Conanoxa–tumulos		?			Vega Alta II Vega Alta I		Cáñamo late			San Pedro I
Initial		2000	?	Conanoxa	?	Tarapacá Group IV	Rinconada?	?		Huelén late	Cáñamo early	?	?	
Preceramic Periods	Hunting–Gathering (Preceramic)	3000 4000 5000	Chinchorro Quiani II Quiani I	Chinchorro Quiani II Quiani I	Chinchorro Pichalo II Pichalo I	Tarapacá Group III Tarapacá Group II		Pukio Núnez ?	Several complexes from Salado–Loa Talabre	Huelén early Chinchorro Quiani I?	Huelén ? ?	Huelén Chinchorro? Abtao Colorado I	Ascotán Cebollar Muasco	Ascotán Miscanti Pelún–Tambillo Tulán–Puripica Gatchi–Talabre
		6000		Tiliviche	Tiliviche	Tarapacá Group I		?			Soronal?			
		7000					Aragón							
		8000			Tiliviche									
		9000							Tuina					San Lorenzo unknown culture
		10,000												

Figure 14.1. Regional chronology of Northern Chile.

counterpart in Tiwanaku deposits in these western regions. On the other hand, the survival of the classic style produces confusions that have made uncertain the chronological situation of the final Formative Phase and the beginning of the Regional Development Phase. This is a fundamental question under discussion at the present time.

4. *Regional Development* (A.D. 1000–1450): The concentration of Formative settlements in our western region could have been generated more or less on the influence of Wankarani culture (1200 B.C.–A.D. 300)—one of the old, standard, farming and animal-breeding cultures of the *altiplano* (Ponce 1970).

The mixture between the early western settlements (maritime adaptation), and Wankarani-Tiwanaku ingredients, plus others of highland (*puna*) origin, permitted the emergence of a Regional Development with specific features that have been well identified at the end of the Tiwanaku stage. The late villages of Arica on the one hand and San Pedro de Atacama on the other provide the best examples of the independent cultural regionalization seen in these late communities, intercepted only by "vertical islands" of late *altiplano* colonies belonging to the immediately pre-Incaic lacustrine "kingdoms" (Murra 1972).

A. Preceramic Period

The earliest radiocarbon dates tend to be concentrated at higher elevations and associated with open campsites, reflecting a special interest in the habitat of hunter-gatherers situated in the inter-Andean valleys between altitudes of 2500 and 4000 m above sea level. From this zone come the majority of the lithic industries giving rise to several artifact complexes. The date of the San Lorenzo Cave, located on the western edge of the Atacama Desert (near Tulan), shows an early occupation but does not reveal specific cultural evidences stratigraphically. Our date, close to 9000 years B.C., could serve as a good estimate for future definition of the cultural contexts associated with the post-Pleistocene peopling of the area (Tuina).

The inter-Andean valleys, having various artifact complexes defined with a tentative chronology based on a comparison with some artifact types that have been fixed chronologically in other regions near Northern Chile, as for example at Intihuasi–Ayampitin. In the western part of the Atacama (*puna*), around the dry lakes, near oases, and at other high-altitude stopping places, a sequence of site types has been determined by ordering the artifacts on the basis of the presence or absence of typological differences.

The Ghatchi Complex near San Pedro de Atacama (Le Paige, 1963) appears to be representative of a group of sites (Fundiciones, Loma Negra, etc.) characterized by the assumed absence of projectile points and the presence of crude artifacts (cores, bifaces, heavy flakes, and cobbles). The identification of such sites has been supported by discovery of the lithic industries of the Salar de Talabre, near Calama, where also occur the large bifaces and a varied assemblage of rather crude artifacts lacking surface association with refined and pressure-flaked points. It is possible that several workshops of heavy bifaces extended over a great part of the Andean region. A broad distribution appears probable, in that newly investigated sites, some very concentrated (like Pukio Núñez in Pica) and others more dispersed (like occasional stopping places such as Pampa in the *quebrada* of Tarapacá), confirm a distribution through several ecological zones in the north of Chile as well as in neighboring regions. The similar distribution in different ecological divisions such as Talabre and Pukio Núñez, and the lithic concentrations can be explained as quarries or workshops. In consequence, we cannot know the forms of the finished artifacts, nor can we deduce the exact relationship between man and the environment. Certainly, it seems likely that the campsites could have been established in other areas more attractive for hunting and gathering. For these reasons, technological and ecological analyses derived from the study of workshops are not sufficient to clarify chronological and cultural situations. The existing tendency to give this supposed biface tradition an early chronological position, based on an early radiocarbon date from Chivateros (Peru), is more intuitive than scientific.

As part of these supposed first lithic industries, an industry of small burins as components of early occupations, has been hypothesized, placed prior to the Biface Horizon, having in mind the model of Oquendo (Peru). Lanning and Patterson (1967) and other investigators have tried to generalize the diffusion of the Chuqui Complex—said to be an early burin industry in some publications—to Northern Chile. However, the Chuqui "industry" is made up of accidental productions; rigorous analysis has established that the forms have not been altered by man, and this certainly invalidates the possibility of early occupations based on an a priori extension of the preceramic scheme for the Central Andes.

In sum, the presence of industries of burins, bifaces, and other crude manufactures included in an apparent "pre–projectile point" horizon all constitute surface evidences; they require a stratigraphic treatment to establish an accurate chronology.

Later in time, a series of sites appear in Atacama sequences in which the presence of projectile points and other associated diagnostic features have provided an ordering for various industries perhaps at a stage of development similar to Lauricocha. These sites, with an undefined time, include the typical artifacts of Tulán, Puripica, Pelún, Tambillo, with lanceolate points, manos, and milling stones (as at Tambillo), and show a stage of development comparable to that of the Ayampitín sites of northwest Argentina (6000 B.C.). However, at such open sites as Tulán, Puripica, and Tambillo, stratified deposits, in situ or in nearby rockshelters are available for examination and will eventually determine their true temporal and technological characteristics, along with the associated lithic components.

In general, the publications on the *puna* of Atacama present several classes of differentiated industries of high density with projectile points; these are without any doubt not all used at the same time. Their chronological ordering continues to be one of the most important problems for the archaeology of the region. In the case of Tulán, an arbitrary separation has been made between sectors with large bifaces (workshops) and those with finer specimens (campsites). Here, there are refuse, milling stones, and a considerable typological variety including scrapers, knives, lanceolate points, and stemmed points. Typical are chips and flakes with pressure-flaked edges. This industry has not been located in stratified deposits of the area, and there is a possibility that some structures are associated with the open camps.[4]

At Puripica a small point with concave base predominates and there is a varied assemblage of stone tools of lanceolate form in presumed association with structures and conical mortars. But there is no stratigraphic relationship, and the more refined artifacts have been grouped under the concept of "Mesolithic," thus eliminating the possibility of mixture, which could affect the a priori taxonomic scheme.

At Tambillo there is a common indicator in small-stemmed and lanceolate points. The small concave-based point becomes common. But, dealing with a site in which milling stones and even human skeletal remains are securely associated, it is essential to conduct test excavations to find deposits with tools associated with organic remains for radiocarbonic proof.

In the sites of the high salt pans, such as Ascotán, there side-notched points predominate, with fewer possibilities of dating due to the rarity of organic remains near the *puna*.

The later preceramic stages of development in the inter-Andean basin are related to the industries of Ascotán, Cebollar, and Miscanti. While no serious chronological evidence exists for believing that these industries are later than others, the diminution of their artifact forms, their concentration on present-day dry lakes, and their absence from the earlier type sites, could suggest that they belong to later and/or independent developments. The presence or absence of traits, and even seriations, have not clarified the problem, since the lithic collections are not from stratified sites and are not associated with radiocarbon dates—indispensable for the application of sophisticated methodologies and for achieving any true sequence in an area.

In the region of the confluence of the Salado and Loa rivers, on the west of

[4]We have taken various carbon samples of these Archaic Andean sites, which are now in process of being analyzed, it is doubtful that they will prove older than the Ayampitín culture of northern Argentina.

the *puna,* a tool assemblage has been identified characterized by artifacts similar to microliths associated with lanceolate forms (projectile points and knives). The Chiu Chiu Complex shows such forms to an extreme degree, associated with organic remains of camelids, birds, rodents, and some Pacific shells. The complex has been dated by Mark Druss of Columbia University at 2165 ± 105 years B.C., from Site RAnL-4-A, on the edge of the present cemetery of Chiu Chiu (Sample I-6741, Teledyne Isotopes). This complex, along with other finds from the Middle Rio Loa, establishes the first preceramic sequence with specific components. About five stratified deposits are known, along with a widespread and abundant lithic industry, now being ordered into a sequence.[5]

Several inter-Andean basin and high valleys between the *altiplano* Tarapaqueño and *puna* Atacameña where preceramic remains are abundant show that at certain seasons of the year conditions were favorable for intensive hunting and collecting. The surface assemblages appear to correspond to open sites (for example, the Huasco Complex, Miscanti Complex) with typologies not necessarily relatable to the campsites of the same population in different microenvironments during a possible seasonal round. A study of seasonal occupations might show that an occupation of the lakes moved in a circuit through many microenvironments, including oases, high valleys, quebradas near Atacama Basin, and pacific in which the people used other basic materials, different techniques of workmanship, and forms with different functions than those of the lake settlements (Transhumance). Certainly this approach would tend to invalidate the "horizontal" sequences developed in the Highland from Northern Chile. The Huasco Complex more or less characterizes the basic industry of the lakes located to the north of the Rio Loa, and it surely forms part of a not yet dated, vigorous hunter–gatherer settlement of the western *altiplano,* making maximum use of the microenvironments of the highlands.

Other preceramic evidences are established in the low elevation dry lakes and quebradas near the coast. Several sites, such as Rinconada, Soronal, and Alto Barranco, attest to the presence of lithic industries with forms similar to those found in the inter-Andean basin, but this time making use of lowland ecological niches (basin) related to the Pampa of Tamarugal, the coastal mountains, and the Pacific Coast. These also lack reasonable chronological placement, and their location in the sequence is comparative and speculative.

Among the valleys or quebradas to the north of the Rio Loa, the preceramic resources have not been properly evaluated. The Pica–Guatacondo column of Figure 14.1 shows clearly the absence of preceramic sites, especially in the *quebrada* of Guatacondo, even though we know that favorable

[5]Recent dating obtained by M. Druss for the Chiuchiu Complex assure a range of time between 2.705 and 2.060 B.C. for the different isolated phases.

resources existed for preagricultural occupations. A similar situation is evident in the Pampa of Tamarugal (Prosopis sp.), where, theoretically, preceramic settlement should have been dense. Nevertheless, peripheral sites have been found, such as Rinconada and Aragón. Rinconada, on the *salar* (dry lake), has yielded heavy artifacts evidently related to local exploitation but without secure dating. Aragón reveals a very dense layered stratification, showing periodic occupations between pacific and oases area, near Pampa, perhaps part of a transhumance pattern (T. Lynch, personal communication).

In these same valleys (for example the projects at Tarapacá), it has been shown that, with a program of large scope, the preceramic remains can be dated by combining statistical seriation with radiocarbon dates from sites with diagnostic artifacts. Group 1 of the Tarapaca sequence might demonstrate the beginning of preceramic settlement, with lanceolate points made about 6000 B.C. Earlier post-Pleistocene occupations no doubt exist but have not been found. The preceramic sequence of the *quebrada* of Tarapacá could serve as a model to be verified in the rest of the valleys and *quebradas* north of the Rio Loa.[6] In the *quebrada* of Tiliviche (in the Camiña region) and Camarones, studies are continuing that will advance knowledge of the context of the lithic industries associated with campsites. The named culture of Conanoxa (Camarones area) has dates that cluster at about 2000 B.C.[7] The excavations carried out at Tiliviche,[8] with several radiocarbon dates in process, are associated with early artifact contexts, including corn, lanceolate, and dentate points, knives, shell fishhooks, manos, and milling stones; this will broaden the preceramic sequence for the *quebradas* near the Pacific Coast. These early groups seem to be part of a transhumance pattern, with differing utilization of the microenvironments of the region (coast-quebradas-Andean region).

Certainly the valleys and *quebradas* located from the *quebrada* of Camarones northward to Lluta (Arica region) ought to contain interior preceramic sites similar to Tiliviche, Conanoxa, Aragón[9] and Tarapacá. However, there are neither radiocarbon dates nor systematic surveys for the valleys and highlands of the extreme north of the country.

Among the preceramic evidences we have so far not mentioned the various sites representing the coastal population, some of them having stratigraphic evidences in the form of shellmounds. The stratigraphic finds of the early shellmounds of the coast so far do not date earlier than 4500 B.C., so

[6]D.L. True *et al.* have proportionate various datings for different occupations with milling stone implements registered at Tarapacá valley. They fluctuate between 4.880 and 1.960 B.C.

[7]H. Niemeyer and V. Schiappacasse have given coherent dates for the Conanoxa culture: 2.070, 2.020, and 1.790 B.C.

[8]We have established the chronological development of the Tiliviche Culture between 7.810 and 4.110 B.C.

[9]The Aragon Site, settled inward from the coast of Pisagua, studied by P. Núñez and V. Zlatar has been temporally placed at between 6.710 and 2.530 B.C.

one can suppose that the early occupations of the interior preceded the earliest coastal settlement. That is to say, until now there is no synchrony between the earliest sites of the Andean region and those along the coast. It is very probable that the earliest coastal sites have been altered by erosion by the sea, or perhaps it has not been known how to prospect for sites older than the known shell middens. There is seemingly a consensus that the coastal settlement could be earlier than the known dates, but this question has not been properly defined.[10] Starting with evidences dated at about 4220 B.C. from the site of Quiani (in the Arica region), a process of specialized adaptation along the coast is apparent through a common series of cultural responses diffused over a wide area under the name of the "Shell Fishhook culture." The exact relationship between this first homogeneous coastal culture and the contemporaneous communities of the inland and Andean areas is a matter of conjecture. It is possible that these settlements formed part of a seasonal nomadism between the microenvironments of the region from the coast to the highland, with a very important maritime adaptation.

Later than the Shell Fishhook culture, along the coast at Arica, Pisagua, and Taltal, a "Second Preceramic Level" has been defined showing an adequate adaptation to marine resources, with a major emphasis on the specialization of such food-producing tools as fishhooks made from cactus spines. This Second Preceramic Level can be related to the expansion of a widespread population characterized by artificial mummification, the Chinchorro Complex. It is accepted that this complex had a broad distribution about 3000 B.C.,[11] extending over a large part of the desert coastline and in areas of river outlets, as well as having contact with the highlands. Several diagnostic cultural features, such as string turbans, were incorporated into the development of later settlements at the end of the preceramic stage and the beginning of the Regional Formative.

The preceramic settlement of the coast has provided a rational dated sequence for its beginnings but the time of its ending is uncertain. There is a gap in the information between 2000 and 1000 B.C.,[12] with an absence of

[10]The preceding footnotes show the development of settlements located inward from the littoral. They are certainly earlier in time than the coast register of Quiani (Area of Arica) with a dating of 4.220 B.C. for the beginning of the occupation.

[11]The determinations of the Chinchorro Complex are obtained from the coast of Pisagua Viejo with a date of 3.050 B.C. Recent studies by M. Rivera and G. Focacci have established that similar practices of burials with artificial mummification persist in the coast of Arica (Site Playa Miller-8) toward 2.140 B.C.

[12]There is actually a manifest tendency to solve this deficit of information. Certainly, some Late Archaic coastal sites near the valleys of Arica were gradually incorporated in the agricultu-ration process established in the lowlands. Investigations by M. Rivera, G. Focacci, and P. Dauelsberg have aided in determining the date of Site Camarones-15, located in the Camarones river outlet, at 1.110 years B.C. It has a similar cultural identification with the preceramic site of Quiani Complex (coast of Arica) dated at 1.640 B.C.

dates that typify the late preceramic contexts; this makes it impossible to see clearly the relation between the local coastal development and the inception of Formative Communities.

Although the coastal stratigraphy has provided fundamental support for the establishment of a first regional sequence, no suitable remains exist for knowing the specific lifeways of the preceramic coastal population. A more specific chronology needs to be attempted on structures associated with the shell middens. At the mouth of the Rio Loa, excavations are currently under way that have determined the existence of a preceramic village (Huelén) dated at about 2800 B.C., with extended burials showing some of the Chinchorroid funerary practices dated at 1800 B.C. The Huelén Complex could extend toward the more central coast, certainly reaching as far as Taltal, where there are similar remains in the pattern of semicircular structures.

On the other hand, on the coast south of the Rio Loa, a stratigraphic sequence has been determined in the shell midden of Abtao, which represents a rather stable population from about 3010–2850 B.C., associated with resources of the slopes, where there are less favorable ecological conditions. Here, old traditions of the Shell Fishhook culture are preserved with later elements. Cañamo and other sites located on the coast south of Iquique are dated at about 2000 B.C., showing a chronological sequence begun after the development of the classic forms of the "Second Preceramic Level." Their cultural contexts appear to be very conservative, without the differentiated phases that would permit demonstration of qualitative changes in the development of the maritime culture. The preceramic history of that part of the coast without river outlets seems to be very low development but show in its final stages the critical changes accompanying the introduction of agricultural foods. The ecology of the slopes along this maritime strip was favorable for the maintenance of small but established populations in preceramic times. Later, with the development of inland agricultural settlements, the sequences tend to show the settlement of small colonies occupying the shore line but dependent on settlements in the interior (Loa River and *puna*).

The coastal south in the region of Antofagasta has a sequence founded on data from the region of Taltal, where a well-defined population was established strongly related to the Shell Fishhook culture (Colorado I) and to the Huelén Complex.

Theoretically one can assume some contact between the end of the preceramic populations and the beginning of controlled agriculture in the well-watered zones at the mouths of rivers, and even in those areas of the coastal slopes capable of being utilized by the new settlements bearing agricultural and ceramic features. However, the chronological sequences have not made clear the nature of the cultural and temporal local changes produced by the expansion of the food-producing societies.

B. Ceramic Period

1. Regional Formative Period

Until recently, the only chronological information on sites with an agricultural economy had been gained from contact with the Inca expansion. However, apart from the efforts of Uhle in relation to the cultural period he called proto-Nazca, new evidences have been identified related to early settlements at a cultural stage in which agriculture was not completely controlled. At present, the Regional Formative encompasses exactly those early sites that succeeded in developing in diverse ecological surroundings, prior to the first expansions of the Tiwanaku culture. It is very probable that a cultural diversification exists in this period because the Formative cultural contributions received in this region had different origins and arrived at different times, in connection with highland cultures (Titicaca-Poopo Area).

In the valleys of the extreme north, between Arica and Camiña, a coastal settlement has been found that could be related to the complex of mounds at Conanoxa (320 B.C.). Probably the Formative settlement of the valleys of Arica had attained some phases that are there represented by such sites as Faldas del Morro, El Laucho, and Alto Ramírez.[13] Such sites have not been dated. Their cultural contexts show a pre-Tiwanaku situation, with a basis of hunting–gathering and some cultivation, which, in Alto Ramírez, attained some importance (sweet potatoes, beans, quinoa, and maize). There appear at these sites the first groups characterized by the use of bulky turbans made from wool cordage, along with crude pottery of limited use (as for example at Faldas del Morro). These assemblages show early cultural elements derived from the earlier maritime preceramic peoples (cactus-spine fishhooks, turbans, interlaced textiles, etc.) that do not survive in the post-Formative sequence. At the terminal occupation, Tiwanaku cultural elements from the classic and expansive periods are superimposed. There are no dates for the arrival of these elements in the extreme north, and this has produced continuing disagreements in the local chronologies.[14] Studies of the seriation of graves show us that the Formative sites, in their final phases, were acculturating by peoples bringing in the Tiwanaku style (examples are Alto Ramírez and Tarapacá 40–B).

Between the valleys of Camarones and Camiña, the first Formative traits

[13]According to M. Rivera and G. Focacci, the El Laucho Site in the coast of Arica has a determination of 530 B.C. On the other side, the funerary mounds of Azapa, basically the Alto Ramírez Site, has been determined to be between 490 and 410 B.C.

[14]Some determinations are available to identify the arrival of the first cultural features of Classic Tiwanaku to the valleys of Arica. M. Rivera and G. Focacci have established a date of A.D. 380 for the Azapa-6 Site (area of Arica) with ceramic types Loreto Viejo-Cabuza. This occupation seems to persist in the village excavated by G. Ampuero in Alto Ramírez (Site Azapa-83) that has been dated by Rivera at A.D. 560.

seem to be linked with the population of the mound complex at Conanoxa and other settlements of "turbaned people" established especially in the fertile lowlands. The rubbish deposits of the coast may show in Punta Pichalo III the incorporation of agriculture and pottery over the preceramic deposit, as a reflection of the new agricultural situation in the interior valleys.

In general, these first Formative populations should have been superimposed on settlements derived from the preceramic Chinchorro Complex, and/or the final phase of Conanoxa (3000–2000 B.C.). But between the two populations and after Conanoxa there is a gap that has not been successfully filled by stratified sites showing the transition toward the establishment of the Formative. In addition, the end of the Formative in the valleys mentioned earlier has an undated acculturation with Tiwanaku elements (as at Pisagua). What is clear is that immediately before A.D. 800 irrigation agriculture (of maize and beans) was extended to these valleys, as shown by the site of Conanoxa–Angostura, before the beginning of Regional Development.

In the *quebrada* of Tarapacá and the Pampa of Tamarugal, Regional Formative is represented by the developing settlement of Caserones village and the early cemeteries of the Tarapacá Complex, characterized by dense groups of turbaned burials. These contexts represent a hunter–gatherer people located for specializing in plant gathering, particularly of *algarrobo* (*prosopis* sp.), and experimenting with the first cultivation of crops. There is a special emphasis on local cultivation of gourds and possibly maize, and on the collection of quinoa in the adjacent *altiplano*.

A chronological alignment of the turbaned burials (Sector A) with the early part of the village site of Caserones is possible, based on the radiocarbon date (360–290 B.C.). There is also an alignment between Sector B, the Tiwanaku part of the Tarapacá complex, tending to confirm that the introduction of agriculture and the emphasis on monochrome pottery was focused in an early village—evidencing a jump from an incipient horticulture to a stable agriculture contemporaneous with the expansion of Tiwanaku at the end of the occupation. In Tarapacá the Formative character is represented by stable settlements dedicated to collection of *algarrobo*, the first agriculture, and the spread of the first plainwares (including black and red-polished types along with the more common brown plainware) associated with maize cultivation (as at Caserones village).

Between the *quebradas* of Quisma and Guatacondo, including the oases of Pica, the first settlements manifesting maize and bean cultivation and monochrome ceramics are represented by the village site of Guatacondo (100 B.C.–A.D. 100), which is also associated with a population of turbaned people. It is not clear whether other occupations occurred between the turbaned people of Guatacondo and the first Tiwanaku contacts in the late settlements of the Pica Complex. It is likely that there was a significant temporal relationship, but it has not as yet been well dated.

Along the Upper and Middle Rio Loa the evidences of the first populations of a Formative character could be represented in the phases Vega Alta I and Vega Alta II, succeeded by the phases Loa I and Loa II,[15] which all show an intensive development of agriculture and animal breeding, along with a proliferation of monochrome pottery. Beginning with Lasana I and Lasana II, there was extensive agriculture, along with the keeping of camelids, characterizing a process of cultural integration in grouping villages together, the best example being the site of Lasana (Regional Development Period of the Middle Loa).

Along the Lower Rio Loa, between Quillagua and the river mouth, the first Formative settlement is represented by the Huelén Complex—mounds with several phases currently under study (450 B.C.–A.D. 250). These groups manifest an agricultural complex (maize), metallurgy, monochrome pottery, and textiles with maritime activities. After, it can be accepted that at the end of this early occupation Tiwanaku was superimposed on the Formative sequence (as at Ancachi).

The Formative occupations that have been dated for the transverse valleys provide considerable information on the surroundings of the favorable zones where rivers empty into the Pacific. Considerable effort is needed to date significant phases that must have developed in the high valleys. In this respect the contributions made in the Rio Salado and Rio Loa provide a better balance of information as between highlands and lowlands.

In the coastal desert the archaeological evidences show less numerous Formative settlements in the areas away from the river outlets. These people developed a specialized adaptation to maritime resources. Formative evidences are present from the coast at Pisagua to the Rio Loa in the latest shellmound deposits (late Cañamo Complex), revealing the incorporation of plain pottery, *algarrobo* and corn at a quite early stage (860 B.C.). It seems that the settlements with mounds had covered some parts of the area at that time. Finally, the spread of the Patache Complex (A.D. 760), on the coast south of Iquique, shows that some groups with pottery similar to that of Caserones had established settlements utilizing the maritime resources (including Tiwanaku style textiles).

It is generally agreed that after the expansion of Tiwanaku there were more or less periodic colonies established in areas west of the *altiplano*, bearing pottery such as that of Chiribaya, Maitas, Huruquilla, Chilpe, and others. From the chronological point of view, the hypothesis related to the "vertical islands" of the Andean area (Murra 1972) permits identification of clearly differentiated ceramic types. These have been placed in sequence without considering that several colonies from the *altiplano* coexisted with local populations, making a time difference between the types unnecessary.

[15]The final phase of Vega Alto Complex has been dated by C. G. Pollard at A.D. 200. He has given a coherent date for the Loa Complex at A.D. 105.

This view should be properly evaluated in the valleys producing the tropical agricultural complex; an excess of surface typologies could well be replaced by test excavations in rubbish corresponding to the village centers, where the chronological possibilities are more realistic.[16]

In the coastal desert and adjacent slopes, the possibilities of development were less and the tendency toward conserving cultural patterns seems to inhibit chronological ordering. Along the coast between the Loa and Taltal, is is probable that the Huelén Complex (funerary mounds) was diffused as well as the evidences of Colorado II, but in general there are no well-defined Formative elements, leaving marked gaps in the local sequence. Still, it must be emphasized that the early ceramic occupations are very similar to Laucho Tradition (Arica Region) and San Pedro de Atacama Tradition.

For the whole *altiplano* from Arica to the Rio Loa, there is an important lack of information in completion of Formative and later cultural chronology. It can be hypothesized that the presence of the Wankarani culture, with early monochrome pottery, agricultural implements (spades), and a village pattern of circular plan, was diffused toward this western margin. However, the records have not been well controlled. It is also logical to suppose that the Tiwanaku culture was superimposed on that of Wankarani in this region, but there are no reliable data.

In the oases of the Atacama Desert, the Formative evidences could correspond to the first settlements with pottery of the type San Pedro red-polished, along with other early associations of the San Pedro I Phase. Possibly the San Pedro II Phase with black polished sherds, and modeled types, can also be included.[17]

Continuing the chronological scheme from the Rio Loa southward, there is no clear relationship between the beginning of the Formative and the end of the preceramic sequence. It is quite possible that the Formative villages of these oases also finally had contact with the Tiwanaku expansion. The archaeological evidence shows the association of many Tiwanaku traits in the San Pedro II Phase (A.D. 200–300). Doubtless the Formative evidences from these oases could fit several phases with a more sophisticated chronol-

[16]There are recent determinations for occupations of colonies depending or related to the Altiplano Highlands with context derivated from the Tiwanaku Pattern. We have dated an influx with Expansive Tiwanaku textiles at the Pica-8 Site at A.D. 1.000 (Pica-Tiwanaku Phase). M. Rivera and C. Focacci dated the Tiwanaku-Chiribaya Phase at A.D. 730 for the valleys of Arica.

[17]G. Le Paige dated the development of the ceramic type "San Pedro Negra Pulida" (San Pedro Black polished) in Quitor-6 Site, at A.D. 250. The date of Solor-6 (A.D. 300) confirms this chronological position. The ceramic components San Pedro Rojo y Negro Pulido (San Pedro Red and Black polished) have been established at A.D. 200 in Quitor-5 Site. Finally, Le Paige has dated the maximum development of the ceramic type San Pedro Rojo Pulido (San Pedro Red polished) and various modeled types in the Toconao-Oriente Site at 580 B.C. The dates of the ceramic type Negra Pulida (Black Polished) suggest that the expansion of Classic Tiwanaku to these oases occurred at an earlier time than is commonly accepted.

ogy, since the history of settlement in these high microenvironments seems to have a very long tradition. The ceramic sequence of the oasis of San Pedro Atacama requires a typological reappraisal; obviously three ceramic types cannot represent the whole complex history of the area.

2. Regional Development Period

Beginning with the Tiwanaku Expansion, cultural developments became regional in accordance with the particular ecological features of the area. Between the valleys of Arica and Camiña,the focus of the Arica culture (with both maritime and agricultural food production) developed the San Miguel Phase (A.D. 1000), which has at least two stages. There were followed by the Pocoma and Gentilar phases.[18] Probably each of these phases has its own differentiated cultural context, but a series of radiocarbon dates is required for better placement of the end of San Miguel and the beginning of Gentilar. In the valley of Camiña, the development of San Miguel met cultural influences from the communities bearing the late monochrome ceramics noted at Pichalo and the groups called Pisagua-Atacameño, of late kinds but with uncertain dating.

Regional Development in the lower part of this valley includes Pisagua, with records of cultural complexes formed out of friction between the Arica polychrome tradition and a tradition of plainware derived from the more central oases and valleys. At the end of the Camiña sequence features of the *altiplano* are introduced, such as some colonies of *chullpas* (as at Nama); although they have not been dated, they appear to exemplify the latest *altiplano* colonies in the western valleys.

In the *quebrada* of Tarapacá friction is again observed, between San Miguel and the monochrome tradition of the Pica Complex.[19] There are several samples for dating which could correspond to cemeteries as well as late villages. It is likely that various phases of Regional Development existed here between the Tiwanaku Expansion and Inca; these require to be systematically dated.

From Tarapacá and neighboring oases, temporary occupations of the Regional Development Period spread to the Pampa of Tamarugal, where rare late pottery types have been found. In general, the Pampa of Tamarugal offers a very incoherent sequence, which requires detailed study. The occupations with pottery seem to have been seasonal without conforming to established communities such as occurred in the neighboring *quebradas,* where control of irrigation was permanent.

Between the valleys and oases of Tarapacá, Pica, and Guatacondo, the

[18]Pocomá-Gentilar Phase, proper of the valleys of Arica, has been situated at A.D. 1.270 H. Niemeyer, V. Schiappacasse, and I. Solimano identified this phase in a village-site at Camarones valley (Camarones-sur).

[19]We determined the time of the Pica Complex at A.D. 1.020 and its persistence reached the Inca contact.

Pica Complex (A.D. 1000), which characterizes the Regional Development of late populations having plainware pottery, was diffused. This pottery is well dated, and might be related to Formative influences derived from Late Wankarani. Two phases are distinguished in this complex: an earlier one associated with Tiwanaku expansion and Charcollo ceramics, and a later one linked with the ceramic types Pica Monochrome, San Miguel, Chilpe,[20] Chiza modeled, and Huruquilla.[21]

Probably the end of the Regional Development Period in all these valleys represented the last waves of late *altiplano* culture which coexisted with the local populations of the western slopes. The pottery types Chilpe, Taltape, and Huruquilla, along with other Khonko–Kollao ingredients, indicate the nature of the latest acculturation from colonies contact influencing the regional sequence, in a late period with few controlled dates.

In the Upper Rio Loa, Regional Development is characterized by the formation of defensive enclosures and settlements associated with pottery bearing a red wash, along with a strong monochrome tradition well shown in the Lasana II and San Pedro III phases. The type site Dupont,[22] near Calama, might represent the final spread of sherds with a black, more or less polished interior, which, together with the pottery of the San Pedro III and Lasana II phases (and derivatives), may represent the last moments of the pre-Inca sequence of the Middle and Upper Loa. It is probable that in this zone also the local sequence was interrupted by settlements with *chullpas* of uncertain date but originating in the *altiplano* (Toconce), and other *altiplano* pattern of tombs at Los Antiquos, near Lasana.

In the Lower Loa, especially in the area around the mouth of the river, there was a possible conflict between the tradition of the Lasana II–San Pedro III Phase, and northern oases with monochrome traditions, and the valleys of the Arica zone with a polychrome tradition. These three traditions form complexes now being studied for arrangement into a sequence which will show intense colonization combined with dependence on inland agrarian centers, in a maritime adaptation.[23]

On the desert coast between Pisagua and the Rio Loa, the late population is characterized by components of the Pica Complex and the San Miguel Phase. From the Rio Loa to the coast of Taltal the San Pedro III and Lasana II

[20]The ceramic type Chilpe Negro sobre Rojo (Chilpe Black over Red) with late altiplanic filiation has been dated at A.D. 1.235 by H. Niemeyer, V. Schiappacasse, and I. Solimano in the Camarones valley (Sabaipugro Site).

[21]G. Le Paige has dated a component of the Negro sobre Blanco (Black over White) style related to the altiplano ceramic type Huruguilla at Quitor-9 Site, with a date of A.D. 1.050. It is associated with the Dupont type characterized by an inner black slip in its initial moment.

[22]The ceramic type Dupont, common in the Middle Loa river, has been dated at A.D. 1.390 for its terminal phase, in the Dupont-1 Site, near Calama.

[23]A late-time village, located in Quillagua, in the Low Loa river, has an initial occupation with components of San Pedro III Phase (Dupont and Roja Violácea types). F. Téllez, M. Cervellino, and I obtained a chronological position of A.D. 1.240.

traditions were found, including ingredients of Dupont clearly contemporaneous with peoples bringing polychrome ceramics, characterized by the presence of San Miguel, Pocoma, and Gentilar (Taltal region) pottery types. Yet there exist neither radiocarbon dates nor stratigraphy to establish a more secure sequence south of the Rio Loa.

For the *altiplano* of the Arica–Loa belt, there is no adequate survey, leaving a considerable gap in the chronological information. Probably the pottery tradition of black-on-red (Chilpe type) is related to late sites of the *altiplano* that could be independent of the Nama type of late occupation with *chullpas*. The lack of an approximate sequence leaves a gap in the regional chronology.

Finally, in the oasis of San Pedro de Atacama, the Regional Development Period is represented by the San Pedro III Phase,[24] which, although lacking radiocarbon dates, may well represent the end of the immediately pre-Inca population.

Next in the sequence is the Inca expansion, and although this has some chronological subphases they can be excluded from this brief survey.

IV. SUMMARY

Scientific archaeology with chronological aims began with the work of Uhle (1919, 1922), applying comparative studies of funerary contexts plus a limited stratigraphic analysis. Beginning with the work of Bird in 1943, full application of stratigraphic methods was begun, leading to formulation of the first cultural sequences. The first stratigraphic excavations of the interior coastal zone were those at Conanoxa (Niemeyer and Schiappacasse 1963) which resulted in the first report based on application of adequate methods.

Beginning in 1961, Gustavo Le Paige began the first concrete attempt to develop a chronology for the ceramic cultural phases of the archaeological district of San Pedro de Atacama (with a date for the cemetery Solor-6). From 1961 to 1973, 49 dates were accumulated in the general area of Northern Chile (provinces of Tarapacá and Antofagasta). Of these dates, only 18 come from stratigraphic cuts, which shows the embryonic status of this approach. For example, it is only in the last 3 years that excavations have been begun of the stratigraphy of preceramic sites, which were traditionally "dated" by the typology of their surface stone artifacts (Nuñez *et al.*, n.d.b)

[24]The San Pedro III Phase, for the oases of San Pedro de Atacama, represent a ceramic group of poor quality as compared with the preceding phases. This is also present in the fortified villages or "pukaras" of the Middle Loa river and the oases of San Pedro de Atacama. C. G. Pollard has dated the Late occupation of the Lasana pukara at A.D. 1.250. G. Le Paige obtained two determinations for the Solor-4 Site with the typical ceramic type of Phase III "Roja Violácea" (red-violet). The dates are A.D. 970 and 1.180.

There has been no application of complementary dating methods, such as obsidian hydration, or dendrochronology, nor have local investigations been conducted to confirm the validity of the radiocarbon determinations—although the dates are not subject to any more doubt than those from other parts of the Andean area.

Bearing in mind the few ongoing long-term investigations into the archeological chronology of Northern Chile, the following observations can be made:

1. Attention is called to the absence of dates prior to 9000 B.C. All the known dates for this early time lack a secure context and archaeologically signify only the presence of man in the area. It must be emphasized that prior to 5000 B.C. there are no dates with cultural references. This lacuna makes very difficult the formulation of chronological stages intermediate between the development of Early Man and the phases of the Regional Archaic.

2. Between 5000 B.C. and 1000 B.C. there are many more dates, making possible the development of a better chronological sequence for the late preceramic settlements. However, between 4000 and 3000 B.C., there are only two controlled samples.

3. From 1000 B.C. to the end of the preceramic period the dates are more numerous and present no extensive gaps; there is a balance between the early stages and the later ones with agriculture and pottery.

4. In sum, by December of 1973 there were 18 preceramic dates and 30 dates corresponding to remains with pottery and agriculture. It is obvious that there is a marked deficit of early preceramic determinations, although the frequency of these sites in known areas is usually greater than for the agricultural sites. Still, there are methodological problems in locating preceramic sites with conditions favorable for dating. On the other hand, the ease in identifying agricultural sites could explain the high frequency of late dates, as well as the fact that in Northern Chile there is a tendency to know best the funerary sites, which generally belong to the Formative and Regional Development periods.

5. The deficiency of dates from the *altiplano,* Puna of Atacama, and high valleys in general is noteworthy. It reflects the lack of knowledge of the chronology of the highlands, producing a one-sided picture compared with the dating of lowland sites. This explains the gaps in information on the ceramic and preceramic periods of the highlands, gaps we are now trying to correct.

6. It is necessary to augment considerably the scientific description of the main archaeological components associated with radiocarbon dates.

7. Dating the large gaps in the preceramic sequence is a high-priority need, along with the need to develop an ordering of the different lithic industries and surface collections of pottery.

8. Where sequences have been developed, it is necessary to date more

precisely the time at which Formative Societies appear. It would also be useful to inquire into some of the abrupt changes for which chronological information is lacking.

9. Concerning establishment of the Regional Formative Period, a more intense study of the sites and stratified deposits is needed to reach a better understanding of the Formative elements that influenced development of the later society.

10. In relation to the Tiwanaku Expansion, the lack of data on structures and site deposits should be mentioned; such data would permit clarification of the true nature of the colonization and its exact temporal relationship to the local settlements. The fact that there is a Classic penetration, another Expansion, and then a derivation from the Expansion, demonstrates the necessity of determining a chronology for the western slopes themselves.

11. The Regional Development Period appears to be composed of several different cultural phases, none of them well dated. This makes it essential to alternate the seriation of graves with chronological techniques linked to village deposits and rubbish heaps.

These deficiencies weaken a chronological–interpretative presentation. However, the following tentative scheme is offered in conclusion.

The cultural manifestations in Northern Chile must have acquired their particular differentiations in response to the environmental zones in which they were developed. The first preceramic settlements seem to have been best adapted to the highlands, extending themselves through time to the valleys, oases, and *quebradas,* as well as to the intermediate lowlands and the Pacific Coast. Later, from about 4206 B.C., a full maritime occupation suddenly appears which shows cultural features very well adapted and specialized for exploitation of the sea (the Shell Fishhook culture).

From about this time on, the peoples of the whole region—Andean, intermediate, and coastal—enter upon multiple relationships as a consequence of occupying a narrow region in which ecological differences are tied to different altitudes in the profile coast–highlands with differentiated natural products. The development of hunter–gatherer occupations seems to continue until the end of the preceramic as a rational use of the differentiated ecological levels.

Various modes of seasonal nomadism are manifested that appear to have attained their maximum expression between 5000 and 2000 B.C. (milling stone). At approximately the end of this epoch, the shift to horticulture in the lowlands begins. However, it is very probable that the first farmers and animal breeders had experimented in the highlands, because of the more favorable vegetational cover in the *altiplano, puna,* and high valleys for development of stock breeding parallel to the domestication and adaptation of economic plants. It can be concluded that in this poorly defined period the social process became diversified through critical changes deriving from the new modes of food production. There is a tendency for human groups to become established in specific favorable niches, where the first foci of Formative Communities (800 B.C. to A.D. 400) can be identified. These groups continue with patterns of seasonal nomadism between the *altiplano* and the coast, through valleys and *quebradas,* but a new development begins, that of nucleated early settlements in zones suitable for the application of farming and stock breeding. This population might be related to waves of pre-Tiwanaku influence which are not definitely known or dated.

Although it is clear that *altiplano* traits continued to influence the local populations through the Regional Development Period, it is important to make clear that cultural development took on a regional character through the organization of groups of culturally independent communities, a more or less homogeneous economic structure composed of tropical agricultural valleys, exploitation of the sea, and farming with animal-breeding between the coast and Andean region.

This historical scheme for Northern Chile is insufficient, but it represents a reasonable beginning.

BIBLIOGRAPHY

Alvarez, L.

1969 Arqueología del Departamento de Arica, Secuencia Cultural del Periódo pre Agroalfarero. *Museo Arqueológico de la Serena, Actas del Congreso Nacional de Arqueología,* 27–32.

Bird, J.

1943 Excavations in Northern Chile. *Anthropological Papers of the American Museum of Natural History* **38**(4):171–316.

1946 The Cultural Sequence in the North Chilean Coast. In Handbook of South American Indians, Vol. 2, edited by J. H. Steward. *Bureau of American Ethnology Bulletin,* 587–594.

1967 Muestras de Radiocarbono de un Basural Precerámico de Quiani, Arica. *Sociedad Arquelógica de Santiago de Chile Boletín* **4:**13–14.

Boisset, G., and A. Llagostera

n.d. Fechas Radiocarbonicas de Caleta Abtao, Comparaciones con otras Fechas de Sitios Costeros. Mimeographed. Congreso Nacional de Arqueología, Universidad de Chile, Santiago.

Boisset, G., A. Llagostera, and E. Salas

1969 Excavaciones Arqueológicas en Caleta Abtao Antofagasta, *Museo Arqueológico de la Serena, Actas del Congreso Nacional de Arqueología,* 60–75.

Capdeville, A.

1923 Un Cementerio Chincha-Atacameño en Punta Grande, Taltal. *Boletín de la Academia Nacional de la Historia,* **18:**1–16.

Dauelsberg, P.

1963 Complejo Arqueológico del Morro de Arica. *Actas del Congreso Internacional de Arqueología en San Pedro de Atacama, Anales de la Universidad del Norte, Chile.* (Resumen).

1972a La Cerámica de Arica y su Situacion Cronológica. *Revista Chungara de la Universidad del Norte* **1:**15–25.

1972b Sobre la Problemática de Arica, Respuesta a L. G. Lumbreras. *Revista Chungara de la Universidad del Norte* **1**:38–44.

1972c Arqueología del Departamento de Arica. *Apartado de la Enciclopedia de Arica*, 161–178.

Dauelsberg, P., L. Alvarez, and S. Chacón

n.d. Investigaciones en Torno a Sitios-Paraderos de Cazadores Tempranos. Unpublished manuscript, Congreso Nacional de Arqueología, Universidad de Chile, Santiago.

Erices, S., and G. Foccaci

n.d. Los Túmulos de San Miguel de Azapa. Unpublished manuscript, Congreso Nacional de Arqueología, Universidad de Chile, Santiago.

Fung, R. P.

1972 El Taller Lítico de Chivateros, valle de Chillón. *Apartado de la Revista del Museo Nacional* **38**:61–72.

Gordon, A.

1967 Fechas Radiocarbónicas (c-14) de la Cronología Arqueologica Chilena. *Sociedad Arqueológica de Santiago Boletín* **4**:43–101.

Laming-Emperaire, A.

1968 Le Site Marassi en Terre de Feu. *Revista Rehue* **1**:133–143.

Lanning, E. P., and T. C. Patterson

1967 Early Man in South America. *Scientific American* **5**(217):44–50.

Le Paige, G.

1963a La Antiguedad de Una Tumba Comprobada por Carbono 14 y el Ambiente Que lo Rodea. *Revista de la Universidad Católica año XLVIII*, 167–176.

1963b Continuedad y Discontinuedad de la Cultura Atacameña. Congreso Internacional de Arqueología en San Pedro de Atacama, *Anales de la Universidad del Norte* **2**:7–25.

1964 Los Cementerios de la Época Agroalfarera en San Pedro de Atacama. *Anales de la Universidad del Norte* **3**:51–91.

Latcham, R. S.

1938 Arqueología de la Región Atacameña. Santiago de Chile: Edicion de la Universidad de Chile.

1941 Fases de la Edad de la Piedra en Chile. *275th Congreso Internacional de Americanistas*, 257–265.

Lumbreras, L. G.

1972 Sobre la Problemática Arqueológica de Arica (carta a L. Núñez). *Revista Chungara de la Universidad del Norte* **1**:27–29.

MacNeish, R. S.

1969 *First Annual Report of the Ayacucho Archaeological Botanical Project*. Andover, Massachusetts: Robert S. Peabody Foundation for Archaeology.

Meighan, C.

1970 Excavations at Guatacondo, Chile, 1969. A Preliminary Report on the Field Activities of N.S.F. Grant GS 2652. Mimeographed, University of California, Los Angeles.

Meltzer, R.

1969 The salar de Talabre, Northern Chile . . . A Tentative Ecological Reconstruction and a Seriation of Archaeological Remains. Paper presented at the conference on Pleistocene man in Latin America, San Pedro de Atacama, Chile.

Montané, J.

1972 Las Evidencias del Poblamiento Temprano de Chile. *Pumapunko* **5**:40–53.

Mostny, G.

1964 Anzuelos de Concha: 6.170 Mas o Menos 220 Años. *Museo Nacional de Historia Natural, Santiago de Chile, Noticiero Mensual* **98.**

1965 Fechas Radiocarbónicas de la Quebrada de Guatacondo. *Museo Nacional de Historia Natural, Sanitago de Chile, Nueticiero Mensual* **105.**

Murra, J. V.
1972 *El Control Vertical de un Máximo de Pisos Ecológicos en la Economía de las Sociedades Andinas*. T-II Visita de la Provincia, León de Huanuco (1562). Huánuco, Perú: Universidad Hermilio Valdizan. Pp. 429–476.
Niemeyer, H., and V. Schiappacase
1963 Investigaciones Arqueológicas en las Terrazas de Conanoxa, Valle de Camarones (provincia de Tarapacá). *Revista Universitaria* **48:**101–166.
Núñez, L.
1970a Algunos Problemas del Estudio del Complejo Faldas del Morro, Norte de Chile. *Sonderdruck aus, ab handlungen und Benchte desstaatlichen museums für volkerkunde* **31:**79–109.
1970b Primer Fechado Radiocarbónico del Complejo Faldas del Morro en el Sitio Tarapacá-40 y Alguna Consideraciones Básicas. *Actas del Congreso Nacional de Arqueología de la Serena*, 47–58.
1971 Secuencia y Cambio en los Asentamientos Humanos de la Desembocadura del Río Loa, Norte de Chile. *Universidad de Chile, Santiago de Chile, Boletín* **112:**3–25.
1972a Sobre el Comienzo de la Agricultura Prehistorica en el Norte de Chile. *Pumapunko* **4:**5–48.
1972b Sobre la Problemática Arqueológica de Arica (Respuesta a L. G. Lumbreras). *Revista Chungara de la Universidad del Norte* **1**:30–37.
n.d.a Complejo Chinchorro en Pisagua Viejo. (Apéndice de un Estudio de J. Munizaga). In press.
n.d.b Dupont-1, un Sitio Tardio del Río Loa Medio. Unpublished manuscript.
n.d.c Asentamientos Campesinos Prehistóricos en los Oasis de Pica (Provincia de Tarapacá). Manuscript in preparation.
Núñez, L., C. Moragas, and C. Staal
n.d.b Excavaciones en el Sitio Tiliviche 1-b (provincia de Tarapacá). Unpublished manuscript.
Núñez, L., and J. Varela
1961–1964 Un Complejo Preagrícola en el Salar del Soronal (cordillera de la costa). *Revista del Instituto de Antropología de la Universidad Nacional de Córdoba* **2-3**:189–204.
1966 Complejo Preagrícola en el Salar del Huasco (Provincia de Tarapacá). *Universidad de Chile Antofagasta*,
Núñez, L., V. Zlatar, and P. Núñez
n.d.a. Caleta Huelén 42: Una Aldea Temprana del Norte de Chile. Paper presented at Congreso Nacional de Arqueología de Santiago, Universidad de Chile, Santiago de Chile.
Núñez, P.
n.d. Informe de Recientes Trabajos en Guatacondo. Unpublished manuscript.
Núñez, P., and V. Zlatar
n.d. Excavaciones en el Sitio Aragón (Provincia de Tarapacá). Unpublished manuscript.
Orellana, M.
1963 Problemas de la Arqueología de San Pedro de Atacama y Sus Alrededores. *Congreso de Arqueología Internacional en San Pedro de Atacama. Anales de la Universidad del Norte* **2:**29–45.
1971 Informe de las Excavaciones de Loa Oeste 3. *Boletín de Prehistoria de Chile* **4**:3–26.
Orellana, M., C. Urrejola, C. Thomas and G. Serracino
n.d. Uso del Sistema de Computacion en los Artefactos Líticos del Río Salado. Paper presented at the 1971 Congreso Nacional de Arqueología. Universidad de Chile, Santiago de Chile.

Pollard, C. G.
1971 Cultural Change and Adaptation in the Central Atacama Desert of Northern Chile. *Nawpa Pacha* **9:**41–64.
Ponce, C.
1961 Breve Comentario Acerca de los Fechados Radiocarbónicos de Bolivia. Paper presented at the Encuentro Arqueológico Internacional de Arica, Universidad de Chile, Arica, Chile.
1970 Las Culturas Wankarani y Chiripa y su Relación Con Tiwanaku. *Academia Nacional de Ciencias de Bolivia Publication* **25.**
Schiappacasse, V., and H. Niemeyer
1969 Comentario a Tres Fechas Radiocarbónicas de Sitios Arqueologicos de Conanoxa (Valle de Camarones, prov. de Tarapacá). *Museo Nacional de Historia Natural, Noticiero mensual* **151.**
n.d. *Apuntes Para el Estudio de la Trashumancia en el Valle de Camarones (Prov. de Tarapaá). Chile.* Antofagasta, Chile: Primer Congreso del Hombre Andino.
Serracino, G., and C. Thomas
1971 Excavación del Yacimiento Confluencia 1. *Boletín de prehistoria de Chile* **4:**49–68.
Soto, P.
n.d. Deformación Craneana en la Fase Cultural El Laucho. Paper presented at the Congreso Nacional de Arqueología de Santiago, Universidad de Chile, Santiago.
Spahny, J. C.
1964 Le cemetière Atacaménien du Pukara de Lasana, Vallée des Rio Loa (Chili). *Journal de la Societie des Americanistes* **53.**
1967a Recherches Archéologiques a l'Embochoure du Rio Loa (Cote du Pacifique Chili). *Journal de la Societie des Americanistes,* 160–179.
1967b Comentario en Radiocarbon. *American Journal of Science* **9.**
Spoueys, O.
n.d. Informe Preliminar de Dos Fechados Para Arica. Paper presented at the Congreso Nacional de Arqueología. Universidad de Chile de Santiago, Santiago de Chile.
Tamers, M. A.
1965 Radiocarbon. *Laboratorio de Radiocarbon, Instituto Venezolano de Investigaciones Científicas, Boletín* No. **7.**
True, D. L., and R. G. Matson
1970 Cluster Analysis and Multidimensional Scaling of Archeological Sites in Northern Chile. *Science* **169:**1201–1203.
True, D. L., and L. Núñez
n.d. Un Piso Habitacional Temprano en el Norte de Chile. In press.
True, D. L., L. Núñez, and P. Núñez
1970 Archaeological Investigation in Northern Chile: Project Tarapacá. Preceramic Resource. *American Antiquity* **35**(2):170–184.
Uhle, M.
1919 La Arqueología de Arica y Tacna. *Sociedad Ecuatoriana de Estudios Históricos Americanos.*
1922 *Fundamentos étnicos y arqueología de Arica y Tacna.* Quito, Ecuador.

A Summary Scan

GORDON R. WILLEY

This summary is written to provide concise synopses of the chronological area presentations in this volume, to offer some brief, critical and other commentaries, and to fill in, however briefly, a number of major area chronology gaps in this New World coverage. Originally, the volume was planned as a complete, hemispherewide treatment of American archaeological areas; but, for the present, this goal has not been attained, leaving several geographical lacunae. My very sketchy remarks on these gaps are in no way adequate substitutes for the detailed chronological discussion and coverage of the kind given in the foregoing area essays. It is to be hoped that the areas in question may be filled in a later and revised edition of this work.

The accompanying chronology charts (Figures 15.1 and 15.2) do present area chronological columns side-by-side and on a time scale, but other than this the present summary scan is not a synthetic "overview" of New World archaeology. Such overviews exist, either culture-historically or developmentally oriented, and the reader is referred to them (Bernal 1964; Gorenstein *et al.*, 1974; Jennings 1974; Lathrop, ms.; Meggers 1963, 1964, 1972; Sanders and Marino 1970; Willey 1966, 1971; Willey and Phillips, 1958) for these types of treatment. The purpose of the present summary, like the volume itself, is essentially factual and narrowly historical—a bringing together in as objective a manner as possible the basic data of space–time systematics in American archaeology.

DATING TECHNIQUES

Before summing up the area presentations, some comment is in order on R. E. Taylor's introductory chapter on dating techniques in archaeology and recent advances. Taylor is concerned with physical and natural science techniques. He notes that of the 12 primary chronimetric methods now available in archaeology only two, dendrochronology and varve studies, were in active use before 1949. That date marked the advent of the radiocarbon method. Taylor is quite correct about its impact on archaeology. Indeed, the "new archaeology" of the 1960s and 1970s owes much to this system of

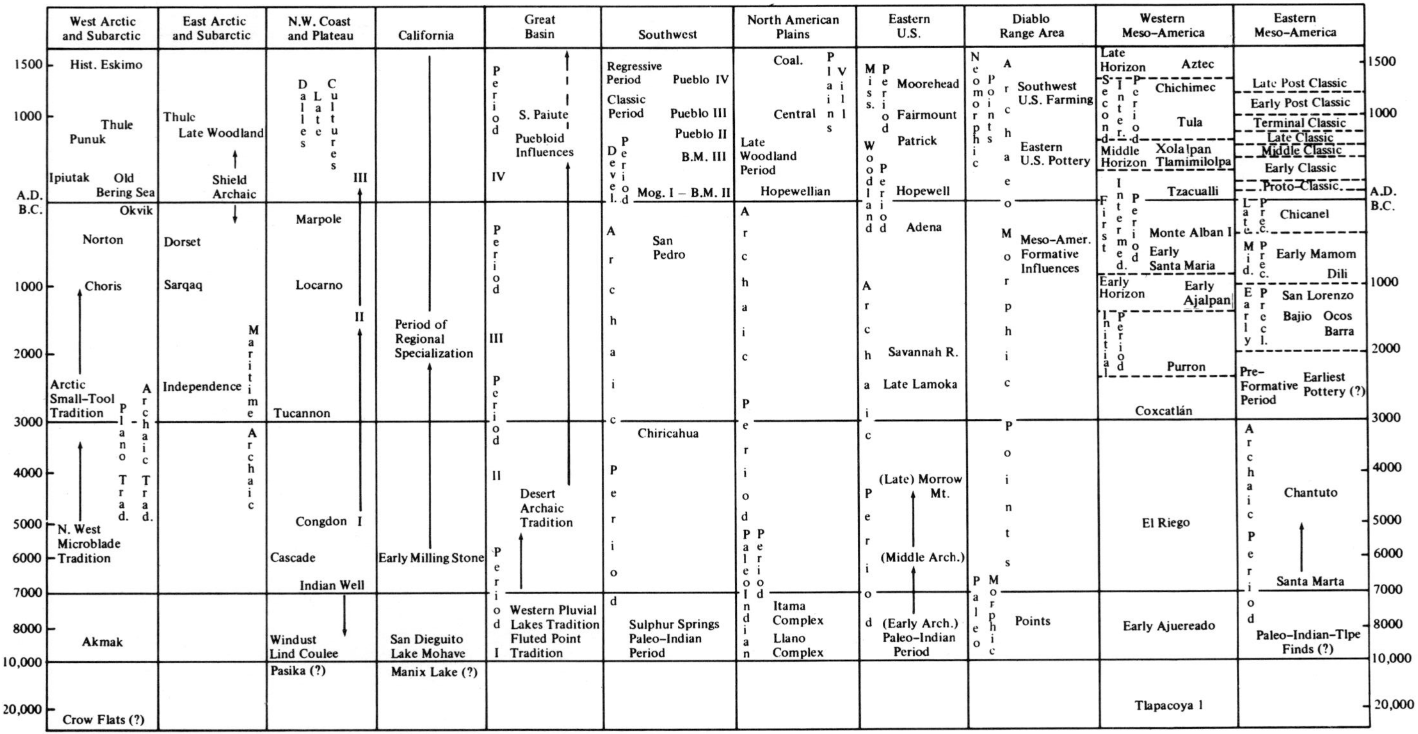

Date	West Arctic and Subarctic	East Arctic and Subarctic	N.W. Coast and Plateau	California	Great Basin	Southwest	North American Plains	Eastern U.S.	Diablo Range Area	Western Meso-America	Eastern Meso-America
1500	Hist. Eskimo		Dalles Late Cultures		Period	Regressive Period; Pueblo IV	Coal.; Plains Village	Miss. Period; Moorehead	Neomorphic; Points; Archaeo	Late Horizon; Aztec; Second Inter. Period; Chichimec	Late Post Classic; Early Post Classic
1000	Thule; Punuk	Thule; Late Woodland			S. Paiute; Puebloid Influences	Classic Period; Pueblo III; Pueblo II; Developed Period; B.M. III	Central; Late Woodland Period	Fairmount; Patrick	Southwest U.S. Farming; Eastern U.S. Pottery	Tula; Middle Horizon; Xolalpan; Tlamimilolpa	Terminal Classic; Late Classic; Middle Classic; Early Classic
A.D.	Ipiutak; Old Bering Sea	Shield Archaic	III		IV	Mog. I – B.M. II	Hopewellian	Woodland Period; Hopewell		First Inter. Period; Tzacualli	Proto-Classic
B.C.	Okvik; Norton	Dorset	Marpole		Period	Archaic; San Pedro	Archaic	Adena	Meso-Amer. Formative Influences	Monte Alban I; Early Santa Maria	Late Prec.; Chicanel; Mid. Prec.; Early Mamom
1000	Choris	Sarqaq	Locarno; II	Period of Regional Specialization	III				Morphic	Early Horizon; Early Ajalpan	Dili; Early Prec.; San Lorenzo; Bajio; Ocos; Barra
2000	Arctic Small-Tool Tradition	Independence; Maritime	Tucannon		Period		Archaic	Archaic; Savannah R.; Late Lamoka		Initial Period; Purron	Pre-Formative Period; Earliest Pottery (?)
3000	Plano Trad.; Archaic Trad.	Archaic				Chiricahua; Period	Period	Period	Points	Coxcatlán	Archaic Period
4000					II; Desert Archaic Tradition			(Late) Morrow Mt.		El Riego	Chantuto
5000	N. West Microblade Tradition		Congdon I								
6000			Cascade	Early Milling Stone	Period		Paleo Period	(Middle Arch.)			
7000			Indian Well						Paleo Morphic		Santa Marta
8000	Akmak		Windust; Lind Coulee	San Dieguito; Lake Mohave	I; Western Pluvial Lakes Tradition; Fluted Point Tradition	Sulphur Springs; Paleo-Indian Period	Paleo-Indian; Itama Complex; Llano Complex	(Early Arch.); Paleo-Indian Period	Points	Early Ajuereado	Paleo-Indian–Tlpe Finds (?)
10,000			Pasika (?)	Manix Lake (?)							
20,000	Crow Flats (?)									Tlapacoya 1	

Figures 15.1 and 2. A hemispheric projection of New World area chronologies: North and Middle America (Figure 15.1) and Lower Central and South America (Figure 15.2). Each area column presents highly synopsized or selected archaeological–chronological data. The B.C.–A.D. dates on the charts are based largely on radiocarbon dates and are the uncorrected renderings of these dates. The heavy horizontal lines that run through the charts, at 10,000 B.C.,

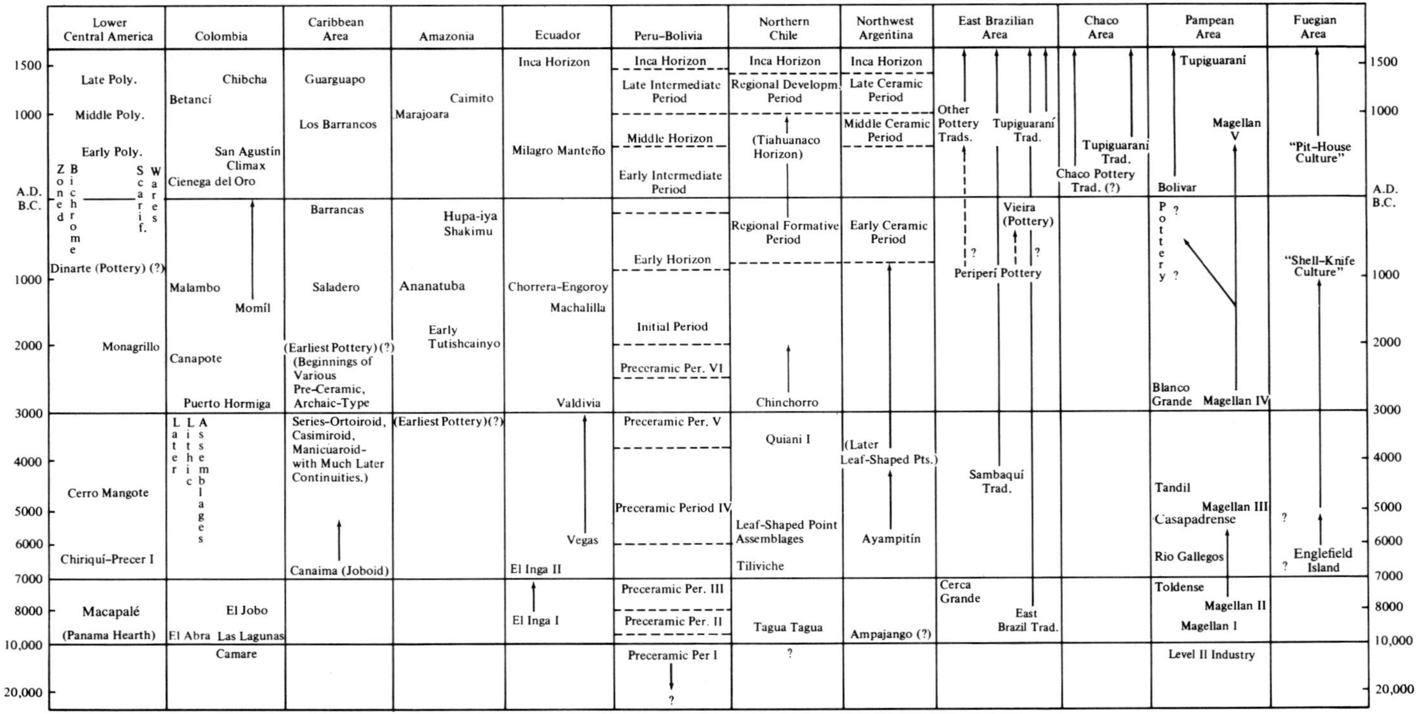

Date	Lower Central America	Colombia	Caribbean Area	Amazonia	Ecuador	Peru–Bolivia	Northern Chile	Northwest Argentina	East Brazilian Area	Chaco Area	Pampean Area	Fuegian Area
1500 1000 A.D.	Late Poly. Middle Poly. Early Poly. Zoned Bichrome Scarified Ware	Chibcha Betancí San Agustín Climax Cienega del Oro	Guarguapo Los Barrancos	Caimito Marajoara	Inca Horizon Milagro Manteño	Inca Horizon Late Intermediate Period Middle Horizon Early Intermediate Period	Inca Horizon Regional Developm. Period (Tiahuanaco Horizon)	Inca Horizon Late Ceramic Period Middle Ceramic Period	Other Pottery Trads. Tupiguaraní Trad.	Tupiguaraní Trad. Chaco Pottery Trad. (?)	Tupiguaraní Magellan V Bolivar	"Pit–House Culture"
B.C. 1000 2000 3000	Dinarte (Pottery) (?) Monagrillo	Malambo Momíl Canapote Puerto Hormiga	Barrancas Saladero (Earliest Pottery)(?) (Beginnings of Various Pre-Ceramic, Archaic-Type	Hupa-iya Shakimu Ananatuba Early Tutishcainyo	Chorrera–Engoroy Machalilla Valdivia	Early Horizon Initial Period Preceramic Per. VI	Regional Formative Period Chinchorro	Early Ceramic Period	? Vieira (Pottery) ? Periperí Pottery		Pottery ? Blanco Grande Magellan IV	"Shell–Knife Culture"
4000 5000 6000 7000	Cerro Mangote Chiriquí–Precer I	Later Lithic Assemblages	Series–Ortoiroid, Casimiroid, Manicuaroid- with Much Later Continuities.) Canaima (Joboid)	(Earliest Pottery)(?)	Vegas El Inga II	Preceramic Per. V Preceramic Period IV	Quiani I Leaf-Shaped Point Assemblages Tiliviche	(Later Leaf-Shaped Pts.) Ayampitín	Sambaquí Trad.		Tandil Magellan III Casapadrense Rio Gallegos	? Englefield Island ?
8000 10,000	Macapalé (Panama Hearth)	El Jobo El Abra Las Lagunas			El Inga I	Preceramic Per. III Preceramic Per. II	Tagua Tagua	Ampajango (?)	Cerca Grande East Brazil Trad.		Toldense Magellan II Magellan I	
20,000		Camare				Preceramic Per I ?	?				Level II Industry	

7000 B.C., 3000 B.C., and at the B.C.–A.D. division point, are for convenience in cross-column comparisons. No cultural periods, stages, or eras are intended. The purpose of the charts is to provide a rapid scan of absolute time scales and archaeological cultures in the Americas.

dating, which is "independent" of the actual phenomena and material that are studied by the archaeologist. Partially freed from his constant concern with chronology, the investigator could turn to problems of context, function, and process.

Taylor reviews the dendrochronological corrections of radiocarbon values. While radiocarbon years and tree-ring years are in essential agreement between A.D. 1 and 1000, they grow increasingly out of synchronization as one proceeds backward in time from A.D. 1, with dendrochronological time (presumably true sidereal time) exceeding that of radiocarbon time. Such differences have been measured back to about 5500 B.C. As the reader will have noted, some of the archaeologists writing for this volume have made observation of this correction; the majority, however, have not. In my comments I will make primary reference to radiocarbon years as these are translated into B.C.–A.D. dates. Corrected sidereal dates, when these have been given by the various authors, will be indicated secondarily or parenthetically. As a general comment, it is probably fair to say that most American archaeologists, while not rejecting the tree-ring and other corrections, are awaiting further clarification on exact scales of correction between radiocarbon and sidereal time.

Lastly, and in this context of dating, I think it should be said that all of the area chronology structures reviewed in this book have had their beginnings not in the context of physical and natural science dating-techniques but in what might be termed "archaeologically independent" dating procedures: stratigraphy, seriation, artifact cross-dating, ethnohistoric documentation, and native calendars. The first of these three are methods of relative dating, rather than of absolute time placement, and they have been used in all parts of the Americas. The fourth method, ethnohistoric documentation (both native and European), has provided absolute datings for the later centuries in most New World areas. The last dating procedure, that derived from native calendars, has had a more restricted application on the New World scene, being confined to the Mesoamerican area. While such a dating technique as radiocarbon has been of tremendous importance to American archaeological chronologies, it does not detract from this importance to emphasize that more traditional archaeological dating procedures still carry the burden of the area chronology structures.

ARCHAEOLOGICAL AREAS

Western Arctic and Sub-Arctic

These territories might be considered as a single culture area, as is done by Douglas Anderson (Chapter 2), or as the western portions of two culture areas (see Willey 1966: Chapter 7). Anderson deals with them in three subareal divisions: (*a*) the Arctic Coast; (*b*) the Interior Arctic and sub-Arctic; and (*c*) the Aleutians and Pacific Coast.

While there are some indications of man's presence in the area as early as 22,000–28,000 B.C., the first technological tradition that can be defined and chronologically placed with any assurance is one that Anderson has called the Paleo-Arctic, represented by the Akmak Complex at Onion Portage and, probably, by the Denali Complex at Mt. Hays. This tradition is radically different from that of the New World Paleo-Indian. It features core bifaces and bifacial knives but not lanceolate or fluted points. Dating is estimated at 9000–7500 B.C. Some scattered typical Paleo-Indian materials have been found in the Arctic, but these have not been dated satisfactorily, so that their presence in Alaska remains open to an interpretation of "back-drift" from midcontinental North America. Finally, with reference to Akmak, Denali, and a Paleo-Arctic industry, it should be pointed out that it would be premature to visualize such a uniform horizon for the area at this time. Discoveries that appear to be equally old, from Healy Lake, the Gallagher Site, and the Aleutian Anangula industry reveal quite different typologies. The "Early Man" situation in the far north remains perplexing.

Anderson notes Archaic-type projectile points in the Arctic Interior and sub-Arctic, and these may relate to Archaic cultures of the Eastern sub-Arctic. Their probable dating range in the west is estimated at 4500–2500 B.C. Although Anderson does not mention them, occasional lanceolate points of Plano or Cordilleran traditions also are found in the western interior and are probably this early or earlier. The principal tradition of the Western sub-Arctic, however, is the one that MacNeish has named the Northwest Microblade. It is a possible forerunner of the later Arctic Small Tool Tradition, and it is also probably ancestral to the Athapaskan Indian cultures of the Western sub-Arctic, although this developmental continuum remains to be demonstrated.

The Arctic Small Tool Tradition is dated at 3000–1000 B.C. Its origins lie either in Siberia or in the Northwest Microblade Tradition mentioned earlier. Arctic Small Tool Tradition cultures appear to be ancestral to the later, more typically Eskimoan cultures; however, this transition in the Western Arctic, which must have taken place between 2000 and 1000 B.C. is still shadowy. After 1000 B.C., the several regional cultures of the Eskimo–Aleut Tradition are reasonably well dated—both relatively and absolutely.

Eastern Arctic and Subarctic[1]

Like the Western Arctic and sub-Arctic, the eastern territory of Northern North America can be considered either as a single culture area or as the eastern portions of two culture areas. The earliest typically Arctic cultures

[1]Area not covered in this volume.

are those pertaining to the Arctic Small Tool Tradition. These are found across northern Canada and into Greenland, Labrador, and Newfoundland. The Independence Phase of Greenland is one of the earliest of the group, dating to 2500 B.C. The succeeding Sarqaq phases of the Melville Peninsula and Greenland are better documented and date to 1000 B.C. The Dorset culture is a later development of the Arctic Small Tool Tradition, arising on the mainland early in the first millennium B.C. Farther east and south, in Greenland and in Newfoundland, it dates somewhat later, lasting until around A.D. 500. Dorset culture was replaced by the more typically Eskimoan Thule culture at about A,D. 1000, and Thule shows a continuity into historic and modern Eskimo (see Jennings 1974: Chapter 8; Willey 1966: Chapter 7).

The dominant cultures of the Eastern sub-Arctic are variants of an Eastern North American Archaic Tradition. There was, however, an interplay between these Archaic Tradition cultures and those of the Arctic Small Tool–Eskimoan lineage. This interplay of alternating occupation and resource exploitation of the same territory has been examined in detail by W. W. Fitzhugh in a monograph (Fitzhugh 1972) on the Hamilton Inlet region of Eastern Labrador. The earliest occupation of the region is identified as a phase of the Maritime Archaic Tradition. This Maritime Archaic Tradition is known from Eastern Canada and Northern New England and is a reformulation and redefinition of a part of what D. S. Byers (1959) referrred to as the "Boreal Archaic." Its beginnings probably go back to 4500–3500 B.C. Forest cover and environmental changes following the climatic optimum probably led to the abandonment of Hamilton Inlet by the Maritime Archaic peoples, and from 800 to 200 B.C. the region was occupied by Dorset culture Eskimos. Another Archaic Tradition culture, this time an expression of the Shield Archaic, defined by J. V. Wright (1970), has a wide distribution in the Northern Canadian Plains, Central Quebec, New Brunswick, and Labrador; and its beginnings, perhaps in the Northern Plains, go back to the beginning of the first millennium B.C. if not earlier. Still later Hamilton Inlet occupations are those of Late Woodland Tradition cultures, dating from about A.D. 1000, and late Thule Eskimo cultures of ca. A.D. 1500.

Northwest Coast and Interior Plateau of Western North America[2]

These two culture areas have their original definitions in ethnography. Their archaeological pasts are somewhat different but related. Chronological research has proceeded on a regional basis in both areas, and, as yet, broad syntheses have been difficult to achieve.

The earliest occupations are known from the Interior Plateau country,

[2]Area not covered in this volume.

both from the Columbia Plateau–Snake River Plain in Washington and Oregon and from the Fraser Canyon in Southern British Columbia. In the former, F. C. Leonhardy and D. G. Rice (1970) outline a long sequence. They place the Paleo-Indian–related Lind Coulee culture at the bottom of this sequence (ca. 10,000–9,000 B.C.). This is followed by a Windust Phase, which they see as developing out of Lind Coulee. Windust has both lanceolate points and Archaic-type, short, broad-stemmed points, plus cobble tools. Their dating estimate is 10,000–7000 B.C., indicating a chronological overlap with Lind Coulee. Jennings (1974:182–188) believes this to be excessive, however, and suggests 8000–6000 B.C. Windust is followed by a Cascade Phase (6000–3000 B.C.) whose diagnostic trait is the bi-pointed, leaf-shaped Cascade point; and Cascade economy is seen as more riverine oriented than was that of Windust. The Tucannon Phase (3000–1 B.C.) has cruder flint chipping and mortars and pestles; the Harder Phase (A.D. 1–1500) is a pit-house complex.

At the Dalles Rapids of the Columbia River, on the very western edge of the Interior Plateau, there is an early cultural level that has been referred to variously as the Early Five Mile Rapids, or Indian Well, Phase. It has typological similarities to Windust and to Cascade and has been dated within the rather broad limits of 9000–5000 B.C., with a date toward the latter half of this range as being the more probable. The Dalles Congdon phases (I–III) follow chronologically in the approximately 5000 B.C.–A.D. 500 span. Dalles later cultures take on from here and extend upward in time to A.D. 1800 (see Willey 1966:397–402).

In the British Columbian Fraser River Canyon, C. E. Borden (1968) has defined a Pasika Phase, which he dates between 10,500 and 9000 B.C. on the basis of geological terrace associations. The Pasika Phase industry is solely that of crude pebble tools (choppers, scrapers, etc.), without bifacial flaking or points. Such pebble or cobble tools are known from the Windust Phase and from Early Five Mile Rapids; however, in both of those contexts they are associated with more advanced flint chipped stone implements, including leaf-shaped points or bipoints. In my opinion, the dating of Pasika remains moot, with a somewhat later time position a possibility. Pasika is succeeded by the Fraser Canyon Milliken Phase. Milliken has bifacial blades and leaf-shaped points. It is dated by radiocarbon at 7500 to 6000 B.C., and Borden relates it to Early Five Mile Rapids. The Milliken Phase economy is notably that of salmon fishing, as is that of Early Five Mile Rapids. The period of the succeeding Fraser Canyon Mazama Phase (6000–4500 B.C.) was marked by a shift toward a drier climate. After a one-thousand-year gap, Borden's Fraser Canyon sequence continues with the Eayem Phase (3500–1500 B.C.), with stemmed points and ground stone artifacts, including the beginnings of the ground slate industry that was to figure more prominently later in both Plateau and Northwest Coast cultures. The Baldwin Phase (1000–350 B.C.) saw a cool, humid climate again, and its artifact inventories emphasize ground stone implements, including mortars and pestles—as in the Columbia Plateau Tucannon Phase. The Fraser Canyon Skamel Phase (350 B.C.–A.D. 200) is attributed to new peoples moving into the region, bringing with them the pit-house trait (see the Columbia Plateau Harder Phase). An Emery Phase (A.D. 200–1200) is characterized by a fusion of Baldwin and Skamel traits with those identified as coastal Marpole derived. A terminal Esilao Phase (A.D. 1200–1808) carries the Fraser Canyon sequence on into the Historic Period.

There are also a number of Northwest Coast sequences, but of these Borden's (1968) for the Fraser River Delta appears to be the most complete. The earliest phase, Locarno Beach, dating only to the first millennium B.C., is much later than any of the Interior Plateau early cultures. Locarno was sea adapted, with toggle harpoons used in the taking of sea mammals and fish, and it has a well-developed slate industry. It partially overlaps with, and is succeeded by, the Marpole Phase, the best known of the Northwest Coast archaeological cultures. Marpole is dated 450 B.C.–A.D. 200. Ground stone and antler woodworking tools are abundant. Villages were large, and there are indications of differential access to wealth and social stratification. The economy was coastal and riverine, presumably with the principal subsistence coming from salmon. In the carved stone sculptures, one sees the beginnings of the great Northwest Coast art style that later was to flourish in woodcarving. Cross-ties are noted with the Baldwin and Skamel cultures of the interior. A Whalen II Phase (A.D. 350–750) continues the tradition, as does a later Stselax Phase (A.D. 1200–1808). The nineteenth century Northwest Coast ethnographically documented cultures follow from this point.

As can be seen from this selective review, the Interior Plateau and Northwest Coast chronologies are still very approximate in absolute dating. Generalizations are difficult. The early cultures of the interior appear to me to be regional adaptations of Paleo-Indian patterns. These adaptations began early and in some places settled into riverine niches. The place of the cobble-tool industry in this early period is still open to question; it might represent a very early occupation of the Plateau, or it might be merely a technological subtradition within the Plateau cultures of the 9000–5000 B.C. period. After 5000 B.C., the Plateau cultures take on a more Archaic-stage cast, with the appearance of new projectile point forms. These may have come in from Desert–Archaic sources in the adjoining Great Basin to the south. The ground slate industry was added to the Plateau cultures after 3500 B.C. Its origins have frequently been cited as northern and boreal, although this remains open to question. After 1000 B.C., the coastal cultures come into the picture; and these, with their own unique developments, interacted with later Plateau cultures. The Northwest Coast way of life, observed in later ethnographic accounts, had taken shape in the coastal regions by the beginning of the Christian era.

The Eastern United States

Early archaeological research in the Eastern United States involved some concern for chronology, although in the general absence of stratigraphic and seriational studies this concern did not move beyond speculation until the 1930s. The great volume of systematic excavation under the federal relief programs of that decade resulted in the first attempts at areawide relative chronologies (which were also culture stage schemes) in the 1940s (Ford and Willey 1941; Griffin 1946). The assignment of absolute dates to these pioneer chronologies was by guess, wlth some minor assists from historic horizon information. In Chapter 3, J. B. Griffin refers to one of the last of the pure guess-dated charts (Phillips, Ford, and Griffin 1951). Since then, ^{14}C determinations have supplemented such guess reckoning. In general, the radiocarbon dates have tended to lengthen Eastern United States chronologies. (Compare the charts in Ford and Willey 1941, with Griffin's present one.) With reference to radiocarbon dates, however, Griffin's remarks bear repeating:

> These problems [concerning radiocarbon dates] and others lead me to believe that at present I am not in a position to identify the best radiocarbon ages of specific cultural events in the East within a narrow time range of 50 years, or in many cases of much longer periods of time. I have normally avoided horizontal lines on chronology charts and have done so with this presentation. If the presentation lacks precision, it does not present a false security [p. 55, this volume].

With but very few exceptions—notably certain dendrochronologically dated cultures in the Southwestern United States and some Classic Maya calendrically dated sites and monuments—this statement holds, with even greater force, for all other American areas.

Griffin's present chronology chart has 12 subareal columns, the Eastern United States, from the Northeast to Florida and the Mississippi Valley to the Atlantic. The sides of the chart are marked off by millennia, and selected culture phases are given chronological placement with the aid of radiocarbon dates, cross-comparisons, and some guessing. No major period or stage lines are indicated on the chart; however, such a scheme is employed in the text presentation.

A Paleo-Indian Period is set at pre–8000 B.C., with dated fluted point findings in the 10,500–8000 B.C. range. Griffin does not accept the "pre–projectile point horizon" or stage for the East.

An Archaic Period falls between 8000 and 1000 B.C. Its earlier subdivision (8000–6000 B.C.) is a time of transition from Paleo-Indian to Archaic-type projectile points; and it also has the stage characteristics of grinding slabs, hammers, and other similar rough tools, although it is without finely ground or polished stone implements. The 6000–4000 B.C. range is marked by the latter (grooved axes, pendants, bannerstones, etc.). The Late Archaic

(4000–1000 B.C.) is the era of adaptation to regional niches, especially those of the rivers and coasts. Fiber-tempered pottery appears as early as 2500 B.C. in South Carolina, according to present radiocarbon readings. Griffin is disinclined to see this as a South American introduction, as some archaeologists have argued. He is also of the opinion that later Woodland pottery (ca. 1500–500 B.C.) is a local development, not an Asiatic transfer.

A Woodland Period is placed after 1000 B.C. No definite terminal date is given for the entire East; however, from his subsequent discussions it is obvious that, from about A.D. 700 on, the rise of agricultural societies and of the Mississippian Tradition describe another important change. There are dates on burial mounds in Michigan that go back to the sixth century B.C., and the earthwork constructions of the Poverty Point Phase of Louisiana have radiocarbon dates that span 1200–400 B.C. Griffin has some doubts, however, that the latter are this early. On his chart, Poverty Point is put at a little after 1000 B.C. The Adena culture is set at 500–100 B.C., overlapping with the beginnings of Hopewellian culture (ca. 200 B.C.–A.D. 400). Gourds, squash, and sunflowers were all cultivated by 1000 B.C. or a little later. Of these, the squash and probably the gourd were introduced to the Eastern United States from areas to the south. Maize makes an appearance at around the beginning of the Christian era, being found in Hopewellian contexts, although it appears to have been a minor economic item at that time.

A Mississippian and Agricultural Period succeeds the Woodland (although Woodland Tradition cultures persist in many places, in the northern and eastern regions of the area, while Mississippian-type cultures are thriving). In the Mississippi Valley, from Vicksburg to St. Louis, the Woodland-to-Mississippian transition was gradual. Details of the Cahokia sequence put a late Woodland phase, the Patrick, as lasting from A.D. 600–800; the 800–900 century sees the first shifts to Mississippian patterns; and the change is solidified in the subsequent Fairmount Phase at A.D. 900–1050. A true agricultural economy, the temple mound-and-plaza site arrangement, ceramic elaborations, and indications of social class distinctions are features of the new Mississippian pattern. This pattern prevailed through much of the East until Historic times.

The Diablo Range Area

The Diablo Range area is the much needed name which E. B. Jelks (Chapter 4) has given to that culture area which lies between the North American Southwest, the Plains, the Eastern United States, and Mesoamerica (see Driver 1961: Map 2, "Northeast Mexico"; Willey 1966: 329–337, "Northeast Mexico–Texas"). It is rugged country, where the aboriginal peoples, for the most part, never converted to farming or the more "advanced" modes of existence.

As in the Great Basin, projectile points are the principal media of archaeological organization. Jelks conceives of three major stylistic stages in points: (*a*) a Paleomorphic, with fluted and other lanceolate points; (*b*) an Archaeomorphic, which, as the name suggests, refers to the stemmed and cornered points of the Archaic and Desert Archaic stages and traditions of other American areas; and (*c*) a Neomorphic, which pertains to small, arrow-type points. The types and series in each of these stylistic stages carry the burden of relative chronology, a chronology that can be related to many individual site stratigraphies and to not a few radiocarbon dates. Absolute dating ranges vary, for we are dealing with stages not periods. In general, Paleomorphic points date before 7000 or 6000 B.C., going back, perhaps, to 10,000 B.C. The Archaeomorphic points fall after 7000–6000 B.C. and continue as late, in some instances, as A.D. 1500. Neomorphic points overlap with them and can be bracketed between A.D. 500 and the nineteenth century.

Research and chronology building has proceeded within seven subareal frameworks: (*a*) Central Texas, (*b*) the Trans-Pecos, (*c*) Coahuila–Chihuahua, (*d*) Nuevo Leon; (*e*) Tamaulipas, (*f*) Lower Rio Grande, and (*g*) Gulf Coast. The details of these chronologies are given in Jelks's several chronology charts. In the Trans-Pecos, farming was assimilated from Southwestern contacts in the latter part of the Neomorphic stage, after A.D. 1000. In interior Tamaulipas, there is evidence of incipient cultivation on the Archaeomorphic level, with pottery and farming established after 500 B.C., the date by which these societies had become a part of the Mesoamerican culture sphere on culture area. At the same time, though, neighboring groups just a little farther north in Tamaulipas remained nonagricultural until historic times. In the other subareas, farming was nonexistent or practiced only in very late times. Pottery, however, made its appearance as early as A.D. 500 in the eastern regions of the Gulf Coast and a few centuries after that in the coastal zones to the west and south. The inspiration for this pottery was, for the more easterly and northerly regions, the Eastern United States; for the more westerly and southerly regions, it was Mesoamerica.

The North American Plains

Plains archaeology received its great impetus when W. D. Strong (1935) demonstrated that the ancestors of the Historic Period horse nomads were, in many instances, settled village farmers. He and W. R. Wedel presented the beginnings of a chronological framework for the area, which the latter has revised at various times. D. J. Lehmer, W. W. Caldwell, and others have continued research in the area, paying considerable attention to the development of culture classification systems that would be more flexible than the Midwestern Taxonomic System which Strong and Wedel had attempted to combine with their direct-historical and chronological approach.

Caldwell and D. R. Henning, in the present volume (Chapter 5), are much concerned with culture classificatory problems, and in the course of this they synthesize a wealth of new data. They focus attention on a Central Plains subarea but also manage to draw in substantial cultural definitional and chronological material from surrounding territories. They offer no chronological chart, but from their discussions we may piece one together as follows:

A Paleo-Indian Period (ca. 9500–5000 B.C.) is borrowed from C. V. Haynes's "Late Paleo-Indian Period" as projected for the New World as a whole. Caldwell and Henning see no clearly defined Plains Technological Tradition for Haynes' "Early" or "Middle Paleo-Indian Periods" (crude lithic industries, pre–projectile point stages, etc.) although some early evidences of man in Oklahoma may date to about 18,000 B.C. Their Late Paleo-Indian Period is defined by the presence of the earlier Llano Complex (of the Clovis points) and the later Itama Series of complexes. The term and concept "Itama" is taken from Henry Irwin's Hell Gap, Wyoming sequence work. Itama subsumes the Plainview, Folsom, Midland, Agate Basin, Hell Gap, and Cody complexes, in that chronological order. A complication arises in that these early hunting traditions are not the only cultural traditions to make an appearance in this Paleo-Indian Period. Cultures of the Plains Archaic Tradition were also extant at that time.

The Archaic Period, however, is fully defined by the Plains Archaic Tradition, and this period is set at ca. 5000 B.C. to the beginning of the Christian era. Some of the better-known cultural units of this period are the Logan Creek, Nebo Hill, and Edwards Plateau of the Southern Plains.

A Woodland Period, characterized by a Woodland cultural tradition can be given the approximate dates of A.D. 1–900. Both dating boundaries are somewhat flexible. Woodland-like traits have their inception later than this in some regions; and the Plains Village pattern, which is definitive of the succeeding period, may begin slightly earlier in some places. The earlier part of the Woodland Period of the Plains is the time of Hopewellian sites and traits. The later part of the period has cultures that relate to Late Woodland manifestations of the Eastern United States. Some of these Woodland cultures of the Plains, particularly those in the north, last later than A.D. 900.

A Plains Village pattern, as Lehmer has designated it, characterizes the latest major period of the Plains chronology. This pattern can be separated into three traditions. The earliest in inception is the Central Plains Tradition, which features such cultures, or culture phases, as the Nebraska, the Upper Republican, and the Smoky Hill. It marks the establishment of farming and settled life in the eastern sectors of the Plains, and it climaxed at ca. A.D. 1000–1300. The Middle Missouri Tradition has beginnings almost as early but climaxes later, and its Terminal phases persist until about A.D. 1675. The Coalescent Tradition starts late in the thirteenth century and continues well into post-Contact times (eighteenth century).

The Great Basin

Projectile point types and type series are the substance of the Great Basin spatial–temporal frameworks. R. F. Heizer and T. R. Hester (Chapter 6) describe such point series and their space–time values, and construct a four-period chronology from these data. The chronology is of a stage type, similar to Meighan's for California.

Period I (10,000 B.C., or earlier, to 5000 B.C.) corresponds, approximately, to Meighan's Early Hunting Stage (his second stage) in that it is an early projectile point period or stage. Heizer and Hester appear to give little credence to the "pre–projectile point" stage, or at least they do not see it as pertinent to the Great Basin. According to them, their Period I was the time of the two major cultural traditions, the Fluted Point and the Western Pluvial Lakes, and the beginning of a third major tradition, the Desert Archaic. Fluted points are widely known in the Basin, but they are anchored by only a single early date, 11,250 B.C., in the lowest stratum of Fort Rock Cave in southwestern Oregon. This is, however, if accepted, the earliest fluted point date in North America. There are other, possibly related, projectile point discoveries—Cougar Mountain Cave 2 (10,000 B.C.), Tule Springs (11,000 B.C.), and Wilson Butte Cave (12,550–13,050 B.C.)—although, if these are subsumed in the same tradition, the definition of such a tradition would have to be broadened somewhat beyond the fluted point trait. The other early tradition for Period I, the Western Pluvial Lakes, is based on the San Dieguito and Lake Mohave complexes of the Southern California Desert, and it is postulated on a desert adaptation to an earlier lacustrine environment. The dating is 9000–6000 B.C., which is backed by various radiocarbon dates. Finally, the Desert Archaic Tradition has its beginnings in Period I, with such assemblages as those of Danger Cave I and II, Hogup Cave, Leonard Rockshelter, and others. Pertinent radiocarbon dates span a range of ca. 9500–5000 B.C.

Period II (5000 to 2000 B.C.) is the period of the Altithermal climatic era. Dates tend to cluster at the beginning and end of this time span; however, the authors are explicit in saying that they do not venture an environmental explanation for the hiatus. The period is dominated by Desert Archaic cultures with their various specialized projectile point forms.

Period III (2000 to 1 B.C.) corresponds, presumably, to the onset of Medithermal climates. A new, or returned, emphasis on lacustrine resources is noted. It has been the practice to conceive of the cultures of this period within the overall framework of the Desert Archaic Tradition; however, some divergence in lifeways is implied.

Period IV (A.D. 1 to the historic present) sees the continuation of the typical Desert Archaic Tradition, together with the lacustrine variant, depending upon the regions considered. It is during this period that Puebloan architecture, ceramics, and farming appear in southern Nevada (A.D. 500–1140) and in the Fremont culture of western Utah (A.D. 700–1000). The Southern Paiute probably entered southern Nevada after A.D. 1000.

The Southwest

Ceramic stratigraphy, seriational studies, systematic classification, and absolute dating (by means of dendrochronology) all enabled the archaeology of the Southwestern United States to take an early lead in the development of finely scaled chronologies. Although other American areas are now catching up, the corpus of well-organized Southwestern data is still impressive. Since 1949 the area has benefited from the radiocarbon method of dating.

Southwestern area chronological schemes began with the Pecos Classification of 1927. This was a period–stage arrangement primarily applicable to the Colorado Plateau–Pueblo subarea. I refer to it by the intentionally ambiguous term *period–stage* because it was never quite clear, to its formulators or its users, whether absolute time or the presence of certain cultural traits were to be the essential criteria of culture unit classification in the scheme. This, of course, is a well-known archaeological dilemma, and it was brought home to Americanists in the Southwest via the impact of tree-ring dates. Arthur Rohn reviews this and other similar classifications, as well as the one of McGregor's that attempts absolute time lines rather than developmental stage criteria. None has proven entirely satisfactory, although the question might be raised as to just how much the archaeologist should expect of such a chronological classification. Rohn also discusses the culture unit classification schemes that were early employed in the Southwest by H. S. Gladwin and H. S. Colton. The phase, or minimal classificatory unit, is still widely used, although the "genetic" implications of these phase classifications have been dropped. Most current research operates within a framework of a subarea chronology, calibrated to an absolute time scale in which phases are placed chronologically and geographically but without prejudice as to their ancestry or their descendants.

Rohn's time chart is so constructed (see Chapter 7). There are the five conventional subarea columns: (*a*) the Colorado Plateau–Pueblo (or Anasazi), (*b*) the Central Arizona–New Mexico–Mogollon, (*c*) the Southern Arizona–Hohokam, (*d*) the Colorado River–"Patayan," and (*e*) the Northern Chihuahua–Casas Grandes. No broad, areawide stages or periods are indicated on the chart; each column is chronologically segmented in terms of its own history of development. While I appreciate the validity of this, there is still some need, in looking at archaeological area chronologies in a hemispheric context, for generalization. I will suggest such a summary of the Rohn chart, designating six major periods. This has certain developmental implications, and I realize that cultural development and absolute chronology are not fully coordinate throughout all of the subareas. Nor do I hold any brief for the names which I will apply to these periods. They are ones in general use in North American archaeology or that have been used in previous Southwestern area classifications, although with not quite the same definitions I am giving to them here.

1. A Paleo-Indian Period dates to before 8000 B.C. The period, as defined, pertains to the remains of that cultural and technological tradition (the Llano Complex, fluted points, etc.).
2. An Archaic Period is set at 8000 to 300 B.C. and is characterized by variants of the North American Desert Archaic Tradition.
3. A Developmental Period pertains to the initiation of farming life and ceramics in the area. The date of 300 B.C. for its inception is Rohn's estimated beginning of the Pioneer Phase of the Hohokam cultural continuum and the first Hohokam pottery. This "floor" for the Developmental Period is, of course, a sloping horizon, with comparable developments in the other subareas being anywhere from one to several centuries later. I would expect, however, that the "Viejo Period," in the Northern Chihuahua column, will prove to be not the earliest farming–pottery-making phase in that part of the Southwest.
4. A Classic Period is placed at A.D. 900 to 1300. This was the period of the maximization of Anasazi, Mogollon, Hohokam, and, probably, the other subarea cultures. The largest towns were maintained, the most impressive architecture constructed, the greatest peak of the arts enjoyed.
5. A Regressive Period, from A.D. 1300 to 1540, is the old Pueblo IV interval of the Pecos Classification. While there were still some large town concentrations in several regions, such as the Rio Grande, there was a general territorial shrinkage of Southwestern cultures and a general cultural retrenchment.
6. The Historic Period is from A.D. 1540 to the present.

California

C. W. Meighan's spatial–temporal organization of California archaeology (Chapter 8) is supported by various site stratigraphies and general typological comparisons, as well as being reinforced by radiocarbon dates. Periodization remains very gross, a circumstance that is due, at least in part, to the gradualness of culture change in the area.

The space–time structure has three key subareas and four major chronological divisions. The subareas are: (*a*) Central California; (*b*) South Coastal California; and (*c*) the Southern California Desert. The additional subareas of the Colorado River drainage and Northwest California also come into the discussions; but these two subareas blend, respectively, into the major culture areas of the Southwest and the Northwest Coast. Meighan's four chronological divisions are stages, rather than strict periods, as their time boundaries are rather loosely defined and their criteria are evolutionary or developmental.

The Pre–Projectile Point Stage, as yet unvalidated, is hypothesized to pertain to those millennia prior to 10,000 B.C. Like its counterpart in other American areas, it is thought to be characterized by rough lithic industries which include some bifacial tools. A variety of evidence concerning such a stage is examined. While all of it is open to some doubt, the Manix Lake and Baker site assemblages may date to before 10,000 B.C. Elsewhere, the collagen dating of human skeletons is suggestive—but no more—of very early habitation in the area.

The Early Hunting Stage, with such complexes as San Dieguito and Lake Mohave, is dated at 10,000–6500 B.C. The presence of lanceolate projectile points, including fluted types in some assemblages, suggests a general contemporaneity and affiliation with classic Paleo-Indian complexes farther to the east. This, a variety of leaf-shaped point forms, and the absence of plant food preparation tools appear to justify the "Early Hunting" terminology.

The Early Milling Stone Stage, dating to after 6500 B.C. and lasting as late as 3000–1500 B.C., is known from such complexes as Oak Grove, Topanga, and La Jolla. It has a "Desert Culture" appearance; the emphasis was on seed and plant foods.

The Regional Specialization Stage carries the California prehistoric record on into historic times. As the name implies, its cultures display diversification and regional adaptation to various ecological niches: the maritime adaptation of the Southern California Coast, or the various land hunters and food collectors of the Central California valleys. In the Colorado River Valley, farming was adopted from Southwestern area cultures; in Northwestern California the adaptation resembles that of the Northwest Coast area.

Western Mesoamerica before A.D. 900

Western Mesoamerica, as Paul Tolstoy treats it (Chapter 9), is one-half or two-thirds of the conventional Mesoamerican culture area. It is not just that portion comprising West and Northwest Mexico that some archaeologists increasingly have come to believe may be a separate culture area sphere. It includes these, but it also takes in the Central Highlands, Oaxaca, and the Gulf Coast. Tolstoy and Lowe divide the Gulf Coastal lowlands somewhere in Olmec country, each making some references to Southern Veracruz–Tabasco sequences.

Tolstoy does not recount the history of the development of archaeological sequences; however, this history is well known in a general way. While very important archaeological and ethnohistorical research was done in Mexico in the nineteenth century, sequence building did not really begin until Manuel Gamio's (1913) excavations in the Valley of Mexico on the eve of World War I. These were followed in the late 1920s by G. C. Vaillant's program of stratigraphic excavation, with the results made known in the 1930s (1930, 1931, 1935). Alfonso Caso (1938) established the outlines of the Monte Albán sequence in Oaxaca at about the same time. From then on work has progressed at a steadily increasing rate throughout the country. As Tolstoy sums it up, the master sequence of the Valley of Mexico is supported by numerous examples of stratigraphy and a great many radiocarbon dates. The Tehuacan (MacNeish, Peterson, and Flannery 1970) chronological column is another well-documented datum, as is the sequence from the Valley of Oaxaca. To this I think we could add the sequence of early culture phases from the Olmec lowlands (M. D. Coe 1970). Elsewhere, as Tolstoy says, sequences suffer from deficiencies in radiocarbon support, incompleteness, and vague phase or culture unit definitions.

As the theme is chronology, Tolstoy makes a fitting effort to be as "chronological" as possible and to eschew stage schemes with their implications of set patterns of cultural evolution. He uses an America-wide periodization of mine (Willey 1966: 473–475, 1971:505–509) for the preceramic cultures. This needs little further comment other than to note that although the data are not organized in a frame of "pre–projectile point," "Paleo-Indian," and "Archaic" stages they may be readily translated into these terms.

The ceramic cultures are marked off in a different set of periods than the ones conventionally used in Mesoamerica. This follows on the recommendations of a recent archaeological conference on chronology and terminology for the Valley of Mexico, which, in turn, were based upon the approach that Rowe (1960) instigated in Peru. The periods are defined in terms of absolute time. A master sequence is selected (in this case the Valley of Mexico sequence), and other subareal and regional sequences are then coordinated with this master sequence by radiocarbon dates and by the cross-matching of culture content. The Mesoamerican periods so devised are as follows. (The dates cited are given in radiocarbon time.)

An Initial Period (2400–1400 B.C.) begins with the first appearance of pottery. In this case an adjustment had to be made to accommodate the fact that the earliest Mesoamerican pottery now known comes from the Tehuacan sequence and the Guerrero Coast rather than from the Valley of Mexico sequence. The period continues to the first appearances of Olmec stylistic influences in the master sequence. The Initial Period thus corresponds, approximately, to the Early Preclassic (or Early Formative) Period of the older chronologies, although most Mesoamericanists have usually retained the earlier Olmec centuries within the Early Preclassic (see Lowe, Chapter 2, this volume).

The Early Horizon Period (1400–950 B.C.) is one of strong Olmec influence in the Valley of Mexico sequence, as well as elsewhere in Mesoamerica. It is, in effect, the main Olmec Horizon.

The First Intermediate Period (950 B.C.–A.D. 165) is the period between this Olmec Horizon and the horizon of Teotihuacan. It corresponds, roughly, to the Middle and Late Preclassic periods of the conventional chronologies. For convenience in cross-dating, Tolstoy segments it into several subperiods.

The Middle Horizon (A.D. 165–700), or the Teotihuacan Horizon, is the period of Teotihuacan dominance and influence in the Valley of Mexico. It begins with the Tlamimilolpa Phase, or the inception of what was once called Teotihuacan III, and closes with the fall and destruction of the city.

The Second Intermediate Period (A.D. 700–1320) is the time between the fall of Teotihuacan and the founding of Tenochtitlan. Tolstoy, in his chapter, is concerned with only the first two centuries of this period, those that span between the end of the Teotihuacan Horizon and the rise of Tula. In this connection, it is of interest that the conference group who proposed this new chronology did not establish a Tula–Toltec Horizon (Tolstoy, personal communication, June 1974).

The Late Horizon (A.D. 1320–1521) is the Aztec Horizon and Empire.

Tolstoy has translated radiocarbon time into sidereal time, following the computations of Suess, although this translation has not been pushed further back than 3000–4000 B.C. For the earlier ceramic periods, the sidereal dates are set as much as 600 years earlier. Thus, the Initial Period radiocarbon dates of 2400–1400 B.C. become the sidereal dates of 3000–1700 B.C. The differential grows progressively less to about the beginning of the Christian era, where it disappears.

Tolstoy justifies his "precision" dating of periods (e.g., 950 B.C.–A.D. 165) by arguing that the false secruity that it might give is more than offset by the conscientious attempt to cross-date regional sequences in accordance with such a time scale, rather than to make the traditional one-to-one phase matchings. While all archaeologists must agree with him about the inadequacy of one-to-one phase correlations, I am, nevertheless, reminded of Griffin's comment about his inability to identify cultural events within time spans of less than 50 years, or even more, within the framework of the archaeological chronologies of the Eastern United States. Although, in some places, Mesoamerican sequences are more complete and better dated than those of Eastern North America, fine date shading of the kind Tolstoy is attempting here is really still largely beyond our power.

This leads to a more general observation about the "new chronology" that has been proposed for Mesoamerica. The separation of absolute time from culture content and culture development is crucial to archaeology. Yet I wonder if the attempt, with its inevitable attendant confusion, is worth the effort at this present point in the course of Mesoamerican archaeology.

Rowe's Peruvian scheme is greatly expedited by the three great horizontal phenomena of that area (the Chavín, the Tiahuanaco–Huari, and the Inca). These are, for the most part, areawide. This is not the case, at least to the same degree, with Olmec, Teotihuacan, and Aztec phenomena in Mesoamerica. Also, Rowe introduced his scheme to Peruvian archaeology when the then current stage schemes (of which there were several) were new and not firmly embedded in the literature. In contrast, the Preclassic–Classic–Postclassic chronology of Mesoamerica is almost universal to the literature. For most researchers, its original evolutionary connotations have been lost and it has become a chronology-defined scheme. With the continuing and increased flow of radiocarbon dates—as well as the potential of other absolute dating methods now in the experimental stage—I wonder if it would not be more practical to go on with the old chronological–terminological structure until chronological scales from all parts of the area can be calibrated in absolute centuries and millennia. These absolute scales could then be employed in conjunction with a variety of developmental–processual schemes as these would pertain to the problems or hypotheses to be examined.

Tolstoy's review of culture complexes and sequences, although necessarily telescoped, is an involved one, a testimony to the very great amount of information that went into his digest. The preceramic evidence involves some of the earliest—and best—claims for very early man in America. The rough stone industries of El Horno and later assemblages in the Valsequillo deposits, as well as Tlapacoya 1, all probably date back before 10,000 B.C. The lanceolate projectile point complexes, of a late Paleo-Indian typology, including Iztapan, Late Ajuereado, and Lerma, come after these. They are followed by the well-known upland cave finds of the hunting–collecting, Archaic-like, and incipient cultivating cultures; and these last, in the third millennium B.C., are coeval with the more recently discovered shellmound complexes of Guerrero, Nayarit, and Veracruz.

For the ceramic levels, the Central Highland master sequence is presented in some detail, with its several new subdivisions of the Early Horizon and the First Intermediate Period. Other sequence columns are then aligned with it. A close study of Tolstoy's complicated charts is recommended. Here, it is possible to call attention to only a few things. One of these is the time of the first appearances of Olmec traits. In the Central Highland master sequence they appear as early as 1400 B.C. On the Gulf Coast, the generally accepted heartland for the style, they are probably almost as early, and Tolstoy believes they date at about the same time in Guerrero. Where did the style originate? I think the question is still open, although there can be no doubt that the first great Olmec ceremonial centers, with monumental art and architecture, were in the Gulf lowlands. Another matter of interest is the Capacha Complex of Colima. A radiocarbon date for it indicates an Early Horizon 1 (1400–1150 B.C.) time position. Capacha ceramics relate to those of the Early Horizon Tlatilco style of the Valley of Mexico, but they may be an extraneous western element injected into the Olmec Tradition. The similarity of Capacha vessel forms to those of Peru may be clues to quite different origins for early West Mexican ceramic cultures than for those of the cultures of Southern and Eastern Mesoamerica. West Mexico, however, is still poorly known. No continuous sequence there can be carried back in time to the Capacha. Also, as has long been recognized, West and Northwest Mexico appear quite different from the rest of Mesoamerica prior to the Teotihuacan Horizon.

Western Mesoamerica after A.D. 900

Chronology in Western Mesoamerica from A.D. 900 to the Spanish Conquest of 1521–1540 is by "dirt" archaeological sequences and native historical traditions. A major problem facing scholars is a reconciliation or concordance between the two. Many attempts have been made in this direction, but, by common consent of the experts involved, there has been no fully satisfactory exegesis. H. B. Nicholson reviews this problem in Chapter 10 of this volume, pointing to the many complexities that beset any effort to coordinate ceramic, artifact, and architectural phases with the political and dynastic histories of the peoples involved. Such histories or record keeping were an important feature of Precolumbian Mesoamerican societies. They were maintained through native writing, calendrical systems, and oral traditions. At the Spanish Conquest, we have only the uppermost branches of these Mesoamerican historiographic trees.

Nicholson is primarily concerned with the histories of Central Mexico, those that pertain to the Aztec and Mixtec dynasties, their contemporaries, and their immediate predecessors. He makes a systematic survey of the documentary materials by region, examining in a critical fashion such records as the *Anales of Cuauhtitlan*, the *Anales of Tlaltelolco*, and many others. What do we know of their origins? How valid are their datings as these are carried in the native year counts? To what archaeological landmarks, as these are known in the material record, might the recorded migrations, wars, and kingly accessions pertain? Nicholson details the difficulties of an archaeological–documentary concordance as a prelude to this critical survey and as a concluding discussion of it. Among these are the disagreements on Mexican–Christian calendrical correlations and, even more troublesome, the high possibility that different year counts were maintained by the several different nations involved. There is also tremendous confusion and contradiction among the sources as these deal with what appear to be the same events. And, as might be expected, the historian–archaeologist's task has not been made easier by the strong inclination on the part of many of the pre-Conquest and Conquest period native historians to "rewrite" histories to portray their particular side in the most favorable light.

Nevertheless, this historical–traditional material is a part of archaeology, an essential dimension to the story if we are to make the most of the available evidence for reconstructing this particular past. In appraising its value, Nicholson makes the following observations (Chapter 10, Table 10.2). As might be anticipated, the traditional accounts are more accurate the closer one comes to the time horizon of the Spanish Conquest. Prior to this, he sees a "watershed" of documentary validity at 1370–1371, the date of the conquest of Tenanyocan and the establishment of the city of Azcapotzalco's supremacy in the western part of the Basin of Mexico. This conquest cleared the way for the expansion of the Tepanec Empire and closed the Chichimec Interregnum. After this time, and until the Spanish Conquest, native sources are reasonably valid. Before 1370, to the founding of Tula, which Nicholson sets as somewhere between 800–1000, there is a considerable falling off in reliability; and for the still earlier time ranges the possibility of accuracy is slight.

That Nicholson did not carry out a standard charting of archaeological phases on the time scale makes his paper less congruent with Tolstoy's than it might have been, but this lack of congruence is mitigated by the fact that the relatively short time span of the Postclassic (A.D. 900–1540) is well known archaeologically in Central Mexico. The problems here, as Nicholson has made clear, have been the relationship of the native historical documents to the "dirt archaeological" framework, and Nicholson's scholarly resumé of these questions is of considerable benefit to Mesoamericanists whose orientation has been that of artifact archaeology.

In order to relate the period 900–1540 in Western Mesoamerica to the more usual kind of time charting, I offer the following observations.

The period 900–1540 is generally referred to as the Postclassic. Tolstoy, of course, used another terminology and chronological breakdown, with his Second Intermediate Period lasting from 700 to 1320 and his Late (or Aztec) Horizon from 1320 to 1521. In the more conventional periodization, the 900–1540 span is usually divided into an Early Postclassic, from 900 to 1200, and a Late Postclassic from 1200 to 1540 (see Porter Weaver 1972: Chart 3). The Early Postclassic is the era of Toltec influence, with the terminal date as the fall of Tula—one of the military–political events that Nicholson discusses. Nicholson is very cautious about assigning a date to this event, although the majority of scholars tend to favor a date somewhere in the mid-to-late twelfth century, so that the A.D. 1200 line for the separation of Early and Late Postclassic is accepted as a reasonable approximation for the end of Toltec hegemony. After this, most scholars assume that the period between the fall of the Tula Toltecs and the rise of the Aztecs, the so-called "Chichimec Period," belongs to the earlier part of the Late Postclassic. The end of the "Chichimec Period" is specified by Nicholson as A.D. 1370, with the rise of the Tepanecs and Azcapotzalco, and the political unification of the Basin of Mexico. In archaeological sequence parlance, this would equate with the Aztec II ceramic styles. Of course, as we have noted, the beginnings of the Late (or Aztec) Horizon go back earlier than this, to 1320. Actually, the Tenochcas, as a political power centered on Tenochtitlan, did not dominate Central Mexico until well after all of this, at ca. 1428.

With these considerations in mind, an archaeological time chart for the Valley of Mexico would go something like this. After the fall of Teotihuacan, the two centuries from A.D. 700 to 900 was the time of proto-Coyotlatelco and Coyotlatelco ceramics. The period from 900 to about 1200 is marked by Tula–Mazapan pottery and by the dominance of Tula. Other ceramic styles, sometimes subsumed under the rubric of Aztec I, pertain to the latter part of that Early Postclassic Period. The Late Postclassic, from 1200 until the Spanish Conquest, was the time of the warring "Chichimec" nations, the rise of the Tepanecs, the rise of Texcoco, and, eventually, the dominance of Tenochtitlan. The usual archaeological phases into which these events are divided are the Aztec II–IV phases.

I shall not attempt here to sketch in the Postclassic sequences in other Mesoamerican subareas. These are well known and are referred to in a number of general sources (see R. Wauchope 1971: various articles in *Handbook of Middle American Indians,* Vol. 11; Porter Weaver 1972).

Eastern Mesoamerica

G. W. Lowe's Eastern Mesoamerica (Chapter 11) is the Maya domain, highland and lowland, together with a marginal strip on the west and another on the east in Honduras and Salvador. He indicates no formal subáreas, although these are suggested by the column designations on his chronology charts.

Following almost a century of exploration, Maya scholars had made sufficient headway by the beginning of the twentieth century to read the hieroglyphic dates on the monuments and to translate these to the Christian calendar. Subsequently, architectural and ceramic sequences were related to these dates, and after 1950 chronologies were lengthened with the aid of radiocarbon dating. While the latter have been of great importance, especially in the Preclassic Period time ranges, they have not yet resolved the debate over the approximately 260-year difference between the generally accepted 11.16.0.0.0 correlation and the alternative 12.9.0.0.0 correlation.

Lowe utilizes Maya calendrical dates (11.16.0.0.0 correlation), ceramic and other "horizon markers," and radiocarbon dates in the relative alignments of his sequence columns. He states that where "horizon marker" evidence conflicts with isolated radiocarbon dates he gives precedence to the former. On the face of it, this seems to contradict Tolstoy's announced procedure; however, I think that a careful reading of the two chapters will make clear that both authors weighed various kinds of evidence, in an *ad hoc* manner, in making the numerous decisions required of them.

Lowe offers a brief discussion of "Paleo-Indian-type" finds in Eastern Mesoamerica, but the first period indicated on his chronological charts is the nonceramic Archaic. It runs from 8000 to 3000 B.C. The finds from the Santa Marta caves belong here. Some coastal shellmound sites may also have their beginnings this early; they definitely extend into his Preformative Period (3000–2000 B.C.). Lowe sees this Preformative Period as a time when late and expanding populations were living in either fishing or farming, and probably prepottery, villages.

For the later cultures, Lowe adheres to the conventional Mesoamerican periodization and terminology—Preclassic, Classic, and Postclassic. These are, however, defined as absolute time periods, without stage or developmental implications. In his use of radiocarbon dates, Lowe refers the reader to MASCA corrections for those dates in the earlier B.C. ranges, and these would correspond, approximately, to Tolstoy's corrected, sidereal dates.

The inception of Lowe's Early Preclassic Period is set at ca. 2000 B.C. (radiocarbon time). This is an estimate, for there are as yet no pottery finds in Eastern Mesoamerica that appear to date as early as the ca. 2400 B.C. occurrences at Tehuacan and on the Guerrero Coast.[3] However, the 2000 B.C. line on the charts is drawn as a wavy one, indicating its very approximate nature. Lowe's earliest ceramic phases are the Barra and Ocos of the Chiapas and Guatemalan Pacific coasts. These have no associated radiocarbon dates, but absolute dating placements are possible through cross-dating extrapolations with the San Lorenzo Site sequence and dates. These suggest an Ocos date of just before 1500 B.C. and a Barra Phase date perhaps as early as 1800 B.C. As such, they would belong to the very end of Tolstoy's Initial Period. Lowe assigns them to his Early Preclassic I Period (2000–1500 B.C.). The ceramics in question have such diagnostic early traits as tecomate and flat-bottomed bowl forms, zoned punctation, color zoning, and rocker stamping. Early Preclassic II (1500–1250 B.C.) includes the San Lorenzo Bajio and Chicharras phases and the Tabascan Pellicer Phase. These belong to Tolstoy's Early Horizon, although in content they are "incipient Olmec" rather than full Olmec. Early Preclassic III (1250–1000 B.C.) is the full Olmec Horizon (San Lorenzo phases), wiith the monumental sculptures. Lowe feels that the ceramics of this 1250–1000 B.C. horizon remain in, and climax, an Early Preclassic pottery tradition, so that this time span is, therefore, more appropriately designated as Early Preclassic than as Middle Preclassic. Earlier, Lowe (Green and Lowe 1967) had made the suggestion that the Olmec Horizon should mark the beginnings of the Middle Preclassic Period.

[3]Since Lowe's first writing, he has revised this to take in the early (ca. 2100 B.C.-RT) date for the Swasey pottery phase of northern Belize.

Lowe's Middle Preclassic is also divided into three subperiods: 1000–800 B.C., 800–600 B.C., and 600–400 B.C. It includes phases such as Dili, Escalera, Xe, and Early Mamom.

In defining a Late Preclassic (400 B.C.–A.D. 100), Lowe begins with Late Mamom. This is an innovation, for Mamom has been for a long time the "typical" Middle Preclassic culture. Lowe justifies this by his arguments for significant cultural changes at this time, such as an initiation of ceramic uniformity over wide areas (continued in Chicanel) and for the beginnings of a fully Preclassic Maya society with its architectural evidences of a hierarchial social order.

The Protoclassic Period (A.D. 100–250) remains as it has been—the prelude to Classic Maya florescence.

Lowe sets an Early Classic Period at A.D. 250–450. This is an attempt to establish a pre-Teotihuacan-influenced Early Classic. It is followed by the innovation of the Middle Classic Period, from A.D. 450 to 650, which is considered to encapsulate Teotihuacan influence in Eastern Mesoamerica and its waning. It is an idea first advanced by L. A. Parsons, who based his arguments largely on events in a Gulf Coast–Pacific Guatemala zone.

Lowe's Late Classic runs from A.D. 650–800. Another innovation then offered is the Terminal Classic Period (A.D. 800–1000). This is the time of Classic decline in the southern Lowlands and of the infiltration of numerous new influences of vaguely "Mexican" character.

The Early Postclassic Period (A.D. 1000–1200) is the time of the more definitively Mexican-influenced Chichen Itza; the Late Postclassic (A.D. 1200–1450) sees the hegemony of Mayapan. This overly brief summary of the Postclassic touches only upon the northern Maya Lowlands. Lowe's charts and text provide much more.

E. W. Andrews V offers an important addendum to Lowe's paper on the correlation of southern and northern Maya Lowland sequences. For years this has been a moot point (for details, see E. W. Andrews IV 1973; Willey and Shimkin 1973). Apparently the matter is now resolved, and the resolution of it can be accommodated to the 11.16.0.0.0 calendrical correlation. Briefly, Tepeu 1 and 2 of the southern Lowland sequences have been demonstrated as pre-Florescent, or prior to the time of the Puuc architectural style. The Puuc style cross-dates with Tepeu 3 (ca. A.D. 800–900), the century in which the Classic Maya civilization of the southern Lowlands was in decline; but the Puuc architectural period also lasts throughout Lowe's Terminal Classic Period, or until about A.D. 1000. After this it was replaced by the Modified Florescent style of Toltec-influenced Chichen Itza.

Lower Central America

Lower Central America is often considered as part of a larger Intermediate area (see Willey 1971: Chapter 5), although it may be treated as a culture area in itself. Systematic chronological knowledge is still spotty for Lower Central America, in spite of the fact that there has been a long tradition of grave digging and collecting in all of these countries. Some important descriptive archaeological works were published in the nineteenth century. C. V. Hartman conducted excavations and surveys in Costa Rica early in the twentieth century. S. K. Lothrop's book on the pottery of Costa Rica and Nicaragua appeared in 1926, and that same author excavated and published on the Coclé culture of Panama in the 1930s. Still, as of the time of World War II, there was no chronological frame of reference for Lower Central America or any of its subareas. Investigations toward this end were begun after the war and have continued up to the present. As a result of these, Wolfgang Haberland is able to offer four subarea chronologies in his Chapter 12: (*a*) Greater Nicoya, (*b*) Central Costa Rica, (*c*) Greater Chiriqui, and (*d*) the Gulf of Panama. While these subareas share many traits, they were never bound together by broad horizonal diffusions, in the manner of Mesoamerican or Peruvian subareas. This, as well as their geographical isolation one from another and the relatively few radiocarbon dates, places limitations on any effort to synthesize an overall Lower Central American archaeological chronology.

There is a case for a ''Paleo-Indian Period'' in Lower Central America. The Macapalé Complex (if scant finds can be dignified by that name) of Panama refers to fluted points found there. There are no dates, but Haberland suggests 8000–7000 B.C. on typological grounds. A radiocarbon date of 10,000 B.C. is reported from a hearth in the Parita district of Panama, indicating man's early presence in the general region, although there are no associated artifacts with this hearth and date.

Archaic-type finds are more numerous. At 4800 B.C. (radiocarbon time—corrected to 6000 B.C. sidereal time) we have the Panamanian Cerro Mangote shellmound site, with its chopping and edge-grinding tools, and the apparently related Sitio Hidalgo. For the Greater Chiriquí subarea, Olga Linares and Anthony Ranere have defined three preceramic phases. These phases appear to be those relating to earlier interior hunters and plant collectors and later coastal peoples. I suspect that the later phases will be shown to affiliate with Cerro Mangote. The chipped stone assemblages are simple and resemble those sometimes attributed to a ''pre–projectile point stage''; but virtually all Lower Central American chipped stone work has this typological aspect. Haberland suggests that the earliest of these Greater Chiriquí phases may begin as early as 6000–7000 B.C. (radiocarbon dates). The latest ends with the first ceramics for the subarea, appearing at ca. 300 B.C.

The ceramic periods are summarized in Haberland's subarea charts, and he also attempts a synthetical chart for all of Lower Central America. So far, Monagrillo pottery, in the Gulf of Panama subarea, is the earliest, with a radiocarbon date of 2100 B.C. (or 3000 B.C. as corrected to sidereal time).

Whether or not pottery was this early farther north in Lower Central America remains to be seen. In this connection, it is to be remembered that pottery dates in Mesoamerica as early as 2400 B.C. (radiocarbon time).

On a later time level of ca. 500 B.C.–A.D. 500, there is a suggestion of a Late Formative Horizon of Zoned Bichrome (combinations of incision and painting) and various Scarified (combinations of incisions, scrapings, brushings, and painting) pottery styles. There are two discernible traditions here. The Zoned Bichrome one, at the northern end of Lower Central America, resembles the Early and Middle Preclassic wares of Mesoamerica in its use of incision outlining color zones and in some of its vessel forms. Its chronological position is, of course, substantially later, and this is attested not only by the radiocarbon dates but by the occasional presence of the Usulutan resist technique on pottery found in Zoned Bichrome Phase contexts. The Scarified Tradition has its representatives in the other three subareas, and the various styles of the tradition are much less Mesoamerican.

Polychrome pottery appears in Lower Central America after the Zoned Bichrome–Scarified ware horizon. It is probably earlier—between A.D. 200 and 500—in Panama than farther north, and the idea of polychrome painting may be of Northern South American inspiration. The polychrome styles farther north may bear some relationship to these Panamanian styles, but, if so, it is relatively slight and of indirect transmission. At the same time, the early polychromes of the Greater Nicoya subarea are not particularly Mesoamerican. In fact, it is probably not until after A.D. 800, or later, that definite Mesoamerican elements can be seen in the Greater Nicoya painted wares. For the Greater Nicoya subarea, Haberland segments a chronology of polychrome pottery into Early (A.D. 500–950), Middle (A.D. 950–1300), and Late (A.D. 1300–1600) periods, and from the field research carried out so far this seems quite valid. But, as the subarea column comparisons indicate, such a periodization has no meaning elsewhere in Lower Central America. Until further work is done, no very effective synthesis can be performed on Lower Central American chronology after the A.D. 500 date except to say that numerous regional polychrome and plastic-decorated styles prevailed.

Colombia[4]

Colombia, as is obvious from its geographical position, is a key area—or will become such—in the linking of Central American and South American sequences. For a long time the archaeology of this part of the Intermediate Area was known mostly from unpublished grave digging, which resulted in many collections, public and private, and from some conscientious but essentially descriptive fieldwork which offered little or nothing in the way of

[4]Area not covered in this volume.

chronology (Mason 1931–39, Preuss, 1931). There were, however, attempts to relate archaeology to ethnohistory and ethnography, especially in the case of the Chibcha nation, known from Spanish accounts of the sixteenth century (Restrepo 1895). Systematic chronological work, backed by demonstrable stratigraphies, was not really begun until after the World War II. The leader in this has been Gerardo Reichel-Dolmatoff, as evidenced from a sample citing of his works (Reichel-Dolmatoff 1954a,b,c, 1955, 1959, 1961, 1965a,b, 1967) and a number of younger researchers have been following this lead.

Unlike Mesoamerica or Peru, Colombia is regionally fragmented in its archaeological cultures with no strong horizonal manifestations to link the regions. For the later Pre-Colombian cultures such regions include: the Caribbean Lowlands, with its Sinú, Lower Magdalena, Coastal, and Rio Ranchería divisions; the Pacific coastal lowlands; the San Agustín-Tierradentro country of the southern interior highlands; and the Chibcha uplands around the present city of Bogotá. These are the best known archaeologically, and virtually all of the chronological information comes from them; however, this leaves many other regions for which there is little or no chronological understanding, such as the Tairona, the Middle and Upper Magdalena Valleys, the Cauca Valley and its tributaries, and the Amazonian and Orinocan sections of Colombia (these latter, however, appear to fit more easily into Lowland South American archaeological spheres). (For a general orientation in Colombian archaeology, see Willey 1971: Chapter 5.)

For an early time horizon there are few data. Discoveries at El Abra, in the highlands near Bogotá, indicate the presence of early hunting groups at ca. 10,000–7000 B.C. There are also some quite different lithic assemblages from a few lowland sites which may date this early but probably fall in the millennia between 6000 and 3000 B.C.

Long pottery sequences have been developed in the Caribbean Lowland regions. These begin as early as 3000 B.C. (radiocarbon time) at Puerto Hormiga and continue through the Canapote, Barlovento, and Malambo phases. The latter, which is dated at ca. 1000 B.C. is believed to be manioc agricultural. The relationship between littoral sites and those of the interior in these early millennia remains problematical. Some Puerto Hormiga pottery is fiber-tempered, and related fiber-tempered wares have been found in the interior, as at San Jacinto. The Puerto Hormiga context is thought to have been shellfish oriented; the San Jacinto may have been manioc oriented. Two interpretations are possible: (*a*) peoples with littoral adaptation moved inland to become root crop farmers; or (*b*) root crop farmers of the interior moved to the coast to become shellfish collectors. Absence of radiocarbon dates from San Jacinto and other interior sites precludes a resolution of the question for the time being.

Another early pottery tradition is also found in the Caribbean Lowlands.

This is known from the Momil Site. This tradition relates to the Machalilla Complex of the Ecuador Coast and also notes resemblances to Mesoamerica. The internal stratigraphy of the Momíl Site suggests a shift from manioc to maize farming, and the question is raised as to whether or not this second pottery tradition may not be linked to the beginnings of maize farming in Colombia. Unfortunately, the important Momíl site and stratigraphy has not been dated by radiocarbon. Reichel-Dolmatoff (Reichel-Dolmatoff and Dussay de Reichel-Dolmatoff 1956) was, at one time, inclined to place it all as no earlier than the first millennium B.C.; more recently however, he has revised this estimate downward for beginnings as early as 1500 B.C. if not before. Sequence details for the Lower Magdalena, relate to the above; those for the Rio Ranchería region are largely later and stand somewhat apart. Pacific Lowland sequences also exhibit regionalism although some phases on the southern Colombian Coast tie to those of coastal Ecuador. A partially radiocarbon-dated sequence from the San Agustín zone begins sometime in the latter part of the first millennium B.C., but the famed sculptures and the culture appear to climax several centuries later. Chibchan and Tairona archaeology is known almost entirely from the late Precolumbian centuries.

There are enormous gaps in systematic knowledge. The 6000–3000 B.C. hiatus is one of these, for any part of the country. Another is the lack of information on what was going on in the Andean interior and upland valleys in the 3000–1000 B.C. time range. Ironically, some of the regions where thousands of pottery specimens and gold and tumbaga ornaments have been looted from graves are still without proper sequences of even the grossest kind. What, for example, is the dating, relative or absolute, of the famous gold styles, such as the Quimbaya or Tolima?

The Caribbean Area

The Caribbean area comprises North and North-Central Venezuela, Northern Guyana, and the West Indies. Compared to either Lower Central America or Colombia, archaeological chronology for the area is well advanced. By the end of the 1930s, Irving Rouse had fashioned an area chronology chart for the islands, and this has gone through subsequent refinements (Rouse 1964). With J. M. Cruxent (Rouse and Cruxent 1963), he has prepared a similar scheme for Venezuela; and Clifford Evans and B. J. Meggers have performed a similar task for Northern Guyana.

The original Rouse and Rouse–Cruxent syntheses operated with a stage–period scheme into which cultural phases, or series of phases (traditions), were placed in the regional–chronological columns. Prior to radiocarbon dating, chronological estimates were essentially guess dates, these began to be replaced with carbon dates after 1950 (numerous radiocarbon assays are presented by Rouse and Allaire in their Chapter 13. The old stage–period scheme fitted to the generally recognized American one of Paleo-Indian, Meso-Indian, Neo-Indian. The Paleo-Indian Period was simply so named in the Caribbean area chronology and set as the time prior to 5000 B.C. The Meso-Indian stage was called Period I (5000–1000 B.C.); Period II (1000 B.C.–A.D. 300) marked the threshold of the Neo-Indian stage, with the advent of agriculture and pottery; Periods III (A.D. 300–1000) and IV (A.D. 1000–1500) were time divisions for later Neo-Indian cultures; and Period V (post–A.D. 1500) was the European invasion horizon. In the application of this scheme, however, an attempt was made to distinguish between absolute time period and degree of cultural development or culture content. Thus, while it was recognized that pottery and farming were present on the Venezuelan mainland as early as the beginning of Period II, it was also recognized that these traits did not occur in the Antilles until well near the end of that period, some several centuries later.

In the present Rouse–Allaire charts (see their Figures 13.1–13.9) the authors have eliminated the old period scheme and have placed cultural phases and series (traditions) in their various regional columns, using radiocarbon dates. In so doing, they have constructed a very sophisticated set of time–space diagrams; however, such a chronological presentation defies succinct presentation or summary in a single, simplified column. In offering such a summary column for my New World chart (see my Figure 15.2), I have been forced to refer to an essentially Orinoco region sequence. Rouse and Allaire have also made another change, this was in terminology. Arguing that there is no one-to-one correlation between technology and economy, they have replaced the old stage names with four "technological ages": (*a*) Lithic (chipped stone technology only), (*b*) Archaic (ground stone technology), (*c*) Ceramic (the presence of pottery), and (*d*) Historic (European period).

In Chapter 13, the Caribbean area is carefully divided up into a number of "regions," which correspond to what I have been calling subareas for the other areas of this volume. The Rouse–Allaire chart presents four (Orinoco, Llanos, Caribbean Mountains, and Coast) of these for Venezuela, two (Lesser Antilles and Greater Antilles) for the West Indies. Pottery is radiocarbon dated as early as 1000 B.C. in the Orinoco and in the Llanos; and the authors have extended this date back to 2000 B.C. by estimate. This refers primarily to the Saladoid ceramic series. Rouse and Allaire suggest that this series originated in either the Amazon Basin or the Intermediate Area. Another ceramic series, the Barrancoid is almost as early as the Saladoid in the Orinoco Basin. In fact, the radiocarbon dating and chronological relationships of the two series still remain somewhat ambiguous. One possible origin point for the Barrancoid pottery (which features deep incision and punctation in contrast to Saladoid painting) is out of the

Puerto Hormiga–Canapote–Barlovento series or tradition in Northern Colombia; however, Rouse and Allaire favor the idea that Barrancoid developed out of Saladoid.

The relationships of these pottery series in time and in space are plotted on the accompanying time charts, along with others such as the Tocuyanoid series of the Caribbean Mountains and the several series of the West Indies. Tocuyanoid pottery, which is also known in Reichel-Dolmatoff's Rio Ranchería region of the Colombian Caribbean Coast, is a very early polychrome decorated ware which may have its origins in a Saladoid–Osoid line of development. The various West Indian ceramic series are thought to have their origins in the Saladoid series, which first penetrated to the Lesser Antilles (presumably carried by Arawakan peoples) at about the beginning of the Christian era.

This kind of "genetic" plotting, lines of artifact development, is not restricted to Ceramic Age cultures but is also a part of the Rouse–Allaire presentation of the Lithic and Archaic Age data. In Western Cuba, an Archaic Age Redondoid artifact series (of shell tools) runs from 1500 B.C. to the Historic Age.

This "genetic" plotting is, of course, not primary chronological work, but it is one kind of hypothesis (a historical–reconstructive one) that can be based upon a chronological–geographical ordering of the data. Only in the Southwestern United States, where there is also a detailed, and generally firm, spatial–temporal framework, have similar attempts at reconstruction been carried to such a degree.

Amazonia[5]

The vast South American lowland area of the Amazon drainage (see Lathrap 1970: various maps; Willey 1971: Fig. 6-29) is known archaeologically from only a relatively few regions. With rare exceptions (e.g., Nordenskiold 1913), stratigraphic and chronology-minded archaeology for the area dates from post–World War II times. There is no generally agreed upon area chronology, although some charts of regional and subareal sequences have been published (Lathrap 1970:14–15; Meggers and Evans 1963: Fig. 16; Willey 1971: Fig. 6-30). Radiocarbon dates are still few. The two longest and best-established sequences are at the opposite ends of the area, on the Upper Amazonian Ucayalí tributary and the Amazon Delta island of Marajó.

D. W. Lathrap has summarized the Ucayalí sequence. It begins with an incised ware pottery style, the Early Tutishcainyo, whose early dating (2000–1600 B.C.) is derived by him from the similarities that this style bears to the nearby Andean highland Waira-jirca pottery of Kotosh, Peru. Waira-jirca is placed by radiocarbon at ca. 1800 B.C. The succeeding Late

[5]Area not covered in this volume.

Tutishcainyo Phase is dated by Lathrap at 1200–1000 B.C. on the basis of its similarity to the radiocarbon-dated Machalilla pottery of the Ecuador Coast. Shakimu, the third phase from the bottom in the Ucayalí sequence, has its own radiocarbon date of 650 B.C.; and Shakimu also appears to have some resemblances to Peruvian Chavín horizon pottery, a circumstance which would not be far out of line with this date. At this point, the continuity in the Ucayalí sequence ceramic tradition is interrupted by the appearance of another tradition, the Barrancoid, in the Hupa-iya Phase (400–1 B.C.). Lathrap believes the Barrancoid tradition to have had its beginnings still earlier than this in the Upper Orinoco–Rio Negro region. Subsequent Ucayalí pottery complexes and phases, in still other traditions, continue this sequence, which is partially dated by radiocarbon, in the A.D. 1–1500 range. One of the latest of these phases is the Caimito, set by Lathrap at a century or two prior to A.D. 1500; it is known from its polychrome ceramics, which have a resemblance to related polychrome wares in the Upper, Middle, and Lower Amazon. The Central Ucayalí master sequence is not the only one in the Ucayalí drainage region, and the reader is referred to the nearby Alto Pachitea sequence (Lathrap 1970: 95–102), which is almost as long and has some radiocarbon dates for the earlier phases.

In commenting upon the Ucayalí sequence, Lathrap is in agreement with the remarks made by Rouse and Allaire (Chapter 13) to the effect that his Tutishcainyo material is to be related to a widespread Amazon–Orinoco Saladero, or Saladoid, pottery tradition; and he would see both the Saladoid and the Barrancoid traditions arising somewhere in these lowlands. Lathrap (1970: 112) further adds the hypothesis that Saladoid beginnings probably go back 1000 to 1500 years earlier (to ca. 3000–3500 B.C.) somewhere in the region of the Upper Amazon–Negro–Madeira confluences.

Clifford Evans, Jr. and B. J. Meggers (1968), who have developed another Upper Amazonian sequence on the Rio Napo, in Eastern Ecuador, interpret their evidence somewhat differently. They relate a Yasuní Phase to Tutishcainyo. This Yasuní Phase, which is their earliest, has a radiocarbon date of ca. 90 B.C., and they hesitate to put the beginnings of either Yasuní or Tutishcainyo as earlier than 500 B.C. (see Meggers and Evans 1963: Fig. 16). It is also their opinion that Shakimu and Hypa-iya are much later than the dates assigned to them by Lathrap. In attempting to synthesize Amazon archaeology they (Meggers and Evans 1961) have formulated a series of horizon markers or styles, patterned on the Peruvian model. Their earliest horizon, the "Zoned Hachure" (referring to incised pottery decoration) is projected by them to subsume Tutishcainyo, Yasuní, and the two early Lower Amazonian complexes, Jauarí and Ananatuba. Lathrap, however, rejects the ceramic affiliations and approximate cross-dating of both Yasuní and Ananatuba with Tutishcainyo.

The Marajó Island sequence, which was developed by Meggers and Evans (1957), begins with the Ananatuba Phase and continues through Mangueiras,

Acauan, Formiga, Marajoara, and Historic Aruã phases. Most of the dating of this sequence has been by estimate, although since the original work there has been a radiocarbon date of 980 B.C. obtained for Ananatuba (see Willey 1971: 407–411 and Fig. 6-30, for summary). The Marajoara Phase is the spectacular painted and relief-decorated burial urn phase which has distant cross-ties with Napo and Caimito on the Upper Amazon, and it is placed by them at about A.D. 1000–1200 (Meggers and Evans 1963: Fig. 16).

Elsewhere, on the Lower and Middle Amazon, there has been some chronological work by P. P. Hilbert (1968). His Jauarí Phase, as indicated, ties to Ananatuba, and he has evidences of a Marajoara-like polychrome horizon (for summary, see Willey 1971:411–416, Fig. 630). The picture, though, is complex, and Meggers–Evans and Lathrap disagree in the interpretation of Hilbert's results, both in dating and in recognitions of ceramic tradition affiliations of his various complexes.

As can be seen from this brief survey, it is extremely difficult for the nonspecialist to come away from the Amazon area with any very coherent picture of its overall archaeological chronology. The apparently earliest pottery style, the Early Tutishcainyo of the Ucayalí, is definitely related to the earliest known pottery from the Andean Huallaga Basin—and these styles date back to about 2000 B.C. Whether other incised decoration styles—Yasuní, Jauarí, Ananatuba—are affiliated with Tutishcainyo is moot; however, it is to be noted that these geographically widely separated pottery complexes all date relatively early—ca. 1000–1 B.C. The presence of Barrancoid ceramic influence in the Amazon Basin cannot be doubted; and, in view of the antiquity of this tradition in the Orinoco drainage, its dating to the middle of the first millennium B.C. in the Ucayalí tributary seems reasonable. The ceramic history of the first millennium A.D. is very confused. Presumably, the elaborate modeled and painted burial urn styles had their beginnings in this period, although their firmest horizon (Marajoara–Napo) does not seem to have been established until after A.D. 1000.

Ecuador[6]

While there were earlier attempts at the formulation of archaeological chronologies for Ecuador—such as those of Jacinto Jijón y Caamaño (1927), who had worked as a colleague of Max Uhle—the first stratigraphically demonstrated sequences were not published until during or after World War II (see Bushnell 1951; Collier and Murra 1943; Evans and Meggers 1957). Important research has been carried out more recently, especially in the coastal subareas, and this has resulted in chronological syntheses (see Lathrap 1975; Meggers 1966 for such summaries and for bibliographic references). One of the things these investigations have shown is that ceramics

[6]Area not covered in this volume.

may be as early on the Ecuadorian Coast as anywhere in the New World and that elements of these early Intermediate area ceramic traditions were diffused or carried from Ecuador to Mesoamerica and to Peru in the second millennium B.C., if not before.

B. J. Meggers (1966) has structured a stage–period chronology for the ceramic cultures of Ecuador; and this scheme, with some of its coastal phases, has been dated (through stratigraphic controls and some radiocarbon assays) as follows:

Formative Period:	
Valdivia Phase	3000–1500 B.C.
Machalilla Phase	2000–1000 B.C.
Chorrera Phase	1500–500 B.C.
Regional Developmental Period:	
Guangala, Bahia, and other phases	500 B.C.–A.D. 500
Integration Period:	
Manteño, Milagro, and other phases	A.D. 500–1550

The early ranges of this chronology have been the focus of considerable debate among authorities. Meggers, Clifford Evans, and Emilio Estrada (1965) have seen the origins of Valdivia Phase pottery in the Japanese Jomon culture, via trans-Pacific contact, and have characterized Valdivia as being primarily sea-dependent in subsistence. D. W. Lathrap (1967, 1973, 1974, 1975), to the contrary, believes that the Valdivia style arose in the South American Tropical Forest and was spread from there to the Ecuadorian Coast by peoples who were basically agricultural (maize and root crops). Radiocarbon dates for the Valdivia Site proper, which is situated immediately upon the littoral edge, fall between 3200 and 1500 B.C. (Meggers, Evans, and Estrada 1965); however, the single 3200 B.C. date is stratigraphically out of context, and Lathrap (1974), by eliminating this date, places that site's earliest pottery at ca. 2600–2700 B.C. Lathrap then notes that the radiocarbon dates for the earliest levels of an inland valley Valdivia culture site (Loma Alta) fall in the 3060–2800 B.C. range; and in his interpretation this indicates an interior riverine origin for Valdivia. This earlier riverine setting, together with other evidences, convinces him of Valdivia's essentially agricultural base. Lathrap's (1975) revised chronology for the Formative phases of the Guayas Coastal subarea is as follows:

Loma Alta (Valdivia culture)	3100–2700 B.C.
Valdivia (subphases 1–8)	2700–1500 B.C.
Machalilla	1500–1100 B.C.
Engoroy (Chorrera)	1100–300 B.C.

In this chronology, Lathrap rejects the Valdivia–Machalilla and Machalilla–Chorrera overlapping arrangement favored by Meggers *et al.* and argues for an essentially straight developmental continuum from Valdivia through Machalilla into Chorrera (Engoroy).

Setting aside the questions of origins and subsistence patterns for the moment, I think it can be affirmed that Valdivia culture and pottery definitely date back to the early centuries of the third millennium B.C. This Valdivia pottery is technically highly competent and simply but gracefully decorated. It in no way represents the crude beginnings of the ceramic craft. Further, it is to be noted that a few ceramics of a quite different tradition, the San Pedro, occur in the very lowest levels of the Loma Alta Site, suggesting still earlier and historically complex beginnings for New World pottery (Lathrap, 1975).

For the highlands, less is known of Formative Period cultures. In the Southern highlands subarea, Meggers (1966) places an Alausí (Early Cerro Narrío) Phase as contemporaneous with Chorrera; but this is opposed by Robert Braun (Ms.) who dates the earliest level of the Cerro Narrío Site as coeval with the beginnings of the Loma Alta–Valdivia cultures of the coast.

The Regional Developmental Period is the time of such ceramically elaborate cultures as the Guangala, Bahía, Jama–Coaque, and Tolita cultures of the coast. Their general datings are supported by a few radiocarbon readings, although the upper and lower boundaries of the period remain very approximate. Estrada and Meggers (1961) see further trans-Pacific influences into the Ecuadorian coastal regions at this time. They, and a number of other authors, agree that Mesoamerican–Ecuadorian coastal contacts were important during the Regional Developmental Period. And, as mentioned earlier, there are evidences that Ecuador–Mesoamerican exchanges of goods and ideas took place in the Formative Period as well (M.D. Coe 1960; Lathrap 1975).

The Integration Period is best known from the Manteño culture of the coast and the Milagro culture of the Guayas Basin. The Manteño capital at Manta, in Manabí Province, was of urban proportions; and the Manteño were great seafarers and traders, almost certainly trading as far north as Western Mexico.

Various cultures of the highlands have been assigned to either the Regional Developmental or Integration Period; however, their definitions and chronological placements remain rather hazy at the present stage of investigation. The local highland cultures were overrun by the Incas in the late fifteenth and early sixteenth centuries, and this Inca influence is recognized in some places as a thin archaeological overlay.

Ecuadorian preceramic evidences are still relatively few. The site of El Inga, in the highlands near Quito, is one source of information (Bell 1965). El Inga I features fishtailed fluted projectile points that are reminiscent of those of Magellan I (Fell's Cave) in extreme Southern South America and also of the North American Paleo-Indian fluted points. The phase has one radiocarbon date of 7000 B.C. Later El Inga phases, with willow-leaf and stemmed points, probably date in the 7000–5000 B.C. range (Willey 1971:45–46, 57–59). On the Ecuadorian Coast the only well-established preceramic horizon is the Vegas, believed to date somewhere in the 6000–3000 B.C. span (see also Willey 1971:262–263).

Peru–Bolivia[7]

The Peru–Bolivia archaeological culture area, comprising the Peruvian Coast and Andes and a highland sector of Bolivia around Lake Titicaca, is a key one in any consideration of New World archaeological chronologies. Our lack of a paper on this area presents us with a serious gap in information in examining South American archaeological chronology as well as in attempting still wider comparisons. Like Mesoamerica, Peru–Bolivia was an area of "high" cultures, and the beginnings of these have been traced back in considerable regional and subareal chronological refinement. The reader is referred to various standard syntheses for this detail (including Bennett and Bird 1964; Gorenstein *et al.* 1974; Lanning 1967; Willey 1971: Chapter 3). Here, in this interim statement, I can refer only to major periods and dates.

The formulation of major periods for the Peru–Bolivia area dates back to Max Uhle's work of the turn of the century; indeed, his was the first New World area chronology (Willey and Sabloff 1974:74–78). He constructed it from grave and architectural superpositions, stylistic seriation, and the cross-matching of styles from one subarea to another. In this last procedure, he utilized the widespread Incaic and Tiahuanacoid horizon markers in pottery, textiles, and other media. Most of the Peru-Bolivia chronology schemes since that time have been based on this structure of Uhle's. This is true of the scheme most currently in use, that fashioned by J. H. Rowe (1960). Rowe's scheme differs from the others, however, in that he has attempted to define his periods in strict chronological terms, eschewing developmental or stage implications. To do this, Rowe used the single regional sequence of the Ica Valley, on the South Coast of Peru, as his basic chronological yardstick. Dates were assigned to his periods by radiocarbon samples or, in the case of the two later periods, by ethnohistoric documentation.

Rowe's chronology, which begins with the first appearance of pottery in his Initial Period, may be outlined as follows. The dates given are his most recent (Rowe 1974) preferences selected from radiocarbon data. These dates have not been adjusted by comparative dendrochronological revisions:

[7]Area not covered in this volume.

Initial Period	2120–2050 to 1500–1300 B.C.
Early Horizon (Chavín influences)	1500–1300 to 420–370 B.C.
Early Intermediate Period	420–370 B.C. to A.D. 540
Middle Horizon (Huari–Tiahuanaco influences	A.D. 540 to 900
Late Intermediate Period	A.D. 900 to 1476
Late Horizon (Inca influences)	A.D. 1476 to 1534

Differences in radiocarbon dates, which Rowe (1965) has discussed at some length, do suggest alternative and somewhat later dates (see Figure 15.2) for the early and middle periods. These may be summarized as follows (see Lanning 1967; Willey 1971: Figs. 3-7, 3-8):

Initial Period	1800–900 B.C.
Early Horizon	900–200 B.C.
Early Intermediate Period	200 B.C.–A.D. 600
Middle Horizon	A.D. 600–1000
Late Intermediate Period	A.D. 1000–1476
Late Horizon	A.D. 1476–1534

For the preceramic era, periodization and dating have been much less formalized. In general, cultural definitions are weaker and radiocarbon dates are fewer and more open to question as to context and significance. One Peru-Bolivia preceramic sequence has been devised by E. P. Lanning (1967) and employed by me (Willey 1971: Figs. 3-7, 3-8), with some modifications. It may be recapitulated, very briefly, as follows.

Preceramic Period I (prior to 9500 B.C.) subsumes all of those early complexes, or claims for such complexes, that precede the bifacially flaked projectile point traditions. It would include the Central Highland Paccaicasa (21,000–14,000 B.C.) and Ayacucho (14,000–11,000 B.C.) industries discovered by R. S. MacNeish and others (1970). Other possible candidates would be the Guitarrero I Complex of the Callejon de Huaylas (Lynch and Kennedy 1970) and the Chivateros Red Zone and Oquendo finds of the Peruvian Central Coast (for summary, see Willey 1971:34–38).

Preceramic Period II (9500–8000 B.C.) then begins with the early projectile point complexes of which MacNeish's (1970) Huanta Phase, with its Fell's Cave type points, is probably the best example. The lozenge-shaped or slightly tanged points of the earlier part of the Guitarrero II Phase (Lynch and Kennedy 1970) might also fall in this time bracket. On the coast this would be the time of Lanning's (1965) Chivateros I industry, with its heavy bifaces.

Preceramic Period III (8000–6000 B.C.) sees the beginnings of the leaf-shaped points in the highlands, with complexes such as Lauricocha I (Cardich 1964) and Guitarrero II (Lynch and Kennedy 1970). On the coast, the Chivateros II Phase points belong to the period.

Preceramic Period IV (6000–4200 B.C.) is the period of Lauricocha II and related complexes in the highlands. Points are the standard willow-leafs. Coastal complexes that date from the period are Paiján, Luz, Canario. In the highlands, there is some incipient cultivation in this period.

Preceramic Period V (4200–2500 B.C.) The coastal adaptation called the Pacific Littoral Tradition begins in this period (Willey 1971: Chapter 3). A fishing economy was supplemented by early cultivation. The Encanto Phase of the Central Coast is one of the best known for the latter part of the period (Moseley 1975:20–21). In the highlands, the Andean Hunting–Collecting Tradition continued.

Preceramic Period VI (2500–1800 B.C.) saw increasing population growth and sedentary trends in the coastal populations, whose economy continued to be based on marine foods. Permanent architecture is noted for a number of sites, and M. E. Moseley (1975) has seen the beginnings of nonegalitarian Peruvian societies at this time. In the highlands, as at Kotosh (Izumi and Sono 1963), populations were becoming increasingly dependent upon crop cultivation.

Northern Chile

Northern Chile, as treated by Lautaro Nuñez (Chapter 15) can also be considered as part of the major South Andes culture area (see Willey 1971: Chapter 4). As Nuñez demonstrates, it contains considerable regional diversity in the cultures of its several coastal, interior valley, and upland mountain basin divisions.

The history of chronological archaeology in Northern Chile begins with Max Uhle, who came there to work shortly before World War I. At that time, Uhle had just completed his almost 20 years of Peruvian archaeological explorations; he approached Chilean archaeology with this background, and also with certain European models in mind. As the result of stratigraphic and grave digging around Arica and Pisagua he devised the following long sequence (Uhle 1919, 1922): (I) the Period of Primordial Man (based on crude lithic tools, which Uhle compared to Old World Lower Paleolithic or "Eolithic" facies—no absolute dates estimated), (II) the Period of the Aborigines of Arica (burial and midden finds of matting, nets, crude textiles—estimated date of the early centuries A.D.), (III) Period Contemporaneous with the Ruins of Chavín (woolen textiles, turbans, weaving designs of "proto-Nazca" affiliation—estimated dates of A.D. 400–600, (IV) Period of Tiahuanaco and Subsequent Epigonal Influences (Tiahuanacoid pottery and woodwork—estimated dates A.D. 600–900), (V) Period of the Civilization of the Atacameña (post-Tiahuanaco pottery of a local style—estimated dates of A.D. 900–1100), (VI) Period of the Chincha–Atacameña (a modification of Period V pottery—estimated dates of A.D. 1100–1350), and (VII) Inca Period (estimated dates of A.D. 1350–1530).

The Uhle Arica sequence is remarkable in a number of ways. Although dealing with data marginal to the Peru–Bolivia area, Uhle's 1919 observation about the chronological priority of Chavín influences with relation to those of Tiahuanaco is, to the best of my knowledge, the earliest published statement on the subject; and I am indebted to Nuñez's paper for calling it to my attention (for other views on the matter, see Lathrap 1973: 1975; and Willey 1971:184). In addition, the Period IV Tiahuanacoid placement has turned out to be not far wide of the mark on absolute dating, although we now know that this horizon did not signal the first appearance of pottery in Northern Chile. Uhle's Period I "Eolithic" culture has not stood up; but the chronological position of Period II has been confirmed, although with somewhat earlier dates. Periods V, VI, and VII were verified by Bird's (1943) later work, but without the Peruvian "Chincha" influences claimed for Period VI.

After Uhle, Ricardo Latcham played an important role in Chilean archaeology, although it was J. B. Bird, in the early 1940s, who introduced modern stratigraphic methods. Bird has been followed by other, younger archaeologists, both foreign and Chilean, and Nuñez is one of the foremost of the latter group in sequence building. Some radiocarbon dates are available; those cited by Nuñez are uncorrected.

Nuñez rejects or reserves judgment about many of the claims for early lithic industries in Northern Chile. This includes the Chuquí Complex and the so-called Andean Biface assemblages. The earliest typologically well-defined and dated horizon is that of the lanceolate, leaf-shaped projectile points resembling those of the Peruvian Lauricocha II and Argentine Ayampitín assemblages. This includes the Tulan, Puripica, and Tambillo materials—upland complexes, with manos and milling stones associated in some cases. There is a long, radiocarbon-dated preceramic sequence in the Tarapaca Quebrada, which begins on this horizon and continues, with projectile point form modifications, up to about 1500 B.C.

On the coast, the Quiani I "Shell Fishhook Culture" has a radiocarbon date of ca. 4200 B.C., and this would seem to mark the time of the shift of the upland populations to the fishing and shellfishing niches.[8] Coastal Chinchorro culture, with its artificial mummification, mats, and nets, is placed at ca. 3000–2000 B.C. This horizon would correspond to Uhle's old Period II.

Nuñez remarks upon a time gap in the evidence from ca. 2000–1000 B.C. It is a crucial gap, for it was in this period that maize agriculture and pottery were introduced to the North Chilean Coast and the interior valleys. These introductions probably came from the north, via the interior. I would guess that the Bolivian *altiplano* was the point of origin, and Nuñez seems to favor some such interpretation.

[8]In footnotes, Nuñez refers to a Tiliviche culture of the coastal regions which dates back to at least 7000 B.C.; however, this culture does not display the same maritime adaptations as Quiani.

Nuñez's Regional Formative Period (800 B.C.–A.D. 1000) subsumes the evidences of the early farming communities: Faldas del Morro, near Arica (Uhle's old Period III), Pichalo III (Bird's "First Pottery Period" at that site), Caserones (with radiocarbon dates of 360–290 B.C.), Guatacondo (at ca. 100 B.C.–A.D. 100); the Huelén Complex (ca. 450 B.C.–A.D. 250); the Canamo Complex (860 B.C.—the earliest date for maize, lima beans, and plain pottery); and the San Pedro I Phase of the upland Atacama Oasis (guess-dated at 1000 B.C.–A.D. 200). These are all sedentary communities. Some of them, such as Guatacondo and Caserones, are walled, compartmented layouts. All have relatively simple, monochrome pottery.

The latter part of the Regional Formative Period (after A.D. 400) is the Tiahuanaco Horizon. Radiocarbon dates are rather few, and the complexes assigned to the period lack clear definition. Many appear to have been formulated on a few grave finds. The most interesting questions that arise in this context involve the processes of dissemination of the Tiahuanaco influences.

The following, Regional Development Period (A.D. 1000–1450) pertains to the well-known later archaeological cultures of Northern Chile, those of San Pedro de Atacama and those of the Arica I and II phases, as well as other regional expressions. Inca influence dates from A.D. 1450 to 1530, a little later than in the Uhle scheme.

Remainder of the South Andes Area[9]

The South Andes culture area has been defined to include all of Chile, down to the southern end of Chiloe Island; a large part of the Bolivian *altiplano;* and the Argentine Andes and immediately bordering lowlands, down as far as Neuquén Province (see Willey 1971: Chapter 4, Fig. 4-1). Within the limits of this definition, Lautaro Nuñez, in Chapter 15, has confined his discussions to the North Chilean, or Atacama, subarea. A brief comment is in order on the several remaining subareas.

For the most part, refined archaeological chronologies are relatively new for these subareas, and wider syntheses have been rare. Working largely through seriations of ceramics, W. C. Bennett, E. F. Bleiler, and F. H. Sommer (1948) attempted such a chronological synthesis of the Argentine subareas prior to the advent of radiocarbon dating. A more inclusive effort was made by A. R. Gonzalez (1963), utilizing the then recent stratigraphic information and some radiocarbon dates (Gonzalez 1961–1964). My own resumé (Willey 1971: Figs. 4-3, 4-4) drew heavily on these earlier schemes, incorporating some new data. Since then, a spate of new work in various parts of the South Andes area necessitates another critical appraisal and

[9]Area not covered in this volume.

review. I cannot pretend that this interim note fills that need. The best I have been able to do is indicate the general outlines of a space–time structure.

Although claims have been made for lithnic industries dating back prior to 8000 B.C.—in particular those pertaining to the "Andean Biface" Tradition as defined for Ampajango in the Argentine northwest and Loma Negra in the Atacama interior—these must be viewed with some skepticism or, at least, reserve until firmer evidence of their antiquity is in hand. For these earlier time ranges, perhaps the best South Andean claim is that from Tagua Tagua, in Central Chile, an assemblage of cores and lamellar flakes, with an associated radiocarbon date of 9400 B.C. (for further references, see Willey 1971: 29, 50). The Tagua Tagua materials are difficult to place typologically. They are not typical of the Andean Biface Tradition, nor can they be securely assimilated into Paleo-Indian projectile point traditions, although the chipping technology as revealed by the lamellar flakes suggests such traditions. The earliest good evidence for preceramic hunting populations is that of the ca. 6000–4000 B.C. horizon, as defined by leaf-shaped Ayampitín and related points. These are inland and upland finds. A key reference for this horizon is that of Gonzalez (1960) on Intihuasi Cave in the Sierras Centrales of Argentina. These leaf-shaped point hunting cultures continue after 4000 B.C., with minor technological modifications in the lithic industry; and at this time their presence is also seen on the Chilean Coast. Nuñez has indicated this with his reference to the North Chilean Quiani complexes; farther south such littoral adaptations are represented by the Guanaqueros cultures of the Valles Transversales subarea and the Las Cenizas of the Chilean Central Valley. These upland hunting and coastal hunting and fishing cultures appear to have persisted until some time into the first millennium B.C.

What Nuñez has designated as his Regional Formative Period corresponds, at least in its earlier centuries, to Gonzalez's (1963) and my (Willey 1971: Chapter 4) Early Ceramic Period. The date of the "floor," or inception, of this period is still uncertain. Nuñez has settled on a date of 800 B.C.; Gonzalez's estimate was 500 B.C. However, as Nuñez states, the time of the introduction of maize agriculture and pottery to the South Andes area probably goes back to the second millennium B.C. Almost certainly, a stage or "sloping horizon" is involved here, with a generally north-to-south gradient; so that the ceramic trait and a farming economy were probably present in the South Bolivian subarea before they appeared farther south. In considering such diffusions, it should also be kept in mind that while farming and pottery have a generally apparent synchroneity there may turn out to be significant time differentials in their first appearances. In general, the earliest ceramics of the South Andes area are competently made, and run to monochromes or incised decoration. This description applies to such complexes as the Faldas del Morro and San Pedro I (Atacama subarea), the El Molle I (Valles Transversales subarea), Cultura de los Tumulos (Southern

Bolivian subarea), Laguna Blanca (Puna–Humuhuaca subarea), Candelaria I (Selvas Occidentales subarea), Tafí I (Valliserrana subarea), and Las Mercedes (Chaco–Santiagueño subarea) (see Willey 1971: Figs. 4-3, 4-4).

The latter part of Nuñez's Regional Formative Period corresponds, but rather approximately, to what has been designated as the Middle Ceramic Period. The distinguishing criteria are ceramics that show what has been considered to be Tiahuanaco Horizon influences. One difficulty here is in distinguishing between traits and influences that might be more appropriately described as pertaining to the Bolivian *altiplano,* in contrast to a distinctly Tiahuanaco Horizon. For instance, a complex such as the Condorhuasi (of the Argentine Valliserrana subarea), which probably dates as early as A.D. 400, may very well be related to pre–Classic Tiahuanaco, rather than Tiahuanaco Horizon, levels. On the other hand, styles closer to the Classic Tiahuanaco may date after A.D. 600. As I have said in my commentary on Nuñez's paper, a Tiahuanaco Horizon for the South Andes is still lacking in definitional and chronological precision.

Nuñez's Regional Development Period, like the Late Ceramic Period construct that Gonzalez and I have employed, is definitely post-Tiahuanaco, and it is the period (A.D. 1000–1450) of the late Chilean and Northwest Argentine painted pottery styles. The Inca Period (A.D. 1450–1550) is represented by that imperial expansion into most (but not all) of the South Andes subareas.

East Brazilian Area[10]

The East Brazilian area (see Willey 1971: Fig. 7-1 map) is in the early stages of the chronological ordering of its archaeology. Much of the work toward this end has been accomplished under the Brazilian *Programa Nacional de Pesquisas Arqueologicas,* which was launched in 1965 (see PRONAPA 1967, 1969a, 1969b, 1970, 1971, 1974). As might be anticipated, the huge area presents considerable environmental and cultural diversity, and research has proceeded in regional contexts under the direction of regional specialists. Sequences have been constructed through artifactual seriations and stratigraphy, and with the aid of some radiocarbon dates. A historic–genetic scheme of cultural classification, with traditions, subtraditions, and phases, is in general use by the archaeologists collaborating in the national program.

There is no generally recognized area chronology scheme. In my textbook treatment (Willey 1971: Chapter 7), I formulated what I called an East Brazilian Upland Tradition, which incorporated the preceramic lithic industries of the interior. These were characterized by percussion-flake tools—cutting edges, punches, scrapers, and other amorphous flake tools. I specu-

[10]Area not covered in this volume.

lated that such a tradition had its beginnings as early as 9000–8000 B.C. I also noted that occasional bifaces, including some lanceolate and stemmed projectile points, were found in these East Brazilian Upland Tradition assemblages. While these were probably made locally, it was suggested that they represented influences from other South American areas and cultures. Among the earliest of such points were those of the Cerca Grande culture of Minas Gerais, with radiocarbon dates of ca. 7700–7000 B.C. (see Hurt and Blasi 1969). I offered the chronological generalization that the earlier cultures of the East Brazilian Upland Tradition (those prior to 3000 B.C.) had fewer projectile points and that more of these tended to be of lanceolate form, whereas the later cultures (after 3000 B.C.) featured more points, especially stemmed points, as well as more semipolished and polished stone axes. Such a generalization still seems to hold (see Lanning in Gorenstein *et al.* 1974: 103–105; E. T. Miller 1974).

Another tentative formulation which I put forward in 1971 was that of a Sambaquí Tradition of the coast. Such a coastal adaptation was conceived of as having its beginnings in the climatic optimum (ca. 5000–4000 B.C.) and as having had its origins in the Upland Tradition. While many of the Brazilian *sambaquís* (shellmounds) are deep and show obvious physical stratification, their excavation has not yet resulted in any very clear-cut cultural stratigraphies. The cultures involved show great technological conservatism, with flake tools persisting throughout. There is, however, some evidence to indicate that polished stone, including some apparent ritual objects, appear only in the later time ranges. The reader is referred to my chronological chart (Willey 1971; Fig. 7-3 for a sampling of cultural complexes, from both the East Brazilian Upland and Sambaquí traditions, as assigned to their presumed chronological positions. One difficulty that confronts the nonspecialist reader is that there are now a bewildering number of regional sequences and culture phase names. (Compare, for example, E. P. Lanning's Chart 4.1, in Gorenstein *et al.* 1974, with mine.)

The later time ranges or the upward chronological limits of the East Brazilian Upland and Sambaquí Tradition cultures are not clearly defined. For many regions it might be held that these traditions persisted into European Colonial times. Simple, plain pottery occurs as early as 880 B.C. (a radiocarbon date) in the Periperí Complex of the Bahía Coast. Several hundreds of miles farther south, in southeastern Rio Grande do Sul, P. I. Schmitz (1973) has published a radiocarbon date of 70 B.C. for his earliest Vieira Phase pottery. Early Vieira pottery, while not the same as that of Periperí, is also an extremely simple ceramic. Thus, there is a case to be made for the diffusion of the idea of simple pottery making, from north to south, on a sloping chronological horizon. On my 1971 chart I suggested such a diffusion, estimating the southern Brazilian terminus at about 500 B.C. This may be too early, although Lanning (in Gorenstein *et al.* 1974:104) speaks of pottery in Rio Grande do Sul as being as early as 400–300 B.C. Regarding cultural tradition definitions, it should be made clear that the archaeologists who have studied these cultures in the field feel that both Periperí and Vieira were nonagricultural and that, in each case, it was simply a matter of the pottery idea being introduced into societies of the old cultural traditions.

Elsewhere in the East Brazilian area, the first appearances of pottery are later than those noted above, falling into a dating range of A.D. 500–1000 or, in places, even later. In some instances these ceramics are of relatively simple styles; in others they belong to the more elaborate Tupiguaraní pottery tradition. The question arises as to whether these later simpler styles are the descendants of the hypothetical Periperí–Vieira Horizon of the first millennium B.C. or whether they are the result of stimulus development in imitation of the Tupiguaraní Tradition. The Tupiguaraní cultures, presumably of ultimate Amazonian area derivation, were known to have been agricultural, and their appearance does mark a break with the East Brazilian and Sambaquí traditions.

The Chaco Area[11]

A Chaco archaeological area deserves no more than a mention, for we have no clear picture of its archaeology or archaeological chronology. I speculated (Willey 1971: 452–458) that a Chacoan pottery tradition may have developed in this area prior to A.D. 500 as the result of influences from the eastern border cultures of the South Andes area (La Candelaria I, Las Mercedes) and, possibly, from an early pottery tradition of the Lower Paraná River. Along the Paraguay River, which flows through the Chaco, there are sites with Tupiguaraní pottery. These sites are generally considered as quite late, and some of them definitely are very late pre-European or even post-European; however, as we noted earlier, Tupiguaraní Tradition influences were present in southern Brazil as early as A.D. 500 and may have reached the Chaco by about this same time.

The Pampean Area[12]

In my textbook summary (Willey 1971: Fig. 7-18) I defined a Pampean culture area to include the Middle and Lower Paraná and Uruguay River drainages, the Pampas proper, Patagonia, and Eastern and Northern Tierra del Fuego. As a construct for ecologically oriented archaeology, this is too gross a definition, embracing, as it does, alluvial lowlands, Pampean grasslands, and Patagonian–Fuegian plateaus. Thus, the hunters, fishers, and

[11,12]Area not covered in this volume.

possibly incipient cultivators of the Paraná–Plate system obviously had a different subsistence adjustment than the guanaco hunters farther south. However, throughout, we are treating with the archaeological remains of essentially nonagricultural, semisedentary peoples, and ceramics and other artifacts indicate an interrelated history of the several subareas making up the whole.

While descriptive archaeology (with accompanying substantial publication of results) has been known for the Pampean area for three-quarters of a century, chronological control is more recent and still very spotty. A key sequence is that of the Strait of Magellan, based on the stratigraphic cave digging of J. B. Bird (1938) in the 1930s. His researchers have been supplemented by those of a French team (Emperaire, Laming-Emperaire, and Reichlen 1963), working there more recently. The earliest period of the sequence, the Magellan I, has radiocarbon dates placing it at 9000–8000 B.C. and is best known from its Fell's Cave type projectile points, a fishtailed, slightly fluted form that relates to the Ecuadorian El Inga I points and, more remotely, to the Clovis-Folsom Tradition of North America. The succeeding Magellan II Period is set at 8000–5000 B.C. Its chipped stone industry is a rough flake one, lacking in points and apparently relating to the North Patagonian Rio Gallegos Complex. However, bifacial projectile point industries were not altogether lacking in Southern South America in this time period. Leaf-shaped and triangular points are known from the Marazzi Site in Northern Tierra del Fuego (Laming-Emperaire, Lavallee, and Humbert 1972) at 7620 B.C. and in the Toldense Phase of Southern Patagonia (Cardich, Cardich, and Hajduk 1973) at 6800 B.C. Magellan III is a leaf-shaped point horizon. It dates from 5000 to 3000–1000 B.C. (see Lanning in Gorenstein *et al.* 1974: Chart 4.1; Willey 1971: Fig. 7-20). Magellan IV is characterized by stemmed dart points. Its terminal date is set at ca. A.D. 500–1000. Magellan V is known from small points, presumably those used in connection with the bow-and arrow.

Mention should also be made of a recently published (Cardich, Cardich, and Hajduk 1973) stratigraphic sequence which presents the first good evidence for a "pre–projectile point" complex from this part of South America. This sequence was found in the Toldos Cave 3, Province of Santa Cruz, Southern Patagonia. The basal industry in this deep cave deposit, dubbed the "Level Eleven Industry" by the excavators, has only large flake scrapers, punches, and other unifacial tools. These are associated with a radiocarbon date of 10,700 B.C. This "Level Eleven Industry" is overlaid by Toldense complex levels, with bifacially flaked leaf-shaped, triangular, and Fell's Cave type points, dating by radiocarbon to 6800 B.C. The Toldense Complex is succeeded, after a sterile layer interval, by a Casapadrense Complex dating to 5300–3500 B.C. This Casapadrense Complex is a flake tool industry with apparent relationships to the Magellan II Phase and to Rio Gallegos. The upper levels of the cave, estimated at ca. 2500 B.C. show stemmed points comparable to those of the later periods of the Magellan sequence.

The preceramic sequences of Northern Patagonia, the Pampas Proper, and the Paraná–Uruguay regions are extremely difficult to synthesize, either typologically or chronologically. The reader is referred to attempts by both Lanning and myself in the works cited earlier, however, neither is very satisfactory. In Northern Patagonia pressure flaking does appear after 5000 B.C. Farther north, as in the Tandil and Blanco Grande cultures of the Pampas, rough flakes industries persist until much later. Pressure-flaked dart points, for example, do not occur in the north until ca. 1000 B.C. Thus, a geographical–chronological trend can be generalized, with pressure flaking and projectile points being earlier in the south and somewhat later in the north.

For ceramics, the trend runs in the opposite direction, with pottery almost certainly earlier in the north. There is considerable uncertainty, however, about the dating of the earliest appearances of pottery. If Pampean area pottery is derived from the East Brazilian area pottery and if pottery is as early as 500–1 B.C. in Rio Grande do Sul, then one would expect it to be about this early in the northern part of the Pampean area. Estimates on its age have varied from ca. 1000 B.C. (Sanguinetti de Bormida 1961–63), to 400 B.C. (Willey 1971: Fig. 7-20, A.D. 1 (Lanning in Gorenstein *et al.* 1974: Chart 4.1). There are a few radiocarbon dates pertinent to the subject, although these add to, rather than clarify, the uncertainty. Some dates on natural beach-line shell deposits, containing water-worn potsherds, are, 2810, 1870, and 1040 B.C. (Cigliano, Schmitz, and Caggiano 1971). The sites in question are in the vicinity of Palo Blanco on the northern coast of Buenos Aires Province. These dates do seem suspiciously early, with the possible exception of the 1040 B.C. one; and I think questions may be raised concerning the association of the dated shells with the pottery (see Willey 1971: Chapter 7, footnote 90). There are three other later radiocarbon dates—A.D. 860, 1055, and 1180—all from the vicinity of Salto Grande, some distance up the Lower Paraná River. They are associated with what is described as a simple incised pottery. In my earlier estimates, I suggested that pottery from this Salto Grande locality might be as early as about 100 B.C. (Willey 1971: Fig. 7-20), but the dates certainly do not confirm this.

Lanning (in Gorenstein *et al.* 1974:106) has made the generalization that earlier Bolivar Phase pottery of Buenos Aires Province is a simple ware whereas the later pottery of this phase is incised and painted. This seems a reasonable developmental assumption, but it still remains to be demonstrated in the field. The typological and phase definitional systematization of some of the younger archaeologists working in the area (e.g., Cigliano, Schmitz, and Caggiano 1971) is a beginning toward this end. We know from the earlier work of Lothrop (1932) and others that incised and painted pottery complexes persisted in the Buenos Aires region until the early sixteenth century, and we also know from these researchers that Tupiguaraní Tradition pottery and sites have this same terminal dating in the vicinity of the Plate delta.

The Fuegian Area[13]

The Fuegian area consists of the Chilean Archipelago, from below Chiloe Island, down to the including the western and extreme southern portions of Tierra del Fuego (Willey 1971: Fig. 7-18). This was the historic territory of the Chono, Alacaluf, and Yahgan tribes. Their marine-oriented subsistence appears to have had its beginnings as early as 5000 B.C. Radiocarbon dates on the Englefield Island Complex are surprisingly early—7200–6500 (± 1500 years) B.C. (Emperaire and Laming 1961). The Englefield Island culture seems to have had an economy divided between land hunting (pressure-flaked willow-leaf points and bolas stones) and marine subsistence (barbed bone harpoons, sea mammal bones, marine shell refuse). Later phases of the Fuegian Tradition are the "Shell-Knife" (Beagle Channel I) and "Pit-House" (Beagle Channel II) phases, with respective estimated datings of 1000 B.C.–A.D. 500, and A.D. 500 to the Historic Horizon (see Lanning in Gorenstein *et al.* 1974: Chart 4.1; Willey 1971: Fig. 7-20). "Shell-Knife" sites appear to be more directly marine-economy associated; "Pit-House" Phase sites give some indication of a partial modification toward land hunting.

BIBLIOGRAPHY[14]

Andrews, E. W., IV

1973 The Development of Maya Civilization after Abandonment of the Southern Cities. In *The Classic Maya Collapse* edited by T. P. Culbert. Mexico: University of New Mexico Press. Pp. 243–269.

Bell, R. E.

1965 *Archaeological Investigations at the Site of El Inga, Ecuador*. Quito: Casa de la Cultura Ecuatoriana. (Bound together with Spanish version.)

Bennett, W. C., and J. B. Bird

1964 *Andean Culture History*. 2nd. and rev. ed. New York: American Museum of Natural History and The Natural History Press.

Bennett, W. C., E. F. Bleiler, and F. H. Sommer

1948 Northwest Argentine Archaeology. *Yale University Publications in Anthropology*, No. **38.**

[13]Area not covered in this volume.

[14]No attempt has been made to provide extensive area bibliographies for this summary chapter. Such reference material is at hand in the other chapters of this volume. Here, I have listed references that document citations on specific points of fact or interpretation, especially for those areas not given detailed exposition in this volume.)

Bernal, I.
1964 Concluding Remarks. In *Prehistoric Man in the New World*, edited by J. D. Jennings and E. Norbeck. Chicago: University of Chicago Press. Chicago. Pp. 559–566.

Bird, J. B.
1938 Antiquity and Migrations of the Early Inhabitants of Patagonia. *Geographical Review* **28** (No. 2):250–275.
1943 Excavations in Northern Chile. *Anthropological Papers, American Museum of Natural History* **38** (Part 4).

Borden, C. E.
1968 Prehistory of the Lower Mainland. In *Lower Fraser Valley: Evolution of a Cultural Landscape*, edited by A. H. Siemens. Vancouver: University of British Columbia and Tantalus Research Ltd., Pp. 9–28.

Braun, R.
Ms. Cerro Narrio Reanalyzed: The Formative as Seen from the Southern Ecuadorian Highlands. Presented at Primer Simposio de Correlaciones Antropologicas Andino-Meso-americano, 2531 July, Salinas, Ecuador. Mimeographed.

Bushnell, G. H. S.
1951 *The Archaeology of the Santa Elena Peninsula in South-West Ecuador*. Occasional Papers, No. 1, Cambridge, England: Cambridge Museum.

Byers, D. S.
1959 The Eastern Archaic: Some Problems and Hypotheses. *American Antiquity* **24:**233–256.

Cardich, A.
1964 *Lauricocha, Fundamentos para una Prehistoria de los Andes Centrales*. Buenos Aires: Centro Argentino de Estudios Prehistoricos, Studia Praehistorica III.

Cardich, A., L. A. Cardich, and A. Hajduk
1973 Secuencia arqueologica y cronologia radiocarbonica de la cueva 3 de Los Toldos (Santa Cruz, Argentina). *Separatas Relaciones* No. **VII.**

Caso, A.
1938 *Exploraciones en Oaxaca, Quinta y Sexta Temporades, 1936–37*. Publicacion 34. Mexico: Instituto Pan-americano de Geografia e Historia.

Cigliano, E. M., P. I. Schmitz, and M. Am. Caggiano
1971 Sitios Ceramicos Prehispanicos en la Costa Septentrional de la Provincia de Buenos Aires y de Salto Grande, Entre Rios, Esquema Tentativo de su Desarrollo. *Anales de la Comision de Investigaciones Cientificas*, Provincia de Buenos Aires, Gobernacion, La Plata, Argentina.

Coe, M. D.
1960 Archaeological Linkages with North and South America at La Victoria, Guatemala. *American Anthropologist* **62:**363–393.
1970 The Archaeological Sequence at San Lorenzo Tenochtitlan, Veracruz, Mexico. *Contributions of the University of California Archaeological Research Facility* No. **8:**21–34.

Collier, D., and J. V. Murra
1943 Survey and Excavations in Southern Ecuador. *Anthropological Series* **35**. Chicago: Field Museum of Natural History.

Driver, H. E.
1961 *Indians of North America*. Chicago: University of Chicago Press.

Emperaire, J., and A. Laming
1961 Les gisements des Iles Englefield et Vivian dans la Mer D'Otway, Patagonia Australie. *Journal de la Société des Américanistes* **50:**7–75.

Emperaire, J. A. Laming-Emperaire, and H. Reichlen
1963 La Grotte Fell et autres sites de la region volcanique de la Patagonie Chilienne. *Journal de la Société des Américanistes* **52:**167–252.

Estrada, E., and B. J. Meggers
1961 A Complex of Traits of Probable Transpacific Origin on the Coast of Ecuador. *American Anthropologist* **63:**913–939.

Evans, C., and B. J. Meggers
1957 Formative Period Cultures in the Guayas Basin, Coastal Ecuador. *American Antiquity* **22:**235–246.

Fitzhugh, W. W.
1972 Environmental Archeology and Cultural Systems in Hamilton Inlet, Labrador. A Survey of the Central Labrador Coast from 3000 B.C. to the Present. *Smithsonian Contributions to Anthropology* No. **16.**

Ford, J. A., and W., G. R.
1941 An Interpretation of the Prehistory of the Eastern United States. *American Anthropologist* **43:**325–363.

Gorenstein, S., R. G. Forbis, P. Tolstoy, E. P. Lanning
1974 *Prehispanic America.* In *St. Martin's Series in Prehistory*, edited by S. Gorenstein and R. Stigler. New York: St. Martin's Press.

Griffin, J. B.
1946 Cultural Change and Continuity in Eastern United States Archaeology. In *Man in Northeastern North America*, edited by F. Johnson. Vol. 3. Andover, Mass: Papers of R. S. Peabody Foundation for Archaeology. pp. 37–95.

Gamio, M.
1913 Arqueologia de Atzcapotzalco, D. F. Mexico. *Proceedings of the 18th International Congress of Americanists*, London. Pp. 180–187.

Gonzalez, A. R.
1960 La Estratigrafia de La Gruta de Intihuasi, (Prov. de San Luis, R. A.) y Sus Telaciones con Otros Sitios Preceramicos de Sudamerica. *Revista del Instituto de Antropologia*, **I.**
1961–1964 La cultura de La Aguada del N. O. Argentino. *Revista del Instituto de Antropologia* **2–3:**205–253. (Spanish version of Gonzalez, 1961).
1963 Cultural Development in Northwestern Argentina. In *Aboriginal Cultural Development in Latin America: An Interpretative Review*, edited by B. J. Meggers, and C. Evans, 103–118. *Smithsonian Miscellaneous Collections*, **140** (No. 1).

Green, D. F., and G. W. Lowe
1967 Altamira and Padre Piedra, Early Preclassic Sites in Chiapas, Mexico, *Papers of the New World Archaeological Foundation.* No. **20** (Publication No. 15).

Hartmann, C. V.
1901 *Archaeological Researches in Costa Rica.* Stockholm: Royal Ethnological Museum.
1907 Archaeological Researchers in the Pacific Coast of Costa Rica. *Memoirs* **3** (No. 1).

Hilbert, P. P.
1968 Archaeologische Untersuchungen am Mittleren Amazonas. *Marburger Studien zur Völkerkunde* **1.**

Jennings, J. D.
1974 *Prehistory of North America.* 2nd ed. New York: McGraw-Hill.

Izumi, S. and T. Sono
1963 *Andes 2: Excavations at Kotosh, Peru, 1960.* Tokyo: Kadokawa Pub.

Jijón y Caamaño, J.
1927 Puruhā. Contribución al Concimiento de los Aborigenes de la Provincia de Chimborazo, de la República del Ecuador. 2 Vols. Reprinted from *Boletín Academia Nacional de Historia de Ecuador* **3** (No. 6); **5** (Nos. 12–14); **6** (Nos. 15–17); **7** (No. 19); **9** (Nos. 24–26).

Laming-Emperaire, A., D. Lavallee, and R. Humbert
1972 Le Site de Marazzi en Terre de Feu. *Objets et Mondes.* **12** (No. 2):225–244.

Lanning, E. P.
1965 Early Man in Peru. *Scientific American* **213** (No. 4):68–76.
1967 *Peru before the Incas*, Englewood Cliffs, N.J.: Prentice-Hall.

Lathrap, D. W.
1967 Review of Early Formative Period of Coastal Ecuador: Valdivia and Machalilla Phases. *American Anthropologist* **69** (No. 1):96–98.
1970 The Upper Amazon. In *Ancient Peoples and Places Series*. London: Thames and Hudson.
1973 Summary or Model Building: How Does One Achieve a Meaningful Overview of a Continent's Prehistory. *American Anthropologist* **75** (No. 6):1755–1767.
1974 The Moist Tropics, the Arid Lands, and the Appearance of Great Art Styles in the New World. In *Art and Environment in Native America*, edited by M. E. King and I. R. Traylor, Jr. Special Publications, No. 7. Texas: The Museum, Texas University. Pp. 115–159.
1975 *Ancient Ecuador: Culture, Clay and Creativity*. Chicago: Field Museum of Natural History.
Ms. Our Father the Cayman, Our Mother the Gourd: Spinden Revisited, or a Unitary Model for the Emergence of Agriculture in the New World. Department of Anthropology, University of Illinois, Urbana. Mimeographed.

Leonhardy, F. C. and D. G. Rice
1970 A Proposed Culture Typology for the Lower Snake River Region, Southeastern Washington. *Northwest Anthropological Research Notes* **4** (No. 1):1–29.

Lothrop, S. K.
1926 Pottery of Costa Rica and Nicaragua. *Contributions*. New York: Museum of American Indian, Heye Foundation.
1932 Indians of the Paraná Delta, Argentina. *Annals of the New York Academy of Sciences* **33**:77–232.

Lynch, T. F. and K. A. R. Kennedy
1970 Early Human Cultural and Skeletal Remains from Guitarrero Cave, Northern Peru. *Science* **169**:1307–1310.

MacNeish, R. S., A. Nelken-Turner, and A. G. Cook
1970 *Second Annual Report of the Ayacucho Archaeological-Botanical Project*. Andover, Mass.: R. S. Peabody Foundation.

MacNeish, R. S., F. A. Peterson, and K. V. Flannery
1970 *Ceramics. The Prehistory of the Tehuacan Valley*. Vol. III. Austin: University of Texas Press.

Mason, J. A.
1931–1939 Archaeology of Santa Marta, Colombia. *Anthropological Papers* **20** (Nos. 1–3).

Meggers, B. J.
1963 Cultural Development in Latin America: An Interpretative Overview. In *Aboriginal Cultural Development in Latin America: An Interpretative Review*, edited by B. J. Meggers and C. Evans. *Smithsonian Miscellaneous Collections*.
1964 North And South American Cultural Connections and Convergences. In *Prehistoric Man in the New World*, edited by J. D. Jennings and E. Norbeck. Chicago: University of Chicago Press. Pp. 511–526.
1966 Ecuador. In *Ancient Peoples and Places*, edited by G. Daniel. No. 49. New York: Frederick A. Praeger.
1972 *Prehistoric America*. Chicago: Aldine-Atherton Press.

Meggers, B. J. and C. Evans
1957 *Archaeological Investigations at the Mouth of the Amazon*. Bulletin 167. Washington, D.C.: Bureau of American Ethnology, Smithsonian Institution.
1961 An Experimental Formulation of Horizon Styles in the Tropical Forest Area of South

America. In *Essays in Pre-Columbian Art and Archaeology*, edited by S. K. Lothrop *et al*. Cambridge, Mass.: Harvard University Press. Pp. 372–388.

Meggers, B. J., C. Evans, and E. Estrada
1965 Early Formative Period of Coastal Ecuador. *Smithsonian Contributions to Anthropology*. **1.**

Miller, E. T.
1974 Pesquisas Arqueologicas em Abrigos-Sob-Rocha No Nordeste do Rio Grande do Sul. *Programa Nacional de Pesquisas Arqueologicas* **5** (No. 26):11–25.

Moseley, M. E.
1974 *The Maritime Foundations of Andean Civilization*. Menlo Park, Calif.: Cummings Pub.

Nordenskiold, E. von
1913 Urnengraber un Mounds im Bolivianischen Flachlande. *Baessler Archiv* **3**:205–255.

Phillips, P, J. A. Ford, and J. B. Griffin
1951 *Archaeological Survey in the Lower Mississippi Alluvial Valley, 1940–47*, (Papers: Peabody Museum; Vol. 25). Cambridge, Mass.: Harvard University.

Porter Weaver, M.
1972 *The Aztecs, Maya, and Their Predecessors*, New York: Seminar Press.

Preuss, K. T.
1931 *Arte Monumental Prehistorico*. 2nd ed., 2 vols. Bogotá: Escuelas Salesianas. (Originally published in German in 1929.)

PRONAPA
1967– Resultados Preliminares, 1965 through 1970. *Programa Nacional de Pesquisas Ar-*
1969a,b *queologicas* Nos. **6, 10, 13, 15, 26.**
1971–
1974

Reichel-Dolmatoff, G.
1954a A Preliminary Study of Space and Time Perspective in Northern Colombia *American Antiquity* **19**:352–366.
1954b Investigaciones arqueólogicas en la Sierra Nevada de Santa Marta. Parts 1 and 2. *Revista Colombiana de Antropología* **2** (No. 2):145–206.
1954c Investigaciones arqueológicas en la Sierra Nevada de Santa Marta. Part 3. *Revista Colombiana de Antropología* **3**:139–170.
1955 Excavaciones en los Conchales de la Costa de Barlovento. *Revista Colombiana de Antropología* **4**:249–272.
1959 The Formative Stage, an Appraisal from the Colombian Perspective *33rd International Congress of Americanists* **1**:152–164.
1961 Puerto Hermiga: Un Complejo Prehistórico Marginal de Colombia. *Revista Colombiana de Antropología* **10**:349–354.
1965a *Colombia*. In *Ancient Peoples and Places Series*. No. 44. New York: Praeger.
1965b *Excavaciones Arqueológicas en Puerto Hormiga, Departamento de Bolivar, Antropología* **2.**
1967 Recientes investigaciones arqueológicas en San Agustín *Razon y Fabula*, No. **2**:35–38.
1972 *San Agustin, A Culture of Colombia*. New York: Praeger.
1975 *Estratigrafia Ceramica de San Agustín, Colombia*, Bogotá: Biblioteca Banco Popular.

Reichel-Dolmatoff, G., and A. Dussan de Reichel
1956 Momíl, excavaciones en el Sinú. *Revista Colombiana de Antropologia* **5**:109–334.

Restrepo, V.
1895 *Los Chibchas antes de la Conquista Española*. Bogotá: Imprenta de La Luz.

Rouse, I.
1964 Prehistory of the West Indies. *Science* **144**:499–514.

Rouse, I., and J. M. Cruxent
1963 Venezuelan Archaeology. In *Caribbean Series* No. **6**.
Rowe, J. H.
1960 Cultural Unity and Diversification in Peruvian Archaeology. In *Men and Cultures, Selected Papers, 5th International Congress of Anthropological and Ethnological Sciences*, edited by A. F. C. Wallace. Philadelphia: University of Pennsylvania Press. Pp. 627–631.
1965 An Interpretation of Radiocarbon Measurements on Archaeological Samples from Peru. In *Proceedings, 6th International Conference of Radiocarbon and Tritium Dating*. Pullman, Wash.: Washington State University. Pp. 187–198.
1974 Kunst in Peru und Bolivien. In *Das Alte Amerika*, edited by G. R. Willey. Propylaen Kunstgeschichte, Band 18. Berlin: Propylaen Verlag. Pp. 285–297.
Sanguinetti de Bórmida, A.
1961–1963 Las Industrias Líticas de Trenque Lauquen (Provincia de Buenos Aires). *Acta Praehistorica* **5–7**:72–95.
Sanders, W. T. and Joseph Marino
1970 New World Prehistory. Archaeology of the American Indian. In *Foundations of Modern Anthropology Series*. Englewood Cliffs, N.J.: Prentice-Hall.
Schmitz, P. I.
1973 Cronologia de las Culturas del Sudeste de Rio Grande do Sul-Brazil. Pub. No. 4. Rio Grande do Sul, Brazil: Univ. Federal do Rio Grande do Sul, Dept. de Ciencias Sociais, Gabinete de Arquelogia.
Strong, W. D.
1935 An Introduction to Nebraska Archaeology. *Smithsonian Miscellaneous Collections*. **93** (No. 10).
Uhle, M.
1919 La Arquelogia de Arica y Tacna. *Boletin de la Sociedad de Estudios Historicos Americanos* **3** (Nos. 7, 8):1–48.
1922 *Fundamentos Etnicos y Arqueología de Arica y Tacna*. 2nd ed. Quito.
Vaillant, G. C.
1930 Excavations at Zacatenco. *Anthropological Papers*. **32** (Part1). New York: American Museum of Natural History.
1931 Excavations at Ticoman. *Anthropological Papers*. **32** (Part 2). New York: American Museum of Natural History.
1935 Excavations at El Arbolillo. *Anthropological Papers*. **35** (Part 2). New York: American Museum of Natural History.
Wauchope, R. (Ed.)
1971 Archaeology of Northern Mesoamerica. *Handbook of Middle American Indians*, edited by G. F. Ekholm and Ignacio Bernal. Vol. 11. Austin: University of Texas Press.
Willey, G. R.
1966–1971 *An Introduction to American Archaeology*. 2 Vols. Englewood Cliffs, N.J.: Prentice-Hall.
Willey, G. R. and P. Phillips
1958 *Method and Theory in American Archaeology*. Chicago: University of Chicago Press.
Willey, G. R. and J. A. Sabloff
1974 *A History of American Archaeology*. London: Thames and Hudson.
Willey, G. R. and D. B. Shimkin
1973 The Maya Collapse: A Summary View. In *The Classic Maya Collapse*, edited by T. P. Culbert. Albuquerque: University of New Mexico Press. Pp. 457–503.
Wright, J. V.
1970 The Shield Archaic in Manitoba: A Preliminary Statement. In *Ten Thousand Years: Archaeology in Manitoba*, edited by W. M. Hlady. Manitoba: Manitoba Archaeological Society.

Index of Places, Sites, and Cultural Terms

B

C

L

M

P

Q

R

T

U

V

W

X

Y

Z

A
B
C 8
D 9
E 0
F 1
G 2
H 3
I 4
J 5

STUDIES IN ARCHEOLOGY

Consulting Editor: Stuart Struever

Department of Anthropology
Northwestern University
Evanston, Illinois

Charles R. McGimsey III. **Public Archeology**

Lewis R. Binford. **An Archaeological Perspective**

Muriel Porter Weaver. **The Aztecs, Maya, and Their Predecessors: Archaeology of Mesoamerica**

Joseph W. Michels. **Dating Methods in Archaeology**

C. Garth Sampson. **The Stone Age Archaeology of Southern Africa**

Fred T. Plog. **The Study of Prehistoric Change**

Patty Jo Watson (Ed.). **Archeology of the Mammoth Cave Area**

George C. Frison (Ed.). **The Casper Site: A Hell Gap Bison Kill on the High Plains**

W. Raymond Wood and R. Bruce McMillan (Eds.). **Prehistoric Man and His Environments: A Case Study in the Ozark Highland**

Kent V. Flannery (Ed.). **The Early Mesoamerican Village**

Charles E. Cleland (Ed.). **Cultural Change and Continuity: Essays in Honor of James Bennett Griffin**

Michael B. Schiffer. **Behavioral Archeology**

Fred Wendorf and Romuald Schild. **Prehistory of the Nile Valley**

Michael A. Jochim. **Hunter-Gatherer Subsistence and Settlement: A Predictive Model**

Stanley South. **Method and Theory in Historical Archeology**

Timothy K. Earle and Jonathon E. Ericson (Eds.). **Exchange Systems in Prehistory**

Stanley South (Ed.). **Research Strategies in Historical Archeology**

John E. Yellen. **Archaeological Approaches to the Present: Models for Reconstructing the Past**

Lewis R. Binford (Ed.). **For Theory Building in Archaeology: Essays on Faunal Remains, Aquatic Resources, Spatial Analysis, and Systemic Modeling**

James N. Hill and Joel Gunn (Eds.). **The Individual in Prehistory: Studies of Variability in Style in Prehistoric Technologies**

Michael B. Schiffer and George J. Gumerman (Eds.). **Conservation Archaeology: A Guide for Cultural Resource Management Studies**

Thomas F. King, Patricia Parker Hickman, and Gary Berg. **Anthropology in Historic Preservation: Caring for Culture's Clutter**

Richard E. Blanton. **Monte Albán: Settlement Patterns at the Ancient Zapotec Capital**

R. E. Taylor and Clement W. Meighan. **Chronologies in New World Archaeology**

Bruce D. Smith. **Prehistoric Patterns of Human Behavior: A Case Study in the Mississippi Valley**

in preparation

Barbara L. Stark and Barbara Voorhies (Eds.). **Prehistoric Coastal Adaptations: The Economy and Ecology of Maritime Middle America**

Lewis R. Binford. **Nunamuit Ethnoarchaeology**

Charles L. Redman (Ed.). **Social Archeology: Beyond Subsistence and Dating**

Bruce D. Smith (Ed.). **Mississippian Settlement Patterns Sarunas Milisauskas. European Prehistory.**

J. Barto Arnold III (Ed.). **The Nautical Archeology of Padre Island. The Spanish Shipwrecks of 1554**

Date	Lower Central America	Colombia	Caribbean Area	Amazonia	Ecuador	Peru–Boliv
1500					Inca Horizon	Inca Horiz
	Late Poly.	Chibcha	Guarguapo			Late Interme Period
		Betancí		Caimito		
1000	Middle Poly.			Marajoara		
			Los Barrancos			
	Early Poly.	San Agustín Climax			Milagro Manteño	Middle Hor
	Zoned Bichrome / Scarif. Wares	Cienega del Oro				Early Interme Period
A.D. / B.C.		↑	Barrancas	Hupa-iya Shakimu		
	Dinarte (Pottery) (?)					Early Hori
1000		Malambo	Saladero	Ananatuba	Chorrera-Engoroy	
		Momíl			Machalilla	
				Early Tutishcainyo		Initial Peri
2000	Monagrillo	Canapote	(Earliest Pottery) (?) (Beginnings of Various Pre-Ceramic, Archaic-Type			Preceramic P
		Puerto Hormiga			Valdivia	
3000		Later Lithic Assemblages	Series-Ortoiroid, Casimiroid, Manicuaroid- with Much Later Continuities.)	(Earliest Pottery)(?)	↑	Preceramic P
4000						
	Cerro Mangote					
5000						Preceramic Pe
6000			↑		Vegas	
	Chiriquí–Precer I		Canaima (Joboid)		El Inga II	
7000					↑	Preceramic P
8000	Macapalé	El Jobo			El Inga I	Preceramic P
	(Panama Hearth)	El Abra Las Lagunas				
10,000		Camare				Preceramic I
20,000						↓ ?